ESSENTIALS OF CONTEMPORARY MANAGEMENT

Third Canadian Edition

Gareth R. Jones
Texas A & M University

Jennifer M. George
Texas A & M University

Michael Rock, Ed.D.
Seneca College of Applied Arts and Technology

J. W. Haddad
Seneca College of Applied Arts and Technology

McGraw-Hill Ryerson
Connect. Learn. Succeed.

Essentials of Contemporary Management
Third Canadian Edition

ISBN-13: 978-0-07096743-4
ISBN-10: 0-07-096743-1

1 2 3 4 5 6 7 8 9 10 WCD 1 9 8 7 6 5 4 3 2 1 0

Statistics Canada information is used with the permission of Statistics Canada. Users are forbidden to copy this material and/or redisseminate the data, in an original or modified form, for commercial purposes, without the expressed permission of Statistics Canada. Information on the availability of the wide range of data from Statistics Canada can be obtained from Statistics Canada's Regional Offices, its World Wide Web site at http://www.statcan.ca and its toll-free access number 1-800-263-1136.

Printed and bound in the USA.

Care has been taken to trace ownership of copyright material contained in this text; however, the publisher will welcome any information that enables them to rectify any reference or credit for subsequent editions.

Vice President, Editor-in-Chief: Joanna Cotton
Senior Sponsoring Editor: Kim Brewster
Marketing Manager: Cathie Lefebvre
Developmental Editor: Lori McLellan
Senior Editorial Associate: Christine Lomas
Supervising Editor: Graeme Powell
Copy Editor: Erin Moore
Proofreader: Rohini Herbert
Production Coordinator: Sharon Stefanowicz
Cover Design: Valid Design
Interior Design: Valid Design
Page Layout: S R Nova Pvt Ltd, Bangalore, India
Printer: Worldcolor Dubuque (U.S.)
Cover Images: Larry Lilac / Alamy

Library and Archives Canada Cataloguing in Publication

Essentials of contemporary management / Gareth R. Jones ... [et al.].—3rd Canadian ed.

Includes index.

First Canadian ed. by: Gareth R. Jones, Jennifer M. George, Nancy Langton; 2nd Canadian ed. by: Gareth R. Jones, Jennifer M. George, Michael Rock and contributor, Jane Haddad.

ISBN 978-0-07-096743-4

1. Management–Textbooks. I. Jones, Gareth R.

HD31.E79 2009   658.4   C2009-905402-7

Brief Contents

Contents

Chapter 9

Chapter 10

About The Authors

Michael Rock has recently retired as a full-time professor at Seneca College of Applied Arts and Technology, Toronto, Ontario. He has been for many years an adjunct professor in the School of Management and Economics at the University of Guelph where he currently teaches Ethics of Leadership in the online M.A. in Leadership Studies program. Professor Rock holds a doctorate in Adult Education from Indiana University (1974) and is a licensed emotional intelligence coach and facilitator with Dr. Reuven Bar-On's Emotional Quotient-Inventory™ or EQ-i™. He has authored over 150 articles in human relations trade journals and magazines and 12 books, such as *EQ Goes to Work, Ethics: To Live By, To Work By* and co-author of *The 7 Pillars of Visionary Leadership*. Currently he is completing Ph.D./D.Th. degrees in Spirituality (in the workplace) and Theology at Saint Paul University and the University of Ottawa. He plans on continuing to provide executive retreats and presentations in the areas of emotional intelligence, ethics, and leadership development.

Jane W. Haddad received her Honours B.A. from Queen's University, Ontario, in 1984 followed by her M.A from the Ontario Institute for Studies in Education at the University of Toronto in 1986. She has taught in the faculties of Sociology and Education at the University of Saskatchewan and the University of Regina, Saskatchewan, and in the Salem International University distance M.B.A. program. In addition to teaching Liberal Studies, Humanities, and Management theory for 20 years, Jane also leads and develops new course curricula as a Professor and Course Director in the School of Business Management at Seneca College of Applied Arts and Technology, Toronto, Ontario. Professor Haddad coordinated a SSHRC funded Community-University Research Alliance (CURA) grant at Seneca from 2000 to 2005 and currently sits on Seneca's Research Ethics Review Board.

Professor Haddad's research interests include youth training and labour markets and barriers to accessing post secondary education. She has presented several academic papers at Learned Society and other conferences across Canada and published her work in journals such as *Canadian Women's Studies Journal* and *The College Quarterly*.

Gareth R. Jones is a Professor of Management in the Lowry Mays College and Graduate School of Business at Texas A&M University. He received his B.A. in Economics/Psychology and his Ph.D. in Management from the University of Lancaster, U.K. He previously held teaching and research appointments at the University Warwick, Michigan State University, and the University of Illinois at Urbana–Champaign.

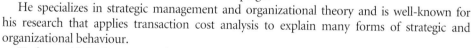

He specializes in strategic management and organizational theory and is well-known for his research that applies transaction cost analysis to explain many forms of strategic and organizational behaviour.

He has published many articles in leading journals and his recent work has appeared in the *Academy of Management Review, Journal of International Business Studies*, and *Human Relations*. He is or has served on the editorial boards of the *Academy of Management Review*, the *Journal of Management*, and *Management Inquiry*.

Jennifer M. George is the Mary Gibbs Jones Professor of Management and Professor of Psychology in the Jesse H. Jones Graduate School of Management at Rice University. She received her B.A. in Psychology/Sociology from Wesleyan University, her M.B.A. in Finance from New York University, and her Ph.D. in Management and Organizational Behavior from New York University. Prior to joining the faculty at Rice University, she was a Professor in the Department of Management at Texas A&M University.

She specializes in Organizational Behavior and is the author of many articles in journals such as the *Academy of Management Journal, Academy of Management Review, Journal of Applied Psychology, Organizational Behavior and Human Decision Processes, Journal of Personality and Social Psychology*, and *Psychological Bulletin*. She is a Fellow in the American Psychological Association, the American Psychological Society, and the Society for Industrial and Organizational Psychology and a member of the Society for Organizational Behavior. Professor George is currently an Associate Editor for the *Journal of Applied Psychology*.

Preface

When groups of people come together to pursue a common goal–often to satisfy their collective needs–various activities have to be structured so that resources can be gathered and used to achieve the goal. The person or people who are assigned the task of keeping the whole group working toward the goal, deciding on timing and strategy, and maintaining the structure of activities and relationships, are those who engage in managing. The activities of managing are critical to any complex cooperative endeavour. Management is both the art and science of arranging and utilizing the physical and human factors of production toward a desired outcome. This book provides you, the student, with an introduction to the management process. As with the second edition, it is designed around the four main sets of activities that managers engage in to achieve organizational goals: Planning, Organizing, Leading, and Controlling.

In **Part 1, Chapter 1: Managers and Managing**, we discuss who managers are, the types and levels of managers found in organizations, their main responsibilities in the organization, the skills needed, and the roles they perform in planning, organizing, leading, and controlling.

Part 2, Chapter 2: Managing the Organizational Environment sets the management process in the environmental context of doing business in Canada and the global economy. The economic, cultural, legal-political, and technological contexts, as well as the immediate agents in the organization's external environment, such as suppliers, customers, distributors, and competitors, are analyzed for the threats and opportunities they present to managers in gaining a competitive advantage. **Chapter 3: Managing Ethics, Social Responsibility, and Diversity** addresses the fundamental challenge facing managers to make optimal and sustainable decisions. Increasingly, this means utilizing and integrating Management Information Systems (MIS).

In **Part 3, Chapter 4: The Manager as a Decision Maker**, we learn about the types of decisions that managers must make, the models they use, and the pitfalls of cognitive biases. **Chapter 5: Managing Planning and Strategy** tackles the process of planning organizational goals and formulating and implementing strategies that are best able to accomplish them. Students learn two common techniques for analyzing the environmental context, which is vital to strategy formulation for a competitive advantage: SWOT and Porters' Five Forces model.

In **Part 4, Chapter 6: Managing Organizational Structures**, we discuss the elements of organizational design and structure. Students learn that the various ways of allocating authority and distributing control over decision making results in different organizational structures. The type of overall organizational structure depends on internal and external organizational factors such as the strategy, technology, and human resources, and the degree of environmental change. **Chapter 7: Managing Culture and Change** explores how an organizational culture is developed, maintained, and changed when an organization's strategy and structure changes. Two models of organizational change are presented.

Part 5, Chapter 8: Managing Motivation discusses the means by which managers can motivate good work effort and performance from employees. Several needs and process theories are discussed and the importance of a total rewards strategy utilizing both intrinsic and extrinsic factors is highlighted. In **Chapter 9: Managing Leadership**, students learn the importance of effective leadership in managing organizational performance. Trait, Behavioural, and Contingency theories are explored and transformational and transactional leadership styles are compared. **Chapter 10: Managing Teams** discusses the types of groups and teams found in contemporary organizations. Students learn the elements of group dynamics, group decision-making techniques, and what managers can do to create high-performing teams in their organizations. **Chapter 11: Managing Human Resources** is focussed on how managers can successfully recruit, select, develop, appraise, and compensate employees in the context of the Canadian legal and regulatory environment. **Chapter 12: Managing Communication, Conflict and Negotiation** deals with developing effective communication, conflict resolution, and negotiation skills for managers.

In **Part 6, Chapter 13: Managing Control and Operations**, students learn how managers monitor and measure the use of resources to make sure the process and products are up to standards throughout the entire value chain. Corporate governance practices are examined in light of recent economic crises. The types of controls that managers use impact the culture and structure of the organization and reflect either innovative or conservative practices.

We have also included an appendix to this edition. Appendix A is a Business Plan template that allows students to apply the principles of management to the writing of a business plan for a new venture or new strategy for an existing organization.

All of the material covered in *Essentials of Contemporary Management*, Third Edition, has a direct application to you as a student of organizational management as well as to any business enterprise you may own, manage, or work for in the future.

Guided Tour
Learning Tools

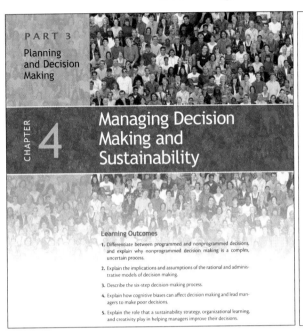

PART 3
Planning and Decision Making

CHAPTER 4

Managing Decision Making and Sustainability

Learning Outcomes

1. Differentiate between programmed and nonprogrammed decisions, and explain why nonprogrammed decision making is a complex, uncertain process.

2. Explain the implications and assumptions of the rational and administrative models of decision making.

3. Describe the six-step decision-making process.

4. Explain how cognitive biases can affect decision making and lead managers to make poor decisions.

5. Explain the role that a sustainability strategy, organizational learning, and creativity play in helping managers improve their decisions.

Summary and Review

1. **THE NATURE OF MANAGERIAL DECISION MAKING** Prog are routine decisions that are made so often that managers ha sion rules to be followed automatically. Nonprogrammed dec response to situations that are unusual or unique; they are non

2. **COMPARING DECISION-MAKING MODELS** The rational moc ing assumes that decision makers have complete information; that information in an objective, rational manner; and make c The administrative model suggests that managers are bounde have access to all the information they need to make optimum d quently satisfice and rely on their intuition and judgment when

3. **SIX STEPS IN THE DECISION-MAKING PROCESS:** Managers for a decision, generate alternatives, assess alternatives, choo tives, implement the chosen alternative, and learn from feedba

4. **BIASES IN DECISION MAKING** Managers are often fairly goo However, problems result when human judgment is adverse operation of cognitive biases. Cognitive biases are caused by s the way decision makers process information to make decisio errors include prior hypotheses, representativeness, the illusi escalating commitment. Managers should undertake a persona become aware of their biases.

5. **IMPROVING DECISION MAKING** Managers can make bett they examine their biases and spend appropriate amounts of ti process. But to make optimum decisions, managers should ad strategy that is transparent, engaging, and economically benefi a large carbon footprint. They must become a learning organi age creativity to ensure that new, innovative ideas are not over

6. **INFORMATION AND MANAGEMENT INFORMATION** Managers must utilize Management Information Systems t quality, timely, relevant and relatively complete information a tions that enable them to make effective decisions.

Learning Outcomes have been highlighted at the beginning of each chapter, and the **Summary and Review** relating to these learning outcomes is included at the end of the chapter.

Business is always evolving. But for those who stand out for being "different," the challenges remain largely the same. Canada is a diverse society. Imagine what we could achieve if our meeting rooms truly reflected this. We have the power to fully engage our workforce by welcoming people and building frameworks to help them succeed. The time to do that is now.

You Be the Manager

1. What else is required in addition to recruiting well?

Expectancy Theory

Expectancy theory, formulated by Victor H. Vroom in the 1960s, states that motivation will be high when employees believe that high levels of effort will lead to high performance and that high performance will lead to receiving desired outcomes. Expectancy theory is one of the most popular theories of work motivation because it focuses on all three parts of the motivation equation: inputs, performance, and outcomes. Expectancy theory identifies three major factors that determine a person's motivation: *expectancy, instrumentality,* and *valence* (see Figure 8.5).[16]

Expectancy

Expectancy is a person's perception about the extent to which effort (an input) will result in a certain level of performance.

expectancy theory
The theory that motivation will be high when employees believe that high levels of effort will lead to high performance and that high performance will lead to the attainment of desired outcomes.

expectancy
In expectancy theory, a perception about the extent to which effort will result in a certain level of performance.

Inco Ltd. has rolled out a front-line planning and scheduling system at its Copper Cliff smelter in Sudbury, Ontario, in which the daily, weekly, and monthly goals for production and maintenance are clearly established every day.

Definitions of Key Terms are highlighted in each chapter and provided in the margins, and a list of these terms with page references is provided at the end of the chapter.

Exhibits are interspersed throughout the text to illustrate concepts and provide a visual framework for students.

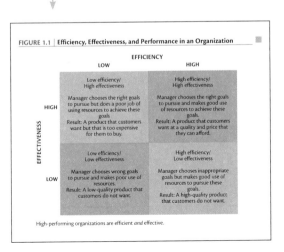

FIGURE 1.1 | Efficiency, Effectiveness, and Performance in an Organization

	EFFICIENCY	
	LOW	HIGH
HIGH	Low efficiency/High effectiveness. Manager chooses the right goals to pursue but does a poor job of using resources to achieve these goals. Result: A product that customers want but that is too expensive for them to buy.	High efficiency/High effectiveness. Manager chooses the right goals to pursue and makes good use of resources to achieve these goals. Result: A product that customers want at a quality and price that they can afford.
LOW	Low efficiency/Low effectiveness. Manager chooses wrong goals to pursue and makes poor use of resources. Result: A low-quality product that customers do not want.	High efficiency/Low effectiveness. Manager chooses inappropriate goals but makes good use of resources to pursue these goals. Result: A high-quality product that customers do not want.

(left axis: **EFFECTIVENESS**)

High-performing organizations are efficient *and* effective.

Rich and Relevant Examples

An important feature of our book is the way we use real-world examples and stories about managers and companies to drive home the applied lessons to students. Moreover, unlike boxed material in other books, we integrate more applied and fewer types of boxes seamlessly into the text; they are an integral part of the learning experience, and not tacked on or isolated from the text itself. This is central to our pedagogical approach.

Each chapter opens with a **Management Snapshot**. These Snapshots pose a chapter-related challenge and then discuss how companies or managers responded to that challenge, bringing to light the many issues surrounding the management process. At the end of the chapter, **So Where Do You Stand?** wraps up the opening in light of the new information gleaned from the chapter.

MANAGEMENT SNAPSHOT

Unto the Seventh Generation[1]

How has it come that we cannot see the value of a forest? And, what does this mean to leaders of our organizations? We live in a time when our corporate leaders manage quarter by quarter and our political leaders tell us they can't be bound by three year plans. Yet, the most pressing problem faced by our planet—the current decline of every living system—requires a multi-generational strategy.—**Gabriel Draven**[2]

In what is called the Cathedral of Temagami, in the near north of Ontario, lies an old growth forest of 150 year-old trees. Plans had been approved to commence clear-cutting of the trees. An elder of the Teme-Augama Anishnabai, the last of his people to homestead on ancestral lands, invited writer Gabriel Draven to visit this area that has served as a gathering place for the elder's people for a thousand years as they sought wisdom and communed with their elders. The area contains the Spirit Forest that lies between Lake Temagami and Lake Obakika. Draven asks why it is that people cannot see the value of a forest and, for our purpose, what does this "not seeing" mean to leaders of today's organizations?

Toronto author Thomas Homer-Dixon,[3] past director of the Trudeau Centre for Peace and Conflict Studies at the University of Toronto, says that our institutions are failing us because they are unable to deal with complex crises like global environmental meltdown, world hunger, peace

Gallop Research? Is it any wonder that disability represents up to 12% of payroll costs in Canada with mental health claims as the fastest growing category of disability, or so according to a major roundtable study completed in 2000 looking at depression in the Canadian workplace?

To be disengaged is to show up physically for work but to be absent mentally.[4] This state of affairs, or disengagement, is called "presenteeism."[5] There is even a website devoted to teaching and helping people to slack off from work. Slackersguild.com bills itself as an "online community made up of people who generally dislike work." It appeals to such a broad range of people that it has offered access to everything from music to contests and interviews. "Our main goal is simple: to give you something to do instead of working," it boasts.[6] Sometimes presenteeism occurs because employees show up for work, even though they may be quite ill! Not only is this an organizational health

SO WHERE DO YOU STAND?

Wrap-Up to Opening Case

We began this chapter on leadership with what could be called "the long view" of leadership. That is, we looked at leadership "unto the seventh generation." There is definitely a need among leaders and society at large to build organizations that serve not only shareholders but also stakeholders, or the wider community. The effect of numerous business scandals has drawn attention to the negative effects of short-term leadership decision making. For example, Ivanhoe Mines Ltd. of Vancouver, believes it has discovered a gigantic copper and gold deposit in South Gobi, Mongolia, and is spending US10 million a month drilling holes, testing results, and pouring a gigantic concrete shaft in preparation for production in about two years. Like other companies in similar situations, time and money are being spent because the consequences of not consulting all the stakeholders can simply be too costly in terms of money and corporate reputation.

Dr. Warren Bennis reminded us that true leaders want to do the right thing. One model that was described

in our opening scenario was that of the Iroquois Confederacy. Leaders in the Confederacy consider the impact of their decisions on the seven generations of people around them: the three that preceded them, the current one, and the three that will follow each leader. In this way, care was a moral duty because of these seventh generation considerations. "Our world is crying—even dying—for such leaders." John Kotter[103] says that "the ultimate act of leadership is to create a culture of leadership."[104] In the spirit of Dr. Margaret Wheatley's thoughts on leader, she believes that in tune with such a culture of leadership is the presence of "the leader-as-host," not the hero-leader. The cult of the hero-leader has created much of the corporate malfeasance that the beginning years of the twenty-first century have experienced from business.[105] Charles Elson, a corporate governance expert at the University of Delaware, puts matters this way: "We're seeing the outcome of a real dramatic shift. It's the destruction of the myth of the imperial CEO."[106]

Think About It with **You Be the Manager** questions are exercises that present a realistic scenario in which a manager or organization faces some kind of challenge, problem, or opportunity and the student plays the role of a management consultant offering advice and recommending a course of action based on the chapter content.

THINK ABOUT IT

Team Players and Scotiabank[33]

Does your boss encourage you to use his office when he is not there? Brian Toda, vice-president of human resources for Scotiabank's compensation group, does. He "invites his employees to use his office when he's not there. They take turns making conference calls from his comfortable black leather chair or holding small meetings at a round table." Sharing office space reflects Scotiabank's team-oriented culture. Roles have certainly changed! Toda explains, "It's not like employees are coming into my space. It's their space, too." He wants to "deliver the best employment experience."

You Be the Manager

1. What is your experience in sharing office space?
2. As a manager, could you easily shift to the role that Toda works from?

Tips for Managers
MANAGING RESOURCES

1. Develop a list of skills that you need to develop now to become not just a good manager but a great one.
2. Make a list of the "hard skills" you still need to develop.
3. Make a list of the "soft skills" you still need to develop.
4. Identify the different levels of managers in an organization you know. Describe why the organization looks as it does.

Tips for Managers distill the lessons that students can take from the chapter and apply to develop their management skills.

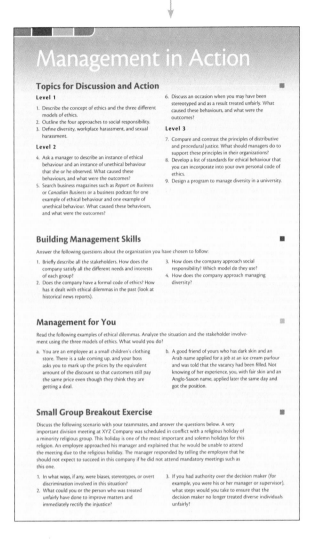

Experiential Learning Features

We have given considerable time and attention to developing state-of-the-art experiential end-of-chapter learning exercises that drive home the meaning of management to students. These exercises are grouped together at the end of each chapter in the section called **Management in Action.**

Topics for Discussion and Action are a set of chapter related questions based on 3 levels of developmental consideration: level 1 tests students' knowledge and comprehension; level 2 tests students' ability for application; and level 3 tests students' synthesis and evaluation skills.

Building Management Skills presents an opportunity for students to follow and analyze an organization of their choice over the semester. Each chapter has an exercise that asks students to evaluate how the issues in the chapter are dealt with by the organization they chose to track.

Management for You is a unique exercise that asks students to internalize concepts from the chapter and apply them to their personal lives and situations at this moment, helping them to grasp the relevance of key chapter ideas and concepts.

Small Group Breakout Exercise is uniquely designed to allow instructors in large classes to utilize interactive experiential exercises in groups of three to four students. The instructor calls on students to form into small groups simply by turning to people around them. All students participate in the exercise in class, and a mechanism is provided for the different groups to share what they have learned with one another.

Managing Ethically is an exercise that presents students with an ethical scenario or dilemma and asks them, either individually or in a group, to think about the issue from an ethical perspective to understand the issues facing practising managers.

Exploring the World Wide Web are two assignments related to chapter content—one is "Specific," directing students to a specific URL with related questions. The second is a more "General" assignment, asking students to find a relevant site to perform research.

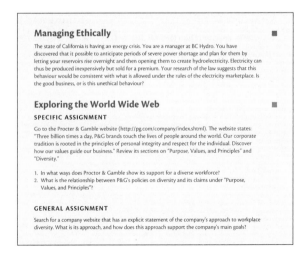

Be the Manager

George Stroumboulopoulos of CBC's *The Hour* initiated a campaign called "One Million Acts of Green,"[85] which is an attempt to get Canadians to engage in something that will prevent greenhouse gas emissions. The act "can be as simple as switching to compact fluorescent lightbulbs, starting a recycling program, or walking to work." As a manager, what decisions could you make that will promote sustainability?

Management Case

Competitive Arousal[84]

If you ever made a decision[87] in the heat of a takeover, labour contract talks, or other high-stakes negotiations and later wondered what you could possibly have been thinking, you fell prey to competitive arousal. In *Harvard Business Review*, academics Deepak Malhotra, Gillian Ku, and J. Keith Murnighan sketch out the three causes of competitive arousal and how to keep it at bay.[86]

Rivalry

Competitive arousal is common—and most powerful—when rivalry is intense, and that usually means a head-to-head rivalry. Research shows individuals are more likely to overbid in auctions when facing only one other bidder, and companies will often dig in their heels in takeovers if a long-time rival is involved.

To defuse rivalry, the first step is to avoid seeing the competitor as an evil nemesis but just as somebody with their own interests at stake, who, like you, is probably smart, reasonably rational, and somewhat emotional (and probably views you as the nemesis).

You should also reconsider the roles of executives who feel this rivalry most strongly, as happened when the NHL and its players' association turned talks over to the second-in-commands because the enmity between commissioner Gary Bettman and players' executive director Bob Goodenow was impeding a settlement.

Be the Manager exercises present a realistic scenario in which a manager/organization faces some kind of challenge, problem, or opportunity and the student plays the role of a management consultant offering advice and recommending a course of action based on the chapter content.

Each chapter contains a **Management Case** dealing with current companies and engaging personalities, one to two pages in length, ending with questions for students to consider.

A **Video Management Case** and questions are included with every chapter to help students make the connections from chapter concepts to real-world applications.

Video Management Case

Could You Go Without Technology for a Week?

Teaching Objective: To consider the role of electronic communication media in work and personal lives.

Video Summary: In this NBC feature, *Forbes* editor Dennis Neal tries to go a week without his cell phone, Blackberry, and email and finds it nearly impossible to do his job, communicate with his family, and manage personal business. His notion that living with technology would help increase face-to-face interaction gives way to total frustration at being unconnected. His experience illustrates how dependent people can become on electronic media and begs the question: Do such media provide convenient communication tools, or do they rule our lives?

Questions to consider

1. How do cell phones and email rank on the information richness scale? When would making a phone call be more effective than sending an email, and vice versa?
2. What are the advantages and disadvantages of using email to communicate?
3. What are some indications—from Dennis Neal's experience and your observations—that people may be too dependent on communications technology?

Integrated Cases help instructors and students alike apply a broad range of theory to the organizational and managerial problems of various companies including NAV Canada air traffic control and Bombardier. These include discussion questions and occur at the end of Parts Two to Six–after Chapters 3, 5, 7, 12, and 13.

Integrated Case

Three Strikes and You're Out[45]

To save Chrysler Group LLC, chief executive Sergio Marchionne has to create a mid-size sedan that can compete with the world's best. It is a three- to five-year job, and he may have two years to do it.

Chrysler, which got a US$15-billion government bailout, may be out of cash in 24 months if he does not return the Auburn Hills (MI)–based company

"He's going to have a much harder-time than at Fiat," said Maryann Keller, president of consulting firm Maryann Keller & Associates in Stamford, Connecticut. She has covered the auto industry since 1972 and said the question is "whether they have time to fix the product problem before they run out of money."

If Marchionne does not successfully rebuild Chrysler, the automaker may not get another chance.

"It has to work this time," said a Chrysler board member. "A patient can only be operated on so many times before he dies."

Discussion Questions

1. What aspects of the different needs theories could apply to this case?

2. "No matter what one's leadership style, a key component of effective leadership is found in the *power* the leader has to affect other people's behaviour and get them to act in certain ways."[46] How are the different types of power illustrated in this case?

3. In what ways does CEO Sergio Marchionne engage in teamwork?

4. How does communication play a role in this case?

The **Developing a Business Plan Appendix** walks students through the steps in preparing a Business Plan that highlights organizational management issues. The appendix can be used with or without business planning software. Developing a Business Plan exercises are found at the end of each chapter as well as online at www.mcgrawhillconnect.ca

Developing a Business Plan APPENDIX A

The Business Plan as an Exercise in the Processes of Management[1]

Writing a business plan may never be a more important exercise than in the context of today's rapidly changing environment. Even if you are not an entrepreneur and do not wish to develop a new original idea and bring it to market, developing a business plan is still a valuable exercise in practising the management processes. It provides a crucial foundation for managing an organization. In this section of the text, we will treat developing a business plan as an exercise in the management processes of planning, organizing, leading, and controlling. By doing the exercises at the end of each chapter, you will have the foundation to put together a plan that will help you develop as a

Student Supplements

Connect™ (www.mcgrawhillconnect.ca): Developed in partnership with Youthography, a Canadian youth research company, and hundreds of students from across Canada, McGraw-Hill Connect™ embraces diverse study behaviours and preferences to maximize active learning and engagement.

With McGraw-Hill Connect™, students complete pre- and post-diagnostic assessments that identify knowledge gaps and point them to concepts they need to learn. McGraw-Hill Connect™ provides students the option to work through recommended learning exercises and create their own personalized study plan using multiple sources of content, including a searchable e-book, multiple-choice and true/false quizzes, chapter-by-chapter learning objectives, interactivities, personal notes, videos, and more. Using the copy, paste, highlight, and sticky note features, students collect, organize, and customize their study plan content to optimize learning outcomes.

McGraw-Hill Connect™—helping instructors and students **Connect, Learn, Succeed!** Authored by Laurel Donaldson, Douglas College.

Essentials of Contemporary Management, Third Edition, offers a complete, integrated supplements package for instructors to address all of your needs.

Instructor Supplements

Connect™ (www.mcgrawhillconnect.ca): McGraw-Hill Connect™ assessment activities don't stop with students! There is material for instructors to leverage as well, including a personalized teaching plan where instructors can choose from a variety of quizzes to use in class, assign as homework, or add to exams. They can edit existing questions and add new ones; track individual student performance—by question, assignment, or in relation to the class overall—with detailed grade reports; integrate grade reports easily with Learning Management Systems such as WebCT and Blackboard; and much more. Instructors can also browse and search teaching resources and text-specific supplements and organize them into customizable categories. All your teaching resources are now located in one convenient place.

McGraw-Hill Connect™—helping instructors and students **Connect, Learn, Succeed!**

Connect also offers instructors downloadable supplements, including an Instructor's Manual, Microsoft® PowerPoint® slides, streaming video cases, as well as access to the Integrator and PageOut, the McGraw-Hill Ryerson Web site development centre. Also included on Connect is a sample of the Group-Video Resource Manual. This online matrix and accompanying manual is available to adopters and contains everything an instructor needs to successfully integrate McGraw-Hill technology and additional group activities into the classroom.

Instructor's Manual: Prepared by Michael Rock, text author, this contains a short topic outline of the chapter and a listing of learning objectives and key terms, a resource checklist with supplements that correspond to each chapter, a detailed lecture outline including marginal notes recommending where to use supplementary cases, lecture enhancers, and critical thinking exercises.

Computerized Test Bank: Prepared by Jane Haddad, text author, the computerized version allows instructors to add and edit questions, save and reload multiple test versions, select questions based on type, difficulty, or key word and use password protection.

Questions test three levels of learning: (1) knowledge of key terms, (2) understanding of concepts and principles, and (3) application of principles.

Microsoft® PowerPoint® Presentations: Prepared by Sean MacDonald of the University of Manitoba, the slideshows for each chapter are based around the learning objectives and include many of the figures and tables from the textbook, as well as some additional slides that support and expand the text discussions. Slides can be modified by instructors with PowerPoint®.

Videos for all Chapters: Complementary videos from CBC programs and customized business segments from the McGraw-Hill Management Library are available on DVD and also can be accessed on the password-protected area of Connect.

Manager's Hot Seat Videos: In today's workplace, managers are confronted daily with issues such as ethics, diversity, working in teams, and the virtual workplace. The Manager's Hot Seat is an online resource that allows students to watch as 15 real managers apply their years of experience to confront these issues. These videos are available as a complementary instructor supplement or for bundling with student textbooks.

The Integrator: Keyed to the chapters and learning objectives of *Essentials of Contemporary Management*, Third Edition, the Integrator is prepared by Sean MacDonald of the University of Manitoba. This tool ties together all of the elements in your resource package, guiding you to where you will find corresponding coverage in each of the related support package components—be it the Instructor's Manual, Computerized Test Bank, PowerPoint® slides, or videos. Link to the Integrator via Connect at www.mcgrawhillconnect.ca.

Business Plan Pro: The Business Plan Pro is available as a bundled option that includes more than 250 sample business plans and 400 case studies to give you a wide variety of examples as you create your own plan. It helps you set up your business by answering questions that help the software customize your plan. You then enter your financial data to generate financial worksheets and statements.

New Business Mentor: For instructors who incorporate a business plan project into their class, the New Business Mentor software can be bundled upon request with student textbooks and includes sample business plans, resources to help you as you start your business, business planning and feasibility planning software, and the "mentor," who will walk you through each step of the business plan. Teaching notes are available.

Management Asset Gallery: McGraw-Hill Ryerson, in conjunction with McGraw-Hill/ Irwin Management, is excited to now provide a one-stop-shop for our wealth of assets making it super quick and easy for instructors to locate specific materials to enhance their course. The Asset Gallery includes our non text-specific management resources (Self-Assessments, Test Your Knowledge exercises, Videos and information, additional group & individual exercises) along with supporting PowerPoint® and Instructor materials.

Create Online: McGraw-Hill's Create Online gives you access to the most abundant resource at your fingertips—literally. With a few mouse clicks, you can create customized learning tools simply and affordably. McGraw-Hill Ryerson has included many of our market-leading textbooks within Create Online for e-book and print customization as well as many licensed readings and cases. For more information, go to www.mcgrawhillcreate.ca.

WebCT and Blackboard

In addition, content cartridges are available for these course management systems. These platforms provide instructors with user-friendly, flexible teaching tools. Please contact your local McGraw-Hill Ryerson *i*Learning Sales Specialist for details.

eInstruction's Classroom Performance System (CPS)

CPS is a student response system using wireless connectivity. It gives instructors and students immediate feedback from the entire class. The response pads are remotes that are easy to use and engage students.

- **CPS** helps you increase **student preparation, interactivity, and active learning** so you can receive immediate feedback and know what students understand.
- **CPS** allows you to administer quizzes and tests, and provide immediate grading.
- With **CPS** you can create lecture questions that can be multiple-choice, true/false, and subjective. You can even create questions on the fly as well as conduct group activities.
- Not only does **CPS** allow you to **evaluate classroom attendance, activity, and grading** for your course as a whole, but CPSOnline allows you to provide students with an immediate study guide. All results and scores can easily be imported into Excel and can be used with various classroom management systems.

CPS-ready content is available for use with *Essentials of Contemporary Management*, Third Edition. Please contact your *i*Learning Sales Specialist for more information on how you can integrate CPS into your classroom.

Superior Service

Service takes on a whole new meaning with McGraw-Hill Ryerson and *Essentials of Contemporary Management*. Rather than just bringing you the textbook, we have consistently raised the bar in terms of innovation and educational research—both in the study of business and in education in general. These investments in learning and the educational community have helped us understand the needs of students and educators across the country and allow us to foster the growth of truly innovative, integrated learning.

*i***Learning Sales Specialist:** Your Integrated Learning Sales Specialist is a McGraw-Hill Ryerson representative who has the experience, product knowledge, training, and support to help you assess and integrate any of the above-noted products, technology, and services into your course for optimum teaching and learning performance. Whether it's how to use our test bank software, helping your students improve their grades, or how to put your entire course online, your *i*Learning Sales Specialist is there to help. Contact your local *i*Learning Sales Specialist today to learn how to maximize all McGraw-Hill Ryerson resources!

Acknowledgements

One never writes a book alone. This is especially true when it comes to acknowledging the contribution of Jane Haddad. In addition to making very insightful comments to improve earlier drafts of this third edition, she also did an outstanding job with the Developing a Business Plan Appendix and accompanying online exercises as well with the Instructor's Test Bank. Thank you, Jane; I deeply appreciate your involvement and input.

I would like to take this opportunity to thank the following people who also walked the path with me as I wrote the third edition: Ed Barter, Johanne Deschamps, Tracey Deagle, Don Green, Daniel Hurtubise, Josée Lajoie, Richard Lemieux, André Nobrega, Conrad Rock, and Siobhán Zych.

Michael Rock

As with all endeavours of this kind, several people have influenced this work, but I want to acknowledge two above all: my father and my father-in-law. My father, John N. Haddad, always put social justice on the agenda. His whole working life was dedicated to alleviating poverty and environmental degradation, and promoting personal dignity for all persons. He had an innate ability to boost his staffs' (and others') confidence and esteem by empowering them to act on their values and ideas. His subtle and unobtrusive ways made him a natural leader. My father-in-law, Josef Ruland, always taught me to examine decisions in terms of their economic consequences. He always asked me "What's the bottom line?" – a question that doesn't always get its rightful place in decision making when social justice and sustainability are primary considerations. He ensured that I always made its relevance a concern. I am grateful to both of them for their teachings.

These two great men have two great messages for management in the 21ˢᵗ Century how to balance economic prosperity with social justice and environmental quality. As manipulators of resources, managers have a central role to play. My hope is that this text, dedicated to these wise men, will make a contribution to this vital project.

Jane W. Haddad

We'd also like to extend thanks to our team at McGraw-Hill Ryerson for keeping the project on track: **Kim Brewster**, Senior Sponsoring Editor; **Lori McLellan**, Developmental Editor; **Graeme Powell**, Supervising Editor; **Sharon Stefanowicz**, Production Coordinator, and **Erin Moore**, Copy Editor.

In the preparation of this edition, we have benefited greatly from the helpful critiques and suggestions of numerous professors across the country. They helped us identify new topics, as well as clarify information, rearrange and delete material, and suggested examples that students would identify with. Their assistance was invaluable, and we extend our many thanks to

David Delcorde	*University of Ottawa*
Ron Shay	*Kwantlen University College*
Sarah Holding	*Vancouver Island University*
Debra Warren	*Centennial College*
Mark Fletcher	*Georgian College*
Susan Thompson	*Trent University*
Donnalu MacDonald	*George Brown College*
Elisabeth Carter	*Douglas College*
Jeff Young	*Mount Saint Vincent University*
Robin Grant	*Kwantlen Polytechnic University*
Valerie Miceli	*Seneca College of Applied Arts and Technology*
John Brownlee-Baker	*Capilano University*
Debby Cleveland	*British Columbia Institute of Technology*
Jai Goolsarran	*Centennial College*
Kate Muller	*Humber College Institute of Technology & Advanced Learning*

PART 1

Management

1

Managers and Managing

Learning Outcomes

1. Describe what management is, what managers do, what organizations are for, and how managers use the resources of their organizations efficiently to achieve organizational goals.

2. Explain how planning, organizing, leading, and controlling (the four principal managerial functions) differ, and how managers' ability to handle each one can affect an organization's performance.

3. Differentiate among the three levels of management, and understand the responsibilities of managers at different levels in the organizational hierarchy.

4. Identify the skills that managers need and the roles that managers perform effectively.

"It was the best of times, it was the worst of times; it was the age of wisdom, it was the age of foolishness; it was the epoch of belief, it was the epoch of incredulity; it was the season of Light, it was the season of Darkness; it was the spring of hope, it was the winter of despair; we had everything before us, we had nothing before us; we were all going directly to Heaven, we were all going the other way." —**Charles Dickens**, from A Tale of Two Cities[1]

Opposable Thinking

Change changed, as they say. We can safely say that we live and work in a much different world than 10 years ago, even five years ago. Current issues then are not current issues now. In the spring of 2008, the oil crisis has taken the price of gasoline to unheard of levels.[2] While the average person and the corporate world seem to be in angst over this state of affairs, others remind us not to panic.[3] So, on the one hand, anxiety fills the air, but on the other hand, we live in a world with unbelievable opportunities and technologies. Globalization surrounds us and comes at us like a two-edged sword, offering both benefits and often unforeseen problems. Economist David Crane writes, "The biggest issue, though, is that societies have to deal with change."[4] To manage organizations efficiently and effectively, supervisors and managers will have to keep the reality of change, with its various dimensions, in mind. This is especially important in relation to the current economic crisis.

Who would have thought we would be facing a food crisis, according to the United Nations (UN)[5] and the International Monetary Fund (IMF).[6] While in the past we might have agreed that there was still much poverty in the world, but that modern technologies would resolve much of that crisis, today this poverty still exists. It is felt even more intensely, so much so, according to experts, that it creates drama and violence around the world because of the interconnectedness and global networks that structure our world now. We *know* about the different crises now—and instantly! What happens in Jakarta can affect what happens in Canada.[7]

Canada is no longer isolated—if it ever was.[8] The following tongue-in-cheek vignette is a scenario of "what a Canadian is" that has changed the way we see and experience ourselves. Journalist Richard Gwyn, in 2005, adds to this by quipping that a Canadian is "someone who is becoming a Canadian."[9]

> A Canadian is a person wearing English tweeds, a Hong Kong shirt and Spanish shoes; who sips Brazilian coffee sweetened with a Philippine sugar from a Bavarian cup while he/she nibbles on Swiss cheese; who sits at a Danish desk over a Persian rug and he/she comes home in a German car from an Italian movie and who writes to their Member of Parliament with a Japanese ballpoint pen on French paper and demands that the Member do something about foreigners taking away Canadian jobs![10]

Managing today has a different feel and a different tone. It can no longer be about "our" company, "our" people, but managing must embrace the global realities of how our world is today.

In this book, we will be discussing the tried-and-true methods that have stood the test of time for managers, such as the key managerial skills that are still critical in the new workplace. For example, Jeffrey R. Immelt, CEO of General Electric Co., is known as a "GE lifer" and manages 300 000 employees in some 160 nations. Yet, for him, even in an age such as ours, with so much change and challenge, he "has never regarded GE as a colossus but as hundreds of businesses, each accountable for its bottom-line performance and development of new products and services."[11] In addition, you will also be introduced to current "hot topics" as we proceed through the story of managing.

Now It's Your Turn

Roger Martin is Dean of the Rotman School of Management, Toronto, Ontario. In his book *The Opposable Mind*[12] he points out that what we need today in business is "opposable" thinking, not "oppositional" thinking. *Opposable* thinking can be considered as integrative thinking. Traditionally, managers have often taken an "either-or" approach to making decisions: examining the relevant features of a situation, seeing the pros and cons, eliminating the cons until one alternative appears most dominant. Because business demands integrative thinking, managers must develop the "**opposable thinking**" style, more along the lines of a "both-and" approach. Tensions in a situation are acknowledged, but not necessarily dismissed. Otherwise we run the risk of seeing that our "correct way" of doing something is the "right way." Such a simplistic mindset is unacceptable in business today.

opposable thinking
The ability to hold opposing viewpoints and be successful with "both-and" or integrative thinking.

Assignment: Think of a situation that involved you in *"opposable* thinking" versus "oppositional thinking." In other words, you did not make a decision simply on "either-or" premises, but accepted the tension of the situation you were in and were patient with the complexities involved; you were able to think differently from those around you; you saw beyond the tension or the contradictions in the situation; and instead, you saw opportunity.

Overview

The opening case illustrates the new thinking that is required for today's business managers. While holding to the traditional core concepts and best practices, managers today must, above all, *think differently*. Managing a company is a complex undertaking, and managers must possess the many kinds of skills and knowledge needed to be effective. With today's emphasis, not only on threshold skills—often called the "hard skills," such as accounting, finance, marketing, and operations management—managers must also excel in the "soft skills," or the human relations skills. We will be addressing such soft skill demands with the topic of human relations skills in this chapter and also in Chapter 10 on "Managing Teams."[13] Managers are paid to make decisions, and this is not always easy; even effective managers make mistakes. Today's managers have to seriously consider the team aspect as well. However, the most effective managers do succeed because they are able to adapt and adjust to new organizational contexts.

In this chapter we look at what management is, what activities or functions are involved in the management process, the types of managers we find in organizations, and the skills and roles that managers need to perform effectively.

LO 1

What Is Management?

When you think of a manager, what kind of person comes to mind? Do you see someone who can determine the future prosperity of a large for-profit company? Or do you see the administrator of a not-for-profit organization such as a school, library, health care organization, or charity? Or do you think of the person in charge of your local McDonald's restaurant or Wal-Mart store? Or is today's manager primarily responsible for corporate social responsibility, both internally and externally?[14] Three of the "grand taboos" of corporate social responsibility, or CSR, as it is known, are: amoral business, continuous economic growth, and the political nature of CSR.[15] Do you realize that even employees are being asked to assume some managerial functions and that management occurs even in informal groups? In other words, these days almost everyone is called upon to manage, although the scope of that responsibility will vary. What, then, does management mean?

Management takes place in **organizations**, which are collections of people who work together and coordinate their actions to achieve a wide variety of goals.[16] **Management** is the planning, organizing, leading, and controlling of resources to achieve goals effectively and efficiently. **Resources** are assets such as people, machinery, raw materials, information, skills, and financial capital. A **manager** is a person responsible for supervising the use of a group's or organization's resources to achieve its goals.

Achieving High Performance: A Manager's Goal

Organizational performance is a measure of how efficiently and effectively managers use resources to satisfy customers and achieve organizational goals. For instance, when an organization, such as Petro-Canada, makes its principal goal the commitment to corporate social responsibility: "we recognize that our interactions with local communities bring opportunity and risk, as well as the potential for significant social change. We also recognize the potential effects that our operations may have on communities and manage our interactions with stakeholders in a manner that balances our business strategies with the immediate and the long-term livelihood of the community"[17]; the principal goal of doctors, nurses, and hospital administrators is to increase their hospital's ability to make sick people well; the principal goal of each McDonald's restaurant manager is to produce burgers, fries, and shakes that people want to eat and pay for. Organizational performance increases in direct proportion to increases in efficiency and effectiveness (see Figure 1.1).

organizations
Collections of people who work together and coordinate their actions to achieve goals.

management
The planning, organizing, leading, and controlling of resources to achieve organizational goals effectively and efficiently.

resources
Assets such as people, machinery, raw materials, information, skills, and financial capital.

manager
A person who is responsible for supervising the use of an organization's resources to achieve its goals.

organizational performance
A measure of how efficiently and effectively a manager uses resources to satisfy customers and achieve organizational goals.

FIGURE 1.1 | Efficiency, Effectiveness, and Performance in an Organization

EFFICIENCY

	LOW	**HIGH**
HIGH	Low efficiency/ High effectiveness — Manager chooses the right goals to pursue but does a poor job of using resources to achieve these goals. Result: A product that customers want but that is too expensive for them to buy.	High efficiency/ High effectiveness — Manager chooses the right goals to pursue and makes good use of resources to achieve these goals. Result: A product that customers want at a quality and price that they can afford.
LOW	Low efficiency/ Low effectiveness — Manager chooses wrong goals to pursue and makes poor use of resources. Result: A low-quality product that customers do not want.	High efficiency/ Low effectiveness — Manager chooses inappropriate goals but makes good use of resources to pursue these goals. Result: A high-quality product that customers do not want.

EFFECTIVENESS

High-performing organizations are efficient *and* effective.

efficiency
A measure of how well or productively resources are used to achieve a goal.

Efficiency is a measure of how well or how productively resources are used to achieve a goal.[18] Organizations are efficient when managers minimize the amount of input resources (such as labour, raw materials, and component parts) or the amount of time needed to produce a given output of goods or services. For example, McDonald's developed a more efficient fat fryer that not only reduces (by 30 percent) the amount of oil used in cooking but also speeds up the cooking of french fries. A manager's responsibility is to ensure that an organization and its members perform, as efficiently as possible, all the activities that are needed to provide goods and services to customers.

effectiveness
A measure of the appropriateness of the goals an organization is pursuing and of the degree to which the organization achieves those goals.

Effectiveness is a measure of the appropriateness of the goals that managers have selected for the organization to pursue and of the degree to which the organization achieves those goals. Management expert Peter Drucker compared the two this way: Efficiency is doing things right; effectiveness is doing the right thing.[19] Organizations are effective when managers choose appropriate goals and then achieve them. Some years ago, for example, managers at McDonald's decided on the goal of providing breakfast service to attract more customers. This goal was a smart choice because sales of breakfast food now account for more than 30 percent of McDonald's revenues. High-performing organizations such as Campbell Soup, McDonald's, Wal-Mart, Intel, Home Depot, IKEA, and the March of Dimes are simultaneously efficient and effective, as shown in Figure 1.1.

Managers who are effective are those who choose the right organizational goals to pursue and have the skills to use resources efficiently. Consider, for example, the way that Ed Clark, CEO of TD Bank, is admired for his management excellence as well as the transparency of his actions.

LO 2

Managerial Functions

THINK ABOUT IT

The Colour of Money Is Increasingly Pink[20]

Today diversity is not just a concept, it is a reality.[21] Business is no exception to this reality. One of the key managerial shifts for some of Canada's biggest banks is the fact that money "is increasingly pink." It is estimated that gay, lesbian, bisexual, and transgendered clients represent a market worth at least $75 billion across the country.[22]

Obviously, banks will be managing their businesses in such a way as to obtain a bigger share of this market. The BMO branch in Toronto's gay district in the summer of 2008 was the first in Ontario to operate seven days a week. Says BMO's vice-president Lily Capriotti, "Clearly when we look at the demographics of this group—they have higher education, higher income levels with more disposable income—we think that is an attractive market for us. In addition, we know that they are heavily involved in philanthropic activities and giving, which, again, aligns with our corporate strategy at the bank." TD bank is also paying attention to its gay and lesbian initiatives and has been doing so since 2004. In speaking to shareholders in 2007, Ed Clark, TD's Harvard-trained president and CEO with a Ph.D., spoke candidly about ensuring that gay and lesbian customers have a "comfortable experience" at TD: "We want to be a place where employees and customers alike feel comfortable and supported in all their diversity—whether they are men, women, people with disabilities, gays, lesbians, or visible minorities."

You Be the Manager

1. It was stated above: "One of the key managerial shifts for some of Canada's biggest banks is the fact that money 'is increasingly pink'." Why would such a shift be important for managers?

The job of management is to help an organization make the best use of its resources to achieve its goals. How do managers accomplish this objective? They do so by performing four essential managerial functions: planning, organizing, leading, and controlling (see Figure 1.2). Henri Fayol first outlined the nature of these managerial activities around the start of the twentieth century in *General and Industrial Management*, a book that remains the classic statement of what managers must do to create a high-performing organization.[23]

Henri Fayol www.lib.uwo.ca/business/fayol.html

Managers at all levels and in all departments—whether in small or large organizations, for-profit or not-for-profit organizations, or organizations that operate in one country or throughout the world—are responsible for performing these four functions, and we will look at each in turn. How well managers perform them determines how efficient and effective their organization is. Individuals who are not managers can also be involved in planning, organizing, leading, and controlling, so understanding these processes is important for everyone.

Planning

Planning is a process used to identify and select appropriate goals and courses of action. There are three steps in the planning process: (1) deciding which goals the

planning
Identifying and selecting appropriate goals and courses of action; one of the four principal functions of management.

FIGURE 1.2 | Four Functions of Management

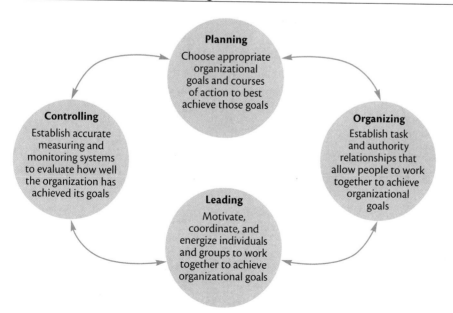

organization will pursue, (2) deciding what courses of action to adopt to attain those goals, and (3) deciding how to allocate organizational resources to attain the goals. How well managers plan determines how effective and efficient their organization is—its performance level.[24] For managers who work for Ed Clark, they know, by observing the way he manages, that preparedness, planning, and candidness are critical in their dealings and management of the bank.

The outcome of planning is a **strategy**, a cluster of decisions concerning what organizational goals to pursue, what actions to take, and how to use resources to achieve goals. For instance, WestJet's strategy is to be a low-cost provider in the Canadian discount airline market. Planning is a difficult activity because, normally, it is not immediately clear which goals an organization should pursue or how best to pursue them. Choosing the right strategy is risky because managers commit organizational resources for activities that could either succeed or fail. The failure of many of the dotcoms is attributable to managers trying to make money quickly, without business plans or a long-term vision. In Chapter 5, we focus on the planning process and on the strategies organizations can select to respond to opportunities or threats.

Organizing

Organizing is a process used to structure workplace relationships in a way that allows members of an organization to work together to achieve organizational goals. Organizing involves grouping people into departments according to the kinds of job-specific tasks they perform. In organizing, managers also lay out the lines of authority and responsibility between different individuals and groups, and they decide how best to coordinate organizational resources, in particular, human resources. When Ed Clark worked in the private sector in Ottawa in the mid-1970s before eventually landing the top job at what is now TD Canada Trust, he realized that he needed a very different set of organizing skills. Says Clark, "Can you imagine running a large organization where you can't fire, you can't hire, and you can't reward people, and yet you have to motivate them to work extraordinarily long hours?"

The outcome of organizing is the creation of an **organizational structure**, a formal system of task and reporting relationships that coordinates and motivates organizational members so that they work together to achieve organizational goals. Organizational structure determines how an organization's resources can best be used to create goods and services.

We examine the organizing process in Chapters 6 and 7. In Chapter 6, we consider the organizational structures that managers can use to coordinate and motivate people and utilize other resources. In Chapter 7, we look at the important roles that an organization's culture, values, and norms play in binding people and departments together so that they work toward organizational goals.

Leading

In **leading**, managers articulate a clear vision and make sure that organizational members understand their individual roles in achieving organizational goals. Leadership depends on the use of power, influence, vision, persuasion, and communication skills for two important tasks: to coordinate the behaviours of individuals and groups so that their activities and efforts are in harmony and to encourage employees to perform at a high level. The outcome of good leadership is a high level of motivation and commitment among organizational members. Before becoming CEO of Toronto-Dominion

strategy
A cluster of decisions about what goals to pursue, what actions to take, and how to use resources to achieve goals.

organizing
Structuring workplace relationships in a way that allows members of an organization to work together to achieve organizational goals; one of the four principal functions of management.

organizational structure
A formal system of task and reporting relationships that coordinates and motivates organizational members so that they work together to achieve organizational goals.

leading
Articulating a clear vision and energizing and empowering organizational members so that everyone understands his or her individual role in achieving organizational goals; one of the four principal functions of management.

Bank, Ed Clark took the job as CEO of Financial Trustco, a struggling conglomerate run by the flamboyant (and now deceased) entrepreneur Gerry Pencer. Although Financial Trustco was widely viewed as a mess, and a career-wrecker in the making, Clark's ability to lead a turnaround made the difference. Previously, in Ottawa, he had earned a reputation "as a consensus-builder, and relied on both that experience and his connections to bring regulators to the bargaining table and buy enough time to unwind Financial Trustco methodically. At the same time, he struck deft agreements with lenders and managed to sell off scattered bits of the company's holdings." He was successful in leading that risky and challenging work.

We discuss the issues involved in managing and leading individuals and groups in Chapters 8 through 12. In Chapters 8 and 9, we examine the best ways to encourage high motivation and commitment among employees. In Chapter 10, we look at the way groups and teams achieve organizational goals, and the coordination problems that can arise when people work together in groups and teams. In Chapter 11, we consider how to manage employees through human resource practices. In Chapter 12, we consider how communication and coordination problems can arise between people and functions, and how managers can try to manage these problems through bargaining and negotiation. Understanding how to manage and lead effectively is an important skill. You might be interested to know that CEOs have just a few short months to prove to investors that they are able to communicate a vision and carry it out. Recent studies suggest that investors and analysts give CEOs only 14 to 18 months to show results.[25]

Controlling

In **controlling**, managers evaluate how well an organization is achieving its goals and take action to maintain or improve performance. For example, managers monitor the performance of individuals, departments, and the organization as a whole to see whether they are all meeting desired performance standards. If standards are not being met, managers take action to improve performance. Individuals working in groups also have the responsibility of controlling because they have to make sure the group achieves its goals and completes its actions. For Ed Clark of TD Canada Trust, controlling involves working closely with his senior managers; he also has very little patience for poor results.

The outcome of the control process is the ability to measure performance accurately and regulate organizational efficiency and effectiveness. In order to exercise control, managers must decide which goals to measure—perhaps goals pertaining to productivity, quality, or responsiveness to customers—and then they must design information and control systems that will provide the data they need to assess performance. These mechanisms provide feedback to managers, and managers provide feedback to employees. The controlling function also allows managers to evaluate how well they themselves are performing the other three functions of management—planning, organizing, and leading—and to take corrective action.

We cover the most important aspects of the control function in Chapter 13, where we outline the basic process of control and examine some control systems that managers can use to monitor and measure organizational performance.

The four managerial functions—planning, organizing, leading, and controlling—are essential to a manager's job. At all levels in a managerial hierarchy, and across all departments in an organization, effective management means making decisions and managing these four activities successfully.

controlling
Evaluating how well an organization is achieving its goals and taking action to maintain or improve performance; one of the four principal functions of management.

Types of Managers[26]

Isabelle Marcoux, Vice-Chair of Transcontinental Inc.

Isabelle Marcoux, is vice-chair of Transcontinental Inc., the Montreal-based printing giant founded and controlled by her father Remi Marcoux.

You carry a heavy load?

I'm lucky that I don't need much sleep. I sleep from 11 to 5, I wake up real early, and the morning is 'my time.' I read the papers, and I run most mornings. I make a point of having breakfast with my kids, who are 10 and 7, although it doesn't always work. I'm at the office by 7:30, and it's a 12-hour shift.

Is it hard being a young female executive in such tough businesses?

I think it is tough being a young mother. I wouldn't say it is tough being a woman because it's what you say more than how you look. You gain respect by your ideas, the amount of work you put in.

So you've had no problems being a woman in this industry?

It is more challenging being the daughter of Remi Marcoux because you are kept to higher standards, higher scrutiny, more pressure. I felt that especially in my first few years at Transcontinental, but now less and less. I think I have delivered. I've met expectations and often surpassed them.

Though everybody knows the reason you are rising?

Yes, but the stages are important and the key is to deliver at each stage. People see you work hard and that also earns respect. I work at least 60 hours a week, and it becomes your life. It's the business and it's family and not much else.

Can you be an effective mother to your young children?

It's an everyday challenge. I try to have breakfast and dinner with them, but last week I had no breakfast with them and two dinners. I don't strive for perfection. Some days you lose, some days you win.

Don't you worry that you will regret you weren't around enough?

All the time. But I have a great help at home, with the same person caring for my kids for the last 10 years. My mother helps a lot, and my husband's mother helps a lot. I'm a BlackBerry addict, which helps working from home.

Who are the most important influences on your career?

Some of our board members have been mentors. Obviously Remi has been a real role model, with his respect for people, integrity, and high standards. And he's a true entrepreneur. I'm more analytical, and he has taught me to take risks.

Will he step back at some point?

He was CEO, and he is now executive chairman. He no longer spends five days a week at the office; it is more like three days, but his influence is still great. So I think when the time is right he will leave his chair. But his heart will be in the business until he dies.

Your younger brother Pierre runs business publications. Isn't he below you in the hierarchy?

We don't think in terms of hierarchy. We are working to build and sustain a great company, which has to adapt to many challenges. We are both doing that in our own spheres, in our own ways. Four family members work as managers in the company, and we complement each other. There is also Patrice [Lacoste], my brother-in-law, and my husband, François [Olivier], who runs the printing business.

I understand this is your first major media interview?

At Transcontinental, we try to do as little of that as possible. I think it is a family tradition. We're humble people. We release our results when we have to—we are transparent—but we're less inclined to talk about ourselves.

What part of the job do you love most?

Acquisitions. I love meeting new people, hearing their stories, understanding their passion, how they've grown their companies. I love figuring out how to continue growing those companies. I negotiate most of our acquisitions. I'm reported to be very tough. Some say "as tough as your father"; others say tougher.

Are you a Type-A personality?

A-plus. Most people in business have a similar character. I just wish there would be a better balance for young mothers, but the reality is I'm not sure you can do that.

You Be the Manager

1. What stands out for you in terms of Isabelle Marcoux's approach to being a manager?

Managers tend to be categorized in terms of their level in the hierarchy, their positions, and their functional (departmental) responsibilities. Top management teams include senior executives. The typical positions found at this level include president, senior vice-president, and vice-president. Functional titles include senior vice-president of marketing, or chief financial officer (CFO).

Middle managers report to top managers and generally hold positions such as director or manager. Functional titles might include operations manager, human resources (HR) manager, sales manager, and finance manager.

First-line managers are accountable to middle managers and supervise non-managerial employees in positions such as supervisor and assistant manager. Functional area titles might include assistant sales manager and assistant operations manager. Each function or **department** is composed of people who work together and possess similar skills or use the same kind of knowledge, tools, or techniques to perform their jobs. As Figure 1.3 indicates, first-line, middle, and top managers, who differ from one another by virtue of their job-specific responsibilities, are found in each of an organization's major departments. Below, we examine why organizations use a hierarchy of managers and group them into departments. We then examine some recent changes that have been taking place in managerial hierarchies.

department
A group of people who work together and possess similar skills or use the same knowledge, tools, or techniques to perform their jobs.

Levels of Management

First-Line Managers

At the base of the managerial hierarchy are **first-line managers** (often called supervisors). They are responsible for the daily supervision and coordination of the nonmanagerial

first-line managers
Managers who are responsible for the daily supervision and coordination of nonmanagerial employees.

■ **FIGURE 1.3** │ **Management Hierarchy**

An entrepreneur founds an organization, takes the role of chief executive officer (CEO), and begins the management task of organizing.

Top managers are hired and together with the CEO become responsible for planning, identifying, and selecting appropriate goals and courses of action.

Middle managers are hired and become responsible for the effective management of organizational resources, including supporting first-line managers.

First-line managers are hired and take on the day-to-day task of leading and controlling nonmanagerial personnel and other resources.

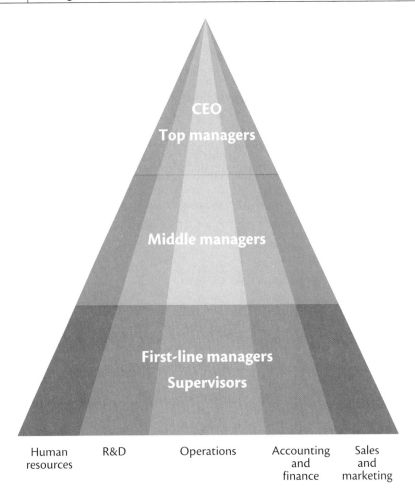

At the same time that the organization is dividing vertically into hierarchical levels, it also divides horizontally into departments: groups of people who work together and possess similar skills or use the same knowledge, tools, or techniques to perform their jobs. Managers and employees become members of a particular department, such as manufacturing, marketing, or research and development.

The final result of this division vertically and horizontally is an organizational structure.

employees who perform many of the specific activities necessary to produce goods and services. First-line managers may be found in all departments of an organization.

Examples of first-line managers include the supervisor of a work team in the manufacturing department of a car plant, the head nurse in the obstetrics department of a hospital, and the chief mechanic overseeing a crew of mechanics in the service department of a new-car dealership.

Middle Managers

Middle managers supervise the first-line managers and have the responsibility of finding the best way to organize human and other resources to achieve organizational goals. To increase efficiency, middle managers try to find ways to help first-line managers and nonmanagerial employees make better use of resources in order to reduce manufacturing costs or improve the way services are provided to customers. To increase effectiveness, middle managers are responsible for evaluating whether the goals that the organization is pursuing are appropriate and for suggesting to top managers ways in which goals should be changed. A major part of the middle manager's job is to develop and fine-tune skills and know-how—manufacturing or marketing expertise, for example—that enable the organization to be efficient and effective. Middle managers also coordinate resources across departments and divisions. Middle managers make the thousands of specific decisions that go into the production of goods and services: Which first-line supervisors should be chosen for this particular project? Where can we find the highest quality resources? How should employees be organized to enable them to make the best use of resources?

Middle managers perform an important role in organizations. For instance, behind a first-class sales force, look for the sales manager responsible for training, motivating, and rewarding salespeople. Behind a committed staff of secondary school teachers, look for the principal who energizes them to look for ways to obtain the resources they need to do an outstanding and innovative job in the classroom.

middle managers
Managers who supervise first-line managers and are responsible for finding the best way to use resources to achieve organizational goals.

Top Managers

In contrast to middle managers, **top managers** are responsible for the performance of all departments.[27] They have cross-departmental responsibilities and they are responsible for connecting the parts of the organization together. Top managers help carry out the organizational vision; they establish organizational goals, such as which goods and services the company should produce; they decide how the different departments should interact; and they monitor how well middle managers in each department use resources to achieve goals.[28] Top managers are ultimately responsible for the success or failure of an organization, and their performance is continually scrutinized by people inside and outside the organization, such as employees and investors.[29]

top managers
Managers who establish organizational goals, decide how departments should interact, and monitor the performance of middle managers.

Top managers report to a company's chief executive officer—for example, WestJet CEO Sean Durfy, who became WestJet's president in September 2006 and added chief executive officer to his title in September 2007. As president and CEO, Durfy is responsible for both the strategic direction of the company and the day-to-day operations of the airline, leading its over 6000 people as they deliver exceptional guest experiences. Other examples are Shaw Communications CEO Jim Shaw, and Quebecor CEO Pierre Karl Péladeau. Or they report to the president of the organization, who is second-in-command. In some organizations, one person holds the title of both CEO and president, such as Lee McDonald at Southmedic and Paul Godfrey at the Toronto Blue Jays. The CEO and president are responsible for developing good working relationships among the top managers who head the various departments (manufacturing and marketing, for example) and who usually have the title vice-president. A central concern of the CEO is the creation of a smoothly functioning

Ray Reiss Photography
Erica Van Kamp, senior product manager at Mattel Canada, rose to her position after starting out as a marketing brand manager at Good Humor-Breyers in 1997.

top-management team
A group composed of the CEO, the president, and the heads of the most important departments.

top-management team, a group composed of the CEO, the president, and the department heads most responsible for helping to achieve organizational goals.[30] The CEO also has the responsibility of setting the vision for the organization.

The relative importance of each of the four managerial functions—planning, organizing, leading, and controlling—to any particular manager depends on the manager's position in the managerial hierarchy.[31] As managers move up the hierarchy, they spend more time planning and organizing resources to maintain and improve organizational performance (see Figure 1.4). Top managers devote most of their time to planning and organizing, the functions that are so crucial to determining an organization's long-term performance. The lower a manager's position in the hierarchy, the more time he or she spends leading and controlling first-line managers or nonmanagerial employees.

FIGURE 1.4 | **Relative Amount of Time That Managers Spend on the Four Managerial Functions**

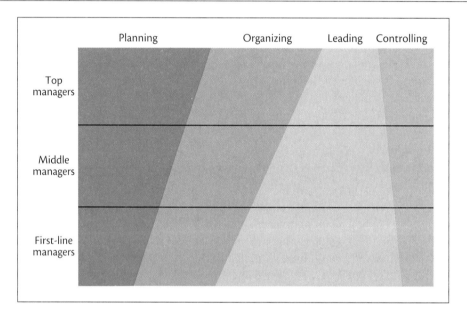

Recent Changes in Managerial Hierarchies

The tasks and responsibilities of managers at different levels have been changing dramatically in recent years. Increasingly, top managers are encouraging lower-level managers to look beyond the goals of their own departments and take a cross-departmental view to find new opportunities to improve organizational performance. Stiff competition for resources—both at home and abroad—has put increased pressure on all managers to improve efficiency, effectiveness, and organizational performance. To respond to these pressures, many organizations have been changing the managerial hierarchy to a flatter, more decentralized structure with fewer levels of management through **restructuring**.[32] Moreover, many organizations have taken two related steps to reduce costs and improve quality. One is the **empowerment** of the workforce, expanding employee's tasks and responsibilities so that they have more authority and accountability. At the Canadian construction company, EllisDon, a new technology platform called Edgebuilder has given the company the confidence to grant greater responsibilities to young employees that they may not have been given otherwise.

restructuring
Downsizing an organization by eliminating the jobs of large numbers of top, middle, and first-line managers and nonmanagerial employees.

empowerment
Expanding employees' tasks and responsibilities.

THINK ABOUT IT

Team Players and Scotiabank[33]

Does your boss encourage you to use his office when he is not there? Brian Toda, vice-president of human resources for Scotiabank's compensation group, does. He "invites his employees to use his office when he's not there. They take turns making conference calls from his comfortable black leather chair or holding small meetings at a round table." Sharing office space reflects Scotiabank's team-oriented culture. Roles have certainly changed! Toda explains, "It's not like employees are coming into my space. It's their space, too." He wants to "deliver the best employment experience."

You Be the Manager

1. What is your experience in sharing office space?
2. As a manager, could you easily shift to the role that Toda works from?

To paraphrase the top management, it is much easier to decide to give someone authority for a project more complex than one they have ever handled when you have IT systems providing management with a transparent overview of how a job is progressing.[34] The other step is the creation of **self-managed teams,** which are groups of employees who are given responsibility for supervising their own activities and for monitoring the quality of the goods and services they provide. At WestJet, former CEO Clive Beddoe created an empowered self-managed workforce. He believes that his "management from the bottom" gives employees pride in fulfilling the company's overall objectives without interference from supervisors. "They are the ones making the decisions about what they're doing and how they're doing it," says Beddoe. Managerial hierarchies are changing.

self-managed teams
Groups of employees who supervise their own activities and monitor the quality of the goods and services they provide.

Tips for Managers

MANAGING RESOURCES

1. Develop a list of skills that you need to develop now to become not just a good manager but a great one.[35]
2. Make a list of the "hard skills" you still need to develop.
3. Make a list of the "soft skills" you still need to develop.
4. Identify the different levels of managers in an organization you know. Describe why the organization looks as it does.

LO4

Managerial Skills and Roles

Managerial Skills

To successfully perform their roles, managers must have certain skills. Research has shown that formal education, training, and experience help managers acquire three principal types of skills: *conceptual*, *human*, and *technical*.[36] As you might expect, the level of these skills that a manager needs depends on his or her level in the managerial hierarchy (see Figure 1.5).

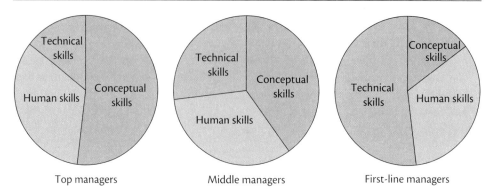

FIGURE 1.5 | Conceptual, Human, and Technical Skills Needed by Three Levels of Management

Top managers   Middle managers   First-line managers

Conceptual Skills

conceptual skills
The ability to analyze and diagnose a situation and to distinguish between cause and effect.

Conceptual skills are demonstrated by the ability to analyze and diagnose a situation and to distinguish between cause and effect. Planning and organizing require a high level of conceptual skill, as does performing the managerial roles discussed above. Top managers require the best conceptual skills because their primary responsibilities are planning and organizing.[37] Conceptual skills allow managers to understand the big picture confronting an organization. The ability to focus on the big picture lets the manager see beyond the situation immediately at hand and consider choices while keeping the organization's long-term goals in mind.

Human Skills

human skills
The ability to understand, alter, lead, and control the behaviour of other individuals and groups.

Human skills include the ability to understand, alter, lead, and control the behaviour of other individuals and groups. The ability to communicate and give feedback, to coordinate and motivate people, to give recognition, to mould individuals into a cohesive team, and to play politics effectively distinguishes effective managers from ineffective managers.

To manage interpersonal interactions effectively, each person in an organization needs to learn how to empathize with other people—to understand their viewpoints and the problems they face. One way to help managers understand their personal strengths and weaknesses is to have their superiors, peers, and subordinates provide feedback about their performance. Managers also need to be able to manage politics effectively so that they can deal with resistance from those who disagree with their goals. Effective managers use political strategies to influence others and gain support for their goals, while overcoming resistance or opposition.

Technical Skills

technical skills
Job-specific knowledge and techniques that are required to perform an organizational role.

Technical skills are the job-specific knowledge and techniques that are required to perform an organizational role. Examples include a manager's specific manufacturing, accounting, or marketing skills. Managers need a range of technical skills to be effective. The array of technical skills a person needs depends on his or her position in the organization. The manager of a restaurant, for example, may need cooking skills to fill in for an absent cook, accounting and bookkeeping skills to keep track of receipts and costs and to administer the payroll, and aesthetic skills to keep the restaurant looking attractive for customers.

Effective managers need all three kinds of skills—conceptual, human, and technical. The absence of even one type can lead to failure. Michael Kavanagh, human resources director for Vancouver-based Crystal Decisions, highlights this point. He

Crystal Decisions
www.crystaldecisons.com

says that at Crystal, a large computer software company, "we place a lot of emphasis on behavioural [human] skills. It's the difference between who gets hired and who doesn't. Your technical skills get you in the door, but your behavioural skills are increasingly the criteria in enhancing your employment opportunities." Management skills, roles, and functions are closely related, and wise managers or prospective managers are constantly in search of the latest educational contributions to help them develop the conceptual, human, and technical skills they need to function in today's changing and increasingly competitive environment.

THINK ABOUT IT

Does an MBA "Cut It"?[38]

If the answer were left up to world-renowned Professor Henry Mintzberg, McGill University management professor, it would be a resounding "No"! Newly minted MBAs—about one million each year!—are simply not ready to assume the role of manager coming out of school. Mintzberg says that they should have a skull-and-crossbones symbol stamped firmly on their foreheads, and the words, "Warning: NOT prepared to manage!"

For Mintzberg, a person filling the role of manager needs to be a seasoned individual, not a typical young MBA who has little experience in managing others. In addition, these graduates tend to be too impatient and too analytical and have too great a need to control to be successful managers. Being skilled in the "hard sciences" of marketing and finance and analysis, for example, often leads to arrogance, an analytical predisposition, and a lack of managerial sensitivity that further advances them to become "calculating" executives. According to Mintzberg, what business needs are "heroic" managers, ones who are skilled in roles that demand solid results, not theatrics, like bold actions and drama, as so many managers exhibit. "Their general lack of success," he says, "is exemplified by the fact that 10 of the 19 superstar MBA graduates listed in one prominent book on the Harvard Business School failed in their jobs, and another four had highly questionable results. Top U.S. business leaders like Bill Gates, Jack Welch, and Warren Buffett don't have MBAs."

You Be the Manager

1. What kinds of roles do seasoned manager play?
2. When you review Mintzberg's managerial roles (below), with which one(s) are you most familiar and comfortable?

Though we might like to think that a manager's job is highly structured and that management is a logical, orderly process in which managers try hard to make rational decisions, being a manager often involves acting emotionally and relying on gut feelings. Quick, immediate reactions to situations rather than deliberate thought and reflection are an important aspect of managerial action.[39] Often, managers are overloaded with responsibilities, do not have time to analyze every nuance of a situation, and therefore make decisions in uncertain conditions without being sure which outcomes will be best.[40] Moreover, for top managers in particular, the current situation is constantly changing, and a decision that seems right today may prove to be wrong tomorrow.

Despite all this flux, however, it is important to note that the roles managers need to play and the skills they need to use have changed little since the early 1970s, when

Henry Mintzberg
www.henrymintzberg.com

McGill University Professor Henry Mintzberg detailed 10 specific roles that effective managers undertake. A **role** is a set of specific tasks that a person is expected to perform because of the position he or she holds in an organization. Although the roles that Mintzberg described overlap with Fayol's model, they are useful because they focus on what managers do in a typical hour, day, or week.[41] Below, we discuss these roles.

Managerial Roles Identified by Mintzberg

Mintzberg examined all the specific tasks that managers need to perform as they plan, organize, lead, and control organizational resources, and he reduced them to 10 roles.[42] Managers assume each of these roles in order to influence the behaviour of individuals and groups inside and outside the organization. People inside the organization include other managers and employees. People outside the organization include shareholders, customers, suppliers, the local community in which an organization is located, and any local or government agency that has an interest in the organization and what it does.[43] Mintzberg grouped the 10 roles into three broad categories: *interpersonal, informational*, and *decisional* (see Table 1.1). Managers often perform several of these roles simultaneously.

TABLE 1.1 | *Managerial Roles Identified by Mintzberg*

Type of Role	Specific Role	Examples of Role Activities
INTERPERSONAL	Figurehead	Outline future organizational goals to employees at company meetings; open a new corporate headquarters building; state the organization's ethical guidelines and the principles of behaviour employees are to follow in their dealings with customers and suppliers.
	Leader	Provide an example for employees to follow; give direct commands and orders to subordinates; make decisions concerning the use of human and technical resources; mobilize employee support for specific organizational goals.
	Liaison	Coordinate the work of managers in different departments; establish alliances between different organizations to share resources to produce new goods and services.
INFORMATIONAL	Monitor	Evaluate the performance of managers in different functions and take corrective action to improve their performance; watch for changes occurring in the external and internal environment that may affect the organization in the future.
	Disseminator	Inform employees about changes taking place in the external and internal environment that will affect them and the organization; communicate to employees the organization's vision and purpose.
	Spokesperson	Launch a national advertising campaign to promote new goods and services; give a speech to inform the local community about the organization's future intentions.
DECISIONAL	Entrepreneur	Commit organizational resources to develop innovative goods and services; decide to expand internationally to obtain new customers for the organization's products.
	Disturbance handler	Move quickly to take corrective action to deal with unexpected problems facing the organization from the external environment, (e.g., a crisis such as an oil spill), or from the internal environment, (e.g., producing faulty goods or services).
	Resource allocator	Allocate organizational resources among different functions and departments of the organization; set budgets and salaries of middle and first-level managers.
	Negotiator	Work with suppliers, distributors, and labour unions to reach agreements about the quality and price of input, technical, and human resources; work with other organizations to establish agreements to pool resources to work on joint projects.

Interpersonal Roles

Managers assume interpersonal roles in order to coordinate and interact with organizational members and provide direction and supervision to employees and to the organization as a whole. A manager's first interpersonal role is to act as a ***figurehead***—the person who symbolizes an organization or a department. Assuming the figurehead role, the chief executive officer determines the direction or mission of the organization and informs employees and other interested parties about what the organization is seeking to achieve. Managers at all levels act as figureheads and role models who establish the appropriate and inappropriate ways to behave in the organization.

A manager's role as a ***leader*** is to encourage subordinates to perform at a high level and to take steps to train, counsel, and mentor subordinates to help them reach their full potential. A manager's power to lead comes both from formal authority, due to his or her position in the organization's hierarchy, and from his or her personal qualities, including reputation, skills, and personality. The personal behaviour of a leader affects employee attitudes and behaviour; indeed, subordinates' desire to perform at a high level—and even whether they desire to arrive at work on time and not be absent often—depends on how satisfied they are with working for the organization.

In performing as a ***liaison***, managers link and coordinate the activities of people and groups both inside and outside the organization. Inside the organization, managers are responsible for coordinating the activities of people in different departments to improve their ability to cooperate. Outside the organization, managers are responsible for forming linkages with suppliers, customers, or the organization's local community in order to obtain scarce resources. People outside an organization often come to equate the organization with the manager they are dealing with, or with the person they see on television or read about in the newspaper.

Business Plan Checklist

- Determine the roles and responsibilities of your management team.
- What skills and experience makes them suitable for the position?
- Decide what type of legal entity or ownership structure is appropriate for your venture: partnership, cooperative, or corporation.
- What are the main risks facing your venture with respect to the above, and how will you minimize them?
- Use this information for section 3 of the business plan, Profile of the Organization in Appendix A.

Informational Roles

Informational roles are closely associated with the tasks necessary to obtain and transmit information. First, a manager acts as a ***monitor*** and analyzes information from inside and outside the organization. With this information, a manager can effectively organize and control people and other resources.

Acting as a ***disseminator***, the manager transmits information to other members of the organization to influence their work attitudes and behaviour. In the role of *spokesperson*, a manager uses information to promote the organization so that people both inside and outside the organization respond positively.

Decisional Roles

Decisional roles are closely associated with the methods that managers use to plan strategy and utilize resources. In the role of *entrepreneur*, a manager must decide which projects or programs to initiate and how to invest resources to increase organizational performance. As a *disturbance handler*, a manager assumes responsibility for handling an unexpected event or crisis that threatens the organization's access to resources. In this situation, a manager must also assume the roles of figurehead and leader to rally employees so that they can help secure the resources needed to avert the problem.

Under typical conditions, *resource allocator* is one of the important roles a manager plays—deciding how best to use people and other resources to increase organizational performance. While engaged as a resource allocator, the manager must also be a *negotiator*, reaching agreements with other managers or groups claiming the first right to resources, with the organization, and with outside groups such as shareholders or customers. Isabelle Marcoux illustrates this role when she acquires new companies.

Tips for Managers
TASKS AND ROLES

1. Think of a manager you know. Estimate what percentage of his or her day is devoted to each of the four tasks just outlined: planning, reorganizing, leading, and controlling. Decide if the balance of these four is appropriate.

2. From your experience, make a list of Mintzberg's roles that managers perform the best.

3. From your experience, make a list of Mintzberg's roles that managers perform the worst.

4. Assume that you are in charge of management education at your local college, identify the necessary steps for managers to have the correct levels of conceptual, technical, and human skills.

Summary and Review

1. **WHAT IS MANAGE MENT?** A manager is a person responsible for supervising the use of an organization's resources to meet its goals. An organization is a collection of people who work together and coordinate their actions to achieve a wide variety of goals. Management is the process of using organizational resources to achieve organizational goals effectively and efficiently through planning, organizing, leading, and controlling. An efficient organization makes the most productive use of its resources. An effective organization pursues appropriate goals and achieves these goals by using its resources to create the goods or services that customers want.

2. **MANAGERIAL FUNCTIONS** According to Fayol, the four principal managerial functions are planning, organizing, leading, and controlling. Managers at all levels of the organization and in all departments perform these functions. Effective management means managing these activities successfully.

3. **TYPES OF MANAGERS** Managers are characterized by level and function. Functions typically include marketing, operations, human resources, accounting and finance, and research and development. Organizations typically have three levels of management. First-line managers are responsible for the day-to-day supervision of nonmanagerial employees. Middle managers are responsible for developing and utilizing organizational resources efficiently and effectively. Top managers have cross-departmental responsibilities. The top managers' job is to establish appropriate goals for the entire organization and to verify that department managers are using resources to achieve those goals. To increase efficiency and effectiveness, some organizations have altered their managerial hierarchies by restructuring, by empowering their workforces, and by using self-managed teams.

4. **RECENT CHANGES IN MANAGERIAL HIERARCHIES** Managers' tasks and responsibilities have been changing dramatically in recent years. Organizations have become flatter, and large numbers of top, middle, and first-line managers have been cut, increasing the managerial responsibilities of those remaining. Some organizations are empowering more employees at all levels, giving them more authority and accountability. Organizations have also introduced self-managed teams, which are responsible for supervising their own activities.

5. **MANAGERIAL SKILLS AND ROLES** Three types of skills help managers perform these roles effectively: conceptual, human, and technical skills. According to Mintzberg, managers play 10 different roles: figurehead, leader, liaison, monitor, disseminator, spokesperson, entrepreneur, disturbance handler, resource allocator, and negotiator.

Key Terms

conceptual skills, p. 16

controlling, p. 9

department, p. 11

effectiveness, p. 6

efficiency, p. 6

empowerment, p. 14

first-line managers, p. 11

human skills, p. 16

leading, p. 8

management, p. 5

manager, p. 5

middle managers, p. 13

opposable thinking, p. 4

organizational performance, p. 5

organizational structure, p. 8

organizations, p. 5

organizing, p. 8

planning, p. 7

resources, p. 5

restructuring, p. 14

role, p. 18

self-managed teams, p. 15

strategy, p. 8

technical skills, p. 16

top-management team, p. 14

top managers, p. 13

Wrap-Up to Opening Case

This is an excellent exercise for you to start "thinking out of the traditional oppositional box." Today, in business, innovation is key; and innovation rests on creativity and seeing where opportunity lies with others seeing only a "this-or-that" solution to a problem. Martin writes, "Human beings ... are distinguished from nearly every other creature by a physical feature known as the opposable thumb. Thanks to the tension we can create by opposing the thumb and the fingers, we can do marvelous things that no other creature can do—write, thread a needle, carve a diamond ... All those actions would be impossible without the crucial tension between the thumb and fingers." Just before this, Martin writes that the leaders he has studied "share at least one trait, aside from their talent for innovation and long-term business success. They have the predisposition and the capacity to hold two diametrically opposing ideas in their heads. And then, without panicking or simply settling for one alternative or the other, they're able to produce a synthesis that is superior to either opposing idea."[44]

The website "Information, Libraries and Provocative Ideas,"[45] has a librarian writing about a breakthrough idea:

> ... let me map that [opposable thinking] back into the library context and onto a conversation I had with my colleague Brian Shepard the other day at lunch at Jimmy John's. We were talking about overdue fines. We know overdue fines are patrons'/users' #1 irritant related to using libraries, yet many libraries (especially public libraries, including my own) still charge them. Here's the evolution of the discussion:

- We could get rid of fines and go to some kind of system where users would not be allowed to take out additional items if they had an item overdue. That would please a lot of people, but there are still many others who don't mind paying a small fraction of one dollar if it allows them to keep their items a few days longer and checkout a few additional items. Which system to go with—what to do?

- Opposable mind breakthrough: Why don't we allow patrons to choose which system they want to participate in?

Most ILS systems should allow any library to create different patron categories that treat different sets of patrons in different ways. We could let some people do away with fines in favour of some other system, and we could let others choose to pay fines (or "extended use charges") to keep the items a little bit longer. And we could let them switch back and forth as often as they would like.

Question

1. How did your "opposable thinking" in the situation you described create a breakthrough for a new or superior idea?

Management in Action

Topics for Discussion and Action

Level 1

1. Describe what management is and what managers do to achieve organizational goals.
2. Describe the difference between efficiency and effectiveness.
3. Describe the primary responsibilities of the three levels of management, and discuss the skills managers use in carrying out their roles and duties.

Level 2

4. Ask a middle or top manager, perhaps someone you already know, to give examples of how he or she performs the management functions of planning, organizing, leading, and controlling. How much time does he or she spend in performing each function?
5. Like Mintzberg, try to find a cooperative manager who will allow you to follow him or her around for a day. List the types of roles the manager plays and how much time he or she spends performing them.
6. Search iTunes for a free podcast on how managers use their time in performing their roles. Write a brief report of your research.

Level 3

7. Evaluate one (real) organization that you believe to be efficient and effective and one organization that you assess to be inefficient and ineffective in its use of resources. Give evidence to support your evaluation.
8. Put yourself in the position of a first-line manager of a retail store such as Zellers. What skills and roles would you use in your daily work?
9. Explain how the managerial functions of planning, leading, organizing, and controlling differ in the three levels of management.

Building Management Skills

You may be asked to follow and analyze an organization over the semester to help you build your management skills. Each chapter will have an exercise that asks you to evaluate how the issues in the chapter are dealt with by your organization. Choose a large, well-known, publicly traded Canadian company that is easy to research through company Web sites, newspapers, the Canadian Securities Administrators' website, SEDAR.com, and company annual reports. Cite all your sources of information using an appropriate method.

Answer the following questions about the organization you have chosen to follow:

1. Give a brief profile of the organization. How large is it in terms of number of employees, annual revenues, profits, location of facilities, and so on? What kinds of products or services does it provide?
2. Give a brief profile of the industry in which it operates. Under what industrial classification does it fall? How many competitors are active? What is their target market?
3. Identify the top management team. Who is the CEO, and what is his or her background? Give examples of the activities of the CEO that illustrate how he or she engages in the management processes of planning, organizing, leading, and controlling.

Management for You

In each chapter, you will find the Management for You *feature, which gives you ideas on how to apply this material to your personal life. We do this to help reinforce the idea that management is not just for managers—all of us manage our lives and can apply many of the concepts in this book.*

Think about where you hope to be in you life five years from now (i.e., your major goal). What is your competitive advantage for achieving your goal? What do you need to plan, organize, lead, and control to make sure that you reach your goal? Looking over Mintzberg's managerial roles (see Table 1.1), which roles do you perform in your daily life? Give examples.

Small Group Breakout Exercise

Assume you and your teammates belong to a fusion rock band. The leader of the group wrote a proposal that will go before city council to get a licence to hold a concert. The band's leader calls a meeting to tell you that it has been accepted by the council with the strict condition that the band ensures that no laws are violated and the safety of all the concert-goers is maintained. Your group accepts the terms and now must figure out how to manage the event.

1. What set of skills did the leader mostly use in creating the proposal?
2. What must now be done to plan this event effectively and efficiently?
3. What kinds of resources must the band use in organizing the event?
4. Identify the managerial role the leader engaged in:
   a. when he or she called the meeting of the band
   b. when he or she met with the council
   c. when the group accepted the terms of the agreement
5. How could the leader of the band lead the group to put on a successful concert?
6. What kind of control measures could the group take to fulfill their agreement with the council?

Business Planning Exercise

Your professor may ask you to write a business plan for a new venture or a strategic plan for an existing venture. At the end of every chapter, you will have an opportunity to apply managerial and organizational concepts to the exercise of writing a business plan. Refer to Appendix A.

OPENING A NEW RESTAURANT

You and two partners are thinking about writing a business plan for a large restaurant in your local community. Each of you can invest $25 000 in the venture, and with a solid business plan you hope to secure an additional investment of $450 000 in the form of a bank loan. You and your partners have little experience in the food industry beyond serving meals or eating in restaurants. But after reading this chapter, you know a little bit more about how you will manage it.

1. Decide what activities and tasks the three levels of management should be responsible for in the restaurant.
2. How should you and your partners go about (a) planning, (b) organizing, (c) leading, and (d) controlling resources effectively in opening the new restaurant?

Managing Ethically

Recently, six global pharmaceutical companies admitted that they had conspired to artificially raise the prices of vitamins on a global basis. This involved a Swiss firm, a German firm, and four others. The decision to inflate the prices came from senior managers in each company through a joint decision. This unethical action resulted in passing on unfair expenses to the customers. In several meetings around the world, they worked out the details that went undiscovered for many years. Once they were caught, there was jail for some and continuing prosecution for others; all were fired.

The result of this situation was that each company agreed to create a special position of ethics officer to oversee behaviour in the organization. Why are some people unethical, while others would not even consider doing what is described above? Is ethics an internal force in each individual, or can you educate people in ethics, or can people be made to be ethical? How do you define "unethical" in this case? Do you think it is possible for businesses to be ethical? What was the gain for the managers?

Exploring the World Wide Web

SPECIFIC ASSIGNMENT

What Makes a Great Manager

Go to the website, and print out Gerard M. Blair's article "What Makes a Great Manager" (www.see.ed.ac.uk/~gerard/Management/art9.html). It is a very down-to-earth article and provides "some common-sense ideas on the subject of great management."

1. What are Blair's specific notions of being a "great manager"?
2. Using Blair's ideas, do a personal write-up about how well you match up to being a "great manager"? Identify your strengths and also your challenges.

GENERAL ASSIGNMENT

Do a search on the Internet and identify a company that you think generally matches up to Blair's ideas of "great management." Be prepared to defend your choice.

1. Why did you choose the company you did?
2. What are the "great manager" strengths that you identified?
3. In what areas would you recommend that they improve?

McGraw-Hill Connect™—Available 24/7 with instant feedback so you can study when you want, how you want, and where you want. Take advantage of the Study Plan—an innovative tool that helps you customize your learning experience. You can diagnose your knowledge with pre- and post-tests, identify the areas where you need help, search the entire learning package for content specific to the topic you're studying, and add these resources to your personalized study plan. Visit www.mcgrawhillconnect.ca to register—take practice quizzes, search the e-book, and much more.

Be the Manager

PLANNING FOR THE UNTHINKABLE[46]

By now, many people have seen the movie *Titanic* and know what an incredible tragedy it all turned out to be.[47] "On April 15, 1912, at 2:10 AM, the mighty ship of dreams, The *R.M.S. Titanic* foundered, bringing with it some 1523 souls into the cold sea."[48] The sinking of the *Titanic* turned out to be the "most infamous disaster of the twentieth century." Each of us asks, "But how could that be? This was a time of optimism, of new materials, of adventure, of safety."

Could the disaster be attributed to bad management practices? Mark Kozak-Holland, in his "Plan for the Unthinkable," writes, "...prestige overtook safety as the primary principle in *Titanic's* design, the ship many thought invincible had a fate that was inevitable. Worse still, the bad guys got away with it."

The business case put forward at the time was that the building of such a ship as the *Titanic* would be a two-year payback project, quite a feat in those days. However, there was a very serious glitch: a competitive frenzy to get the ship out on the water. Executives overrode the architects' plans for "safety, performance, stability, security, maintainability, and the environment to ensure the ship delivered its functions." In practice, this meant that operating the *Titanic* put everyone at risk. The ship's performance, therefore, was severely compromised. Pride got in the way as well. The architects gave in to the executives' demands to get the ship afloat and have the "ultimate passenger experience" because of their overconfidence in the ship's design. "The lifeboats were viewed as an added safety feature, useful if *Titanic* had to rescue another ship in distress." Planning for testing was also compromised because of time and investment pressures. The net result was the perception that the *Titanic* was invincible. Reputations, corporate and personal, were at stake. Testing was sporadic and inadequate at best. However, management philosophy literally was "full-steam ahead"!

Think now what kind of a manager you would be as the planning was being done to get the *Titanic* ready to sail.

Questions

1. What suggestions would you have made for planning and controlling? Refer to www.gma.org/space1/titanic.html

Management Case

He Was the "Wisest of the Old Mandarins"[49]

Arthur Kroeger, one of the last great Canadian mandarins, a public servant extraordinaire whose "high ethical compass" and professionalism was a symbol of the plain-speaking, independent and non-partisan public servant, died Friday, May 9, 2008, at age 75. He was a Companion of the Order of Canada, and a deputy minister of numerous federal departments in a distinguished career spanning 34 years. From 1993 to 2002, he was also the chancellor of Carleton University in Ottawa, Canada.

He was ahead of his time in many ways, and one of his defining legacies was his role in advancing the rights of women in public service. He was fearless and not afraid to go against the establishment even in retirement, if he felt the cause was right.

"I think it is fair to say that he was the last of a great and extraordinary generation of public servants who, you could say, were co-architects of the new Canada," said Gilles Paquet, senior research fellow at the University of Ottawa's School of Public and International Affairs. "He was probably the wisest of the old mandarins. He represented the ultimate wise mandarin who was capable of working with any government." Jim Roche, a senior official in the office of the Minister of Transport when Kroeger was deputy minister, said, "He was a great leader and public servant. He had a great belief in the good the government can do for the country, and he inspired a whole generation of public servants. Before it was even fashionable, he opened the door to women in public service. He sought them out, he nurtured them, and he promoted them. It is one of his defining legacies." He could manage the delicate balance between his own convictions and serving his political masters.

Questions

1. In view of some of the ideas in this chapter, what supports the basis of the story of Kroeger as a wise leader?
2. What are some qualities of Kroeger's life that you would want to emulate?

Part 1: Integrated Case

How Do I Manage a Mobile Workforce?[50]

There can be tremendous advantages to having a mobile workforce. However, if you manage a mobile workforce with the traditional brick-and-mortar business mindset and old-school management style, there is a good chance you will not get the most out of your employees. Key competencies required for mobile working include adaptability, good communication, and planning, organizational, and relationship-building skills.

Once the decision has been made and the employee goes mobile, it is time to let go. A common complaint from mobile workers is excessive scrutiny from their managers, which leads to higher stress and lower productivity. Deborah Hurst, associate professor, Centre for Innovative Management at Athabasca University, says, "The command-and-control approach to management simply doesn't work very well in a distributed workforce." Gail Rieschi, president of Toronto-based VPI, says, "They need to manage through trust and measure performance more on outputs than on conformity to prescribed work protocols."

In keeping with the notion of the "*opposable* mind" mentioned earlier, a manager needs to step outside the old bricks-and-mortar management mindset and think instead in terms of building strong, reliable relationships among the mobile employees, their manager or managers, and the rest of the company. Again, it is not "either-or," but "both-and."

Technology is also essential in managing a mobile workforce and is always determined by answering the question why one needs a mobile workforce in the first place.

Question

1. What kind of management mindset and style are required to manage a mobile workforce?

Sticking With His Team

CEO TV had the chance to spend sometime with former Argonauts player and long time coach Michael "Pinball" Clemons. His journey has taken him off the football field and behind the desk, as its new CEO. *July 7, 2008.*

1. What are Pinball Clemons' qualities as a leader?
2. How will he measure his success in the competitive world of pro football?
3. What made him decide to go into the corporate world?

Video Management Case

BusinessWeek TV's Destination CEO
Name: Motorola
CEO of Company: Ed Zander

One of the first things Ed Zander did after being named Motorola CEO was to knock down the wood-paneled walls of his executive suite and move his desk to a smaller interior space. He set up lunch meetings in the company cafeteria. Zander, who came from Sun Microsystems, has been described as no-nonsense and execution oriented. He replaced CEO Chris Galvin, grandson of Motorola founder Paul Galvin. The 80-year old Motorola, once known as the global leader in communications, was out of innovative ideas and slow to get new phones to market.

1. How did Zander transform Motorola?

Zander's job was to regain lost market share on Nokia by transforming the company culture into one of accountability, execution, and speed. Motorola had lost its dominant mobile phone market share to competitor Nokia in the 1990s. Zander executed a massive company reorganization which included thousands of layoffs worldwide. In addition, Motorola had also established a reputation for unreliability of its products. Under Zander's command, Motorola introduced the Razr and the Slvr, two sleek and high-profile cell phones. The Q, a multimedia device that includes smart phone technology and notebook computer functionality, was also introduced to compete with Blackberry mobile devices.

While Zander still has much work to do at Motorola before it regains its once-held position as the global leader in communication devices, his efforts to date have shown positive results. Motorola trades under the symbol MOT on the NYSE.

Note: During 2007, Samsung overtook Motorola as the number 2 mobile phone manufacturer. http://www.theaustralian.news.com.au/story/0,25197,22105589-36375,00.html

PART 2

The Environment of Management

CHAPTER

2

Managing the Organizational Environment

Learning Outcomes

1. Explain why being able to perceive, interpret, and respond appropriately to the organizational environment is crucial for managers' success.

2. Identify the main forces in an organization's *task* environment and the challenges that these forces present to managers.

3. Identify the main forces in an organization's *general* environment and the challenges that these forces present to managers.

4. Discuss the ways managers can minimize threats and uncertainty from the external environment.

5. Discuss the major challenges managers face in gaining a competitive advantage in the global economy.

Adapting, in Good Times and in Tough Times[1]

Floform Industries Ltd., in Winnipeg, manufactures countertops. Even in these times of economic downturns, new homes, new condos, and new rental apartments all need kitchens. And what does every kitchen need? Of course, a countertop.

Floform is on its way to becoming the largest maker of countertops on the Prairies—and maybe even all of northwestern North America, if current plans continue apace. In 2007, the Winnipeg factory and satellite sites in Saskatoon, Calgary, and Edmonton turned out $24.25-million worth of laminate and stone countertops.

And the nice thing about this business is that it does not just depend on that boom in new housing. When housing starts drop, renovation projects kick in. Owner Ted Sherritt says, "A healthy economy all across the West means there is lots of money for renovations. And when times get tough, people look to improving their homes." When people want to fix up their homes to enhance sale prices, they often start with the kitchen. And that usually means starting with a new countertop. They are relatively inexpensive and can give the room a brand new look and feel.

In 2007, sales increased by about 27.5 percent, and annual growth since 2005 has averaged more than 20 percent. Sherritt attributes part of that

(c) The McGraw-Hill Companies, Inc./Jill Braaten, photographer.

growth to the introduction of the new stone countertop line that "has taken off like a shot."

Sherritt joined the company as a partner in 1995. He saw a good business opportunity, and he bought a 20-percent interest from the original owner-brothers. He bought out both brothers by 2000 and currently owns an 80-percent interest, with the balance spread among key managers.

What made his rapid growth possible? The ability to recruit and retain talented managers. "Great managers are gold. You can't grow a company as fast as we have grown this one without super competent people," says Sherritt. He also sees the company moving west into the Vancouver market and into the northwest United States as well.

One of his greatest challenges is keeping up with the demand from his more than 3000 customers. "While stone countertops are still a relatively small part of the overall revenues, the growth has been phenomenal," he says.

Will he ever look east and move in that direction as well? "That's not in the plans," he says. "We have always been, and will likely stay, a Western company. What we will do, however, is start moving into the major, much more competitive big city markets, I would think. As I said, we have that strong management team, and that can take us to the next level."

Now It's Your Turn

1. What are the three factors, from the reading of the story, that work in favour of Floform Industries Ltd. as it learns to adapt and manage in this new global environment?

2. What are some additional current issues that may impact Floform Industries' organizational environment?

▪▪▪▪ Overview

The global digital economy has profoundly changed how we do business. No longer can managers ignore the forces operating in their environments; otherwise, they will simply go out of business. Perhaps the main challenging characteristic of this shift from the Industrial Age model of doing business to the new global model is the shift from a world where business was vertically integrated to one now where business web integration is horizontal. This new reality has profound impact not only on how business does business (its internal processes) but also on the effects this shift has on customers, distributors, competitors, and suppliers. Survival of the organization is at stake here, and most managers know this and are learning to shift as well.

In this chapter, we examine the organization's external environment in detail. We describe it and identify the principal forces—both task and general—that create pressure and influence managers and thus affect the way organizations plan, organize, lead, and control. We conclude with a study of several methods that managers can use to help organizations adjust and respond to forces in the organizations' environments. By the end of the chapter, you will understand the steps managers must take to ensure that organizations adequately address and appropriately respond to their external environment.

What Is the Organizational Environment?

organizational environment
The set of forces and conditions that can affect the way an organization operates.

internal environment
The forces operating within an organization and stemming from the organization's structure and culture.

external environment
The forces operating outside an organization that affect how the organization functions.

stakeholders
Persons, groups, and institutions directly affected by the activities and decisions of an organization.

task environment
The set of forces and conditions that start with suppliers, distributors, customers, and competitors and affect an organization's ability to obtain inputs and dispose of its outputs, because they influence managers on a daily basis.

The **organizational environment** is a set of forces and conditions, such as technology and competition, that can affect the way the organization operates and the way managers engage in planning and organizing.[2] One interesting reality in mid-2008 was the class project by MIT computer science students: they designed open cell phone systems. Professor Hal Abelson said, "This class is a glimpse of the future, and what's nice, the not-so-distant future."[3] This means that wireless companies are now being pressured "to loosen the control they have maintained over what devices do." In addition, "phones will soon challenge the Internet as a source of innovation." These forces change over time and thus present managers with *opportunities* and *threats*. The organizational environment can be divided into the internal environment and the external environment. The **internal environment** consists of forces operating within an organization and stemming from the organization's structure and culture, including the strategy, human resources, and technology capabilities. The **external environment** consists of forces operating outside an organization that affect how an organization functions. We generally divide the organization's external environment into two major categories: the task environment and the general environment. All of these environments are shown in Figure 2.1. All the persons, groups, and institutions that are directly affected by the internal and external environments are known as the **stakeholders** of the organization.

The **task environment** is a set of external forces and conditions that start with suppliers, distributors, customers, and competitors and affect an organization's ability to obtain inputs, or raw materials, and dispose of its outputs, or finished products. When managers turn on the radio or television, arrive at their offices, open their mail, or look at their computer screens, they are likely to learn about problems facing them because of changing conditions in their organization's task environment.

FIGURE 2.1 | Forces in the Organizational Environment

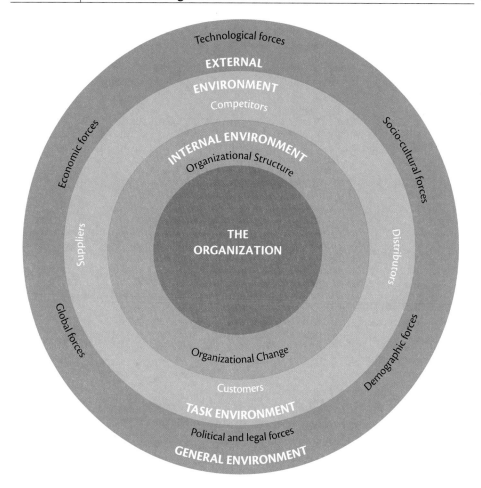

The **general environment** is a wide-ranging set of external factors—including economic, technological, socio-cultural, demographic, political and legal, and global forces—that affect the organization and its task environment directly or indirectly. For the individual manager, opportunities and threats resulting from changes in the general environment are often more difficult to identify and respond to than are events in the task environment. In Chapter 5, we examine how managers analyze their environment, using SWOT (strengths, weaknesses, opportunities, and threats) analysis and Porter's five forces of competitive analysis, and Porter's Five Forces competitive analysis.

Some changes in the external environment, such as the introduction of new technology or the opening of foreign markets, create opportunities for managers to obtain resources or enter new markets and thereby strengthen their organizations. In contrast, the rise of new competitors, an economic recession, or an oil shortage poses a threat that can devastate an organization if managers are unable to obtain resources or sell the organization's goods and services. The ability of managers to perceive, interpret, and respond to forces in the organizational environment is critical to an organization's performance.

Although the task, general, and internal environments influence each other, we leave detailed discussion of how to manage the internal environment until Parts 3 and 4. In this chapter, we explore the nature of the external forces and consider how managers can respond to them.

general environment
The economic, technological, socio-cultural, demographic, political and legal, and global forces that affect an organization and its task environment.

L O 2

The Task Environment

The *task* or *specific* environment includes several groups, organizations, and persons whom the organization deals with directly in its daily operations and who have an immediate effect on the operations and performance levels of the organization. Forces in the task environment result from the actions of suppliers, distributors, customers, and competitors (see Figure 2.1). These four groups affect a manager's ability to obtain resources and distribute outputs on a daily, weekly, or monthly basis and thus have a significant impact on short-term decision making. We discuss each of these factors in turn.

THINK ABOUT IT

Global Trends Affect Change[4]

For Canadian entrepreneurs, the twenty-first century seems to be proving the adage that "change is the only constant." The usual concerns about government—taxes, spending, and regulation—and the cost of inputs such as energy are still top of mind. But, there is growing recognition that three powerful global trends—competition from new economic powerhouses, the greying of the population, and the greening of environmental policies—are changing the way we do business.

A clear sign of the change to the **competitive landscape** is China supplanting Canada as top supplier to the U.S. market in the second half of 2006. Low-cost producers in emerging nations are bound to continue gaining market share in mature nations as their export base broadens in areas such as autos. Mexico, for example, is ramping up vehicle production at a time when its NAFTA partners are realigning and, in aggregate, cutting output. At the same time, robust growth in countries such as China and India will underpin Canada's energy and industrial commodity sectors, keeping growth "best in the West" for the remainder of the decade. Canada's service industries are more insulated from foreign competition than are manufacturing industries and have accounted for more than 90 percent of net job gains since the beginning of the decade. Even here, the performance of outward-oriented services such as tourism has lagged, aided by a 35-percent decline in U.S. visitors since a peak in 1999—a trend likely to continue as the United States tightens its entry regulations.

For Canadian entrepreneurs, these competitive challenges come with new opportunities. Businesses producing for or servicing the local market can use their market capabilities to distribute an expanding array of imports. High growth Asian and Latin American countries require a wide array of specialized advisory services and niche products. With some repositioning and a strong marketing strategy, Canada's tourism sector also has a great opportunity to serve the rapidly growing ranks of well-to-do travellers from emerging nations.

Canada and other mature industrialized nations are also wrestling with the implications of an **aging population**. The retirement bulge will put enormous pressure on health care and create markets for advisory services and lifestyle products. In less than a decade, there will be only four working-age Canadians for every person 65-plus, down from a 6:1 ratio in the early 1990s. The impending drop in workforce participation is likely to aggravate labour and skills shortages, keeping unemployment rates low.

The competition for workers will put upward pressure on pay and benefit incentives to keep older Canadians working longer and to induce younger ones to start working earlier. As well, immigration levels will have to increase to augment labour

---

competitive landscape
The competitive environment within which a company operates.

---

aging population
When the average age of a country's population increases; popularly known as the emerging "silver tsunami" to indicate a large wave of people with greying hair in the population.

supply. These trends point to a rapidly expanding market for training, retraining, and temporary placement services, often to meet highly specialized requirements. Tight public education budgets suggest the private sector will have to do some of the heavy lifting, opening up business opportunities in the training field.

Heightened **environmental consciousness** and the associated greening of public sector policy will also have a profound impact on production processes here and abroad. Canada is still largely in the design phase of forming a comprehensive and coordinated strategy to increase energy efficiency and curb pollution. However, two things are clear: First, policy decisions made here about what will be required, who will pay, and how much will be paid relative to the decisions made in other countries will have a big impact on Canadian businesses and their competitiveness; second, the unleashing of enormous demand for environmental products and services provides entrepreneurs with a golden opportunity to become part of a solution to a global problem.

> **environmental consciousness**
> The awareness that people have of environmental and ecological issues and realities and their dependence on ecosystems.

You Be the Manager

1. How will the three global trends affect Canada's competitive presence in the new global economy?
2. What opportunities do the three global trends bring to today's managers?

Suppliers

Suppliers are the individuals and organizations that provide an organization with the input resources (such as raw materials, component parts, or employees) that it needs to produce goods and services. In return, the supplier receives compensation for those goods and services. An important aspect of a manager's job is to ensure a reliable supply of input resources. In the digital economy, with networked technologies, organizations can often be picky and choose suppliers who will provide the security and dependence they need. Tapscott and Agnew write, "Around the globe, commercial enterprises are scrambling to avoid not only being left in the dust of the upstarts but also being made irrelevant as suppliers and customers alike embrace new ways of doing business."[5]

> **suppliers**
> Individuals and organizations that provide an organization with the input resources that it needs to produce goods and services.

Changes in the nature, number, or types of suppliers lead to opportunities and threats that managers must respond to if their organizations are to prosper. Often, when managers do not respond to a threat, they put their organization at a competitive disadvantage. For example, when Joan Fisk was managing the Tiger Brand Knitting Co., she relied too heavily on the strength of the low Canadian dollar at the time. Meanwhile, all this meant was that the dollar was simply buying the company time because "Wal-Mart was demanding price cuts from its suppliers. And all the while China was tooling up to fill the vacuum left by those who couldn't comply."[6]

One major supplier-related threat that confronts managers arises when suppliers have a strong bargaining position with an organization. They can then raise the prices of the inputs they supply to the organization. A supplier's bargaining position is especially strong if (1) the supplier is the sole source of an input and (2) the input is vital to the organization.[7] For example, the Canadian gift store chain Bowring, operated by Tereve Holdings Ltd., known to many Canadians because it once had 64 stores operating across Canada for the past 50 years, filed for bankruptcy protection in August 2005. The reason? It faced tremendous competition and was not perceived as the preferred choice for many people any longer. "Chains like Winners' Home Sense,

Hudson's Bay Co.'s Home Outfitters, Linens N' Things, Caban, and Pottery Barn have opened in Canada to capitalize on a boom in the home-renovation and housing markets." In addition, nontraditional merchants, such as Loblaw Cos. and Costco, started competing with Bowring as well.[8]

Distributors

distributors
Organizations that help other organizations sell their goods or services to customers.

Distributors are organizations that help other organizations sell their goods or services to customers. The decisions that managers make about how to distribute products to customers can have important effects on organizational performance. For many years, Apple Computer refused to let others sell its computers, which meant that customers had to buy directly from Apple. Thus, potential customers who shopped at large computer stores with a variety of products were less likely to buy an Apple computer, since it would not be sold there.

The changing nature of distributors and distribution methods can also bring opportunities and threats for managers. If distributors are so large and powerful that they can control customers' access to a particular organization's goods and services, they can threaten the organization by demanding that it reduce the prices of its goods and services.[9] For example, before Chapters was taken over by Indigo Books & Music, publishers complained that Chapters had used its market share to force them into dropping their wholesale prices to the book retailer. Because Chapters was the largest distributor of books to customers in Canada, publishers felt compelled to comply with Chapters' demands.

In contrast, the power of a distributor may be weakened if there are too many options. Demand for service from regional phone companies has declined greatly with the advent of cellphones and the larger number of service providers.

Customers

customers
Individuals and groups that buy the goods and services that an organization produces.

Customers are the individuals and groups that buy the goods and services that an organization produces. Dell Canada's customers can be divided into several distinct groups: (1) individuals who purchase personal computers, or PCs, for home use, (2) small companies, (3) large companies, (4) government agencies, and (5) educational institutions. Changes in the numbers and types of customers or changes in customers' tastes and needs result in opportunities and threats. An organization's success depends on its response to customers. Amazon.ca is a good example of how customer responsiveness—or what is called **"customer-centricity"**—pays off. Not only does it ask customers to review its products, it also summarizes these comments with evaluations from the customers.

customer-centricity
The awareness and focus that a company has of a customer's needs, wants, desires, and behaviours.

The rapid growth of the Internet and supporting technologies has given consumers increased strength in the customer–company relationship. As customers have grown in power, so have their expectations, and their expectations are your real competition. Whatever you want to call it, this growth in popularity of customer-centricity is taking hold in a variety of industries. The believers are investing serious time and resources into understanding customer expectations and improving their value and relevancy to their customers. It's paying off.[10]

Competitors

competitors
Organizations that produce goods and services that are similar to a particular organization's goods and services.

One of the most important forces that an organization confronts in its task environment is competitors. **Competitors** are organizations that produce goods and services that are similar to a particular organization's goods and services. In other words, competitors are organizations that are vying for the same customers. Statistics Canada indicates that

40 percent of successful businesses identified more than 20 competitors each. "Think of the *benefit* of your product and service and then consider who else can provide that same *benefit* to your customers. There is only so much money in a consumer or business budget, and a family or company must decide how best to spend it. Your competition is every company that is in some way vying for those same 'benefit' dollars."[11]

Rivalry between competitors can be the most threatening force that managers must deal with. A high level of rivalry often results in price competition, and falling prices reduce access to resources and cause profits to decrease. Today, competition in the personal computer industry is intense as all the major players battle to increase their market share by offering customers better-equipped machines at lower prices.

Barriers to Entry

The rivalry between existing competitors is a major threat, and so is the possibility that new competitors will enter the task environment. In general, the potential for new competitors to enter a task environment (and thus boost the level of competition) depends on barriers to entry.[12] **Barriers to entry** are factors that make it difficult and costly for an organization to enter a particular task environment or industry.[13] The higher the barriers to entry, the smaller is the number of competitors in an organization's task environment and thus the lower the threat of competition. With fewer competitors, it is easier to obtain customers and keep prices high. Airlines are the classic example of an industry with barriers to entry. Montreal-based Air Canada operates as a near monopoly because of the high cost of establishing an airline. In 2001 alone, Royal Airlines and CanJet were swallowed up by Canada 3000, and Roots Air was bought out by Air Canada after only one month of operation. Canada 3000 then went out of operation at the end of 2001. In mid-March 2005, Jetsgo also met its demise. "High fuel prices, brutal fare wars, and safety concerns all weighed on Jetsgo."[14] Competitors such as Tango, Jazz, and Porter Airlines have since appeared and have also struggled to gain market share.

Barriers to entry result from two main sources: economies of scale and brand loyalty (see Figure 2.2). **Economies of scale** are the cost advantages associated with large operations. Economies of scale result from factors such as being able to manufacture products in large quantities, buy inputs in bulk, or be more effective than competitors at making use of organizational resources by fully utilizing employees' skills and knowledge. If organizations already in the task environment are large and enjoy significant economies of scale, then their costs are lower than the costs of potential entrants will be, and newcomers will find it very expensive to enter the industry.

Brand loyalty is customers' preference for the products of organizations that currently exist in the task environment. If established organizations enjoy significant brand loyalty, then a new entrant will find it extremely difficult and costly to obtain

barriers to entry
Factors that make it difficult and costly for an organization to enter a particular task environment or industry.

Air Canada
www.aircanada.ca

economies of scale
Cost advantages associated with large operations.

brand loyalty
Customers' preference for the products of organizations that currently exist in the task environment.

FIGURE 2.2 | Barriers to Entry and Competition

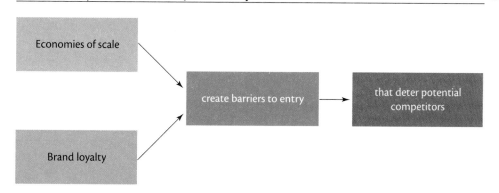

(c) John Woods
Bob Silver, president of Western Glove Works, makers of Silver and 1921 jeans, in his Winnipeg company's sewing room, looking over some new lines with sewing machine operator Adelaida Ebreo.

a share of the market. Newcomers must bear the huge advertising costs for building customer awareness of the good or service they intend to provide.[15] Western Glove Works Ltd. of Winnipeg, Manitoba, is a company that fosters brand loyalty. It is considered "a powerhouse in blue jeans."[16] When, in 1977, it came out with Ziggy, which became a very successful fashion line, Loblaw Cos. in 1982–83 objected because it had prior rights to the name "Ziggy," its specialty delicatessen products. Western then took its own family name, "Silver," and used it as a brand: the Silver Jeans line. Said Bob Silver, company president, "What we learned from all this was the value of brand loyalty. It is a very tough business, indeed, to create a brand and then establish brand loyalty among consumers, but we knew it as something we had to do if we were going to continue to prosper." Read the "Timbit Affair" (see below) and the importance of brand reputation.

In some cases, government regulations function as a barrier to entry. For example, until the late 1980s, government regulations prohibited third parties from reselling long-distance service in Canada. This prevented competition with the established long-distance companies—Bell Canada, SaskTel, and NBTel. When the regulations were amended to allow other companies to compete, the opportunities and threats facing companies in the telephone industry changed. Even more competition opened up when the Canadian Radio-Television and Telecommunications Commission (CRTC) allowed for competition in long-distance calls to areas outside of Canada. The government has also established regulations that make it difficult to establish new private hospitals.

In summary, high barriers to entry create a task environment that is highly threatening and causes difficulty for managers trying to gain access to customers and other resources an organization needs. Conversely, low barriers to entry result in a task environment where competitive pressures are more moderate and managers have greater opportunities to acquire customers and other resources for their organizations to be effective.

LO3

The General Environment

Managers not only must concern themselves with finding suppliers and customers, they must also pay attention to the larger environment around them. Economic, technological, demographic, political, and legal forces in an organization's general environment can have profound effects on the organization's task environment, effects that may be ignored by some managers. For example, technology in the telecommunications industry has made it possible for companies to offer their customers a variety of products. In the past, consumers simply chose the cheapest long-distance package or the best telephone system, but now they are looking at enhanced communication products—such as local calling, cellphone options, long distance, Internet access, and video-conferencing—that are offered as part of the package. Telephone providers who failed to expand their range of offerings quickly have had difficulty keeping customers.

THINK ABOUT IT

The Timbit Affair[17]

In managing the external environment, one of the key forces that managers and supervisors must manage is the demographic one, for example, the changing attitudes in people's expectations about how companies treat them. According to Wolf Blitzer of CNN, "United Breaks Guitars," the YouTube sensation[18] in July 2009, was a "nightmare"[19] for United Airlines when singer and guitarist Dave Carroll did not get what he felt was good customer service, when his $3500 Taylor guitar was broken by its baggage handlers at Chicago's O'Hare Airport. He wrote the song and posted it on YouTube. In the space of two weeks, over 2.5 million viewers watched and listened to his 4.54-minute video—a public relations disaster for United. The Internet, now in its role as a demographic force in the external environment, has obviously placed power in the hands of the consumer.[20]

Another example is one expensive Timbit that caused a public relations problem for Tim Hortons as well. Employee Nicole Lilliman gave a free Timbit to an 11-month-old fussy baby; the baby's mother was a regular customer; Lilliman had been working at the London, Ontario, store for three years; she was a single mother with four children. Her $10/hr paycheque was very important to her. However, she was fired over giving away one Timbit—a 16-cent blob of fried dough! "When I told my daughter I lost my job, she started crying. She's only six, and she doesn't know. She said, 'We won't have any food any more.'"[21]

For Tim Hortons, the fallout from the Timbit incident made any revenue lost from the giveaway of a bite-sized doughnut laughable by comparison. Costs associated with handling this type of problem can escalate "very, very quickly," according to Penny Bonner, senior partner at Ogilvy Renault LLP. "It would certainly be in the tens of thousands," said Bonner, chairwoman of the company's recall and crisis-management practice team. "Clearly, you want to put procedures in place to ensure something like that doesn't happen again." Clearly, also, external demographic forces in society today carry weight.

When news emerged that an employee had been fired after giving away the Timbit, the company's corporate headquarters surged into overdrive as officials scrambled to repair the damage. The franchise owner, along with head office, offered the woman apologies and promptly reinstated her in her job, at a different location. At the same time, company officials were tied up in conference calls well into the night in order to be briefed on the issue and develop a strategy for handling the negative publicity.

The company publicly apologized for the manager's "poor judgment" in firing Nicole Lilliman for breaking a policy to not give away food. The company also reimbursed the woman's wages for two days of missed work, according to spokeswoman Rachel Douglas. People today—the new demographic reality and force in our external environment—have clout.

You Be the Manager

1. What would you have done if you were the manager at Tim Hortons?

When organizations have for years had a monopoly environment to work in—such as the phone companies until recently (e.g., Bell Canada), and the electrical companies (e.g., New Brunswick Power and Ontario Hydro)—and then find themselves facing the reality of operating in a deregulated environment, their managers will have to constantly analyze the forces impacting the new environment in order to manage effectively. Their decisions and planning will have long-term effects. Below we examine each of the major forces in the general environment in turn, exploring their impact on managers and on the organization's task environment and examining how managers can deal with them. In Chapter 5, we examine one of the major tasks involved in planning—the careful and thorough analysis of forces in the general environment.

Economic Forces

Economic forces affect the general health and well-being of a nation or the regional economy of an organization. They include interest rates, inflation, unemployment, and economic growth. Economic forces produce many opportunities and threats for managers. Low levels of unemployment and falling interest rates mean a change in the customer base: more people have more money to spend, and as a result organizations have an opportunity to sell more goods and services. Good economic times affect supplies: Resources become easier to acquire, and organizations have an opportunity to flourish.

In contrast, worsening macroeconomic conditions pose a threat because they limit managers' ability to gain access to the resources their organization needs. Profit-oriented organizations such as retail stores and hotels have fewer customers for their goods and services during economic downturns. Not-for-profit organizations such as charities and colleges receive fewer donations during economic downturns. Even a moderate deterioration in national or regional economic conditions can seriously affect performance.

Poor economic conditions make the environment more complex and managers' jobs more difficult and demanding. Managers may need to reduce the number of individuals in their departments and increase the motivation of remaining employees, and managers and workers alike may need to identify ways to gain and use resources more efficiently. Successful managers realize the important effects that economic forces have on their organizations, and they pay close attention to changes in the national and regional economies in order to respond appropriately.

But when a global economic crisis occurs, as it did in October 2008, dire consequences result for managers, especially in the financial industry. That global financial crisis demonstrated that too much risk-taking and not enough oversight and governance of economic forces can severely derail economic growth. The credit crunch, precipitated by the largest housing bubble in U.S. history, saw many innovative financial products derived from mortgage-backed securities. When the value of the products collapsed as the bubble broke and houses were foreclosed on, several investment banks in the United States collapsed. The trading of these debt instruments led to the worst economic collapse and the largest intervention in the market by governments since the stock market crash of 1929 and the Great Depression.

> *In two tumultuous weeks the Federal Reserve and the Treasury between them nationalized the country's two mortgage giants, Fannie Mae and Freddie Mac; took over AIG, the world's largest insurance company; in effect extended government deposit insurance to $3.4 trillion in money-market funds; temporarily banned short-selling in over 900 mostly financial stocks; and, most dramatic of all, pledged to take up to $700 billion of toxic mortgage-backed assets on to its books.*[22]

While the unregulated financial instruments called into question banking systems around the world, Canada's banks, which had relatively little exposure to the new and complicated debt products, were ranked the worlds' most sound with a score of 6.8.[23] Canada inched ahead of the banks in five other countries—Sweden, Luxembourg, Australia, Denmark, and the Netherlands—all of which received a score of 6.7 percent. The United States, was ranked 40th with a score of 6.1 out of 7.[24]

Technological Forces

Technology is the combination of skills and equipment that managers use in the design, production, and distribution of goods and services. **Technological forces** are outcomes of changes in the technology that managers use to design, produce, or distribute goods and services. Technological forces have increased greatly since the Second World War because the overall pace of technological change has sped up so much.[25] Computers have become increasingly faster and smaller. Transportation speed has increased. Distribution centres are able to track goods in ways that were unthinkable even 10 years ago with technologies such as Radio-Frequency Identification (RFID) systems.

Technological forces can have profound implications for managers and organizations. Technological change can make established products obsolete overnight—for example, eight-track tapes and black-and-white televisions—forcing managers to find new products to make. Although technological change can threaten an organization, it also can create a host of new opportunities for designing, making, or distributing new and better kinds of goods and services. Managers must move quickly to respond to such changes if their organizations are to survive and prosper.

Changes in information technology also are changing the very nature of work itself within organizations, and the manager's job. Telecommuting and teleconferencing are now everyday activities that provide opportunities for managers to supervise and coordinate employees working from home or other locations. Even students engage in telecommuting, communicating with classmates and instructors via email or discussion forums, and completing assignments at home. This has changed the way instructors do their jobs.

Demographic Forces

Demographic forces are outcomes of changes in, or changing attitudes toward, the characteristics of a population, such as age, gender, ethnic origin, race, sexual orientation, and social class. In 2006, with regard to the aging population, the Auditor General of Canada stated: "*The* demographic die is cast: there is little we can do to reverse or even slow the aging of Canada's population over the coming decades. But it is certainly within our power to plan better for it. And better planning begins with better information concerning the long-term fiscal implications of the coming demographic shift."[26] Like the other forces in the general environment, demographic forces present managers with opportunities and threats and can have major implications for organizations. "A projection from the Urban Futures Institute sees Canada requiring nearly 20.6 million people in the labour force in 2017, a 14-percent increase from 2006. Overall, the female workforce will grow by 15 percent while the male contingent grows by 13 percent."[27] As well, "[O]ver the past 30 years, women have made spectacular inroads in business and all of the professions. They now make up nearly 60 percent of university graduates. They outnumber men in the lower managerial ranks, and they'll soon outnumber men in medicine and law."[28] The dramatic increase in the number of working women has focused public concern on issues such as equal pay for equal

technology
The combination of skills and equipment that managers use in the design, production, and distribution of goods and services.

technological forces
Outcomes of changes in the technology that managers use to design, produce, or distribute goods and services.

demographic forces
Outcomes of changes in, or changing attitudes toward, the characteristics of a population, such as age, gender, ethnic origin, race, sexual orientation, and social class.

work and sexual harassment at work. One issue in particular that managers will have to address more and more is the lack of women in top positions. This concern is important because managers are responsible for attracting and making full use of the talents of female employees. According to Catalyst Canada, women account for only 14.4 percent of corporate officer positions in the top 500 companies. This is about the same percentage as it was in 2002, a "disturbingly low" number, according to Catalyst. At this rate, women ascending to the top ranks will not reach a critical mass of 25 percent until 2025! According to *The Globe and Mail* journalist Margaret Wente, there are reasons to explain this circumstance: the mommy track (having families), sex and hormones (the differences between male and female biology), and the reality of boredom for women in the corporate ranks. "Women are more interested in emotionally fulfilling lives than in being leader of the pack."[29] New information from Catalyst in May 2008 showed the following: "On average, companies with the highest representation of women in corporate-officer positions financially outperformed those with the lowest representation. In fact, return on equity was 35.1 percent higher. Total return to shareholders was 34 percent higher. The numbers jumped for women serving as directors on Fortune 500 boards. On average, return on equity was 53 percent higher for those boards with a high representation of women than those with the least women; return on sales was 42 percent higher; and return on invested capital was 66 percent higher."[30] Needless to say, managers must factor in these kinds of circumstances into their decision making. We discuss the important issue of workforce diversity at length in Chapter 3.

Changes in the age distribution of a population are another example of a demographic force that affects managers and organizations. Currently, most industrialized nations are experiencing the aging of their populations as a consequence of falling birth and death rates and the aging of the baby boom generation, whereas emerging nations are not. The aging of the population is increasing opportunities for organizations that cater to older people; the recreation and home health care industries, for example, are seeing an upswing in demand for their services.

The aging of the population also has several implications for the workplace. Most significant are a relative decline in the number of young people joining the workforce and an increase in active employees willing to postpone retirement past the traditional retirement age of 65. These changes suggest that organizations will need to find ways to motivate older employees and use their skills and knowledge, an issue that many Western societies have yet to tackle.

Political and Legal Forces

political and legal forces Outcomes of changes in laws and regulations, such as the deregulation of industries, the privatization of organizations, and increased emphasis on environmental protection.

Political and legal forces result from political and legal developments within society and significantly affect managers and organizations. Political processes shape a society's laws; for instance, public pressure for corporations to be more environmentally conscious has strengthened pollution laws in Canada. Laws constrain the operations of organizations and managers and thus create both opportunities and threats.[31] For example, in much of the industrialized world, there has been a strong trend toward deregulation of industries previously controlled by the state and privatization of organizations once owned by the state.

Deregulation and privatization are just two examples of political and legal forces that can create challenges for organizations and managers. Others include increased emphasis on safety in the workplace and on environmental protection and the preservation of endangered species. Successful managers carefully monitor changes in laws and regulations in order to take advantage of the opportunities they create and counter the threats they pose in an organization's task environment.

The Competition Act of 1986 provides more legislation that affects how companies may operate. Under this Act, the Bureau of Competition Policy acts to maintain and encourage competition in Canada. For example, when companies merge, they face intense scrutiny from the bureau to make sure there is no unfair competitive advantage to customers, employees, and other stakeholders. Even though Ellis Jacob, CEO of Cineplex Galaxy LP, had the "deal of a lifetime" with a $500-million purchase of rival movie theatre exhibition chain Famous Players from Viacom Inc., he had to sell theatres to meet the demands of regulators: "The federal Competition Bureau sought to maintain competition in pricing and choice by making it a condition of the deal that Cineplex sell 35 theatres in 17 cities across Canada, which would have brought in about 11 percent of the companies' combined revenue of $874 million."[32] In early 2005, the Competition Bureau declared that Sears Canada Inc. breached federal laws by pitching exaggerated savings on automobile tires in its ads and asked that they pay a $500 000 fine. In the summer of 2004, Forzani Group Ltd., the country's largest sporting goods retailer, agreed to pay a record $1.7 million to settle allegations that it misled consumers about prices. And a year earlier, clothier Suzy Shier agreed to pay a $1-million penalty in a similar matter.[33]

The Competition Act
http://laws.justice.gc.ca/
en/C-34

Business Plan Checklist

- Conduct an environmental, scan of the forces that directly affect your venture. Who are your potential competitors, suppliers, distributors, and customers?
- What are the trends in the forces in the general environment, and how do they impact your industry and venture?
- Research the North American Industrial Classification System (NAICS) code to determine your 'venture's' industrial sector.
- What are the major threats to your venture, and how will you minimize them?
- Use this information for section 4 of the business plan, Profile of the Industry in Appendix A.

Global Forces

Global forces are outcomes of changes in international relationships, changes in nations' economic, political, and legal systems, and changes in technology. Perhaps the most important global force affecting managers and organizations is the increasing economic integration of countries around the world.[34] Developments such as the North American Free Trade Agreement (NAFTA), the free-trade agreements enforced by the World Trade Organization (WTO), and the growth of the European Union (EU) have led to a lowering of barriers to the free flow of goods and services between nations.[35]

Falling trade barriers have created enormous opportunities for organizations in one country to sell goods and services in other countries. But by allowing foreign companies to compete for an organization's domestic customers, falling trade barriers also pose a serious threat because they increase competition in the task environment. After NAFTA was signed, one of the major challenges facing Canadian managers was how to compete successfully against American companies moving into this country. Zellers and The Bay, for instance, faced strong challenges from Wal-Mart as well as smaller boutique operations.

global forces
Outcomes of changes in international relationships; changes in nations' economic, political, and legal systems; and changes in technology, such as falling trade barriers, the growth of representative democracies, and reliable and instantaneous communication.

totalitarian regime
A political system in which a single party, individual, or group holds all political power and neither recognizes nor permits opposition.

representative democracy
A political system in which representatives elected by citizens and legally accountable to the electorate form a government whose function is to make decisions on behalf of the electorate.

command economy
An economic system in which the government owns all businesses and specifies which and how many goods and services are produced and the prices at which they are sold.

mixed economy
An economic system in which some sectors of the economy are left to private ownership and free-market mechanisms, and others are owned by the government and subject to government planning.

free-market economy
An economic system in which private enterprise controls production, and the interaction of supply and demand determines which and how many goods and services are produced and how much consumers pay for them.

Despite evidence that countries are becoming more similar to one another and that the world is on the verge of becoming a "global village," countries still differ across a range of political, legal, economic, and cultural dimensions. When an organization operates in the global environment, it confronts a series of forces that differ from country to country and world region to world region.

The Impact of Political and Economic Forces

In recent years, two large and related shifts in political and economic forces have taken place globally (see Figure 2.3).[36] One is the shift away from **totalitarian regimes**, where those in charge allow no opposition, toward more democratic regimes. This change has been most dramatic in Eastern Europe and the former Soviet Union, where totalitarian communist regimes collapsed during the late 1980s and early 1990s. There is, of course, debate going on as to how authentic these reforms are, given how then Russian President Vladimir Putin treated Yukos oil company CEO Mikhail Khodorkovsky: he had him incarcerated, and the wealth of his oil company—billions—went into government coffers. "Vladimir Putin is an economically ignorant new Czar who seeks to expropriate these more productive assets so that Russia can frighten people again." The concept and reality of the rule of law is absent in Russia; "In Russia, the ruler is Vladimir Putin."[37] The other shift—toward **representative democracy**, where voters elect a government that makes decisions on their behalf—has occurred from Latin America to Africa.

Accompanying this change in political forces has been a worldwide shift away from **command economies** (where the government owns all businesses) and **mixed economies** (where only some sectors are government owned) and toward **free-market economies** (where competition determines prices).[38] This economic shift began with the realization that government involvement in economic activity often blocks economic growth. Thus, a wave of privatization and deregulation has swept

FIGURE 2.3 | Changes in Political and Economic Forces

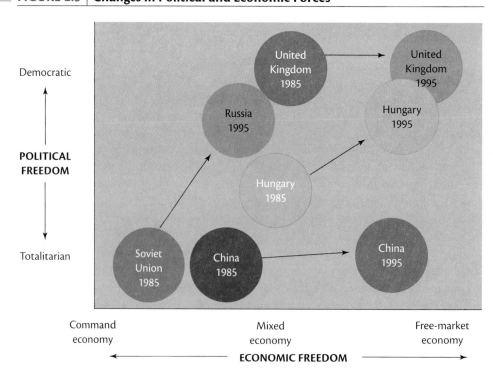

over the world, from the former communist countries to Latin America, Asia, and Western Europe.

These trends are good news for managers of global organizations because they result in the expansion of opportunities for exporting and investment abroad. The managers of many Western companies have had a lot of trouble establishing business operations in Eastern Europe and China, however. For example, when the Chiquita banana company entered the Czech Republic in 1990, it found that Czech citizens apparently had difficulty understanding why something of better quality should cost more. Chiquita was forced to switch to lower quality bananas after discovering that consumers were unwilling to pay higher prices for superior bananas.[39]

The Impact of National Culture

Differences among national cultures have important implications for managers. First, management practices that are effective in Canada might not work in Japan, Hungary, or Mexico because of differences in national culture. For example, pay-for-performance systems used in Canada, which emphasize the performance of individuals alone, are less suitable in Japan, where individual performance in pursuit of group goals is the value that receives emphasis.

A culturally diverse management team can be a source of strength in the global marketplace. Organizations that employ managers from a variety of cultures better appreciate how national cultures differ than do organizations with culturally similar management teams, and they tailor their management systems and behaviours to the differences. Arcelor Mittal (India) and Lenovo (China) are good examples of top multinational companies with international management teams and are poised to become role models for all global companies.[40]

To be an effective global manager, according to research done by McGill University professors Karl Moore and Henry Mintzberg, the most important characteristics are to be able to understand, empathize, and work with multiple cultures.[41] As we shall see in our discussion of diversity in Chapter 3, businesses increasingly face customers and clients who are culturally different. Doing business internationally necessitates an understanding of these differences. "For example, business in Latin America is based very much on relationships of personal trust: One gets to know a Mexican or Argentinean boss before one presents him with a formal contract. In France, one deals directly with the powerful patron at the top. In Germany, on the other hand, written rules and procedures are all-important: A foreign manager seeking to speak to a German CEO will immediately be directed to the appropriate department head. In contrast to Germany's strict written rules, the Japanese operate on strict *unwritten* rules, known as *kata*. Job security is considered in America to produce a mediocre employee, but in Japan, the *lack* of job security will do the same. The French admire intellectual prowess and the Americans short-term success; Australians are often wary of both."[42]

The research of Geert Hofestede provides us with a framework for understanding how national cultures differ on the basis of five dimensions (see Figure 2.4). Nations such as Japan, which ranks #2 in the world's multinational corporations according to *Fortune 500*, has a very low score on Hofestede's Individualism versus Collectivist dimension, suggesting that the interests of the "group" take precedence over individual self-interest. However, diversity is very low in Japan and consequently, "only natives can scale the heights within Japanese companies, which dramatically reduces the interest of ambitious young foreigners, cutting off Japanese multinationals from a critical source of new ideas and making it difficult for them to truly understand foreign markets and develop a cadre of global managers."[43] On the other hand, nations

■ FIGURE 2.4 | Cultural Dimensions[44]

Cultural Dimension	Meaning	Examples of Nations
Power Distance (PD)	The degree to which the least powerful people accept the unequal distribution of power. A high PD score indicates a tolerance and acceptance of inequality.	High PD: Argentina Low PD: USA
Individualism (IDV) versus collectivism	Individualistic countries have a lower reliance on the community or society and a stronger reliance on immediate family in providing well-being. Countries that have a low IDV score, show strong group cohesion and loyalty and respect among members of the group.	High IDV: USA Low IDV: Japan
Masculinity (MAS) versus femininity	The degree to which the nation values "assertiveness" (which Hofestede called masculinity) over 'caring' (which he called femininity).	High MAS: Austria Low MAS: Denmark
Uncertainty Avoidance Index (UAI)	The degree to which the nation is anxious and uncomfortable with uncertain and unknown situations. A low UAI score indicates a greater acceptance of uncertainty.	High UAI: Greece Low UAI: UK
Long-Term Orientation (LTO) versus short-term focus	The degree to which the nation values traditions and customs. A high LTO score indicates a strong adherence to social norms and obligations.	High LTO: Japan Low LTO: USA

that are not the largest players in the global economy but have a great deal of diversity produce great global managers. According to Moore and Mintzberg, these countries include Canada, Switzerland, Belgium, Singapore, Norway, Sweden, the Netherlands, Denmark, Australia, and Finland.[45]

 ## Tips for Managers

FORCES IN THE ENVIRONMENT

1. Identify key forces from the environment that act as threats or opportunities for managers today.

2. List the forces that you feel are the most important for managers to work with.

3. Finally, choose the #1 force you believe is affecting most managers today as they grapple with their organizational environment.

LO 4

Managing The External Environment

As previously discussed, an important task for managers is to understand how forces in the task and general environments create opportunities for, and threats to, their organizations. To analyze the importance of opportunities and threats in the external environment, managers must measure (1) the level of complexity in the environment and (2) the rate at which the environment is changing. With this information, they can plan better and choose the best goals and courses of action.

THINK ABOUT IT

New Age, New Rules, New Capitalism[46]

One of the most interesting business books in 2007 was *Firms of Endearment: How World-Class Companies Profit from Passion and Purpose*. The authors, experts in marketing, consumer behaviour, and global competition, have an opening Prologue with a quote from Valentine Coverly in Tom Stoppard's play *Arcadia*:[47]

> *The future is disorder. A door like this has opened up only five or six times since we got up on our hind legs. It's the best possible time to be alive, when almost everything you thought you knew is wrong.*

The authors believe this quote to be a very apt one because it signals the end of an era. We are entering an era where *meaning* is becoming paramount, where the "share of wallet" will not determine market share, but the "share of heart."[48] They believe that this search for meaning "is changing the very soul of capitalism." There is now a major shift occurring from a *having* society to a *being* society. The book is not a "bleeding heart" book at all, but one grounded in "hard" data results stemming from key humanistic companies they have researched—which they call **"firms of endearment"** (or FoEs)—such as Amazon, BMW, Costco, Google, Harley-Davidson, Honda, IKEA, New Balance, Patagonia, and Starbucks, to name a few. For example,

> *The public FoEs returned 1026 percent for investors over the 10 years ending June 30, 2006, compared to 122 percent for the S&P 500; that's more than an 8-to-1 ratio! Over five years, the ratio is even higher because the FoEs returned 128 percent, while the S&P 500 only gained 13 percent. Over three years, FoEs returned 73 percent versus 38 percent for the S&P 500.*[49]

What is emerging now is what they call the Age of Transcendence[50] whereby "materialistic" influences of the twentieth century are giving way (slowly perhaps) as "experiential" influences become stronger.[51] They buttress their argument with mainstream words in business today: *affection, love, joy, authenticity, empathy, compassion,* and *soulfulness.* The first cultural movement has been the Age of Empowerment, which linked democracy with capitalism to create a new world from the eighteenth century on. This age was followed by the Age of Knowledge (roughly 1880) with the invention of the telephone by Alexander Bell and the phonograph, incandescent light bulb, and the first central electrical power system by Thomas Edison.

We are now entering globally the Age of Transcendence or the "Self-Actualization of Capitalism."

"firms of endearment" Humanistic companies—companies with "soul"—that seek to maximize their value to society as a whole, not just to their shareholders.

You Be the Manager

1. If the authors' claim in *Firms of Endearment* that the Age of Transcendence is now emerging is correct, what do you think is the impact of this paradigm shift on how managers will need to manage the organizational environment for the future?

The complexity of the external environment depends on the number and potential impact of the forces that managers must respond to in the task and general environments. A force that seems likely to have a significant negative impact is a potential threat to which managers must devote a high level of organizational resources. A force likely to have a marginal impact poses little threat to an organization and requires only a minor commitment of managerial time and attention. A force likely to make a significant positive impact warrants a considerable commitment of managerial time and effort to take advantage of the opportunity. When Starbucks went to Vienna, the company had to think carefully about its no-smoking policy, since it would be the only coffee shop in the city to ban smoking.

In general, the larger an organization is, the greater is the number of environmental forces that managers must respond to. Consider, for example, the external environment facing the manager of a place like Johnny's Hamburgers on Victoria Park just north of Highway 401 in Toronto. Johnny's has been in its current location for years. This small "burger joint" is known to many people. Their customers cannot eat on the premises; they order and receive full portions of reasonably priced and, according to many, delicious food, which they eat in their cars or at their offices or homes. Johnny's has had regular customers for years; it does the same thing it has done for years; people come and go, but Johnny's remains more or less the same. Consider Tim Hortons as it keeps expanding. Now, of course, it is owned by Wendy's International Inc. Each year it must consider, to take just one example, the environmental issue of its coffee cups when it announces its "Roll Up the Rim" contest. For some people, as in Edmonton, it is a chance to win an SUV; for environmentalists, however, these cups represent a serious biodegradable hazard; they also litter the environment.[52] "I don't think it's socially responsible to have a promotion which creates massive waste," said Ronald Colman, executive director of GPI Atlantic, a non-profit group that researches environmental and quality-of-life issues.[53] He has a very strong point here: In Nova Scotia, for example, "a government-sponsored study showed Tim Hortons and fast-food rival McDonald's alone account for one-third of all litter in that province. Tim Hortons' packaging accounted for 22 percent and McDonald's for 10.1 percent of all identifiable litter."

Thus, in addition to determining how to distribute food supplies to restaurants in the most efficient ways, managers have to ensure that the organization's practices do not discriminate against any ethnic groups or older workers, and respond to customers' preferences for different types of foods. Tim Hortons and other restaurants must also deal with ecological forces in the environment and move toward more sustainable decision-making practices as discussed in Chapter 4.

environmental change
The degree to which forces in the task and general environments change and evolve over time.

Environmental change is the degree to which forces in the task and general environments change and evolve over time. Change is problematic for an organization and its managers because the consequences of change can be difficult to predict.[54] Managers can try to forecast or simply guess about future conditions in the task environment, such as where and how strong the new competition may be. But, confronted with a complex and changing task environment, managers cannot be sure that decisions and actions taken today will be suitable in the future. This uncertainty makes their jobs especially challenging. It also makes it vitally important for managers to understand the forces that shape the external environment.

To manage the external environment, managers need to:

1. List the types and relative strengths of the forces that affect their organizations' task and general environments the most.
2. Analyze the way changes in these forces may result in opportunities or threats for their organizations.
3. Draw up a plan indicating how they propose to take advantage of those opportunities or counter those threats, and what kinds of resources they will need to do so.

An understanding of the external environment is necessary so that managers can anticipate how the task environment might look in the future and decide on the actions to pursue if the organization is to prosper. McDonald's is a good example of how adaptive an organization must be to remain successful. With the aging population, and the emphasis on low-fat foods, McDonald's began changing its menu by including salads and wraps that had less fats and carbohydrates. It is also aware of people with food allergies and other food sensitivities and has made adjustments accordingly.[55] The fact that Charlie Bell, McDonald's

CEO, died of colorectal cancer in early 2005 at the age of 44, has only heightened awareness of this need for low-fat foods, if for no other reason than its corporate reputation.[56] However, one commentator put it this way: "I also know that the human body is designed to live well past 100. To die at any age under 50 requires a sustained poisoning effort: like consuming soft drinks, fried foods, red meat, refined white flour, added sugars, hydrogenated oils, and so on. ... I wonder what ingredients are in a Big Mac these days."[57]

Reducing the Impact of Environmental Forces

Finding ways to reduce the number and potential impact of forces in the external environment is the job of all managers in an organization.

- The principal task of the CEO and the top-management team is to devise strategies that will allow an organization to take advantage of opportunities and counter threats in its general and task environments (see Chapter 5 for a discussion of this vital topic).

- Middle managers in an organization's departments collect relevant information about the task environment, such as (1) the future intentions of the organization's competitors, (2) the identity of new customers for the organization's products, and (3) the identity of new suppliers of crucial or low-cost inputs.

- First-line managers find ways to use resources more efficiently to hold costs down or to get close to customers and learn what they want.

Managers at all three levels and in all functional areas are responsible for reducing the negative impact of environmental forces as they evolve over time (see Figure 2.5).

Managers as Agents of Change

It is important to note that although much of the change that takes place in the external environment is independent of a particular organization (e.g., basic advances in

FIGURE 2.5 | Managing Forces in the Organizational Environment

Level in the Hierarchy	Responsibility for Reducing the Impact of Environmental Forces
CEO and Top Management	Devise strategies to explore opportunities and counter threats posed by forces in the general environment
Middle Managers	Gather relevant information on forces in the task environment for implementing strategies for growth
First-Line Managers	Find ways to use resources efficiently and add value for the customer to build brand loyalty
Functional Area Managers	**Role in Managing the Forces in the Organizational Environment**
Sales and Service	Ensure customer satisfaction and brand loyalty
Research and Development	Deal with technological forces
Marketing and Strategy	Deal with pressures from competitors
Accounting and Finance	Handle economic forces
Legal and Public Relations	Deal with political and legal forces
Operations and Materials Management	Deal with pressures from suppliers

FIGURE 2.6 | Uncertainty in the Environment and Managerial Action

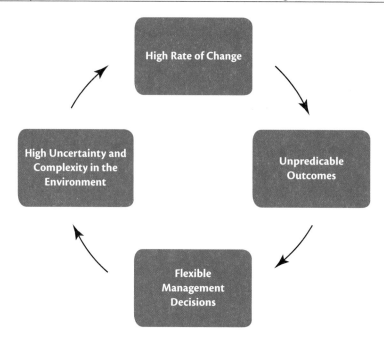

biotechnology or plastics), a significant amount of environmental change is the direct consequence of actions taken by managers within organizations.[58] An organization is an open system: It takes in inputs from the environment and converts them into goods and services that are sent back to the environment. Thus, change in the environment is a two-way process. Often, however, the choices that managers make about which products to produce and even about how to compete with other organizations affect the system as a whole. Our ability to predict and control the course of events is determined by the rate of change in the environment and the complexity of the environment (see Figure 2.6).

Many decisions managers make in response to the forces in the environment are made under conditions of **uncertainty** and risk. As we will see in Chapter 4, it is very difficult to know all the possible outcomes of adopting a particular alternative or strategy. The more complex and dynamic the environment, the greater are the uncertainty and risk. Strategies and organizational structures must be somewhat flexible to be able to accommodate change. However, when managers act under conditions of **certainty,** there is less risk and more complete knowledge of the possible outcomes of their decisions. Management must try to minimize any threats from changes in the task and general environmental forces while capitalizing on the opportunities they present by adopting flexible organizational structures and work processes (see Figure 2.7).

uncertainty
The state of environmental forces that is so dynamic that managers cannot predict the probable outcomes of a course of action.

certainty
The state of environmental forces that is stable enough to predict possible outcomes of decisions.

Tips for Managers

MANAGING THE EXTERNAL ENVIRONMENT

1. Describe the level of complexity and uncertainty that exists in organizational environments today.

2. Make a list of suggestions you would make to managers to help them respond to their customers, competitors, and suppliers.

3. Itemize your own personal strengths, weaknesses, opportunities, and threats as you prepare to work in this new global environment.

FIGURE 2.7 | Uncertainty Matrix

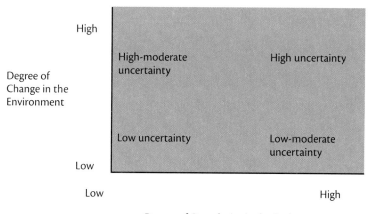

High

Degree of
Change in the
Environment

High-moderate uncertainty   High uncertainty

Low uncertainty   Low-moderate uncertainty

Low

Low   High

Degree of Complexity in the Environment

L O 5

Challenges for Management in a Global Environment

Canadian firms are less likely to operate only within their own borders these days. Not only do firms face competition domestically, but they also face global competition. The rise of **global organizations**—organizations that operate and compete in more than one country—has put severe pressure on many organizations to improve their performance and to identify better ways to use their resources. The successes of Indian metals industry giant Arcelor Mittal, German chemical companies Schering and Hoechst, Italian furniture manufacturer Natuzzi, Korean electronics companies Samsung and Lucky Goldstar, and Brazilian plane maker Empresa Brasileira de Aeronautica SA (Embraer)—all global companies—are putting pressure on organizations in other countries to raise their level of performance in order to compete successfully.

global organizations
Organizations that operate and compete in more than one country.

THINK ABOUT IT

Mobility and Flexibility: Key to Increasing Globalization[59]

Prem Benimadhu, vice-president of the Conference Board of Canada, a non-profit group in Ottawa that monitors economic trends, public policy, and organizational performance, says the workplace of the future will have an international cohort of employees. "The nine-to-five concept will go the way of the dodo bird. There's going to be even more blurring of work and life, given the different time zones people will have to work with."

Example: Even though it is 7 p.m. in Toronto, Monika Morrow is just about to dial in to a conference call. Morrow is vice-president and national practice leader of transition services for the Canadian operation of Right Management Inc., a human resources consulting firm and subsidiary of Wisconsin-based Manpower Inc. The call is coming in from Australia, where it is only 7 a.m. Behold the global workplace in action.

Cross-border mergers and acquisitions have certainly soared in recent years, with worldwide activity hitting more than US$716 billion in 2005, compared with about US$300 billion in 2003. "The global economy is increasingly becoming integrated," says Morris Kleiner, co-author of a published academic paper titled "Governing the Global Workplace"

(c) Comstock/Jupiter Images

and industrial relations professor at the Hubert H. Humphrey Institute of Public Affairs at the University of Minnesota in Minneapolis.

Canada's vision of the future workforce: Kleiner says that even if employees are working in Canada, they will not think of themselves as part of the Canadian workforce. Why is this vision so dynamic? Since "talented employees will see themselves as members of a global workforce," says Prem Benimadhu, "that will be challenging for companies in terms of employee retention because they not only will have to compete with other employers in the country, they also have to worry about the company in Beijing or Australia who might poach their employees away from them."

A shadow side: As more Canadian companies are swallowed up by larger companies in the United States or Europe, many workplaces in Canada could turn into mere branch offices. There is also the problem that these same technologies will also continue to erode the demarcation between the work day and personal time.

The key for people like Monika Morrow is the willingness to be mobile. For those employees who are members of Generation Y and, unlike boomers and Gen-Xers, will find that not so eager to travel for work, technology will make it possible for companies to go global without employees having to be mobile.

Ms. Morrow adds, "We need to be equipped with great change-management skills and the ability to reinvent ourselves."

You Be the Manager

1. How can managers make sure they are doing enough to recruit local Canadians for their companies?
2. Is Canada better off "going where the talent is" rather than trying to "grow talent at home"?

The list of the top 100 Global Companies of 1998 did not include any Canadian firms. Ten years later, in 2008, 14 of the 500 Global Companies were Canadian. More than three times as many Canadian companies rank in the world top five in their industry as did 20 years ago.[60] Today, managers who make no attempt to learn and adapt to changes in the global environment find themselves reacting rather than innovating, and their organizations often become uncompetitive and fail.[61] Three major challenges stand out for Canadian managers in today's global economy: building a competitive advantage, maintaining ethical standards, and utilizing new kinds of information systems and technologies.

Building a Competitive Advantage

If Canadian managers and organizations are to reach and remain at the top of the competitive environment, they must build a **competitive advantage**, which is the ability of one organization to outperform other organizations because it produces desired goods or services more efficiently and effectively than its competitors. The four building blocks of competitive advantage are superior *efficiency, quality, innovation,* and *responsiveness to customers* (see Figure 2.8).

Increasing Efficiency

Organizations increase their efficiency when they reduce the quantity of resources (such as people and raw materials) they use to produce goods or services. In today's competitive environment, organizations are constantly seeking new ways to use their resources to improve efficiency. Many organizations are training their workers in new skills and techniques to increase their ability to perform many new and different tasks. Canada could do more on the training front, however. Japanese and German companies invest far more in training employees than do Canadian companies.

New technological solutions to project management are another way companies can increase efficiency. EllisDon, one of Canada's largest construction companies, developed a software platform technology to help it deal with the "mountains of documents—forms, correspondence, quotes, contracts, schedules, purchase orders, architectural drawings, drawing revisions, photographs, meeting minutes, payroll time sheets, permits, safety inspection reports, and anything else one could think of with respect to building structures in a way that involved clients, consultants, and innumerable subtrades."[62] The result was that the company grew by 50 percent without having to increase their staff.

In addition to training staff and introducing new technologies, companies can sometimes work together to increase efficiency. Creating alliances and partnerships, where two companies with their own relative strengths cooperate to produce results that neither could have achieved alone, can result in positive synergies and cost savings. (These kinds of networked structures and B2B relationships are discussed in more detail in Chapter 6.) Spin Masters, a Canadian toy company, has achieved efficiencies through creating alliances in all aspects of its operations, from designing new products to manufacturing and retailing. The flexibility of outsourcing everything has allowed Spin Masters to concentrate on what they do best—bringing products to market faster than

competitive advantage
The ability of one organization to outperform other organizations because it produces desired goods or services more efficiently and effectively than competitors do.

FIGURE 2.8 | Building Blocks of Competitive Advantage

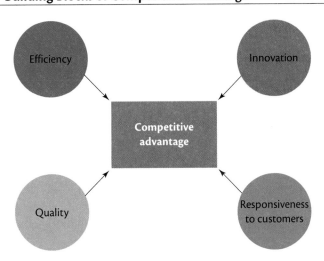

BananaStock/Jupiter Images

Holland College[64]

ISO 9001:2000 Certified

"Dedicated to excellence in performance, Holland College is committed to providing quality educational opportunities and services that meet or exceed the needs of learners, industry/business and our community."

Holland College Statement of Mission

any of the big companies, such as Hasboro and Mattel, could ever do. Take for example, the deal to manufacture and market Catch-a-Bubble in 2002. "Six months after the first meeting in Hong Kong, Spin Master shipped 7 million units and invoiced $15 million."[63] Gaining a competitive advantage in the global economy demands that organizations achieve efficiencies in order to provide affordable merchandise to their customers.

Increasing Quality

The challenge from global organizations such as Korean electronics manufacturers, Mexican agricultural producers, and European marketing and financial firms has also increased pressure on companies to improve the quality of goods and services delivered. One major thrust to improve quality has been to introduce quality-enhancing techniques known as *total quality management* (TQM). Employees involved in TQM are often organized into quality control teams and are given the responsibility of continually finding new and better ways to perform their jobs; they also are given the responsibility for monitoring and evaluating the quality of the goods they produce.

Increasing Innovation

innovation
The process of creating new goods and services or developing better ways to produce or provide goods and services.

Innovation—the process of creating new goods and services that customers want, or developing better ways to produce or provide goods and services—poses a special challenge. Managers must create an organizational setting in which people are encouraged to be innovative. Typically, innovation takes place in small groups or teams; management passes on control of work activities to team members and creates an organizational culture that rewards risk-taking. Understanding and managing innovation and creating a work setting that encourages risk-taking are among the most difficult managerial tasks. Dr. Michael Rachlis, an associate professor at the University of Toronto's department of health care policy and author of *Prescription for Excellence: How Innovation is Saving Canada's Health Care System*, points out how a few years ago, the innovative Sault Ste Marie Group Health Centre in Ontario assigned a home-care nurse to visit every heart-failure patient, a practice that reduced re-admissions by 70 percent. In another case, the Northwest Territories' diabetes program ensures comprehensive follow-up and, at least partly as a result, no one with diabetes has suffered the loss of kidney function due to complications from the disease.[65]

Research In Motion (RIM) is particularly good at innovation. Founded in 1984 and headquartered in Waterloo, Ontario, RIM is a leading designer, manufacturer, and marketer of innovative wireless solutions for the worldwide mobile communications market. It first developed in 1999 the BlackBerry device that had the capability of sending wireless email. After a lengthy battle with NTP, a Virginia-based company, over patent infringement, the case was settled in 2006 with RIM paying NTP $612.5 million. The company has not looked back since in terms of developing innovative wireless services and applications. Its new SureType and SurePress technologies in its smart phones provide users with an integrated keyboard that combines a traditional telephone keypad and the facility to type single fingered or double thumbed without changing the interface. Moreover, the software recognizes the words as you type them.

The legal and political environments again put RIM in the news in 2009 when Nortel Networks Corporation received a bid from the world's largest wireless network firm Swedish LM Ericsson to purchase its wireless technology assets and patents for US$1.13 billion. Nortel was Canada's leading telecommunications company until bankruptcy forced the sale of its assets under court supervision. RIM had been in talks with Nortel about purchasing its key intellectual property patents such as its CDMA technology (code division multiple access technology) but did not end up participating in the auction of assets on July 24, 2009. Nortel's CDMA system still widely deployed by mobile-phone carriers and other essential patents will not remain in Canadian hands; after approval by government regulators, the Swedish firm will benefit by having won the auction. CDMA is widely used in emerging markets like Asia.[66]

Increasing Responsiveness to Customers

Organizations use their products and services to compete for customers, so training employees to be responsive to customers' needs is vital for all organizations, and particularly for service organizations. Retail stores, banks, and restaurants, for example, depend entirely on their employees to give high-quality service at a reasonable cost.[67] As Canada and other countries move toward a more service-based economy (in part because of the loss of manufacturing jobs to China, Malaysia, and other countries with low labour costs), managing behaviour in service organizations is becoming increasingly important.

Take for example, Harry Rosen, a high-end menswear retailer. In today's global economy, innovations in the fashion industry are quickly replicated at lower costs by knock-off manufacturers in emerging markets. It is not enough to sell uniqueness at premium prices. CEO Larry Rosen explains, "Quality for the customer becomes less a question of what you sell than of how you sell it. When you get to a price point at Rosen, it's the experience you're buying. We don't perceive ourselves as being in the clothing business. We don't just sell suits and sport jackets. It's a relationship-based business. My business is to get to know you, to have you build a relationship with one of my highly trained associates. I want to be your clothier for life. The whole key to our business is loyal clients. I strongly believe we have a corporate culture that has a love of quality and a love of clients. And building customer relationships is a managed process."

Maintaining Ethical Standards

While mobilizing organizational resources, all managers are under considerable pressure to increase the level at which their organizations perform. For example, top managers receive pressure from shareholders to increase the performance of the entire organization in order to boost stock prices, improve profits, or raise dividends. In turn, top managers may then pressure middle managers to find new ways to use organizational resources to increase efficiency or quality in order to attract new customers and earn more revenues.

Pressure to improve performance can be healthy for an organization because it causes managers to question the organization's operations and encourages them to find new and better ways to plan, organize, lead, and control. However, too much pressure to perform can be harmful.[68] It may induce managers to behave unethically in dealings with individuals and groups both inside and outside the organization.[69] For example, a purchasing manager for a large retail chain might buy inferior clothing as a cost-cutting measure. Or to secure a large foreign contract, a sales manager in a large defence company might offer bribes to foreign officials. Or overzealous stock brokers might trade in Credit Default Swaps and other securities derivatives to make a fast buck without due consideration of the risk of total financial collapse as almost happened in the crisis of 2008–2009.

When managers act unethically, some individuals or groups may obtain short-term gains, but in the long run the organization and people inside and outside the organization will pay. In Chapter 3, we discuss the nature of ethics and the importance of managers and all members of an organization behaving ethically as they pursue organizational goals.

Utilizing New Information Systems and Technologies

Another important challenge facing Canadian managers is the pressure to increase performance through new information systems and technologies.[70] Canadian companies have been slower to adopt new technologies than their American counterparts, lagging behind the United States by two decades when it comes to corporate and government spending on information technology, a Conference Board of Canada report found. As a result, the United States enjoys higher productivity and economic growth rates.[71] The importance of information systems and technologies is discussed in greater detail in Chapter 4.

Summary and Review

1. **WHAT IS THE ORGANIZATIONAL ENVIRONMENT?** The organizational environment is the set of forces and conditions that affect a manager's ability to acquire and use resources. The organizational environment has two components: the internal environment and the external environment. The external environment can be divided into the task environment and the general environment.

2. **THE TASK ENVIRONMENT** The task environment is the set of forces and conditions that originate with suppliers, distributors, customers, and competitors and that influence managers on a daily basis.

3. **THE GENERAL ENVIRONMENT** The general environment includes wider-ranging economic, technological, demographic, political and legal, and global forces that affect an organization and its task environment.

4. **MANAGING THE EXTERNAL ENVIRONMENT** Two factors affect the nature of the opportunities and threats that organizations face: (1) the level of complexity in the environment and (2) the rate of change in the environment. Managers must learn how to analyze the forces in the environment in order to respond effectively to opportunities and threats. Managers at all three levels and in all functional areas are responsible for reducing the negative impact of environmental forces as they evolve over time.

5. **CHALLENGES FOR MANAGEMENT IN A GLOBAL ENVIRONMENT** Today's competitive global environment presents three main challenges to managers: Building a competitive advantage by increasing efficiency, quality, innovation, and responsiveness to customers; behaving ethically toward stakeholders inside and outside the organization; and utilizing new information systems and technologies.

Key Terms

aging population, p. 32

barriers to entry, p. 35

brand loyalty, p. 35

certainty, p. 48

command economy, p. 42

competitive advantage, p. 51

competitive landscape, p. 32

competitors, p. 34

customer-centricity, p. 34

customers, p. 34

demographic forces, p. 39

distributors, p. 34

economic forces, p. 38

economies of scale, p. 35

environmental change, p. 46

environmental consciousness, p. 33

external environment, p. 30

"firms of endearment", p. 45

free-market economy, p. 42

general environment, p. 31

global forces, p. 41

global organizations, p. 49

innovation, p. 52

internal environment, p. 30

mixed economy, p. 42

organizational environment, p. 30

political and legal forces, p. 40

representative democracy, p. 42

stakeholders, p. 30

suppliers, p. 33

task environment, p. 30

technological forces, p. 39

technology, p. 39

totalitarian regime, p. 42

uncertainty, p. 48

SO WHERE DO YOU STAND?

Wrap-Up to Opening Case

1. What are the three factors from the reading of the story that work in favour of Floform Industries Ltd. as it learns to adapt and manage in this new global environment?

   One factor, which is a key one in thinking strategically and how the external environment may affect the business, is that both in *good* times and in *tough* times consumers turn to home renovations.

   A second, and key, factor is the fact that Floform Industries is a well-managed and well-financed company. Owner Ted Sherritt said that it was the ability to recruit and retain talented managers that allowed Floform Industries to grow as rapidly as it did.

   A third factor is that while Mr. Sherritt states that Floform Industries has always been and will "likely stay" a Western company, he also leaves open the door to "start moving into the major, much more competitive big city markets."

2. What are some additional current issues that may impact Floform Industries' organizational environment?

   With the unprecedented rise in oil prices in 2008, Floform Industries needed to factor in more dynamically the cost of importing its machines from China and Brazil. Airlines began adding on surcharges, fuel charges, and any other charges that would help make up the loss in revenue from the oil crisis.

Management in Action

Topics for Discussion and Action

Level 1

1. Identify and describe the forces found in an organization's task and general environments.
2. Identify and describe the two factors in the organizational environment that affect the nature of opportunities and threats that a firm faces.
3. Describe what each level of manager can do to reduce the impact of the forces in the organizational environment.

Level 2

4. Ask the manager of an organization to discuss the types and strengths of forces in the organization's task environment. What are the current opportunities and threats resulting from competitors, customers, and suppliers?
5. Scan the environmental forces affecting local businesses by reading the business section of today's newspaper or listening to a business podcast. Explain the impact of the forces on local business' ability to acquire and use resources.

6. Go to the library and gather information that allows you to compare and contrast the political, economic, demographic, and cultural systems of the United States, Mexico, and Canada. How might the similarities and differences affect the management of an enterprise such as Wal-Mart, which does business in all three countries?

Level 3

7. Illustrate how each force in the organization's task environment can pose an opportunity and a threat for a manager of a Tim Hortons' restaurant wishing to expand into the United States.
8. Put yourself in the position of a first-line manager of a retailer such as Zellers. What suggestions would you make to your boss on how to use the four building blocks to gain a competitive advantage?
9. Which organization is likely to face the most complex task environment: a biotechnology company trying to develop a cure for cancer, or a large retailer such as Zellers or The Bay? Explain why this is the case with reference to each force in the organization's task environment.

Building Management Skills

Answer the following questions about the organization you have chosen to follow:

1. Describe the main forces in the task environment that are affecting the organization.
2. Describe the main forces in the general environment that are affecting the organization.
3. Try to determine whether the organization's task and general environments are relatively stable or changing rapidly.

4. Explain how these environmental forces affect the job of an individual manager within this organization. How do these forces determine the opportunities and threats that managers must confront?
5. How does the organization utilize the four building blocks of a competitive advantage?

Management for You

You are considering organizing an event to raise funds for a special cause (e.g., children living in poverty, breast cancer research, literacy, or something of your choice). Think about who you might invite to this event (i.e., your "customers"—those who will buy tickets to the event). What type of event might appeal to them? What suppliers might you approach for help in organizing the event? What legal issues might you face in setting up this event? After considering all these issues, how difficult is the environment you face in holding this event?

Small Group Breakout Exercise

Assume you and your teammates run a management consultancy company. Two of your clients, a multinational pharmaceutical company and a home construction company, are concerned about changing demographic trends in Canada. The population is aging because of declining birth rates, declining death rates, and the aging of the baby boom generation.

1. What might be some of the implications (opportunities and threats) of this demographic trend for your clients?

Business Planning Exercise

After reading this chapter, you start to realize you have to analyze the forces in the organizational environment to determine the impact of the opportunities and threats from the forces in the task and general environment for your business plan. This analysis will form an important part of the Profile of the Industry (Section 4, Appendix A).

1. Who are your customers? Research the characteristics of your target market. For example, what is their demographic profile and size of population in your community (age, income, amount of disposable income spent on eating out, etc.)?
2. Who are your competitors? Research the numbers and the strengths and weaknesses of your competitors. What degree of threat do they pose?
3. Where will you obtain all the inputs you will need to run your business? For the restaurant example, who will supply the food, kitchen equipment, tables, cutlery, etc.?

4. What kind of legal and political factors do you need to address? Which types of licences are needed, and where can you obtain them?
5. Are there any significant socio-cultural forces in your community that might present an opportunity or a threat that should be discussed in your business plan?
6. Illustrate how the building blocks of competitive advantage could be used to help your restaurant succeed.

Managing Ethically

You are a manager for a drug company that has developed a pill to cure river blindness, a common disease in Africa. It was a quick and easy solution, but there were no buyers because the people afflicted or who could be afflicted are too poor to buy the pills. Should you shelve the pills and wait until the market can pay the price? What other alternatives might you have?

Exploring the World Wide Web

SPECIFIC ASSIGNMENT

Go to the website of Mountain Equipment Co-op: http://www.mec.ca, and describe the firm's organizational environment.

1. Click on "About our Co-op" and "Ethical Sourcing Blog." Describe the following environmental forces that MEC faces: Customers and Suppliers.
2. From your analysis of its website, how well is MEC managing its opportunities and challenges? Discuss.

GENERAL ASSIGNMENT

Search for the website of a company that has a complex, rapidly changing environment. What forces in its environment are creating the strongest opportunities and threats? How are managers trying to respond to these opportunities and threats?

McGraw-Hill Connect™—Available 24/7 with instant feedback so you can study when you want, how you want, and where you want. Take advantage of the Study Plan—an innovative tool that helps you customize your learning experience. You can diagnose your knowledge with pre- and post-tests, identify the areas where you need help, search the entire learning package for content specific to the topic you're studying, and add these resources to your personalized study plan. Visit www.mcgrawhillconnect.ca to register—take practice quizzes, search the e-book, and much more.

Be the Manager

THE "PERSONAL TOUCH"[72]

As a communications expert, you have just read that research shows that friendlier workers are more productive. You found this very interesting because you will shortly be providing consultation to a company that wants to make its workplace friendlier. Until now this company has felt that it is more professional to stay impersonal at work, but, as mentioned above, research is showing that friendlier employees are more productive. A comparison of the American work ethic to approaches in other countries shows that keeping an emotional distance may not be the most effective way to get the job done. Friendly workers pay attention to indirect meanings, work well with other cultures, and are perceived as trustworthy, the research found.

> *An impersonal style tends to restrict the bandwidth of information a person attends to in the workplace. What is literally said will be followed closely but information about the context in which the information is conveyed—information often critical for task success and productivity—is lost. This impersonal attitude at work is rooted in Protestant beliefs of putting emotion aside at the office. The American style of keeping things impersonal at the workplace is virtually confined to the United States. Workers in South Korea, Japan, and India and especially Latin American countries place high importance on personal relationships at work. Latin Americans become friends with people they are doing business with first and then move on to the work, while Americans work first and then become friends.*

Question

1. Which force in the organizational environment does this research illustrate? What do you recommend managers do to overcome this potential threat from the general environment?

Management Case

The Future of the Future[73]

Alan M. Webber, founding editor of *Fast Company* magazine, speaks of *five revolutions* affecting all of us globally:

1. **WORK:** The rise of China and India is an integral part of the powerful revolution that is reinventing the dynamics of business, work, and wealth creation.

2. **POLITICAL CULTURE:** The convergence of politics, religion, and culture is acting as a powerful force for national and international identity and change.

3. **SCIENCE AND TECHNOLOGY:** At a remarkable gathering [in August 2005] hosted by the Waldzell Institute in Vienna, Craig Venter, the man who

cracked the human genome code, described his next project: to learn how to create life from scratch.

4. *ART:* A revolution is taking place in self-expression. Daniel Pink, in his book *A Whole New Mind: Moving from the Information Age to the Conceptual Age,*[74] talks about the shift in business now from the left brain (or rational perspective) to the right brain (or the more emotional, intuitive, perspective).[75] According to Pink, companies must learn to connect now to the six senses: "*Design:* paying attention to aesthetics when carrying out any task. *Story:* conveyance of information to consumers, employees, and others through storytelling techniques. *Symphony:* the ability to put together pieces to create a holistic picture; synthesis is a good synonym. *Empathy:* identifying with and understanding another person's circumstances, feelings, and motives. *Play:* putting fun into every activity to enhance both pleasure and creativity. *Meaning:* extending the value of an activity beyond the moment and self."[76]

5. *MEANING:* There is a global search for meaning in our world. "What was once presumed to be reserved as a privilege for the wealthy is now a global consideration, as widely shared as the thirst for personal freedom and national independence. People around the world not only want to put food on the table, find good work, and have safety in their homes—they want to have meaning in their lives."

Webber says that these five revolutions are happening concurrently in our world today and are every bit as powerful as the ones of 100 years ago. He draws out four "operating rules" from the five revolutions (above):

1. "If you want to lead in the future, you have to unleash your organization's capacity to innovate and create."

2. "If we want to see the future, we will have to ask the right questions about it."

3. Increasingly the future that is emerging requires cross-disciplinary thinking, the ability to work across categories and at the boundaries of expertise. The future will be born where art meets business; the MFA (Master of Fine Arts) is the new MBA.

4. The future will emerge as we master the art of creating a "both-and" world, a world where we thrive on individual and collective creativity and action, where inspiration comes from sources within and without our own lives and our own cultures, where we can have conservation of our most important traditions and heritages, and the constant creation of new art, new science, and new technology.

Video Management Case

The Environment of Business

The video, "The Environment of Business," showcases the Trek Bicycle Corporation. The video illustrates how linking quality to managing well creates a high-performance work environment for business. Trek realized that quality and standards would be the new mantra. The company grew 700 percent as a result. Trek's comeback was absolutely amazing. Employees were also empowered to make good judgment calls as they went about their work each day. If something on the line was not right, they could stop production, work with others, and fix the problem. As preparation for watching the video, go to their website and get a "feel" for the company: www.trekbikes.com. Go through the various options at the website as well. Now watch the video, "The Environment of Business."

Questions to consider

1. What's your sense of the company?

2. Would you want to work for such a company as Trek? Why? Why not?

3. What is Trek's environment for doing business?

4. What are the challenges that managers at Trek face in the global marketplace?

5. How successful do you think Trek will be?

CHAPTER 3

Managing Ethics, Social Responsibility, and Diversity

Learning Outcomes

1. Describe the concept of ethics and the different models of ethics.

2. Detail the ways in which organizations can encourage ethical behaviour among managers and employees.

3. Describe four approaches to corporate social responsibility.

4. Define diversity, and explain why the effective management of diverse employees is both an ethical issue and a means for an organization to improve its performance.

5. Identify instances of workplace harassment, and discuss how to prevent its occurrence.

Don't Look Now[1]

Harvard Business School professor Max Bazerman and his colleagues, in their paper "See No Evil: When We Overlook Other People's Unethical Behaviour"[2] write, "We believe that these scandals [at Enron, WorldCom, Parmalat,[3] and Tyco International] would not have occurred if leaders and employees within these firms had taken note of the unethical behaviour of their colleagues rather than overlooking such behaviour."[4]

The authors discuss a concept called *bounded ethicality*.

> Just as bounded rationality refers to the fact that people have cognitive limitations that affect the choices they make based on their own preferences, bounded ethicality refers to the tendency of people to engage in behaviour that is inconsistent with their own ethical values. That is, bounded ethicality refers to situations in which people make decision errors that not only harm others but are inconsistent with their own consciously espoused beliefs and preferences—decisions they would condemn upon further reflection or greater awareness.[5]

Most of us would be horrified at the idea of cheating a customer or selling bad-quality goods, much less making money out of another person's suffering.

But it happens all the time. We engage in behaviours that are inconsistent with our own ethical values, decisions we would condemn in others and in ourselves, if only we thought about it long enough. And we regularly look the other way when others engage in ethically questionable behaviour on our behalf.

Sound far-fetched? What about the manager who tells his sales staff to "do what it takes" to achieve goals or get a client? Perhaps you work for a company that outsources production to subcontractors with substandard hiring practices or environmental standards, or for a company that "gets creative" with business practices in order to retain a client. There are subtle ways, says writer Donna Nebenzahl, a professor of journalism at Concordia University,

(c) Digital Vision

Montreal, and author of *Womankind*,[6] whereby we can end up "on the dark side," and that is a reality that should make all employers and employees sit up and take note.

In her write-up "See No Evil," in the Harvard Business School paper, Nebenzahl summarizes its key ideas:

First, there's something they call "motivated blindness,"[7] which describes our tendency to overlook the unethical behaviours of others if it might cause us harm. If you work with a boss, for instance, who is unethical, there is huge incentive to see him or her in a favourable light. With your own security or survival at stake, it stands to reason you would have difficulty accurately assessing that person's behaviour.

Auditors are a classic example of people who can be in conflict between acting in their own interests and acting ethically, the researchers note. In one study, participants were asked to assess a company's value, and they did so entirely differently depending on whether they worked for the seller or the buyer. So when Arthur Andersen audited Enron, the pressure would have been huge to turn a blind eye to the behaviour of the company that paid it millions in fees.

Research indicates "humans are biased to selectively see evidence supportive of the conclusion they would like to reach, while ignoring evidence that goes against their preferences or subjecting it to special scrutiny," they write.[8]

We also, it seems, are able to forgive others who benefit from delegating unethical behaviour, as seen in the case of pharmaceutical company Merck, which in 2005 sold off a couple of cancer drugs it had developed to a smaller firm, Ovation, while continuing to manufacture the drugs. It turned out the smaller company raised the wholesale price of the drug tenfold, allowing Merck to avoid the headline of increasing cancer drug prices, yet making money from this transaction. "The public and press fail to condemn people and firms that use an intermediary to do their dirty work," the authors state.[9]

The result, recent evidence shows, is people who allow it eventually grow comfortable with unethical behaviour, a condition the authors call "change blindness." This is the classic slippery slope, especially when we allow small incremental unethical transgressions to occur over time.

Another roadblock to acting ethically in the business world, they point out, is our tendency to value outcomes over processes, which can easily affect one's judgment. If, for instance, someone manipulated pharmaceutical research in some small way and the drug that ended up on the market killed a number of patients, we would be quick to condemn them. But suppose the drug did not kill anyone. In that case, studies show we are much less likely to condemn the manipulation of the research.

"We believe executives should ... be held responsible for the harm that their organizations predictably created, with or without intentionality or awareness," Prof. Bazerman and his colleagues conclude.[10]

Now It's Your Turn

1. The authors of "See No Evil" in our opening case write elsewhere: "Most people value ethical decisions and behaviour and strive to be good. Yet psychological processes sometimes lead them to engage in questionable behaviours that are inconsistent with their own values and beliefs."[11] Why do employees engage in behaviours that are inconsistent with their own values and beliefs?

▪▪▪▫ Overview

Mention was made in our opening case of Italy's disgraced Parmalat Finanziara SpA company referred to as "Europe's Enron."[12] Marc Caira, a graduate of Seneca College's Marketing Administration Program, was CEO of Parmalat Dairy & Bakery Inc. in Canada from 2004 to January 26, 2006. For some managers, it is their refusal to accept what has happened that exacerbates the unethical behaviour. For Caira, it was his vision, ethics, and business acumen that made the difference in Canada.

It is easy to see that in spite of his what was labelled the "Aw-Shucks" defence, Bernie Ebbers, ex-WorldCom boss, was found guilty of a record-breaking US$11-billion fraud and conspiracy for his role in the biggest corporate blow-up in U.S. corporate history. Ebbers defence was the "Aw-shucks, I'm-not-sophisticated defence," as one prosecutor defined it, also known as the Canadian defence, and also known as the Sgt. Schultz "I-know-nothing" defence. The jury at his trial in 2005 did not accept that defence. Journalist Jennifer Wells describes his defence this way: "In the words of that great American cultural icon, Gomer Pyle, 'Well, Golly'."[13] Ebbers was sentenced to 25 years in prison.

When Caira discovered what was happening, he immediately took steps to rectify matters. He began working on managing what he had to do to protect the Canadian operation. He did this in spite of the fact that he was not at all involved in the scandal at head office in Italy, a scandal that revealed US$11.7 billion in unaccounted funds! Because of his transparency, good management skills, and ethical vision, he saved the Canadian operation from scandal; indeed, he even made it profitable!

The ways in which managers view their responsibilities to the individuals and groups that are affected by their actions are central to the discussion of ethics and social responsibility and to the discussion of organizational performance as well. In this chapter, we explore what it means to behave ethically. We describe how managers and organizations can behave in a socially responsible way toward the individuals and groups in their organizational environment.

We then focus on one particular aspect of ethical behaviour that is receiving increasing attention today: how to manage diversity to ensure that everyone an organization employs is fairly and equitably treated. Managers' ability and desire to behave ethically and to manage diversity effectively are central concerns in today's complex business environment. Increasingly, if managers ignore these issues or fail to act appropriately, their organizations are unlikely to prosper in the future.

We also discuss workplace harassment, which is both unethical and illegal, and a behaviour that managers and organizations—military as well as civilian—must confront and respond to in a serious manner. By the end of the chapter, you will appreciate why ethics, diversity, and workplace harassment are issues that make a manager's job both more challenging and more complex.

LO 1

What Are Ethics?

THINK ABOUT IT

Like a Child in a Candy Store?[14]

Paul Coffin, in Montreal, was the first person convicted of 15 counts of fraud in the federal government's sponsorship contracts scandal. He was also the first ad executive to reimburse some of the money improperly paid in federal contracts, by handing back $1 million of the $1.6 million he admitted he owed taxpayers; this agreement was reached as an out-of-court settlement in the civil suit Ottawa filed in spring 2005 against 19 individuals and firms involved in the scandal.

In the courtroom, he asked for clemency when being sentenced. The crown attorney said he deserved at least 34 months in prison even though he made amends; Justice Jean-Guy Boilard of the Quebec Superior Court said that the fraud was quite elaborate and that Coffin had truly betrayed the public's trust.

Coffin's defence lawyer said that Coffin was "like a child in a candy store." Raphael Schachter, Coffin's lawyer, said blame should be placed on the federal government's shoulders in Ottawa for tempting his client with the lax way it administered the sponsorship program. This laxness made it virtually impossible for him to avoid the temptation of the fraud, even if it was $1.6 million he admitted he owed taxpayers!

Coffin said that he was an honest man who strayed only once, that he was raised by law-abiding parents, including a mother who told him to return a wallet he had found when he was a boy because "honesty is the best policy." He indicated that he had already contacted Montreal's four universities and offered to give business students lectures on ethics. "My objective is to give back to the community I betrayed," he said.

The Crown prosecutor did not want to accept Coffin's contrition. He said that if Coffin did not go to jail, it would be like telling the students: "For nearly five years, I sent false invoices, invoices that were paid with your money, I lived well, and now I'm before you, a citizen who isn't behind bars—don't do as I did." This, according to the prosecutor, would be sending the wrong message.[16]

Coffin's intention is to spend the rest of his life, if necessary, in paying off his debts to the people he defrauded. Said Coffin, "I feel very ashamed of what I've

(c) Ryan Remioz
After admitting at the Gomery inquiry to blatantly inflating costs and filing false invoices, Communications Coffin president Paul Coffin became the first person to face criminal charges in connection with the sponsorship scandal. In May 2005, he pleaded guilty to 15 counts of fraud and was handed a conditional sentence that requires him to lecture students about business ethics. Coffin and his company are now also on the list of 11 firms and eight individuals that the federal government has instructed to pay back misappropriated sponsorship funds.[15]

done ... I want to make restitution. I want to come clean ... I want to clear my name and feel better with my family."

You Be the Manager

1. Do you accept Paul Coffin's defence lawyer's claim that his client was really like "a child in a candy store"?
2. What would you recommend as an appropriate sentence for Coffin's fraudulent behaviour?

ethics
Moral principles or beliefs about what is right or wrong.

The questions raised about Paul Coffin's fraudulent role in the sponsorship contracts scandal highlight ethical concerns to which managers need to pay attention. **Ethics** are moral principles or beliefs about what is right or wrong. These beliefs guide individuals in their dealings with other individuals and groups who have a concern in a particular situation (stakeholders), and they provide a basis for deciding if a behaviour is right and proper.[17] Ethics help people determine moral responses to situations in which the best course of action is unclear.

Managers often experience an ethical dilemma when they confront a situation that requires them to choose between two courses of action, especially if each decision is likely to serve the interests of one particular stakeholder group to the detriment of another.[18] To make an appropriate decision, managers must weigh the competing claims or rights of the various stakeholder groups. Sometimes, making a decision is easy because some obvious standard, value, or norm of behaviour applies. In other cases, managers have trouble deciding what to do.

Making Ethical Decisions

Philosophers have debated for centuries about the specific criteria that should be used to determine whether decisions are ethical or unethical. Three models of what determines whether a decision is ethical—the *utilitarian*, *moral rights*, and *justice* models—are summarized in Table 3.1.[19] In theory, each model offers a different and complementary way of determining whether a decision or behaviour is ethical, and all three models should be used to sort out the ethics of a particular course of action. Ethical issues are seldom clear-cut, however, and the interests of different stakeholders often conflict, so it is often extremely difficult for a decision maker to use these models to identify the most ethical course of action. That is why many experts on ethics propose the following practical guide to determine whether a decision or behaviour is ethical.[20] A decision is probably acceptable on ethical grounds if a person can answer "yes" to each of these questions:

ethical decision
A decision that reasonable or typical stakeholders would find acceptable because it aids stakeholders, the organization, or society.

1. Does my decision fall within the accepted values or standards that typically apply in the organizational environment?
2. Am I willing to see the decision communicated to all stakeholders affected by it— for example, by having it reported in newspapers or on television?
3. Would the people with whom I have a significant personal relationship, such as family members, friends, or even managers in other organizations, approve of the decision?

unethical decision
A decision that a manager would prefer to disguise or hide from other people because it enables a company or a particular individual to gain at the expense of society or other stakeholders.

From an organizational perspective, an **ethical decision** is a decision that reasonable or typical stakeholders would find acceptable because it aids stakeholders, the organization, or society. By contrast, an **unethical decision** is a decision that a person would

TABLE 3.1 | *Utilitarian, Moral Rights, and Justice Models of Ethics*

Model	Managerial Implications	Problems for Managers
Utilitarian Model An ethical decision is a decision that produces the greatest good for the greatest number of people	Managers should compare and contrast alternative courses of action based on the benefits and costs of those alternatives for different organizational stakeholder groups. They should choose the course of action that provides the most benefits to stakeholders. For example, managers should locate a new manufacturing plant at the place that will most benefit its stakeholders.	How do managers decide on the relative importance of each stakeholder group? How are managers to measure precisely the benefits and harms to each stakeholder group? For example, how do managers choose among the interests of stockholders, employees, and customers?
Moral Rights Model An ethical decision is a decision that best maintains and protects the fundamental rights and privileges of the people affected by it. For example, ethical decisions protect people's rights to freedom, life and safety, privacy, free speech, and freedom of conscience.	Managers should compare and contrast alternative courses of action based on the effect of those alternatives on stakeholders' rights. They should choose the course of action that best protects stakeholders' rights. For example, decisions that would involve significant harm to the safety or health of employees or customers are unethical.	If a decision will protect the rights of some stakeholders and hurt the rights of others, how do managers choose which stakeholder rights to protect? For example, in deciding whether it is ethical to snoop on an employee, does an employee's right to privacy outweigh an organization's right to protect its property or the safety of other employees?
Justice Model An ethical decision is a decision that distributes benefits and harms among stakeholders in a fair, equitable, or impartial way.	Managers should compare and contrast alternative courses of action based on the degree to which the action will promote a fair distribution of outcomes. For example, employees who are similar in their level of skill, performance, or responsibility should receive the same kind of pay. The allocation of outcomes should not be based on arbitrary differences such as gender, race, or religion.	Managers must learn not to discriminate between people because of observable differences in their appearance or behaviour. Managers must also learn how to use fair procedures to determine how to distribute outcomes to organizational members. For example, managers must not give people they like bigger raises than they give to people they do not like or bend the rules to help their favourites.

prefer to disguise or hide from other people because it enables a company or a particular individual to gain at the expense of society or other stakeholders. The sponsorship contracts scandal incident highlights how easy it can be, even for seasoned managers and executives, to become involved in shady deals and, in Coffin's case, in serious fraudulent behaviour. We saw that even though Paul Coffin demonstrated contrition, agreed to pay back as much as he could, and indicated he would spend the rest of his life making amends, he still left it to his lawyer to argue that the temptation to commit fraud was just too great for his client and hence Coffin was at the mercy of the forces, such as a child would be "in a candy store." Ethics and accountability must go hand in hand. The authors of the Harvard Business School paper "See No Evil" conclude their paper with the following words: "They [executives] should be held responsible for the harms that their organizations predictably create, with or without intentionality or awareness" because "we believe that executives should face a higher hurdle."[21] People will always ask, "Was Paul Coffin really at the mercy of the forces, as his lawyer suggests—like a child in a candy store—or was this defence simply a way to avoid accountability—and prison?" If it was, it also trivialized the seriousness of the charges.

Codes of Ethics

Codes of ethics are formal standards and rules, based on beliefs about right or wrong, that managers can use to make appropriate decisions in the best interests of their stakeholders.[22] Ethical standards embody views about abstractions such as justice, freedom, equity, and equality (see Table 3.1). An organization's code of ethics derives from three main sources in the organizational environment: (1) **societal ethics**, governing how everyone deals with each other on issues such as fairness, justice, poverty, and the rights of the individual; (2) **professional ethics**, governing how members of

codes of ethics
Formal standards and rules, based on beliefs about right or wrong, that managers can use to make appropriate decisions in the best interests of their stakeholders.

societal ethics
Standards that govern how members of a society deal with each other on issues such as fairness, justice, poverty, and the rights of the individual.

professional ethics
Standards that govern how members of a profession make decisions when the way they should behave is not clear-cut.

■ **FIGURE 3.1 | Sources of an Organization's Code of Ethics**

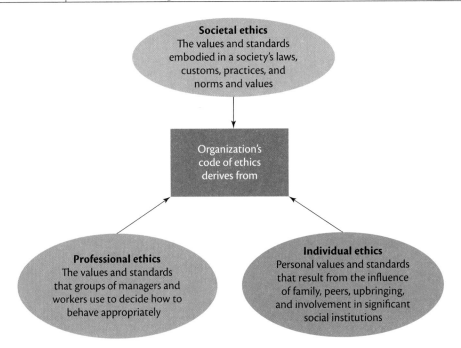

the profession make decisions when the way they should behave is not clear-cut; and (3) the **individual ethics**, or personal standards for interacting with others, of the organization's top managers (see Figure 3.1).

The code of ethics for the Canadian Timber Company, for example, is guided by Biblical principles. According to their website, they say the following:[23]

individual ethics
Personal standards that govern how individuals interact with other people.

> *These principles have shown themselves to be true in all of recorded history and continue to be foundational for successful living in both the personal and corporate world. We believe that both our company and customers benefit from our endeavouring to honour these principles.*
>
> *We will strive to hold to the highest standards of honesty, integrity, and responsibility in all of our business dealings with you by:*

- *Writing contracts and warranties that are clear, honest, and fair to all parties involved;*

- *Honouring all contractual obligations in a timely manner;*

- *Adhering strictly to the highest quality standards of manufacturing;*

- *Being fiscally responsible and honouring all legitimate financial obligations;*

- *Maintaining required insurances;*

- *Maintaining and promoting safe and healthy workplaces;*

- *Promoting only those products and services that are of proven quality and value;*

- *Quickly acting on and attempting to resolve all customer complaints.*

On the other hand, the code of ethics approved by its board of directors in July 2003 for the Canadian Investor Relations Institute (CIRI) states:[24]

> *As a member of the Canadian Investor Relations Institute, I will:*
>
> 1. *Practise investor relations within the highest legal, regulatory, and ethical standards.*
> 2. *Exercise independent professional judgment in the conduct of my duties and responsibilities.*

3. *Attempt to avoid even the appearance of professional impropriety in the conduct of my investor relations responsibilities.*

4. *Keep up to date regarding the affairs of my company/clients, as well as the laws, regulations, and principles affecting the practice of investor relations.*

5. *Maintain the confidentiality of information acquired in the normal course of business.*

6. *Not use confidential information acquired in the normal course of business for my personal advantage, nor for the advantage of others, except in the legitimate performance of my duties on behalf of my company/clients.*

7. *Report to company authorities, the board of directors, or appropriate securities regulators, if I suspect or recognize fraudulent or illegal acts.*

8. *Recognize that the integrity and credibility of the capital markets is based on complete, timely, and nonselective disclosure of financial and nonfinancial corporate information and, to the best of my ability and knowledge, work to ensure that my company or client communicates such information on a timely basis.*

Canadian shareholders were just as affected by the financial crisis as others around the world, even with the code of ethics of the Canadian Investor Relations Institute (CIRI). Friday, October 22 2009, was the 80th anniversary stock market crash. It began on Thursday and accelerated the following week on days that have come to be known as Black Monday and Black Tuesday.[25]

Recently, stock markets around the world saw dramatic declines calling into question the ability of free market capitalism to self-regulate and balance the interests of all stakeholders. Ex-chairman of the U.S. Federal Reserve Alan Greenspan declared, in a testimony delivered to the House Oversight Committee into the causes of the financial crisis, that there was a "flaw" in "free market ideology." He said he was "in a state of shocked disbelief" because he "looked to the self-interest of lending institutions to protect shareholder's equity" but they did not.[26] Greenspan blamed "infectious greed" and called for more regulation of the financial system to address the breakdown of the market.[27]

Environmentalists, consumers, nonprofit organizations, and governments are increasingly vocal in lobbying, campaigning, and directing managerial efforts toward socially responsible and sustainable decisions. Ecologically sound decisions are ethical decisions, as the management of the large oil company Syncrude found out in 2008. In April 2008, in the Alberta Tar Sands, Syncrude Canada failed to put sufficient deterrents for migrating birds on one of its ponds that contained the oily waste water from the oil extraction process. The result was that 500 ducks died after landing on

Many ethical issues arise for mining companies who do business in countries without infrastructure in South Gobi, Mongolia. Would safety standards compare well with mines in North America?

organizational stakeholders
Shareholders, employees, customers, suppliers, and others who have an interest, claim, or stake in an organization and in what it does.

the toxic tailing pond. The company was charged by both the Alberta and federal governments after a 10-month investigation. The maximum penalty under Canada's Migratory Birds Convention Act, is a fine of $300 000 and/or six months in jail. Under the Alberta Environmental Protection and Enhancement Act, the maximum penalty is $500 000. Critics said the penalties amounted to nothing more than a slap on the wrist and that the company put profit first and protecting people and the environment second. Higher standards for preventing such occurrences from happening again have since been enforced in Alberta.[28]

Ethics and Stakeholders

The individuals and groups that have an interest, claim, or stake in an organization and in what it does are known as **organizational stakeholders**.[29] Organizational stakeholders include shareholders, managers, nonmanagerial employees, customers, suppliers, the local community in which an organization operates, and even citizens of the country in which an organization operates. To survive and prosper, an organization must effectively satisfy its stakeholders.[30] Stockholders want dividends, managers and employees want salaries and stable employment, and customers want high-quality products at reasonable prices. If stakeholders do not receive these benefits, they may withdraw their support for the organization: Stockholders will sell their stock, managers and workers will seek jobs in other organizations, and customers will take their business elsewhere.

Managers are the stakeholder group that determines which goals an organization should pursue to benefit stakeholders most, and how to make the most efficient use of resources to achieve those goals. In making such decisions, managers often have to juggle the interests of different stakeholders, including themselves.[31] Managerial decisions that may benefit some stakeholder groups and harm others involve questions of ethics. For example, South Gobi, Mongolia, is the exploration site of Ivanhoe Mines Ltd. of Vancouver, which has discovered a huge copper and gold deposit there. It is also spending US$10 million a month drilling holes, testing results, and pouring a gigantic concrete shaft in preparation for production. Mongolia is a country without infrastructure. Issues that have to be addressed include power generation, transportation, and smelting, water, and dust control. To overcome these obstacles, world-class companies must negotiate who is going to pay for what and when. Meeting these challenges is a time-consuming process because all stakeholder concerns must be met. "This is what goes on everywhere," said Ivanhoe chairman Robert Friedland. "It is in everyone's interest that the deal is fair to the government and citizens in order to have a sustainable development franchise."[32]

Ethics and National Culture

Views about what is ethical vary among societies. For example, ethical standards accepted in Canada and the United States are not accepted in all other countries. In many economically emerging countries, bribery is standard practice to get things done—such as getting a telephone installed or a contract awarded. In Canada and many other Western countries, bribery as part of doing business is considered unethical and often illegal in one's home country. Bribing foreign public officials is widespread, however. The U.S. government reported that between 1994 and 2001, bribery was uncovered in more than 400 competitions for international contracts.[33] A recent study found that some Asian governments were far more tolerant of corruption than others. Singapore, Japan, and Hong Kong scored relatively low on corruption (0.83, 2.5, and 3.77 out of 10, respectively), and Vietnam, Indonesia, India, the Philippines, and Thailand scored as the most corrupt of the 12 Asian countries surveyed.[34]

In April 2008, the chairman of the Samsung Group, Lee Kunhee, was indicted on charges of evading taxes on billions of dollars that he hid in stock accounts under the names of his aides.[35] He ended up resigning a few days after that.[36] Kim Yong-chul, a former chief legal counsel at Samsung, became a whistleblower and said that Samsung ran a bribery network, filling the pockets of prosecutors, bureaucrats, and politicians with cash gifts. Kim said he personally delivered some of these bribes; he named as bribe takers several former and incumbent senior prosecutors, who gained powerful posts under the country's new president Lee Myung-bak, currently the 17th president of Korea.[37]

While Canada has no national laws regarding codes of ethics, in 1997 a coalition of Canadian companies developed a new international code of ethics. The code is voluntary and deals with such issues as the environment, human rights, business conduct, treatment of employees, and health and safety standards. Supporters of the Canadian code include the Alliance of Manufacturers & Exporters Canada, the Conference Board of Canada, and the Business Council on National Issues. Alcan Inc., Komex International Ltd., Shell Canada Ltd., and Talisman Energy Inc. are among the companies that have signed the code. Former foreign affairs minister Lloyd Axworthy hailed the code as a way of putting Canadian values into the international arena.[38]

The Global Corruption Report for 2008 predicts that by 2020, between 75 and 250 million people in Africa alone will be exposed to increased water scarcity due to climate change. "As water becomes scarce and more precious, corruption becomes more lucrative and widespread. Less water and more corruption is a lethal combination, and the poor are likely to be the hardest hit. Conflicts such as in Darfur, Sudan, are increasingly linked to corrupt governance and local water shortages intensified by climate change."[39]

Initiatives such as the UN Global Compact and its 10th Principle against Corruption are promoting voluntary codes of conduct by raising awareness on business integrity and on ways to counter bribery in emerging economies as well as rich ones such as Canada.[40]

What Behaviours Are Ethical?

A key ethical decision for managers is how to divide harms and benefits among stakeholder groups.[41] Suppose a company has a few very good years and makes high profits. Who should receive these profits—managers, employees, stockholders, or customers? For example, as oil prices soared throughout the world in 2008, Canadian oil industry profits reached record highs. Customers, whose heating bills rose greatly, thought they should get some of their money back in rebates.

The decision about how to divide profits among managers, employees, stockholders, and even customers might not seem to be an ethical issue, but it is—in the same manner as how to apportion harms or costs among stakeholders when things go wrong.[42] For instance, it is not unusual for companies to engage in restructurings—resulting in massive layoffs—to improve their bottom line and perhaps increase returns to stockholders, who are the legal owners of a corporation. Are layoffs of managers and employees ethical? Managers at some companies try to make the layoffs less painful by introducing generous early retirement programs that give employees full pension rights if they retire early. Employees are sometimes paid a month's or several months' salary for each year of service to the company.

The question whether layoffs are ethical took on a new light in 2008, when Lehman Brothers, the 150-year-old U.S. investment bank declared bankruptcy and employees and shareholders lost just about everything, while its CEO Richard Fuld Jr. had taken home about $350 million in salary since 2000. In front of a committee of Congress Fuld argued that the demise of the company was a result of short-selling securities related to the subprime mortgage market. While Lehman was not bailed out by the U.S. government, the huge insurance company AIG was, with $85 billion to help it cope with the "credit crunch"—the inability to borrow funds necessary for operations. While the ethical issue of executive pay has become highly contentious in times of recession, layoffs, and bankruptcies, so too has the ethics of executive expenditures. CEO Robert Willumstad and former CEO Martin Sullivan were summoned to the same Congressional committee and asked to explain—among other things—how the company could spend US$480 000 for a week-long executive retreat (including tens of thousands of dollars in charges for massages, manicures, and pedicures) just days after the U.S. government committed the funds to bail out the troubled insurance company.[43]

The very question of whether governments should intervene in a free market economy to subsidize huge corporations with taxpayers' money is certainly questionable. The US$700-billion bailout package implemented by the U.S. government raised such questions in 2008.

Managers also face ethical dilemmas when choosing how to deal with other stakeholders. For example, suppliers provide an organization with its inputs and expect to be paid within a reasonable amount of time. Some managers, however, consistently delay payment to make the most use of their organization's money. This practice can hurt a supplier's cash flow and threaten its very survival. Heather Reismans' Chapters and Indigo big-box bookstores were accused of such behaviour early in this century in Canada.

An organization that is a powerful customer and buys large amounts of particular suppliers' products is in a position to demand that suppliers reduce their prices. Wal-Mart is famous for such practices. If an organization does this, suppliers earn lower profits and the organization earns more. Is this behaviour just "business as usual," or is it unethical?

In addition to suppliers and distributors, customers are a critical stakeholder group because, as noted in Chapter 1, organizations depend on them for their very survival. Customers have the right to expect an organization to provide goods and services that will not harm them. As well, local communities and the general public have an interest or stake in whether the decisions that managers make are ethical. The quality of a city's school system or police department, the economic health of its downtown area, and its general level of prosperity all depend on choices made by managers of organizations.

In summary, managers face many ethical choices as they deal with the different and sometimes conflicting interests of organizational stakeholders. Deciding what behaviour is ethical is often a difficult task that requires managers to make tough choices that will benefit some stakeholders and harm others.

Promoting Ethics

A 2000 ethics survey by KPMG found that nearly two-thirds of Canadian firms promote values and ethical practices. However, more than half the companies surveyed had not designated a senior manager responsible for ethical issues. Only 14 percent evaluated their employees in terms of ethical performance.[44] Despite a seeming lack of commitment to concrete actions by Canada's companies, there are many ways in which managers can communicate their desire for employees at all levels to behave ethically toward organizational stakeholders. The irony of this KPMG survey is that in August 2005 eight former executives of KPMG LLP were indicted on the largest criminal tax case ever filed, which allowed the firm's clients to avoid $2.5 billion in taxes! To avoid a situation where KPMG might collapse, as did Arthur Anderson, a former Big Four account firm competitor, KPMG agreed to pay US$456 million in penalties and admitted to helping wealthy clients fraudulently avoid billions in taxes.[45]

A 2005–2006 KPMG Integrity Survey,[46] based on responses from 4056 U.S. employees, spanning all levels of job responsibility, 16 job functions, 11 industry sectors, and four thresholds of organizational size, found the following: *Nearly three out of four employees reported that they had observed misconduct in the prior 12-month period, with half of employees reporting that what they had observed was serious misconduct that could cause "a significant loss of public trust if discovered."*

Between 2000 and 2005, employees reported:

- Consistent levels of overall misconduct, with 74 percent reporting in 2005 that they had observed misconduct, compared with 76 percent in 2000;

- Consistent levels of serious misconduct, with 50 percent in 2005 characterizing the misconduct they had observed as serious, compared with 49 percent in 2000.

But the survey does go on to talk about some positive factors as well: *Although the level of observed misconduct has remained constant, employees reported that the conditions that facilitate management's ability to prevent, detect, and respond to fraud and misconduct within companies are improving.*

Between 2000 and 2005, employees reported the following positive changes in conditions and attitudes:

- Pressure to engage in misconduct to meet business objectives has decreased.

- The adequacy of resources available to meet targets without cutting corners has improved.

- Apathy and indifference toward codes of conduct have declined.

- Comfort level in using a hotline to report misconduct has risen.

- Confidence that appropriate action would be taken in response to alleged improprieties has increased.

- Confidence that whistleblowers would be protected from retaliation has increased.

- Perception of chief executive officers and other senior executives as positive role models has improved.

- The perception that top management is approachable if employees have questions about ethics or need to deliver bad news has improved.

- The perception that business leaders would respond appropriately if they became aware of misconduct has improved.

Establishing Ethical Control Systems

Perhaps the most important step to encourage ethical behaviour is to develop a code of ethics that is given to every employee and published regularly in company newsletters and annual reports. The "Integrity Program" at Calgary-based Nexen

Inc. (formerly Canadian Occidental Petroleum Ltd.) covers such issues as business conduct, employee and human rights, and the environment. Each division at Nexen has an integrity leader who is supposed to make sure that the message about the company's commitment to ethics spreads throughout the organization.[47] At UPS Canada, employees must develop an action plan around their codes of conduct. Managers are assessed on such matters as integrity and fair treatment.[48]

ethics ombudsperson
An ethics officer who monitors an organization's practices and procedures to ensure that they are ethical.

The next step is to provide a visible means of support for ethical behaviour. Increasingly, organizations are creating the role of ethics officer, or **ethics ombudsperson**, to monitor their ethical practices and procedures. The ethics ombudsman is responsible for communicating ethical standards to all employees, for designing systems to monitor employees' conformity to those standards, and for teaching managers and nonmanagerial employees at all levels of the organization how to respond to ethical dilemmas appropriately.[49] Because the ethics ombudsperson has organizationwide authority, organizational members in any department can discuss instances of unethical behaviour by their managers or co-workers without fear of retribution. This arrangement makes it easier for everyone to behave ethically. In addition, ethics ombudspersons can provide guidance when organizational members are uncertain about whether an action is ethical. Some organizations have an organizationwide ethics committee to provide guidance on ethical issues and help write and update the company code of ethics.

Developing an Ethical Culture

An organization can also communicate its position on ethics and social responsibility to employees by making ethical values and norms a central part of its organizational culture. A number of companies try to encourage ethical behaviour through their corporate culture, emphasizing such values as honesty, trust, respect, and fairness. (We discuss organizational culture in detail in Chapter 7.) It is important to note that when organizational members abide by the organization's values and norms, those values and norms become part of each individual's personal code of ethics. Thus, an employee who faces an ethical dilemma automatically responds to the situation in a manner that reflects the ethical standards of the organization. High standards and strong values and norms help individuals resist self-interested action and recognize that they are part of something bigger than themselves.[50]

The manager's role in developing ethical values and standards in other employees is very important. Employees naturally look to those in authority to provide leadership, and managers become ethical role models whose behaviour is scrutinized. If top managers are not ethical, their subordinates are not likely to behave in an ethical manner. They may think that if it is all right for a top manager to engage in ethically dubious behaviour, it is all right for them, too.

The US$700-billion bailout passed by the U.S. Congress in 2008 made sure to embed strong ethical values that would protect the taxpayer's interest by stipulating that the money in the Treasury's Troubled Asset Relief Program (TARP funds) could not be used to compensate senior executives of failing banks and insurance and mortgage companies.[51]

Ethical control systems such as codes of ethics and regular training programs help employees and managers learn an organization's values. However, only a third of Canadian businesses provide managers with such training, and it is generally less than one hour a year.[52] Moreover, strong codes of ethics and good governance practices still do not guarantee ethical behaviour. Enron and Arthur Andersen, the accounting

The Case of Satyam

- Employs 53 000 people, operates in 66 countries

- Won 2008 global award for excellence in corporate governance by World Council for Corporate Governance (WCFCG)

- Became official IT services provider for the FIFA World Cups 2010 and 2014

- Ramalinga Raju, Satyam's founder and chairman, won Ernst & Young's 2007 entrepreneur of the year award

company that certified and audited Enron's fraudulent accounts, both had codes of ethics. Even companies that are recognized and rewarded for good governance can be ethically deceptive.

In 2008, Satyam, India's fourth largest software development company, was awarded the global award for excellence in corporate governance by the World Council for Corporate Governance (WCFCG). In 2009, it was the subject of the largest scandal in the global economy since Enron's bankruptcy in 2001.[53] Ramalinga Raju, the founder and chairman of Satyam, in a statement sent to the stock exchange, admitted to "inflating profits" and the shares of the company immediately plunged by 82 percent. He said "[w]hat started as a marginal gap between actual operating profits and the one reflected in the books of accounts continued to grow over the years … It was like riding a tiger, not knowing how to get off without being eaten."

Tips for Managers
CHAMPIONING ETHICAL BEHAVIOUR

1. Identify the ways that managers can make decisions that will not adversely affect stakeholders more effectively and with an ethical rationale for their actions.

2. Think of an organization you have worked for that you know does not have a code of ethics. Design one, and make recommendations on how employees can live up to its ideals.

3. List ways to show how managers can help employees develop ways to resolve the ethical dilemmas they encounter in their day-to-day work.

4. Make a list of ways to ensure that managers serve as role models for their employees.

Social Responsibility

L O **2**

There are many reasons why it is important for managers and organizations to act ethically and do everything possible to avoid harming stakeholders. However, what about the other side of the coin? What responsibility do managers have to provide benefits to their stakeholders and to adopt courses of action that enhance the well-being of society at large? The term **social responsibility** refers to a manager's duty or obligation to make decisions that nurture, protect, enhance, and promote the welfare and well-being of stakeholders and society as a whole. Many kinds of decisions signal an organization's interest in being socially responsible (see Table 3.2).

social responsibility
A manager's duty or obligation to make decisions that promote the well-being of stakeholders and society as a whole.

TABLE 3.2 | *Forms of Socially Responsible Behaviour*

Managers are being socially responsible and showing their support for their stakeholders when they:

- Provide severance payments to help laid-off workers make ends meet until they can find another job;
- Provide workers with opportunities to enhance their skills and acquire additional education so they can remain productive and do not become obsolete because of changes in technology;
- Allow employees to take time off when they need to and provide extended health care and pension benefits to employees;
- Contribute to charities or support various civic-minded activities in the cities or towns in which they are located;
- Decide to keep open a factory whose closure would devastate the local community;
- Decide to keep a company's operations in Canada to protect the jobs of Canadian workers rather than move abroad;
- Decide to spend money to improve a new factory so that it will not pollute the environment;
- Decline to invest in countries that have poor human rights records;
- Choose to help poor countries develop an economic base to improve living standards.

THINK ABOUT IT

The $15 000 Crib![54]

The purpose of introducing this rather different case example is to have you reflect on the question: When does social responsibility say "enough is enough"?

Consider PoshTots, an American online company that prides itself on purveying "the most extraordinary children's furnishing in the world."

Do you want to be astonished?

Plush Studios/Getty images

Then visit the PoshTots website[55] and shell out $15 000 for a crib. Writer Julie Mason calls this the "new lows in an age of excess."

Or is it?

Why can't people who have the money shell out almost $15 000 for a crib? You can also buy and have your wee one play in a luxury theme park. You can purchase a Chuckwagon Toddler Bed with canvas roof and western-style changing table for $13 995!

PoshTot petites spend their earliest days coddled in a Fantasy Carriage Crib ($14 995) with faux leather seats and a round mattress. Little PoshTot buckaroos bounce their baby butts on a hand-carved mahogany rocking horse ($2400). You are up to $32 395 already. Get ready to throw in the Lighthouse Bedroom Set ($14 500) that includes an entertainment system in the lighthouse and laundry hamper in the keeper's house. Of course, do not forget the ultimate good: a Fantasy Coach Bed ($47 000) that resembles Cinderella's pumpkin coach minus the footmen.

So, where are we? Oh yes: $93 895 and counting!

Writer Julie Mason says that it is easy to make fun of PoshTots; however, they "are making pots of money catering to PoshParents who are paying pots of money to buy this stuff. And as parents, haven't we all been just a little guilty of overindulging with Bugaboo strollers or Baby Gap sleepers?"

However, Mason said that when she clicked on the PoshTots website, she "couldn't help but think about my day job, which is raising money for some of the world's neediest kids. The cost of the Chuckwagon Toddler Bed would buy a medical clinic;

the Mermaid Costume would pay annual school fees for 25 boys and girls; the Tumble Outpost would feed 250 starving children a life-saving breakfast and lunch for two years. Just so you know."

You Be the Manager

1. What is your reaction to the PoshTots story?
2. For you, what is socially acceptable—or not—about PoshTots?

Approaches to Social Responsibility

The strength of organizations' commitment to social responsibility ranges from low to high (see Figure 3.2).[56] At the low end of the range is an **obstructionist approach**. Obstructionist managers choose not to behave in a socially responsible way. Instead, they behave unethically and illegally and do all they can to prevent knowledge of their behaviour from reaching other organizational stakeholders and society at large.

A **defensive approach** indicates at least a commitment to ethical behaviour. Managers adopting this approach do all they can to ensure that their employees behave legally and do not harm others. But when making ethical choices, these managers put the claims and interests of their shareholders first, at the expense of other stakeholders.

Some economists believe that managers in a capitalist society should always put stockholders' claims first. They suggest that if such choices are unacceptable or are considered unethical to other members of society, then society must pass laws and create rules and regulations to govern the choices managers make.[57] From a defensive point of view, it is not managers' responsibility to make socially responsible choices; their job is to abide by the rules that have been legally established.

But increasingly, going beyond what is legislated may be the only way to do any business at all. Indian mining giant, Vedanta Resources, was told by the Supreme Court of India that its application to mine bauxite in the pristine Nyuamgiri hills in one of India's poorest states would be turned down by the Supreme Court unless it participated in a joint venture with the state-owned Orissa Mining Corporation to spend 100 million rupees (US$2.4 million) a year or 5 percent of its operating profits, whichever is greater, on fighting poverty and protecting wildlife and the tribal people.[58]

An **accommodative approach** is an acknowledgment of the need to support social responsibility. Accommodative managers agree that organizational members ought to behave legally and ethically, and they try to weigh the interests of different stakeholders against one another so that the claims of one group of stockholders are seen in relation to the claims of other stakeholders. Managers adopting this approach want to make choices that are reasonable in the eyes of society and want to do the right thing when

obstructionist approach
Disregard for social responsibility; willingness to engage in and cover up unethical and illegal behaviour.

defensive approach
Minimal commitment to social responsibility; willingness to do what the law requires and no more.

accommodative approach
Moderate commitment to social responsibility; willingness to do more than the law requires, if asked.

FIGURE 3.2 | Approaches to Social Responsibility

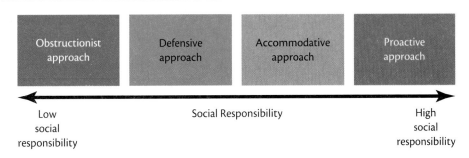

U.S. Air Force
As Hurricane Katrina struck Air Force Base, rising waters swallowed cars parked along streets.

called on to do so. Wal-Mart Canada has been criticized for its policy of doing business with third-party suppliers—such as Hampton Industries, Sutton Creations, Global Gold, Stretch-O-Rama, Cherry Stix, and By Design—who import goods from Myanmar (Burma), which engages in forced labour, including that of children. In defence of the company's actions, Wal-Mart Canada spokesman Andrew Pelletier noted, "We have a policy we are looking at, of monitoring vendors sourcing from other countries."[59] The company started with a defensive approach, focusing on not doing anything illegal, but has moved to a more accommodative style. Even the ex-president of the famous environmental group the Sierra Club is now "working with the enemy." *Fast Company* magazine writes, "Once the youngest president of the Sierra Club, Adam Werbach used to call Wal-Mart toxic. Now the company is his biggest client. Does the path to a greener future run through Bentonville?"[60] Something else: Who did the most to help victims of Hurricane Katrina? Yes, it was Wal-Mart, the company everyone loves to hate,[61] according to a new study by Steven Horwitz, an Austrian-school economist at St. Lawrence University in New York.[62]

> As the president of the brutalized Jefferson Parish put it in a Sept. 4 [2005] Meet the Press interview, speaking at the height of nationwide despair over FEMA's confused response: "If [the U.S.] government would have responded like Wal-Mart has responded, we wouldn't be in this crisis." This benevolent improvisation contradicts everything we have been taught about Wal-Mart by labour unions and the "small-is-beautiful" left. We are told that the company thinks of its store management as a collection of cheap, brainwashable replacement parts; that its homogenizing culture makes it incapable of serving local communities; that a sparrow cannot fall in Wal-Mart parking lot without orders from Arkansas; that the chain puts profits over people. The actual view of the company, verifiable from its disaster-response procedures, is that you can't make profits without people living in healthy communities. And it's not alone: As Horwitz points out, other big-box companies such as Home Depot and Lowe's set aside the short-term balance sheet when Katrina hit and acted to save homes and lives, handing out millions of dollars' worth of inventory for free.[63]

proactive approach
Strong commitment to social responsibility; eagerness to do more than the law requires and to use organizational resources to promote the interests of all organizational stakeholders.

Managers taking a **proactive approach** actively embrace the need to behave in socially responsible ways, go out of their ways to learn about the needs of different stakeholder groups, and are willing to use organizational resources to promote the interests of stockholders as well as other stakeholders. Taking a proactive approach does not seem to be the case when Hardee's introduced its 1420-calorie Monster Thickburger; the Center for Science in the Public Interest called the burger a "fast-food pornographic snuff film." Hardee's defended its actions this way when Bruce Frazer, vice-president of marketing, said, "We didn't know how people would react to something that was basically a monument to decadence … It turned into a phenomenon." The burger has two Angus beef patties, four strips of bacon, three slices of cheese, and mayo on a bun slathered with butter.[64]

On the other hand, a proactive approach is easily demonstrated by Paul Tsaparis, president and chief executive of Hewlett-Packard (Canada) Co. He writes that those who are going to lead our corporations in the decades to come must understand that there are no substitutes for the fundamentals of business leadership. His recipe for being proactive and socially responsible includes the following:

• A CEO should manage the company, not the share price.

• Managing means balancing short-term returns with long-term investment.

• It is a CEO's job to think about a decade, not just a quarter.

- Real profit and real cash flow and real balance sheets matter.

- Trust, integrity, transparency, accountability, and responsibility matter.[65]

In a talk at the Canadian Club of Toronto, Tsaparis announced that for Canadians, the best way forward lay in learning from their past: their "propensity to embrace and support those qualities that Canadians are recognized for globally."[66] "True competitiveness must be inclusive of an organization's effect on the community in which it lives and reflect the values of its society."[67]

The Husky Injection Moulding Company constructed a state-of-the-art injection moulding facility on the Moose Deer Point reserve in Ontario called Niigon, which means "future" in Ojibway. Niigon is fully owned by the Moose Deer Point First Nations people, and all employees are residents of the First Nations community. The development was the first of its kind in Canada for several reasons: It is a joint venture among private industry, First Nations, and governments, and it is modelled on proactive socially responsible principles and practices.

"For Husky, it meets all four of the company's values—it makes a contribution, is environmentally proactive, exercises the company's passion for excellence and honesty, and sets bold goals. For the Moose Deer Point First Nations community, Niigon is a win-win situation—it gives a tremendous boost to local economic development by providing close to 70 jobs in the first five years of operation. And the $7.5-million commitment is a winning investment for Aboriginal Business Canada and the Department of Indian Affairs and Northern Development. It stands as a model of successful business development—demonstrating a new way in which the public and private sectors can work together to assist in the development of viable Aboriginal communities."[68]

Why Be Socially Responsible?

There are several advantages to social responsibility by managers and organizations. First, employees and society benefit directly because organizations (rather than the government) bear some of the costs of helping employees. Second, it has been said that if all organizations in a society were socially responsible, the quality of life as a whole would be higher.[69] Indeed, several management experts have argued that the way organizations behave toward their employees determines many of a society's values and norms and the ethics of its citizens. Experts point to Japan, Sweden, Germany, the Netherlands, and Switzerland as countries where organizations are socially responsible and where, as a result, crime and unemployment rates are relatively low, the literacy rate is relatively high, and socio-cultural values promote harmony among different groups of people. Other reasons for being socially responsible are that it is the right thing to do and that companies that act responsibly toward their stakeholders benefit from increasing business and see their profits rise.[70]

Jason Mogus, president of Communicopia.Net, finds that being socially responsible is a competitive advantage: "The times that we are in right now are tough times for a lot of high-tech firms, and the ones that are thriving are the ones that really did build community connections and have strong customer and employee loyalty," says Mogus. "If everyone's just there for the stock price and it goes underwater, then what you have is a staff of not very motivated workers."[71]

Given these advantages, why would anyone quarrel over organizations and their managers pursuing social responsibility? One response is that a commitment to social responsibility could benefit some stakeholders and not others. For instance, some shareholders might think they are being harmed financially when organizational resources are used for socially responsible courses of action. Some people argue that business has only one kind of responsibility: to use its resources for activities that increase its profits and thus reward its stockholders.[72] See Figure 3.3.

FIGURE 3.3 | Why Be Socially Responsible?

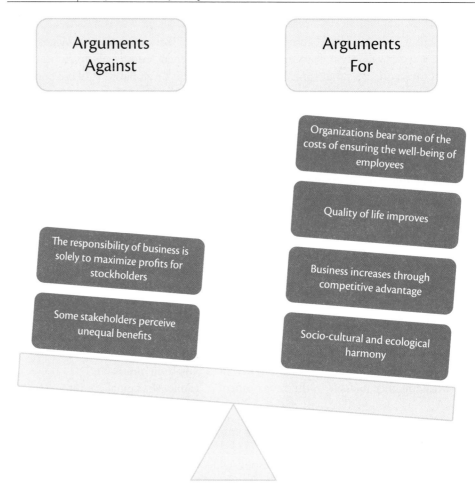

How should managers decide which social issues they will respond to, and to what extent their organizations should trade profits for social gain? Obviously, illegal behaviour should not be tolerated, and all managers and workers should be alert to its occurrence and report it promptly. The need to behave legally is only one of the criteria managers can use to decide which social actions to undertake. **A social audit** allows managers to consider both the organizational and the social effects of particular decisions. The audit ranks various courses of action according to both their profitability and their social benefits.

Evidence suggests that in the long run, managers who behave in a socially responsible way will most benefit all organizational stakeholders (including stockholders). It appears that socially responsible companies, in comparison with less responsible competitors, are less risky investments, tend to be somewhat more profitable, have a more loyal and committed workforce, and have better **reputations**; these qualities encourage stakeholders (including customers and suppliers) to establish long-term business relationships with the companies.[73] Socially responsible companies are also sought out by communities, which encourage such organizations to locate in their cities and offer them incentives such as property-tax reductions and the construction of new roads and free utilities for their plants. Thus, there are many reasons to believe that, over time, strong support of social responsibility brings the most benefits to organizational stakeholders (including stockholders) and society at large.

social audit
A tool that allows managers to analyze the profitability and social returns of socially responsible actions.

reputation
The esteem or high repute that individuals or organizations gain when they behave ethically.

LO 3

Managing an Increasingly Diverse Workforce

One of the most important issues in management to emerge over the past 30 years has been the increasing diversity of the workforce. In Chapter 2, we addressed issues of diversity that result from organizations' expansion into the global environment.

THINK ABOUT IT

Business Schmoozing with a Decidedly Indian Flavour[74]

Sanjay Tugnait is the head of the Canadian, Caribbean, and Latin American operations for Satyam Computer Services—an international consulting and information technology global sourcing company headquartered in Hyderabad, India. It is listed on the New York Stock Exchange with $1 billion in revenues worldwide and 21 000 employees in 46 countries.

Call it "doing business with an Indian twist" when one meets Tugnait, 38, in his regal silk kurta; he also lectures at the University of Toronto's Rotman School of Management. He set up Satyam's Toronto office in 2003 with a handful of employees. "I feel very proud of my Indian heritage. That's what differentiates us from others, so we shouldn't be shying away from our roots." Satyam employs 130 people in Canada with offices in Calgary and Vancouver as well. In wooing clients, such as General Electric Co. and Citibank, he does what he calls "business schmoozing with a decidedly Indian flavour."

He takes clients or potential clients to top-end Indian restaurants. He helps Western clients understand unfamiliar menu items, with his wife Karishma acting as co-host; clients' spouses are always invited. After dinner, he might take clients to a Bollywood show featuring megastars Shah Ruk Khan or Hrithik Roshan or to hear new age guru Deepak Chopra, whenever these celebrities are in town. "I don't take them for golf or basketball or any of that. That's left for the competition. ... They love the food. They love the diversity. They love the culture. It's a total change for them."

You Be the Manager

1. What is Sanjay Tugnait doing in promoting a culture of diversity?
2. Why is diversity so important in today's new workplace?

Here, we address diversity as it occurs closer to home—in an organization's workforce. **Diversity** is dissimilarity—differences—among people due to age, gender, race, ethnicity, religion, sexual orientation, socio-economic background, and capabilities or disabilities (see Figure 3.4). Diversity raises important ethical issues and social responsibility issues as well. It is also a critical issue for organizations, one that if not handled well can bring an organization to its knees, especially in our increasingly global environment.

Canada has become a truly diverse country, although this might not be apparent to everyone. More than 200 different ethnic origins were reported in the 2006 Census. An estimated 5 068 100 individuals were members of the visible minority population. They represented 16.2 percent of the total population in 2006, up from 13.4 percent in 2001.[75] The numbers of the visible minority population vary widely across the country. The largest number of people identifying themselves as visible minorities

diversity
Differences among people in age, gender, race, ethnicity, religion, sexual orientation, socio-economic background, and capabilities or disabilities.

▨ **FIGURE 3.4 | Sources of Diversity in the Workforce**

are found in Ontario with almost 3 million, or 23 percent, of the population. British Columbia, with just over one million, represents about one-quarter of its population. Next highest is Alberta with approximately 14 percent of its population identifying themselves as visible minority, followed by Manitoba with almost 10 percent; Quebec has about 9 percent; Northwest Territories have 5.5 percent; Nova Scotia and Yukon both have approximately 4 percent; and finally, Newfoundland and Labrador, New Brunswick, Prince Edward Island, and Nunavut all have 2 percent or less of the population themselves identifying as visible minorities.

There are many more women and minorities—including people with disabilities and gays and lesbians—in the workforce than ever before, and most experts agree that diversity is steadily increasing.

Age diversity also presents managers with unique challenges. Older workers are staying longer in the labour force and retiring later at the same time that **Generation Y** is entering the labour force. Table 3.3 presents some of the myths about Generation Y and the positive strategies managers can adopt to help integrate them into the labour force.

Why is diversity such a pressing issue both in the popular press and for managers and organizations? There are several reasons:

- There is a strong ethical imperative in many societies to see that all people receive equal opportunities and are treated fairly and justly. Unfair treatment is also illegal.

- Effectively managing diversity can improve organizational effectiveness. When managers manage diversity well, they not only encourage other managers to treat diverse members of an organization fairly and justly but also realize that diversity is an important resource that can help an organization gain a competitive advantage.

- Embracing diversity encourages employee participation and thus encourages differences of opinions or ideas that are beneficial to the organization.

One website that can be of immense help in thinking through and finding valuable information on hiring immigrants, work, and diversity issues is the website www.hireimmigrants.ca. It is still a struggle for many highly skilled immigrants to find adequate and well-paying jobs in Canada. "Recent immigrant men holding a

Generation Y
Also known as Millennials, refer to people born between 1981 and 1992.

TABLE 3.3 | *Perceptions of Generation Y and Management Strategies to Deal with Them*[76]

Perceptions	Why?	Positive Strategies
Disrespectful and vocal if dissatisfied	Gen Ys were raised in a less authoritarian manner. Parents and teachers were addressed by their first names, family decisions were made collectively, and they have always been encouraged to express their feelings and opinions. They will question everything.	1. Engage Gen Ys—explain how and why things are done. 2. Provide opportunities for employees to voice opinions and share ideas and concerns. 3. Their respect will be earned by engaging and listening to them.
Lack a strong work ethic	There is not the same pressure to succeed as they are entering a workforce in which they are being sought out. They value the work-life balance.	1. Find out how they define work ethic, and share your expectations. 2. Determine what motivates them. 3. Challenge them.
Not loyal	Gen Ys saw their parents and grandparents downsized after years of loyal service. They are prepared to change jobs as new opportunities arise.	Gen Ys will stay with a company: 1. That engages in meaningful work that makes a difference. 2. Where co-workers share their values. 3. That meets their personal goals. 4. That has a strong sense of social corporate responsibility.
High maintenance	Gen Ys have been raised with high expectations of success and achievement. This generation tends to be more tech savvy, and better educated than any previous generation.	They expect: 1. Constant learning experiences. 2. New challenges. 3. Open lines of communication.
Technologically dependent	Gen Ys were raised in the computer age. They can instantly access, collect, and share information.	1. Use technology in new and innovative ways. 2. Young people need stimulation to stay engaged.
Sense of entitlement	Due to the ease of information access, Gen Ys are aware of what jobs should pay and are likely to question the effort-reward equation. Be prepared to discuss salary.	Gen Ys will work for the organization that has: 1. The greater sense of corporate responsibility. 2. Provides professional development. 3. Provides opportunities and supports work-life balance.
Supportive relationships	Many Gen Ys had a full schedule of sports, music, and special-interest lessons. Coaches and teachers have always played a key role in terms of providing guidance and feedback.	Before a job begins: 1. Clearly outline the parameters. 2. Give them space to tackle the task. 3. Provide constant feedback. 4. Debrief once the task is completed.

degree earned only 48 cents for each dollar their university-educated, Canadian-born counterparts did. Some 30 percent of male immigrants with a university degree worked in jobs that required no more than a high-school education—more than twice the rate of those born in Canada."[77] To take a specific city in Canada: "In Calgary, 223 700 people of working age are not actively participating in the workforce. Certain groups participate less than others, and some groups experience higher rates of unemployment than others. A reasonable increase in participation rates combined with reduced unemployment in these groups could provide additional labour."[78]

The Calgary, Alberta, Economic Development Report puts things this way: "These increases depend upon thoughtful consideration as to how to address the barriers to more fulsome participation. For example, attitudes and beliefs about older workers currently impact employability. Older workers can be perceived to be less productive, less flexible, and less skilled than recent graduates and have more health issues. Hence both employer perceptions and worker perceptions would need to be modified in order to attract and retain older workers."[79]

But visible minorities are gaining, and the understanding of diversity is becoming more nuanced as well. Navdeep Bains, MP for Mississauga-Brampton South and one of the 10 South Asians in the House of Commons, believes that diversity should not be limited to the colour of one's skin. "You want to have representation reflected in your institutions that ultimately reflects your diversity. ... I think diversity goes well beyond just the typical definition of just looking different. I think it has to do with being open to the ideas and concerns of others."[80] Markham, Ontario, however, has the largest population of visible minorities: 65 percent. "In what's known as the census metropolitan area of Toronto, 42.9 percent of the population identified themselves as a visible minority. A total of 27.8 percent of the visible minority population was born in Canada. The largest visible minority population was South Asian (684 070), followed by Chinese (486 325) and black (352 220)."[81] "Canada accepts about 250 000 immigrants a year, a figure that has increased since the Conservatives took office. The backlog of applications grew from 50 000 when the Liberal Party took office in 1993 to around 500 000 in 2000. By the time the Conservatives came to power in early 2006, it was around 800 000, and in the past two years that number has grown to around 875 000.[82] In 2017, visible minorities will become the majority in Canada. In addition, Aboriginal entrepreneurs are also growing in number and moving beyond their roots. The Aboriginal birth rate is already 1.5 times that of non-Aboriginals. These fast-changing realities also change the face of business. Orrin Benn is president of the newly formed Canadian Aboriginal and Minority Supplier Council (CAMSC) and wants to help these entrepreneurs succeed in growing their businesses because he does not want Canada to lose out on talent. CAMSC offers Aboriginal and minority entrepreneurs the opportunity to enter mainstream business in a way they have never been afforded in the past. For example, John Bernard, president and founder of Donna Cona Inc., Canada's largest Aboriginal-owned technology firm, designed the infrastructure for Nunavut residents to communicate across Canada's largest territory.

In the rest of this section, we examine why effectively managing diversity makes sense. Then we look at the steps that managers can take to manage diversity effectively in their organizations.

L O 4

The Ethical Need to Manage Diversity Effectively

Effectively managing diversity not only makes good business sense but is also an ethical obligation in Canadian society. Two moral principles provide managers with guidance when they try to meet this obligation: distributive justice and procedural justice.

THINK ABOUT IT

Two Images, Two Different Realities

Canada is known for its multicultural mosaic as opposed to the melting pot that the United States has long been. U.S. president Richard Nixon told Canadians in a 1972 address to our House of Commons, "Mature partners must have autonomous, independent policies: Each nation must define the nature of its own interests, decide the requirements of its own security, the path of its own progress.

The soundest unity is that which respects diversity, and the strongest cohesion is that which rejects coercion."[83]

Canada has different management challenges to face as it proceeds into this century. Toronto, for example, may be the only city in the country that can claim a "visible majority" rather than "visible minorities."[84] Gordon Nixon, who is CEO of RBC Financial Group, points out that since Canada has such a small population, in order to grow and prosper, it must attract new immigrants, and they must also be better integrated into our communities, workforce, and economy. Says Nixon, "Canada's standard of living has lagged behind that of the United States for the last 25 years. Our competitive advantage is no longer driven by the resource industry, or by capital assets like plants, equipment, and machinery. It is being driven by our ability to tap human capital so we can develop technology, improve productivity, and develop creatively."

For businesses, diversity represents both a great opportunity and the right thing to do. Senior managers must exhibit a strong commitment to such diversity. In that way, all employees get a chance to unleash their potential. Finally, says Nixon, "In so doing, we'll provide our country with both a competitive advantage and a source of national pride."

You Be the Manager

1. What has been your experience of diversity in the workplace?
2. Why does managing diversity matter in an organization?
3. In your experience, what makes Canada unique?

Distributive Justice

The principle of **distributive justice** dictates that the distribution of pay raises, promotions, job titles, interesting job assignments, office space, and other organizational resources among members of an organization be fair. The distribution of these outcomes should be based on the meaningful contributions that individuals have made to the organization (such as time, effort, education, skills, abilities, and performance levels) and not on irrelevant personal characteristics over which individuals have no control (such as gender, race, or age).[85] Managers have an obligation to ensure that distributive justice exists in their organizations. This does not mean that all members of an organization receive identical or similar outcomes; rather, it means that members who receive more outcomes than others have made much greater or more significant contributions to the organization.

Is distributive justice common in organizations in corporate Canada? Probably the best way to answer this question is to say that things are getting better. Fifty years ago, **overt discrimination** (knowingly and willingly denying diverse individuals access to opportunities and outcomes in an organization) against women and minorities was not uncommon; today, organizations are inching closer toward the ideal of distributive justice. Statistics comparing the treatment of women and minorities with the treatment of white men suggest that most managers would need to take a proactive approach in order to achieve distributive justice in their organizations. For instance, Calgary-based Enbridge Inc., Canada's largest gas utility, supports the career development of women employees through their woman@enbridge program. "The program provides peer coaching, mentorship opportunities, and leadership training in an effort to increase the

distributive justice
A moral principle calling for the distribution of pay raises, promotions, and other organizational resources to be based on meaningful contributions that individuals have made and not on personal characteristics over which they have no control.

overt discrimination
Knowingly and willingly denying diverse individuals access to opportunities and outcomes in an organization.

representation of women in senior management positions, encourage their participation on company boards, and retain women employees."[86] Thirty percent of employees and 27 percent of managers are women. In 2008, Enbridge was recognized as one of Canada's best diversity employers for working diligently to advance women through the ranks as well as working closely with First Nations groups to create employment opportunities for Aboriginal peoples.[87]

In many countries, managers have not only an ethical obligation to strive to achieve distributive justice in their organizations but also a legal obligation to treat all employees fairly. Managers risk being sued by employees who feel that they are not being fairly treated.

Procedural Justice

procedural justice
A moral principle calling for the use of fair procedures to determine how to distribute outcomes to organizational members.

The principle of **procedural justice** requires managers to use fair procedures to determine how to distribute outcomes to organizational members.[88] This principle applies to typical procedures such as appraising subordinates' performance, deciding who should receive a raise or a promotion, and deciding whom to lay off when an organization is forced to downsize.

Procedural justice exists, for example, when managers (1) carefully appraise a subordinate's performance; (2) take into account any environmental obstacles to high performance beyond the subordinate's control, such as lack of supplies, machine breakdowns, or dwindling customer demand for a product; and (3) ignore irrelevant personal characteristics, such as the subordinate's age or ethnicity. Like distributive justice, procedural justice is necessary not only to ensure ethical conduct but also to avoid costly lawsuits.

A significant challenge for managers in Canada today is to ensure that the principles of distributive and procedural justice are maintained to avoid discrimination. Each year a significant number of immigrants come to Canada but cannot find suitable employment because their credentials are not recognized. The process to have their experience and education recognized is onerous and lengthy; many end up being underemployed, even when companies are in need of their services. Organizations like UMA Foundation are working with governments at all levels to try to speed up the process of recognizing international accreditation that would help integrate skilled new immigrants into the Canadian economy.[89]

Human Rights Act
http://laws.justice.gc.ca/
en/H-6

Employment Equity Act
http://laws.justice.gc.ca/
en/E-5.401

Effectively Managing Diversity Makes Good Legal Sense

A variety of legislative acts affect diversity management in Canada. Under the Canadian Human Rights Act, it is against the law for any employer or provider of service that falls within federal jurisdiction to make unlawful distinctions based on the following prohibited grounds: race, national or ethnic origin, colour, religion, age, sex (including pregnancy and childbirth), marital status, family status, mental or physical disability (including previous or present drug or alcohol dependence), pardoned conviction, or sexual orientation. Employment with the following employers and service providers is covered by the Human Rights Act: federal departments, agencies, and Crown corporations; Canada Post; chartered banks; national airlines; interprovincial communications and telephone companies; interprovincial transportation companies; and other federally regulated industries, including certain mining operations.

In addition to the Human Rights Act, Canada's Employment Equity Act of 1995 lists four protected categories of employees: Aboriginal peoples (whether Indian, Inuit, or Métis); persons with disabilities; members of visible minorities (non-Caucasian in race or nonwhite in colour); and women. The reasoning behind the Employment Equity Act is that individuals should not face employment barriers due to being a woman, a person with a disability, an Aboriginal person, or a member of a visible minority.

For example, employers must provide "reasonable accomodation" for persons with ability challenges that include making facilities accessible. Thus the federal legislation aims at ensuring that members of these four groups are treated equitably. Employers affected by the Canadian Human Rights Act are also covered by the Employment Equity Act.

A number of provinces have their own legislation, including employment equity acts, governing employers in their provinces. Many companies have difficulty complying with equity acts, as recent audits conducted by the Canadian Human Rights Commission show. In an audit of 180 companies, only Status of Women Canada; Elliot Lake, Ontario-based AJ Bus Lines; the National Parole Board; Canadian Transportation Agency; and Les Méchins, Quebec-based Verreault Navigation were found to be compliant on their first try.[90]

Effectively Managing Diversity Makes Good Business Sense

Though organizations are forced to follow the law, the diversity of organizational members can be a source of competitive advantage in more than a legal sense, as it helps an organization provide customers with better goods and services.[91] In fact, Cirque du Soleil, headquartered in Montreal, Quebec, has made diversity part of its global brand. Its international cast of performers, gymnasts, and artists has given the Canadian company a reputation for unique and quality entertainment experiences in every corner of the world. Cirque du Soleil's competitive advantage is its embodiment of diverse cultures.[92] The variety of points of view and approaches to problems and opportunities that diverse employees provide can improve managerial decision making. Just as the workforce is becoming increasingly diverse, so too are the customers who buy an organization's goods or services.

Diverse members of an organization are likely to be attuned to what goods and services diverse segments of the market want and do not want. Major car companies, for example, are increasingly assigning women to their design teams to ensure that the needs and desires of female customers (a growing segment of the market) are taken into account in new car design.

Effectively managing diversity makes good business sense for another reason. More and more, consumer and civil rights organizations are demanding that companies think about diversity issues from a variety of angles. For instance, Toronto-based Royal Bank of Canada found its efforts to acquire North Carolina-based Centura Banks Inc. under attack by Inner City Press/Community on the Move (ICP), a U.S. civil rights group. In April 2001, the group asked American and Canadian regulators to delay approval of the acquisition to allow further investigation of alleged abusive lending practices carried out by Centura. "Centura's normal interest rate lending disproportionately denies and excludes credit applications from people of colour," said Matthew Lee, ICP executive director.[93] ICP alleged that in two American cities, Centura denied applications for home purchase from Black people three times more frequently than applications from White people. The group wanted Royal Bank to guarantee that it would end the alleged unfair lending practices.

(c) 2009 Jupiter Images Corporation
Women wearing the hajib, the traditional head cover of Muslim women, face discrimination when they look for jobs in Canada. A recent study found that 40 percent of the time when visibly Muslim women asked if jobs were available, they were either told there were not or were not given a chance to apply for a job.

In the province of Quebec, a debate on the reasonable accommodation of how religious and ethnic minorities should be integrated into the province was front and centre in 2007 when the premier of the province initiated hearings into the issue. The state commission quickly revealed sentiments that polarized the population on whether Muslim religious symbols, including wearing the hijab, should be allowed in public service. Christian symbols and practices were not part of the debate, leading the Muslim minority to charge the government with overt racism toward nondominant cultures and calling into question the view of Canada as tolerant of cultural diversity.[94]

In 2009, Canada's largest supermarket chain Loblaw purchased the Asian food retailer T&T Supermarket Inc. to take advantage of the growing ethnic food business. T&T serves South Asian and Chinese families in Ontario, Alberta, and British Columbia. In 2008, this segment of the market spent 23 percent more than the average on groceries and accounted for about one-third of grocery spending in Vancouver and Toronto. Allan Leighton, president of Loblaw, said, "The ethnic market opportunity in Canada is vast. Today we have a relatively small share. Our objective is to be the #1 player. T&T gives us the platform to build to this objective."[95]

Being aware of diversity issues extends beyond employees to include the issues of suppliers, clients, and customers. Nestlé Canada recently announced that it was planning to do away with its nut-free products because trying to keep the production area free of nut products seemed more costly than it was beneficial. Nestlé Canada was soon deluged with protests from Canadian families who had relied upon such products as Kit Kat, Mirage, Coffee Crisp, and Aero chocolate bars and Smarties. Between 1 and 2 percent of all Canadians, and perhaps as many as 8 percent of children, are allergic to peanuts and other nuts, which is why the protest was so vocal. Within a month, Nestlé Canada announced that it would go back to producing these candies in a nut-free facility to cater to its consumers with this particular disability. Nestlé's initial decision factored in "a growing public demand for chocolate with nuts, as well as the need to protect jobs at its Toronto plant."[96] Nestlé senior vice-president Graham Lute still wants to expand Nestlé's manufacturing in Canada but says, "We'll just execute it in a different way, but not as attractive a way as it would have been before, from a sheer business point of view."[97] In other words, the attention to this particular diversity issue has caused the company to rethink part of its business strategy.

Increasing Diversity Awareness

It is natural to see other people from your own point of view because your feelings, thoughts, attitudes, and experiences guide how you perceive and interact with others. The ability to appreciate diversity, however, requires people to become aware of other perspectives and the various attitudes and experiences of others. Many diversity awareness programs in organizations strive to increase managers' and employees' awareness of (1) their own attitudes, biases, and stereotypes and (2) the differing perspectives of diverse managers, subordinates, co-workers, and customers. Diversity awareness programs often have these goals:[98]

- Providing organizational members with accurate information about diversity

- Uncovering personal biases and stereotypes

- Assessing personal beliefs, attitudes, and values and learning about other points of view

- Overturning inaccurate stereotypes and beliefs about different groups

- Developing an atmosphere in which people feel free to share their differing perspectives

- Improving understanding of others who are different from oneself

The Royal Canadian Mounted Police's Canadian Law Enforcement Training Unit in Regina, Saskatchewan, has as its mission "to provide the highest quality of training via experienced professionals, as well as state-of-the-art methodology, facilities and technology."[99] The emphasis is on meeting the changing needs of the different communities they serve. In addition, "the Aboriginal Heritage Room, found in D Block, was designed so that Aboriginal candidates at the Academy could attend and experience an area of Aboriginal culture and spiritual significance. The artifacts and photo prints on display are from the RCMP Centennial Museum, and reflect the rich diversity of Aboriginal culture. The room may be used by any candidate in training, as well as members of the RCMP."[100]

Techniques for Increasing Diversity Awareness and Skills

Many managers use a varied approach to increase diversity awareness and skills in their organizations: Films and printed materials are supplemented by experiential exercises to uncover any hidden **bias** (the systematic tendency to use information about others in ways that result in inaccurate perceptions) or **stereotype** (simplistic and often inaccurate belief about the typical characteristics of particular groups of people). Sometimes simply providing a forum for people to learn about and discuss their differing attitudes, values, and experiences can be a powerful means for increasing awareness. Also useful are role-playing exercises in which people act out problems that result from lack of awareness and then indicate the increased understanding that comes from appreciating others' viewpoints. Accurate information and training experiences can debunk stereotypes. Group exercises, role plays, and diversity-related experiences can help organizational members develop the skills they need to work effectively with a variety of people.

Managers sometimes hire outside consultants to provide diversity training. For instance, Trevor Wilson, president of Toronto-based Omnibus Consulting, has presented employment equity programs to such clients as IBM Canada Ltd., Molson Inc., and National Grocers Co. Ltd.[101] Some organizations have their own in-house diversity experts such as Maureen Geddes at Union Gas, based in Chatham, Ontario.

bias
The systematic tendency to use information about others in ways that result in inaccurate perceptions.

stereotype
Simplistic and often inaccurate beliefs about the typical characteristics of particular groups of people.

THINK ABOUT IT
Accommodating Muslim Employees During Ramadan[102]

On September 13, people of the Muslim faith began observing the holy month of Ramadan. To describe it very simply, during Ramadan, Muslims fast from sunrise to sundown (no food or drink). After sundown, the fast is broken each night with a special meal, prayer, and gathering with family. At the end of Ramadan, a special feast is held, and more praying occurs.

Under human rights legislation in Canada, employees are protected from discrimination in the workplace on the basis of religion. This means that employers have the duty to accommodate employees whose religious requirements come into conflict with the requirements of the workplace. As a result, an employer would be required to resolve the employees' conflict to enable them to meet their religious needs by making changes to the workplace requirements subject to undue hardship. So, for example, Muslim employees might require flexibility in their work schedules during Ramadan.

While the concept of undue hardship will be discussed in a future post, for now, I would say that undue hardship represents the limit of how far an employer is required to go to accommodate the needs of any employee when those needs are tied to a protected ground under human rights legislation (for example, religion, sex, disability, etc.). What amounts to undue hardship in a given situation is determined on a case-by-case basis. Some of the factors that are usually taken into account in determining undue hardship are cost, disruption to a collective agreement, size of the business, safety, interchangeability of the workforce and facilities and problems of morale of other employees (but note, though, in provinces such as Ontario, the factors considered are limited to cost, health and safety, and the availability of outside sources of funding). Based on the undue hardship factors and how the courts are interpreting them, in most instances employers will not reach the undue hardship limit when it comes to accommodating religion in the workplace. In other words, employers should assess requests for religious accommodation from the starting point that, somehow, they ought to be able to modify the workplace to meet the employee's needs.

For employees who require religious accommodation, they should follow any policy their employer has in place setting out how to make accommodation requests.

You Be the Manager

1. What can employees who require religious accommodation do?
2. What should employers do?

The Importance of Top-Management Commitment to Diversity

When top management is truly committed to diversity, top managers embrace diversity through their actions and example, spread the message that diversity can be a source of competitive advantage, deal effectively with diverse employees, and are willing to commit organizational resources to managing diversity. That last step alone is not enough. If top managers commit resources to diversity (such as providing money for training programs) but as individuals do not value diversity, any steps they take are likely to fail.

Some organizations recruit and hire women for first-level and middle-management positions, but after being promoted into middle management, some of these female managers quit to start their own businesses. A major reason for their departure is their belief that they will not be promoted into top-management positions because of a lack of commitment to diversity among members of the top-management team. As Professor David Sharp of the Richard Ivey School of Business notes, "It seems that some Canadian women entrepreneurs are neither born nor made. They are pushed."[103] Enbridge is an example of an organization that has been very proactive in making sure women will not leave, through its efforts to aggressively promote women to upper-management positions.

By now, it should be clear that managers can take a variety of steps to manage diversity effectively. Many companies, such as Enbridge, Air Canada, and others that were recognized by MediaCorp Inc. in 2008 for exceptional diversity and inclusive programs, and their managers continue to develop and experiment with new diversity initiatives to meet this ethical and business challenge.[104] Although some steps prove unsuccessful, it is clear that managers must make a long-term commitment to diversity. Training sessions oriented toward the short term are doomed to failure: Participants quickly slip back into their old ways of doing things. The effective management of diversity, like the management of the organization as a whole, is an ongoing process: It never stops and never ends.

Tips for Managers
MANAGING AN INCREASINGLY DIVERSE WORKFORCE

1. Align your decisions with the values of distributive and procedural justice.
2. Pay attention to managers who overtly or indirectly favour certain ethnic groups over others.
3. Make sure your commitment to diversity management is clear and acknowledged by those who work for you.
4. Provide training in diversity management.

L O 5

Harassment in the Workplace

Harassment in the workplace can take many forms. It refers to any behaviour directed toward an employee that is known to be or ought to be known to be offensive and unwelcome. According to Service Canada, "[i]t comprises objectionable conduct, comment or display made on either a one time or continuous basis that demeans, belittles, or causes personal humiliation or embarrassment to an employee of the department. It includes harassment within the meaning of the Canadian Human Rights Act, that is based on any of the prohibited grounds of discrimination listed in that Act."[105] Abuse of authority and sexual harassment are two common forms of **workplace harassment,** which we will discuss here. Abuse of authority occurs when the legitimate power vested in a position is used improperly to influence the behaviour of an employee. Threats that intimidate and coerce employee behaviour are examples of abuse of authority, as is blackmail. When "an individual improperly uses the power and authority inherent in his or her position to endanger an employee's job, undermine the performance of that job, threaten the economic livelihood of the employee, or in any way interfere with or influence the career of the employee," they are committing an abuse of authority.[106] Bullying is a form of abuse of authority when committed by a boss. "Over 72 percent of bullies are bosses, some are co-workers, and a minority of employees bullies higher-ups. A bully is equally likely to be a man or a woman."[107]

Sexual harassment is defined by the Supreme Court of Canada as unwelcome behaviour of a sexual nature in the workplace that negatively affects the work environment or leads to adverse job-related consequences for the employee. In 1987, the court ruled that employers will be held responsible for harassment by their employees. The court also said that the employers should promote a workplace free of harassment. The court recommended that employers have clear guidelines to prevent harassment, including procedures to investigate complaints.

Although women are the most frequent victims of sexual harassment—particularly those in male-dominated occupations, or those who occupy positions stereotypically associated with certain gender relationships (such as a female secretary reporting to

workplace harassment
Any behaviour directed toward an employee that is known to be or ought to be known to be offensive and unwelcome.

sexual harassment
Unwelcome behaviour of a sexual nature in the workplace that negatively affects the work environment or leads to adverse job-related consequences for the employee.

a male boss)—men can be victims, too. Several male employees at Jenny Craig in the United States said that they were subject to lewd and inappropriate comments from female co-workers and managers.[108] To date, there have been no media reports of women sexually harassing either men or women in Canada.

Sexual harassment seriously damages the victims as well as the reputation of the organization. It is not only unethical but also illegal. Beyond the negative publicity, sexual harassment can cost organizations large amounts of money. Managers have an ethical obligation to ensure that they, their co-workers, and their subordinates never engage in sexual harassment, even unintentionally.

Forms of Sexual Harassment

There are two basic forms of sexual harassment: *quid pro quo sexual harassment* and *hostile work environment sexual harassment.* **Quid pro quo sexual harassment** occurs when a harasser asks or forces an employee to perform sexual favours to keep a job, receive a promotion or raise, obtain some other work-related opportunity, or avoid receiving negative consequences such as demotion or dismissal.[109] This "Sleep with me, honey, or you're fired" form of harassment is the more extreme form and leaves no doubt in anyone's mind that sexual harassment has taken place.[110] A study conducted by York University in 1999 found that only 3 percent of working Canadian women reported having experienced quid pro quo sexual harassment.[111]

Hostile work environment sexual harassment is more subtle. It occurs when organizational members are faced with an intimidating, hostile, or offensive work environment because of their gender.[112] Lewd jokes, sexually oriented comments, displays of pornography, displays or distribution of sexually oriented objects, and sexually oriented remarks about someone's physical appearance are examples of hostile work environment sexual harassment. About 45 percent of working Canadian women reported this form of harassment in the recent study at York University. Barbara Orser, a researcher with the Conference Board of Canada, noted that "sexual harassment is more likely to occur in workplace environments that tolerate bullying, intimidation, yelling, innuendo, and other forms of discourteous behaviour."[113]

A hostile work environment interferes with organizational members' ability to perform their jobs effectively and has been deemed illegal by the courts. Managers who engage in hostile work environment harassment or allow others to do so risk costly lawsuits for their organizations, as was the experience of Magna International Inc. based in Aurora, Ontario.[114] Sexual harassment is against the law. "Sexual harassment in the workplace is an abuse of power in working relationships. Like other forms of sexual violence, sexual harassment both reflects and reinforces the inequality between men and women in our society. No employee is safe if sexual harassment is ignored! Organizations are responsible to address and investigate all complaints of sexual harassment."[115]

Steps Managers Can Take to Eradicate Workplace Harassment

Managers have an ethical obligation to eradicate workplace harassment in their organizations. There are many ways to accomplish this objective. Here are four initial steps that managers can take to deal with the problem.[116]

• *Develop and clearly communicate a workplace harassment policy endorsed by top management.* This policy should include prohibitions against both general workplace and sexual harassment. It should contain: (1) examples of types of behaviour

---

quid pro quo sexual harassment
Asking or forcing an employee to perform sexual favours in exchange for some reward or to avoid negative consequences.

hostile work environment sexual harassment
Telling lewd jokes, displaying pornography, making sexually oriented remarks about someone's personal appearance, and other sex-related actions that make the work environment unpleasant.

that are unacceptable, (2) a procedure for employees to use to report instances of harassment, (3) a discussion of the disciplinary actions that will be taken when harassment has taken place, and (4) a commitment to educate and train organizational members about sexual harassment.

- *Use a fair complaint procedure to investigate charges of workplace harassment.* Such a procedure should (1) be managed by a neutral third party, (2) ensure that complaints are dealt with promptly and thoroughly, (3) protect and fairly treat victims, and (4) ensure that alleged harassers are fairly treated.

- *When it has been determined that workplace harassment has taken place, take corrective actions as soon as possible.* These actions can vary depending on the severity of the harassment. When harassment is extensive, prolonged over a period of time, of a quid pro quo nature, or severely objectionable in some other manner, corrective action may include firing the harasser.

- *Provide workplace harassment education and training to organizational members, including managers.* Managers at DuPont, for example, developed DuPont's "A Matter of Respect" program to help educate employees about workplace harassment and prevent it from happening.

Barbara Orser, a researcher with the Conference Board of Canada, noted that most large Canadian organizations have harassment policies on paper. However, many lack a clear resolution process.

Summary and Review

1. **WHAT ARE ETHICS?** Ethics are moral principles or beliefs about what is right or wrong. These beliefs guide people in their dealings with other individuals and groups that have an interest in the situation at hand (stakeholders) and provide a basis for deciding whether a behaviour is right and proper. Many organizations have a formal code of ethics derived mainly from societal ethics, professional ethics, and the individual ethics of the organization's top managers.

2. **PROMOTING ETHICAL BEHAVIOUR** Managers can apply ethical standards to help themselves determine the proper way to behave toward organizational stakeholders. Social responsibility refers to a manager's duty to make decisions that nurture, protect, enhance, and promote the well-being of stakeholders and society as a whole. Managers generally take one of four approaches to the issue of socially responsible behaviour: obstructionist, defensive, accommodative, or proactive. Promoting ethical and socially responsible behaviour is a major managerial challenge. Written codes of ethics help managers make good decisions.

3. **APPROACHES TO SOCIAL RESPONSIBILITY** Managers generally take one of four approaches to the issue of socially responsible behaviour; obstructionist, defensive, accommodative, or proactive. Proactive approaches benefit both organizational stakeholders and create a competition advantage by promoting sustainable practices that are popular and socially sustainable.

4. **MANAGING AN INCREASINGLY DIVERSE WORKFORCE** Diversity refers to differences among people due to age, gender, race, ethnicity, religion, sexual orientation, socio-economic background, and capabilities or disabilities. Effectively managing diversity is an ethical obligation that makes good business sense. Diversity can be managed effectively if top management is committed to principles of distributive

and procedural justice, values diversity as a source of competitive advantage, and is willing to devote organizational resources to increasing employees' diversity awareness and diversity skills. Managers need to ensure that they and their subordinates appreciate the value that diversity brings to an organization, understand why diversity should be celebrated rather than ignored, and have the ability to interact and work effectively with men and women who are physically challenged or are of a diverse race, age, gender, ethnicity, nationality, or sexual orientation.

5. **WORKPLACE HARASSMENT** Workplace harassment is any conduct that is known or ought to be reasonably known to be offensive and unwelcome. It can take the form of abuse of authority, bullying, and harassment. Steps that managers can take to halt harassment include developing and communicating a workplace harassment policy endorsed by top management, using fair complaint procedures; ensuring prompt corrective action when harassment occurs; and training and educating organizational members on workplace harassment.

Key Terms

accommodative approach, p. 75

bias, p. 87

codes of ethics, p. 65

defensive approach, p. 75

distributive justice, p. 83

diversity, p. 79

ethics, p. 64

ethical decision, p. 64

ethics ombudsperson, p. 72

Generation Y, p. 80

hostile work environment sexual
   harassment, p. 90

individual ethics, p. 66

obstructionist approach, p. 75

organizational stakeholders, p. 68

overt discrimination, p. 83

proactive approach, p. 76

procedural justice, p. 84

professional ethics, p. 65

quid pro quo sexual harassment, p. 90

reputation, p. 78

sexual harassment, p. 89

social audit, p. 78

social responsibility, p. 73

societal ethics, p. 65

stereotype, p. 87

unethical decision, p. 64

workplace harassment, p. 89

SO WHERE DO YOU STAND?

Wrap-Up to Opening Case

The authors of "See No Evil" in our opening case write elsewhere: "Most people value ethical decisions and behaviour and strive to be good. Yet psychological processes sometimes lead them to engage in questionable behaviours that are inconsistent with their own values and beliefs."[117] What are some work situations when you experienced "questionable behaviours," which were "inconsistent with their own values and beliefs"?

The authors of "See No Evil" discuss some key psychological processes that can lead to questionable behaviours. Can you identify with some of them?

First, there is "motivational blindness": our tendency, writes journalism professor Donna Nebenzahl, to overlook the unethical behaviours of others if it might cause us harm. For example, if you work with a boss who is unethical, there is huge incentive to see him in a favourable light. With your own security or survival at stake, it stands to reason you would have difficulty accurately assessing that person's behaviour.

Second, we explore how readily people forgive others who benefit from delegating unethical behaviour as in the case of the pharmaceutical company Merck, which in 2005 sold off a couple of cancer drugs it had developed to a smaller firm, Ovation, while continuing to manufacture the drugs. It turned out the smaller company raised the wholesale price of the drug tenfold, allowing Merck to avoid the headline of increasing cancer drug prices, yet making money from this transaction. Say the authors, "The public and press fail to condemn people and firms that use an intermediary to do their dirty work."[118]

Third, there is a situation the authors call "change blindness." In other words, gradual moral decay leads people to grow comfortable with unethical behaviour. Such a classic slippery slope allows small incremental unethical transgressions to occur over time. "The boiling frog story," for examples, "states that a frog can be boiled alive if the water is heated slowly enough—it is said that if a frog is placed in boiling water, it will jump out, but if it is placed in cold water that is slowly heated, it will never jump out."[119]

Fourth, we have a tendency to value outcomes over processes that can affect our assessments of the ethicality of others' choices. As our opening case states, "If, for instance, someone manipulated pharmaceutical research in some small way and the drug that ended up on the market killed a number of patients, we would be quick to condemn them. But suppose the drug didn't kill anyone. In that case, studies show we are much less likely to condemn the manipulation of the research."

How to Make an Ethical Decision

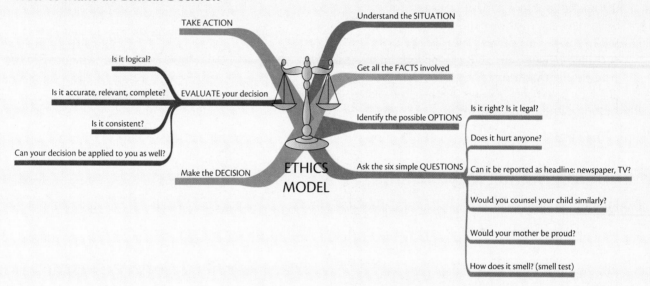

Management in Action

Topics for Discussion and Action

Level 1

1. Describe the concept of ethics and the three different models of ethics.
2. Outline the four approaches to social responsibility.
3. Define diversity, workplace harassment, and sexual harassment.

Level 2

4. Ask a manager to describe an instance of ethical behaviour and an instance of unethical behaviour that she or he observed. What caused these behaviours, and what were the outcomes?
5. Search business magazines such as *Report on Business* or *Canadian Business* or a business podcast for one example of ethical behaviour and one example of unethical behaviour. What caused these behaviours, and what were the outcomes?

6. Discuss an occasion when you may have been stereotyped and as a result treated unfairly. What caused these behaviours, and what were the outcomes?

Level 3

7. Compare and contrast the principles of distributive and procedural justice. What should managers do to support these principles in their organizations?
8. Develop a list of standards for ethical behaviour that you can incorporate into your own personal code of ethics.
9. Design a program to manage diversity in a university.

Building Management Skills

Answer the following questions about the organization you have chosen to follow:

1. Briefly describe all the stakeholders. How does the company satisfy all the different needs and interests of each group?
2. Does the company have a formal code of ethics? How has it dealt with ethical dilemmas in the past (look at historical news reports).

3. How does the company approach social responsibility? Which model do they use?
4. How does the company approach managing diversity?

Management for You

Read the following examples of ethical dilemmas. Analyze the situation and the stakeholder involvement using the three models of ethics. What would you do?

a. You are an employee at a small children's clothing store. There is a sale coming up, and your boss asks you to mark up the prices by the equivalent amount of the discount so that customers still pay the same price even though they think they are getting a deal.

b. A good friend of yours who has dark skin and an Arab name applied for a job at an ice cream parlour and was told that the vacancy had been filled. Not knowing of her experience, you, with fair skin and an Anglo-Saxon name, applied later the same day and got the position.

Small Group Breakout Exercise

Discuss the following scenario with your teammates, and answer the questions below. A very important division meeting at XYZ Company was scheduled in conflict with a religious holiday of a minority religious group. This holiday is one of the most important and solemn holidays for this religion. An employee approached his manager and explained that he would be unable to attend the meeting due to the religious holiday. The manager responded by telling the employee that he should not expect to succeed in this company if he did not attend mandatory meetings such as this one.

1. In what ways, if any, were biases, stereotypes, or overt discrimination involved in this situation?
2. What could you or the person who was treated unfairly have done to improve matters and immediately rectify the injustice?
3. If you had authority over the decision maker (for example, you were his or her manager or supervisor), what steps would you take to ensure that the decision maker no longer treated diverse individuals unfairly?

Business Planning Exercise

After reading this chapter, you and your group should discuss who the stakeholders are in your new venture, how competing interests should be balanced, and what set of values and professional ethics should be incorporated into your business plan.

1. Write a values statement and a code of ethics that you can incorporate into your vision and mission statements.

Managing Ethically

The state of California is having an energy crisis. You are a manager at BC Hydro. You have discovered that it possible to anticipate periods of severe power shortage and plan for them by letting your reservoirs rise overnight and then opening them to create hydroelectricity. Electricity can thus be produced inexpensively but sold for a premium. Your research of the law suggests that this behaviour would be consistent with what is allowed under the rules of the electricity marketplace. Is the good business, or is this unethical behaviour?

Exploring the World Wide Web

SPECIFIC ASSIGNMENT

Go to the Procter & Gamble website (http://pg.com/company/index.shtml). The website states: "Three billion times a day, P&G brands touch the lives of people around the world. Our corporate tradition is rooted in the principles of personal integrity and respect for the individual. Discover how our values guide our business." Review its sections on "Purpose, Values, and Principles" and "Diversity."

1. In what ways does Proctor & Gamble show its support for a diverse workforce?
2. What is the relationship between P&G's policies on diversity and its claims under "Purpose, Values, and Principles"?

GENERAL ASSIGNMENT

Search for a company website that has an explicit statement of the company's approach to workplace diversity. What is its approach, and how does this approach support the company's main goals?

McGraw-Hill Connect™—Available 24/7 with instant feedback so you can study when you want, how you want, and where you want. Take advantage of the Study Plan—an innovative tool that helps you customize your learning experience. You can diagnose your knowledge with pre- and post-tests, identify the areas where you need help, search the entire learning package for content specific to the topic you're studying, and add these resources to your personalized study plan. Visit www.mcgrawhillconnect.ca to register—take practice quizzes, search the e-book, and much more.

Be the Manager

EXPENSIVE LESSON IN USING DISCIPLINE[120]

Rather than shrieking with delight, Christine Pynaker's heart sank upon receiving a bouquet of flowers and a gold necklace. Yet again, Wayne Brazeau, 25 years her senior, was after her. For more than three years, Brazeau had showered Pynaker with gifts, including flowers, jewellery—even an airline ticket to visit her parents in Spain—accompanied by romantic cards and emails.

Pynaker's attempts at rebuffing Brazeau, who, like her, was employed as an international representative for the International Brotherhood of Electrical Workers (IBEW), were futile. Although she accepted many of the presents, she also told Brazeau that his conduct was offensive. Finally, after more than three years, Pynaker flatly told Brazeau that he was too old; that no relationship could ever materialize between them; and that she regarded his behaviour as sexual harassment.

Brazeau, properly, immediately ceased directing any attention toward Pynaker. But, improperly, he also ceased being as supportive of her as he had been in the past. Over the next several years, Brazeau was episodically hostile to Pynaker: failing to provide her with the materials and information required to effectively do her work; making disparaging remarks about her sex life; and accusing a male colleague of flirting with her.

Believing that Brazeau was retaliating for her earlier rebuff, Pynaker lodged a complaint of sexual harassment with her employer.

Questions

1. You are the manager. What would you do?
2. What other alternative actions could Pynaker have taken?

Management Case

Is It Right to Use Child Labour?

In recent years, the number of Canadian and U.S. companies that buy their inputs from low-cost foreign suppliers has been growing, and concern about the ethics associated with employing young children in factories has been increasing. In Pakistan, children as young as six years work long hours in deplorable conditions to make rugs and carpets for export to Western countries. Many children in poor countries throughout Africa, Asia, and South America work in similar conditions.

Opinions about the ethics of child labour vary widely. Some believe that the practice is totally reprehensible and should be outlawed on a global level. Another view, championed by *The Economist* magazine (www. economist.com), is that while nobody wants to see children working in factories, citizens of rich countries need to recognize that in poor countries a child is often the family's only breadwinner. Thus, denying children employment would cause whole families to suffer, and correcting one wrong (child labour) might produce a greater wrong (poverty). Instead, *The Economist* favours regulating the conditions under which children are employed and hopes that over time, as poor countries become richer, the need for child employment will disappear.

Many Canadian and U.S. retailers buy their clothing from low-cost foreign suppliers, and managers in these companies have had to take their own ethical stance on child labour. In Chapter 1, we discussed how Mountain Equipment Co-op (www.mec.ca) was facing demands from some of its members to discontinue manufacturing clothing in China. Wal-Mart Canada (www.walmart. com) has been criticized for its policy of doing business with third-party suppliers—such as Hampton Industries, Sutton Creations, Global Gold, Stretch-O-Rama, Cherry Stix and By Design—that import goods from Myanmar (Burma), which engages in forced labour, including that of children. In defence of the company's actions, Wal-Mart Canada spokesman Andrew Pelletier noted, "We have a policy we are looking at, of monitoring vendors sourcing from other countries. ... For other corporations, our expectation is that they would take their direction from the Canadian government, that's what we would recommend they would do."

At present, the Canadian government, unlike the U.S. government, does not have regulations governing the use of child labour in foreign countries by Canadian companies.

Questions

1. Should Canada develop regulations governing the use of child labour in foreign countries by Canadian companies?

2. You are the manager of a company considering setting up a factory in a foreign country that allows child labour. What would be the benefits to your company for deciding not to use child labour?

3. You are the manager of a company considering setting up a factory in a foreign country that allows child labour. Should you simply rely on the laws of that country when deciding what to do about child labour? Why, or why not?

Video Management Case   ■

Bakery with a Conscience

Teaching Objective: Illustrate how a company's values can lead to a competitive advantage and build a corporate culture that emphasizes social responsibility.

Summary: Dancing Deer is an inner-city Boston baking company that makes all-natural cookies, cakes, and other sweets sold through mail-order, the Internet, and stores such as Whole Foods, Wild Oats, and Williams-Sonoma. The company is exceptional in its commitment to employees and the community. All workers get health and disability insurances, education reimbursements, matching IRAs, and stock options. CEO Trish Carter believes that giving everyone a stake in the company makes it better. The bakery also donates millions of dollars to local nonprofits that work with impoverished people.

Questions to consider

1. What values provide the foundation for Dancing Deer Baking? How do these values benefit the company?

2. How does Dancing Deer meet the expectations of its various stakeholders?

3. How does Trish Carter illustrate a commitment to a diverse workforce?

Part 2: Integrated Case

Generation NGO[121]

Unimpressed with the bureaucracy of big charities, twenty-somethings are going the DIY route and launching their own nonprofits. Are they brats who do not play well with others—or just misunderstood? Keep in mind that NGOs are as much organizations as are for-profit organizations.

Two years ago, a University of Manitoba undergrad named Jesse Hamonic began feeling pangs of status guilt as he travelled to and from economics classes. He had the trickle-down theory and Keynesian economics down cold. But passing by homeless people in Winnipeg, he saw little evidence of theory in practice. "Here I am paying $6000 for a good education and a bright future," he remembers thinking, "and these people can't even afford to eat."

He tried volunteering at a few well-established local charities. To his shock, they turned him away. "It's like pulling teeth trying to volunteer for them," he recalls. "You need reference letters. You need to fill out all kinds of paperwork. It was like applying for university all over again."[122] So Hamonic followed a path blazed by hundreds of other students in recent years. He began his own charity, a nationwide organization of university food banks called Student Harvest. "One man's idea turns into many people's effort."[123]

In 2007 he launched two more groups: StudentCharities.ca[124] links established charities with a large pool of student volunteers who want to avoid the application rigmarole that Hamonic faced; and Wave of Hope[125] gives students a pair of workboots and sends them to New Orleans for a week. Hamonic, 22, is now working on nonprofit number four, which will place high-school volunteers with food banks and organizations such as Habitat for Humanity. And, oh yeah, he just started law school.

Both his age and audacity place Hamonic firmly among Generation Y—the headstrong, attention-weak cohort born between 1980 and 1995 that is reinventing the way we volunteer. They are bemused by the dense bureaucracies and regimented campaigns of big non-profits such as Amnesty International, the Red Cross, and the World Wildlife Fund. But rather than fight the power, they are stealing it, forming small, nimble charities that rely on blogs and Facebook networks rather than on onerous mail campaigns and donor drives. They are smart. They are driven. And for some, they are a little vexing.

"One thing that bothers me is that they're missing the wisdom that existing nonprofits have spent generations picking up," says Linda Graff, a nonprofit consultant and author of several books on volunteer management. "Those who run charities, they know a thing or two. The upstarts don't realize this." With about 150 000 registered charities already operating across the country, the sudden addition of hundreds more will ultimately put the squeeze on nonprofits, according to Graff. "All these new charities, combined with the dying off of old charities, will undoubtedly create chaos in the nonprofit sector."

That spectre has prompted some to question the Gen Y motives. A recent Youthography-MySpace poll showed that while four out of five youths aged 15 to 24 had supported a charity in the last year, 68 percent of them wanted more recognition for their good deeds.

So are they self-centred brats who do not play well with others—or just misunderstood? "I've heard that I'm doing this just to pad my résumé." says Jess Sloss, a business student at Capilano College in Vancouver, who is launching Watch for Change, a nonprofit video site with advertising revenue going entirely to charity. "But this is about making a difference. The option of volunteering for a big organization and licking stamps all day is not that appealing. We want to show what we can do."

Teachers in Capilano College's Global Stewardship Program, which trains students for NGO work, have noticed a flood of this bold optimism in recent years. Several current and former students in the small program have formed their own nonprofits after dismal experiences working for larger organizations. "They're taking up the call for action in ways that my generation hasn't," says program coordinator Rita Isola, 40. "They're natural leaders. And if the NGOs won't let them lead right away, then, dammit, they'll go out and lead themselves."

The barriers to starting a nonprofit are lower than ever. Gen-Yers with broad networks of online contacts can reach thousands with little more than an Internet connection. "All you do," says Hamonic, "is throw up a website, put out a couple press releases, get picked up on a few blogs around the world and, all of a sudden, you have a firestorm of phone calls. I couldn't imagine doing this kind of work 30 or 40 years ago."

Still, he does encounter some resistance. "The student unions especially have frowned on us, saying they have their own food banks and that all the collected food should stay on campus."

Some established NGOs have already started changing recruiting strategies to accommodate the new wave of entrepreneurial volunteers. Rather than pull student volunteers in to stuff envelopes, Oxfam Canada encourages some interested students to stay home and talk up the charity online. They have also launched a social networking site specifically for its campus groups across the country. In two years, the number of campus Oxfam groups has gone from 2 to 13.

Most charities, however, have not adapted their recruitment initiatives. "Most nonprofits don't have the slightest idea what volunteers want and what they will do and won't do," says Graff. "They're completely out of tune. They keep offering the same old jobs without understanding that the entire volunteer labour force is undergoing a huge transition."

In working with nonprofits across the country, Graff has noticed that new volunteers tend have seasonal, episodic work patterns and that older, stalwart volunteers are creeping into their eighties. "That's going to be the death of some charities," she says. "But we need to let some of them die off. If the issue is important enough, one of these young people will come along and reincarnate it."

Discussion Questions

1. What is the ethical motivation for Jesse Hamonic in setting up Student Harvest?
2. How is the "new generation" making its impact on traditional management practices?

CHAPTER

4

Managing Decision Making and Sustainability

Learning Outcomes

1. Differentiate between programmed and nonprogrammed decisions, and explain why nonprogrammed decision making is a complex, uncertain process.

2. Explain the implications and assumptions of the rational and administrative models of decision making.

3. Describe the six-step decision-making process.

4. Explain how cognitive biases can affect decision making and lead managers to make poor decisions.

5. Explain the role that a sustainability strategy, organizational learning, and creativity play in helping managers improve their decisions.

6. Explain how the utilization of information and Management Information Systems (MIS) can be vital to a manager's decision-making processes.

Contextual Intelligence

Managers are paid to make decisions, but not just any decisions. A key to making good decisions is the ability to read the context. Anthony J. Mayo and Nitin Nohria of the Harvard Business School, in their book *In Their Time: The Greatest Business Leaders of the 20th Century*, discuss *contextual intelligence*, that ability to understand and make sense of the situation one is in and to maximize opportunities that it presents. Great leadership is also born of such a mix of abilities. The Latin poet Horace (65–8 BCE),[1] from ancient Roman times, wrote a poem entitled "Carpe Diem," or "Seize the day." Implied in this image is knowing when to say yes and when to say no. More than ever, today's managers have to be particularly astute in seizing opportunities because of the complexity of events, both local and global. For example, in the spring of 2008, when oil prices were skyrocketing every day, managers had to access their contextual intelligence on a daily, if not hourly, basis. The context seemed one of "oil mania."[2] One of the questions for managers at that time was a keen ability to factor "mania" into their decision making. On Tuesday, May 21, 2008, American Airlines became the first airline to begin charging passengers a US$15 fee for the first bag checked. Was this decision born from contextual intelligence or simply a reaction or, even more simply, a way to earn more profits?

The decision-making question becomes one of how to "see" and understand if a mania is actually at work in the context. As far back as March 2008, Chen Zhao, global investment strategist at Bank Credit Analyst in Montreal, was advising his clients that oil was a candidate for a classic financial mania. And then on Wednesday, May 21, 2008, when oil set a new record of US$133.72 a barrel, "Zhao said that with global growth slowing and supplies relatively stable, there was no economic reason the price should be setting new highs. However, mania could take it higher still. Every day the thing is going up. We know demand is not exceeding supply on a daily basis, no way." In Zhao's estimation and with his contextual intelligence, "it's got to be something else. It's definitely a building mania."[3] Related to the oil crisis, in reading the context and obviously seeing the ethical implications of not being transparent with its advertising, Monte Brewer, CEO of Air Canada, wanted the airline to be more "transparent" about its

pricing and so decided to include "details of the fuel surcharge" in its ads that began running on May 20, 2008.[4] Just a week before this, Ross Marowits of the Canadian Press had written:

> Air Canada ... failed the test of transparency by not being up front enough in informing the public about new fuel surcharges, industry observers said Friday. Unlike rival WestJet, Canada's largest airline has made little mention of the reintroduction of a substantial increased cost of flying. The primary reference is buried in the link on its website once consumers establish the final cost of their travel. ... Air Canada spokeswoman Isabelle Arthur said the airline has not hidden the fuel surcharge. "It's at the forefront of everyday life for everyone ... and our fuel surcharges are indicated at the time when you buy your airfare." While the airline has noted on its website policy changes regarding unaccompanied minors and additional baggage charges, it has failed to mention the surcharge. "We don't put out press releases for every policy or fare change," Arthur added.[5]

On reflecting on the inclusion of ethics in business practices, it is obvious from the above scenario on oil pricing that transparency is very much part of being ethical; lack of it is the slippery slope to abuse of entrusted power and corruption.[6] "We ... consider the term relational transparency to be more descriptive than the phrase relational authenticity because it better reflects the open and transparent manner whereby authentic leaders and followers are posited to share information with each other and close others."[7] Decision making, therefore, is always a contextual matter—hence the need for contextual intelligence.

When managers realize how their commitments shape the direction, limitations, and opportunities of their departments and organizations, they can make those decision-making choices that will align themselves more deliberately and effectively to fulfilling their commitments. Before making important decisions, a manager needs to ask, "Is this a process or relationship that is being decided upon something I can live with in the future? Am I locking myself into a course of action—and hence the organization—that we'll come to regret?" Managers are truly known, therefore, by their commitments and the decisions that lead to fulfilling such commitments.

Ryan McVay/Getty images

Now It's Your Turn

Think of a time in your life when you had to make some important decisions.

1. *Why* were you making these decisions? (This question speaks to the *context* you had in mind.)

2. Were you clear as to *why* you were making the decisions?

3. What were the results of your decisions?

4. Depending on whether you felt successful in your decision-making efforts, to what extent was knowing *why* (the context) you were making the decisions helpful?

■■■■ Overview

The opening scenario in this chapter allows us to see that a manager's job basically is to make decisions. But we kept asking the question, "Making decisions in view of what end?" Such a question introduced the idea that managers make decisions in view of the commitments they have agreed to or envisioned as important for their department or organization. Commitments, therefore, frame the *context* within which managers make decisions. To the best of their ability, managers align their decisions with the end-result in mind: their commitments.

The purpose of this chapter is to examine how managers make decisions and to explore how individual, group, and organizational factors affect the quality of the decisions they make and thus determine organizational performance. We discuss the nature of managerial decision making and examine some models of the decision-making process that help reveal the complexities of successful decision making. Then we outline the main steps of the decision-making process; in addition, we explore the biases that may cause capable managers to make poor decisions both as individuals and as a group. We then examine how managers can promote sustainability, organizational learning and creativity and improve the quality of their decision making. Finally, we look at how management systems (MIS) are changing the way managers utilize technology in decision making. By the end of this chapter, you will understand the crucial role that decision making plays in creating a high-performing organization.

LO 1

The Nature of Managerial Decision Making

THINK ABOUT IT

Bounded Rationality and Bounded Emotionality

In 1976, Herbert Simon, an economist who won the Nobel memorial prize in 1978, wrote about an idea called *bounded rationality*.[8] By that he meant that being rational and making rational decisions has its limits. In other words, we are not always rational in the way we make our decisions. He termed this limitation, or contextual factor in our decision making, "bounded rationality." In other words, our rationality has "bounds," or limits. Such boundedness occurs because of the very nature of the human mind, and when we make decisions, at our best, we do the best we can. This he called "satisficing." At the time, this was a major new shift and challenge in understanding what was known as the "rational man." The so-called "rational man" did not always make the most rational of decisions.

Simon factored in two reasons for his theory: uncertainty about the future and costs in acquiring information in the present. We saw in our opening Management Snapshot how relevant these reasons are in view of the oil crisis mania of 2008. Thus, according to Simon, instead of being fully rational about making decisions—what he called "maximization"—managers do their best—what he called "satisficing, or setting an aspiration level which, if achieved, they will be happy enough with, and if they do not, they try to change either their aspiration level or their decision. These "rules of thumb" are the utmost that agents can achieve in the "bounded" and uncertain real world."[9]

Dennis K. Mumby and Linda L. Putnam, in their article "The Politics of Emotion: A Feminist Reading of Bounded Rationality,"[10] have added an important contemporary factor to the concept of bounded rationality: emotion. In a time that considered males to be managers and rationality to be their stronghold, Simon had first published the so-called claim to rationality with his theory of bounded rationality. Now Mumby and Putnam introduce, from a feminist perspective, the role of emotion—**bounded emotionality**—into the decision-making mix. This concept not only challenges the patriarchal structure inherent in management practices, especially that of organizing, but it also "opens up possibilities for alternative ways of organizing and for rewriting organizational theory."[11]

Mumby and Putnam write:

> The concept of bounded emotionality refers to an alternative mode of organizing in which nurturance, caring, community, supportiveness, and interrelatedness are fused with individual responsibility to shape organizational experiences. Individualizing is joined with relatedness. The term bounded shifts in meaning to incorporate the intersubjective limitations or the constraints that individuals must exercise in a community (see Table 4.1). Bounded, then, refers to an individual being able to recognize another person's subjectivity, a state that is necessary for producing understanding or interrelatedness. Individuals are constrained by their commitment or responsiveness to others. These constraints differ markedly from Simon's view of bounded as limitations in decision making based on simple rules of thumb. Boundedness is, thus, a necessary condition for understanding organizational experiences.[12]

They contrast both types of boundedness in Table 4.1 below:

bounded emotionality
Sometimes called the management of emotion, that is, the inclusion of emotional expression in organizations for the purposes of productivity.

TABLE 4.1 | *A Comparison of Bounded Rationality and Bounded Emotionality*

Bounded Rationality	Bounded Emotionality
Organizational limitations	Intersubjective limitations
Reduction of ambiguity through satisficing	Tolerance of ambiguity
Hierarchy–Means-end chain	Heterarchy of goals and values
Mind-body dualism	Integrated self-identity
Fragmented labour	Community
Gendered and occupational feeling rules	Relational feeling rules

With bounded emotionality, therefore, a greater tolerance of ambiguity could be accepted; and rather than always attempting to reduce such ambiguity, organizations could learn to recognize and embrace "divergent and even contradictory positions,"[13] thus enhancing flexibility and adaptation to a changing environment.

You Be the Manager

1. As a manager, how would you personally manage both types of boundedness?

Every time a manager acts to plan, organize, direct, or control organizational activities, he or she makes a stream of decisions. In opening a new restaurant, for example, managers have to decide where to locate it, what kinds of food to provide to customers, what kinds of people to employ, and so on. In Chapter 1, where we considered Mintzberg's managerial roles, we described four decision-making roles managers have. We also noted in Chapter 1 the importance of managers having conceptual skills. Decision making is a basic part of every task in which a manager is involved, and in this chapter we study how decisions are made.

decision making
The process by which managers analyze the options facing them and make decisions about specific organizational goals and courses of action.

Decision making is the process by which managers analyze the options facing them and make determinations, or decisions, about specific organizational goals and courses of action. Good decisions result in the selection of suitable goals and courses of action that increase organizational performance; bad decisions result in lower performance.

Programmed and Nonprogrammed Decision Making

Regardless of the specific decision that a manager is responsible for, the decision-making process is either programmed or nonprogrammed.[14]

Programmed Decision Making

programmed decision making
Routine, virtually automatic decision making that follows established rules or guidelines.

Programmed decision making is a routine, virtually automatic process. Programmed decisions are decisions that have been made so many times in the past that managers have been able to develop rules or guidelines to be applied when certain situations inevitably occur. Programmed decision making takes place for much of the day-to-day running of an organization, for example, when the office manager needs to order supplies. He or she can rely on long-established decision rules such as these:

- *Rule 1.* When the storage shelves are three-quarters empty, order more paper.

- *Rule 2.* When ordering paper, order enough to fill the shelves.

This decision making is called "programmed" because the office manager does not need to make judgments constantly about what should be done. Managers can develop rules and guidelines to regulate all kinds of routine organizational activities.

Nonprogrammed Decision Making

nonprogrammed decision making
Nonroutine decision making that occurs in response to unusual, unpredictable opportunities and threats.

Nonprogrammed decision making occurs when there are no ready-made decision rules that managers can apply to a situation. Why are there no rules? The situation is unexpected, and managers lack the information they would need to develop rules to cover it. Examples of nonprogrammed decision making include decisions to invest in a new kind of technology, to develop a new kind of product, to launch a new promotional campaign, to enter a new market, or to expand internationally. In the remainder of this chapter, when we talk about decision making, we are referring to nonprogrammed decision making because it is the kind that causes the most problems for managers.

Comparing Decision-Making Models

The rational and the administrative decision-making models reveal many of the assumptions, complexities, and pitfalls that affect decision making. We compare and contrast them below.

THINK ABOUT IT

"Head" and "Heart" Decisions

French artist Joseph Roux (1725–1793) once remarked, "We distrust our heart too much and our head not enough."[15]

For companies that manage not only with the "head" but also with the "heart" dividends are readily apparent. "Among many tangible and intangible benefits, they claim that opening the purse strings, or giving their employees time to volunteer for a good cause, increases worker satisfaction and reduces turnover."[16] Seventy-nine percent of employees in a 2002 GlobeScan survey said that "the more socially responsible my company becomes, the more motivated/loyal an employee I become." "Head" decision making is not, therefore, the only way to run a business; the "heart" must also be involved. For example, when the pharmaceutical company GlaxoSmithKline allowed employees the option to determine where some of the money for social causes should go, they noticed an increase in motivation, productivity, and loyalty. Similarly at the Bank of Montreal (or BMO) which, in 2003, donated about $25 million to different charities. Said BMO spokesperson Michael Edmonds, "And one of the reasons why employees have shown loyalty to us is they see us as a good corporate citizen." Because employees buy into the vision of the company, said Mark Federman, a consultant and University of Toronto lecturer on new approaches to business strategy, it is important, as we noted in our opening case scenario, that employees know *why* managers are making the decisions they are making. In other words, employees are asking of managers, "What are you committed to? When we notice that you base your decisions not only on 'head' choices but also on 'heart' choices, we can support you, and this kind of employee support will show up in terms of increased loyalty and bottom line profits." A suggested book for all managers to read that interrelates profit, passion, and purpose is Rajendra S. Sisodia, David B. Wolfe, and Jagdish N. Sheth's *Firms of Endearment: How World-Class Companies Profit from Passion and Purpose.*

You Be the Manager

1. What are your feelings about working for an organization that has both "head" and "heart"?

2. What was your experience of working for an organization that did not make "head" as well as "heart" decisions?

rational decision-making model
A prescriptive approach to decision making based on the idea that the decision maker can identify and evaluate all possible alternatives and their consequences and rationally choose the most suitable course of action.

The Rational Model

One of the earliest models of decision making, the **rational model** (also referred to as the *classical model*), is prescriptive, which means that it specifies how decisions *should*

(c) J.P. Moczulski
"Corporate fool" Guy Laliberté receives a leadership award for his achievements at the World Leaders Awards.

optimum decision
The best decision in light of what managers believe to be the most desirable future consequences for their organization.

be made. Managers using the rational model make a series of simplifying assumptions about the nature of the decision-making process (see Figure 4.1). The idea behind the rational model is that once managers recognize the need to make a decision, they should be able to make a complete list of *all* alternatives. For each alternative they should be able to list all consequences, and they can then make the best choice. In other words, the rational model assumes that managers have access to *all* the information they need to make the **optimum decision**, which is the best decision possible in light of what they believe to be the most desirable future consequences for their organization. Furthermore, the rational model assumes that managers can easily list their own preferences for each alternative and rank them from least to most preferred in order to make the optimum decision. While we can agree that making decisions rationally is an important task for managers, we can also agree with the Scottish poet Robert Burns (1759–1796), in his poem "To a Mouse," that "the best laid plans of mice and men" will often go off the tracks, precisely because managers do not have all the information they need at the time to make a totally and fully informed rational decision.[17] Because managers do not always have all the information at their fingertips, additional tools such as "social software" are now starting to show up in organizations. For example, Jon Husband is a Vancouver-based social software and blogging guru, who has coined the word: "wirearchy." He says, "Instead of having a few people up at the top make the decisions for all of us, the concept of wirearchy is a two-way flow of power and authority based on knowledge, credibility, trust, and results enabled by interconnected people and technology."[18] This concept of "wirerarchy" is related to the earlier discussion of bounded rationality and emotionality. The social architecture of our new wired world is becoming increasingly important.[19]

■ **FIGURE 4.1 | The Rational Model of Decision Making**

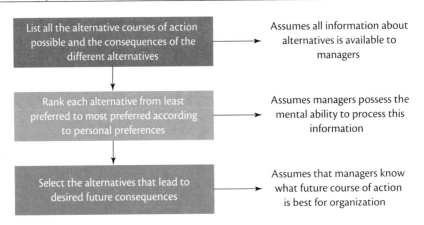

administrative model
An approach to decision making that explains why decision making is basically uncertain and risky and why managers usually make satisficing rather than optimum decisions.

The Administrative Model

James March and Herbert Simon were aware that many managers do not have access to all the information they need to make a decision. Moreover, they pointed out that even if all information were readily available, many managers would lack the mental or psychological ability to absorb and evaluate it correctly. As a result, March and Simon developed the **administrative model** of decision making to explain why decision making is always basically an uncertain and risky process—and why managers can rarely make decisions in the manner prescribed by the rational model. The administrative model is based on three important concepts: *bounded rationality*, *incomplete information*, and *satisficing*.

Bounded Rationality

March and Simon pointed out that human decision-making capabilities are bounded by people's limitations in their ability to interpret, process, and act on information.[20] **Bounded rationality** thus describes the situation in which the number of alternatives and the amount of information are so great that it is difficult for the manager to evaluate everything before making a decision.[21]

bounded rationality
Cognitive limitations that constrain one's ability to interpret, process, and act on information.

Incomplete Information

Even if managers did have an unlimited ability to evaluate information, they still would have incomplete information. Information is incomplete because the full range of decision-making alternatives is unknowable in most situations, and the consequences are uncertain.[22] Because of **uncertainty**, the probabilities of alternative outcomes cannot be determined, and future outcomes are *unknown*. Another reason why information may be incomplete is that much of the information that managers have at their disposal is **ambiguous information**. Its meaning is not clear—it can be interpreted in multiple and often conflicting ways.[23]

uncertainty
Unpredictability.

ambiguous information
Information that can be interpreted in multiple and often conflicting ways.

Satisficing

Faced with bounded rationality and incomplete information, March and Simon argue, managers do not try to discover every alternative. Rather, they use a strategy known as **satisficing**, exploring a limited sample of possible alternatives.[24] In 1978, Herbert Alexander Simon (1901–1985) won the Nobel Prize for this concept called "satisficing"—finding results that are very good instead of looking for the perfect option, which would take longer and might bankrupt firms. Simon, who trained as a political scientist, questioned the mainstream economists' view of the economic manager as "a lightning-quick calculator of costs and benefits."[25] Instead the manager had to also deal with constraints, such as not knowing all the details before making a decision. When managers satisfice, they search for and choose acceptable, or satisfactory, ways to respond to problems and opportunities, rather than trying to make the best decision.[26] For instance, the purchasing manager for Ford Canada would likely engage in a limited search to identify supplies. This might involve asking a limited number of suppliers for their terms, trusting that they are representative of suppliers in general, and making a choice from that set. Although this course of action is reasonable from the point of view of the purchasing manager, it may mean that a potentially superior supplier is overlooked.

satisficing
Searching for and choosing acceptable, or satisfactory, ways to respond to problems and opportunities, rather than trying to make the best decision.

March and Simon pointed out that managerial decision making is often more art than science. In the real world, managers must rely on their intuition and judgment to make what seems to them to be the best decision in the face of uncertainty and ambiguity.[27] **Intuition** is a person's ability to make sound decisions based on past experience and immediate feelings about the information at hand. Intuition, of course, has a long history, with its relationship to wisdom and, in turn, wisdom's relationship to ethics.[28] Dr. Margaret Somerville, founding director of the Centre for Medicine, Ethics, and Law at McGill University in Montreal and author of *The Ethical Imagination: Journeys of the Human Spirit*, says, "Our multiple ways of human knowing, in addition to reason, that are essential to ethics include human memory (history, looking back seven generations); imagination and creativity (looking forward seven generations to

intuition
Ability to make sound decisions based on past experience and immediate feelings about the information at hand.

hold our world in trust for them); intuition—especially moral intuition; experiential knowledge; and 'examined' emotions."[29]

judgment
Ability to develop a sound opinion based on one's evaluation of the importance of the information at hand.

Judgment is a person's ability to develop a sound opinion because of the way he or she evaluates the importance of the information available in a particular context. Both functional and dysfunctional signs of judgment are constantly occurring, for example, as society adjusts to the ubiquity of new technology, such as with cellphone cameras, says Dr. Liss Jeffrey, director of the McLuhan Global Research Network at the University of Toronto. What we sometimes end up with currently is a culture of recording the moment versus experiencing it, often as a result of bad judgment calls where people's privacy is invaded. In the hours before police publicly identified a 36-year-old Toronto woman killed by a drunk driver in July [2008], several teenage gawkers captured images of the woman's maimed body on their cellphone cameras. When police lifted the tarp off her body, the teens jostled for a better angle from which to shoot and zoom in with their phones. Seconds later, they began discussing their favourite fast-food restaurants with little regard for the mother who had hours earlier died on her way home from the park where she had been flying a kite with her son. Says Dr. Jeffrey, "You don't need to have a member of the media absolutely everywhere. We all become members of the media. ... But not everybody has ethics, or professional standards, or an editor back there who's going to say, 'No this shouldn't run.' Instead, you can be 13 years old and have no sense or judgment and post it on YouTube."[30] For reasons that we examine later in this chapter, both intuition and judgment are often flawed and can result in poor decision making.

L O 3

Steps in the Decision-Making Process

The conditions for an optimum decision rarely exist. To help managers make the best decision possible, researchers have developed a step-by-step model of the decision-making process and the issues and problems that managers confront at each step. There are six steps that managers should consciously follow to make a good decision (see Figure 4.2).[31] We review them in this section.

Recognize the Need for a Decision

The first step in the decision-making process is to recognize the need for a decision. Managers face decisions that arise both internally and as a consequence of changes in the external environment.[32] Once a decision maker recognizes the need to make a

FIGURE 4.2 | Six Steps in Decision Making

Step 1: Recognize the need for a decision

Step 2: Generate alternatives

Step 3: Assess alternatives (according to weighted criteria)

Step 4: Choose among alternatives

Step 5: Implement the chosen alternative

Step 6: Learn from feedback

decision, he or she will need to diagnose the issue or problem in order to determine all the factors underlying the problem. Take for example, the following scenario:

> A middle manager of a medium sized company, Linda, must make a decision as to what type of vehicles she should purchase for her sales team. The existing fleet of Ford Escort's is old, inefficient and the employees no longer feel safe in them while on the road. Many of the company's customers are located in rural areas that are not supported by public transportation such as airplanes, buses and trains and so purchasing vehicles appears to be her only option for reaching them. She recognizes the problem and formulates the following decision question: What type of vehicle should she purchase? Recognizing the need to make a decision is an important part of the process that generally involves two steps: stating the problem and formulating the decision question. The identification of the problem involves analyzing the current state of affairs and what the future state of affairs should be. It does not suggest a solution.

Tools to help assess the accuracy of the problem statement and decision question

- Make sure the current state of the situation is stated clearly and that it does not reflect the symptom of the problem.

- At this point, you are not asking "why" there is a problem on which a decision has to be made. But you should be asking: Who does it affect? What does it affect? How does it affect? When does it affect? And where is it a problem?

- Ask yourself what the desired future state would look like. What is the goal of the project? Where do you want to be?

- Make sure you focus on only one problem.

- Make sure the problem statement does not suggest a solution or assign any blame.

- The decision question follows from the combined statement of the current situation and the desired future state, or problem statement.

- The decision question avoids asking "Why" but can be formulated as "What" or "How" questions.

In our example, the current situation for Linda is that the fleet of cars that her salesforce uses is no longer dependable. The desired future state or goal is to have a reliable fleet of vehicles that will meet the travel needs of the sales team. The question that flows from this problem is what type of vehicles should Linda purchase?

Generate Alternatives

Having recognized the need to make a decision, a manager must generate a set of feasible alternative courses of action to take in response to the opportunity or threat. The failure to properly generate and consider different alternatives is one reason why managers sometimes make bad decisions.[33] In our example, the manager comes up with three alternatives: Ford Escort, Toyota Corolla, and Suburu Legacy.

Linda believes these alternatives, once examined and assessed according to the criteria that are important to the decision (Step 3), will meet her original expectations and solve the problem of the aging fleet. Should none of these alternatives end up meeting expectations, Linda would have to begin again with the entire process.

■ **FIGURE 4.3** | **General Criteria for Evaluating Possible Courses of Action**

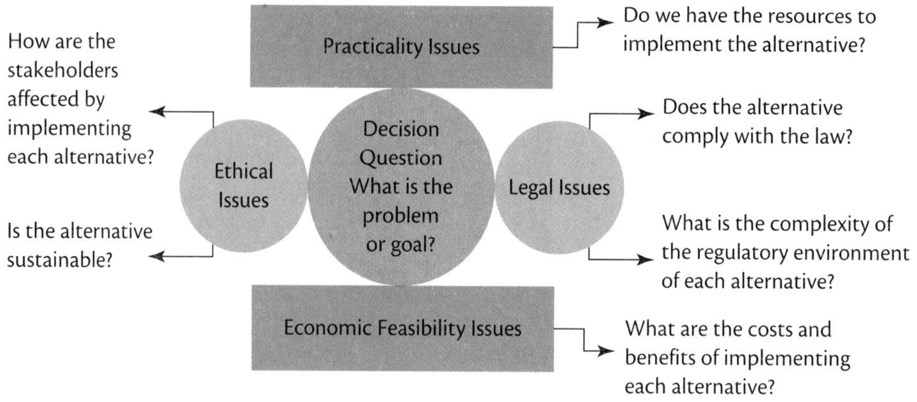

Assess Alternatives

Once managers have listed a set of alternatives, they must evaluate the advantages and disadvantages of each one.[34] The key to a good assessment of the alternatives is being able to define the opportunity or threat exactly, and then specifying the criteria that *should* influence the selection of alternative ways of responding to the problem or opportunity.

One reason for bad decisions is that managers often fail to specify the criteria that are important in reaching a decision.[35] In general, successful managers use four criteria to evaluate the pros and cons of alternative courses of action (see Figure 4.3):

1. *Practicality.* Managers must decide whether they have the capabilities and resources to implement the alternative, and they must be sure that the alternative will not threaten the ability to reach other organizational goals.
2. *Economic feasibility.* Managers must decide whether the alternatives make sense economically and fit the organization's performance goals. Typically, managers perform a cost-benefit analysis of the various alternatives to determine which one is likely to have the best financial payoff.
3. *Ethicality.* Managers must ensure that a possible course of action is ethical and that it will not unnecessarily harm any stakeholder group. Many of the decisions that managers make may help some organizational stakeholders and harm others (see Chapter 3).
4. *Legality.* Managers must ensure that a possible course of action is legal and will not violate any domestic and international laws or government regulations.

In order to arrive at a reasonable decision about which car to purchase, Linda consulted with her team and made a list of the features and criteria that were important to make the best decision. The new vehicle had to have the following features to meet the needs of the salesforce:

> Have all-wheel (AW) drive
> Have the full automatic package
> Be fuel efficient
> Be equipped with automatic braking system (ABS)
> Be reasonably priced
> Maintain good value over time
> Be easy and convenient to service, with a good warranty policy
> Be manufactured by a reputable and reliable company

Linda then categorized the requirements into four broad categories of criteria. Linda then categorized the requirements into the categories of criteria. While she recognized that some of the requirements could fall into more than one category, she decided to combine the ethical and legal concerns into one, and assigned it a relative value or weight of 30%. She gave the practical concerns a weight of 50% and the economic feasibility concerns a value of 20%. See below.

Criteria	Weight
Practicality—50%	
AW drive	20%
Fully loaded	15%
Fuel efficient	10%
ABS	5%
Economic Feasibility—20%	
5-year residual value	11%
On-the-road price	9%
Ethical and Legal Criteria—30%	
Service record/warranty	11%
Dealer reputation	10%
Dealer accessibility	9%
Total	100%

Next, Linda began to research how the alternatives measured up to the criteria in order to arrive at a score out of 10 points. She displayed her analysis in a Decision Preference Matrix (see Figure 4.4)

- The Subaru Legacy had AW drive, the Toyota Corolla and the Ford Focus did not, and therefore out of a possible score of 10, she rated Subaru Legacy 10, the Ford Focus 0, and Corolla 0.

- All cars could be bought fully loaded, although the Subaru Legacy had a few extras such as heated side mirrors and windshield wipers, as well as heated front seats, and the Focus had lower quality finishings, so she gave Subaru 10, Corolla 9, and the Focus 7.

- The Corolla had slightly better fuel efficiency over Subaru and the Focus, thus a score of 10 for Corolla, 8 for Subaru, and 6 for the Focus.

- All cars had ABS and seemed to have the same rating from most reviewers; thus all cars scored a 10 out of 10.

- For cost, most reviewers mentioned that both Corolla and Subaru held their values very well; but Corolla had a slight edge for resale, thus a score of 10 for Corolla and 9 for Subaru. Ford Focus had the lowest five-year residual value and thus scored 5.

- When Linda priced the cars, Focus was the cheapest. Corolla was cheaper than Subaru but in fairness was not quite as big or as powerful as Legacy. However, Ford

■ **FIGURE 4.4** | **Decision Preference Matrix**

	Weight	Corolla Score (1-10)	Weighted score	Subaru Score (1-10)	Weighted score	Ford Focus Score (1-10)	Weighted score
Practicality—50%							
AW drive	20%	0	0	10	200	0	0
Fully loaded	15%	9	135	10	150	7	35
Fuel efficient	10%	10	100	8	80	6	60
ABS	5%	10	50	10	50	10	50
Practicality Subtotal	**50**		**285**		**480**		**145**
Economic Feasibility—20%							
5-year residual value	11%	10	110	9	99	5	55
On-the-road price	9%	9	81	8	72	10	90
Economic Feasibility Subtotal	**20**		**191**		**171**		**145**
Ethical and Legal Criteria—30%							
Service record/warranty	11%	10	110	8	88	8	88
Dealer reputation	10%	10	100	8	80	6	60
Dealer accessibility	9%	9	81	9	81	10	90
Ethical and Legal Criteria Subtotal	**30**		**291**		**249**		**238**
Totals	**100%**		**767**		**900**		**528**

was more amenable when it came to trade-in values for the fleet of old cars—thus 9 for Corolla, 8 for Subaru, and 10 for Ford.

- From experience and fact gathering, Linda was confident that the service record of Corolla was slightly superior to those of Ford and Subaru in terms of price and customer service—thus 10 for Corolla, 8 for Subaru, and 8 for Ford.

- The Japanese manufacturers have a very enviable reputation relative to North American manufacturers, but Toyota sells many more cars than does Subaru— therefore 10 for Corolla, 8 for Subaru, and 6 for Ford.

- Both Toyota and Subaru dealerships are within 5 km from Linda's office, and both are relatively easy to get to for the salespeople, therefore both received a score of 9 out of 10; but Ford has a dealership just 2.5 km from the office, thus gets a score of 10.

Choose Among Alternatives

Once the set of alternative solutions has been carefully evaluated, the next task is to rank the various alternatives (using the criteria discussed in the previous section) and make a decision. When ranking alternatives, managers must be sure that all of the available information is brought to bear on the problem or issue at hand. Identifying all relevant information for a decision does not mean that the manager has complete information. In most instances, information is incomplete.

In our example, Linda's research leads her to the Subaru Legacy as the highest-ranking alternative car for her salespeople. She takes her research and results to her manager so that the decision can be acted upon.

Implement the Chosen Alternative

Once a decision has been made and an alternative has been selected, the alternative must be implemented and many subsequent and related decisions must be made. Although the need to make further decisions may seem obvious, many managers make the initial decision and then fail to act on it.[36] This is the same as not making a decision at all.

Managers often fail to get buy-in from those around them before making a decision. However, successful implementation requires participation. One study found that participation was used in only 20 percent of decisions, even though broad participation in decisions led to success 80 percent of the time. By contrast, the most common form of decision-making tactics, power of persuasion, used in 60 percent of decisions, is successful in only one of three decisions.[37]

To ensure that a decision is implemented, top managers must let middle managers participate in decisions, and then give them the responsibility to make the follow-up decisions necessary to achieve the goal. They must give middle managers enough resources to achieve the goal, and they must hold the middle managers accountable for their performance. Linda's manager is very impressed with the thoroughness of her decision-making process and is prepared to support the implementation of the outcome. Linda is given the budget she requested, and she goes ahead and purchases the new Subarus for her team.

Learn from Feedback

The final step in the decision-making process is learning from feedback. Managers who do not evaluate the results of their decisions do not learn from experience; instead they stagnate and are likely to make the same mistakes again and again.[38] To avoid this problem, managers must establish a formal procedure for learning from the results of past decisions. The procedure should include these steps:

1. Compare what actually happened to what was expected to happen as a result of the decision.
2. Explore why any expectations for the decision were not met.
3. Develop guidelines that will help in future decision making.

Individuals who always strive to learn from past mistakes and successes are likely to continuously improve their decision making. It is known that managers and executives at Hewlett-Packard, for example, "manage by wandering around, gathering feedback in hallways and cafeterias."[39] Their focus is on continually making better decisions. Daniel Goleman, Richard Boyatzis, and Annie McKee, in their book *Primal Leadership: Realizing the Power of Emotional Intelligence*, use the term "CEO disease" for those executives and managers who are unaware of or do not want feedback about their performance. The opposite of that is the emotionally intelligent executive or manager who actively seeks out feedback.[40] In our example, Linda seeks feedback from the salespeople who have been driving the new Subarus for a number of months to determine if her choice of vehicle is meeting their needs and has solved the initial problem of which type of vehicle to purchase.

 Tips for Managers

MANAGING THE DECISION-MAKING PROCESS

1. Be the best you can be with the information you have at hand. If you wait for the "best timing" for your decisions, the opportunity will probably be gone.

2. Be at the "top of your game" by continually scanning your environment, being proactive, identifying the key trends and opportunities, and knowing when best to make decisions.

3. Know your audience and the purpose of the decision you are about to make.

4. Learn to treat successes and failures as stepping stones in your decision-making practice.

Business Plan Checklist

- Use the steps in the decision-making process to determine the type of venture for your business plan.

L O 4

Biases in Decision Making

THINK ABOUT IT

Ignoring the Writing on the Wall?

What are known as our cognitive biases—preferences for a decision to be one way or another—can often create great stress and problems for us.[41] For example, one close-to-home example of a cognitive bias is that an expensive item, beer, for example, is "better" than a less expensive item (beer). "This finding holds true even when prices and brands are switched; putting the high price on the normally relatively inexpensive brand is enough to lead subjects to perceive it as tasting better than the beer that is normally more expensive. One might call this 'price implies quality' bias."[42] Everyone learns in life, sooner or later, that the reality of dying and death refocuses our cognitions and minimizes our biases because we all know we will die; we cannot fool ourselves in this regard. The philosopher scientist Bertrand Russell (1872–1970) once remarked, "It has been said that man is a rational animal. All my life I have been searching for evidence which could support this."[43]

In their book *Decision Traps*, Dr. J. Edward Russo and Dr. Paul J. H. Schoemaker reveal the 10 most common mistakes in decision making, many of which are related to cognitive bias:[44]

1. **Plunging in**: Beginning to gather information and reaching conclusions too early.
2. **Frame Blindness**: Creating a mental framework for your decision.
3. **Lack of Frame Control**: Failing to define the problem in more than one way.
4. **Overconfidence in Your Judgment**: Failing to gather key factual information.
5. **Shortsighted Shortcuts**: Relying inappropriately on "rules of thumb."
6. **Shooting from the Hip**: Failing to follow a systematic procedure when making the final decision.
7. **Group Failure**: Failing to manage the group decision-making process.
8. **Fooling Yourself about Feedback**: Failing to interpret the evidence from past outcomes correctly.
9. **Not Keeping Track**: Failing to keep systematic records to track the results of your decisions.
10. **Failure to Audit Your Decision Process**: Failing to create an organized approach to understand your own decision making.

Cognitive biases and organizational pressures to play up the positive mar our decision making. For example, we exaggerate our project's potential benefits and downplay its risks. We then cling to our initial forecasts—refusing to adjust them to account for subsequent (and more negative) market and financial analyses. The project flounders because no one anticipated the full range of likely problems. We also tend to seek only the information that supports our points of view. And we exaggerate our abilities and control over events.

You Be the Manager

1. What biases do people typically have when they "really" want a job they find interesting?
2. How do biases affect the way people make decisions?

In the 1970s, two psychologists, Daniel Kahneman and Amos Tversky, suggested that because all decision makers are subject to bounded rationality, they tend to use **heuristics**, rules of thumb that simplify the process of making decisions.[45] Kahneman and Tversky argued that rules of thumb are often useful because they help decision makers make sense of complex, uncertain, and ambiguous information. Sometimes, however, the use of heuristics can lead to systematic errors in the way decision makers process information about alternatives and make decisions. **Systematic errors** are errors that people make over and over again and that result in poor decision making. Because of cognitive biases, which are caused by systematic errors, otherwise capable managers may end up making bad decisions.[46] Four sources of bias that can negatively affect the way managers make decisions are prior hypotheses, representativeness, the illusion of control, and escalating commitment (see Figure 4.5).

heuristics
Rules of thumb that simplify decision making.

systematic errors
Errors that people make over and over again and that result in poor decision making.

■ **FIGURE 4.5 | Cognitive Biases in Decision Making**

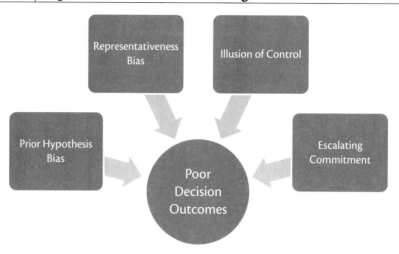

Prior Hypothesis Bias

prior hypothesis bias
A cognitive bias resulting from the tendency to base decisions on strong prior beliefs even if evidence shows that those beliefs are wrong.

Decision makers who have strong prior beliefs about the relationship between two variables tend to make decisions based on those beliefs *even when presented with evidence that their beliefs are wrong*. In doing so, they are falling victim to **prior hypothesis bias**. Moreover, decision makers tend to seek and use information that is consistent with their prior beliefs and to ignore information that contradicts those beliefs. Parents know all about prior hypothesis bias even though they might not call it that. Think back to your childhood. Many adults remember being "stubborn" when faced with new choices their parents were making. This is especially true of teenagers when one or both parents have to move because of work. The teenagers cannot imagine the new location and new home, for example, as being "better" than the vision of the one they now have. From a business strategic perspective, "a CEO who has a strong prior belief that a certain strategy makes sense might continue to pursue that strategy, despite evidence that it is inappropriate or failing."[47] Michael Cowpland, founder of Corel software, seemed to have that when he tried to "overtake" Microsoft as the #1 supplier of office software. Thomas Hobbes (1588–1679), English political philosopher, in his book *The Leviathan*, wrote that the life of a person is "solitary, nasty, brutish, and short."[48] So it was for Corel, according to ZDNet.co.uk, when it described the fight as "a fight that left Corel bloodied and battered." Microsoft purchased $135 million of Corel stock and settled their legal differences as well.[49]

Representativeness Bias

representativeness bias
A cognitive bias resulting from the tendency to generalize inappropriately from a small sample or from a single vivid case or episode.

Many decision makers inappropriately generalize from a small sample or even from a single vivid case or episode. An interesting example of the **representativeness bias** occurred as more and more investors perceived that Amazon.com was going to be the next great business model and invested in dot-com companies that had no serious business plans. The investors made the mistake of thinking that marketing on the Internet would be good for any new company.

Illusion of Control

illusion of control
A source of cognitive bias resulting from the tendency to overestimate one's own ability to control activities and events.

Other errors in decision making result from the **illusion of control**, the tendency of decision makers to overestimate their ability to control activities and events. Top-level managers seem to be particularly prone to this bias. Having worked their way to the top of an organization, they tend to have an exaggerated sense of their own worth and are overconfident about their ability to succeed and to control events.[50] The illusion of control causes managers to overestimate the odds of a favourable outcome and, consequently, to make inappropriate decisions. For example, in the 1980s, Nissan was run by Katsuji Kawamata, an autocratic manager who thought he alone had the skills to run the car company. He made all the decisions—decisions that resulted in a series of spectacular mistakes, including changing the company's name from Datsun to Nissan—and Nissan's share of the North American market fell dramatically. "Perceptions of power also have an impact on which expectations and commitments can be judged as realistic, and therefore the issue of power is central for the normative discussion about corporate social responsibility" (discussed in Chapter 3).[51]

Escalating Commitment

Having already committed significant resources to a course of action, some managers commit more resources to the project *even if they receive feedback that the project is failing.*[52] Feelings of personal responsibility for a project apparently bias the analysis of decision makers and lead to **escalating commitment**. They decide to increase their investment of time and money in a course of action and ignore evidence that it is illegal, unethical, uneconomical, or impractical (see Figure 4.3). Often, the more appropriate decision would be to "cut and run." It is now known that **self-fulfilling prophecy** and escalating commitment can cause an organizational crisis.[53]

A tragic example of the result of escalating commitment is the Columbia shuttle disaster. Apparently, managers were so anxious to keep the shuttle program on schedule that they ignored or discounted any evidence that falling debris might seriously compromise the shell of the shuttle. Thus, information about potential disaster was downplayed, even during the flight of the doomed shuttle.

escalating commitment
A source of cognitive bias resulting from the tendency to commit additional resources to a project even if evidence shows that the project is failing.

self-fulfilling prophecy
A person's prediction in their way of thinking and feeling that actually causes, directly or otherwise, for something to come true.

Improving Decision Making

L O 5

How can managers avoid the negative effects of cognitive biases and improve their decision-making and problem-solving abilities? They must uncover their biases and use their time wisely, but the quality of decision making ultimately depends on innovative responses to opportunities and threats in the environment. Managers can increase their ability to make nonprogrammed decisions by adopting a *sustainability strategy*, becoming a *learning organization* that promotes individual and group creativity, and utilizing *Management Information Systems (MIS)* effectively.

Uncover Biases and Manage Time Wisely

Individual managers as well as whole companies often have difficulty identifying their own biases and assumptions and seeking help from networks outside of their firms such as from consulting and marketing firms to help them uncover their biases.[54] More and more openness and transparency in revealing and sharing decision-making challenges are becoming popular among progressive companies. For example, Timberland is engaging in frank and candid discussions of its sourcing decisions with its stakeholders and networks in an effort to examine the criteria it uses to assess and evaluate the ethicality of alternative courses of action and if any cognitive biases and heuristics were used to arrive at the chosen options.[55]

Often managers fail to allocate enough time, let alone other resources, to the decision-making process. The development of time-management skills is essential. Experts suggest it can be helpful to managers to recall two recent decisions, one that turned out well and one that turned out poorly, and analyze the decision process. Examine how much time was spent on each of the six steps in the decision-making process to see if it was sufficient.[56] Make sure enough and uninterrupted time is devoted to important activities in the decision-making process.

Adopt a Sustainability Strategy

sustainability
Decisions that protect the environment, promote social responsibility, respect cultural differences, and provide an economic benefit.

www.saatchi.com

Sustainability is a way to make decisions that meet the needs of the current generation without sacrificing the future generation's ability to do so. The strategy must show how it can serve the core competencies of the business to create, innovate, and enter new markets. A **sustainability** strategy must have four elements: it must protect the environment, promote social responsibility, respect different cultures, and have an economic benefit. Sustainability not only has to have the support of the top management of the organization but also has to engage the employees. Everyone must internalize the individual responsibility for the good of the whole.

One way that employees are encouraged to engage in sustainable strategies at Saatchi and Saatchi is to have them embark on their own personal projects inside and outside the office. This might mean making the decision to park as far away from the door of the shopping mall as possible, to get a little walk in for exercise while shopping. Or it might mean deciding to bicycle to work rather than driving. Such forms of engagement create sustainable practices and make for good decision making in every area of life.

Making sustainable decisions becomes particularly important when managers consider the choice of source of their inputs. Chef Robert Clark of Vancouver's C Restaurant promotes sustainable fishing practices in British Columbia through the Ocean Wise program at the Vancouver Aquarium. Part of the program includes purchasing direct from fishers who use organic means of growing, selective harvesting, and exclusive production techniques that support and maintain the diverse marine ecosystem.[57] As of September 2008, Compass Group Canada and Sea Choice Canada, as partners with Ocean Wise, expanded the program nationwide to include new purchasing standards, internal compliance mechanisms, and chef and public education and awareness. "As the Canadian leader in food and support services, we are proud to embrace a sustainable seafood policy that will support the health of our oceans. Our purchasing shift can make a significant impact and it is clearly the right thing for us to do."[58] Says Jack MacDonald, CEO of Compass Group Canada.

Many universities and colleges are making the decision to not purchase eggs from caged hens because it severely limits the ability of the hens to engage many of their natural behaviours such as wing stretching, walking, dust bathing, standing on solid ground, or laying eggs in a nest. The European Union will ban the practice of caged hens by 2012. More than 300 universities and colleges in North America, including the University of Guelph, the University of British Columbia, Langara College, and the BC Institute of Technology, have already stopped purchasing eggs from suppliers that cage their hens.[59]

FIGURE 4.6 | Sustainability Decisions at Timberland[60]

Pillar #1	To become carbon neutral by 2010
Pillar #2	To design recyclable product
Pillar #3	To create fair, safe, and nondiscriminatory workplaces
Pillar #4	To engage in community greening campaigns

Firms also need to become more transparent about their efforts to create a sustainability strategy. The organizations that are open about their challenges with sustainability issues are gaining respect and market share. Take for example, again, Timberland. Timberland's "Just Means" website campaign is a powerful communication tool dedicated to reporting on its CSR activities, making Timberland one of the most transparent companies with a sustainability strategy (see Figure 4.6).

Consumers still have trouble identifying the leaders in sustainability.[61] A recent study by IMC2 on how effectively S&P 100 companies are communicating their sustainability efforts found that financial, media, and entertainment companies had the worst practices and policies related to communicating with the outside world about their sustainability issues, while the automotive and forestry industries were the best.[62]

www.justmeans.com
www.timberland.com

Become a Learning Organization

Organizational learning is the process through which managers seek to improve employees' desire and ability to understand and manage the organization and its task environment so that employees can make decisions that constantly raise organizational effectiveness.[63] A **learning organization** is one in which managers do everything possible to maximize the ability of individuals and groups to think and behave creatively and thus maximize the potential for organizational learning to take place. At the heart of organizational learning is **creativity**, the ability of a decision maker to discover original ideas that lead to feasible alternative courses of action. Encouraging creativity among managers is such a pressing organizational concern that many organizations hire outside experts to help them develop programs to train their managers in the art of creative thinking and problem solving.

organizational learning
The process through which managers seek to improve employees' desire and ability to understand and manage the organization and its task environment.

learning organization
An organization in which managers try to maximize the ability of individuals and groups to think and behave creatively and thus maximize the potential for organizational learning to take place.

creativity
A decision maker's ability to discover original and novel ideas that lead to feasible alternative courses of action.

THINK ABOUT IT

How to Think about the Problem

"When asked what single event was most helpful in developing the theory of relativity, Albert Einstein is reported to have answered, 'Figuring out how to think about the problem'."[64] Thomas Jefferson stated, "If nature has made any one thing less susceptible than all others of exclusive property, it is the action of the thinking power called an idea, which an individual may exclusively possess as long as he [sic] keeps it to himself [sic]."[65] Today, more than ever, organizations desperately want to have their employees share their ideas and be engaged in what they are doing. They look for creativity among employees. For example, "Modern teams are typically made up of knowledge workers whose competitive advantage lies in their combined ability to out-know other groups. Therefore, the knowledge resources of the team must be supported and protected by the team leader."[66]

For some organizations, the issue of young people downloading music files or sharing music files across the Internet is cause for litigation. One author sees things differently and uses the notion that if these same organizations used more creativity, a new vision would be possible. "The lesson the music industry should be taking from iTunes is not that selling MP3s is viable, it's that the digital music file is the perfect loss leader. Its marginal cost of production is zero. Use it to sell something that cannot be copied (fan merchandise, live performances, endorsements, collectibles). The medium (an MP3 file) is not the product. The gold lies in the emotional connection between performer and audience."[67] At the internationally renowned Montreal-based Cirque du Soleil, boss Guy Laliberté asked François Gourd, known as a "corporate fool," to inject this kind of energy into his employees as a way to get them to be more creative. Gourd said Laliberté used the following exact words, "Contaminate my company. You have carte blanche. Surprise me."[68]

You Be the Manager

1. What would you do to develop more creativity in your company?

Promote Individual Creativity

Research suggests that individuals are most likely to be creative when certain conditions are met. First, people must be given the opportunity and freedom to generate new ideas. Creativity declines when managers look over the shoulders of talented employees and try to "hurry up" a creative solution. How would you feel if your boss said you had one week to come up with a new product idea to beat the competition? Creativity results when individuals have an opportunity to experiment, to take risks, and to make mistakes and learn from them. Companies that have a lot of innovation foster that through their formal structure and expectations. For instance, in one recent year, 3M launched more than 200 new products. To encourage this level of development, managers are told that 30 percent of sales are expected to come from products less than four years old.[69]

Once managers have generated alternatives, creativity can be encouraged by providing employees with constructive feedback so that they know how well they are doing. Ideas that seem to be going nowhere can be eliminated and creative energies refocused in other directions. Ideas that seem promising can be promoted, and help from other managers can be obtained as well.[70] Sometimes a manager misses a good opportunity because of decision-making biases, as discussed earlier in this chapter, and sometimes it happens because they do not share their concerns about an idea with others and simply reject it outright. Sharing challenges and getting feedback from a wide variety of channels, including other firms through networking, can help managers make sure they do not miss out on a good idea as did Hewlett-Packard, when they decided not to develop one of their employee's ideas. The result: Steve Wozniak went off with his device to co-found Apple Computer. Other examples are shown in Figure 4.7.

It is also important for top managers to stress the importance of looking for alternative solutions and to visibly reward employees who come up with creative ideas. Being creative can be demanding and stressful. Employees who believe that they are

FIGURE 4.7 | Some of the Biggest Mistakes Managers Have Ever Made

- Alexander Graham Bell invented the telephone in 1876, but he had a hard time attracting backers. President Rutherford B. Hayes used a prototype telephone and remarked, "That's an amazing invention, but who would ever want to use one of them?" Bell approached Western Union Telegraph Company and offered to sell them the patents. Their decision: They had no use for an electrical toy.

- A young inventor, Chester Carlson, took his idea to 20 corporations, all of whom turned him down. He finally got a small New York company named Haloid Co. to purchase the rights to his electrostatic paper-copying process. Haloid became Xerox Corporation, and Carlson's process made both Xerox and Carlson very rich.

- In 1962 four musicians played for executives of Decca Recording Company. One executive later explained that his company just did not like the group's sound, noting that guitar groups were on their way out. Four other record companies turned them down. The Decision Making Hall of Fame will have a special place for Decca, which turned down the Beatles.

- Hewlett-Packard's decision not to develop a product created by an employee: Steve Wozniak went off with his device to co-found Apple Computer.

working on important, vital issues will be motivated to put forth the high levels of effort that creativity demands.

Despite the importance of fostering creativity in organizations, in a recent survey of 500 CEOs, only 6 percent felt that they were doing a great job at managing their creative people. John MacDonald, co-founder of MacDonald Dettwiler & Associates Ltd. (MDA), based in Richmond, BC, suggests that "managing creative people is a bit like riding herd on a thousand prima donnas. They are all highly individual people who don't follow the herd, so managing them is a challenge."[71]

L O 6

Utilizing Information and Management Information Systems (MIS)

THINK ABOUT IT

"Men Are from Canon, Women Are from Kodak"[72]

Managers need information to make decisions. The question is: what types of information? "In an age of hyperchange, seeing our way to the future is harder and harder."[73] If you are the Eastman Kodak Co., having the right information at the right time to make decisions is absolutely essential. Kodak got its information correctly: Women had traditionally bought film from the company; they were the targeted audience for decades. When the digital camera came along, men jumped on the bandwagon, and film met a hasty death. Rather than die, Kodak gathered information that its cameras should be "female-friendly" if it wanted to be and stay competitive. "The company's research showed that women wanted digital photography to be simple and that they desired high-quality prints to share with family and friends." So, what did Kodak do with this new information? "Kodak revamped its digital cameras, stressing simple controls and larger display screens. It invented a new product category, the compact stand-alone photo printer, which could be used to easily make prints without a computer. And it pushed to make digital-image printing simpler through retail kiosks and an online service." And the result, "Today, Kodak is clawing its way to the top of the digital world by bringing its best customers into that world with it."

You Be the Manager

1. How important is information in the work you do?

In order for managers to generate and assess their alternatives in making a decision, they need access to data and information both from inside the organization and from external stakeholders. When deciding how to price a seat sale, for example, the WestJet marketing manager needs information about how consumers will react to different prices. She needs information about unit costs because she does not want to set the price below the costs of flying. She also needs data about how many people (and what class of flyer—business or vacation) are likely to fly on any given day. WestJet also needs information about competitors' prices, since its pricing strategy should be consistent with its competitive strategy. Some of this information can come from outside the organization (e.g., from consumer surveys) and some from inside the organization (information about flight costs from operations). As this example suggests, managers' ability to make effective decisions rests on their ability to acquire and process information.

data
Raw, unsummarized, and unanalyzed facts.

information
Data that are organized in a meaningful fashion.

information technology
The mean by which information is acquired, organized, stored, manipulated, and transmitted.

Information is not the same as data.[74] **Data** are raw, unsummarized, and unanalyzed facts such as volume of sales, level of costs, or number of customers. **Information** is data that are organized in a meaningful fashion such as in a graph showing the change in sales volume or costs over time. The distinction between data and information is important because one of the uses of information technology is to help managers transform data into information in order to make better managerial decisions. **Information technology** is the means by which information is acquired, organized, stored, manipulated, and transmitted. Rapid advances in the power of information technology—specifically, through the use of computers—are having a fundamental impact on information systems and on managers and their organizations.[75]

Attributes of Useful Information

When we evaluated the rational decision-making process earlier in this chapter, we noted that it is often difficult for individuals to have access to all possible information needed to make a decision. While information is still collected from individuals, much information is now accessed through information technology (websites, databases, and the like). Regardless of how it is acquired, individuals need to decide whether the information is useful. Four factors determine the usefulness of information: quality, timeliness, completeness, and relevance (see Figure 4.8).

Quality

Accuracy and reliability determine the quality of information.[76] The greater the accuracy and reliability, the higher is the quality of information. For an information system to work well, the information that it provides must be of high quality. If managers conclude that the quality of information provided by their information system is low, they are likely to lose confidence in the system and stop using it. Alternatively, if managers base decisions on low-quality information, poor and even disastrous

FIGURE 4.8 │ Factors Affecting the Usefulness of Information

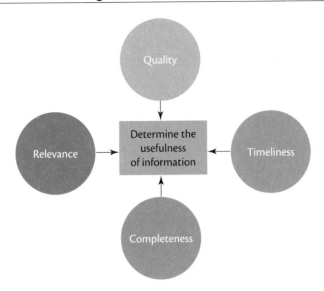

decision making can result. For example, the partial meltdown of the nuclear reactor at Three Mile Island in Pennsylvania during the 1970s was the result of poor information caused by an information system malfunction. The information system indicated to engineers controlling the reactor that there was enough water in the reactor core to cool the nuclear pile, although this was, in fact, not the case. The consequences included the partial meltdown of the reactor and the release of radioactive gas into the atmosphere.

Timeliness

Information that is timely is available when it is needed for managerial action, not after the decision has been made. In today's rapidly changing world, the need for timely information often means that information must be available on a real-time basis.[77] **Real-time information** is information that reflects current conditions. In an industry that experiences rapid changes, real-time information may need to be updated frequently. Airlines use real-time information on the number of flight bookings and competitors' prices to adjust their prices on an hour-to-hour basis to maximize their revenues.

real-time information
Frequently updated information that reflects current conditions.

Completeness

Information that is complete gives managers all the information they need to exercise control, achieve coordination, or make an effective decision. We have already noted that because of uncertainty, ambiguity, and bounded rationality, managers have to make do with incomplete information.[78] One of the functions of information systems is to increase the completeness of the information that managers have at their disposal.

Relevance

Information that is relevant is useful and suits a manager's particular needs and circumstances. Irrelevant information is useless and may actually hurt the performance of a busy manager who has to spend valuable time determining whether information is relevant. Given the massive amounts of information that managers are now exposed to and the limited information-processing capabilities of humans,

Management Information Systems (MIS)
Electronic systems of interconnected components designed to collect, process, store, and disseminate information to facilitate management decision making, planning, and control.

the people who design information systems need to make sure that managers receive only relevant information.

Computer-based information gathering and processing systems are central to the operation of most organizations today. **Management Information Systems (MIS)** are designed to specifically to help managers make efficient and effective decisions when planning, leading, organizing, and controlling. The following are types of Management Information Systems:

- Decision Support Systems (DSS)

- Enterprise Resource Planning Systems (ERP)

- Supply Chain Management Systems

- Customer Relationship Management Systems

- Human Resources Information Systems (HRIS)

In the recent past, the software designed to do this had to be purchased by individual firms which were granted licences to use the closely guarded programs. In the last decade, many of the kinds of service applications that were once distributed privately, at a very large expense to individuals and companies, are increasingly becoming available on the Internet for a fraction of the cost. It is referred to as "cloud computing." Web-based services include everything from managing supply chains and human resources, to data storage and digital content creation. Almost all software can be offered as a service that can be merged and intertwined with other applications, effectively being tailored to a firm's specific needs. These Web services allow online offerings to connect and synchronize their data. According to a study by *The Economist*,[79] "it is unlikely that the software cloud will end up as a vast nebula of thousands of specialized services." Rather, two clumps of services are emerging: integrated suites of applications, such as Google Apps and Zoho, which offer about 20 applications including word processing, project management and customer-relationship management (CRM), and platforms, similar to operating systems used today, providing consumer services such as the social network Facebook. The competition is so fierce in cloud computing, some suggest the platform war will rival that of the epic fights between Microsoft and Apple. Between 2006 and 2011 annual compound growth is predicted to be 29.1 percent.

As a result of this growth, data centres are becoming "factories of computing services on an industrial scale; software is increasingly being delivered as an online service; and wireless networks connect more and more devices to such offerings," making large IT departments in firms obsolete.[80] Moreover, the increase in data centres will have an enormous ecological imprint on the environment. According to EMC2, a marketing firm that helps companies figure out their carbon footprint and how to offset it, "energy consumption tied to data centres doubled between 2001 and 2006 and could do so again by 2011, according to a recent study by the Environmental Protection Agency (EPA). This energy consumption already accounts for an estimated 2 percent of the world's carbon emissions, an impact equivalent to air travel."[81]

Summary and Review

1. **THE NATURE OF MANAGERIAL DECISION MAKING** Programmed decisions are routine decisions that are made so often that managers have developed decision rules to be followed automatically. Nonprogrammed decisions are made in response to situations that are unusual or unique; they are nonroutine decisions.

2. **COMPARING DECISION-MAKING MODELS** The rational model of decision making assumes that decision makers have complete information; are able to process that information in an objective, rational manner; and make optimum decisions. The administrative model suggests that managers are boundedly rational, rarely have access to all the information they need to make optimum decisions, and consequently satisfice and rely on their intuition and judgment when making decisions.

3. **SIX STEPS IN THE DECISION-MAKING PROCESS:** Managers recognize the need for a decision, generate alternatives, assess alternatives, choose among alternatives, implement the chosen alternative, and learn from feedback.

4. **BIASES IN DECISION MAKING** Managers are often fairly good decision makers. However, problems result when human judgment is adversely affected by the operation of cognitive biases. Cognitive biases are caused by systematic errors in the way decision makers process information to make decisions. Sources of these errors include prior hypotheses, representativeness, the illusion of control, and escalating commitment. Managers should undertake a personal decision audit to become aware of their biases.

5. **IMPROVING DECISION MAKING** Managers can make better decisions when they examine their biases and spend appropriate amounts of time engaging in the process. But to make optimum decisions, managers should adopt a sustainability strategy that is transparent, engaging, and economically beneficial without leaving a large carbon footprint. They must become a learning organization and encourage creativity to ensure that new, innovative ideas are not overlooked.

6. **INFORMATION AND MANAGEMENT INFORMATION SYSTEMS (MIS)** Managers must utilize Management Information Systems that provide high-quality, timely, relevant and relatively complete information and service applications that enable them to make effective decisions.

Key Terms

administrative model, p. 106
ambiguous information, p. 107
bounded emotionality, p. 103
bounded rationality, p. 107
creativity, p. 119
data, p. 122
decision making, p. 104
escalating commitment, p. 117
heuristics, p. 115
illusion of control, p. 116
information, p. 122
information technology, p. 122
intuition, p. 107
judgment, p. 108
learning organization, p. 119

Management Information
  Systems (MIS), p. 124
nonprogrammed decision making, p. 104
optimum decision, p. 106
organizational learning, p. 119
prior hypothesis bias, p. 116
programmed decision making, p. 104
rational decision-making model, p. 105
real-time information, p. 123
representativeness bias, p. 116
satisficing, p. 107
self-fulfilling prophecy, p. 117
sustainability, p. 118
systematic errors, p. 115
uncertainty, p. 107

Wrap-Up to Opening Case[82]

We are known by the commitments we make. In the opening case scenario, we showed how decisions must be tied to commitments to be in alignment. Commitment focuses the decision maker on what, how, and why to decide.

Fernando Flores was Chile's minister of finance at one time—and, later, a political prisoner under president and dictator of Chile Augusto Pinochet Ugarte (1973–1990). His three years in solitary confinement transformed him. Now he teaches companies how to use assessments and commitments to transform the way they do business. The outcome: executives who speak and act with intention. In 1984, Flores founded Action Technologies to develop software that can track the fulfillment of promises and commitments in day-to-day work operations. Flores says that he wants to open up people's moral imagination. By doing this, they will have a strategic advantage in business, in politics, and in their personal lives.

It was while doing his Ph.D. after he got out of prison in Chile that he studied the German philosopher Martin Heidegger. "From Heidegger, Flores learned that language conveys not only information but also commitment and that people act by expressing assessments and promises."

Talk all you want to, Flores says, but if you want to act powerfully, you need to master "speech acts": language rituals that build trust between colleagues and customers, word practices that open your eyes to new possibilities. Speech acts are powerful because most of the actions that people engage in—in business, in marriage, in parenting—are carried out through conversation. But most people speak without intention; they simply say whatever comes to mind. Speak with intention, and your actions take on new purpose. Speak with power, and you act with power.

Ask Yourself

1. When I am making decisions, do I see the "big picture" and the commitment I must first make that will shape my process of decisionmaking?

2. How do people know that when you give your word, you mean it?

3. What are you committed to in your business practice?

Management in Action

Topics for Discussion and Action

Level 1

1. Define and describe the two types of decisions.
2. Describe the six steps that managers should take to make the best decisions.
3. Describe the difference between data and information. What are the characteristics of useful information?

Level 2

4. Ask a manager to recall the best and the worst business decisions he or she ever made. Try to determine why these decisions were so good or so bad.
5. Ask a manager to describe the main kinds of information systems that he or she uses on a routine basis at work.
6. Listen to the podcast "Sustainability—The Only Strategy" from Harvard Business Ideacast 111, September 11, 2008, and describe how managers use the "TEN" cycle to promote sustainability, creativity, and organizational learning.

Level 3

7. Compare and contrast the assumptions underlying the rational and administrative models of decision making.
8. You are a first-line manager of a grocery store that has a home delivery service. You tell your boss that you have found a cheaper supplier of insurance for the drivers with the same amount of coverage. Your boss continues to use the more expensive insurer. What decision-making bias is your boss suffering from?
9. When a manager is asked to judge an alternative in terms of a cost-benefit analysis, which criterion are they weighting most highly?

Building Management Skills

Answer the following questions about the organization you have chosen to follow:

1. Try to find some evidence that managers at the organization made a few poor decisions over the past decade.

2. If poor decisions were made, what role, if any, did decision-making biases play?

Management for You

HOW DO YOU MAKE DECISIONS?

Pick a decision that you have made recently that has had important consequences for you. This decision may be your decision concerning which college to attend, which major to select, which part-time job to take, or even whether or not to take a part-time job. Using the material in this chapter, analyze the way in which you made the decision:

1. Identify the criteria you used, either consciously or unconsciously, to guide your decision making.
2. List the alternatives that you considered. Were these all the possible alternatives? Did you unconsciously (or consciously) ignore some important alternatives?
3. How much information did you have about each alternative? Did you base the decision on complete or incomplete information?
4. Try to remember how you reached a decision. Did you sit down and consciously think through the implications of each alternative, or did you make a decision on the basis of intuition? Did you use any rules of thumb to help you make the decision?
5. Do you think that your choice of decision alternative was shaped by any of the cognitive biases discussed in this chapter?
6. Do you think in retrospect that you made a reasonable decision? What, if anything, might you do to improve your ability to make good decisions in the future?

Small Group Breakout Exercise

BRAINSTORMING

Form groups of three or four people, and appoint one member as the spokesperson who will communicate your findings to the whole class when called on by the instructor. Then discuss the following scenario:

Assume your group is charged with solving the problem of replacing the obsolete desktop computer monitors for the human resources department. You must purchase seven new monitors, but are struggling over the decision of what brand to buy. Apply the steps in the decision-making process.

1. State the decision question.
2. Brainstorm the brands of computer monitors available.
3. a. List the factors that are important in making the decision, and fit them into the four categories of criteria.
   b. Assign a value or weight to each of the criteria categories and subfactors.
   c. Discuss the advantages and disadvantages of each of the brands in terms of the decision criteria and assign them a score out of 10 (0 is low).
   d. Make a Decision Preference Matrix (see Figure 4.4) to display the weighted scores.
4. Which brand will you choose, and why?
5. How will you go about implementing your decision?
6. How will you know if you made a good decision?

Business Planning Exercise

You and your teammates want to make the best decision possible about the type of restaurant on which you will be writing the business plan. You have to keep several important factors in mind when making this decision, for example, your business plan must demonstrate to the investor that the venture is worth their while. You decide to use the six step decision-making model to help you make a choice that is likely to succeed.

Step 1: Recognize the need to make a decision as to the type of restaurant you should develop your business plan on.

Step 2: Generate alternatives.
Make a list of all of your options and place these in the columns across the top of a table as column headings.

Step 3: Assess the alternatives using a Decision Preference Matrix (see Figure 4.4).
a. Make a list of all the factors that are important to the decision, that is, the criteria that fall under the four categories outlined in the text. Place these in rows on the left-hand side of the table. Put all the factors that are important to the decision under the appropriate category of criteria as a subheading.
b. Next, weight the four categories of criteria by working out their relative importance to the decision. For example, you might believe the category of Economic Feasibility should carry the most weight (say 50 percent), followed

by Practical Issues (30 percent), and Legal and Ethical Criteria (10 percent each).
c. Assign each decision variable a score based on information you gathered through research. Show these as numbers from, say, 0 to 10, where 0 means that the factor is absolutely unimportant or has the least beneficial outcome in the final decision, and 10 meaning that it is very important or has the most favourable outcome. (It is perfectly acceptable to have factors with the same level of importance.) For example: Your research may suggest that a restaurant with entertainment may require more complicated permits and licences to operate than a restaurant that serves only breakfast. Under the criteria of Legal Issues, the breakfast option scores higher than the nightclub, say, 10 to 2, in terms of licensing because it is less legally complicated. However, when considering Economic Feasibility, the nightclub has greater potential to earn revenue

than does the breakfast option and thus would have a greater score, say 9 to 1.

d. Create another column for the weighted scores. Working down the columns of options, multiply the score on each decision variable by the value assigned to its relative importance. In our example, under Legal Issues, the nightclub option's weighted score is $2 \times 10 = 20$ for licensing, whereas the breakfast option has a weighted score of $10 \times 10 = 100$. Under Economic Feasibility, the nightclub scores $9 \times 50 = 450$, while the breakfast option scores $1 \times 50 = 50$ for potential to generate revenue.

e. Finally, add up these weighted scores for each of your options.

Step 4: Choose among the alternatives.
The option that scores the highest is the one you will choose for your business plan.

Step 5: Implement the alternative.
Now that you have decided which type of restaurant, you must create an action plan to manage the project of writing the business plan. You might consider using a Gantt Chart to manage the tasks and timelines in completing the business plan project.

Step 6: Learn from feedback.
You will know if you made a good decision when you present your business plan to an investor (or your professor) and it is favourably received.

Managing Ethically

MANAGERS STRUGGLE WITH ETHICAL DECISIONS[83]

It is hard to do the right thing as a manager—especially when you are not sure what the "right thing" is. Sometimes you must balance your own sense of ethics with organizational pressures.

Take the case of employees at a cabinet manufacturing company. A number of them routinely work on their own projects on company time. The manager is aware of this. But there is a labour crunch in the booming construction sector, and she is concerned about retaining staff. So she turns a blind eye. The organization tacitly supports the manager's decision not to stop the practice because labour is hard to find. Nevertheless, the manager is uncomfortable. The decision does not sit right, and she has noticed that allowing the practice has affected other workers. People are taking longer lunches and breaks and talking on the phone during company time. Productivity is starting to slide. How do you think the manager should deal with this situation?

Exploring the World Wide Web

SPECIFIC ASSIGNMENT

Go to the website for the consulting firm 5i Strategic Affairs (www.5istrategicaffairs.com/index.htm). Review the site. Click on the button "Philosophy/Principles." Then click on "Philosophy/Process," and read about the issues involved in the 5i process. Click on the button "About 5i," and read the following: "5i is perfectly fluid, with teams being assembled as required to meet the specific needs of each mandate. Our consulting team comprises only experienced independent professionals, each possessing formidable experience in a given field of expertise, which includes strategy implementation, organizational design, marketing communications and project management. Each mandate is led personally by company founder Mark Hollingworth."[84]

1. What from the 5i website resonates with some of the key ideas in this chapter?

GENERAL ASSIGNMENT

Search for a website that describes a company whose managers have just made a major decision. What was the decision? Why did they make it? How successful has it been?

McGraw-Hill Connect™—Available 24/7 with instant feedback so you can study when you want, how you want, and where you want. Take advantage of the Study Plan—an innovative tool that helps you customize your learning experience. You can diagnose your knowledge with pre- and post-tests, identify the areas where you need help, search the entire learning package for content specific to the topic you're studying, and add these resources to your personalized study plan. Visit www.mcgrawhillconnect.ca to register—take practice quizzes, search the e-book, and much more.

Be the Manager

George Stroumboulopoulos of CBC's *The Hour* initiated a campaign called "One Million Acts of Green,"[85] which is an attempt to get Canadians to engage in something that will prevent greenhouse gas emissions. The act "can be as simple as switching to compact fluorescent lightbulbs, starting a recycling program, or walking to work." As a manager, what decisions could you make that will promote sustainability?

Management Case

Competitive Arousal[86]

Jupiter Images/Brand X/Alamy

If you ever made a decision[87] in the heat of a takeover, labour contract talks, or other high-stakes negotiations and later wondered what you could possibly have been thinking, you fell prey to competitive arousal. In *Harvard Business Review*, academics Deepak Malhotra, Gillian Ku, and J. Keith Murnighan sketch out the three causes of competitive arousal and how to keep it at bay.[88]

Rivalry

Competitive arousal is common—and most powerful—when rivalry is intense, and that usually means a head-to-head rivalry. Research shows individuals are more likely to overbid in auctions when facing only one other bidder, and companies will often dig in their heels in takeovers if a long-time rival is involved.

To defuse rivalry, the first step is to avoid seeing the competitor as an evil nemesis but just as somebody with their own interests at stake, who, like you, is probably smart, reasonably rational, and somewhat emotional (and probably views you as the nemesis).

You should also reconsider the roles of executives who feel this rivalry most strongly, as happened when the NHL and its players' association turned talks over to the second-in-commands because the enmity between commissioner Gary Bettman and players' executive director Bob Goodenow was impeding a settlement.

Another option: If your ego is at stake, admit it, and quantify how much you are willing to pay to beat your rival, since that might be less than what you would pay if your unchecked emotions ran away from you.

Time Clocks

Ticking clocks in auctions, negotiations, takeovers, and disputes can overwhelm us with the desire to win. Emotions take over, the ability to find needed information is decreased, and decision-making heuristics turn simplistic as we become increasingly fixated.

Take a vacation if you can, or otherwise look to extend or eliminate arbitrary deadlines you have set for yourself or those that others have established but are more flexible than it appears. Union and management will sometimes, wisely, take this route in labour negotiations to avoid a premature breakdown. Ask yourself: "Do I really have to decide this today?"

The Spotlight

The presence of an audience passing judgment on you—be it your boss wondering whether you can hold on to a shaky customer or the media reporting on a prospective merger—can also lead to mistakes. Individuals are more likely to overbid in public auctions, where the auctioneer singles them out for attention in front of a crowd, than in private, Internet auctions.

Try to spread responsibility in such situations across team members, so no one person is in the glare. Judge people on their overall performance rather than on one specific account. In acquisitions, calculate how high you are willing to go before the story hits the newsstands and other players react to your strategy.

Questions

1. In your own terms, what are the three causes of competitive arousal?
2. How has competitive arousal affected you in making decisions?

Video Management Case

Anne Mulcahy: How to Make Decisions

Teaching Objective: To help students appreciate the importance of making timely decisions, even if they involve risk on the part of the decision maker, and to provide examples of how one CEO makes tough decisions.

Summary: Since Anne Mulcahy became CEO of Xerox in 2001, she orchestrated what some have called the turnaround of the century. She accomplished this by taking risks and making quick, tough decisions. Mulcahy believes that when you take no risks and make no mistakes, you end up not making enough decisions. Even though some decisions did not turn out the way she would have liked, she learned from her mistakes and moved on.

Questions

1. Why is it so critical to make decisions sooner rather than later?
2. What biases should a manager like Anne Mulcahy avoid in making decisions?
3. How can managers make sure the tough decisions they make are ethical?

Managing Planning and Strategy

Learning Outcomes

1. Describe what planning is, who does it, types of plans, why it is important, and what qualities make plans effective.

2. Describe Scenario planning and Crisis Management

3. Describe planning as a five-step process involving the following:

   a. Determining an organization's vision, mission, and goals

   b. Analyzing the forces in the organizational environment

   c. Formulating strategy

   d. Implementing strategy

   e. Evaluating strategy

4. Explain how managers use SWOT and Porter's Five Forces model to evaluate the opportunities and threats in the organization's environment.

5. Differentiate among corporate-level, business-level and functional-level strategies.

6. Describe the steps in implementing and evaluating the success of the strategy to achieve the organization's mission and goals.

Strategist: "I Did It My Way"[1]

Ted Rogers died in the fall of 2008 at the age of 75.

Most Canadians are familiar with Rogers Communication Inc. (RCI) in one way or another. Even when Ted Rogers was in his early seventies, the "king" of cable, wireless, and media in Canada was not about to surrender his throne—yet. His son, Edward Rogers, now in his thirties, seemed poised to take over as top strategist and planner for the future of the $30-billion family business—but not yet! He was seen as one of several candidates for the top job at Rogers, but not the clear-cut favourite; and he knew it. Said Edward, "I keep my head down and work." The critics, however, did not think he had the "right stuff" to take over from his father.

Edward Rogers is an enigmatic figure in one of Canada's best known companies, the quiet son—often called shy—who came up in the shadow cast by his famous father. He has held a variety of jobs inside the company, gaining a reputation as a hard worker. Yet through it all, he is viewed by some only as Ted's son—rather than his successor.

Ted Rogers' 37-year-old daughter Melinda is also another key contender.

By age 33, son Edward had moved into his first high-profile post, being appointed chief operating officer of the cable unit, taking over from John Tory, who became the leader of the Ontario Conservatives; but during his tenure, the cable unit's operating profit jumped from $563.5 million in 2002 to $1 billion in 2007. Tory said Edward won the job because of his cable credentials, not his name.

Nevertheless, Ted, the father, remained, as ever, heavily involved in the cable business.

When planning for the future at the time, Ted Rogers said, "The next 10 years depends really on, once we have the company improved, what do we do for growth? Do we do growth in Canada, and is there any growth possibilities in Canada, or do we look south of the border? I was south of the border before

with cable. We had a million customers. We had to sell them in order to finance the wireless."

John Tory, the leader of the Ontario Progressive Conservative Party, who formerly ran RCI's cable division, said that Ted Rogers had an incredible ability to look into the future and see what people needed before they knew they needed it. In 2008, Ted Rogers reached the milestone that he set for himself: to work until age 75 as chief executive officer and then pass on the reins. However, in 2008, he changed those plans and decided instead to leave his departure from the company open-ended. Like moving out of a leased apartment, Ted's new plan in 2008 was to give the board six months' notice when he decided to vacate the company. He insisted then that he harboured no immediate plans to go! On December 2, 2008, Ted Rogers died.

What is known now is that the cable industry is in transition. The market changed dramatically since Ted Rogers first started in the cable business some 40 years ago. Rogers no longer just sells a utility-like basic TV service each month. Instead, it offers lucrative digital TV, wireless, and Internet services. In 2005, the cable industry added local phone service to that mix, taking on old telecom foes Bell Canada and Telus Corp.

One thing Ted Rogers was sure of in planning for the future of RCI was that the top person "had to be a leader. You can get a consensus, but there's a danger to too much consensus. The consensus is the common denominator, and there's no leadership. ... The CEO has to make the final decision. He has to listen to people and consider all views, but the danger is you know that somebody is very much against a move that you know would be very good for the company."

And the stock price over the years? December 31, 1989: $7.77; May 23, 2008: $44.28.

Ted Rogers did it "his way"!

Photo: CP

20081203; ON; Business; B1—Ambitious Ted: TV cable magnate Ted Rogers displays some of the equipment that will be the focal point of an ambitious high-tech program in which $1.1 billion will be allocated to increase cellular telephone coverage and prepare for the age of high-definition television. Photo taken by Frank Lennon/Toronto Star March 29, 1989.

Now It's Your Turn

Think of a time (or research a case) when you were involved in a work or organizational situation that included the context as described in the opening story about Rogers Communications Inc.: planning a strategy for the future when the founding entrepreneur sent out mixed signals about who was going to be in charge and when that would occur.

1. What was the background to your own case situation?

2. What were some of the challenges involved for staff?

3. What, if any, final resolution occurred? (As you develop your answer, track strategy from two years ago to two years from now.)

Overview

The opening scenario to this chapter allows us to see that even with successful companies such as Rogers Communications Inc. (RCI), planning often reflects the dynamics operating at the very senior levels. This is especially true in the case of RCI because of the strong and often autocratic leadership provided over the years by founder Ted Rogers, who kept putting out mixed signals for his retirement over the years. Deloitte & Touche, LLP, United Kingdom, points out that planning to have the right people in place can be more challenging given the opportunity many have today to jump from job to job.[2] And even if succession planning has occurred and the new person is in charge, the "meddlesome predecessor"[3] can sometimes impact the planning process by making comments or by interfering in the process as a now-outsider. This seemed to be the case for the new CEO of General Electric (GE), Jeffrey Immelt, "when Jack Welch, the former chief executive officer of General Electric Co., let loose criticisms of the way his successor has been handling the job." As leadership coach Nick Pollice, an instructor for the Canadian Management Centre in Toronto, puts it, "All of these meddlers continue to think they know best how to do your job. And in many cases, they may be openly critical of your performance, intentionally or unintentionally undercutting you."

In an uncertain competitive environment, managers must engage in thorough planning to find a strategy that will allow them to compete effectively. This chapter explores the manager's role both as planner and as strategist. We first discuss what planning is, who does it, why its important for high performance, and what qualities make effective plans. We then discuss the five main steps in the planning process: a) Determining an organization's vision, mission and goals and communicating these to the members of the organization through Management by Objectives (MBO); b) analyzing the forces in the organizational environment by applying SWOT and Porter's Five Forces model; c) formulating strategy at the corporate, business and functional level; d) implementing strategy; and finally, e) evaluating the success of the strategy in achieving the mission and goals of the organization. See Table 5.1.

An Overview of the Planning Process

THINK ABOUT IT

Business Plan Competitions and Real-World Experience[4]

Rob Warren, director of the Centre for Entrepreneurship at the University of Manitoba's Asper School of Business says, "We put a lot of emphasis on business plan competitions and have worked to make it our signature piece." What is interesting about what he says is that in the past seven years, six businesses have been started as a result of entering business plans into competitions. This is truly real-world experience. Students in Professor Warren's business planning class put strategy and planning together and, as has been shown, come out with winning business plans that create viable businesses. At this Manitoba school, the students are responsible for writing, editing, and constantly revising their own plans—with a little guidance from their professor.

An example of a winning competition was the one by Kevin Michaluk and Michal Miller, both of whom met at a conference months earlier and then met in Professor Warren's class. They formed PlasiaTEK, a startup medical technology enterprise that has already won $75 000 in business plan competitions across Canada and the United States and has gone on to raise more than US$200 000 in investment capital, and whose product is just months away from hitting the U.S. market.

Professor Warren comments, "With a business plan, you have to come up with a real concept, develop the technology, and then write up a plan so someone would want to invest in it. To win, it can't just be an academic exercise. You have to go out and recruit key executive members, develop a sales and marketing plan, and prove that the market will pay for your product."

You Be the Manager

1. Why is planning so important?
2. When it comes to developing a successful business, what role does a business plan play?

Planning, as we noted in Chapter 1, is a process that managers use to identify and select suitable goals and courses of action for an organization.[5] It is also one of the four managerial functions identified by French manager Henri Fayol. The organizational plan that results from the planning process details the goals of the organization and specifies how managers intend to attain those goals. The cluster of decisions and actions that managers take to help an organization attain its goals is its **strategy**. Thus, planning is both a goal-making and a strategy-making process.

Who Plans?

In large organizations, planning usually takes place at three levels of management: corporate, business or division, and department or functional.[6] GE has three main levels of management: corporate level, business level, and functional level (see Figure 5.2). At the corporate level are CEO and Chairman Jeffrey Immelt, three

planning
Identifying and selecting suitable goals and courses of action; one of the four principal functions of management.

strategy
A cluster of decisions about what goals to pursue, what actions to take, and how to use resources to achieve goals.

■ **FIGURE 5.1** | **Steps in the Planning Process**

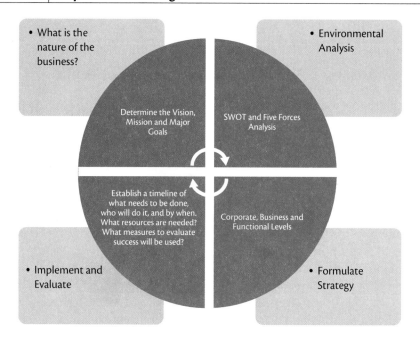

■ **FIGURE 5.2** | **Levels of Planning at General Electric**

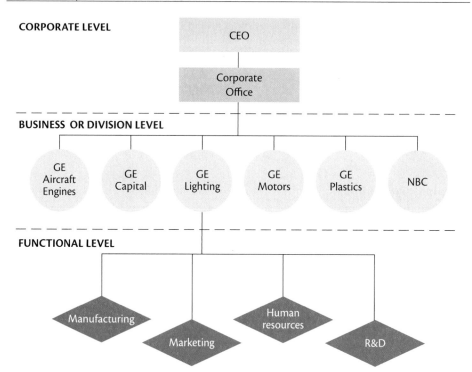

General Electric Company
(GE) www.ge.com.

division

A business unit that has its own set of managers and functions or departments and competes in a distinct industry.

other top managers, and their corporate support staff. Below the corporate level is the business level. At the business level are the different divisions of the company. A **division** is a business unit that competes in a distinct industry; GE has more than 150 divisions, including GE Capital, GE Aircraft Engines, GE Lighting, GE

Motors and Industrial Systems, GE Plastics, and NBC. Each division has its own set of **divisional managers**. In turn, each division has its own set of functions or departments—manufacturing, marketing, human resources, research and development (R&D), and so on. Thus, GE Aircraft Engines has its own marketing function, as do GE Lighting, GE Motors, and NBC.

divisional managers
Managers who control the various divisions of an organization.

Even though corporate-level planning is the responsibility of top managers, lower-level managers can be and usually are given the opportunity to become involved in the process. At GE and many other companies, divisional and functional managers are encouraged to submit proposals for new business ventures to the CEO and top managers, who evaluate the proposals and decide whether to fund them.[7] Corporate-level managers are also responsible for approving business- and functional-level plans to ensure that they are consistent with the corporate plan.

An important issue in planning is ensuring *consistency* in planning across the three levels. Functional goals and strategies should be consistent with divisional goals and strategies, which, in turn, should be consistent with corporate goals and strategies, and vice versa. Once complete, each function's plan is normally linked to its division's business-level plan, which, in turn, is linked to the corporate plan. Although many organizations are smaller and less complex than GE, most do their planning as GE does and have written plans to guide managerial decision making.

Time Horizons of Plans

Plans differ in their **time horizons**, or intended durations. Managers usually distinguish among long-term plans with a horizon of five years or more, intermediate-term plans with a horizon between one and five years, and short-term plans with a horizon of one year or less.[8] Typically, corporate- and business-level goals and strategies require long- and intermediate-term plans, and functional-level goals and strategies require intermediate- and short-term plans.

time horizon
The intended duration of a plan.

Although most organizations operate with planning horizons of five years or more, it would be inaccurate to infer from this that they undertake major planning exercises only once every five years and then "lock in" a specific set of goals and strategies for that period. Most organizations have an annual planning cycle, which is usually linked to their annual financial budget (even though a major planning effort may be undertaken only every few years).

Although a corporate- or business-level plan may extend over five years (or more), it is typically treated as a *rolling plan,* a plan that is updated and amended every year to take into account changing conditions in the external environment. Thus, the time horizon for an organization's 2010 plan might be, but it might be reviewed and amended in 2011, 2012, 2013 and 2014. The use of rolling plans is essential because of the high rate of change in the environment and the difficulty of predicting competitive conditions five years in the future. Rolling plans allow managers to make any mid-course corrections that environmental changes warrant or to change the thrust of the plan altogether if it no longer seems appropriate. The use of rolling plans allows managers to plan flexibly, without losing sight of the need to plan for the long term.

Standing Plans and Single-Use Plans

Another distinction often made between plans is whether they are standing or single-use plans. Managers create standing and single-use plans to help achieve an organization's specific goals. *Standing plans* are used in situations where programmed decision making is appropriate. When the same situations occur repeatedly, managers develop

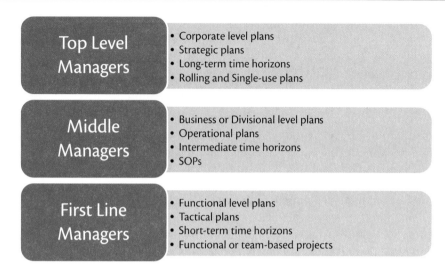

■ **FIGURE 5.3** | **Level of Manager Responsible for Types of Plans**

Top Level Managers
- Corporate level plans
- Strategic plans
- Long-term time horizons
- Rolling and Single-use plans

Middle Managers
- Business or Divisional level plans
- Operational plans
- Intermediate time horizons
- SOPs

First Line Managers
- Functional level plans
- Tactical plans
- Short-term time horizons
- Functional or team-based projects

standard operating procedures (SOPs)
Written instructions describing the exact series of actions that should be followed in a specific situation.

policy
A general guide to action.

rule
A formal, written guide to action.

policies, rules, and **standard operating procedures (SOPs)** to control the way employees perform their tasks. A **policy** is a general guide to action; a **rule** is a formal, written guide to action; and an *SOP* is a written instruction describing the exact series of actions that should be followed in a specific situation. For example, an organization may have a standing plan about the ethical behaviour of employees. This plan includes a policy that all employees are expected to behave ethically in their dealings with suppliers and customers; a rule that requires employees to report any gift worth more than $10 that is received from a supplier or customer; and an SOP that obliges the recipient of the gift to make the disclosure in writing within 30 days. In Chapter 2, mention was made of the YouTube video "United Breaks Guitars." Because of the increasingly negative publicity for United Airlines in the summer of 2009, the airline knew it would have to revise how it handled feedback as a result of the new social media reality. With no effective policy in place for dealing with such a viral video, United was brought to its knees, given that more than 5,655,585 people had watched the video and commented 30 000 times online … most comments expressing unhappiness with United Airlines.

In contrast, *single-use plans* are developed to handle nonprogrammed decision making in unusual or one-of-a-kind situations. Examples of single-use plans include *programs* (integrated sets of plans for achieving certain goals), and *projects* (specific action plans created to complete various aspects of a program). One of NASA's major programs was to reach the moon, and one project in this program was to develop a lunar module capable of landing on the moon and returning to earth. See Figure 5.3 for the levels of managers responsible for various types of plans.

Why Planning Is Important

Essentially, planning is determining where an organization is at the present time and deciding where it should be in the future and how to move it forward. When managers plan, they must consider the future and forecast what may happen in order to take action in the present, and gather organizational resources to deal with future opportunities and threats. As we have discussed in previous chapters, however, the external environment is uncertain and complex, and managers typically must deal with incomplete information and bounded rationality. This is one reason why planning is so complex.

Almost all managers engage in planning, and all *should* do so because planning helps predict future opportunities and threats. The absence of a plan often results in hesitation, false steps, and mistaken changes of direction that can hurt an organization or even lead to disaster. Planning is important for four main reasons:

1. It is a useful way of getting managers to take part in decision making about the appropriate goals and strategies for an organization.
2. It is necessary to give the organization a sense of direction and purpose.[9] By stating which organizational goals and strategies are important, a plan keeps managers on track so that they use the resources under their control effectively.
3. A plan helps coordinate managers of the different functions and divisions of an organization to ensure that they all pull in the same direction. Without a good plan, it is possible that the members of the manufacturing function will produce more products than the members of the sales function can sell, resulting in a mass of unsold inventory.
4. A plan can be used as a device for controlling managers within an organization. A good plan specifies not only which goals and strategies the organization is committed to but also who is responsible for putting the strategies into action to attain the goals. When managers know that they will be held accountable for attaining a goal, they are motivated to do their best to make sure the goal is achieved.

Effective Plans

Effective plans have four qualities:[10]

- *Unity*. At any one time, only one central guiding plan should be put intooperation.

- *Continuity*. Planning does not just happen once. Rather, plans are built, refined, and modified so that at all levels—corporate, business, and functional—fit together into one broad framework.

- *Accuracy*. Managers need to make every attempt to collect and use all available information at their disposal in the planning process.

- *Flexibility*. Plans should be altered if the situation changes.

By making sure that plans have these characteristics, planners ensure that multiple goals and plans do not cause confusion and disorder. Managers must recognize that it is important not to be bound to a static plan, as situations change. They must also recognize that uncertainty exists and that information is almost always incomplete, so one does the best planning possible and then reviews the plans as situations change or more information becomes available.

Scenario Planning

One of the most difficult aspects of making plans is predicting the future, which can be very uncertain. In the face of uncertainty, one of the most widely used planning techniques is scenario planning. **Scenario planning** (also known as *contingency planning*) is the generation of multiple forecasts of future conditions followed by an analysis of how to respond effectively to each of those conditions.

Scenario planning generates "multiple futures"—or scenarios of the future—based on different assumptions about conditions that *might prevail* in the future, and then develops different plans that detail what a company *should do* in the event that any of these scenarios actually occur. Managers use scenario planning to generate different

scenario planning
The generation of multiple forecasts of future conditions followed by an analysis of how to respond effectively to each of those conditions; also called *contingency planning*.

future scenarios of conditions in the environment. They then develop responses to the opportunities and threats facing the different scenarios and create a set of plans based on these responses. The great strength of scenario planning is its ability not only to anticipate the challenges of an uncertain future but also to educate managers to think about the future—to think strategically.[11]

Paul J. H. Schoemaker with George Day, in a *BusinessWeek* article "Peripheral vision: Detecting the weak signals that will make or break your company,"[12] points out the following:

Traditional forecasting and budgeting systems produce linear projections insufficient for risky, uncertain times. What's needed is scenario planning, where companies stress-test their strategies and processes against a wide range of future scenarios to identify their vulnerabilities. Thus informed, the companies can adjust them to be more responsive and resilient. But scenario planning often takes a backseat to more immediate concerns: developing new products, fighting an aggressive competitor, meeting earnings targets. So when large-scale external events hit, their impact is seismic.[13]

One of Schoemaker's strategies to deal with uncertainty is called "future-proofing." A classic case is of Randall Oliphant, an executive dubbed the "boy wonder," who had no future proofing and was summarily dismissed in 2003 after 16 years, the final four as president, by Peter Munk, chairman and founder of Barrick Gold Corp. The upside of his being fired, even without a plan, was that he realized how he had lost touch with the common experiences of life. In his case, not having a contingency plan—his Achilles' heel—was, in fact, to become a stepping stone for him to get reconnected with his wife and 10-year-old daughter and to play regular games of squash with his buddies. Of course, unlike many others who have very little when they are "dumped" from the company payroll, he left with a hefty severance package worth $6.4 million US! This allowed him to buy time and perspective to think about the rest of his life. "But he now appreciates the unreality of life at the top, with its perks and handlers. 'It's like being locked inside a Four Seasons Hotel,' he says. The surroundings are very nice, but it can be a delicious trap." His wife's reaction to his firing? "Thank goodness!" There is a silver lining at times to having no contingency plan!

Crisis Management

In many cases, managers cannot predict the conditions that might give rise to a contingency plan. In cases where unpredictable and unforeseeable conditions prevail, usually a disaster that can seriously damage the organization is in the making. The degree to which the organization can recover from such a crisis largely hinges on how transparent and open the top managers are with the stakeholders. **Crises management plans** are formulated to deal with possible future crises. Management crisis software can help formulate a response that minimizes the potential damage to reputation and consumer confidence that comes along with a disaster. Several companies have faced crises that had to be managed for damage control. See Figure 5.4.

In two Toronto-based cases, two very different approaches to crisis management were used, resulting in two very different outcomes. Maple Leaf Foods recalled the entire stock of meat products, 220 products, from one of its plants that was shut down after being found to be the source of food-borne bacteria called *Listeria monocytogenes*. The listeriosis outbreak caused several deaths and illnesses. How did CEO Michael McCain handle the crisis? In an effort to protect the company and its customers, he gave press releases, media interviews, and posted up-to-date information on the efforts the company was taking to get rid of the bacteria. His highly apparent candour about the situation won him praise from the public. Communication

crises management plans are formulated to deal with possible future crises.[14]

FIGURE 5.4 | Notable Corporate Responses to Crisis Management[15]

1. Johnson & Johnson's response to the case of tampered Tylenol is widely cited as the gold standard response to a crisis. In 1982, in Chicago, seven people died after taking extra-strength Tylenol that had been laced with cyanide. The company yanked the product off the shelves across the United States It would ultimately introduce three-way, tamper-proof pill bottles. Within a year, Tylenol had regained its market share.

2. U.S.-based toy giant Mattel issued an extraordinary apology to China in September 2007 over the recall of millions of Chinese-made toys, taking the blame for design flaws and saying it had recalled more lead-tainted toys than justified. Mattel ordered three high-profile recalls in the summer of 2007 involving more than 21 million Chinese-made toys, including Barbie doll accessories and toy cars due to concerns about lead paint and tiny magnets that could be swallowed.

3. In March 2007, the president of Canadian pet food company Menu Foods apologized to pet owners amid a recall of products found to contain Chinese-supplied wheat gluten laced with poisonous melamine. Company shares dropped following deaths of cats and dogs. Executives were asked to take pay cuts, and the company downsized its workforce after millions of packages of pet food were recalled and dozens of lawsuits were launched. The recall cost Menu Foods an estimated $55 million.

was the key to their crisis management strategy. What could have ruined the business turned out to be a short-lived crisis with a quick recovery.

On the other hand, the blast at the Sunrise Propane plant in North York, Ontario, which caused the deaths of two people and the evacuation of some 12 000 residents, was handled quite differently. The company kept a very low profile "in order to avoid prejudicing themselves, or to create problems for themselves later if there are legal proceedings."[16] These illustrate two very different approaches to managing crises.

Tips for Managers

PLANNING

1. Question yourself as to whether you have a contingency plan or not. Ask yourself: Would I be able to bounce back—even if it took years—from a dramatic fall from grace?

2. Do not allow yourself to suffer from what is called "paralysis by analysis," that is, you take too much time mulling over your plans and do not come to a decision.

3. Do remember that plans were made to assist you; do not become a slave to plans.

4. Plans serve as guides and give you parameters on how you should be engaged and take action with your projects.

5. It has been said that "those who fail to plan, plan to fail." There is much wisdom in that expression.

Five Steps in the Planning Process

In most organizations, planning is a five-step process (see Figure 5.1). The first step is *determining the organization's vision, mission, and goals.*

- A **vision statement** reveals the big picture of the organization, its dream for the future. When Bill Gates founded Microsoft, his vision was "a computer on every desk, in every home, and in every office." Steve Ballmer, Microsoft's current CEO,

vision statement
A broad declaration of the big picture of the organization and/or a statement of its dreams for the future.

sees this vision as insufficient in today's high-tech world and has developed a new vision: "Empower people anytime, anywhere, on any device."[17]

mission statement
A broad declaration of an organization's purpose that identifies the organization's products and customers and distinguishes the organization from its competitors.

- A **mission statement** is a broad declaration of an organization's overriding purpose; this statement is intended to identify an organization's products and customers, as well as to distinguish the organization in some way from its competitors.

- A **goal** is a desired future outcome that an organization strives to achieve. Generally, the goals are set based on the vision and mission of the organization.

goal
A desired future outcome that an organization strives to achieve.

The second step involves analyzing the forces in the organizational environment to determine where the opportunities lie and how to counter the threats to profitability. We use two techniques to *analyze the current situation:* SWOT and Porter's Five Forces analysis.

The third step is *formulating strategy*. Managers analyze the organization's current situation and then conceive and develop the strategies necessary to attain the organization's mission and goals.

The fourth step is *implementing strategy*. Managers decide how to allocate the resources and responsibilities required to implement the chosen strategies among individuals and groups within the organization.[18] The last step is *evaluation*. In subsequent sections of this chapter, we look in detail at the specifics of each of these steps.

THINK ABOUT IT

Determining a Policy[19]

Good Samaritan scolded after buying a homeless, pregnant woman food—then leaving her to eat it

No good deed involving doughnuts, it appears, goes unpunished.

Two weeks after an employee at a Tim Hortons in London was fired, then rehired, after she gave a child a free Timbit, Toronto investment manager Teresa Lee bought breakfast Wednesday for a pregnant homeless woman at a Tim Hortons downtown—then was scolded by a restaurant employee who was unhappy that the homeless woman stayed in the restaurant to eat.

The employee, Lee said, told her the Tim Hortons at King and Victoria Streets does not let homeless people eat inside, even if they are eating Tim Hortons food, because they "make a mess."

"I said, 'She purchased the goods, there's no reason she shouldn't be able to eat in the store,'" said Lee. "He said, 'No, she didn't purchase it, you purchased it.' I said, 'They were purchased. There's no reason she doesn't have the right to eat it in the store.' He said, 'No, she's going to make a mess, who's going to clean up that mess? Are you going to clean up that mess?'"

The homeless woman, Tim Hortons spokesperson Rachel Douglas wrote in an email yesterday, had been "disruptive to customers and staff" on "several" occasions in the past. But Douglas did not say the woman had caused any problems Wednesday morning, and she apologized later to Lee—though Lee was unsatisfied with what Douglas said.

Walking to her office Wednesday around 8 a.m., Lee, 34, said she saw the homeless woman lying on a grate on King St. When the woman got upset after police told her to move, Lee asked her if she was hungry.

Lee bought her a sandwich, a Boston cream doughnut, and chocolate milk. The woman, Lee said, sat down at a corner table to eat, "not bothering anybody". When Lee walked out the door, the employee followed her out to admonish her.

Douglas said the homeless woman, who could not be located later for comment, had been asked to leave the restaurant on several previous occasions. Tim Hortons, she said, does not have a policy on the treatment of the homeless; it is up to franchisees to "make delicate judgment decisions when dealing with any disruptive customers to ensure the store is pleasant, comfortable, and safe."

But she acknowledged that the woman had not been disruptive that Wednesday before the employee rebuked Lee. "What happened here was the act of a Good Samaritan, and we agree it was not handled in the best of manners. We have since apologized to the customer."

Lee, who works at an investment firm at Yonge and King Streets, said that the apology was inadequate. Douglas appeared to apologize only for how the restaurant treated her, she said, not the homeless woman. "I don't think she directly admitted what they did was wrong," Lee said.

The Lee incident Wednesday and the Timbit controversy two weeks earlier illustrates the challenges companies like Tim Hortons face in protecting their brand images from negative publicity created by the decisions of their franchisees.

Ninety-five percent of the Canadian stores in the Tim Hortons chain are owned by independent franchisees who pay annual fees to the company, not by Tim Hortons itself. The company, "a Canadian icon of best practices from a franchising perspective," extensively trains franchisees on the treatment of customers, said Perry Maisonneuve, the principal at Northern Lights Franchise Consultants in Mississauga. "But it comes down to judgment. Somebody is Johnny-on-the-spot, they're there at that time, and they're going to react."

Maisonneuve said a specific company policy on the treatment of the homeless would probably be "too narrow"; Tony Wilson, a franchise lawyer at Boughton Law Corp. in Vancouver, said "it's just common sense" to most restaurant owners that they should not evict homeless customers.

But after another public controversy, Wilson said, "I'll bet you dollars to navy beans Tim Hortons is developing a policy right now on it."

You Be the Manager

1. What recommendations would you make to Tim Hortons as they design a policy?

Determining the organization's vision, mission, and goals is the first step of the planning process. Once these are agreed upon and formally stated in the corporate plan, they guide the next steps by defining which strategies are appropriate at all three levels.[20]

Defining the Vision

Vision differs from other forms of organizational direction setting in several ways:

A vision has clear and compelling imagery that offers an innovative way to improve, which recognizes and draws on traditions, and connects to actions that people can take to realize change. Vision taps people's emotions and energy. Properly articulated, a vision creates the enthusiasm that people have for sporting events and other leisure time activities, bringing that energy and commitment to the workplace.[21]

The organization's vision is generally set by the CEO. When Bill Gates founded Microsoft, his vision was "a computer on every desk, in every home, and in every office." Steve Ballmer, Microsoft's current CEO, broadened the vision to: "Empower people anytime, anywhere, on any device."

Nonprofit organizations also have vision and mission statements.

For example, the vision statement of Point Pleasant Lodge in Halifax, Nova Scotia, is: "Point Pleasant Lodge will provide an affordable hotel alternative for those undertaking medical-related travel in our region. We strive to live the response to the question, Am I my brother's keeper?"

Its mission statement is: "In order to realize our Vision, our Mission, since 1975, is to provide clean, safe, and basic accommodations at the most reasonable rates for those facing the additional financial burden of medical-related travel."

Setting the Mission

The organization's mission is supposed to flow from the vision for the organization. To determine an organization's mission, managers must first define its business so that they can identify what kind of value they will provide to customers. To define the business, managers must ask three questions:[22] (1) Who are our customers? (2) What customer needs are being satisfied? (3) How are we satisfying customer needs? These questions identify the customer needs that the organization satisfies and the way the organization satisfies those needs. Answering these questions helps managers identify not only what customer needs they are satisfying now but what needs they should try to satisfy in the future and who their true competitors are. All of this information helps managers determine the mission and then establish appropriate goals. The mission statements of Montreal-based Gildan Activewear Inc.; Toronto-based The Body Shop Canada; and Montreal-based Bombardier Inc. are presented in Figure 5.5.

FIGURE 5.5 | Three Mission Statements

COMPANY	MISSION STATEMENT
Bombardier	Bombardier's mission is to be the leader in all the markets in which it operates. This objective will be achieved through excellence in the fields of aerospace, rail transportation equipment, recreational products, financial services, and services related to its products and core businesses.
The Body Shop Canada	**Our Reason for Being** To dedicate our business to the pursuit of social and environmental change. To Creatively balance the financial and human needs of our stakeholders: employees, franchisees, customers, suppliers and shareholders. To Courageously ensure that our business is ecologically sustainable: meeting the needs of the present without compromising the future. To Meaningfully contribute to local, national and international communities in which we trade, by adopting a code of conduct which ensures care, honesty, fairness and respect. To Passionately campaign for the protection of the environment, human and civil rights, and against animal testing within the cosmetics and toiletries industry. To Tirelessly work to narrow the gap between principle and practice, whilst making fun, passion, and care part of our daily lives.
Gildan Activewear	Gildan Activewear is dedicated to being the lowest-cost manufacturer and leading marketer of branded basic activewear to wholesale channels of distribution both in North America and internationally. To attain this goal, we will deliver the best in quality, service, and price to our customers and, ultimately, to the end-users of our activewear products.

FIGURE 5.6 | Qualities of Good Goal Formulation: Make them SMART

- **S**pecific
- **M**easurable
- **A**ssignable (Achievable, Attainable, Action oriented, Acceptable, Agreed-upon, Accountable)
- **R**ealistic (Relevant, Result-Oriented)
- **T**ime-related (Timely, Time-bound, Tangible, Traceable)

Establishing Major Goals

Once the business is defined, managers must establish a set of primary goals to which the organization is committed. Developing these goals gives the organization a sense of direction or purpose. Effective goals have five characteristics represented by the acronym "SMART."[23] See Figure 5.6.

The best statements of organizational goals are ones that are demanding, that is, they stretch the organization and require managers to improve organizational performance capabilities.[24] Although goals should be challenging, they should be realistic. Challenging goals give managers an incentive to look for ways to improve an organization's operation, but a goal that is unrealistic and impossible to attain may prompt managers to give up.[25] The period in which a goal is expected to be achieved should be stated. Time constraints are important because they emphasize that a goal must be reached within a reasonable period; they inject a sense of urgency into goal attainment and act as a motivator.

For example, in an effort to reduce energy use, Timberland set itself the goal of becoming carbon-neutral by 2010.[26] Furthermore, they will:

- Use 60 percent renewable energy by 2015.

- Reduce employee travel emissions by 25 percent by 2010.

http://gildan.com/distributors/home.cfm
www.thebodyshop.ca/
www.bombardier.com/

www.timberland.com

Communicating Goals: Management by Objectives

To allow managers to monitor progress toward achieving goals, many organizations use some version of management by objectives (MBO). **Management by objectives** is a system of evaluating subordinates for their ability to achieve specific organizational goals or performance standards.[27] Most organizations make some use of management by objectives because it is pointless to establish goals and then fail to communicate the goals and their measurement to employees. Management by objectives involves three specific steps:

- Step 1. *Specific goals and objectives are established at each level of the organization.*

Management by objectives starts when top managers establish overall organizational objectives, such as specific financial performance targets. Objective setting then cascades down throughout the organization as managers at the divisional and functional levels set their own objectives to achieve the corporate objectives.[28] Finally, first-line managers and workers jointly set objectives that will contribute to achieving functional goals.

- Step 2. *Managers and their subordinates together determine the subordinates' goals.*

An important characteristic of management by objectives is its participatory nature. Managers at every level sit down with the subordinate managers who report directly to them, and together they determine appropriate and feasible goals for the subordinate and bargain over the budget that the subordinate will need so as to achieve his or her goals. The participation of subordinates in the objective-setting process is a way of strengthening their commitment to achieve their goals.[29] Another reason why it is so

management by objectives
A system of evaluating subordinates for their ability to achieve specific organizational goals or performance standards.

important for subordinates (both individuals and teams) to participate in goal setting is to enable them to tell managers what they think they can realistically achieve.[30]

- Step 3. *Managers and their subordinates periodically review the subordinates' progress toward meeting goals.*

Once specific objectives have been agreed upon for managers at each level, managers are accountable for meeting those objectives. Periodically, they sit down with their subordinates to evaluate their progress. Normally, salary raises and promotions are linked to the goal-setting process. (The issue of how to design reward systems to motivate managers and other organizational employees is discussed in Chapter 8.) The evaluation of whether goals were achieved is part of the control process, which we discuss in Chapter 13.

L O 4

Formulating Strategy

THINK ABOUT IT

SWOT Analysis of eBay[31]

Strengths

eBay is the leading global brand for online auctions, a giant marketplace used by more than 100 million people to buy and sell all manner of things. It was started by Pierre Omidyar, a French entrepreneur, when he was just 28. It was founded in September 1995 and is The World's Online Marketplace®. Today, the eBay community includes more than a hundred million registered members from around the world. People spend more time on eBay than any other online site, making it the most popular shopping destination on the Internet.

The company exploits the benefits of Customer Relationship Management (CRM). Buyers and sellers register with the company and data is collected by eBay on individuals. This is the Business-to-Consumer (B2C) side of their business. However, the strong customer relationships are founded on a Consumer-to-Consumer (C2C) business model, where strong interrelationships occur, for example, where buyers and sellers leave feedback for each other and whereby awards are given to the most genuine of eBayers.

Weaknesses

eBay works tremendously hard to overcome fraud, but its model does leave it open to a number of fraudulent activities, even though the company deals with such activities very quickly. Unscrupulous individuals can exploit the C2C business model. As with many technology companies, systems breakdowns could disturb the trading activities of eBay. In the past, both eBay and its payment brand PayPal have encountered shutdowns and outages.

Opportunities

Acquisitions provide new business strategy opportunities. eBay seized the opportunity to buy online telephone company Skype Technologies on September 12, 2005, for a total upfront consideration of approximately €2.1 billion, or approximately US$2.5 billion, plus potential performance-based consideration.[32] New and emerging markets provide opportunities in countries such as China and India. There, consumers are becoming richer and have more leisure time than previous generations. There are also still opportunities in current markets such as Western Europe and the United States, which still have many potential consumers yet to discover the benefits of online auctions.

Threats

As with many of the global Internet brands, success attracts competition. International competitors competing in their domestic markets may have the cultural experience that could give them a competitive advantage over eBay. Attack by illegal practices is a threat. Also, some costs cannot be controlled by eBay, for example, delivery charges and credit card charges. If fuel prices or credit card rates were to rise, the cost is passed on to the consumer in terms of delivery and postal fees.

You Be the Manager

1. In your own words, what are the existing strengths, weaknesses, opportunities, and threats (SWOT) in the eBay scenario?
2. From your own experience, what additional features would you include for each section of the SWOT analysis?

Strategy formulation includes analyzing an organization's current situation and then developing strategies to accomplish the organization's mission and achieve its goals.[33] Strategy formulation begins with managers analyzing the factors within an organization and outside—in the task and general environments—that affect or may affect the organization's ability to meet its current and future goals. *SWOT analysis* and the *Five Forces Model* are two techniques managers use to analyze these factors.

strategy formulation
Analysis of an organization's current situation followed by the development of strategies to accomplish the organization's mission and achieve its goals.

SWOT Analysis

SWOT analysis is the first step in strategy formulation at any level. It is a planning exercise in which managers identify organizational strengths (S) and weaknesses (W), and environmental opportunities (O) and threats (T). Based on a SWOT analysis, managers at the different levels of the organization select corporate-, business-, and functional-level strategies to best position the organization to achieve its mission and goals (see Figure 5.7).

SWOT analysis
A planning exercise in which managers identify organizational strengths (s) and weaknesses (W), and environmental opportunities (O) and threats (T) relative to the competition.

FIGURE 5.7 | Environmental Assessment and Strategy Formulation

SWOT Analysis
Porter's Five
Forces Model

Corporate-Level Strategy
A plan of action to manage the growth and development of an organization so as to maximize its long-run ability to create value

Business-Level Strategy
A plan of action to take advantage of favourable opportunities and find ways to counter threats so as to compete effectively in an industry

Functional-Level Strategy
A plan of action to improve the ability of an organization's departments to create value

The first step in SWOT analysis is to identify an organization's strengths and weaknesses that characterize the present state of their organization, *relative to their competition*, and then consider how the strengths will be maintained and the weaknesses overcome.

Take the example of Starbucks. It recently underwent significant restructuring after seeing a decline in comparable sales in company-operated stores throughout the United States. Upon assessing their strengths and weaknesses (see Figure 5.8), Starbucks engaged in a significant re-architecture of its corporate-level strategy to position itself to take advantage of emerging opportunities and counter significant threats.

According to the company, "As Starbucks moves from fiscal 2008, a year of significant transition for the company, it is well positioned to deliver in fiscal 2009 with the following foundational planks in place:

- A re-architectured cost structure to allow for long-term operating margin expansion

- A healthier store portfolio achieved through closure of underperforming stores

- A stronger value and rewards platform—consistent with Starbucks premium brand

- A renewed emphasis and investment around coffee leadership

- A galvanized company with a common purpose."[34]

FIGURE 5.8 | SWOT Analysis of Starbucks[35]

Strengths	Weaknesses
Starbucks Corporation is a very profitable organization. The company generated revenue of $10.4 billion in 2008, a 10-percent increase over 2007.	Starbucks has a reputation for new product development and creativity. However, they remain vulnerable to the possibility that their innovation may falter over time.
It is a global coffee brand built upon a reputation for fine products and services. Until recently, it had almost 9000 cafes in almost 40 countries.	The organization has a strong presence in the United States with more than three quarters of their cafes located in the home market. It is often argued that they need to look for a portfolio of countries, in order to spread business risk.
Starbucks was one of the *Fortune Top 100 Companies to Work For* in 2005. The company is a respected employer that values its workforce.	In 2008, it closed 61 underperforming stores in Australia and 600 in the United States Profit fell by 53 percent over 2007 as a whole and 97 percent in the last quarter of 2008.
Its rewards program and Gold card program have gained customer loyalty.	The organization is dependent on a main competitive advantage, the retail of coffee. This could make them slow to diversify into other sectors when the economy falters and consumer spending on luxury retail declines as it did in the last quarter of 2008.
The organization has strong ethical values and an ethical mission statement as follows, "*Starbucks is committed to a role of environmental leadership in all facets of our business.*"	

Opportunities	Threats
Starbucks is very good at taking advantage of opportunities. In 2004 the company created a CD-burning service in their Santa Monica (California, U.S.) cafe with Hewlett Packard, where customers create their own music CD.	Who knows if the market for coffee will grow and stay in favour with customers, or whether another type of beverage or leisure activity will replace coffee in the future? Starbucks is exposed to rises in the cost of coffee and dairy products.
New products and services can be retailed in their cafes, such as Fair Trade products.	Since its conception in Pike Place Market, Seattle, in 1971, Starbucks' success has lead to the market entry of many competitors and copy-cat brands that pose potential threats. "You sell $4 cups of coffee, not $500 dresses. You're not on the same playing field relative to other luxury retailers," said Patricia Edwards, retail consultant and founder of Seattle-based Storehouse Partners LLC. "I am concerned, especially in this environment that they are going to have a real tough time making earnings."[36]
The company has the opportunity to expand its global operations. New markets for coffee such as India and the Pacific Rim nations are beginning to emerge. International sales were up by 2 percent in comparable stores sales in 2008 over 2007.	
Co-branding with other manufacturers of food and drink, and brand franchising to manufacturers of other goods and services both have potential. Specialty revenues grew 14 percent in 2008 to $1.6 billion from $1.4 billion in fiscal 2007.	

FIGURE 5.9 | SWOT Analysis of Tim Hortons[37]

Strengths	Weaknesses
Begun in 1964 in Hamilton, Ontario, Tim Hortons is the largest coffee and baked goods chain in Canada with approximately 3000 locations. In 2008, it had 500 stores operating in the United States.[38] Franchise licensees, once approved, must engage in a comprehensive training program to ensure the standards of the company are upheld. A Corporate Culture study in 2008 polling Canadian executives, rated Tim Hortons as #9 of the Top 10 Most Admired Canadian Corporate Cultures. It has iconic branding of its coffee blend and significant market share in Canada. Tim Hortons has a strong commitment to supporting socially responsible community and charitable work. Very popular "Roll-up-the-Rim-to-Win" contest has strengthened brand loyalty. The Tim Hortons approach to coffee sustainability is to be directly involved with coffee producing communities.	Strong presence limited to North America, particularly Canada. The organization is dependent on a main competitive advantage, the retail of coffee. This could make them slow to diversify into other sectors when the economy falters and consumer spending on luxury retail declines as it did in the last quarter of 2008. The operator of the Tim Hortons chain, TDL Group Corp. may have difficulty in controlling licensees. Criticism of the Roll-up-the-Rim contest has centred on the pollution caused by using non-biodegradable coffee cups.
Opportunities	**Threats**
Continued expansion into the United States, including in areas where Starbucks has retrenched, such as Detroit, Michigan.[39] Tim Hortons has iconic brand recognition. Tim Hortons has the opportunity to expand its program of working with suppliers (farmers) to enhance their sustainability strategy through community partnership programs. In 1995, Tim Hortons merged with Wendy's International, Inc., giving new focus and impetus to the expansion of the Tim Hortons concept in the United States. Tim Hortons locations can presently be found in Michigan, Maine, Connecticut, Ohio, West Virginia, Kentucky, Pennsylvania, Rhode Island, Massachusetts, and New York, with responsible expansion continuing in these core markets. The Canadian operation is 95 percent franchise—owned and operated—and plans in the United States call for the same key strategy to be implemented as expansion progresses.	A potential threat for Tim Hortons is that preference for the consumption of coffee will decline. Recent negative press coverage of managerial treatment of employee discipline has bruised their reputation. If Tim Hortons' commitment to reducing waste and using recyclable materials and packaging is not strengthened, it may jeopardize brand loyalty. Competitors such as Country Style now offer similar products that could easily substitute those offered by Tim Hortons.

Comparing U.S.-based Starbucks with Canadian-based Tim Hortons' SWOT (see Figure 5.9), illustrates how companies within the same industry may develop very different strategies based on the environmental threats and opportunities. Tim Hortons' corporate-level strategy involves a steady penetration of the U.S. market through franchise owner/operator partnerships. It differentiates itself on the basis or providing convenient customer service with its many locations, as well as offering value to customers, by providing good quality food and beverages for reasonable prices. Starbucks on the other hand, offers its customers leisure and relaxation, rather than fast and convenient service. It targets people with more discretionary income to spend on luxury beverages and upscale snacks.

Identifying the strengths of an organization involves an analysis of the things it does well. When conducting a SWOT on a competitor, the manager looks at the internal organizational forces such as the strategy, resources (assets and people), management competencies, organizational structure, capacity and capabilities, location, trademarks and patents, length of time in business, source of competitive advantage. When identifying weaknesses, managers look at the internal organizational forces that are done poorly, such as: gaps in capabilities, lack of competitive strength, financials (debt to equity, ROI), reputation, level of employee morale, lack of management competencies. Opportunities are found in the external organizational environment. Opportunities are chances for increasing market share and growth. Managers look for things in the organizational environment that present such opportunities. Threats are things in the external environment that hinder profitability and growth such as shifts in market demand and legal and political changes. See Table 5.1.

TABLE 5.1 | *Elements Managers look for in a SWOT analysis of a competitor*

Strengths
- capabilities
- competitive advantages
- resources
- location
- management capacities
- trademarks and patents

Weaknesses
- gaps in capabilities
- lack of competitive strength
- financial management
- reputation
- employee morale
- management capacity
- high turnover rates

Opportunities
- market developments
- competitors vulnerabilities
- demographic and lifestyle trends
- partnerships and licensing agreements
- international expansion
- vertical and horizontal integration

Threats
- legal and political forces
- sociocultural forces
- demographic and lifestyle changes
- technological forces
- declining market demand
- cash flow and long tern financing

When managers are able to identify potential opportunities and threats in their environments that affect the organization at the present and may affect it in the future, they can then consider how to take advantage of the opportunities for growth and overcome any threats. For Starbucks, this type of analysis lead to massive store closures and a renewed corporate strategy. For Tim Hortons, it lead to aggressive expansion into the US market.

The Five Forces Model

Porter's Five Forces Model
A technique managers use to analyze the potential profitability of entering and competing in a particular industry.

Michael **Porter's Five Forces Model** is a widely used technique for analyzing the potential profitability of entering and competing in a particular industry (see Figure 5.10). It helps

FIGURE 5.10 | **Porter's Five Forces Competition Model**

Level of Rivalry	Increased competition results in lower profits.
Potential for Entry	Easy entry leads to lower prices and profits.
Power of Suppliers	If there are only a few suppliers of important items, supply costs rise.
Power of Customers	If there are only a few large buyers, they can bargain down prices.
Substitutes	More available substitutes tend to drive prices and profits.

managers isolate particular forces in the external environment that are potential threats. Porter identified five factors (the first four are also discussed in Chapter 2) that are major threats because they affect how much profit organizations that compete within the same industry can expect to make:

- *The level of rivalry among organizations in an industry.* The degree of rivalry is the extent of the competition—the more that companies compete against one another for customers. For example, by lowering the prices of their products or by increasing advertising, the lower is the level of industry profits. Low prices mean less profit. For example, in the telecommunications industry, price wars among wireless companies in Europe and the United States have made it difficult for companies to make a profit. The degree to which firms vigorously compete with one another used to be conceptualized in terms of the entire operation of one firm against another. Recently, as Peter Drucker predicted,[42] firms have begun to swallow their pride and cooperate in specific areas while maintaining fierce competition in others. Automobile manufacturers and airlines have long since adopted these networked strategic alliances to achieve economies of scale by collaborating on vehicle platforms and sharing check-in facilities, but recently industries such as media and courier companies have increased their cooperation, coined **co-opetition** by professors at Yale University.[43] For example, New York newspaper arch enemies, the *New York Post* and the *Daily News* owned by media moguls Robert Murdoch and Mortimer Zuckerman, respectively, are talking about consolidating printing, distribution, and back-office operations while still competing for readership through separate editorial and advertising sales operations.[44] Similarly, in a 10-year deal, the German-owned parcel-delivery company DHL would pay American UPS to carry its packages in the United States, Canada, and Mexico to reduce its losses in North America while taking advantage of UPS's excess capacity. "When this deal is finalized, nothing will change the fact that we are a rabid competitor of DHL," says a UPS executive.[45]

  co-opetition
  Arrangements in which firms compete vigorously with one another, while also cooperating in specific areas to achieve economies of scale.

- *The potential for entry into an industry.* This indicates how easy it is for another firm to enter the industry. The easier it is for companies to enter an industry—because, for example, barriers to entry are low (see Chapter 2)—the more likely it is for industry prices and therefore industry profits to be low. For example, there are huge barriers to entry in the oil and aerospace industries because of the large investment of capital needed to start up and operate. Moreover, brand loyalty, such as that enjoyed by Coke, protects profits. Industries that rely on the difficulty of change such as Microsoft's Windows Operating System and drug companies that enjoy long-term patents on proprietary drugs make it harder for new firms to compete, create large barriers to entry, and thus enjoy a stronger potential for profits.

- *The power of suppliers.* If there are only a few suppliers of an important input, then (as discussed in Chapter 2) suppliers can drive up the price of that input, and expensive inputs result in lower profits for the producer. For example, the airline industry suffers from threats posed by the suppliers of expensive fuel. Electricity suppliers, such as BC Hydro reaped very large profits by supplying hydro-electricity energy at premium prices to captive customers such as California during their energy crisis in 2001.[46]

- *The power of customers.* The bargaining power of your customers is affected by their size and how much revenue they generate for your company. If only a few large customers are available to buy an industry's output, they can bargain to drive down the price of that output. As a result, producers make lower profits. For example, Wal-Mart, as the largest retailer in the global economy, has a huge impact on firms that supply it with goods to sell. If Wal-Mart refuses to carry a company's products, it would be unlikely for the company to become successful in the global economy. Wal-Mart is so large and it purchases it so much inventory and accounts for such a large proportion of a supplier's revenue that most companies will do anything to protect their business with them.

- *The threat of substitute products.* Often, the output of one industry is a substitute for the output of another industry (e.g., plastic may be a substitute for steel in some applications). Companies that produce a product with a known substitute cannot demand high prices for their products, and this constraint keeps their profits low. On the other hand, industries that have few, if any, substitutes can command very high profits as long as there remains a demand for the product. For example, there is no known substitute for oil. If gasoline prices go too high, people may stop driving or pay the high price because they cannot easily find something else to substitute gasoline. But, if the price of designer clothing goes up, people have the option of buying cheaper no-name brands.

Porter argued that when managers analyze opportunities and threats, they should pay particular attention to these five forces because they are the major threats that an organization will encounter. It is the job of managers at the corporate, business, and functional levels to formulate strategies to counter these threats so that an organization can respond to both its task and general environments, perform at a high level, and generate high profits.

L O 5

Levels of Strategies

THINK ABOUT IT

Less and More Strategy: Both Head *and* Heart[47]

When people hear the word "strategy," they often associate it with another word: "boring." The noted Professor Henry Mintzberg and his colleagues do not think things have to be that way. Strategy can be "novel, creative, inspiring, sometimes even playful." In their book, *Strategy Bites Back: It Is Far More, And Less, Than You Ever Imagined ...*, the authors take a serious look at the idea of strategy and then conclude that it is time for strategy to "bite back." In what they call "bytes" (interesting, educative ideas) and "bites" (stimulating jabs at traditional thinking on strategy), the authors have produced a book that offers "heart" in a field of study—strategy—that has so much "head." Head and heart need to go together. It is a conclusion that Harvard's John Kotter reached also:

Our main finding, put simply, is that the central issue is never strategy, structure, culture, or systems. All those elements, and others, are important. But the core of the matter is always about changing the behaviour of people, and behaviour change happens in highly successful situations by speaking to people's feelings. This is true even in organizations that are very focused on analysis and quantitative measurement, even among people who think of themselves as smart in an M.B.A. sense. In highly successful change efforts, people find ways to help others see the problems or solutions in ways that influence emotions, not just thought. Feelings then alter behaviour sufficiently to overcome all the many barriers to sensible large-scale change. Conversely, in less successful cases, this seeing-feeling-changing pattern is found less often, if at all.[48]

Some key nuggets from the book:

- Jeanne Liedtka of the University of Virginia, "No strategy is ever 'true'—all strategies are inventions. They are man-made designs. Business is not governed by natural laws—our strategies are not 'discovered' truths, like $e = mc^2$."

- Strategy helps everyone shape—not delude or manipulate—an image of a shared corporate future.

- The five Ps of strategy are the following:
  - Strategy is a *plan*—a consciously intended course of action and guideline to deal with the situation facing an organization
  - Strategy can be a *ploy*—a manoeuvre to outwit a competitor.
  - Strategy is a *pattern*—a stream of actions, providing consistency in behaviour.
  - Strategy is a *position*—a means of locating an organization in its environment, such as a market niche.
  - Strategy is *perspective*—an ingrained way of perceiving the world by the organization. "Strategy in this respect is to the organization what personality is to the individual," he says.

Strategy, therefore, can act as a flexible guide, or like blinders on horses such that the organization keeps going in a straight line but does not have access to its peripheral vision and, as a result, does not see the whole picture.

You Be the Manager

1. What does Jeanne Liedtka, of the University of Virginia, mean when she says, "No strategy is ever 'true'—all strategies are inventions. They are man-made designs. Business is not governed by natural laws—our strategies are not 'discovered' truths, like $e = mc^2$"?
2. What's an example of an organization that has "blinders" for its strategy?

Corporate-Level Strategy

Corporate-level strategy is a plan of action concerning which industries and countries an organization should invest its resources in to achieve its mission and goals. In developing a corporate-level strategy, managers ask: How should the growth and development of the company be managed in order to increase its ability to create value for its customers (and thus increase performance) over the long run? Managers of most organizations have the goal to grow their companies and actively seek out new opportunities to use the organization's resources to create more goods and services for customers. This is precisely what Mintzberg et al. described in their book *Strategy Bites Back: It Is Far More, And Less, Than You Ever Imagined.* Seeking out new opportunities occurs when companies and their strategies are able to adapt to changing circumstances.

In addition, some managers must help their organizations respond to threats due to changing forces in the task or general environment. For example, customers may no longer be buying the kinds of goods and services a company is producing (manual typewriters, eight-track tapes, black-and-white televisions), or other organizations may have entered the market and attracted customers away (this happened to Xerox when its patents expired and many companies rushed into the market to sell photocopiers). Or the markets may become saturated, as happened in the telecommunications

corporate-level plans
Top management's decisions relating to the organization's mission, overall strategy, and structure.

industry recently, when more high-speed fibre optic networks were built than the market demanded. Top managers aim to find the best strategies to help the organization respond to these changes and improve performance. **Corporate level plans** contain decisions relating to the organization's mission and goals, overall or grand strategy, and structure that facilitate growth.

The principal corporate-level strategies that managers use to help a company grow, to keep it on top of its industry, and to help it retrench and reorganize in order to stop its decline are: *concentration on a single business; diversification; international expansion;* and *vertical integration.*

These four strategies are all based on one idea: An organization benefits from pursuing a strategy only when it helps *further increase the value of the organization's goods and services for customers.* To increase the value of goods and services, a **corporate-level strategy** must help an organization, or one of its divisions, differentiate and add value to its products either by making them unique or special or by lowering the costs of value creation. Sometimes formulation of a corporate-level strategy presents difficult challenges. This is what Mintzberg et al. are suggesting when they discuss how some companies and their strategies are more like "blinders" on horses; they keep charging straight head and are prevented from seeing what is going on around them. This rigid singleness of purpose can be detrimental to a company.

corporate-level strategy
A plan that indicates the industries and national markets in which an organization intends to compete.

Concentration on a Single Business

Most organizations begin their growth and development with a corporate-level strategy aimed at concentrating resources in one business or industry in order to develop a strong competitive position within that industry. Tom Peters, in his best-selling book, *In Search of Excellence,* pointed out that excellent companies "stick to the knitting," that is, focus on what they do best and keep doing it.[49] For example, in 2005, Winnipeg-based Peak of the Market, one of Canada's premier grower-owned vegetable suppliers and winner of the 2002 Outstanding Manitoba Ambassador award,[50] bought Winnipeg-based Stella Produce because it would allow the cooperative to increase its packaging capacity while adding another recognized brand name. This decision by Peak of the Market's president and CEO, Larry McIntosh, continued the company's concentration on a single business while bringing it new growth opportunities. Similarly, even a well-established company such as BCE Inc. was attempting to tie together many loose threads with its strategy. Chief Michael Sabia said BCE has to first engage in what he called "self-inflicted creative destruction" by "blowing up the culture and structures of its Bell Canada unit to prepare for a world when technological boundaries between landline, TV, and wireless networks will disappear." He believed this was necessary because if Bell did not do its own creative destruction around its torn-worn strategy, "somebody else will," and that "somebody else" was Rogers Communications Inc. Sabia explained his singleness of purpose and strategy this way: "If we've changed anything, the perspective is now don't diversify away from Bell—reposition Bell, fix Bell, transform Bell, add to Bell, strengthen those capabilities because that is what you know as an organization, that is what you are good at." Call this a vision "to build one of the world's greatest telecommunications companies" with "an image of convergence that carries echoes of his predecessor's dreams, although without the grandiose and expensive scale."[51]

Sometimes, concentration on a single business becomes an appropriate corporate-level strategy when managers see the need to reduce the sizes of their organizations in order to increase performance. Managers may decide to get out of certain industries, for example, when particular divisions lose their competitive advantage. Managers may sell off those divisions, lay off workers, and concentrate remaining organizational resources in another market or business to try to improve performance. In contrast, when organizations are performing effectively, they often decide to enter new industries in which they can use their resources to create more value.

Diversification

Diversification is the strategy of expanding operations into a new business or industry and producing new goods or services.[52] Examples of diversification include PepsiCo's diversification into the snack-food business with the purchase of Frito-Lay, Time-Warner's diversification into Internet services with the acquisition of AOL, and Quebecor Media Inc.'s move into broadcasting with its acquisition of Vidéotron ltée. There are two main kinds of diversification: related and unrelated.

diversification
Expanding operations into a new business or industry and producing new goods or services.

Related Diversification

Related diversification is the strategy of entering a new business or industry to create a competitive advantage in one or more of an organization's existing divisions or businesses. Related diversification can add value to an organization's products if managers can find ways for its various divisions or business units to share their valuable skills or resources so that synergy is created.[53] **Synergy** is obtained when the value created by two cooperating divisions is greater than the value that would be created if the two divisions operated separately.

related diversification
Entering a new business or industry to create a competitive advantage in one or more of an organization's existing divisions or business.

synergy
Performance gains that result when individuals and departments coordinate their actions.

In pursuing related diversification, managers often seek to find new businesses where they can use the existing skills and resources in their departments to create synergies, add value to the new business, and hence improve the competitive position of the company. Alternatively, managers may acquire a company in a new industry because they believe that some of the skills and resources of the *acquired* company might improve the efficiency of one or more of their existing divisions. If successful, such skill transfers can help an organization lower its costs or better differentiate its products because they create synergies between divisions.

The merger of Molson Inc. with Adolph Coors Co. to create Molson Coors Brewing Co. was built on the hope that the brewer's flagging fortunes could be reversed. Key questions were in the air about the merger in 2004: "The merger ensures that Molson will keep its lucrative arrangement to brew and sell Coors Light in Canada. That's the good news. The bad news is both Molson Canadian and Coors Light are losing share in their main markets, and the deal presents a new marketing problem for each. Can a company run by an American from Colorado sell 'I am Canadian'? Will consumers still think Coors Light is Rocky Mountain fresh if it's brewed in Toronto?"[54]

So, what happened with the strategy and merger? "The company is now one of the largest brewers in the world, with leading positions in three of the world's largest and most profitable beer markets." To accomplish its objective, Molson Coors enlisted the help of an innovative ally: EDS. "By converting existing applications and systems to a globally integrated solution, the brewer was able to reduce application maintenance costs. By consolidating its SAP® environment, they gained operational synergy and optimization."[55]

Unrelated Diversification

Managers pursue **unrelated diversification** when they enter new industries or buy companies in new industries that are not related in any way to their current businesses or industries. One of the main reasons for pursuing unrelated diversification is that sometimes managers can buy a poorly performing company, transfer their management skills to that company, turn its business around, and increase its performance, all of which creates value.

unrelated diversification
Entering a new industry or buying a company in a new industry that is not related in any way to an organization's current businesses or industries.

Another reason for pursuing unrelated diversification is that buying businesses in different industries lets managers use a *portfolio strategy*, which is dividing financial resources among divisions to increase financial returns or spread risks among different businesses, much as individual investors do with their own portfolios. For instance, managers may transfer funds from a rich division (a "cash cow") to a new and promising division (a "star") and, by allocating money appropriately between divisions, create value. At the start of the Second World War, E.D. Smith & Sons Ltd. acquired the Canadian rights to H.P. Sauce Ltd. of Britain and in 1948 the latter's subsidiary Lea & Perrins Ltd. On October 15, 1948, E.D. Smith died. The private company bearing his name was sold to Imperial Capital in 2001.[56] In this specific example, when Imperial Capital bought E.D. Smith & Sons Ltd. in 2001, it was following what it described as "an acquisition strategy that identifies recession-resistant niche businesses in profitable, low-risk industries poised for consolidation."[57] Toronto-based Brascan Corp. is one of the last large Canadian conglomerates that continues to pursue this diversified strategy. As an asset management company, it focuses on the real estate and power generation sectors. Brascan owns over 70 office properties in North America and owns nearly 130 power generating plants in Europe.[58] Under CEO Bruce Flatt, previously president and CEO of Brookfield Properties Corporation,[59] it has focused its development on three of its multiple lines: real estate (Toronto-based Brookfield Properties), financial services (Toronto-based Brascan Financial), and power generation (Masson-Angers, Quebec-based Brascan Power).[60] Also, the company owns Toronto-based Noranda Inc., a mining subsidiary, and Toronto-based Nexfor Inc., a paperboard company. Though used as a popular explanation in the 1980s for unrelated diversification, portfolio strategy started running into increasing criticism in the 1990s.[61] Today, many companies and their managers are abandoning the strategy of unrelated diversification because there is evidence that too much diversification can cause managers to lose control of their organizations' core business so that they end up reducing value rather than creating it.[62] Since the 1990s, there has been a trend among many diversified companies to sell off unrelated divisions and concentrate organizational resources on their core business and related diversification.[63] For instance, Toronto-based George Weston Ltd., the food processing and supermarket giant, announced in February 2001 that it would sell Blacks Harbour, New Brunswick-based Connors Bros., a fish processing operation, so that it could acquire Bestfoods Baking Co. Chairman Galen Weston explained that the move would allow the company "to go forward in the baking and the supermarket business."[64] The company did not feel that it held a competitive advantage in the fish processing industry. With the acquisition of Bestfoods Baking, George Weston inherited one of the nation's largest and most efficient DSD (direct-store-delivery) systems, distributing fresh bakery products to more than 60 000 customers on almost 5000 delivery routes. The company's product line includes such grain-based food products as sweet baked goods, doughnuts, soft cookies, breakfast bars, soft breadsticks, pizza crusts, English muffins, rolls, pan bread, pita bread, and pasta.[65]

International Expansion

As if planning the appropriate level of diversification were not a difficult enough decision, corporate-level managers also must decide on the appropriate way to compete internationally. When E.D. Smith & Sons decided to move into the American market, it was partnered with Toronto-based Loblaw Cos. Ltd., which was intending to sell E.D. Smith jams to Wal-Mart. Unfortunately Loblaw was not successful in getting a contract from Wal-Mart, and E.D. Smith's expansion to the United States did not pay off.

A basic question confronts the managers of any organization that competes in more than one national market: To what extent should the organization customize features of its products and marketing campaign to different national conditions?[66] When managers decide that their organization should sell the same standardized product in each national market in which it competes and use the same basic marketing approach, they adopt a **global strategy**.[67] Such companies undertake very little, if any, customization to suit the specific needs of customers in different countries. Such is the case with Tim Hortons. Its corporate strategy of expanding into the United States

involves little if any customization. It has adopted a global strategy based on a global brand. But if managers decide to customize products and marketing strategies to specific national conditions, they adopt a **multidomestic strategy**. Japan's Matsushita Electric has traditionally pursued a global strategy, selling the same basic TVs and VCRs in every market in which it does business and often using the same basic marketing approach. However, even McDonald's has had to customize its food products for the global market. When McDonald's went to India, it had to sell chicken burgers and mutton burgers rather than beef burgers.

Both global and multidomestic strategies have advantages and disadvantages. The major advantage of a global strategy is the significant cost savings associated with not having to customize products and marketing approaches to different national conditions. The major disadvantage of pursuing a global strategy is that by ignoring national differences, managers may leave themselves vulnerable to local competitors that do differentiate their products to suit local tastes.

The advantages and disadvantages of a multidomestic strategy are the opposite of those of a global strategy. The major advantage of a multidomestic strategy is that by customizing product offerings and marketing approaches to local conditions, managers may be able to gain market share or charge higher prices for their products. The major disadvantage is that customization raises production costs and puts the multidomestic company at a price disadvantage because the company often has to charge prices higher than the prices charged by competitors pursuing a global strategy. Obviously, the choice between these two strategies calls for trade-offs.

Vertical Integration

When an organization is doing well in its business, managers often see new opportunities to create value by either producing their own inputs or distributing their own outputs. Managers at E.&J. Gallo Winery, for example, realized that they could lower Gallo's costs if they produced their own wine bottles rather than buying them from a glass company. As a result, Gallo established a new division to produce glass bottles. Similarly, Starbucks began roasting its own coffee beans and had three roasting plants by 1998. By investing in this type of backward vertical integration, Starbucks could better control the quality of the beans by discarding batches that were not up to par.[68]

Vertical integration is the corporate-level strategy through which an organization becomes involved in producing its own inputs (backward vertical integration) or distributing and selling its own outputs (forward vertical integration).[69] A steel

global strategy
Selling the same standardized product and using the same basic marketing approach in each national market.

multidomestic strategy
Customizing products and marketing strategies to specific national conditions.

vertical integration
A strategy that allows an organization to create value by producing its own inputs or distributing and selling its own outputs.

company that supplies its iron ore needs from company-owned iron ore mines is using backward vertical integration. When Steve Jobs announced in 2001 that Apple Computer would open 25 retail stores to sell Macintosh machines directly to consumers, he showed that Apple was engaging in forward vertical integration. Starbucks uses a forward vertical integration strategy through a mail order and Internet distribution service.[70]

Figure 5.11 illustrates the four main stages in a typical raw-materials-to-consumer value chain; value is added at each stage. Typically, the primary operations of an organization take place in one of these stages. For a company based in the assembly stage, backward integration would involve establishing a new division in intermediate manufacturing or raw-material production, and forward integration would involve establishing a new division to distribute its products to wholesalers or to sell directly to customers. A division at one stage receives the product made by the division in the previous stage, transforms it in some way—adding value—and then transfers the output at a higher price to the division at the next stage in the chain.

Consider how Cisco Systems, for example, makes only a small proportion of the computer networking products that are its stock-in-trade. Instead it coordinates the efforts of other distributors, manufacturers, and suppliers in its business web while applying its own special expertise in marketing and managing customer relationships. "Guided by a primary company, the aim of this type of business web is to manage the contributions of the different members to create a product or service that has a greater value than the sum of its parts."[71]

A major reason why managers pursue vertical integration is that it allows them either to add value to their products by making them special or unique or to lower the costs of value creation. For example, SunOpta Inc.'s headquarters is located in a red brick farmhouse north of Toronto, Ontario. It also has a nice, folksy tradition: Executives plant a tree each time they complete an acquisition. If you look around the property, you will notice a "mall forest" of saplings that illustrates the company's acquisitions. SunOpta had a stated goal of reaching US$1 billion in sales by the end of 2007; to do so, it had to execute 30 acquisitions during 2005–2007. "We plant trees to symbolize growth for the company," says chief executive Jeremy Kendall. "Look around, you'll see trees everywhere." He then goes on to say that he wanted to created a "vertically integrated" food producer offering products "from the field to the table." For example, Coca-Cola and PepsiCo, in a case of forward vertical integration

FIGURE 5.11 | Stages in a Vertical Value Chain

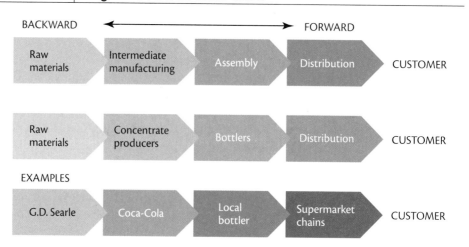

to build brand loyalty and enhance the differentiated appeal of their colas, decided to buy up their major bottlers to increase control over marketing and promotion efforts—which the bottlers had been handling.[72] An example of using forward vertical integration to lower costs is Matsushita Electric's decision to open company-owned stores to sell its own products and thus keep the profit that independent retailers otherwise would earn.[73]

Even though vertical integration can help an organization to grow rapidly, it can be a problem when forces in the organizational environment conflict with the strategies of the organization and make it necessary for managers to reorganize or retrench. Vertical integration can make an organization less flexible in responding to changing environmental conditions. For example, IBM used to produce most of its own components for mainframe computers. Doing this made sense in the 1960s, but it became a major handicap for the company in the fast-changing computer industry of the 1990s. The rise of organizationwide networks of personal computers has meant slumping demand for mainframes. As demand fell, IBM found itself with an excess-capacity problem, not only in its mainframe assembly operations but also in component operations. Closing down this capacity cost IBM more than $7.75 billion in 1993 and clearly limited the company's ability to pursue other opportunities.[74] When considering vertical integration as a strategy to add value, managers must be careful because sometimes vertical integration will actually reduce an organization's ability to create value when the environment changes.

Something managers need to consider when deciding on possible expansion strategies is the human costs of consolidating operations. While Air Canada initially projected $880 million in "synergies" from merging with Canadian Airlines, that figure was at least $150 million less because of the difficulty of bringing the two employee groups together. CEO Robert Milton noted that it was "an emotionally charged process ... perceived to create winners and losers."[75] Management from the two merged companies can also clash, creating political struggles, as was seen in the public battle between the management of Montreal-based Abitibi-Consolidated Inc., a pulp and paper giant, and Montreal-based Quebecor.

Business-Level Strategies

THINK ABOUT IT

Concentrating on What We Do Best![76]

In July 2005 grocer Quebec-based Metro Inc. bought the assets of A&P Canada in a $1.7-billion deal and beat out larger rival Sobeys Inc. to clinch the winning bid. This deal transformed the company into the country's third-largest supermarket chain with 579 stores. This strategic acquisition could place Metro Inc. eventually into the #2 spot in Canada. Sobeys' 2004 sales were $12.2 billion; Metro and A&P's combined were $10.6 billion. Metro chief executive Pierre Lessard said, "It could happen, surely. We would like to be number two (behind Loblaw Cos.). We have the volume to be competitive. But our goal now is to be the best food retailer in Canada and be a very profitable food retailer." Sales in the second quarter of 2006 soared by more than 75 percent to $2.42 billion. Metro said it would concentrate on finding savings from the A&P acquisition: $35 million in savings in 2006 and $25 million in 2007. The company also announced it had extended the contract of CEO Pierre Lessard until April 2008. Lessard has been Metro's CEO since 1990.[77]

When A&P decided to sell, Metro Inc. saw this opportunity to acquire the company as a very important strategic move. Metro Inc. understood the A&P company and found its goals and culture to be quite similar to Metro's. Further, when Metro's team met A&P's management team, they felt more at ease because it realized that the nature of such a large deal ($1.7 billion) rested on how well the management teams got along. Metro Inc. also felt that its offer was the best one. Said Lessard, "We managed to convince them that a dollar of Metro shares was worth more than a dollar of cash, and if you look at the result of the transaction the stock went up about $5. A&P has about 18 million shares so on top of the offer we made, they have already made about $90 million."

Lessard hopes to cut out $60 million in annual costs at the end of 2007, with a good part coming from procurement synergies as well as distribution efficiencies and some additional administrative costs.

You Be the Manager

1. What kinds of factors went into Metro Inc.'s strategy?

Rob Melnychuk/Getty Images

business-level strategy
A plan that indicates how a division intends to compete against its rivals in an industry.

business-level plan
Divisional managers' decisions relating to divisions' long-term goals, overall strategy, and structure.

cost-leadership strategy
Driving the organization's costs down below the costs of its rivals.

Michael Porter, the researcher who developed the Five Forces Model discussed earlier, also formulated a theory of how managers can select a **business-level strategy** and a **business-level plan** to gain a competitive advantage in a particular market or industry.[78] According to Porter, managers must choose between the two basic ways of increasing the value of an organization's products: higher quality or lower costs. Porter also argues that managers must choose between serving the whole market or serving just one segment or part of a market. Given those choices, managers choose to pursue one of four business-level strategies: *cost-leadership, differentiation, focused low-cost,* or *focused differentiation* (see Table 5.2).

Cost-Leadership Strategy

With a **cost-leadership strategy**, managers try to gain a competitive advantage by focusing the energy of all the organization's departments or functions on driving the organization's costs down below the costs of its rivals. This strategy means manufacturing managers must search for new ways to reduce production costs, R&D managers must focus on developing new products that can be manufactured more cheaply, and marketing managers must find ways to lower the costs of attracting

TABLE 5.2 | *Porter's Business-Level Strategies*

Strategy	Number of Market Segments Served	
	Many	Few
Cost-leadership	✓	
Focused low-cost		✓
Differentiation	✓	
Focused differentiation		✓

customers. According to Porter, organizations following a low-cost strategy can sell a product for less than their rivals sell it and yet still make a profit because of their lower costs. Thus, organizations that pursue a low-cost strategy hope to enjoy a competitive advantage based on their low prices.

Differentiation Strategy

With a **differentiation strategy**, managers try to gain a competitive advantage by focusing all the energies of the organization's departments or functions on distinguishing the organization's products from those of competitors in one or more important dimensions, such as product design, quality, or after-sales service and support. For instance, Ganong Bros. Ltd., based in St. Stephen, New Burnswick, is a small player in the chocolate market in Canada. It differentiates itself from bigger boxed-chocolate makers by focusing on the assorted chocolates market, where it ranks second in Canada. Its Fruitfull brand, made with real fruit purée and packaged like chocolates, has a 43-percent share of fruit jelly sales.[79]

differentiation strategy
Distinguishing an organization's products from the products of competitors in dimensions such as product design, quality, or after-sales service.

Often, the process of making products unique and different is expensive. This strategy, for example, often requires managers to increase spending on product design or R&D to make the product stand out, and costs rise as a result. However, organizations that successfully pursue a differentiation strategy may be able to charge a *premium price* for their products, a price usually much higher than the price charged by a low-cost organization. The premium price allows organizations pursuing a differentiation strategy to recoup their higher costs.

Don Watt is known as one of the smartest retail brand designers in the country. In terms of differentiation strategies, he was the brains behind Loblaw's President's Choice and No Name labels, designed many of its supermarkets, and has helped behemoth Wal-Mart develop its superstores and private labels. Watts says, "It really isn't rocket science. This is remarkably simple stuff. I've often been amazed that people would pay me for this because it's so simple … It's not just a package at a time—it's taking a broad approach to a category and how you differentiate one category from another in a store."[80] Dave Nichol, a former president of two Loblaw divisions and a private label guru in his own right, says of Watt, "He understands the big idea, something that really hits consumers between the eyes, something they can't ignore. The way that Michael Jordan shoots a basketball, the way that Tiger Woods hits a golf ball—that's the way that Don deals with design. He's just an intuitive genius."

Business Plan Checklist

- Create the vision, mission, and goal statements for your venture.
- To analyze the current environment, conduct a SWOT based on your direct competitor.
- To analyze industry trends (section 4), apply Porter's Five Forces analysis to your sector.
- Base your business-level strategy on the environmental analysis. Is it more appropriate for your venture to adopt a differentiation strategy or a cost leadership strategy? Should you focus on the whole market or a single segment or niche market?
- Profile your target market. Create a promotion and marketing plan.
- What are the major risks associated with the above, and how will you minimize them?
- Use this information for section 6 of the business plan, the Marketing Plan in Appendix A.

"Stuck in the Middle"

According to Porter's theory, managers cannot simultaneously pursue both a cost-leadership strategy and a differentiation strategy. Porter identified a simple correlation: Differentiation raises costs and thus necessitates premium pricing to recoup those high costs. What Best Buy Co. Inc. does to offset these costs—or not incur them—is to focus on customer service, and it does this with their employees. "Service," believe it or not, turned out to be their bold new strategy, and it worked! This strategy aligns itself with the new "customer-centricity" stores,[81] which aim to woo shoppers with more personalized service. Brian Postol of AG Edwards, a full-service brokerage firm, in St. Louis, Missouri, said that Best Buy's strategy allowed them to differentiate its offerings from those of gargantuan Wal-Mart Stores Inc., as well as rivals Target, Dell, and Amazon. According to Porter, managers must choose between a cost-leadership strategy and a differentiation strategy. He says that managers and organizations that have not made this choice are "stuck in the middle." According to Porter, organizations stuck in the middle tend to have lower levels of performance than do those that pursue a low-cost or a differentiation strategy. To avoid being stuck in the middle, top managers must instruct departmental managers to take actions that will result in either low cost or differentiation.

However, exceptions to this rule can be found. In many organizations, managers have been able to drive costs down below those of rivals and simultaneously differentiate their products from those offered by rivals.[82] For example, Toyota's production system is reportedly the most efficient in the world. This efficiency gives Toyota a low-cost strategy vis-à-vis its rivals in the global car industry. At the same time, Toyota has differentiated its cars from those of rivals on the basis of superior design and quality. This superiority allows the company to charge a premium price for many of its popular models.[83] Thus, Toyota seems to be simultaneously pursuing both a low-cost and a differentiated business-level strategy. This example suggests that although Porter's ideas may be valid in most cases, very well-managed companies such as Toyota, McDonald's, and Compaq may have both low costs and differentiated products.

Focused Low-Cost and Focused Differentiation Strategies

Both the differentiation strategy and the cost-leadership strategy are aimed at serving most or all segments of the market. Porter identified two other business-level strategies that aim to serve the needs of customers in only one or a few market segments.[84]

focused low-cost strategy
Serving only one segment of the overall market and being the lowest-cost organization serving that segment.

A company pursuing a **focused low-cost strategy** serves one or a few segments of the overall market and aims to be the lowest-cost company serving that segment. This is the strategy that Cott Corporation adopted. Cott focuses on large retail chains and strives to be the lowest-cost company serving that segment of the market. A major reason for Cott's low costs is the fact that the company does not advertise, which allows Cott to underprice both Coke and Pepsi.

focused differentiation strategy
Serving only one segment of the overall market and trying to be the most differentiated organization serving that segment.

By contrast, a company pursuing a **focused differentiation strategy** serves just one or a few segments of the market and aims to be the most differentiated company serving that segment. BMW pursues a focused strategy, producing cars exclusively for higher-income customers. Sleeman has followed this strategy in producing its premium beers.

As these examples suggest, companies pursuing either of these focused strategies have chosen to specialize in some way—by directing their efforts at a particular kind of customer (such as serving the needs of babies or affluent customers) or even the needs of customers in a specific geographical region (customers on the East Coast or the West Coast).

Functional-Level Strategies

As discussed earlier in the chapter, a **functional-level strategy** is a plan of action to improve the ability of an organization's departments to create value that is consistent with the business-level and corporate level strategies. It is concerned with the actions that **functional managers** of individual departments (such as manufacturing or marketing **functions**) can take to add value to an organization's goods and services and thereby increase the value customers receive.

There are two ways in which departments can add value to an organization's products:

1. Departmental managers can lower the costs of creating value so that an organization can attract customers by keeping its prices lower than its competitors' prices.
2. Departmental managers can add value to a product by finding ways to differentiate it from the products of other companies.

For instance, the marketing and sales departments at Molson-Coors value by building brand loyalty and finding more effective ways to attract customers. General Electric's Lighting division's strategy to drive costs down might translate into a **functional-level plan** for the manufacturing department to "reduce production costs by 20 percent over three years." The functional-level strategy to accomplish this might include (1) investing in state-of-the-art European production facilities and (2) developing an electronic global business-to-business network to reduce the cost of inputs and inventory-holding costs. Each organizational function has an important role to play in lowering costs or adding value to a product (see Table 5.3).

functional-level strategy
A plan that indicates how a function intends to achieve its goals.

functional managers
Managers who supervise the various functions—such as manufacturing accounting and sales—within a division.

function
A unit or department in which people have the same skills or use the same resources to perform their jobs.

functional-level plan
Functional managers' decisions relating to the goals that they propose to pursue to help the division reach its business-level goals.

TABLE 5.3 | *How Functions Can Lower Costs and Create Value or Add Value to Create a Competitive Advantage*

Value-creating Function	Ways to Lower the Cost of Creating Value (Low-cost Advantage)	Ways to Add Value (Differentiation Advantage)
Sales and marketing	• Find new customers • Find low-cost advertising methods	• Promote brand-name awareness and loyalty • Tailor products to suit customers' needs
Materials management	• Use just-in-time inventory system/computerized warehousing • Develop long-term relationships with suppliers and customers	• Develop long-term relationships with suppliers to provide high-quality inputs • Reduce shipping time to customers
Research and development	• Improve efficiency of machinery and equipment • Design products that can be made more cheaply	• Create new products • Improve existing products
Manufacturing	• Develop skills in low-cost manufacturing	• Increase product equity and reliability
Human resource management	• Reduce turnover and absenteeism • Raise employee skills	• Hire highly skilled employees • Develop innovative training programs

In trying to add value or lower the costs of creating value, all functional managers should pay attention to these four goals:[85]

1. *To attain superior efficiency.* Efficiency is a measure of the amount of inputs required to produce a given amount of outputs. The fewer the inputs required to produce a given output, the higher is the efficiency and the lower the cost of outputs.
2. *To attain superior quality.* Here, quality means producing goods and services that are reliable—they do the job they were designed for and do it well.[86] Providing high-quality products creates a brand-name reputation for an organization's products. In turn, this enhanced reputation allows the organization to charge a higher price.
3. *To attain superior innovation.* Anything new or unusual about the way in which an organization operates or the goods and services it produces is the result of innovation. Innovation leads to advances in the kinds of products, production processes, management systems, organizational structures, and strategies that an organization develops. Successful innovation gives an organization something unique that its rivals lack. This uniqueness may enhance the value added and thereby allow the organization to differentiate itself from its rivals and attract customers who will pay a premium price for its product.
4. *To attain superior responsiveness to customers.* An organization that is responsive to customers tries to satisfy their needs and give them exactly what they want. An organization that treats customers better than its rivals treats them provides a valuable service for which customers may be willing to pay a higher price.

The important issue to remember here is that all of these techniques can help an organization achieve a competitive advantage by lowering the costs of creating value or by adding value above and beyond that offered by rivals.

LO 6

Implementing and Evaluating Strategy

THINK ABOUT IT

Mergers, Differentiations, Success![87]

The Centre for Addiction and Mental Health (CAMH) in Toronto was created in 1998 through the successful merger of the former Addiction Research Foundation, the Clarke Institute of Psychiatry, the Donwood Institute, and the Queen Street Mental Health Centre. With its 2003–2006 Strategic Plan, CAMH plans to continue being successful in implementing its strategy around the following four mandates: client-centred care, education, health promotion/prevention, and research. It will also update its mission and vision statements to reflect CAMH's increased emphasis on health promotion and the determinants of health as an essential part of its work and to be more clearly and actively focused on improving the lives of people and building healthy communities.

How has CAMH's strategy been practically implemented? It has been able to:

• Launch a multi-year public education strategy.

• Establish provincial priorities in the areas of youth, concurrent disorders, and diversity.

• Acquire a new Positron Emission Tomography (PET) scanner—one of only two in Canada.

Additional highlights include:

- Average length of stay decreased from 87 days to 47 days.
- Professional education increased by over 30 percent, to 9000 providers/year.
- Over 30 percent increase in volunteers.
- Research funding increased by close to 60 percent to $28 million per year.
- Fundraising increased from $3 million to $6 million per year, and the donor base from 2280 donors to 4964 donors.

You Be the Manager

1. How does strategy relate to implementation?

After conducting a SWOT analysis and analyzing the forces in the organization's industry using Porter's Five Forces Model, managers formulate appropriate strategies at the corporate, business, and functional level that support the organization's vision, mission, and goals. The next step in the planning process, implementation, now confronts managers with the challenge of how to put those strategies into action. Strategy implementation is a five-step process.

1. Allocating responsibility for implementation to the appropriate individuals or groups
2. Drafting detailed action plans that specify how a strategy is to be implemented
3. Establishing a timetable for implementation that includes precise, measurable goals linked to the attainment of the action plan. A **Gantt chart** can be used to manage the project.[88]
4. Allocating appropriate resources to the responsible individuals or groups
5. Holding specific individuals or groups responsible for reaching corporate, divisional, and functional goals

Gantt chart
A graphic bar chart managers use to schedule tasks in a project showing what tasks need to be done, who will do them, and by what timeframe.

www.smartdraw.com

As the case of CAMH illustrates, the planning process goes beyond the mere identification of strategies; it also includes actions taken to ensure that the organization actually implements its strategies.

Evaluating Strategy

The last step in the process of planning is evaluating whether or not the strategy has been successful in achieving the major goals set out in step one. How do managers know when they are successful? In evaluating the success of a strategy, managers must monitor progress, evaluate performance levels, and make corrective adjustments if there is a substantial gap between the goal and the actual performance. This is essentially the controlling process more fully discussed in Chapter 13. Managers monitor and measure actual performance levels and compare the results with the initial goal for a particular strategy. For example, following a corporate-level strategy of international expansion, the CIBC decided to enter the U.S. retail banking market by putting branches in grocery stores. But after about a decade of losses amounting to hundreds of millions of dollars, the strategy was abandoned. CIBC largely pulled out of the United States after this strategy failed. At the time this text went to press, the CIBC was in discussions about buying a stake in a troubled Irish bank. Looking overseas to expand internationally may, in part, be because of its disastrous venture into the United States.[89] When goals are unmet, strategy must be rethought in such a way as to stay true to the vision and mission of the organization.

It should be noted that the plan for implementing a strategy may require radical redesign of the structure of the organization, the adoption of a program for changing the culture of the organization and the development of new control systems. We address the first two issues in the next two chapters. We discuss the issues of control in Chapter 13.

Tips for Managers

STRATEGY

1. Take time for reviewing your corporate strategy.

2. Ask yourself if you have a strategy with "blinders" or if you include "peripheral vision" and see what is occurring around you as well?

3. Make sure you clearly see the link between your strategy and how it is implemented.

4. Ask yourself if your strategy will be incurring costs that will negate the bold dream you have for the company.

Summary and Review

1. **WHAT IS PLANNING, WHO DOES IT, AND WHY IS IT IMPORTANT?** Planning is setting goals and finding the best strategy to achieve them. This is done by management at all three levels of the organization: top-level managers are responsible for long-term strategic planning and strategizing, middle-level for intermediate planning, and first-line for functional-level planning. Planning serves to give direction and purpose to the organization, it coordinates different functions and divisions, and it allows managers to control the use of resources. *Scenario or contingency planning* is managers forecasting what may happen in the future and then gathering resources to meet these anticipated needs, opportunities, and threats. *Crisis management* occurs when unanticipated and unplanned contingencies arise.

2. **PLANNING AS A FIVE STEP PROCESS**
   a. Determining an organization's vision, mission, and goals
   b. Analyzing the forces in the organizational environment
   c. Formulating strategy
   d. Implementing strategy
   e. Evaluating strategy

3. **DETERMINING THE ORGANIZATION'S VISION, MISSION, AND GOALS** requires managers to define the nature of the business of the organization and establish and communicate major goals.

4. **CONDUCTING AN ANALYSIS OF THE ORGANIZATIONAL ENVIRONMENT** to evaluate how the internal and external forces impact the organization by creating opportunities and threats. SWOT analysis examines the internal strengths and weaknesses of the organization, while Porter's Five Forces analyzes the potential for profitability within a particular industry by looking at the degree of competitive rivalry, the ease of entry, the power of buyers, the power of suppliers, and the threat of substitute products. Managers use these two techniques to evaluate what strategy would gain them a competitive advantage.

5. **FORMULATING STRATEGY** At the corporate level, organizations use strategies such as concentration on a single business, diversification, international expansion, and vertical integration to help increase the value of the goods and services provided to customers. At the business or divisional level, managers are responsible for developing a low cost or differentiation strategy, either for the whole market or for a particular segment of it (focus strategy). At the functional level, departmental managers try to add value to the product or service by differentiating them or increasing efficiencies by reducing costs.

6. **IMPLEMENTING AND EVALUATING STRATEGY** requires managers to allocate responsibilities to individuals or groups, draft detailed action plans that specify how a strategy is to be implemented, establish a timetable for implementation that includes specific measurable goals, allocate necessary resources, and hold the individuals or groups accountable for reaching goals. Managers monitor the progress of goal achievement and make corrective adjustments when strategies fail.

Key Terms

business-level plan, p. 160
business-level strategy, p. 160
co-opetition, p. 151
corporate-level plans, p. 154
corporate-level strategy, p. 154
cost-leadership strategy, p. 160
crises management plans, p. 140
differentiation strategy, p. 161
diversification, p. 155
division, p. 136
divisional managers, p. 137
focused differentiation strategy, p. 162
focused low-cost strategy, p. 162
function, p. 163
functional-level plan, p. 163
functional-level strategy, p. 163
functional managers, p. 163
Gantt chart, p. 165
global strategy, p. 157
goal, p. 142

management by objectives, p. 145
mission statement, p. 142
multidomestic strategy, p. 157
planning, p. 135
policy, p. 138
Porter's Five Forces Model, p. 150
related diversification, p. 155
rule, p. 138
scenario planning, p. 139
standard operating procedures (SOPs), p. 138
strategy, p. 135
strategy formulation, p. 147
SWOT analysis, p. 147
synergy, p. 155
time horizon, p. 137
unrelated diversification, p. 155
vertical integration, p. 157
vision statement, p. 141

Wrap-Up to Opening Case[90]

Rogers Communications Inc. (RCI) continues to push ahead with its strategic vision for the future. It is hoping now that more and more Canadians will replace their land-line phones with a cellphone—of course, linked with RCI services! According to Statistics Canada, about 6.4 percent of households have replaced their land lines with cellphones. The company's cellphone business, Rogers Wireless, announced that it will begin to roll out a so-called "unlicensed mobile access" (UMA), which will give users unlimited calling in their homes through a connection to the Internet. "Instead of having a few phones that you pay for, you can have one phone, one voice mail service, one caller ID, one address box," said John Boynton, Rogers' chief marketing officer. "This one phone becomes the phone for everything." Feeling the threat from Telus Corp. and, of course, the popular iPhone smartphone device from Apple Inc., Rogers is targeting the youth market. "For teenagers, students and young adults, a cellphone is their primary phone," Mr. Boynton said. "Since about 30 percent of cellphone calls are done at home, this is a way to save about $35 per month by eliminating the need for a home phone if it's not being used."

On December 2, 2008, Ted Rogers died. Taking a line from Rogers' own biography, *Toronto Star* writer Moira Welsh wrote: "If my life has a lesson for others, I think it is that everyone has a shot. Don't follow your dream; live it. No matter what it is you want, take your best shot. Be passionate, work hard, maybe harder than you've ever dreamt, but the opportunity is there."[91]

On Monday, March 30, 2009, Nadir Mohamed was named president and chief executive officer of Rogers Communications Inc.

Ask Yourself

1. If you were Nadir Mohamed, what would be going through your mind?

Management in Action

Topics for Discussion and Action

Level 1

1. Describe the five steps in the planning process. Explain how they are related.
2. Discuss who plans, the time horizons of plans, the difference between standing and single-use plans, and why planning is important. What are the qualities of effective plans?
3. Describe scenario planning. How can scenario planning help managers predict the future?

Level 2

4. Ask a manager to identify the corporate-, business-, and functional-level strategies used by his or her organization.
5. Watch the video on Porter Airlines at www.youtube.com/watch?v=xnhExEZvJNI . Identify the airline's mission. What type of business-level strategy is it pursuing? Give evidence to support your answer.

6. Go to the website of Bombardier. Identify the vision, mission, and major goals for the company. What corporate level strategy is it engaged in? What is the business-level strategy of its largest division?

Level 3

7. Research a well-known company that you can easily find information about. What is the main industry that the company competes in? Apply Porter's Five Forces model to this industry to determine its profitability.
8. Present an argument for having lower-level managers participate in the company's strategic planning process. What might happen if they were to have no input?
9. Research two firms in the same industry, and perform a competitive SWOT analysis. What type of corporate-, business-, and functional-level strategies would you recommend for the firms, and why?

Building Management Skills

Answer the following questions about the organization you have chosen to follow:

1. Identify the vision, mission, and major goals of the organization.
2. What is the corporate-level strategy of the company?
3. What is the business-level strategy of the company?
4. Have the strategies supported the vision and mission? How so?

5. Has there been a significant shift in strategy over the past decade? If yes, describe it, and try to determine why the organization made the changes.
6. How successful is the organization's planning process?

Management for You

Think ahead to five years from now to consider what it is that you might like to be doing with your life. Develop your own vision and mission statements. Establish a set of goals that will help you achieve your vision and mission.

Develop a SWOT analysis for considering what you want to be doing in five years. What are your strengths and weaknesses? What are the opportunities and threats in carrying out this plan?

Develop a five-year plan that maps out the steps you need to take in order to get to where you want to be in your life at that time.

Small Group Breakout Exercise

Form groups of three or four, and appoint one member as the spokesperson who will communicate your findings to the class when called on by the instructor. Then discuss the following scenario:

You are a team of management consultants hired by a grocery store chain to plan the feasibility of opening a store in your community. You must answer all the questions below and report back to your clients.

1. List the major supermarket chains in your city, and identify their strengths and weaknesses relative to one another. What opportunities and threats exist for each chain?
2. What business-level strategies are these supermarkets currently pursuing?

3. What kind of supermarket strategy would do best against the competition?
4. What would you recommend to your clients, and why?

Business Planning Exercise

In Chapter 4, your team made a decision on what type of venture you will write a business plan on. Now the planning must begin. You must create a Profile of the Organization and Industry. Using the planning tools in this chapter, do the following:

1. Write the vision and mission statements for your venture.
2. Formulate two major goals for the business. These could relate to revenue within the first year or market share or number of customers served.
3. Find out the NAICS code for your industry. Research the trends in the industry.
4. Analyze the competitive environment by applying Porter's Five Forces model to the industry. What

threats exist for your venture, and how will you minimize the risks?
5. Conduct a SWOT analysis of your venture relative to one direct competitor.
6. What strategy will your venture pursue to gain a competitive advantage over your rival?

Managing Ethically

A major department store has received repeated criticism for selling clothes that are produced at low cost in developing countries. The CEO of the department store knows that suppliers are paying 5 percent better than the going rate of wages in these countries and feels that this is fair enough. Working conditions at suppliers' factories are no worse than at other factories in those countries. The CEO has come to you to check her assumptions that as long as the suppliers are buying from manufacturing plants that have better-than-average working conditions for the country where the company is located, nothing further needs to be done. What would you advise her? How would you justify your advice?

Exploring the World Wide Web

SPECIFIC ASSIGNMENT

This exercise follows up on the activities of McDonald's Corporation (www.mcdonalds.com), which is vertically integrating on a global level. Research McDonald's website to get a feel for this global giant. In particular, focus on McDonald's most recent annual report and its descriptions of the company's goals and objectives.

1. What are the main elements of McDonald's strategy at the corporate, business, and functional levels?
2. How successful has the company been recently?
3. Has the strategy of McDonald's Canada been any different from its parent operation's?

GENERAL ASSIGNMENT

Search for a website that contains a good description of a company's strategy. What is the company's mission? Use the concepts and terminology of this chapter to describe the company's strategy to achieve its mission.

McGraw-Hill Connect™—Available 24/7 with instant feedback so you can study when you want, how you want, and where you want. Take advantage of the Study Plan—an innovative tool that helps you customize your learning experience. You can diagnose your knowledge with pre- and post-tests, identify the areas where you need help, search the entire learning package for content specific to the topic you're studying, and add these resources to your personalized study plan. Visit www.mcgrawhillconnect.ca to register—take practice quizzes, search the e-book, and much more.

Be the Manager

BEYOND THE GREEN DOOR

The Green Door restaurant is a vegetarian restaurant in Ottawa, Canada, with an "eye and palette ... focused on nourishment drawn from the local, organic, seasonal, natural, wholesome, comforting and colourful."[92] The restaurant is situated directly across from Saint Paul University[93] (part of the University of Ottawa and home to about 1000 undergraduate and graduate students in such disciplines as spirituality, philosophy, human sciences, pastoral counselling, and conflict studies). OttawaPlus.ca considers the Green Door the "heaven for vegetarians" and an Ottawa institution.[94]

Questions

1. Name some vegetarian restaurants in the city where you live. Do a SWOT analysis as to their strengths and weaknesses.
2. Look up reviews on the Green Door on the Internet. If the Green Door wanted to expand, what kind of business-level strategy should it pursue?

Management Case

Strategy, Moses Znaimer, and Foretelling the Future[95]

Moses Znaimer does not really know how old he is. At 25, Znaimer was a wunderkind producer at CBC. By 30, he was running CITY-TV. He said, "People get fixated by counting. We get older by counting. I never understood the point." He also explains that growing up in the harrowing years of the Second World War people made up dates; the issue was survival, not counting! He is probably 66-ish at this point.

In Toronto, the name 'Moses Znaimer' is quite well known. For many years he served up the "media's tastiest empty calories: MuchMusic, Fashion Television, The shaky cam." He built up CITY-TV, which he never fully controlled, and was forced out in 2003. "His downfall in that instance was a failure to control the means of production through ownership." His experience since then is that strategists and visionaries "exist only at the bottom or the top. In the middle, where he's living right now, they're better described as pitchmen." And so, in July 2009, he found himself making a pitch at the lakeside Boulevard Club to a roomful of about 200 Procter & Gamble reps that people over 55 still count.

While his earlier visions and strategies helped make CITY-TV a roaring success, now he had the chance to test his new vision—that older people have lives—and develop a strategic plan from there. He has now "added a small boutique of television channels—including the flagship religious service Vision TV—to his growing Zoomer lifestyle and media brand—a concept he kicked off in 2005." However, unlike before, today he is a major shareholder, not "just the guy at the top of the flow chart."

Can he now foretell the future again? That older people, over 55, have lives also and that it is good for business as well? At the lakeside Boulevard Club in Toronto, convincing a room filled with younger people that his vision was a real one was his immediate piece of strategy, and it needed money. His presentation was "in the form of a video, a slick presentation of stats demonstrating how much money the aging have (a lot) and how largely they figure in the plans of advertisers (a very little)."

His presentation centred around a "$25-million Vision package—which includes the flagship station, a stake in One: The Mind, Body and Spirit channel, and a pair of local religious channels in Winnipeg and Vancouver"— but "it also brings with it access to something in the neighbourhood of 10 million households."

Perhaps a key, if not *the* key, ingredient in the strategic direction that Znaimer has taken might be in the comment by Marilyn Lightstone, the artist who has been Znaimer's longtime companion: "We were both born Jewish, but neither of us believes in organized religion. I think what Moses is doing is almost rabbinic, almost Talmudic. The purpose of being Jewish is to save the world, to make it a better place. If (Moses) is Jewish in any way, it's that."

The strategic issue now seems to be: "Now it's about the ever-after. Has Moses Znaimer forsaken the profane for the sacred?" Znaimer responds to this question: "Yes, there's a certain rhythm to it, one that may be visible in hindsight. There were (other channels) I could have acquired, but something has led me here. Part of it is opportunity, happenstance. But you may be right."

Sometimes people raise their eyebrows at Znaimer's new "spiritual" direction, given the "racy" overtones to his former work initiatives and personal charisma. Ross Mayot, a former TVO exec who worked with Znaimer in educational television and recruited back to work with him again, said the plan is to remove the sermons and massage the message. "It's a question of existence," says Mayot. "If you don't exist on television, you live in the shadows." According to Cathal Kelly of the *Toronto Star*, "Znaimer's image of Godhead rests somewhere in mass media, and the television set in particular."

Perhaps strategy and foretelling the future lie in Znaimer's own words: "I know you're going to hold this against me, but that's why all religions are, at some level, at war with show business. Before the advent of show business, where could you get a good show? Once a week, good music, guys wearing costumes, incense ... I think I can act as a useful bridge between these two worlds."

Says Cathal Kelly again: "Perhaps. But in the end, it comes down to the most basic spiritual need of all."

Question

1. What seem to be Moses Znaimer's vision and strategy?

Video Management Case   ■

Panera Bread Company

Teaching Objective: To observe how a fast-casual restaurant chain delivers value to customers, builds loyalty, and achieves a competitive advantage.
Video Summary: Panera Bread Co. combines some of the best aspects of fast food and sit-down venues. Its bakery-cafés offer quick meals throughout the day and a casual, sit-down place where customers are welcome to linger. Panera prides itself on high-quality food, the inviting atmosphere, and great customer service provided by managers and employees empowered

to make decisions that increase responsiveness to customers. The Panera formula leads to high levels of employee commitment and customer satisfaction and has fueled tremendous growth for the company.

1. How do Panera Bread's corporate vision and strategy lead to a competitive advantage in the restaurant industry?

2. How does Panera achieve responsiveness to customers?

3. How does its corporate culture help make Panera Bread a high-performing company?

Part 3: Integrated Case

Sour Notes for Bronfman Jr.[96]

(c) Lennox McLendon

For Edgar Bronfman Jr., heir to the legendary Seagram fortune, the moment of "three strikes and you're out" appears nigh. Losses had deepened and were accompanied by a suspension of Warner's dividend in order to cope with a huge debt-service burden. And this after about 400 layoffs last year at the New York-based Warner, whose acts include Madonna, Nickelback, R.E.M., Green Day, and Simple Plan. There was a second-quarter loss—US$37 million, but of more concern was the loss of 11 cents a share, a sign the company no longer had a grasp of industry conditions.

Warner stock dived as much as 22 percent on the May 7, 2008 news, to as low as just under $7. Among the boo-birds on Internet message boards was an observer who contrasted recent pay raises for Warner's top brass, Bronfman included, with the firm's difficult finances

under their stewardship. Warner is the global industry's third-largest label and yet commands a market cap of just $800 million or so and is bloated with about $2.6 billion in debt. Bronfman himself, in disclosing the dividend suspension, insisted that he felt "totally comfortable" with Warner's ability "to meet our debt covenants." That is the sort of thing a CEO says when things have turned bad enough that solvency is widely in doubt.

Bronfman is the grandson of Seagram liquor-dynasty co-founder Sam Bronfman who had the chance to consolidate the high end of the global booze business that Seagram already dominated with prized brands such as Crown Royal, Glenlivet, and Möet & Chandon when handed the CEO's reins by his father in the 1990s.

Instead, the part-time songwriter (for Céline Dion and Dionne Warwick, among others) let that business languish, leaving it to Britain's Diageo PLC and France's Pernod Ricard SA to eclipse what had been the world's biggest liquor combine for much of the twentieth century.

Having let its prowess weaken, Bronfman could then point to liquor's underwhelming financial performance to convince his father, Edgar Sr., and uncle Charles to reinvent Seagram as an entertainment purveyor, buying the Universal movie and TV studios and theme parks and PolyGram, a music leader.

Frustrated with the box-office and Billboard-chart vagaries of that business, though, Bronfman drank deeply of the "media convergence" Kool-Aid of the late 1990s and impulsively exchanged his family's entire firm—booze, music labels, TV production contracts, U.S. theme parks, and all—for stock in a venerable French sewer and filtration outfit intent on transforming itself into a global entertainment conglomerate.

The convergence euphoria collapsed almost immediately after that 2000 deal. Vivendi stock plunged. And an estimated two-thirds of the fortune accumulated since Sam and his brothers' bootlegging days in the 1920s was wiped out.

Few corporate strategists with that kind of track record get a third chance. But in 2004, Edgar Jr. was able to put together a group of institutional investors to buy the substantial music operations of Time Warner Inc., itself in the midst of a fire sale after its own spectacular disaster in merging with a wildly overpriced America Online Inc. Bronfman got a steal in what became the Warner Music Group. And it seemed he had finally found his métier, carving $250 million in costs from the long-neglected outpost of the Time Warner conglomerate.

Indeed, for a brief shining moment Bronfman was a golden boy. Warner stock was trading well above its 2005 initial public offering price. Bronfman's partners had doubled their money. And the Warner board—confident of better things to come—spurned a rich 2006 takeover offer of $31 a share from British rival EMI.

Then the Bronfman Jr. curse reappeared. The traditional music business was roiled by increasingly widespread illegal music downloading on the Internet (the vocation of an estimated 8 million enthusiasts globally). Lucrative CD sales went into irreversible decline. And power shifted from artists and retailers to fans. The rampant piracy that began in the 1990s with rogue file-sharing site Napster killed off traditional record shops, which toed the line with record companies for fear of losing out on the hottest new release.

Today's leading music vendors, Apple Inc.'s number one iTunes (from a standing start in 2003) and number two Wal-Mart Stores Inc., with the likes of Zellers, J.C. Penney, and even Starbucks Corp. big in the game, now call the shots in a merchandise category that is for them a mere sideline. Wal-Mart negotiates pinched margins from Warner no differently than it does on volume purchases of Procter & Gamble Co.'s Tide and Prell.

Apple's iTunes, while now selectively relenting on its simple one-price formula for everything it sells, remains staunchly averse to the labels' preference for "variable pricing"—simply, the ability to charge more for a hot-selling new CD than for a collection of mouldy oldies.

Musicians, meanwhile, are increasingly calling their own shots. Garnering the bulk of their income from concerts, they increasingly bypass record labels to promote their shows, recordings, and merchandise on social-networking sites MySpace, YouTube, and Facebook. This enables them to establish strong ties with fans. It beats hoping a decent portion of a label's promotion budget will be devoted to an act's latest release.

And consumers are so enamoured of singles over more profitable CDs in their online purchases that Amazon.com recently adopted the iTunes formula that enables shoppers to spend $3 on three tunes from three CDs rather than laying out $30 for those three CDs.

The industry, now in an eight-year CD revenue slide, has not helped itself by pursuing high-profile lawsuits against 13-year-old fans caught illegally downloading tracks from popular file-sharing sites. Artists who initially shared the labels' concern about lost royalties now regard such moves as a bullying that risks breaking the bond between artist and fan.

A new trend of pay-what-you-please began last fall with Radiohead's long-awaited and well-received "In Rainbows" CD. By this spring, 62 percent of folks who downloaded "In Rainbows" paid nothing, in keeping with the stubborn Internet culture that online content should be free.

The industry also blundered with encryption devices installed in CDs for the past five years, intended to thwart illicit copying. But rather than curbing piracy, the effect of encryption in preventing music from being played on multiple devices—from traditional CD players to iPods—has simply alienated customers, leading to EMI's decision last year to end the five-year practice.

Then there are Warner's own blunders. These include writing off $18-million on a bizarre investment in Bulldog Entertainment Group, an outfit that staged intimate concerts in the Hamptons on Long Island starring the likes of Billy Joel with absurd $3000 admission prices. Critics feasted on determining just how much Edgar Bronfman Jr. was willing to pay to hobnob with Tom Petty, James Taylor, and Prince at the sparsely attended events.

A little more mind-boggling was the $73 million Warner spent to buy Roadrunner Records simply to acquire artist Nickelback. Warner neglected to read the fine print under which Nickelback could ankle after just one more CD for the label. Warner was obliged to kick in additional "elephant bucks," as one music blog put it, to avoid that embarrassment.

Even ring tone sales are slipping. As long as the traditional industry's survival depends on selling enough $1 downloads to compensate for the slow death of the $20 CD market, this is a business model the angel Gabriel could not save.

What irks most investors is that Bronfman could have seen the fading treble clef on the wall and sold to EMI at $31 a share, almost four times what Warner stock now fetches.

But having been burned in a cash-and-stock deal with Vivendi, Bronfman and his board were wary of what they regarded as funny money in EMI's offer. And, fair enough, EMI has since hit the skids. But a more prescient Bronfman, grasping the dismal prospects for the industry, would have pushed EMI for an all-cash deal.

Of the world industry's "big four," Warner alone is almost wholly reliant on music, the others being appendages of book and magazine publishers and electronics makers (Sony/BMG), and broadcasting, publishing, and sewer maintenance (Universal Music). EMI owns the world's largest music-publishing business.

Bronfman, more than his peers, has to live with the import of the Warren Buffett dictum that when you have even a well-run company in a lousy industry, it is the reputation of the industry that remains intact.

Discussion Questions

1. What are some key decisions that Bronfman needs to make?
2. What are the particular threat and opportunity that Bronfman faces?

PART 4

Organizing

CHAPTER

6

Managing Organizational Structure

Learning Outcomes

1. Identify the elements involved in designing organizational structures.

2. Explain how managers group tasks into jobs that are motivating and satisfying for employees.

3. Explain how jobs are grouped into functional, divisional and networked structures.

4. Explain the ways that managers allocate authority and coordinate activities.

5. Explain the factors that managers consider when deciding on a formal or flexible overall structure.

Structure and Common Sense

Change has changed.

All around us people and organizations are going through massive changes. These changes are not only local but global as well. Some refer to our time as a time of paradigm shifts; for others it is adapting to globalization. At one moment it is "all global"; then an oil crisis occurs, as it did in the spring of 2008, and the emphasis shifts again. Organizations are now very sensitive to what happens globally as well as locally.

Such ongoing change and changes as we have been experiencing for over a decade also means that organizations are in this process as well; so are their structures. In the past, organizations usually had fixed—and often inflexible—policies and procedures for work times, vacations, retirement, and so on.

Flexibility is demanded from *everyone* and *everything*. And that includes organizations. According to the UK's Chartered Institute of Personnel and Development (CIPD), allowing employees to take gap-year breaks and unpaid leave seems beneficial for all parties involved. Obviously such allowances will affect an organization's structure. Organizational change impacts everything and everyone. CIPD research adviser Vanessa Robinson said employers are beginning to realize that in order to retain the best people, structures must now be flexible—adding that more and more people were opting to take time out to travel. "It makes sense for the employer to say, 'Yes that's ok, we'll give you that time as unpaid leave because we value you, and it's better for us that you come back in six months and work with us again than having to recruit somebody new,' " she explained.[1] In addition, such time off, says Robinson, also helps boost employability.

Another change affecting organizational structures is flexible working patterns. Such organizational flexibility is aimed at recruiting the best people. Caroline Waters, director of employment policy at British Telecommunications, said employers have to move with the times and adapt to what the labour force wants. "We want them to commute, and they want to work from home—just in this country alone, 1.1 billion hours are spent just in getting to work. Does that sound like an economy

Adam Crowley/Cartesia/PhotoDisc Images/Getty Images

for the twenty-first century? I don't think so," she commented. According to a joint study by Work Wise UK and the Automobile Association, the average worker in the UK spends 29 days a year commuting to his or her place of employment every year—which equates to five years over the course of a working life.[2]

According to authors and consultants, Gary Neilson, a senior vice-president with Booz Allen Hamilton in Chicago and co-author of *Results: Keep What's Good, Fix What's Wrong, and Unlock Great Performance* and Jack McGrath, a senior vice-president with Booz Allen in Cleveland, Ohio, "Successful transformation requires the common sense of experienced management. Unfortunately, the ability to apply that common sense, especially over the long time frame of a serious change in organizational culture, is all too rare." They suggest a 10-point checklist that can help leaders of large-scale transformation put their wisdom into practice:[3]

1. ***The CEO must make a strong case for change by clearly and persuasively articulating the factors that are driving it.*** Most people in organizations understand that today's highly competitive global marketplace shapes business in unpredictable and often punishing ways. As a result, stakeholders will support large-scale change if they are truly convinced that such change is essential. But for this to happen, the CEO must personally make the case, starting with a compelling analysis of the business climate that makes it bracingly clear why the organization must embark upon radical change.

2. ***Senior leaders must set an aggressive, enterprisewide target. Big goals are the key to driving big actions.*** For example, an audacious, market-mandated target ("We have to get US$1 billion out of the cost of this enterprise, or we'll lose out to the low-cost provider within two years") sends the message that transformation is not a matter of incremental changes, like trimming finance or putting HR on a diet. It will require a fundamental rethinking of current priorities, market position, and strategic intent.

3. ***Senior management must be firmly aligned.*** The CEO of a transforming organization is responsible for bringing the top levels of management on board in strong support of both the targets articulated and the reasoning behind them. Every individual on the leadership team needs to have a stake in the transformation effort as a whole, rather than focusing only on the piece related to his or her business or function. As one CEO said, "Everyone has to own the problem, even if they don't like doing so. They've got to understand it, believe it, suck it up, and move ahead."

4. ***An integrated enterprisewide program for change must be put in place.*** Cross-functional business solutions enable people to live out the new business model instead of remaining locked in the concerns of their day-to-day responsibilities. To achieve this, the organization has to mix things up, putting a finance person in charge of new footprints, assigning a sales representative or plant manager to a product launch team, pulling a legal person over into a marketing project, or creating one common functional solution across several businesses. This kind of mixing up is not the same as creating a formal matrix, which implies a hardwired structure, but rather identifying people who can take collective ownership of the transformation effort and putting them physically together with others in temporary working groups—especially when two or more traditional silos are involved in rethinking a common endeavour.

5. ***Senior leaders must focus on augmenting capabilities along with cutting costs.*** The prospect of working to create a better future is highly motivating for most employees, whereas the prospect of cutting costs is not. As a result, efforts to massively change the cost structure of an organization must always be set within the positive context of building new skills. The bottom-line part of the change equation can be clearly quantified, which is one reason many senior leaders emphasize it. But articulating a commitment to building new capabilities is equally important and provides a much greater incentive for people to support change.

6. ***"Moments of truth" must be recognized and shared in order to demonstrate commitment.*** A "moment of truth" is a revelatory incident or event, either deliberately engineered or recognized when it occurs, that highlights precisely what needs to change in an organization. These often originate with executive leaders and later cascade down through layers of the organization via retelling of the story. For one CEO, the moment came at a meeting when the transformation team unveiled its first progress report. It was focused on cutting capabilities as a corollary to cutting costs. The CEO (as he later recalled it) suddenly saw that this solution would drain the organization of the very skills it needed to survive the change. "Wait a minute," he said. "I thought our strategy was to do *more* with less, not less with less."

7. ***A detailed plan must provide the blueprint.*** After senior leadership identifies targets and articulates a comprehensive vision for the future, leaders must start the work of developing a comprehensive guide to the changes ahead. This blueprint specifies the steps that will enable the organization to meet its targets, sets aggressive yet achievable timelines, addresses the change management issues that occur at every stage, and identifies new roles for people throughout the organization without getting too tied up in trying to detail the management chart.

8. ***Enabling triggers must be built in from the start.*** The detailed map for the transformation should identify in advance triggering events that will clearly be important in moving the process of change forward. For example, one of our clients stopped budgeting for

a number of smaller, declining brands; logic suggested they would have to be eliminated later. Subsequently, when the changes were announced, the difficult work of shutting down these product lines had already begun, and there was more time to design the implementation. At another company we worked with, redundant staff were encouraged to take early retirement before the change initiative was formally announced; when the work streams were cut, the people who had been doing those jobs were already gone. Building in these kinds of advance measures helps ensure that transformation timelines will be met. Timing departures ahead of making overall cuts in functions also minimizes the shock to the company. The focus of employees is shifted from feeling the loss to adapting to the new approach.

9. ***Communication must be proactive and ongoing.*** Skillful internal and external communication linked to a strategic vision is essential to large-scale change. Internal communications should be blunt and realistic about the market imperative driving transformation. They should be consistent throughout the enterprise but should also be flexible enough to address the concerns of specific businesses and functions.

10. ***The results of change must be sustained.*** Transformation is as much a way to change behaviours and practices as to reconfigure costs and strategy. New capabilities for achieving accountability, distributing benefits, allocating incentives, and tracking results must therefore remain in place even after financial targets are met.

Now It's Your Turn

1. What would be the first change in organizational structure you would personally want for yourself when you begin establishing your own career? Why would such an option be important for you?

2. Which points in the 10-point checklist that authors and consultants, Gary Neilson and Jack McGrath, have outlined above would you find challenging if you were the CEO of an organization? Why?

▪▪▪▪ Overview

The opening scenario to this chapter allows us to see that change is impacting organizations and their structures because of the change in global and local needs. As well, a 10-point checklist—prerequisites for success and commonsense items—that a CEO must adhere to was also presented.

In Part 4, we examine how managers can organize human and other resources to create high-performing organizations. To organize, managers must design an organization that makes the best use of resources to produce the goods and services customers want.

By the end of this chapter, you will be familiar not only with various organizational structures but also with various factors that determine the organizational design choices that managers make. Then in Chapter 7, we examine issues surrounding the organization's culture and what it takes for an organization to achieve change.

L O 1

Designing Organizational Structure

Executive Overview[4]

The problems America's organizations are facing are not due to temporary downturns in the economy. They are a vivid testimony to the fact that organizations of the nineteenth and twentieth centuries are obsolete. We need radically new kinds of organizations to meet the extreme challenges of today's world and tomorrow's. Keep in mind also that traditional organizational structure was bureaucratic, and now there is a shift toward flatter organizations, especially in innovative, creative organizations.

In the past, organizations have been structured around largely autonomous, self-contained, traditional functions such as accounting, finance, human resources, law, marketing, strategic planning, and so on. While important, they are no longer the building blocks of today's organizations. Today's environment has produced new challenges—crisis management, issues management, global competitiveness, total quality management, environmentalism, and ethics programs, for which the traditional functions are largely inadequate.

To meet tomorrow's challenges, according to organizational structure experts, Mitroff and Mason, they propose that organizations be structured around five new organizational entities:

- Knowledge/Learning Centre
- Recovery/Development Centre
- World Service/Spiritual Centre
- World Class Operations Centre
- Leadership Institute

The world is going through a transition—many would say a fundamental revolution—that is as profound as that from the Agrarian Age to the Industrial Age. Indeed, we have already moved from the Industrial Age to the Information/Knowledge/Systems Age. One sure sign of revolution is the inability of old institutions, old functions, and core competencies to adapt to and cope with new issues.

The environment of business is more volatile than ever and grows more so every day. To meet this challenge, the dominant response of ... business has unfortunately been the adoption of one quick-fix and band-aid approach after another: thus, budgets have been slashed, departments cut, the workforce reduced, early retirements forced, divisions moved offshore, whole departments and functions eliminated or outsourced, and on and on. While many of these actions are necessary, and even help for a while, they do not respond to the real source of the problem.

The fundamental problem is that the basic structure of ... business is outmoded and has outlived its usefulness. While quick fixes and band-aids stop the hemorrhaging for a while, they do not constitute a viable strategy for responding to the true forces prompting change. Nothing less than a radical redesign is required.

You Be the Manager

1. What is your response to the five new organizational entities that the authors propose?

TABLE 6.1 | *Organizational Design Questions and Answers*

Questions to Consider	Design Options	Criteria
How should tasks be grouped into jobs?	• Job Design: Creating an initial division of labour • Job Enlargement: Increasing the number of tasks • Job Simplification: Reducing the number of tasks • Job Enrichment: Adding responsibility and control	• Based on the most efficient way to produce the product/service and serve the customer.
How should jobs be grouped into units?	• Functional Structure: Departments such as Operations, Finance, HR, Sales, and Marketing • Divisional Structures: Product, Geographic, Market • Matrix and Product Team Structures • Strategic Alliances and Network Structures • Outsourcing	• Based on matching the organization's environment, HR, technology and strategy with the organization's size and resources.
How should authority be distributed so that the organization can coordinate and control its activities?	• Hierarchy of Authority: Tall or flat • Centralized or Decentralized Control over Decision Making	• Based on the Minimum Chain of Command principle, which states that the managerial hierarchy should have the fewest levels necessary to use organizational resources efficiently and effectively.
Should the overall organizational structure be formal or flexible?	• Mechanistic Structures: Formal, stable, and rigid • Organic Structures: Fluid, dynamic, and flexible	• Depends on the degree of change in the organizational environment, the use of industrial or new technology, the use of skilled or unskilled labour and the type of strategy (low cost or differentiation).

Organizing is the process by which managers establish the structure of working relationships among employees to allow them to achieve organizational goals efficiently and effectively. **Organizational structure** is the formal system of task and reporting relationships that determines how employees use resources to reach organizational goals.[5] **Organizational design** is the process by which managers make specific organizing choices that result in the construction of a particular organizational structure.[6] See Table 6.1.

How do managers design a structure? The way an organization's structure works depends on the organizing choices managers make about four issues:

- How to group tasks into individual jobs

- How to group jobs into functions and divisions

- How to coordinate and allocate authority in the organization among jobs, functions, and divisions

- Whether to pursue a more formal or flexible structure

organizational structure
A formal system of both task and reporting relationships that coordinates and motivates organizational members so that they work together to reach organizational goals.

organizational design
The process by which managers make specific organizing choices that result in a particular kind of organizational structure.

LO 2

Grouping Tasks into Jobs

THINK ABOUT IT

Design: Competitive Weapon, Innovation Driver[7]

Dr. Roger Martin, Dean of the University of Toronto's Rotman School of Management, says that design "has emerged as a new competitive weapon and key driver of innovation for organizations." He goes on to say that "leveraging the power of design across all aspects of a business can establish and sustain an organization's unique competitive advantage."

According to *Fast Company* magazine, in the real world of design, designers frequently cross disciplines, from architecture to graphic arts to industrial design to film to animation. The purpose of this interrelationship of disciplines is to reflect its sense of boundarylessness and from this perspective to embrace and reframe it in a new way. Design is like business and must be in the service of solving problems. That is why Martin says that "design skills and business skills are converging." Design, therefore, matters to all employees because of its impact beyond the organization. For example, think of an organization's design efforts as they impact sales and marketing efforts. The implications are huge.

You Be the Manager

1. What are some additional implications of the organization design?
2. Can you think of an example where poor organization had disastrous consequences?

---

job design
The process by which managers decide how to divide tasks into specific jobs.

The first step in organizational design is **job design**, the process by which managers decide how to divide tasks into specific jobs. Managers at McDonald's, for example, have decided how best to divide the tasks required to provide customers with fast, cheap food in each McDonald's restaurant. After experimenting with different job arrangements, McDonald's managers decided on a basic division of labour among chefs and food servers. Managers allocated all the tasks involved in actually cooking the food (putting oil in the fat fryers, opening packages of frozen french fries, putting beef patties on the grill, making salads, and so on) to the job of chef. They allocated all the tasks involved in giving the food to customers (such as greeting customers; taking orders; putting fries and burgers into bags; adding salt, pepper, and serviettes; and taking money) to food servers. They also created other jobs—the job of dealing with drive-through customers, the job of keeping the restaurant clean, and the job of shift manager responsible for overseeing employees and responding to unexpected events. The result of the job design process is a **division of labour** among employees, one that McDonald's and other managers have discovered through experience is most efficient.

division of labour
The overall result of job design among employees in an organization.

Establishing an appropriate division of labour among employees is a critical part of the organizing process, one that is vital to increasing efficiency and effectiveness. At McDonald's, the tasks associated with chef and food server were split into different jobs because managers found that for the kind of food McDonald's serves, this approach was most efficient. When employees are given fewer tasks to perform (so that their jobs become more specialized), they become more productive at performing the tasks that constitute their jobs.

A strict division of labour is not the only way to organize jobs in a fast food restaurant, however. At Subway sandwich shops, there is no division of labour among the people who make the sandwiches, wrap the sandwiches, give them to customers, and take the money. The roles of chef and food server are combined into one role. This different division of tasks and jobs is efficient for Subway and not for McDonald's because Subway serves a limited menu of mostly submarine-style sandwiches that are prepared to order. Subway's production system is far simpler than McDonald's because McDonald's menu is much more varied and its chefs must cook many different kinds of foods.

Managers of every organization must analyze the range of tasks to be performed and then create jobs that best allow the organization to give customers the goods and services they want. In deciding how to assign tasks to individual jobs, however, managers must be careful not to go too far with **job simplification**—the process of reducing the number of tasks that each employee performs.[8] Too much job simplification may reduce efficiency rather than increase it if workers find their simplified jobs boring and monotonous, become demotivated and unhappy, and as a result perform at a low level.

job simplification
Reducing the number of tasks that each worker performs.

Job Enlargement and Job Enrichment

Researchers have looked at ways to create a division of labour and design individual jobs to encourage employees to perform at a higher level and be more satisfied with their work. Based on this research, they have proposed job enlargement and job enrichment as better ways than job simplification to group tasks into jobs.

Job enlargement increases the *number of different tasks* in a given job by changing the division of labour.[9] For example, because Subway food servers make the food as well as serve it, their jobs are "larger" than the jobs of McDonald's food servers. The idea behind job enlargement is that increasing the range of tasks performed by an employee will reduce boredom and fatigue and may increase motivation to perform at a high level—increasing both the quantity and the quality of goods and services provided.

job enlargement
Increasing the number of different tasks in a given job by changing the division of labour.

Job enrichment increases the *degree of responsibility* a worker has over his or her job by, for example, (1) empowering employees to experiment to find new or better ways of doing the job, (2) encouraging employees to develop new skills, (3) allowing employees to decide how to do the work and giving them the responsibility for deciding how to respond to unexpected situations, and (4) allowing employees to monitor and measure their own performance.[10] The idea behind job enrichment is that increasing employees' responsibility increases their involvement in their jobs and thus increases their interest in the quality of the goods they make or the services they provide.

job enrichment
Increasing the degree of responsibility a worker has over his or her job.

In general, managers who make design choices that increase job enrichment and job involvement are likely to increase the degree to which workers behave flexibly rather than rigidly or mechanically. Narrow, specialized jobs are likely to lead people to behave in predictable ways; employees who perform a variety of tasks and who are allowed and encouraged to discover new and better ways to perform their jobs are likely to act flexibly and creatively. For example, in November 2008, Ubisoft and Allen Carr teamed up to publish the video game based on the successful "Allen Carr's Easyway to Stop Smoking" method.[11] Thus, managers who enlarge and enrich jobs create a flexible organizational structure, and those who simplify jobs create a more formal structure. If employees are also grouped into self-managed work teams, the organization is likely to be flexible because team members provide support to each other and can learn from one another.

For example, the video-game development industry has earned a reputation as a sweatshop. However, the design of how work gets done is beginning to change, says Cédric Orvoine, Canadian spokesperson for Ubisoft, whose largest studio is in Montreal, Québec. For him, "It's all a matter of doing your planning and your milestones efficiently so you can get your game done in time without burning out people." Trevor Fencott, president of Toronto games publisher Groove Games, says that although a passion for video games drives many workers to put in long hours voluntarily, two years ago Ubisoft Montreal established a *bureau de project*, a workplace design involving a team of 60 people dedicated to planning and streamlining game production. Instead of a single producer being responsible for each project, now each management team also includes a human resources staffer and a planner. "We're working really hard to make sure that the crunch periods are as short as possible," Orvoine says. In addition, he says, the company offers bonuses and time off at the end of the project to compensate for crunch time.[12]

L O 3

Grouping Jobs into Functional, Divisional, and Networked Structures

THINK ABOUT IT

Becoming More Like Design Shops[13]

Design skills and business skills are converging. To be successful in the future, business people will have to become more like designers—more "masters of heuristics" than "managers of algorithms."—Dr. Roger Martin, Dean of the University of Toronto's Rotman School of Management

A heuristic is the ability to visualize and invent; it is both an art and a science. We could say that Wayne Gretzky in playing hockey did so heuristically. The science was in his ability to understand the game of hockey and to play it well; the art was in his ability to know where the puck would be, not where it was at.

Roger Martin (Dean of the Rotman School at the University of Toronto) is once again reminding us that we need more heuristics—a way of understanding the world and the people in it—than algorithms—packaging or routinizing a solution in a certain way; we need a greater sense of discovery than simply to solve what is right in front of us. Key companies that succeeded with these kinds of solution-driven algorithms were McDonald's (mass-produced hamburgers), Procter & Gamble (brand management success), and Wal-Mart stores (superior processes). We could say that these companies "took the mystery" out of hamburgers, brands, and processes, and developed very efficient formulae (algorithms).

Today, in designing organizations, developing *perspective* is more important than "Is this your final answer?" In a world that is constantly changing, the older "formula-producing" design (or code) for company success is now too static. In an effort to get customers back into their stores, for example, they have had to try different approaches with different menus precisely because the old formula or algorithm is running out of steam. As for our future designs, Roger Martin says, "I believe we are transitioning into a twenty-first century world in which value creation is moving back to the world of taking mysteries and turning them into heuristics. ... The twenty-first century presents us with an opportunity to delve into mysteries and come up with new heuristics."

Some of the "mysteries" that organizations are now facing include such questions as: What do customers really want? How do we as an organization enable our employees to become "masters of heuristics" more than "masters of algorithms"?

These question harken back to William Thorsell, former editor of The *Globe and Mail*, who reminded us that we need "more Shakespeare" (mysteries/heuristics) and "less Adam Smith" (algorithms/code). Table 6.2 shows how this shift will look.[14]

You Be the Manager

1. What are some "design" conclusions you can make from what Roger Martin says?
2. Review Table 6.2. What are some implications of grouping jobs into functions and divisions?

TABLE 6.2 | *Modern Firms Must Become More Like Design Shops*

Feature	From "Traditional Firm ..."	... To "Design Shop"
Flow of Work	Ongoing tasks	Projects
Life	Permanent assignments	Defined Terms
Source of Status	Managing big budgets and large staffs	Solving "wicked problems"
Style of Work	Defined roles Wait until it is "right"	Collaborative Iterative
Mode of Thinking	Deductive Inductive	Deductive Inductive Abductive
Dominant Attitude	We can only do what we have budget to do Constraints are the enemy	There is nothing that cannot be done Constraints increase the challenge and excitement

Once managers have decided which tasks to allocate to which jobs, they face the next organizing decision: how to group jobs together to best match the needs of the organization's environment, strategy, technology, and human resources. Most top-management teams decide to group jobs into departments and develop a functional structure to use organizational resources. As the organization grows, managers design a divisional structure or a more complex matrix or product team structure.

Choosing a structure and then designing it so that it works as intended is a significant challenge. As noted in Chapter 5, managers reap the rewards of a well-thought-out strategy only if they choose a suitable type of structure initially and then execute the strategy. The ability to make the right kinds of organizing choices is often what sets effective and ineffective managers apart.

Functional Structure

A function is a group of people, working together, who possess similar skills or use the same kind of knowledge, tools, or techniques to perform their jobs. Manufacturing, sales, and research and development are often organized into functional departments. A **functional structure** is an organizational structure composed of all the departments that an organization requires to produce its goods or services. Pier 1 Imports, a home furnishings company, uses a functional structure to supply its customers with a range of goods from around the world to satisfy their desires for new and innovative products.

Pier 1's main functions are finance and administration, merchandising (purchasing the goods), stores (managing the retail outlets), logistics (managing product distribution), marketing, human resources, and real estate. Each job inside a function exists

functional structure
An organizational structure composed of all the departments that an organization requires to produce its goods or services.

because it helps the function perform the activities necessary for high organizational performance. Thus, within the logistics department are all the jobs necessary to distribute and transport products efficiently to stores. Inside the marketing department are all the jobs (such as promotion, photography, and visual communication) that are necessary to increase the appeal of Pier 1's products to customers.

There are several advantages to grouping jobs according to function. First, when people who perform similar jobs are grouped together, they can learn from watching one another. Thus they become more specialized and can perform at a higher level. The tasks associated with one job often are related to the tasks associated with another job, which encourages cooperation within a function. Second, when people who perform similar jobs are grouped together, managers can monitor and evaluate their performance more easily.[15] Finally, as we saw in Chapter 2, managers like functional structure because it allows them to create the set of functions they need for scanning and monitoring the task and general environments.[16]

As an organization grows, and its strategy changes to produce a wider range of goods and services for different kinds of customers, several problems can make a functional structure less efficient and effective.[17] First, managers in different functions may find it more difficult to communicate and coordinate with one another when they are responsible for several different kinds of products, especially as the organization grows both domestically and internationally. Second, functional managers may become so preoccupied with supervising their own specific departments and achieving their departmental goals that they lose sight of organizational goals. If that happens, organizational effectiveness will suffer because managers will be viewing issues and problems facing the organization only from their own, relatively narrow, departmental perspectives.[18] Both of these problems can reduce efficiency and effectiveness.

Divisional Structures: Product, Geographic, and Market

As the problems associated with growth and diversification increase over time, managers must search for new ways to organize their activities to overcome the problems linked with a functional structure. Most managers of large organizations choose a **divisional structure** and create a series of business units to produce a specific kind of product for a specific kind of customer. Each division is a collection of functions or departments that work together to produce the product. The goal behind the change to a divisional structure is to create smaller, more manageable units within the organization. There are three forms of divisional structure (see Figure 6.1).[19]

divisional structure
An organizational structure composed of separate business units within which are the functions that work together to produce a specific product for a specific customer.

When managers organize divisions according to the type of good or service they provide, they adopt a *product* structure. When managers organize divisions according to the area of the country or world they operate in, they adopt a *geographic* structure. When managers organize divisions according to the types of customers they focus on, they adopt a *market* structure.

Product Structure

product structure
An organizational structure in which each product line or business is handled by a self-contained division.

Using a **product structure** (see Figure 6.1A), managers place each distinct product line or business in its own self-contained division and give divisional managers the responsibility for devising an appropriate business-level strategy to allow the division to compete effectively in its industry or market.[20] Each division is self-contained because it has a complete set of all the functions—marketing, R&D, finance, and so on—that it needs to produce or provide goods or services efficiently and effectively. Functional managers report to divisional managers, and divisional managers report to top or corporate managers.

FIGURE 6.1 | Product, Market, and Geographic Structures

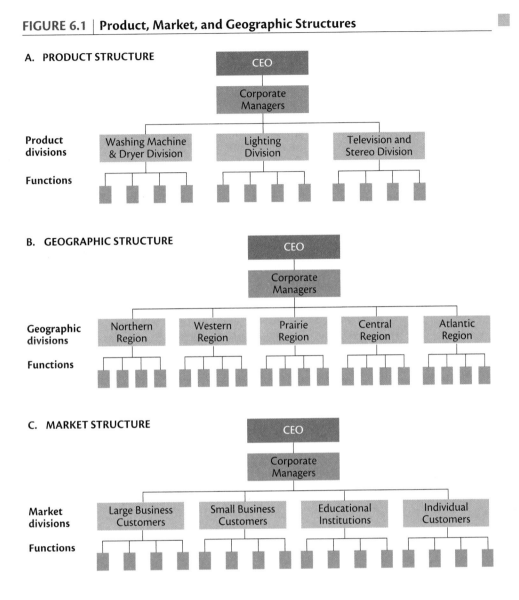

A. PRODUCT STRUCTURE

CEO
Corporate Managers

Product divisions: Washing Machine & Dryer Division | Lighting Division | Television and Stereo Division

Functions

B. GEOGRAPHIC STRUCTURE

CEO
Corporate Managers

Geographic divisions: Northern Region | Western Region | Prairie Region | Central Region | Atlantic Region

Functions

C. MARKET STRUCTURE

CEO
Corporate Managers

Market divisions: Large Business Customers | Small Business Customers | Educational Institutions | Individual Customers

Functions

Grouping functions into divisions focused on particular products has several advantages for managers at all levels in the organization. First, a product structure allows functional managers to specialize in only one product area, so they are able to build expertise and fine-tune their skills in this particular area. Second, each division's managers can become experts in their industry; this expertise helps them choose and develop a business-level strategy to differentiate their products or lower their costs while meeting the needs of customers. Third, a product structure frees corporate managers from the need to supervise each division's day-to-day operations directly; this latitude allows corporate managers to create the best corporate-level strategy to maximize the organization's future growth and ability to create value. Corporate managers are likely to make fewer mistakes about which businesses to diversify into or how best to expand internationally, for example, because they are able to take an organizationwide view.[21] Corporate managers also are likely better evaluate how well divisional managers are doing, and they can intervene and take corrective action as needed.

The extra layer of management, the divisional management layer, can improve the use of organizational resources. Moreover, a product structure puts divisional managers close to their customers and lets them respond quickly and appropriately to the changing task environment. Organizations sometimes change their divisional strategy because of market changes. Even though organizations in the past were generally organized as functional bureaucracies of manufacturing, sales, and R&D, which were coordinated and controlled at the top, today organizations use a complex mix of these structures. For example, AT&T is split into three companies on the basis of product but continues to use the mix of markets, products, regions, and functions and processes. Its Network Services Division is structured according to processes such as provisioning, maintenance, leadership, and human resource management.[22] As well, the City of Toronto and its Water Supply and Water Pollution Control Sections, in response to its challenges from new technologies, operations and maintenance practices, and to its business-oriented organizational structures, established the Works Best Practices Program (WBPP) in 2002. The City designed, restructured, and implemented a unique Performance and Operations Management System (POMS) that now consolidates information at all levels, including unit processes, complete plant facilities, and the entire Water Supply and Water Pollution Control Sections. The result: $36 million annual savings.[23]

Business Plan Checklist

- Determine the kind of organizational structure which best suits your venture.
- Create an organizational chart. Include this in section 7 of the business plan, the Organization Plan in Appendix A.

Geographic Structure

When organizations expand rapidly both at home and abroad, functional structures can create special problems because managers in one central location may find it increasingly difficult to deal with the different problems and issues that may arise in each region of a country or area of the world. In these cases, a **geographic structure**, in which divisions are broken down by geographical location, is often chosen (see Figure 6.1B). To achieve the corporate mission of providing next-day mail service, Fred Smith, chair, president, and CEO of Federal Express, "with transportation in his blood,"[24] chose a geographic structure and divided up operations by creating a division in each region. Large retailers often use a geographic structure. Since the needs of retail customers differ by region—for example, umbrellas in Vancouver and down-filled parkas in the Prairies and the East—a geographic structure gives regional retail managers the flexibility they need to choose products that best meet the needs of regional customers.

geographic structure
An organizational structure in which each region of a country or area of the world is served by a self-contained division.

Market Structure

Sometimes, the pressing issue managers face is how to group functions according to the type of customer buying the product, in order to tailor the organization's products to each customer's unique demands. Telus, based in Burnaby, BC, is structured around six customer-focused business units: Consumer Solutions, focused on households and individuals; Business Solutions, focused on small- to medium-sized businesses and entrepreneurs; Client Solutions, focused on large organizations in Canada; Partner Solutions, focused on Canadian and global carriers into and within Canada; Wireless

Telus Communications Inc.
www.telus.com

Solutions, focused on people and businesses on the go; and Telus Québec, a Telus company for the Quebec marketplace.

To satisfy the needs of diverse customers, Telus adopts a **market structure** (also called a *customer structure*), which groups divisions according to the particular kinds of customers they serve (see Figure 6.1C). A market structure allows managers to be both responsive to the needs of their customers and able to act flexibly to make decisions in response to customers' changing needs.

market structure
An organizational structure in which each kind of customer is served by a self-contained division; also called "customer structure."

Matrix and Product Team Designs

Moving to a product, market, or geographic divisional structure means managers can respond more quickly and flexibly to the particular set of circumstances they confront. However, when the environment is dynamic and rapidly changing, and uncertainty is high, even a divisional structure may not provide managers with enough flexibility to respond to the environment quickly enough. When technology or customer needs are changing rapidly and the environment is very uncertain, managers must design the most flexible organizational structure available: a matrix structure or a *product team structure* (see Figure 6.2).

FIGURE 6.2 | Matrix and Product Team Structures

A. MATRIX STRUCTURE

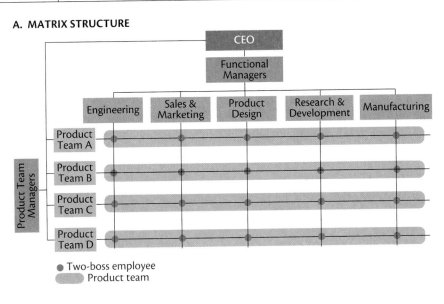

B. PRODUCT TEAM STRUCTURE

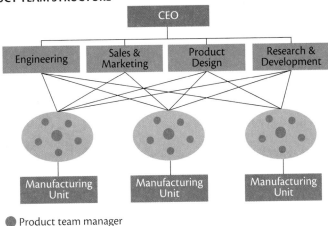

matrix structure
An organizational structure
that simultaneously groups
people and resources by
function and by product.

Matrix Structure

In a **matrix structure**, managers group people and resources in two ways simultaneously: by function and by product.[25] Employees are grouped into *functions* to allow them to learn from one another and become more skilled and productive. Employees are also grouped into *product teams*, in which members of different functions work together to develop a specific product. The result is a complex network of reporting relationships among product teams and functions that makes the matrix structure very flexible (see Figure 6.2A). Each person in a product team reports to two managers: (1) a functional manager, who assigns individuals to a team and evaluates their performance from a functional point of view, and (2) the manager of the product team, who evaluates their performance on the team.

The functional employees assigned to product teams change over time as the specific skills that the team needs change. At the beginning of the product development process, for example, engineers and R&D specialists are assigned to a product team because their skills are needed to develop new products. When a provisional design has been established, marketing experts are assigned to the team to gauge how customers will respond to the new product. Manufacturing personnel join when it is time to find the most efficient way to produce the product. As their specific jobs are completed, team members leave and are reassigned to new teams. In this way, the matrix structure makes the most use of human resources.

To keep the matrix structure flexible, product teams are empowered and team members are responsible for making most of the important decisions involved in product development.[26] The product team manager acts as a facilitator, controlling the financial resources and trying to keep the project on time and within budget. The functional managers try to ensure that the product is the best that it can be in order to make the most of its differentiated appeal.

High-tech companies have been using matrix structures successfully for many years. These companies operate in environments where new product developments happen monthly or yearly and the need to innovate quickly is vital to the organization's survival. The matrix structure provides enough flexibility for managers to keep pace with a changing and increasingly complex environment. For this reason, matrixes also have been designed by managers who want to control international operations as they move abroad and face problems of coordinating their domestic and foreign divisions.[27] Motorola, for example, operates a global matrix structure because it hopes to obtain synergies from cooperation among its worldwide divisions.

A global matrix structure allows an organization's domestic divisions to supply its foreign divisions quickly with knowledge about new R&D advances in order to help the foreign divisions gain a competitive advantage in their local markets. Likewise, the foreign divisions can transmit new product marketing ideas to domestic divisions that may give the domestic divisions an advantage in the domestic market. The expression "Think locally and act globally" describes the way managers in global matrix structures should behave.[28]

Product Team Structure

The dual reporting relationships that are at the heart of a matrix structure have always been difficult for managers and employees to deal with. Often, the functional manager and the product manager make conflicting demands on team members, who do not know which manager to satisfy first. Also, functional and product team managers may come into conflict over precisely who is in charge of which team members and for how long. To avoid these problems, managers have devised a way of organizing people and resources that still allows an organization to be flexible but makes its structure easier to operate: a product team structure.

The **product team structure** differs from a matrix structure in two ways: (1) It does away with dual reporting relationships for employees, and (2) functional employees

product team structure
An organizational structure
in which employees are
permanently assigned to a
cross-functional team and
report only to the product
team manager or to one of his
or her direct subordinates.

are permanently assigned to a cross-functional team that is empowered to bring a new or redesigned product to market. A **cross-functional team** is a group of individuals brought together from different departments to perform organizational tasks. When individuals are grouped into cross-departmental teams, the artificial boundaries between departments disappear, and a narrow focus on departmental goals is replaced with a general interest in working together to achieve organizational goals. The results of such changes have been dramatic: For example, Chrysler Canada's use of cross-functional teams has reduced the time it takes to retool for a new product from months to just weeks.

Members of a cross-functional team report only to the product team manager or to one of his or her direct subordinates. The functional managers have only an informal, advisory relationship with members of the product teams. These managers counsel and help cross-functional team members, share knowledge among teams, and provide new technological developments that can help improve each team's performance (see Figure 6.2B).[29]

cross-functional team
A group of individuals from different departments brought together to perform organizational tasks.

THINK ABOUT IT

Native Communities with Cash; Big Banks Seeking Alliances[30]

Anticipated and unprecedented economic development is in the air as a result of native communities, flush with cash from land claim deals—almost $1.2 billion in the hands of First Nations groups, says Margot Geduld, a spokesperson for Indian and Northern Affairs Canada. Perhaps it is not the best motivation in the world, but the big banks know about this and are seeking to make alliances with them. The only bank branch on the Wikwemikong native reserve—located on a picturesque island in Lake Huron, a six-hour drive north of Toronto—closed in 1999. When its 3000 permanent residents left to do banking elsewhere, they did their shopping away from the reserve as well. For Walter Manitowabi and his family, this spelled trouble, since they ran the supermarket, hardware store, gas station, and a handful of other businesses. Finding another bank became a priority. In 2001, an "agency" bank arrangement with Royal Bank Canada (RBC) became a reality. Residents then started using Walter's services again.

Canada's biggest banks all took an interest in developing business relationships with Aboriginal groups in the mid-1990s when the prospect of land claim settlements and self-government promised large pools of money for First Nations groups, located on 2900 reserve lands, that would be spent on business and infrastructure development. RBC's Ms. Carla Woodward, national manager of Aboriginal banking at RBC who is herself Métis, says these initiatives are integral to relationship building. "It's beyond corporate citizenship," she says. "It's a smart business decision."

You Be the Manager

1. What is so smart about the decision RBC made?

Recently, innovations in organizational structure—strategic alliances, joint ventures, and network structures—have been sweeping through Canadian, American, and European businesses. These structures allow for considerably more flexibility by creating links outside the organization. We cover each of these in turn.

Strategic Alliances and Joint Ventures

Many people use the terms *strategic alliance* and *joint venture* interchangeably, but technically they are different. A **strategic alliance** is a formal agreement that commits two or more companies to exchange or share their resources in order to produce and

strategic alliance
An agreement in which managers pool or share their organization's resources and know-how with a foreign company, and the two organizations share the rewards and risks of starting a new venture.

joint venture
A strategic alliance among two or more companies that agree to establish jointly and share the ownership of a new business.

network structure
A series of strategic alliances that an organization creates with suppliers, manufacturers, and distributors to produce and market a product.

boundaryless organization
An organization whose members are linked by computers, faxes, computer-aided design systems, and video teleconferencing, and who rarely, if ever, see one another face to face.

iGen Knowledge Solutions Inc.
www.igeninc.com

business-to-business (B2B) networks
A group of organizations that join together and use software to link themselves to potential global suppliers to increase efficiency and effectiveness.

market a product.[31] A **joint venture** is a strategic alliance among two or more companies that agree to establish jointly and share the ownership of a new business.

Japanese car companies such as Toyota and Honda have formed a series of strategic alliances with suppliers of inputs such as car axles, gearboxes, and air-conditioning systems. More and more Canadian, American, and European organizations are relying on strategic alliances to gain access to low-cost foreign sources of inputs. This approach allows managers to keep costs low.

Network Structure

A **network structure** is a series of strategic alliances that an organization creates with suppliers, manufacturers, and distributors to produce and market a product. For instance, Handspring, which is known for its PDAs (personal digital assistants), does not actually make them. A network of partner companies manufacture, design, ship and support Handspring's products. Handspring's role is to manage the network. Network structures allow an organization to bring resources (workers especially) together on a long-term basis in order to find new ways to reduce costs and increase the quality of products—without experiencing the high costs of operating a complex organizational structure (such as the costs of employing many managers).

The ability of managers to develop networks to produce or provide the goods and services customers want, rather than creating a complex organizational structure to do so, has led many researchers and consultants to popularize the idea of a **boundaryless organization** composed of people who are linked by computers, faxes, computer-aided design systems, and video teleconferencing, and who rarely, if ever, see one another face to face. This structure is also referred to as *network organizations, learning organizations,* or *virtual corporations.*[32] People are used when their services are needed, much as in a matrix structure, but they are not formal members of an organization. They are functional experts who form an alliance with an organization, fulfill their contractual obligations, and then move on to the next project.

iGEN Knowledge Solutions Inc., based in New Westminster, BC, operates as a virtual organization to bring technical solutions to its business clients. Associates work from home offices connected by wireless technologies and the Internet and collaborate to solve client problems. The virtual model allows fast cycle times for idea implementation, service delivery, and product development. The model also makes it easy to set up operations in different regions of the country without large overhead costs.

Leadership in virtual organizations may be more important and more difficult than in conventional organizations. A study of a number of successful virtual organizations found that the most important factor was a leader organization with a strategically important core competence.[33] The leader of the organization manages and inspires the other organizational relationships. Because virtual organizations have similar characteristics to voluntary organizations, leaders need to be able to build trust while recognizing that they do not have authority or full control over partners.

The push to lower costs has also led to the development of electronic **business-to-business (B2B) networks**, in which most or all of the companies in an industry (e.g., car makers) use the same software platform to link to each other and establish industry specifications and standards. Then, these companies jointly list the quantity and specifications of the inputs they require and invite bids from the thousands of potential suppliers around the world. Suppliers also use the same software platform so that electronic bidding, auctions, and transactions are possible between buyers and sellers around the world. The idea is that high-volume standardized transactions can help drive down costs at the industry level. Canada's Mediagrif has B2B networks in nine areas: electronics components, wines and spirits, computer equipment, telecommunications equipment, automotive aftermarket parts, truck parts, government e-tendering (which includes the MERX electronic tendering system used by the federal government of Canada), medical equipment, and IT parts and equipment.[34]

Outsourcing

In a study of 22 industries in Canada, 15 increased their use of inputs from other industries between 1986 and 2002, most by a significant amount. This increase is a measure of how industries are specializing in their core competency while farming out the manufacture of parts or the provision of services to other firms. This process is commonly called **outsourcing**.

BusinessWeek named Canada as the #1 outsourcing destination nation out of 30 nations in the world based on our ability to compete.[35] See Figure 6.3. Australia and Ireland tied for second place with 42 points, and Singapore came in third with 40 points. India tied for fifth place with New Zealand with 38 points. China scored 27 points ranking it 19th. Ukraine was last with 20 points. Whether outsourcing to other firms in Canada, or *offshoring* to firms around the globe, the motivation is the same—to boost efficiency and lower costs. Two of the four industries where outsourcing fell were education and the nonprofit sector, which are relatively insulated from the market forces pushing for more efficiency.[36]

FIGURE 6.3[37] | **Outsourcing: Canada versus China**

No. 1—Canada Total Score: 43	
Criterion	**Rating**
Language	Excellent 5
Government support	Good 3
Labour pool	Very good 4
Infrastructure	Excellent 5
Educational system	Very good 4
Cost	Fair 2
Political and economic environments	Excellent 5
Cultural compatibility	Excellent 5
Global and legal maturity	Excellent 5
Data and intellectual property security and privacy	Excellent 5
No. 19—China Total Score: 27	
Criterion	**Rating**
Language	Fair 2
Government support	Good 3
Labour pool	Good 3
Infrastructure	Very good 4
Educational system	Good 3
Cost	Very good 4
Political and economic environments	Good 3
Cultural compatibility	Fair 2
Global and legal maturity	Fair 2
Data and intellectual property security and privacy	Poor 1

outsourcing
Using outside suppliers and
manufacturers to produce
goods and services.

The use of **outsourcing** is increasing rapidly as organizations recognize the many opportunities that the approaches offer to reduce costs and increase organizational flexibility. Canadian Pacific Railway (CPR) outsources the maintenance of applications for which it does not need to develop in-house expertise. For example, it has outsourced the maintenance of some of its legacy applications to RIS and also outsources its mainframe infrastructure to IBM. When CPR did the work itself in-house everything was not running smoothly. Allen Borak, vice-president for information services at CPR in Calgary, said, "I would say that part of our business wasn't well managed." The decision to outsource has left CPR free to concentrate on what it does best.[38] Stephen Libman, president of Libman Chimo Travel in Montreal, has a similar story. He has gained 90 percent of his time back after he outsourced to another Montreal company, Eternitee Systems Inc., Libman's desktop hardware and software and its network for a fixed monthly fee. Libman says he spends about the same amount of money on technology as before but has gained his time back.[39]

Companies that specialize in outsourced work, such as EDS Corporation—which manages the information systems of large organizations such as Xerox, Eastman Kodak, and even the Central Bank of Canada[40]—are major beneficiaries of this new approach. While many companies use outsourcing, not all have been successful at implementing it. Managers should be aware of the following concerns when considering its use: (1) choosing the wrong activities to outsource, (2) choosing the wrong vendor, (3) writing a poor contract, (4) failing to consider personnel issues, (5) losing control over the activity, (6) ignoring the hidden costs, and (7) failing to develop an exit strategy (for either moving to another vendor or deciding to bring the activity back in-house.)[41] A review of 91 outsourcing activities found that writing a poor contract and losing control of the activity were the most likely reasons for an outsourcing venture to fail. Designing organizational structure is becoming an increasingly complex management function. To maximize efficiency and effectiveness, managers must carefully assess the relative benefits of having their own organization perform a functional activity versus forming an alliance with another organization to perform the activity.

L O 4

Allocating Authority and Coordinating Activities

THINK ABOUT IT

Bureaucracy's Radical Reno[42]

Is it possible that Canada's federal government can act more like businesses on Bay Street? That seems to be what is now taking place—at least when it comes to its procurement policy: public-sector employees behaving more like their private-sector brethren. In practice, this will mean that the government, similar to what Wal-Mart does, will attempt to flex its purchasing power muscle in order to get the best deal from suppliers. Scott Brison, Minister of Public Works, whose department is in charge of procurement reform, said, "What we are doing as a government is what large companies did 20 years ago. We can't defend antiquated, expensive, inefficient practices to our neighbours and friends outside of government."

The way the bureaucracy has gone about its business is now being challenged with this initiative. Mike Murphy, senior vice-president at the Canadian Chamber of Commerce, said, "You can't help but agree that this is the right philosophy. These initiatives reflect that the way Ottawa has been doing things needs to change. They have to do things much smarter." Obviously a new management culture will result from these changes to the organizational structure. The challenges will be immense, of course: reducing the amount of paperwork that businesses, large and small, file with bureaucrats; maximizing the value of its real estate properties; and overhauling a regulatory system to ensure harmonization among departments, provinces, and trading partners, most notably the United States.

> Up until now, individual government departments or agencies—and there are close to 100 of them—purchased supplies required for its employees. But under the changes envisaged, Public Works would be responsible for a coordinated purchase of goods. Supplies needed would be grouped into roughly 40 commodity buckets, with each bucket managed by a council composed of relevant industry groups and federal procurement specialists.

You Be the Manager

1. Why is the federal government seeking to make changes to its organizational structure?
2. What are some of the challenges that these changes will evoke?

In organizing, managers group functions and divisions and create the organizational structure best suited to the contingencies they face. Managers' next task is to ensure that there is sufficient coordination among functions and divisions so that organizational resources are used efficiently and effectively. Having discussed how managers divide organizational activities into jobs, functions, and divisions to increase efficiency and effectiveness, we now look at how they put the parts back together.

Allocating Authority

As organizations grow and produce a wider range of goods and services, the size and number of their functions and divisions increase. To coordinate the activities of people, functions, and divisions, and to allow them to work together effectively, managers must develop a clear hierarchy of authority.[43] **Authority** is the power vested in a manager to make decisions and use resources to achieve organizational goals by virtue of his or her position in an organization. The **hierarchy of authority** is an organization's chain of command—the relative authority that each manager has—extending from the CEO at the top, down through the middle managers and first-line managers, to the nonmanagerial employees who actually make goods or provide services. Every manager, at every level of the hierarchy, supervises one or more subordinates. The term **span of control** refers to the number of subordinates who report directly to a manager.

authority
The power to hold people accountable for their actions and to make decisions concerning the use of organizational resources.

hierarchy of authority
An organization's chain of command, specifying the relative authority of each manager.

span of control
The number of subordinates who report directly to a manager.

Tall and Flat Organizations

As an organization grows in size (normally measured by the number of its managers and employees), its hierarchy of authority normally lengthens, making the organizational structure taller. A *tall* organization has many levels of authority relative to company size; a *flat* organization has fewer levels relative to company size (see Figure 6.4).[44] As a hierarchy becomes taller, problems may result that make the organization's structure less flexible and slow managers' response to changes in the organizational environment.

FIGURE 6.4 | Tall and Flat Organizations

A. FLAT ORGANIZATIONAL HIERARCHY
(3 LEVELS IN THE HIERARCHY)

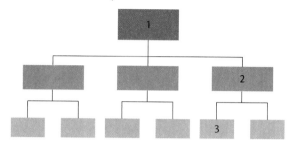

B. TALL ORGANIZATIONAL HIERARCHY
(7 LEVELS IN THE HIERARCHY)

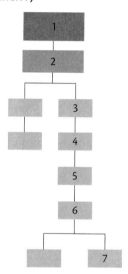

For instance, communication problems may arise. When an organization has many levels in the hierarchy, it can take a long time for the decisions and orders of upper-level managers to reach managers further down in the hierarchy, and it can take a long time for top managers to learn how well their decisions worked out. Feeling out of touch, top managers may want to verify that lower-level managers are following orders and may require written confirmation from them. Middle managers, who know they will be held strictly accountable for their actions, start devoting more time to the process of making decisions in order to improve their chances of being right. They might even try to avoid responsibility by making top managers decide what actions to take.

Another communication problem that can result is the distortion of commands and orders being transmitted up and down the hierarchy, which causes managers at different levels to interpret differently what is happening. Distortion of orders and messages can be accidental, occurring because different managers interpret messages from their own narrow functional perspectives. Or it can be intentional, when managers low in the hierarchy decide to interpret information to increase their own personal advantage.

Another problem with tall hierarchies is that usually they indicate an organization is employing too many managers, and managers are expensive. Managerial salaries, benefits, offices, and secretaries are a huge expense for organizations. Large companies such as IBM and General Motors pay their managers billions of dollars a year. Throughout the 1990s, hundreds of thousands of middle managers were laid off as companies tried to reduce costs by restructuring and downsizing their workforces.

The Minimum Chain of Command

To ward off the problems that result when an organization becomes too tall and employs too many managers, top managers need to work out whether they are employing the right number of middle and first-line managers, and to see whether they can redesign their organizational structure to reduce the number of managers. Top managers might well follow a basic organizing principle—the principle of the minimum chain of command—which states that top managers should always construct a hierarchy with the fewest levels of authority necessary to use organizational resources efficiently and effectively.

Effective managers constantly scrutinize their hierarchies to see whether the number of levels can be reduced—for example, by eliminating one level and giving the responsibilities of managers at that level to managers above and empowering employees below. This practice has become more common in Canada and the United States as companies that are battling low-cost foreign competitors search for new ways to reduce costs.

One organization that is trying to empower staff is Ducks Unlimited Canada of Stonewall, Manitoba, a private nonprofit charitable organization founded by sportsmen, that is devoted to preserving wetlands and associated waterfowl habitats.[45] The company recently went through a reorganization, flattening its management structure. The 330 staff members have been divided into groups to focus on different areas critical to the future of the organization. They are examining such issues as performance, development, and job classification.

Ducks Unlimited Canada
www.ducks.ca

Gary Goodwin, past director of human resources, explains that "the reorganization was essentially to help empower employees, making it easier for people working in the field to make decisions quickly without having to go up and down the proverbial power ladder."

Deborah Hurst, associate professor, Centre for Innovative Management at Athabasca University, says, "It's the human element that is key to every successful mobile workforce. Technology enables the collaboration and facilitates the transfer of ideas, knowledge and practices, but it is the company's individuals and team members who work together to deliver results. The command-and-control approach to management simply does not work very well in a distributed workforce." While there is technology available to control the work routines of mobile workers, and BlackBerrys that allow managers to constantly and instantly check up on their workers, the most effective mobile workforce management, experts say, focuses on employee empowerment. "They need to manage through trust and measure performance more on outputs than on conformity to prescribed work protocols," says Gail Rieschi, president of Toronto-based vpi, a firm specializing in career and employment management.[46]

Centralization and Decentralization of Authority

Another way in which managers can keep the organizational hierarchy flat is to decentralize authority to lower-level managers and nonmanagerial employees.[47] If managers at higher levels give lower-level employees the responsibility to make important decisions and only manage by exception, then the problems of slow and distorted communication noted previously are kept to a minimum. Moreover, fewer managers are needed because their role is not to make decisions but to act as coach and facilitator and to help other employees make the best decisions. In addition, when decision making is done at the low level in the organization and near the customer, employees are better able to recognize and respond to customer needs.

Decentralizing authority allows an organization and its employees to behave flexibly even as the organization grows and becomes taller. This is why managers are so interested in empowering employees, creating self-managed work teams, establishing cross-functional teams, and even moving to a product team structure. These design innovations help keep the organizational structure flexible and responsive to complex task and general environments, complex technologies, and complex strategies.

While more organizations are taking steps to decentralize authority, too much decentralization has certain disadvantages. If divisions, functions, or teams are given too much decision-making authority, they may begin to pursue their own goals at the expense of organizational goals. Managers in engineering design or R&D, for example, may become so focused on making the best possible product that they fail to realize that the best product may be so expensive that few people will be willing or able to buy it. Also, with too much decentralization, lack of communication among functions or among divisions may prevent possible synergies among them from ever materializing, and organizational performance suffers.

Top managers have to look for the balance between centralization and decentralization of authority that best meets the organization's needs. If managers are in a stable environment, using well-understood technology, and producing staple kinds of products (such as cereal, canned soup, books, or televisions), there is no pressing need to decentralize authority, and managers at the top can maintain control of much of the organizational decision making.[48] However, in uncertain, changing environments where high-tech companies are producing state-of-the-art products, top managers must empower employees and allow teams to make important strategic decisions so that the organization can keep up with the changes taking place.

Procter & Gamble chose to centralize rather than decentralize its management structure. Global operations were divided into four main areas—North America, Europe, the Middle East and Africa, and Asia. In each area, P&G created a new position—global executive vice-president—and made the person in that position responsible for overseeing the operations of all the divisions within his or her world region. Each global executive vice-president is responsible for getting the various divisions within his or her area to cooperate and to share information and knowledge that will lead to synergies; thus, authority is centralized at the world area level. All of these new executive vice-presidents report directly to the president of Procter & Gamble, further centralizing authority.

Tips for Managers
CHOOSING A DIVISIONAL STRUCTURE

1. Describe what appeals to you more as a consumer: a product structure or a geographic structure.

2. In today's new economy, evaluate which structure (product or geographic) will allow the organization to be more competitive.

3. Describe what, for you, are the advantages of a divisional structure.

Choosing a Formal or Flexible Structure Overall

THINK ABOUT IT

Grizzled Workaholics, the BlackBerry, the New Breed[49]

Canadians are spending fewer hours than ever before at work; civil servants are building firewalls to protect themselves from home invasion by BlackBerry. For many, overtime has become more trouble than it is worth. What is behind this new (not) work ethic? What does it mean for Canadian companies? and for our collective future?

For example, Ottawa's Liz Vavasour, 55, is one of the baby boomers who has cut back on her workweek during 2007–2008. She took advantage of a federal program that allows public servants to reduce their workweek within two years of retirement without losing benefits or pension credits. Known as a pre-retirement transition leave, it allows Ms. Vavasour to work three days a week in advance of her retirement in November 2009. "At this stage of my life, I just want a bit more breathing room," she says. "I've found that I have more time to go out for lunch with friends, take yoga in the morning, and help my mother."

(c) Beatham/Corbis

Statistics suggest that aging workaholics and their central faith, the Protestant work ethic, are fast losing office space to a new breed committed to the doctrine of work-life balance. In 2008, Statistics Canada reported that the average worker put in 36.5 hours a week in 2006, down from 38.6 hours three decades earlier.[50] There is even a fledgling backlash against that Trojan Horse of technology, the BlackBerry, ingeniously designed to invade workers' homes and family time. In an effort to repel that incursion, Citizenship and Immigration Canada has implemented a BlackBerry blackout between 7 p.m. and 7 a.m. "People want to find a way of doing their work and having a real life, getting to enjoy time with their families, their kids and aging parents," says Patty Ducharme, national executive vice-president of the Public Service Alliance of Canada. Employers will increasingly have to address the fact that fewer and fewer workers—both men and women—will be willing to sacrifice their home lives for the corporate good.

Carleton University's Linda Duxbury, a professor in the Sprott School of Business in Ottawa, believes this is a time of "transformative organizational change." With "workhorse" baby boomers moving into retirement, and with younger workers dedicated to more balanced lives coming in, businesses will no longer be able to simply load more onto their employees. "The generation-Xers have seen what these incredibly long hours have done to their parents: They saw their parents on Prozac, on stress leave, getting divorced. So they are not prepared to work the long hours." Meanwhile, Ms. Duxbury says, many older baby boomers have burned out and are essentially retired on the job. "They're saying, 'I'm not going to bust my butt for you anymore'." The result, she says, is that organizations will no longer be able to boost profits and productivity simply by demanding more from fewer employees. "We're moving from a buyer's market in labour to a seller's market. And it's going to really be a big shakeup," she says. "Organizations have long exploited their workers' desire for a job and promotion. And now it's coming back to haunt them: we're seeing a decline in hours, a decline in loyalty, and a decline in engagement. All of these things are coming together."

You Be the Manager

1. In your own words, what are your views on how many hours you see as fitting in order to balance home and work?
2. In what ways is the "generational issue" creating new challenges to the flexible versus business-as-usual organizational structure?

Earlier in this chapter, we discussed the choices managers make in deciding how tasks should be organized into jobs and jobs should be grouped into departments. Managers also need to determine how formal or flexible they want the organization to be.

Burns and Stalker proposed two basic ways in which managers can organize and control an organization's activities to respond to characteristics of its external environment: They can use a formal *mechanistic structure* or a flexible *organic structure*.[51] Figure 6.5 illustrates the differences between these two types of structures. After describing these two structures, we discuss what factors managers consider when choosing between them.

Mechanistic Structures

mechanistic structure
An organizational structure in which authority is centralized at the top of the hierarchy, tasks and roles are clearly specified, and employees are closely supervised.

When the environment around an organization is stable, managers tend to choose a mechanistic structure to organize and control activities and make employee behaviour predictable. In a **mechanistic structure**, authority is centralized at the top of the managerial hierarchy, and the vertical hierarchy of authority is the main means used to control subordinates' behaviour. Tasks and roles are clearly specified, subordinates are closely supervised, and the emphasis is on strict discipline and order. Everyone knows his or her place, and there is a place for everyone. A mechanistic structure provides the most efficient way to operate in a stable environment because it allows managers to obtain inputs at the lowest cost, giving an organization the most control over its conversion processes and enabling the most efficient production of goods and services with the smallest expenditure of resources. This explains McDonald's mechanistic structure.

Organic Structures

organic structure
An organizational structure in which authority is decentralized to middle and first-line managers and tasks and roles are left ambiguous to encourage employees to cooperate and respond quickly to the unexpected.

In contrast, when the environment is changing rapidly, it is difficult to obtain access to resources. Managers need to organize their activities in a way that allows them to cooperate, to act quickly to obtain resources (such as new types of wood to produce new kinds of furniture), and to respond effectively to the unexpected. In an **organic structure**,

FIGURE 6.5 | Mechanistic versus Organic Organizations

Characteristic of the Environment	Appropriate Type of Structure
Stable →	**Mechanistic** • Centralized authority • Vertical communication flows • Strict rules and procedures
Changing →	**Organic** • Decentralized authority • Horizontal communication flows • Cross-departmental cooperation

authority is decentralized to middle and first-line managers to encourage them to take responsibility and act quickly to pursue scarce resources. Departments are encouraged to take a cross-departmental or functional perspective, and authority rests with the individuals and departments best positioned to control the current problems the organization is facing. Control in an organic structure is much looser than it is in a mechanistic structure, and reliance on shared norms to guide organizational activities is greater. This is somewhat representative of Blue Water Café, where restaurant staff are dependent on what is fresh and available each day to create their menus.

Managers in an organic structure can react more quickly to a changing environment than can managers in a mechanistic structure. However, an organic structure is generally more expensive to operate, so it is used only when needed—when the organizational environment is unstable and rapidly changing. Organic structures may also work more effectively if managers establish semistructures that govern "the pace, timing, and rhythm of organizational activities and processes." In other words, introducing a bit of structure while preserving most of the flexibility of the organic structure may reduce operating costs.[52]

Factors Affecting Choice of Overall Organizational Structure

Organizational structures need to fit the factors or circumstances that affect the company the most and cause them the most uncertainty.[53] Thus, there is no "best" way to design an organization: Design reflects each organization's specific situation. Four factors are important determinants of organizational structure: the nature of the organizational environment, the type of strategy the organization pursues, the technology the organization uses, and the characteristics of the organization's human resources (see Figure 6.6).[54]

The Organizational Environment

In general, the more quickly the external environment is changing and the greater the uncertainty within it, the greater are the problems a manager faces in trying to gain access to scarce resources. In this situation, to speed decision making and communication and make it easier to obtain resources, managers typically make organizing choices that bring flexibility to the organizational structure.[55] They are likely to decentralize authority and empower lower-level employees to make important operating decisions. In contrast, if the external environment is stable, if resources are readily available, and if uncertainty is low, then less coordination and communication among

FIGURE 6.6 | **Factors Affecting Overall Organizational Structure**

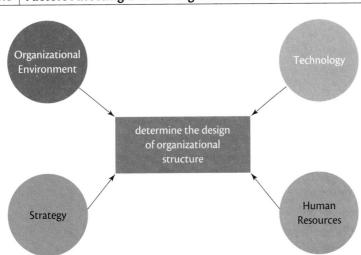

people and functions is needed to obtain resources, and managers can make organizing choices that bring more formality to the organizational structure. Managers in this situation prefer to make decisions within a clearly defined hierarchy of authority and use extensive rules and standard operating procedures to govern activities.

As we discussed in Chapter 2, change is rapid in today's marketplace, and increasing competition both at home and abroad is putting greater pressure on managers to attract customers and increase efficiency and effectiveness. Thus, there has been growing interest in finding ways to structure organizations—such as through empowerment and self-managed teams—to allow people and departments to behave flexibly. A case in point is media executive Kathleen Dore, president of television and radio at CanWestMedia Works, and her unique empowerment management style. In a world dominated by men, she has become a role model for other women. She uses a term "force multiplier," which focuses "on using your skills, abilities, and experience as a magnet which pulls others toward you and makes them want to engage in the undertaking you're about."[56]

Strategy

As discussed in Chapter 5, once managers decide on a strategy, they must choose the right means to implement it. Different strategies often call for the use of different organizational structures. For example, a differentiation strategy aimed at increasing the value customers perceive in an organization's goods and services usually succeeds best in a flexible structure. Flexibility assists a differentiation strategy because managers can develop new or innovative products quickly—an activity that requires extensive cooperation among functions or departments. In contrast, a low-cost strategy that is aimed at driving down costs in all functions usually fares best in a more formal structure, which gives managers greater control over the expenditures and actions of the organization's various departments.[57]

In addition, at the corporate level, when managers decide to expand the scope of organizational activities by, for example, vertical integration or diversification, they need to design a flexible structure to provide sufficient coordination among the different business divisions.[58] As discussed in Chapter 5, many companies have been divesting businesses because managers have been unable to create a competitive advantage to keep them up to speed in fast-changing industries. By moving to a more flexible structure, such as a product division structure, divisional managers gain more control over their different businesses.

Finally, expanding internationally and operating in many different countries challenges managers to create organizational structures that allow organizations to be flexible on a global level.[59] As we discuss later, managers can group their departments or functions and divisions in several ways to allow them to pursue an international strategy effectively.

Technology

Technology is the combination of skills, knowledge, tools, machines, computers, and equipment that are used in the design, production, and distribution of goods and services. As a rule, the more complicated the technology that an organization uses, the more difficult it is for managers and employees to impose strict control on technology or to regulate it efficiently.[60] Thus, the more complicated the technology, the greater is the need for a flexible structure to enhance managers' and employees' ability to respond to unexpected situations and give them the freedom to work out new solutions to the problems they encounter. In contrast, the more routine the technology, the more appropriate a formal structure is because tasks are simple and the steps needed to produce goods and services have been worked out in advance.

The nature of an organization's technology is an important determinant of its structure. Today, there is a growing use of computer-controlled production, and a movement toward using self-managed teams (groups of employees who are given the responsibility for supervising their own activities and for monitoring the quality of the goods and service they provide) to promote innovation, increase quality, and reduce costs. As a result, many companies are trying to make their structures more flexible to take advantage of the value-creating benefits of complex technology.

Human Resources

A final important factor affecting an organization's choice of structure is the characteristics of its human resources. In general, the more highly skilled an organization's workforce and the more people are required to work together in groups or teams to perform their tasks, the more likely is the organization to use a flexible, decentralized structure. Highly skilled employees or those who have internalized strong professional values and norms of behaviour as part of their training usually desire freedom and autonomy and dislike close supervision. Accountants, for example, have learned the need to report company accounts honestly and impartially, and doctors and nurses have absorbed the obligation to give patients the best care possible.

Flexible structures, characterized by decentralized authority and empowered employees, are well suited to the needs of highly skilled people. Similarly, when people work in teams, they must be allowed to interact freely, which also is possible in a flexible organizational structure. Thus, when designing an organizational structure, managers must pay close attention to the workforce and to the work itself.

In summary, an *organization's external environment, strategy, technology,* and *human resources* are the factors to be considered by managers seeking to design the best structure for an organization. The greater the level of uncertainty in an organization's environment, the more complex its strategy and technology, and the more highly qualified and skilled its workforce, the more likely managers will design a structure that is flexible. The more stable an organization's environment, the less complex and better understood its strategy or technology, and the less skilled its workforce, the more likely managers will design an organizational structure that is formal and controlling.

Tips for Managers

DESIGNING STRUCTURE AND JOBS

1. Monitor the challenges an organization faces as it structures its design to meet those challenges.
2. When new structures are implemented, new roles and responsibilities as well as job descriptions will occur.
3. Flexible structures need enriched jobs and a corporate culture that sees value in its organizational flexibility.
4. When managers rethink jobs, roles, and responsibilities, there is always room to build in a sense of empowerment.

Summary and Review

1. **DESIGNING ORGANIZATIONAL STRUCTURE** Organizational structure is the formal system of both task and reporting relationships that determines how employees use resources to achieve organizational goals. The way organizational structures work depends on how tasks are grouped into individual jobs; how jobs are grouped into functions and divisions; how coordination and allocating authority are accomplished; and whether the structure is formal or flexible.

2. **GROUPING TASKS INTO JOBS** Job design is the initial process by which managers group tasks into jobs. To create more interesting jobs, and to get workers to act flexibly, managers can enlarge and enrich jobs.

3. **GROUPING JOBS INTO FUNCTIONAL, DIVISIONAL, AND NETWORKED STRUCTURES** Managers can choose from many kinds of organizational structures to make the best use of organizational resources. Depending on the specific organizing problems they face, managers can choose from functional, divisional (based on product, geography, or market segment), matrix, product team, strategic and network alliances, and outsourcing structures.

4. **ALLOCATING AUTHORITY TO COORDINATE ACTIVITIES** No matter which structure managers choose, they must decide how to distribute authority in the organization, how many levels to have in the hierarchy of authority, and what balance to strike between centralization and decentralization to keep the number of levels in the hierarchy to a minimum. As organizations grow, managers must increase integration and coordination among functions and divisions.

5. **OVERALL STRUCTURE: FORMAL OR FLEXIBLE?** Overall organizational structure is determined by conditions of the environment. When the environment is stable, a mechanistic structure is appropriate. When the environment is changing rapidly, an organic structure is more appropriate. An organic structure is more flexible. To avoid many of the communication and coordination problems that emerge as organizations grow, managers are adopting more flexible structures. The four main determinants of organizational structure are the external environment, strategy, technology, and human resources. In general, the higher the level of uncertainty associated with these factors, the more appropriate is a flexible, adaptable structure as opposed to a formal, rigid one.

Key Terms

authority, p. 195

boundaryless organization, p. 192

business-to-business (B2B)
    networks, p. 192

cross-functional team, p. 191

division of labour, p. 182

divisional structure, p. 186

functional structure, p. 185

geographic structure, p. 188

hierarchy of authority, p. 195

job design, p. 182

job enlargement, p. 183

job enrichment, p. 183

job simplification, p. 183

joint venture, p. 192

market structure, p. 189

matrix structure, p. 190

mechanistic structure, p. 200

network structure, p. 192

organic structure, p. 200

organizational design, p. 181

organizational structure, p. 181

outsourcing, p. 194

product structure, p. 186

product team structure, p. 190

span of control, p. 195

strategic alliance, p. 191

Wrap-Up to Opening Case[61]

We began this chapter with a discussion on the changing workplace. We indicated how such change is not only local but global as well. Vanessa Robinson, of the UK's Chartered Institute of Personnel and Development (CIPD), said that employers had to seriously start implementing new flexible structures in order to attract the best people. That not only made sense, but it also supported effective recruiting. Caroline Waters, director of employment policy at British Telecommunications, pointed out that in the UK alone, 1.1 billion hours were spent just in getting to work. She then asked, "Does that sound like an economy for the twenty-first century?" And, of course, her answer was clear, "I don't think so."

We then shifted our attention to what the CEO must think about and do regarding organizational change and transformation. A 10-point checklist to help leaders of large-scale transformation put their wisdom into practice was highlighted:

1. The CEO must make a strong case for change by clearly and persuasively articulating the factors that are driving it.
2. Senior leaders must set an aggressive, enterprisewide target. Big goals are the key to driving big actions.
3. Senior management must be firmly aligned.
4. An integrated enterprisewide program for change must be put in place.
5. Senior leaders must focus on augmenting capabilities along with cutting costs.
6. "Moments of truth" must be recognized and shared in order to demonstrate commitment.
7. A detailed plan must provide the blueprint.
8. Enabling triggers must be built in from the start.
9. Communication must be proactive and ongoing.
10. The results of change must be sustained.

The more traditional structural elements of organizations, such as product and geographic structures, matrix organizational and teambased designs, tall versus flat organizations, issues of authority, and chain of command, will certainly continue.

The immediate future for business is not going to see a reduction of these issues. Indeed, organizational design and structure will be in the forefront of managers' thinking as they attempt to stay current, hire and maintain the best employees, and remain competitive.

Ask Yourself

1. Which organizational structure is more appealing to you: one with more structure or one with less structure? Before you answer this question, keep in mind also your own personal style and preferences. Why is the structure you feel is more appealing important to you?
2. What will happen to organizations that will not adapt to changing circumstances?

Management in Action

Topics for Discussion and Action

Level 1

1. When and under what conditions might a manager change from a functional structure to (a) a product, (b) a geographic, or (c) a market structure?
2. How do matrix structures and product team structures differ? Why is the product team structure more widely used?
3. How might a salesperson's or secretary's job be enlarged or enriched to make it more motivating?

Level 2

4. Google's organizational structure has been described as being similar to the "Brownian motion," the way the molecules of food colouring move through water in a bottle. View the following video on YouTube, and describe Google's organizational structure: www.youtube.com/watch?v=Q1qoDY-gjKY&eurl=http://www.2-speed.com/2007/03/andy-grove-describes-googles-organizational-structure-as-brownian-motion/
5. Identify a manager and the kind of organizational structure that his or her organization uses to coordinate people and resources. Discuss the distribution of authority. Does the manager think that decentralizing authority and empowering employees is appropriate?
6. Research the organizational structure of Branson's Virgin Group Investments Ltd. Would you characterize the Branson empire as mechanistic or organic in overall structure?

Level 3

7. Compare the pros and cons of using a network structure to perform organizational activities and performing all activities in-house (within one organizational hierarchy).
8. Would a flexible or a more formal structure be appropriate for these organizations: (a) a large department store, (b) a big accounting firm, (c) a biotechnology company? Explain your reasoning.
9. When and under what circumstances would it be appropriate for a manager to consider outsourcing and/or offshoring some of its activities?

Building Management Skills

UNDERSTANDING ORGANIZING

Answer the following questions about the organization you have chosen to follow:

1. Describe the organizational structure of the firm.
2. Does the enterprise have centralized or decentralized control over decision making?
3. How many levels are present in the hierarchy of authority? Is the structure tall or flat?
4. Is the structure suitable for the strategy, technology, human resources, and organizational environment in which the firm operates? If not, suggest ways in which it could better align its structure to support its mission.

Management for You

Choose an organization for which you have worked. How did the structure of your job and the organization affect your job satisfaction? Did the tasks within your job make sense? In what ways could they be better organized? What structural changes would you make to this organization? Would you consider making this a taller or flatter organization? How would the changes you have proposed improve responsiveness to customers and your job satisfaction?

Small Group Breakout Exercise

BOB'S APPLIANCES

Form groups of three or four, and appoint one member as the spokesperson who will communicate your findings to the whole class when called on by the instructor. Then discuss the following scenario:

Bob's Appliances sells and services household appliances such as washing machines, dishwashers, stoves, and refrigerators. Over the years, the company has developed a good reputation for the quality of its customer service, and many local builders are customers at the store. Recently, some new appliance retailers, including Circuit City and Future Shop, have opened stores that also sell numerous appliances. In addition to appliances, however, to attract more customers, these stores carry a complete range of consumer electronics products, including television sets, stereos, and computers. Bob Lange, the owner of Bob's Appliances, has decided that to stay in business he must widen his product range and compete directly with the chains.

In 2006, he decided to build a new 1800-square-metre store and service centre, and he is now hiring new employees to sell and service the new line of consumer electronics. Because of his company's increased size, Lange is not sure of the best way to organize the employees. Currently, he uses a functional structure; employees are divided into sales, purchasing and accounting, and repair.[62]

You are a member of a team of local consultants that Bob has called in to advise him as he makes this crucial choice. Which structure would you recommend? Why?

FUNCTIONAL STRUCTURE

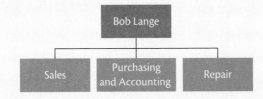

PRODUCT STRUCTURE

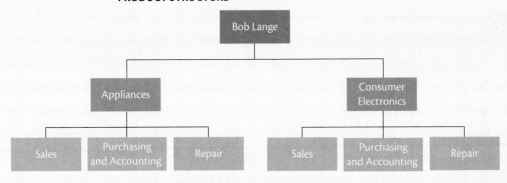

Business Planning Exercise

After reading this chapter, begin to think about how your new venture should be designed and structured to achieve your mission and goals. You need to think about the following questions for your business plan:

1. How should you design the jobs that need to be done?
2. How should you best group jobs and processes together?
3. Describe your venture in terms of:
   a. Centralized versus decentralized decision making
   b. Span of control

4. Create and draw organizational charts for Year One and Year Three of your venture.
   a. How might they change as the business grows?

b. Is a tall, mechanistic structure or a flat organic structure more suited to your venture in the first year? Why?

Managing Ethically

In many businesses—such as chicken-processing plants, small engineering companies, furniture makers, warehouses, and offices—unskilled workers perform the same repetitive tasks for many hours a day, day in and day out, and often for years if they stay at the same job. Boredom is common, as is the development of physical ailments such as skin problems, muscle fatigue, and carpal tunnel syndrome. Is it ethical for managers to allow workers to perform repetitive tasks for long periods of time? What kinds of standards would you use to settle this issue? To what degree should job redesign be used to change such a situation and enrich jobs if it also would raise costs and make a company less competitive? How could organizational structure be redesigned to make this problem less prevalent?

Exploring the World Wide Web

SPECIFIC ASSIGNMENT

Go to the website of Onex Corp. (www.onex.com). Onex is one of Canada's largest companies that acquires attractive businesses and builds them up in partnership with management. "Since 1983, we acquire attractive companies at fair prices and, in partnership with operating managers, we grow them and ultimately realize on the value we've created through a variety of strategies."[63] Review the Onex Corp. website.

1. What are Onex Corp.'s mission and corporate goals?
2. What kind of organizational structure does Onex Corp. have?
3. What is Onex Corp.'s approach to managing its structure (its approach to decentralization, delegation, etc.)

GENERAL ASSIGNMENT

Search for a website that tells the story of how an organization changed its structure in some way to increase its efficiency and effectiveness.

McGraw-Hill Connect™—Available 24/7 with instant feedback so you can study when you want, how you want, and where you want. Take advantage of the Study Plan—an innovative tool that helps you customize your learning experience. You can diagnose your knowledge with pre- and post-tests, identify the areas where you need help, search the entire learning package for content specific to the topic you're studying, and add these resources to your personalized study plan. Visit www.mcgrawhillconnect.ca to register—take practice quizzes, search the e-book, and much more.

Be the Manager

As a management consultant, you try to keep current by reading some of the best books on managing and strategy. Recently you read *Peripheral Vision*[64] and were quite excited about the ideas the authors (from the Wharton School of Business) presented. Their research has shown that less than 20 percent of firms have developed peripheral vision in sufficient capacity to remain competitive.[65] They claim that while companies need to focus on their planned strategic growth, often they may be unaware of a competitor "lurking" on the side, hence the need for peripheral vision to avoid any surprises. To raise managers' vigilance, they propose the following solution to developing peripheral vision:

- **Scoping:** the skill of determining how broadly to look. "If your scope is too narrow, you can still be blindsided, but if the scope is too wide you risk being overwhelmed by unimportant signals."[66]

- **Scanning:** the skill of practising more active searching, being more "detective-like."

- **Interpreting:** the skill of making sense of the puzzle that emerges as you go about your work.

- **Probing:** the skill of exploring more closely what seems to be occurring in the patterns emerging, an activity that will often involve experimenting and testing the market, perhaps in unique ways.

- **Acting:** the skill of exploiting any new possibilities uncovered or avoiding any imminent threats determined.

Question

1. Your new business client has asked you to show how the idea of peripheral vision could enhance the business of developing strategic alliances for her. What would you say?

Management Case

The Core Group[67]

What purpose are most organizations seeking to fulfill? ... Art Kleiner asserts that the primary purpose is not—as many of us believe—meeting customers' needs, fostering innovation, or making a better world. Rather, organizations are set up, first and foremost, to fulfill the perceived desires and priorities of a "core group" of people. As such, the success or failure of the organization is determined by the behaviour of this key set of individuals.[68]

[Author Art Kleiner] ... asserts that core groups exist in every organization, large or small, for-profit or not-for-profit, private or public sector. Members of this elite set take their power not from their position in the hierarchy but from the way they influence decisions at every level of the hierarchy. Every organization, at any given moment, has its own unique core group pattern; the most influential people might be high-profile shareholders, critical technology specialists, key suppliers, major customers, or members of the company's founding family. Core groups often include "bottlenecks," people who control or manage essential parts of operations, such as the graphic design and production staff of a publishing company or the veteran school bus administrator of a local school system. In other words, the core group does not necessarily comprise just people with hierarchical authority but those who are, for whatever reason, perceived as central to the enterprise by the people who work there.

Managing Organizational Complexity

According to Kleiner, core groups are not inherently bad or good; they are simply part of the nature of organizational systems. Without them, it would be impossible for organizations to exist, simply because the complexity of most organizational environments would be too great to manage effectively. Art says that just as a baby instinctively recognizes human faces, most of us in organizations are instinctively attuned to the people whom we have come to believe are important. Instead of making decisions based on the balance of customer and shareholder priorities, we say to ourselves, "I don't want to be the one to walk into Cheryl's office and say we can't do that." We let Cheryl, whom we probably know only slightly, represent the full range of factors affecting the decision we have to make.

Art asks those of us who resist the idea of a core group to examine our thinking when faced with a complex decision. Do we consider how it will sit with our boss, our boss's boss, or someone else entirely? If so, then we are basing our choices on the needs of the core group. The reason that the influence of these key people "trumps all other concerns," the author explains, "is not because of some mystical resonance but simply because of the cumulative effect of the decisions made throughout the organization. If people believe the core group needs and wants something to happen, they assume that making it happen is part of their job." As such, those who do make it happen often get rewarded and recognized, while those who act on the basis of other criteria usually get left behind.

Creating Great Core Groups

One of the reasons that Art developed the core group theory was his awareness of the rapid proliferation of organizations in the world. "If we are going to act effectively in a society of organizations," he says, "we need a theory that helps us see organizations clearly, as they are." Organizations in which core groups behave in self-serving and exploitative ways, such as Enron, are dismal places to work in and often end in failure. Organizations in which decision makers expand the core group by creating structures that take into account the welfare and development of everyone in the enterprise, such as Springfield Remanufacturing Corporation and Southwest Airlines, are typically high-performing work environments with deeply committed workforces. In other words, behind every great organization is a great core group.

By understanding the characteristics and principles of core groups in their organizations, people can act far more effectively. Employees, for example, can decide if they are interested in building a career in an organization even if they never get into the core group. People trying to change the organization from within can increase their chances of success by seeking sponsorship from core group members. And those at the top of the organization can consider how to galvanize spirit and effectiveness among employees by creating the conditions for the core group to expand to a larger group of people. When leaders guide core groups to work in the best interests of everyone in the organization, they can amplify the capabilities of their enterprise and create a legacy they can be proud of.

Questions

1. What are the main elements in Kleiner's approach to organizational design?
2. What organizational problems might emerge from his approach?

Video Management Case

General Motors Global Research Network

Teaching Objective: To see how a large, traditional organization changed the structure of its research and development function to focus on innovation and globalization

Video Summary: GM's top managers realized that the organization was too self-contained and that to increase its competitiveness, they needed to change the company's business model. They restructured GM to create a global team environment for research and development. By building an extensive network of engineers that allows it to tap into R&D expertise around the globe, GM aims to reach the level of innovation required to differentiate itself from its competitors.

Questions to consider

1. How does technology influence organizational structure at GM? What other factors should managers at GM consider when selecting a structure?
2. What organizational structures do you equate with GM's old model of research? Which structures do you equate with the new model?
3. What must GM managers consider as they move from the old structure to the new structure?

CHAPTER 7

Managing Organizational Culture and Change

Learning Outcomes

1. Explain organizational culture and how a strong culture is created and sustained.

2. Explain how members of an organization learn its culture.

3. Explain how successful organizational change, whether induced or imposed, requires altering the organization's culture.

4. Explain the processes involved in managing organizational change.

5. Describe two models of organizational change.

6. Explain how managers deal with organizational change in unionized environments.

Strategy, Heart, Execution

A company is not only top management, nor is it only middle management. A company is everyone from the top to the front lines. And it is only when all the members of an organization are aligned around a strategy and support it, for better or for worse, that a company stands apart as a great and consistent executor. Overcoming the organizational hurdles to strategy execution is an important step toward that end. It removes the roadblocks that can put a halt to even the best of strategies.

But in the end, a company needs to invoke the most fundamental base of action: the attitudes and behavior of its people deep in the organization. You must create a culture of trust and commitment that motivates people to execute the agreed strategy—not to the letter, but to the spirit. People's minds and hearts must align with the new strategy so that at the level of the individual, people embrace it of their own accord and willingly go beyond compulsory execution to voluntary cooperation in carrying it out.[1]

Strategy and heart and execution. All three are needed. Strategy brings focus and direction; heart brings willingness and commitment; and execution brings completion and fulfillment. As we have seen in previous chapters, the global workspace today brings new challenges and new opportunities; it also means that new mindsets are needed. In *Blue Ocean Strategy: How to Create Uncontested Market Space and Make the Competition Irrelevant,*

Jupiter Images

authors W. Chan Kim and Renée Mauborgne argue that companies must shift from what they call a red ocean strategy to a blue ocean strategy. While they acknowledge that red ocean strategies are still important, increasingly the success of a company's initiatives will reside with blue ocean strategies. Red ocean strategies seek to compete in the *same* market space; blue ocean strategies compete in *new* market spaces. They use the example of Cirque du Soleil and its realization "that to win in the future, companies must stop competing with each other. The only way to beat the competition is to stop *trying* to beat the competition."[2] Current industries represent the red oceans; blue oceans envision industries *not* in existence today. The authors illustrate this difference in highlighting Cirque du Soleil because the heart and soul of blue ocean strategy is its dedication to *value innovation.*

Authors Kim and Mauborgne describe a reality they call *fair process,* or what has also been called procedural justice. In other words, not only is the outcome important but also *how* the outcome happens or is expected to occur. This brings to mind the Scottish poet Robert Burns' line "The best laid plans of mice and men often go awry" in his poem "To a Mouse" written in November 1785. In other words, in the case of organizational culture and change, to neglect or to forget to factor in the people dimension is a sure-fire recipe for failure. Fair process matters because intellectual and emotional recognition of employees is essential.

Now It's Your Turn

Think of a time (or research a case) when you were involved in a work or organizational situation that included a "red ocean" context and one that included a "blue ocean" context.

1. What was the background to your own case situation?

2. What were some of the challenges involved for staff in both contexts?

3. What, if any, final resolution occurred?

■■■■ Overview

Over a decade ago, Harvard professors John Kotter and James Heskett showed, through empirical research at more than 200 companies such as Hewlett-Packard, Xerox, and Nissan, how the culture of a corporation powerfully influences its economic performance, for better or for worse. Their thesis is that adaptive cultures—not necessarily strong ones on certain dimensions—are more likely to survive. For example, K-Mart's lack of a customer-service ethos cost it dearly when it had to compete with Wal-Mart.[3] Different cultures in organizations will be shaped by the different ways that managers interact with their employees. That is why the power of words is so important—a reality brought forth so vividly by the movie *What the Bleep Do We Know?* in its presentation of positive versus negative words. If, as we saw in Chapter 6, organizational structure provides an organization with a skeleton, organizational culture provides the muscles, sinews, nerves, and sensations that allow managers to regulate and govern the organization's activities. Organizational culture also affects the ability of the organization to engage in change and adapt to new environments when necessary. K-Mart was ineffective at doing precisely this in relation to Wal-Mart.

In this chapter, we look at how culture works, and how it is taught to organizational members. This continues our discussion from the previous chapter about how managers organize human and other resources to create high-performing organizations. We will examine why culture can inspire employees to achieve great goals and why it can also lead to organizational failure. We will look at how to manage change successfully, in the face of strong culture, and how to overcome resistance to change. By the end of this chapter, you will understand how culture helps convey meaning and purpose to employees. You will also understand the vital role that change plays in building competitive advantage and creating a high-performing organization.

L O 1

Organizational Culture

THINK ABOUT IT

"Basically, It's Common Sense"[4]

So says Toronto psychologist, Barbara Moses, Ph.D., when discussing how workplace training, environment and corporate culture are critical to boosting productivity. She goes on to point out how work today is a "constant audition," or a theatre in which no one can rest on his/her laurels—hence, the necessity of employers to provide personal and professional development learning opportunities to employees. What is "common sense" to Dr. Moses are the fundamentals: appreciating a job well done, providing recognition, and giving employees a sense of accomplishment as a result of their efforts. These factors contribute to the making and shaping of the organizational culture. She also points out that the "new worker" today is not simply the young person starting out who wants a job but also the ordinary employee who knows that to stay competitive in today's workplace demands an attitude of employability, that fundamentally the employee must take responsibility for his or her career. Managers must mentor and create a culture in which people take responsibility for ensuring this employability.

You Be the Manager

1. How prepared are you for the new workplace?
2. What would you expect a manager to do for you to create a healthy workplace culture?

Organizational culture refers to a system of shared meaning held by organizational members that distinguishes the organization from other organizations.[5] Culture is the "glue" that keeps organizational members together, and guides their behaviour. New employees learn the organizational culture from their managers and other employees.

Culture can be viewed as something that both helps employees make sense of the organization and guides employee behaviour. In essence, culture defines the rules of the game:

> Culture by definition is elusive, intangible, implicit, and taken for granted. But every organization develops a core set of assumptions, understandings, and implicit rules that govern day-to-day behaviour in the workplace. Until newcomers learn the rules, they are not accepted as full-fledged members of the organization. Transgressions of the rules on the part of high-level executives or front-line employees result in universal disapproval and powerful penalties. Conformity to the rules becomes the primary basis for reward and upward mobility.[6]

Organizational culture can control individuals and groups in an organization through shared values, norms, standards of behaviour, and expectations. **Values** are the stable, long-lasting beliefs about what is important. **Norms** are unwritten rules or guidelines that prescribe appropriate behaviour in particular situations. Norms emerge from values.[7]

Organizational culture is not an externally imposed system of constraints, such as direct supervision or rules and procedures. Rather, employees internalize organizational values and norms and then let those values and norms guide their decisions and actions. Just as people in society at large generally behave in accordance with socially acceptable values and norms, such as lining up at the checkout counters in supermarkets, so are individuals in an organizational setting mindful of the force of organizational values and norms.

Levels of Culture

Culture exists at two levels in an organization: the visible level and the invisible level. We see culture through its **artifacts**. These are what you see, hear, and feel when you are within an organization. For instance, organizations have different dress policies, have different ways of organizing office space, and have different ideas of what should be displayed on company walls. The things you see reveal the organization's culture.

At the invisible level of culture are the values, beliefs, and assumptions that make up the organizational culture. **Beliefs** are the understandings of how objects and ideas relate to each other. **Assumptions** are the taken-for-granted notions of how something should be. Because of basic assumptions that are held by organizational members, it can be difficult to introduce change. For example, John Ralston Saul, in his book *The Collapse of Globalism and the Reinvention of the World*[8] and Thomas Friedman in *The Lexus and the Olive Tree* present radically different assumptions. Friedman presents a "globalization-worshipping" account, whereas Saul refers to what he calls the "globalist ideology" that emerged in the 1970s and that would brook no alternative approach to economics. Saul does this "by singling out what he sees as

organizational culture
A system of shared meaning held by organization members that distinguishes the organization from other organizations.

values
The stable, long-lasting beliefs about what is important.

norms
Unwritten rules or guidelines for appropriate behaviour in particular situations.

artifacts
Aspects of an organization's culture that one sees, hears, and feels.

beliefs
The understandings of how objects and ideas relate to each other.

assumptions
The taken-for-granted notions of how something should be in an organization.

two disturbing and flawed assumptions: the inevitability of global economic forces (and thus the absence of public-policy choice and leadership) and the fact that society and, indeed, all civilization must be viewed through an economic prism."[9]

The values and assumptions of an organization are not easily observed. Thus, we look to organizational artifacts (i.e., the things we can observe) to help us uncover the values and assumptions. For instance, managers' and employees' behaviour often reveals the organization's values and assumptions. When employees continue talking to each other in front of a waiting customer, they signal that employees are more important than customers to this organization.

Creating a Strong Organizational Culture

Culture is created and sustained in three ways:[10]

1. The founders and/or senior managers of the organization hire and keep only employees who think and feel the way they do.
2. The management indoctrinates and socializes these employees to their way of thinking and feeling.
3. Top managers serve as role models. By observing their behaviour, employees identify with them and internalize their beliefs, values, and assumptions.

In an organization, values and norms make it clear to organizational members what goals they should pursue and how they should behave to reach those goals. Thus, values and norms perform the same function as formal goals, written rules, or direct supervision. Research shows that having a strong culture usually pays off, except in times of a changing environment.[11] Those companies with stronger cultures tend to have better returns on investment, higher net income growth, and larger increases in share price than firms with weaker cultures. However, strong culture can be a liability when the environment is changing. Organizations with strong cultures have greater difficulty adapting to change.

Managers can influence the kinds of values and norms that develop in an organization. Some managers might cultivate values and norms that let subordinates know they are welcome to perform their roles in innovative and creative ways. Employees are thus encouraged to be entrepreneurial and are willing to experiment and go out on a limb even if there is a significant chance of failure. At organizations such as Lucent Technologies and 3M Canada, top managers encourage employees to adopt such values in order to support organizational commitment to innovation as a source of competitive advantage.

Other managers, however, might cultivate values and norms that let employees know that they should always be conservative and cautious in their dealings with others. Thus, these employees should always consult with their superiors before making important decisions and should always put their actions in writing so they can be held accountable for whatever happens. In any setting where caution is needed—nuclear power stations, large oil refineries, chemical plants, financial institutions, and insurance companies—a conservative, cautious approach to making decisions might be highly appropriate.[12] When used inappropriately, however, caution may stifle employees' ability to innovate or communicate. One interesting merger that people looked at a few years ago was the one of Molson Inc. of Montreal and Colorado's Adolph Coors Co. Some asked at the time if a culture shock was the main thing on the horizon.[13] However, the merger proved successful. Chairman Pete Coors said, "We've known each other for a long time, we respect them as brewers, they respect us as brewers, we respect each other from a marketing perspective.

You can't put two people together and expect perfect harmony, but this is as harmonic as I think you can possibly get putting two companies together." Was he just putting on a brave face? When three executives each "at random" picked up a bottle of either Coors or Molson to toast the successful conclusion of the merger, the eldest Coors swivelled slowly toward the meeting and said, "I'd stick with Coors Light if I were all of you."

Difficulties arise when two organizations with different cultures merge. For instance, when Calgary-based TransCanada PipeLines Ltd. and Nova Corporation merged in 1998, cultural differences led to conflicts in bringing the two companies together. Nova and TransCanada treated their employees very differently. TransCanada had a more traditional, top-down management control structure. Nova relied on its culture of empowering employees to govern their behaviours. One Nova employee described the merger as "GI Joe meets the Care Bears."[14] Three years later, the two companies had still not completely resolved their cultural differences.

TransCanada PipeLines
Limited
www.transcanada.com

Nova Chemicals
Corporation
www.novachem.com

L O 2

Learning Organizational Culture

Managers deliberately cultivate and develop the organizational values and norms that are best suited to their task and general environments, strategy, or technology. Organizational culture is transmitted to and shared with organizational members through the values of the founder, the process of socialization, ceremonies and rites, and stories and language (see Figure 7.1).

Values of the Founder

One manager who has a very important impact on the kind of organizational culture that emerges in an organization is the founder. An organization's founder and his or her personal values and beliefs have a substantial influence on the values, norms, and standards of behaviour that develop over time within the organization.[15] Founders set the stage for the way cultural values and norms develop because they hire other managers to help them run their organizations. It is reasonable to assume that founders select managers who share their vision of the organization's goals and what it should be doing. In any case, new managers quickly learn from the founder what values and norms are appropriate in the organization and thus what is desired of them. Subordinates imitate the style of the founder and, in turn, transmit his or her values and norms to their subordinates. Gradually over time, the founder's values and norms permeate the organization.[16]

FIGURE 7.1 | Factors in Learning Organizational Culture

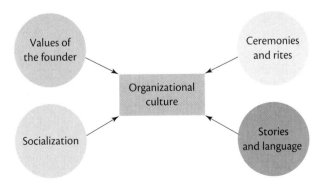

Frank Stronach, Magna International
www.magnaint.com/
magnaweb.nsf/webpages/

Richard Branson, Virgin Group
www.virgin.com/aboutus/
autobiography/

A founder who requires a great display of respect from subordinates and insists on such things as formal job titles and formal modes of dress encourages subordinates to act this way toward their subordinates. Often, a founder's personal values affect an organization's competitive advantage. Frank Stronach, founder of Magna Corporation, based in Aurora, Ontario, believes that his employees should show a "strong sense of ownership and entrepreneurial energy." He practises this belief by diverting 10 percent of pre-tax profit to profit-sharing programs for his employees. Similarly, managers' salaries are deliberately set "below industry standards" so that managers will earn more through profit-sharing bonuses. To further emphasize managerial responsibility, Magna's managers are given considerable autonomy over buying, selling, and hiring. Through these policies of profit-sharing and empowerment, Stronach has developed a workforce that has made Magna one of the largest and most profitable companies in the country.

Similarly, Richard Branson of the Virgin Group, known for his entrepreneurial style, challenges his managers to act like him. All of his small companies are headed by managing directors who have a stake in the company they run. He wants his managers to operate the companies as if they were their own. Branson's style of management has made Virgin a success in a number of different markets it has entered.

Another success story in living the dreams and upholding the values of the founder is the innovative Canadian company Cirque du Soleil. Every travelling Cirque du Soleil show has its own creative director who makes sure the production stays true to the vision and passion of its co-founder Guy Laliberté.[17]

Socialization

Over time, organizational members learn from each other which values are important in an organization and the norms that specify appropriate and inappropriate behaviours. Eventually, organizational members behave in accordance with the organization's values and norms—often without realizing they are doing so. **Organizational socialization** is the process by which newcomers learn an organization's values and norms and acquire the work behaviours necessary to perform jobs effectively.[18] As a result of their socialization experiences, organizational members internalize an organization's values and norms and behave to fit in with them, not only because they think they have to but also because they think that these values and norms describe the right and proper way to behave.[19]

Most organizations have some kind of socialization program to help new employees "learn the ropes"—the values, norms, and culture of their organization. The military, for example, is well known for the rigorous socialization process it uses to turn raw recruits into trained soldiers. Many organizations put new recruits through a rigorous training program to provide them with the knowledge they need not only to perform well in their jobs but also to represent the company to its clients. Thus, through the organizational socialization program, the founder and top managers of an organization can transmit to employees the cultural values and norms that shape the behaviours of organizational members.

organizational socialization
The process by which newcomers learn an organization's values and norms and acquire the work behaviours necessary to perform jobs effectively.

Ceremonies and Rites

Another way in which managers can try to create or influence an organizational culture is by developing organizational ceremonies and rites—formal events that recognize incidents of importance to the organization as a whole and to specific employees.[20] The most common rites that organizations use to transmit cultural norms and values to their members are rites of passage, of integration, and of enhancement (see Table 7.1).[21]

Business Plan Checklist

- Be sure to incorporate your principles and values into your vision, mission, and goals.
- Determine the licences, trademarks, and other branding measures you require to make your product/service unique and to run the business.
- What future innovations and developments can you pursue for your venture?
- What are the risks, and how will you deal with them?
- Use this information for Section 5 of the business plan, the Profile of the Product/Service in Appendix A.

TABLE 7.1 | *Organizational Rites*

Type of Rite	Example of Rite	Purpose of Rite
Rite of passage	Induction and basic training	Learn and internalize norms and values
Rite of integration	Office Christmas party	Build common norms and values
Rite of enhancement	Presentation of annual award	Motivate commitment to norms

Rites of passage determine how individuals enter, advance within, or leave the organization. At Cirque du Soleil, an annual training event is held at the Montreal headquarters studio for all new recruits who come from all over the world. For many, it is a major adjustment on two cultural fronts: First, it is a new country for most; and second, to fully integrate the values of the organization, the athletes must shift their focus from a world of competition to a world of expression. The socialization programs developed by all organizations are rites of passage. Likewise, the ways in which an organization prepares people for promotion or retirement are rites of passage.

Sometimes, rites of passage can get out of hand. Fraternities, sororities, sports teams, and even the military have been known to use hazing to initiate members. Activities can include "sleep deprivation, public nudity and childish pranks or, at worst, extreme drunkenness, gross racial slurs, even beatings."[22] The videotaped hazing rituals at CFB Petawawa caused the Airborne Regiment to be disbanded in 1995. While the goal of the hazing might have been to desensitize new recruits to the brutality of war, many Canadians felt that the practice had gone too far. In Australia, a court held an organization liable for assault after a teenager, who was wrapped in cling film during a hazing ritual, prosecuted a company and two of its directors for assault under workplace safety laws.

His shoes and bag were then filled with sawdust and he was placed on a work trolley. He was covered with sawdust, and his co-workers squirted wood glue in his shoes, over his body and into his mouth. "Doyle, an asthmatic, coughed, choked and was unable to breathe," said New South Wales Chief Industrial Magistrate George Miller. "What started out as a simple episode of bullying got out of control, leading to a serious physical threat to Doyle's health and safety." Employees were not disciplined, and a company director knew in advance the hazing would take place.[23]

Rites of integration, such as office parties, company cookouts, and shared announcements of organizational successes, build as well as reinforce common bonds among organizational members. Southwest Airlines is well known for its efforts to develop ceremonies and rituals to bond employees to the organization by showing them that they are valued members. Southwest holds cookouts in the parking lot of its Dallas headquarters, and Herb Kelleher, the founder and chair, personally attends each employee Christmas party throughout the country. Because there are so many Christmas parties to attend, Kelleher often finds himself attending parties in July!

Rites of enhancement, such as awards dinners, newspaper releases, and employee promotions, let organizations publicly recognize and reward employees' contributions and thus strengthen their commitment to organizational values. By bonding members within the organization, rites of enhancement help promote group cohesiveness.

Stories and Language

Stories and language also communicate organizational culture. Stories (whether fact or fiction) about organizational heroes and villains and their actions provide important clues about values and norms. Such stories can reveal the kinds of behaviours that are valued by the organization and the kinds of practices that are frowned on.[24] Stories about Ted Rogers, the person (hero) who made Rogers Communications the company it is today, shed light on many aspects of Rogers Communications' corporate culture. Stories also about Bill Newnham, founder of Seneca College in Toronto, speak volumes about his spirit and how this spirit lives on in the organizational culture of the college.[25] Language—through slogans, symbols, and jargon—is used to help employees come to know expectations while bonding with one another.

http://www.ford.com/
www.husky.ca

Material Symbols

The organization's layout is a material symbol, and so are the size of offices; whether individuals wear uniforms or have a dress code; and the kinds of cars that top executives are given.[26] Material symbols convey to employees who is important, how much distance there is between top management and employees, and what kinds of behaviour are appropriate. For example, at Toronto-based Willow Manufacturing, everyone from the CEO down wears a uniform to convey the message that everyone in the company is part of a team.

Similarly, Alain Batty, the current director, European Sales Staffs, Ford of Europe, when he was president and CEO of Ford Motor Company of Canada, Limited from 2001–2005, had the same kind of huge desk in his office in Toronto as William Clay Ford Jr., chair and CEO of Ford Motor Company, and every other Ford divisional head. The office buildings for all of Ford's operations are also similar. Founder Henry Ford believed it was more efficient to organize office space this way.[27] At Husky Injection Molding Systems, based in Bolton, Ontario, employees and management share the parking lot, dining room, and even washrooms, conveying the sense of an egalitarian workplace.

The concept of organizational language encompasses not only spoken language but also how people dress, the offices they occupy, the cars they drive, and the degree of formality they use when they address one another. IBM Canada, long known for its dark-blue suits, introduced less formal clothing in 1993 so that customers would feel more comfortable when interacting with the company.[28] When employees "speak" and understand the language of their organization's culture and they know how to behave in the organization and what attitudes are expected of them.

Organizational Culture and Change

THINK ABOUT IT

Bliss of Bowing[29]

In *Religion and the Workplace: Pluralism, Spirituality, Leadership*, author Douglas A. Hicks states that dignity and equal respect as well as voluntariness are among the key elements necessary to create a place of *worth* in the workplace.[30] The framework of respectful pluralism allows individuals the opportunity to express (within the constraints of accommodation) their religious, political, cultural, spiritual, and other commitments while on the job.

Diana L. Eck, a Harvard professor of Comparative Religion and Indian Studies and director of The Pluralism Project,[31] says plurality of religious traditions and cultures has come to characterize every part of the world today. Here are her four main points:

(c) Digital Vision

- First, pluralism is not diversity alone, but *the energetic engagement with diversity*. Diversity can and has meant the creation of religious ghettoes with little traffic between or among them. Today, religious diversity is a given, but pluralism is not a given; it is an achievement. Mere diversity without real encounter and relationship will yield increasing tensions in our societies.

- Second, pluralism is not just tolerance, but *the active seeking of understanding across lines of difference*. Tolerance is a necessary public virtue, but it does not require Christians and Muslims, Hindus, Jews, and ardent secularists to know anything about one another. Tolerance is too thin a foundation for a world of religious difference and proximity. It does nothing to remove our ignorance of one another and leaves in place the stereotypes, the half-truths, the fears that underlie old patterns of division and violence. In the world in which we live today, our ignorance of one another will be increasingly costly.

- Third, pluralism is not relativism, but *the encounter of commitments*. The new paradigm of pluralism does not require us to leave our identities and our commitments behind, for pluralism is the encounter of commitments. It means holding our deepest differences, even our religious differences, not in isolation, but in relationship to one another.

- Fourth, pluralism is *based on dialogue*. The language of pluralism is that of dialogue and encounter, give and take, criticism and self-criticism. Dialogue means both speaking and listening, and that process reveals both common understandings and real differences. Dialogue does not mean everyone at the "table" will agree with one another. Pluralism involves the commitment to being at the table—with one's commitments.

When we examine cultural practices such as greeting with a bow, as is the practice in Korea, for example, we can see the encounter of commitments as complementary to a respectful work environment. Traditional Korean thought has been influenced by a number of religious and philosophical systems over the years: Shamanism, Buddhism, Confucianism, Taoism, and Christianity; bowing is the active seeking of understanding across lines of difference that each citizen voluntarily shares. Although bowing is the cultural tradition for greeting, it is not reserved only for this purpose. Bowing is a gesture of respect, and different bows are used for gratitude or apologies and to express different emotions, humility, sincerity, remorse, or deference. In Korea, bowing spans a variety of traditional arts and religious ceremonies and is a prime example of energetic engagement with diversity.

Basic bows are performed with the back straight and the hands at the sides, and with the eyes down. Bows originate at the waist. Generally, the longer and deeper the bow, the stronger is the emotion.

Bows can be generally divided into three main types: informal, formal, and very formal. Informal bows are made at about a 15-degree angle and more formal bows at about 30 degrees. Very formal bows are deeper.

When dealing with non-Koreans, many Koreans will shake hands. Since many non-Koreans are familiar with the custom of bowing, this often leads to a combined bow and handshake. This combination demonstrates awareness based on dialogue, respect, and accommodation. As Eck points out, the new paradigm of pluralism does not require us to leave our identities and our commitments behind; it means holding our deepest differences, even our religious differences, not in isolation but in relationship to one another.

You Be the Manager

1. Can you highlight a cultural influence in your own life that could fit the definition of respectful pluralism?

induced change
New institutional arrangements made to gain a competitive advantage.

imposed change
New institutional arrangements made to comply with regulations.

e-business
Using the Internet and intranet applications to communicate with employees, suppliers, customers, and other stakeholders.

There are two types of organizational change: imposed and induced. **Induced change** refers to new institutional arrangements in terms of strategy, technology, human resources, and organizational structure in response to changes in the task and general organizational environments made to gain a competitive advantage. **Imposed change** can be viewed as new institutional arrangements set out by changes in legislation and law that force change in order to comply with the new rules. For example, when the city of Toronto legislated a ban on smoking in restaurants, all organizations had to accept that change and implement alternative strategies that targeted smokers, even though it had been imposed rather than induced. Even induced change that comes from within the organization is risky and challenging. In March and April 2008 the Economist Intelligence Unit[32] conducted an online survey and interviewed 600 global leaders about change and business transformation. Fifty-eight percent of the respondents said that over the past five years, half or fewer of their change initiatives had been successful. For the United States, the participant experience was worse, with 75 percent stating that half or fewer of their change initiatives had been successful. The most frequently cited barrier was winning over the hearts and minds of employees at all levels (51 percent). Management buy-in (31 percent) and cultural issues (27 percent) were featured as major barriers. Organizations that want to move in a new direction, such as mergers, acquisitions, divestitures, global expansion, must alter structures, policies, behaviours, and beliefs in order to get from "how we've always done it" to how things will be done in the future. Thus all changes in the organization need to be carried out within the context of examining and changing the organization's culture. Moreover, the necessity to become an **e-business** is one of the greatest challenges facing business today. Transforming a traditional "bricks and mortar" company into a "clicks and mortar" company demands vast changes in the organization's culture, as it fundamentally changes the way it views, serves, and satisfies customers. Changes in any organizational activities may well result in resistance.

While it is difficult to analyze organizational change that is imposed from outside, in the next part of this chapter we look at how the dimensions of organizational culture are transformed when organizational change is induced from within. Then we compare two approaches to organizational change: Kurt Lewin's three-stage model and Ralph Stacey's ideas on complexity theory. Finally, we end our discussion with how managers deal with change in a unionized organizational setting.

Managing Organizational Change

THINK ABOUT IT

Are You Ready?[33]

Position your firm to navigate leadership crisis.

If recruiting for future leaders is not on the top of your firm's to-do list, then it may be too late. Because if you are not already facing a scarcity of talent at the leadership level, it is just a matter of time.

It is not just the initial attraction. A company with an employment brand that clearly articulates its corporate culture is essential in keeping tomorrow's leaders. Understanding how a new employee will mesh with your corporate culture all comes down to "fit."

Corporate culture was something rarely discussed by Canadian leaders in the past. But with changing demographics and the void of readily available and skilled leadership candidates, things have changed dramatically.

Today, many leading organizations believe corporate culture is the most important weapon in the push to be an employer of choice. The figures are alarming. In two years, a staggering 40 percent of North America's workforce—the baby boomers—will start hitting retirement age. Already, 43 percent of North American companies say a shortage of skills is the top business concern, and yet a quarter of all companies freely admit they are not ready for this mass exodus of retirees.

Make no mistake, we are on the brink of a leadership crisis. As organizations face a shrinking labour pool and global competition, Canada's looming talent shortage is a primary issue being discussed around boardroom tables across the country.

Boomers have a large array of options and just as many reasons to lure them out of senior management roles. They often are bringing in two incomes and have invested well and received inheritances, and senior roles are more demanding than ever before.

As these experienced leaders permanently head for the cottages, there will be an intense competition for the best new leaders. These future leaders—coming from Generations X and Y—are a different breed than most of us have yet seen, and they come with unique recruitment and retention challenges. To start with, there are fewer of them. They are most definitely not their parents' generation: They want more than a paycheque. They want balance in their lives, and they want to work for a firm with a solid track record. More importantly, they actively seek out values and behaviours that mirror their own.

As it turns out, those values—known as corporate culture—can be a competitive advantage. A healthy corporate culture is your firm's employee value proposition, and it is a powerful tool to attract the best and brightest people.

Culture determines fit because it is a reflection of values. Employee values drive their behaviour, and it is their behaviour that determines whether you will achieve your business plans and goals. Firms leading the way in corporate culture offer customized compensation plans, flex benefits systems, enhanced training initiatives, and vacation policies, along with recruitment incentives galore, hoping to find and keep candidates who fit their culture.

They also are spending more than ever before on recruitment efforts. Unfortunately, few do this in a systematic way that aligns their culture to attracting candidates who represent the behavioural characteristics they need.

WestJet does: The company's compensation system, which includes a profit-share plan and stock ownership for every employee, is a good example of how companies can attract people who value teamwork, belonging, interdependency,[34] and frugality. WestJet has had a culture department since its humble beginnings in 1997. The company contends that if you hire, reward, and celebrate employees who act in accordance with the organizational values, results will follow.

The carrier has an average three-year revenue growth of 105 percent and a three-year asset growth of 85 percent. In the same period, the TSX 60 Composite Index had average growth of 15 percent and 13 percent, respectively.

This is staggering information, considering airlines are one of the most competitive industries worldwide and that the capital markets are coming off record performances. Firms taking corporate culture seriously are well positioned to safely navigate the troubled skies ahead, brought on by the impending leadership crisis. WestJet, for example, represents a unified and consistent voice to "WestJetters" present and future. And in doing so, you can bet that it will continue to outperform its peers across many key business indicators.

You Be the Manager

1. What makes working for WestJet such an attractive proposition?

Deciding how to change an organization is a complex matter, not least because change disrupts the status quo and poses a threat, prompting employees to resist attempts to alter work relationships and procedures. Several experts have proposed a model that managers can follow to introduce change successfully while effectively managing conflict and politics.[35] Figure 7.2 outlines the steps that managers must take to manage change effectively.

FIGURE 7.2 | Four Steps in the Organizational Change Process

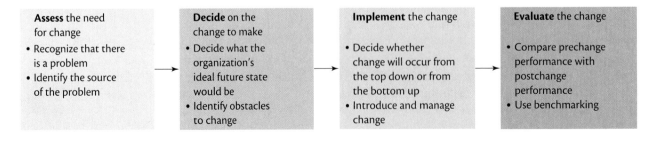

Assess the need for change
- Recognize that there is a problem
- Identify the source of the problem

Decide on the change to make
- Decide what the organization's ideal future state would be
- Identify obstacles to change

Implement the change
- Decide whether change will occur from the top down or from the bottom up
- Introduce and manage change

Evaluate the change
- Compare prechange performance with postchange performance
- Use benchmarking

Assessing the Need for Change

Assessing the need for change calls for two important activities: recognizing that there is a problem and identifying its source. This is not always easy. NASA generally has been reluctant to address management failures after problems arise, and more willing to look for and address mechanical failures. When the Columbia Accident Investigation Board issued its report in the summer of 2003, it listed many of the same management failures that were identified after the Challenger disaster of 1983. NASA is not unique in this approach. Sometimes the need for change is obvious, such as when an organization's performance is suffering. Often, however, managers have trouble determining that something is going wrong because problems develop gradually; organizational performance may slip for a number of years before it becomes obvious. This is what happened at NASA. Thus, during the first step in the change process, managers need to recognize that there is a problem that requires change.

Often, a gap between desired and actual performance signals that there is a problem. By looking at performance measures—such as falling market share or profits, rising costs, or employees' failure to meet their established goals or stay within budgets—managers can see whether change is needed. These measures are provided by organizational control systems (discussed in Chapter 13).

If there is a gap between desired performance and actual performance, managers need to discover the source of the problem. They do this by looking both inside and outside the organization. Outside the organization, they must examine how changes in environmental forces may be creating opportunities and threats that are affecting internal work relationships. In the era of e-business, rapid technological changes are forcing traditional land-based, bricks-and-mortar business to radically change the way it operates to compete in an environment of low overheads, process automation, and downward pressure on prices.

Deciding on the Change to Make

Once managers have identified the source of the problem, they must decide what they think the organization's ideal future state would be. In other words, they must decide where they would like their organization to be in the future—what kinds of goods and services it should be offering, what its business-level strategy should be, how the organizational structure should be changed, and so on. During this step, managers also must engage in planning how they are going to attain the organization's ideal future state. Companies transforming to e-business must create customer value by using networked computing to improve internal communications among employees and external communications with customers, suppliers, and strategic partners. Ideally, the hybrid "clicks and mortar" company will serve customers better through customized products, lower turnaround times, and lower costs. But moving from a "bricks and mortar" to a "clicks and mortar" organization presents significant challenges to today's managers. See Figure 7.3.[36]

This step in the change process also includes identifying obstacles or sources of resistance to change. Managers must analyze the factors that may prevent the company from reaching its ideal future state. Obstacles to change are found at the corporate, divisional, departmental, and individual levels of the organization.

Corporate-level changes in an organization's strategy or structure—even seemingly trivial changes—may significantly affect how divisional and departmental managers behave. Suppose that to compete with low-cost foreign competitors, top managers decide to increase the resources spent on state-of-the-art machinery and reduce the resources spent on marketing or R&D. The power of manufacturing managers would

FIGURE 7.3 | Transformation of the Large, Land-based Enterprise

Today		Tomorrow
• Customer problems viewed as annoyances • Customer insights derived from demographics • Delayed reaction to customer purchasing activity • Standard products and services • Mass mailing and promotions • Intense conflict between physical and electronic channels	**Expand customer management competencies** ⟶	• Customer problems prompt Web-driven solutions • Deep customer insights obtained from ability to predict their behaviour • Specialized products and services based on individual customer profitability • Personalized promotions based on individual needs • Strategies for physical and electronic channels coordinated to reduce conflict
• Customer and price lists closely guarded • Information on product availability and specifications kept internally • Supplier ensures that inventory levels remain adequate • Customer and supplier data in different information systems • Goal is to increase operating efficiency	**Manage business intelligence** ⟶	• Web enables customers and suppliers to see business structure • Information on product availability and specifications on the Web • Customer configures own product on the Web and sends order directly to supply network • Integrated value chain information • Goal is to increase productivity and knowledge of customers, distributors, and salespeople
• Supply-curve pricing mediated by intermediary • Competition based on price • Dependence on expensive salesforce	**Understand firm economics** ⟶	• Demand-curve pricing driven by buyer/seller relationship • Competition based on customer service innovation • Strategic investment shifts to Web-based sales and business intelligence tools

Source: FILJ.

increase, and the power of marketing and R&D managers would fall. This decision would alter the balance of power among departments and might lead to increased politics and conflict as departments start fighting to retain their status in the organization. An organization's present strategy and structure are powerful obstacles to change.

Organizational culture also can make change easier or harder. Organizations with entrepreneurial, flexible cultures, such as high-tech companies, are much easier to change than are organizations with more rigid cultures such as those sometimes found in large bureaucratic organizations, for example, the military or General Motors.

The same obstacles to change exist at the divisional and departmental levels as well. Division managers may differ in their attitudes toward the changes that top managers propose and will resist those changes if their interests and power seem threatened. Managers at all levels usually fight to protect their power and control over resources. Given that departments have different goals and time horizons, they may also react differently to the changes that other managers propose. When top managers are trying to reduce costs, for example, sales managers may resist attempts to cut back on sales expenditures if they believe that problems stem from the manufacturing managers' inefficiencies.

At the individual level, too, people are often resistant to change because change brings uncertainty, and uncertainty brings stress. For example, individuals may resist the introduction of e-business technology because they are uncertain about their abilities to learn it and effectively use it.

These obstacles make organizational change a slow process. Managers must recognize these potential obstacles to change and take them into consideration. Some obstacles can be overcome by improving communication so that all organizational members are aware of both the need for change and the nature of the changes being made. Empowering employees and inviting them to take part in the planning for change also can help overcome resistance and reduce employees' fears. Emphasizing big-picture goals, such as organizational effectiveness and gaining a competitive advantage, can make organizational members who resist a change realize that the change is ultimately in everyone's best interests because it will increase organizational performance. The larger and more complex an organization is, the more complex is the change process.

Introducing the Change

Generally, managers can introduce and manage change from the top down or from the bottom up.[37] **Top-down change** is implemented quickly: Top managers identify the need for change, decide what to do, and then move quickly to introduce the changes throughout the organization. For example, top managers may decide to restructure and downsize the organization and then give divisional and departmental managers specific goals to achieve. With top-down change, the emphasis is on making the changes quickly and dealing with problems as they arise.

Bottom-up change is typically more gradual. Top managers consult with middle and first-line managers about the need for change. Then, over time, these low-level managers work with nonmanagerial employees to develop a detailed plan for change. A major advantage of bottom-up change is that it can reduce uncertainty and resistance to change. The emphasis in bottom-up change is on participation and on keeping people informed about what is going on.

For example, to understand the changes a traditional land-based business must make to transform to doing e-business, we can look at how a strictly dot-com company operates. Born out of a website, the virtual business must outsource everything. They depend on Web-enabled networks of third-party suppliers, warehouses, distributors, and payment processors that together provide reliable products or services when, where, and how the customer needs them. A common strategy has been to concentrate on unmet customer demand for customized products at lower costs than traditional companies have been able to provide with their high overhead costs. An example of this is TD Waterhouse, an online discount brokerage firm aimed at customers who do not want to pay high commission fees for advice from a financial advisor. An account with such a firm allows the customer to trade in the stock market relatively cheaply and quickly. Dot-com companies are simply facilitators and intermediaries. They facilitate commerce by using the Web to coordinate suppliers on the customer's behalf.

Evaluating the Change

The last step in the change process is to evaluate how successful the change effort has been in improving organizational performance.[38] Using measures such as changes in market share, profits, or the ability of managers to meet their goals, managers compare how well an organization is performing after the change with how well it was performing before.

Managers also can use **benchmarking**, comparing their performance on specific dimensions with the performance of high-performing organizations to decide how successful the change effort has been. For example, when Xerox was doing poorly in

top-down change
Change that is introduced quickly throughout an organization by upper-level managers.

bottom-up change
Change that is introduced gradually and involves managers and employees at all levels of an organization.

benchmarking
Comparing performance on specific dimensions with the performance of high-performing organizations.

the 1980s, it benchmarked the efficiency of its distribution operations against those of L.L. Bean, the efficiency of its central computer operations against those of John Deere, and its marketing abilities against those of Procter & Gamble. Those companies are renowned for their skills in those different areas, and by studying how they performed, Xerox was able to dramatically increase its own performance.

 ## Tips for Managers
INTRODUCING CHANGE

1. No one likes change forced on them. However, sometimes change is the only alternative. Think through why change is necessary in the work you do and the people you manage.

2. Ponder the following statement: "Change is the only constant."

3. Ponder the following statement: "Change changed."

L O 5

Models of Organizational Change

In this section we examine two models of organizational change: Lewin's Three Stage Model and Complexity Theory.

Lewin's Three-Stage Model of Change

Kurt Lewin identified a three-step process that organizations could use to manage change successfully: *unfreeze* the status quo, *move* to a new state, and *refreeze* the new change to make it permanent.[39]

Organizations in their ordinary state reflect the status quo. To move toward a new state, unfreezing is necessary. Unfreezing, the process by which an organization overcomes the resistance to change, can occur in one of three ways, as shown in Figure 7.4.

FIGURE 7.4 | Lewin's Model of Change

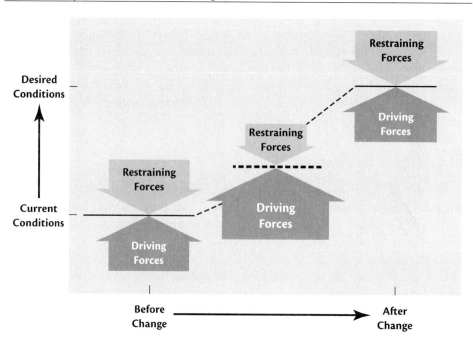

Driving forces, which direct behaviour away from the status quo, can be increased. **Restraining forces**, which hinder movement from the existing equilibrium, can be decreased. One can also combine the first two approaches.

driving forces
Forces that direct behaviour away from the status quo.

restraining forces
Forces that prevent movement away from the status quo.

Individuals generally resist change, and therefore managers must take steps to break down that resistance. They can increase the driving forces by promising new rewards or benefits if employees work toward the change. Managers can also remove some of the restraining forces. For instance, if employees fear change because they do not know how to use the new technology, training could be given to reduce that fear. When resistance to change is extremely high, managers may have to work on both the driving forces and the restraining forces for unfreezing to be successful.

Moving involves getting the change process itself underway. Once change has been implemented, the behaviours have to be refrozen so that they can be sustained over time. Otherwise, change is likely to be short-lived, and employees are likely to go back to the previous state. Refreezing balances the driving and restraining forces to prevent the old state from arising again.

To refreeze the change, managers need to put permanent driving forces into place. For instance, the new bonus system could reinforce specific new changes. Over time, the norms of the employee work groups and managers will also help solidify the change if senior managers have sufficiently reinforced the new behaviour.

Complexity Theory and Organizational Change

Typically, to embrace a strategy for a competitive advantage, a company has to learn new behaviours and practices until they become second nature. The new behaviours and cultural practices must be refrozen to match the new strategy. This alignment positions the firm to take advantage of internal strengths and counter any external threats. However, Ralph Stacey suggests that too much "fit" can prevent an organization from making the necessary changes that would allow it to compete in a dynamic organizational environment. **Complexity theory** suggests that organizations respond best to fundamental change if they are poised on the "edge of chaos," that is, not perfectly aligned with their environments. To achieve this state, managers have to do the following:

complexity theory
Organizations respond best to change if they are not perfectly aligned with their environment.

- Increase the channels of communication to promote informal and spontaneous self-organization—people coming together because they are motivated to find new ways of doing things, not because their department has detailed them to attend a particular committee.

- Not dictate agendas or set specific objectives but identify problems or pose paradoxes for groups to resolve. For example, how can we be both a successful innovator and a low-cost producer? Set rules and establish the constraints for the debate; do not try to predict outcomes.

- Rotate people regularly so that they do not get stale and can both disseminate their own expertise and gain insights from other parts of the business. Bring in outsiders with different backgrounds and cultures. Involve people at the periphery of the organization who have not yet been fully absorbed into the culture.

- Avoid over-reliance on an incumbent management team. In many firms, the further up the hierarchy you go, the greater is the attachment to the existing dominant logic and the closer the adherence to the status quo. We should therefore identify change agents below the top.

- Tolerate parallel developments. In a world where the future is inherently unknowable and everything is to play for, sticking too closely to the knitting can be disastrous. Permit experimentation and learn from failure.

- Avoid excessive "fit." To challenge the status quo, there needs to be enough organizational slack for the firm to develop the future "recipe" alongside the existing one.

- Try to reduce anxiety. Since change is threatening and likely to induce anxiety and defensive behaviour, fear needs to be reduced by offering realistic terms: for example, continued employment in return for total flexibility.[40]

Complexity theory suggests that fixed notions such as mission statements, developing core competencies, and leadership may be suitable for firms operating in a stable environment but have little relevance to those confronting the necessities for fundamental change to remain competitive today. It focuses more on processes and organizational dynamics that question the traditional notion that strategy can be planned and programmed.

LO 6

Managing Change in a Unionized Environment

THINK ABOUT IT

Featherbedding and All That![41]

The British created a civil service job in 1803 that required a man to stand on the cliffs of Dover with a spyglass. He was supposed to ring a bell if he saw Napoleon coming. The job was abolished in 1945.

Featherbedding refers to "the practice of requiring an employer to hire more workers than are needed or to limit their production in keeping with a safety regulation or union rule."[42] Can that same requirement be justified or tolerated in an age such as ours with so much rapid change, downsizing, and outsourcing? That is the question facing both managers and union officials. Some even ask if there is a future for unions? "But the deep question is whether unions have any chance of regaining power in a world of computerization and globalization. So, are unions capable of delivering real value to postmodern workers, or are they just gangs of conspiratorial spongers who smother the occasional business to death as a means of clinging to relevance?"[43]

Statistics Canada shows that Canada's "union density," as it is called, for the year 2004 was 28.6 as a percentage of the civilian labour force and 30.4 as a percentage of nonagricultural paid workers. While the civilian labour force statistics have remained relatively stable over a 14-year period (28.7% for 1990 vs. 28.6% for 2004), the nonagricultural paid workers statistics have shown a decrease (34.8% for 1990 vs. 30.4% for 2004).[44]

It is claimed that the union density is high because of public service employees. The Canadian union movement is also dominated by the "bloated public sector," according to Colby Cosh, Canadian commentator, writer, and editor, and "since the Canadian union movement is dominated by the public sector, most of its leaders are decades away from perceiving this as a problem."

University of Ottawa economics professor Gilles Paquet paints an unflattering economic portrait of Canada, depicting it as a risk-averse nation on the brink of becoming an ageing society. Canada, he wrote in *Policy Options* magazine, is "plagued by social rigidities that prevent it from adapting smoothly and quickly to meet the new [economic] challenges. ... Such an ageing economy is marred by a decline in risk-taking, clinging to old techniques when new and more economical ones are available, resistance to rationalization, [and] a propensity to feather-bedding."[45]

You Be the Manager

1. How will managers engage unions in meaningful ways that involve changes for the future of the workplace?

When managers work in a unionized environment, they may have some other considerations to face. Two consultants who have worked with a number of Canadian organizations in recent years note four essential elements for managing change in a unionized environment.[46]

- *An effective system for resolving day-to-day issues.* Employees should have alternatives to the formal grievance process so that they feel they can be heard easily. If the workplace is open to hearing workers' issues, this will underscore a commitment to participation and empowerment.

- *A jointly administered business education process.* Because union leaders and their members become uneasy about the effects of change on jobs, education can help employees understand the need for change. Making them more aware of company performance helps them better understand the decisions the company makes.

- *A jointly developed strategic vision for the organization.* Giving union members the opportunity to be involved in setting the vision lets them focus on how change can be made, rather than whether it should be made. The vision "should describe performance expectations, work design, organizational structure, the supply chain, governance, pay and rewards, technology, education and training, operating processes, employee involvement, employment security, and union-management roles and relations."[47]

- *A nontraditional, problem-solving method of negotiating collective agreements.* Managers need to create an atmosphere of tolerance and willingness to listen. Expanding the traditional scope of bargaining to include complex issues such as strategic plans is also helpful. Management resists bargaining over these issues, but when managers do bargain, it communicates a commitment to working jointly with unionized employees.

Summary and Review

1. **ORGANIZATIONAL CULTURE** Organizational culture is the set of values, norms, standards of behaviour, and common expectations that guide how individuals and groups in an organization interact with each other and work to achieve organizational goals. Culture guides individuals and groups through shared values, norms, standards of behaviour, and expectations. A strong culture is created and sustained by the values of the founder and senior managers who serve as role models for employees.

2. **LEARNING ORGANIZATIONAL CULTURE** Organizational culture is transmitted to employees through the values of the founder, the process of socialization, organizational ceremonies and rites, and stories and language. The way managers

perform their management functions influences the kind of culture that develops in an organization.

3. **ORGANIZATIONAL CULTURE AND CHANGE** When organizational change is either induced from inside the organization or imposed from outside, changes in the culture of the organization are necessary in order to be successful.

4. **MANAGING ORGANIZATIONAL CHANGE** Managing organizational change is one of managers' most important and difficult tasks. Four steps in the organizational change process are assessing the need for change, deciding on the change to make, introducing the change, and evaluating how successful the change effort has been.

5. **CHANGE MANAGEMENT THEORY** Developed by Kurt Lewin, it suggests a three-step process where the status quo is unfrozen, the organization moves to the desired state, and the changes are refrozen to make them permanent. Complexity theory suggests that to effectively deal with change, managers must create flexible systems that teeter on the "edge of chaos" rather than rigid, permanent structures that perfectly align the strategy and the environment.

6. **MANAGING CHANGE IN A UNIONIZED ENVIRONMENT** To manage change in a unionized environment it is important to resolve day-to-day issues, provide education about the change, work together on developing a vision for the organization, and establish new problem-solving arrangements.

Key Terms

SO WHERE DO YOU STAND?

Wrap-Up to Opening Case

Our opening case began with a discussion on blue ocean strategy versus red ocean strategy. Blue ocean strategy aims for value innovation and as such demands responsiveness from a healthy corporate culture. By its very nature, as we saw in this chapter, culture is elusive, it is intangible, and we simply take it for granted. We also take the air we breathe for granted—until we are deprived of it! Culture takes in our assumptions, understandings, and the implicit rules and expectations we have around our lives and our workplace. Words connect us, one to the other. The adage that "sticks and stones may break your bones, but words will never hurt you" is simply untrue. Words can truly hurt; words can truly heal as well.

When managers, therefore, seek to create positive, life-giving corporate cultures, what they say and how they say it become critical to that health. Culture represents the "way we do things around here."

Organizational culture can be the life-blood to an extremely effective workplace, but it can also cause incredible harm. So much depends on the how managers go about creating their corporate realities. Most of us are familiar with, or have experienced, bosses whose work habits have created pain and anguish in the workplace. Many administrative assistants can validate how destructive some managers can be while creating the building blocks of corporate cultures. A woman named Lisa shared this story with Susan Bourette, the *Globe and Mail* reporter:

He'd [manager] lose it if his pickles weren't sliced properly. He'd lose it if the freshly squeezed grapefruit juice she served him had settled. He lost it for 45 minutes the day she replaced a broken coffee maker with one that wasn't in the company colours. And once, when he was left waiting at the airport for 10 minutes, he called the office, shouting: "How dare you keep me waiting here. *Don't you know I'm the most important man in the world?"*[48]

Luckily, there are also effective managers who do create engaging corporate cultures, such people as Darwin Smith, CEO at paper-products maker Kimberly-Clark.[49] According to Jim Collins, author of *From Good to Great*, he created not just a "good" company but a "great" company, in all respects of this term. What singles out "great" leaders are two factors: will and humility. "Out of 1435 Fortune 500 companies that renowned management researcher Jim Collins studied, only 11 achieved and sustained greatness—garnering stock returns at least three times the market's—for 15 years after a major transition period."

Organizational culture matters because people matter. That declaration not only is ethically correct, it is also the only profitable way to do business.

Management in Action

Topics for Discussion and Action

Level 1

1. What is organizational culture? How does it guide behaviour in organizations? How is corporate culture created and maintained?
2. Explain how members of an organization learn corporate culture.
3. Describe the four steps in the managing organizational change.

Level 2

4. View the following videos on YouTube:
   a. www.youtube.com/watch?v=aOZhbOhEunY.
   b. www.youtube.com/watch?v=vd6BPhJjYL4.
   c. Evaluate the culture at Google. What kinds of green initiatives make up the culture at Google? How does this company entrench its culture?
5. Interview some employees of an organization, and ask them about their organization's values, norms, socialization practices, ceremonies and rites, and special language and stories. Referring to this information, describe the organization's culture.
6. Interview a manager about a change effort that he or she was involved in. What issues were involved? What problems were encountered? What was the outcome of the change process?

Level 3

7. Analyze the difficulties managers face when trying to introduce organizational change? How might they overcome some of these difficulties?
8. Go to the iTunes Store, and listen to the (free) Harvard Business Ideacast number 109, broadcast on August 8, 2008, entitled "Pixar and Collective Creativity." Describe how the co-founder Ed Catmull fosters a creative culture at Pixar. How will the culture be maintained when he leaves the company?
9. Discuss and evaluate the importance of complexity theory in change management.

Building Management Skills

Answer the following questions about the organization you have chosen to follow:

1. Describe the organizational culture of the firm you are following.
2. How does this organization socialize its managers into its cultural values?
3. Has the organization undergone a significant change in the last decade? Describe the driving and restraining forces that operated in this change.
4. If the organization was to experience a significant change in the future, what steps could be taken to ensure that the change takes hold?

Management for You

Think of something that you would like to change in your personal life. It could be your study habits, your fitness and nutrition, the way you interact with others, or anything else that is of interest to you. What values and assumptions have encouraged the behaviour that currently exists (i.e., the one you want to change)?

What driving and restraining forces can you address in order to make the desired change?

Small Group Breakout Exercise

REDUCING RESISTANCE TO ADVANCES IN INFORMATION TECHNOLOGY

Form groups of three or four, and appoint one member as the spokesperson who will communicate your findings to the whole class when called on by the instructor. Then discuss the following scenario:

You are a member of a team of managers in charge of information and communications in a large consumer products corporation. Your company has already introduced many advances in information technology. Managers and employees have access to voice mail, email, the Internet, your company's own intranet, and groupware.

Many employees use the new technology, but the resistance of some is causing communication problems. For example, all managers have email addresses and computers in their offices, but some refuse to turn their computers on, let alone send and receive email. These managers feel that they should be able to communicate as they have always done—in person, over the phone, or in writing. Thus, when managers who are unaware of their preferences send them email messages, those messages are never retrieved.

Moreover, the resistant managers never read company news sent by email. Another example of the resistance that your company is encountering concerns the use of groupware. Members of some work groups do not want to share information with others electronically.

Although you do not want to force people to use the technology, you want them at least to try it and give it a chance. You are meeting today to develop strategies for reducing resistance to the new technologies.

1. One resistant group of employees is made up of top managers. Some of them seem computer-phobic. They have never used, and do not want to start using, personal computers (PCs) for any purpose, including communication. What steps will you take to get these managers to give their PCs a chance?

2. A second group of resistant employees consists of middle managers. Some middle managers resist using your company's intranet. Although these middle managers do not resist the technology per se and use their PCs for multiple purposes, including communication, they seem to distrust the intranet as a viable way to communicate and get things done. What steps will you take to get these middle managers to take advantage of the intranet?

3. A third group of resistant employees is made up of members of groups and teams that do not want to use the groupware that has been provided to them. You think that the groupware could improve their communication and performance, but they seem to think otherwise. What steps will you take to get these members of groups and teams to start using groupware?

Business Planning Exercise

The culture of your organization is reflected in every aspect of the operation—from the art that hangs on the walls, to how open and transparent the management is with the stakeholders. In planning your business, you aim to embed your values and principles in the norms and material symbols of the organization. Think about these issues and what to include in the organizational plan component of your business plan.

1. Develop a set of values and principles or philosophy that you want your venture to follow.

2. Describe the organizational culture you want to foster.

3. How will you teach the managers and staff to internalize these norms and values?

Managing Ethically

Some organizations, such as Arthur Andersen and Enron, seem to have developed norms and values that caused their members to behave in unethical ways. When and why might a strong norm that encourages high performance become one that can cause people to act unethically? How can organizations prevent their values and norms becoming "too strong"?

Exploring the World Wide Web

SPECIFIC ASSIGNMENT

Enter the website of Dupont Canada at www2.dupont.com, and search and download the pdf called Safety Management:
www2.dupont.com/Energy_Sources/en_GB/assets/downloads/Safety%20Managment.pdf.

1. Describe Dupont's strategy of creating "Safety as an Independent Culture."
2. Illustrate the changes that occur as a company moves from a reactive, to dependent, to independent, and finally interdependent culture within an organization.

GENERAL ASSIGNMENT

Search for the website of a company that actively uses organizational culture to build competitive advantage. What kind of values and norms is the culture based on? How does it affect employee behaviour?

McGraw-Hill Connect™—Available 24/7 with instant feedback so you can study when you want, how you want, and where you want. Take advantage of the Study Plan—an innovative tool that helps you customize your learning experience. You can diagnose your knowledge with pre- and post-tests, identify the areas where you need help, search the entire learning package for content specific to the topic you're studying, and add these resources to your personalized study plan. Visit www.mcgrawhillconnect.ca to register—take practice quizzes, search the e-book, and much more.

Be the Manager

THE PERSONAL TOUCH[50]

You have been called in to help with a five-year-old plastics company. This company has grown enormously since its inception and been very successful financially. It has expanded rapidly and now has over 100 employees. The company has come to realize that while it has a very "hands-on" culture as far as technical expertise goes, this approach to working with employees alienated some of the newer employees. As a matter of fact, the company recently lost three of its best employees. In exit interviews, they said they found the company had become very "impersonal" and they did not want to work in such an organization.

Questions

1. What would be some suggestions you could make to create a more "personal" corporate culture?
2. How would you go about helping managers develop a team performance culture as well?

Management Case

New Workers, New Employers[51]
Workplace training, environment, and culture are critical to boosting productivity

Companies will be more productive if senior managers respond to the needs of the "new worker," says Barbara Moses, an author and career expert.

Contrary to expectation, this "new worker" is not the young and the restless twenty-something armed with a master of business administration (MBA) degree and a

Blackberry. Instead, it is the person trying to get ahead in a tough, competitive marketplace while dealing with the stress of trying to achieve work–life balance.

"The new worker is independent of age," says Moses. "Today, everybody has to take responsibility for their own employability."

Work today is a constant audition, she says, a theatre in which no one can rest on [his/her] laurels. That is why employers who offer personal and professional development and who provide learning opportunities stand to reap rewards.

New workers crave everything from formal training and online learning to cross-departmental movement opportunities, says Moses, who emphasizes that professional development should be provided in good times and bad, not just when staff retention is an issue. "Managers need to give people the tools by which they can take charge of their own careers, so they can identify what they need and want."

Here are some ways to keep new workers motivated—and more productive:

Managers who want to advance productivity would be wise to coach and counsel their employees. "People can benefit from the opportunity to be counselled in everything from career development to how to solve tricky political problems," Moses says. "The best way to ensure that someone feels good about having a career inside this company is to give them the skills so they know that, no matter what happens, they are equipped. That also means mentoring and creating a culture in which people take responsibility for ensuring their own employability."

Provide a life-friendly environment. "The bar is very high in the workplace, but, at the same time, people are overwhelmed in their personal lives," Moses says. "If you are asking people to work 110 percent all the time, they will have nothing left and are not going to be productive. Ironically, if you don't have a culture of overwork, then people are more productive."

Although small and mid-sized companies may not be able to provide the bonanza of benefits—such as on-site daycare or help with elder care—offered by giant corporations, they still can be more sensitive to the needs of all staff, regardless of their age and whether or not they are parents.

Smaller organizations need not wait for policies in order to effect change. A company president with young children may decide that work–life balance is a priority, and his attitude can permeate an entire organizational culture. "If anything, the opportunity to leverage things in small- to medium-sized companies is there more than in larger organizations," Moses says. "A policy may be unnecessary."

Create a more intimate culture, an environment where people can feel more closely aligned to their work and its results, Moses advises. "If you're running an organization of 65 000 people, there can be a more alienating experience,

and employees tend to identify more with their work unit," Moses says. A smaller company's personality also can be influenced by the personality of its owner: If that person is motivational, inspiring, and positive, the result can be a terrific work environment.

The opposite is also true in that an egotistical or temperamental leader can wreak havoc and misery. And it is not just a leader's personality that impacts on an organization but also his or her management style. For instance, if the president controls all aspects of the company and is reluctant to let professional managers do their jobs, the results can be disastrous.

Micromanagers can be a real turn-off, Moses notes, especially since today's workers want opportunities to own a project, to have the same kinds of experiences they might have if they were running their own business.

Managers will get the best from their employees if they recognize the unique needs of each and every one of them.

While we all work for money, Moses observes, we also work to be intellectually engaged, to make a difference, to satisfy our needs for connection to others, to refine our craft, to be appreciated for our contribution, or to satisfy deeply held personal values.

Some of these reasons are more important to some employees than others: Ideally, with input from employees, a manager should be able to understand the unique needs of individuals who report to them.

Senior managers on the lookout for ways to improve productivity in others are themselves often under-nurtured. The result is job apathy—a threat to the productivity of both themselves and those they manage. "Many feel caught in a rut. You can't expect them to be models promoting inspiring behaviour for others if they feel overworked, underappreciated, or resentful," Moses says.

She says senior managers should closely examine their own needs and motivations before looking for a new job. "Sometimes you will be able to make minor shifts, to act on the one or two things that are really bothering you within your own organization."

Employees often are motivated by fundamental things such as appreciation for a job well done and some recognition. "Give them the opportunity to make a contribution and feel a sense of accomplishment, and provide them with the kind of training they need to manage their career," Barbara Moses says. "Basically, it's common sense."

Questions

1. What are some new factors in the new corporate culture?
2. Of the new norms and values, which ones will make it easy or difficult to create or change an already existing organizational culture?

Video Management Case

Wendy's Restaurants of Canada

Employees at Wendy's Restaurants of Canada are about to be swept up in a tide of extraordinary change. To boost profits, Wendy's wanted to break down the military style of management and, in its place, create a culture of vulnerability and trust. To launch this change process, Wendy's brought together 160 restaurant managers from across Canada to an Ontario resort where New Mexico-based Pecos River guided them to a new way of working with their employees. This classic CBC video program takes the viewer through the Pecos River program, then transports us to Winnipeg where district manager Craig Stapon is responsible for getting his managers on-board the change process. Although this program was filmed in the early 1990s, it remains one of the best video clips to illustrate the trials and tribulations of introducing change in the workplace.

Questions to consider

1. What changes did executives at Wendy's Restaurants of Canada expect to result from the Pecos River program? Did these changes occur in the Winnipeg restaurants?
2. Was there any resistance to change among the Winnipeg restaurant managers? If so, what form of resistance did it take?
3. What change management strategies did Craig Stapon use among the Winnipeg managers? Were these strategies effective? Why or why not?

Source: From the website of Hill and McShane, Principles of Management (New York: McGraw-Hill/Irwin, 2008). See Management gallery.

Part 4: Integrated Case

Organizations, Like People, Have Personalities[52]

In one particularly funny episode of *Seinfeld*, Jerry goes to a restaurant where his car is parked by a valet who has body odour.

When Jerry picks up the car later, it stinks. He tries everything to get the smell out—he washes the upholstery, cleans the carpet, even changes the seats. Nothing works. The car still stinks.

When I think of some organizational cultures, I am reminded of that episode.

There are five particularly "stinky" organizations to which I have had repeated exposure over the past 20 years.

Although these organizations have been continuously re-engineered, reinvented, reimagined, restructured, redesigned, and every other "re" you can think of, like Jerry Seinfeld's car, they still stink.

Tellingly, when I ask experienced consultants who have had broad corporate exposure about their worst clients, the names of these same companies invariably pop up.

Organizations, like people, have personalities. Go into an organization and, within about 10 minutes, you can get a general sense of what it is like to work there.

At the core, I would describe these "stinky" companies as rigid, arrogant, and cold. People look fed up. Their staffs have that determined look of one who has to catch the commuter train in three minutes and is running late. Their speech is abrupt.

In contrast, when you go into a great work environment, you see and hear people talking as if they really want to be in on the conversation.

There is laughter in the background. People ask their co-workers how projects are going and make offers of help, and some talk about personal life events.

So what makes for a great organization? Obviously, people work for and are motivated by different things, whether it be money, career advancement, collegial work relationships, flexibility, or perfecting a craft.

But at the foundation, we all want the same thing: the opportunity to do work in sync with our values, that plays to our strengths, provides a sense of accomplishment, makes us feel valued, and still leaves something in time and emotional resources to give to other parts of our lives.

What makes the difference is whether the organizational culture truly promotes in employees the sense that they can accomplish their work to a level of personal satisfaction and still go home with energy and a sense of well-being.

People today are hungry—for time, recognition, and appreciation. And when these needs are not met, they are not productive.

Anger ("I'm working too hard for too little reward"), resentment ("my boss gets the best of me, my family gets the dregs") and deprivation ("I have nothing left for me") are not a recipe for employee engagement.

Organizations today talk about the need to promote innovation. But to be creative, people need to feel good about themselves and what they are accomplishing, and an environment that allows them the resources to get their work done. They will not generate innovative ideas when they are exhausted or have a sense of helplessness.

Managers who simultaneously lament looming skills shortages while piling on the work and not providing training, resources, or time are operating as if staff will have collective amnesia when talent again becomes scarce, which it surely will.

Do managers think they can come into work one day and say, "Hey, guys, the skills shortage is here. We've got to start to be nice to people from today on."

Remember Jerry Seinfeld. Once the stink sets in, you cannot get it out. People have an acute sense of smell—and long memories.

Workplace wisdom

Here are some ways that organizations can promote a positive employee experience:

Recognize the diminishing returns from excessive demands. No one can be effective working at full blast all the time.

Demonstrate understanding of the overcommitted lives of staff both in small ways, such as saying thank you, and larger ones, such as meaningful work–life balance opportunities.

Make every employee feel like a unique and valued human being. The acid test: They should be able to answer the question "What is in it for me to work here?" in a simple and compelling way. Show appreciation for individual differences in psychological motivators, life stage needs, and strengths.

Enable staff to have a sense of accomplishment. This means providing sufficient resources, from being able to get information and support to the time required to finish work to a satisfactory level. When people talk about feeling good about themselves and their work, this is often the major reason; that is also conversely the case when they feel demoralized.

Equally important, allow people time "to experience their experience." Most people are actually accomplishing more than they realize, but they have no time to reflect and therefore to digest what they have accomplished. No sooner have they finished something than something else is thrown at them.

Promote learning opportunities. About 70 percent of today's managers and professionals are personal developers, motivated by opportunities to learn, be challenged, and improve their professional skills. Learning can come from conferences, on-the-job training, working with a mentor, or participation in a project that stretches skills.

Provide psychologically meaningful rewards. As one thirty-something woman commented: "Why do they always want us to play golf? It means I have to buy expensive golf clothes and give up time with my kids. How about a nice massage?"

Provide autonomy. For example, let individuals see a project through to experience outcomes associated with their work initiatives, and show trust in their competencies to do it right.

Promote career self-management. Provide staff with tools to enable them to make informed career and life decisions about how they want to spend their time, and design work that plays to their strengths and supports their values and needs. Ask people what they need to feel good about their work experience.

Value all workers regardless of their employment relationship and age. Part-time contract student workers, for example, may become your future full-time employees; older workers, many of whom now are just weighing up how soon they can retire, might also well be a future talent pool, not to mention a valuable mentoring resource, if treated with a degree of respect for their experience and offered opportunities for phased retirement.

Develop a culture that is disdainful of the quick, hurried, and abrupt. Encourage an extra minute to have a conversation that is not goal-directed.

Be an organization that people can be proud to be a part of. Be ethical and a good corporate citizen.

Discussion Questions

1. Choose five factors listed by Dr. Moses that contribute to a great company culture? Why did you choose those five?

2. What are today's workers looking for in their work experiences?

3. What is the most important factor contributing to a healthy corporate culture?

CHAPTER 8

Managing Motivation

Learning Outcomes

1. Describe the nature of motivation and how it leads to the attainment of intrinsic and extrinsic outcomes.

2. Explain how *needs theories* of motivation help managers determine the needs of employees and provide outcomes that satisfy them.

3. Describe how *process theories* of motivation help managers explain high and low performance levels.

4. Explain how managers use reward systems to increase employee motivation.

Made to Stick[1]

We choose to go to the moon in this decade and do the other things, not because they are easy but because they are hard, because that goal will serve to organize and measure the best of our energies and skills, and because that challenge is one that we are willing to accept, one we are unwilling to postpone, and one which we intend to win, and the others, too ... Many years ago the great British explorer George Mallory, who was to die on Mount Everest, was asked why he wanted to climb it. He said, "Because it is there." Well, space is there, and we're going to climb it, and the moon and the planets are there, and new hopes for knowledge and peace are there.[2]

Reach for the moon, and motivate staff to succeed!

When U.S. President John F. Kennedy decided to commit his country to the space race in the early 1960s, he could have addressed the nation the way an experienced chief executive might address his staff.

It would have gone something like this: "Our mission is to become the international leader in the space industry through maximum team-centred innovation and strategically targeted aerospace initiatives."

But Kennedy knew he needed to present an idea that would fire the imagination.

So, at the end of his address to Congress on how the United States could gain the upper hand in the Cold War, Kennedy said: "I believe that this nation should commit itself to achieving the goal, before the decade is out, of landing a man on the moon and returning him safely to Earth. If we make this judgment affirmatively, it will not be one man going to the moon, it will be an entire nation. For all of us must work to put him there."

The mission succeeded, as we know, and Kennedy's man-on-the-moon speech is one of the more famous of his presidency. It continues to inspire today, business writers Chip and Dan Heath say, because it contains all the components of an idea presented in such a way that it genuinely inspires a call to action. For the Heath brothers—one a professor of organizational behaviour at Stanford University, the other a consultant at Duke Corporate

StockTrek/Getty Images
U.S. President John F. Kennedy's address to Congress (May 25, 1961) inspired the American public to put the first man on the moon (July 16, 1969).

Education—Kennedy's words fall into the category of "ideas that stick."

They adhere, according to the Heaths, to these six principles:

"Simple? Yes. Unexpected? Yes. Concrete? Amazingly so. Credible? The goal seemed like science fiction, but the source was credible. Emotional? Yes. Story? In miniature."

These principles, argue the Heaths, who collected hundreds of so-called "sticky ideas" for their book titled (naturally) *Made to Stick*,[3] are the reason why some ideas will inspire and motivate and others will not. And do not dismiss this as a marketer's tactic that has little to do with the workplace, Dan Heath said in a recent interview.

"The No. 1 skill of a manager is communication because, by definition, as a manager you have left the role of being an individual contributor and are now judged by your effectiveness in motivating and aligning other people," he pointed out. "We live in a world where no one has been trained on how to design an idea."

Not rocket science, any of this. While all of these principles appear so much like common sense, the authors are left wondering: "Why aren't we deluged with brilliantly designed sticky ideas? Why is our life filled with more process memos than proverbs?"

One big reason is "the curse of knowledge."

It is beautifully illustrated by a study done in 1990 by Stanford Ph.D. student Elizabeth Newton using a simple game in which she assigned people to be tappers—who tapped out assigned songs like "Happy Birthday to You" by knocking on a table—and listeners, who were to guess the song, based on the rhythm being tapped. Over the course of Elizabeth Newton's experiment, 120 songs were tapped out.

Before they got the score, Newton's tappers predicted that the odds were 50 percent of the songs would be guessed correctly. In reality, instead of getting the song 1 time in 2, the tappers got them 1 time in 40. Listeners guessed only 2.5 percent of the songs. The discrepancy, Newton realized, was that the tappers were hearing the songs in their heads. The listeners were only hearing tap-tap-tap, and the tappers could imagine what it was like not to hear the song.

This is the curse of knowledge, and this experiment is "re-enacted every day across the world," the Heaths wrote. "The tappers and listeners are CEOs and front-line employees, teachers and students, politicians and voters, marketers and customers, writers and readers."

They all need ongoing communication but instead are faced with utter lack of understanding. "When a CEO discusses 'unlocking shareholder value,' there is a tune playing in her head that the employees can't hear." This is the top villain in our need to communicate. "I do think it's this nasty paradox," Dan Heath said. "The smarter you get at something and the better at solving problems, the harder it is to communicate." Communication is even more relevant now, as the business world faces unprecedented change due to economic demands and technological imperatives. So what is a manager to do?

First, Heath said, you have to help people see the new direction in a very concrete way. "Change is always about defining a new destination. If employees can see clearly where you're headed, they're more able to act." This is about being concrete, allowing all employees to buy into the success of the company. "Part of giving a concrete goal is that you can create a mental picture of what success looks like," Heath said. "There's so much complexity during a time of change that delivering new ideas that stick is even more important. It's pivotal that everyone shares a common picture of what this change looks like," he said.

How important is this? "There are an infinite number of great ideas that disappear every day," Heath said. "They must be made to stick."

Now It's Your Turn

What would be five "sticky ideas" that would so catch your attention in a job as to motivate you?

1. _____
2. _____
3. _____
4. _____
5. _____

■■■■ Overview

Over 200 years ago, the Scottish poet and writer Robert Burns (1759–1796) wrote about "the best-laid plans of mice and men." His idea was that people's plans are no more secure than those of mice. This same notion can be applied to life in organizations as well. That is, even with the best strategy in place and an appropriate organizational architecture, an organization will be effective only if its members are motivated to perform at a high level. In any organization leadership is critical to ensure that every member is motivated to perform highly and help the organization achieve its goals. Effective leadership ensures that an organization has a highly motivated workforce. The key, however, is for managers to get to know the employees well to perform at a high level.

FIGURE 8.1 | **Important Theories of Motivation**

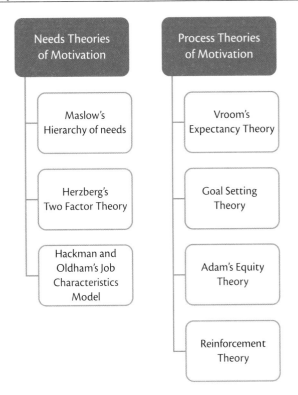

In this chapter, we describe what motivation is, where it comes from, and why managers need to promote high levels of it for an organization to be effective and achieve its goals. In Figure 8.1 we list important theories of motivation.

Each of the theories found in Figure 8.1 provides managers with important insights about how to motivate organizational members. The theories are complementary in that each focuses on a somewhat different aspect of motivation. We begin this chapter with a discussion of the nature of motivation; what it is and how it leads to intrinsic and extrinsic outcomes that are desired by employees. We then look at *needs theories* of motivation. These theories help managers understand how human needs motivate us to act to satisfy them. *Process theories* help managers explain why people act the way they do and thus help managers understand the roots of high and low performance levels among employees. We end the chapter with a discussion of a *total reward strategy* which managers use to encourage high levels of motivation throughout an organization.

LO 1

The Nature of Motivation

THINK ABOUT IT

Spend Time with Your Employees!

Carol Pamasiuk is the executive vice-president and general manager of Cohn & Wolfe Canada,[4] which has offices in Toronto and Montreal and more than 50 employees. It is an affiliate of Cohn & Wolfe, a leading marketing and communications firm with clients around the world. Says Pamasiuk, "Maybe you didn't start out in the mailroom and then work your way to the top, but if you truly want to understand your employees, spend some time doing their jobs and working with them. Unless you've done some of these jobs yourself, you'll never truly appreciate what your employees do, how they do it, what motivates them, and how they see themselves contributing to the organization. Also, standing in your employees' shoes will help you to gain insights into your customers' experiences in interacting with your company, and you may even get some ideas on how to make your business run more efficiently."[5]

You Be the Manager

1. Identify a situation where you spent some time with someone doing his or her job. What happened, and how did you feel?
2. Why would "standing in your employees' shoes" help you gain insights into your customers' experiences in interacting with your company?

motivation
Psychological forces that determine the direction of a person's behaviour in an organization, a person's level of effort, and a person's level of persistence.

intrinsically motivated behaviour
Behaviour that is performed for its own sake.

extrinsically motivated behaviour
Behaviour that is performed to acquire material or social rewards or to avoid punishment.

The term "**motivation**" refers to the psychological forces that determine the *direction* of a person's behaviour in an organization, a person's level of *effort*, and a person's level of *persistence* in the face of obstacles.[6] People are motivated to obtain certain outcomes that they desire. An outcome is anything a person gets from a job or organization. Some outcomes, such as autonomy, responsibility, a feeling of accomplishment, and the pleasure of doing interesting or enjoyable work, result in intrinsically motivated behaviour. Other outcomes, such as pay, job security, benefits, and vacation time, result in extrinsically motivated behaviour. **Intrinsically motivated behaviour** is behaviour that is performed for its own sake; the source of motivation is actually to perform the behaviour, and motivation comes from doing the work itself. **Extrinsically motivated behaviour** is behaviour that is performed to acquire material or social rewards or to avoid punishment; the source of motivation is the consequences of the behaviour, not the behaviour itself.

Organizations hire people to obtain important inputs. An input is anything a person contributes to his or her job or organization, such as time, effort, education, experience, skills, knowledge, and actual work behaviours. Inputs such as these are necessary for an organization to achieve its goals. Managers strive to motivate members of an organization to contribute inputs—through their behaviour, effort, and persistence—that help the organization achieve its goals. They do this by making sure that members of an organization obtain the outcomes they desire when they make valuable contributions to the organization.

This alignment between employees and organizational goals as a whole can be described by the motivation equation shown in Figure 8.2. Managers aim to ensure that people are motivated to contribute important inputs to the organization, that these inputs are put to good use or focused in the direction of high performance, and that high performance results in employees obtaining the outcomes they desire.

The main theories of motivation that we cover in this chapter fall into one of two categories: needs theories and process theories. *Needs theories* focus on the types of needs individuals have that will lead them to be motivated, and *process theories* explore how one actually motivates someone by explaining common workplace behaviours, such as why some people perform well while others perform poorly. Process theories can also explain high absenteeism, lack of punctuality, and high turnover rates. Each of the theories of motivation we discuss focuses on one or more aspects of the motivation equation in Figure 8.2. Together, the

FIGURE 8.2 | **The Motivation Equation**

INPUTS FROM ORGANIZATIONAL MEMBERS	PERFORMANCE	OUTCOMES RECEIVED BY ORGANIZATIONAL MEMBERS
Time Effort Education Experience Skills Knowledge Work behaviours	Contributes to organizational efficiency, organizational effectiveness, and the attainment of organizational goals	Pay Job security Benefits Vacation time Job satisfaction Autonomy Responsibility A feeling of accomplishment The pleasure of doing interesting work

theories provide a comprehensive set of guidelines for managers to follow to promote high levels of employee motivation. Effective managers tend to follow many of these guidelines, whereas ineffective managers often fail to follow them and seem to have trouble motivating organizational members.

LO 2

Needs Theories of Motivation

THINK ABOUT IT

"Echo Employees": Coddled, Confident, and Cocky![7]

Managers today have to manage "echo employees"! They may not particularly appreciate these employees, precisely because of their demographic identity. The challenge for such managers is to learn how to motivate them.

Echo employees, born since the 1980s, are the children of the baby boomers. So, who are they?

Tomi/Photo Link/Getty Images
Echo employee confidently exhibiting her own style.

This is the first postwar generation that, on the whole, has not rebelled against their parents' or society's values, nor against a work environment they view as withholding opportunities. ...

Gen-Yers were raised by guilty, work-obsessed, hovering parents who made their kids' feelings and success their hobby. They worshipped at the altar of promoting self-esteem and tried to make up for the lack of time spent with their kids by lavishing them with travel experiences, clothes, and electronic toys.

As kids, Gen-Yers were told they were brilliant because they could program the VCR. They were given the vote on almost everything, from where to go on vacation to the colour of the family car. It is not surprising they believe their feelings matter, that they should feel good about their work, and that they should be able to express themselves. People used to think about work only when it felt bad, if they thought about it at all. Now, as a result of heightened work consciousness, this generation asks, "Does this feel good?" They use a finely nuanced vocabulary to describe their work and are more thoughtful about their careers and work. And when they are not happy, much to management's regret, they are vocal about it.

You Be the Manager

1. What are the two most important concerns for "echo employees"?
2. What advice would you give an older manager on how to motivate "echo employees"?

---

need
A requirement or necessity for survival and well-being.

needs theories
Theories of motivation that focus on what needs people are trying to satisfy at work and what outcomes will satisfy those needs.

A **need** is a requirement or necessity for survival and well-being. The basic premise of need theories is that people are motivated to obtain outcomes at work that will satisfy their needs. **Needs theories** suggest that in order to motivate a person to contribute valuable inputs to a job and perform at a high level, a manager must determine what needs the person is trying to satisfy at work and ensure that the person receives outcomes that help satisfy those needs when the person performs at a high level and helps the organization achieve its goals.

We discuss three needs theories below: Abraham Maslow's *hierarchy of needs*, Frederick Herzberg's *two-factor motivator-hygiene theory*, and Hackman and Oldham's *job characteristics approach* to motivation. These theories describe needs that people try to satisfy at work. In doing so, the theories provide managers with insights about what outcomes will motivate members of an organization to perform at a high level and contribute inputs to help the organization achieve its goals.

Maslow's Hierarchy of Needs

Maslow's hierarchy of needs
An arrangement of five basic needs that, according to Maslow, motivate behaviour. Maslow proposed that the lowest level of unmet needs is the prime motivator and that only one level of needs is motivational at a time.

Psychologist Abraham Maslow proposed that everyone aims to satisfy five basic kinds of needs: physiological needs, safety needs, belongingness needs, esteem needs, and self-actualization needs (see Table 8.1).[8] He suggested that these needs constitute a **hierarchy of needs**, with the most basic or compelling needs—physiological and safety needs—at the bottom. Maslow argued that these lowest-level needs must be met before a person will strive to satisfy needs higher up in the hierarchy, such as self-esteem needs. Once a need is satisfied, he proposed, it no longer is a source of motivation, and needs at the next highest level become motivators.

Although Maslow's theory identifies needs that are likely to be important sources of motivation for many people, research does not support his contention that there is a needs hierarchy or his notion that only one level of needs is motivational at a time.[9] Nevertheless, a key conclusion can be drawn from Maslow's theory: People differ in what needs they are trying to satisfy at work. To have a motivated workforce that achieves goals, managers must determine which needs employees are trying to satisfy in organizations and then make sure that individuals receive outcomes that will satisfy their needs when they perform at a high level and contribute to organizational effectiveness.

In an increasingly global economy, it is also important for managers to realize that citizens of different countries might differ in the needs they try to satisfy through work.[10] Some research suggests, for example, that people in Greece and Japan are especially motivated by safety needs and that people in Sweden, Norway, and Denmark are motivated by belongingness needs.[11] In poor countries with low standards of living, physiological and safety needs are likely to be the prime motivators of behaviour. As countries become wealthier and have higher standards of living, it is likely that needs

TABLE 8.1 | *Maslow's Hierarchy of Needs*

	Needs	Description	Examples of How Managers Can Help People Satisfy These Needs at Work
Highest-level needs	**Self-actualization needs**	The needs to realize one's full potential as a human being	By giving people the opportunity to use their skills and abilities to the fullest extent possible
	Esteem needs	The needs to feel good about oneself and one's capabilities, to be respected by others, and to receive recognition and appreciation	By granting promotions and recognizing accomplishments
	Belongingness needs	Needs for social interaction, friendship, affection, and love	By promoting good interpersonal relations and organizing social functions such as company picnics and holiday parties
Lowest-level needs (most basic or compelling)	**Safety needs**	Needs for security, stability, and a safe environment	By providing job security, adequate medical benefits, and safe working conditions
	Physiological needs	Basic needs such as food, water, and shelter that must be met in order for a person to survive	By providing a level of pay that enables a person to buy food and clothing and have adequate housing

The lowest level of unsatisfied needs motivates behaviour; once this level of needs is satisfied, a person tries to satisfy the needs at the next level.

related to personal growth and accomplishment (such as esteem and self-actualization) become important as motivators of behaviour.

Herzberg's Motivator-Hygiene Theory

According to **Herzberg's motivator-hygiene theory**, also known as the two-factor theory, people have two sets of needs or requirements: motivator needs and hygiene needs.[12] *Motivator needs* are related to the nature of the work itself and how challenging it is. Outcomes such as interesting work, autonomy, responsibility, being able to grow and develop on the job, and a sense of accomplishment and achievement help satisfy motivator needs. In order to have a highly motivated and satisfied workforce, Herzberg suggested, managers should take steps to ensure that employees' motivator needs are being met.

Hygiene needs are related to the physical and psychological context in which the work is performed. Hygiene needs are satisfied by outcomes such as pleasant and comfortable working conditions, fair pay, job security, good relationships with co-workers, and effective supervision. According to Herzberg, when hygiene needs are not met, workers will be dissatisfied, and when hygiene needs are met, workers will not be dissatisfied, that is, they will be neutral. For satisfaction to occur, the motivator needs must be met. Herzberg measures dissatisfaction and satisfaction on two different continuums because the factors causing each are different. According to Herzberg, the opposite of satisfaction is not dissatisfaction but, rather, *no* satisfaction. Similarly, the opposite of dissatisfaction is *no* dissatisfaction. Hygiene factors must be adequate for employees to feel no dissatisfaction, while jobs must be sufficiently empowered in order for employees to feel satisfaction. This is illustrated in Figure 8.3. Pazmac's owner, Steve Scarlett, exhibits his understanding of Herzberg's theory. To satisfy motivator needs, he provides opportunities for his employees to be involved in decision making and ensures good relationships among employees. He also shows concerns about employees' hygiene needs. Usually machine

Herzberg's motivator-hygiene theory
A needs theory that distinguishes between motivator needs (related to the nature of the work itself) and hygiene needs (related to the physical and psychological context in which the work is performed). Herzberg proposed that motivator needs must be met in order for motivation and job satisfaction to be high.

Pazmac Enterprises
www.pazmac.com

FIGURE 8.3 | Herzberg's Motivation-Hygiene Theory

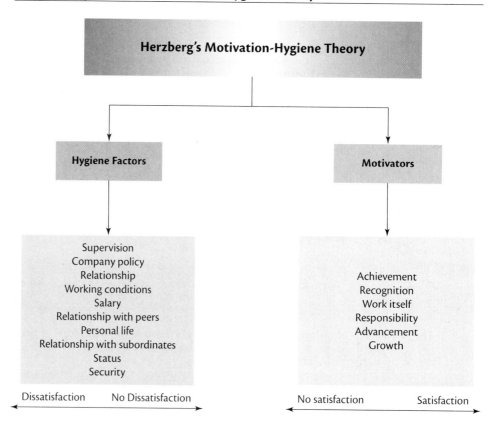

shops are noisy and messy, the floors are covered with oil, and employees wear dirty overalls. Pazmac, however, is spotlessly clean. The lunchroom is tastefully designed, and the men's washroom is plush, with potpourri bowls and art on the walls.

Many research studies have tested Herzberg's propositions, and, by and large, the theory fails to receive support.[13] Nevertheless, Herzberg's formulations have contributed to our understanding of motivation in at least two ways. First, Herzberg helped researchers and managers focus attention on the important distinction between intrinsic motivation (related to motivator needs) and extrinsic motivation (related to hygiene needs), covered earlier in the chapter. Second, his theory prompted researchers and managers to study how jobs can be designed or redesigned so that they are intrinsically motivating.

Hackman and Oldham's Job Characteristics Model

Hackman and Oldham's job characteristic model
States that when employee growth needs are strong, integrating core job dimensions into their work, leads to positive personal and job outcomes.

Hackman and Oldham's job characteristics model (see Figure 8.4) outlines five core job dimensions that when incorporated into the design of a job can lead to positive personal and organizational outcomes. Jobs that require the employee to do a broad range of tasks instead of a narrow range of tasks have a high level of *skill variety*. *Task identity* is the degree to which one associates oneself with the work or profession. The extent that one controls the entire process of production or simply a small part of it determines the task identity. Jobs that involve conceptualizing the product and executing the tasks involved in its production have high levels of task identity. *Task significance* is the degree to which the job is socially relevant and important. The above three core job dimensions have the potential to create a sense of meaningfulness for employees and generally result in positive personal and organizational outcomes.

FIGURE 8.4 | Job Characteristics Model

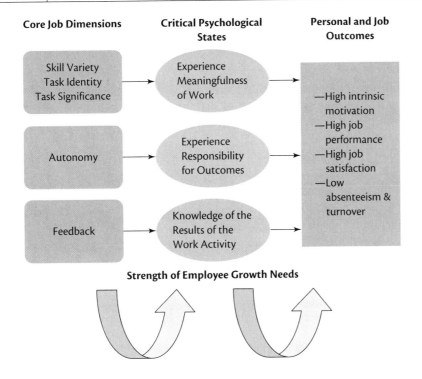

When *autonomy* is built into a job, employees direct their own work. The results of the work activity are known to the employee from the degree of *feedback* they get from doing the work itself. The degree of feedback can be high or low. See Table 8.2 for examples.

The degree to which the core job characteristics should be built into the design of the job depends on the state of the employee's need for growth, that is their desire and ability to take on responsibility and challenging goals. Employees with a strong growth need will be motivated to perform well when the job design has high levels of the core job characteristics, while an employee who has a low need for growth, perhaps due to stress and burnout, will not be motivated to perform well if given additional responsibility.

TABLE 8.2 | *Job Characteristics Model Examples*

Job Characteristics	Example of High Levels	Example of Low Levels
Skill Variety	A worker at Subway sandwiches who bakes the buns, makes the customer's sandwich, and processes the payment for the order	A worker at MacDonald's who grills hamburgers for the entire shift
Task Identity	A seamstress or tailor who designs a suit, creates the pattern, selects the cloth, and sews the garment	A worker in a textile factory who operates a machine that cuts cloth
Task Significance	A firefighter who rescues people and property from devastation	A cashier at a coffee shop
Autonomy	An electrician who decides which jobs to do, when to do them, and how best to fix any problems that arise	An automotive assembly-line worker
Feedback	A chef who cooks and tastes the dish and adjusts the seasonings	A kitchen hand who peels potatoes but has no role in preparing a dish with them and tasting it

Other Needs

Clearly, more needs motivate employees than the those described by these theories. For example, more and more employees are feeling the need for work–life balance and time to take care of their loved ones while also being highly motivated at work. Interestingly enough, recent research suggests that being exposed to nature (even just by being able to see some trees from your office window) has many beneficial effects and that a lack of such exposure can actually impair well-being and performance.[14] Thus, having some time during the day when one can at least see nature may be another important need.

Managers of successful companies often strive to ensure that as many of their valued employees' needs as possible are satisfied in the workplace.

Needs theories address the different needs that individuals have that could be used to motivate them. **Process theories**, which we cover below, focus on the more concrete ways of actually motivating someone. Within the process theories, we cover *expectancy theory, goal-setting theory, reinforcement theory,* and *equity theory.*

process theories
Theories of motivation that explore how one actually motivates someone.

LO 3

Process Theories of Motivation

THINK ABOUT IT

Hiring Is Just the First Step[15]

Diverse workers will need to become leaders

Canada's universities boast a wonderful mosaic of cultures and traditions. At Ernst & Young, we are inspired by the increasingly diverse student bodies we encounter nationwide. We are proud to recruit from this rich pool of bright individuals, and our workforce reflects this diversity. But it is also important to help people feel included once they enter our environment. If we do not motivate them to grow and develop, we will fail our people and our business.

When my husband and I moved here from South Africa in 1987, we were excited about building a new life. Canada has always been a country with great potential and a bright future. But we face real challenges in achieving that potential and reaching that future.

Canada's workforce is changing: The baby boom generation is hitting retirement age, the national birth rate is dipping, and industries are feeling the first pains of a true talent crunch. Our reaction to these changes will set the pace for business in the twenty-first century.

As a woman who often finds herself presenting to all-male audiences in an accent different from theirs, I know what it feels like to stand on the outside looking in. More than 20 years ago, I arrived here armed with four degrees, enthusiasm, and the will to make a contribution. I sent out countless resumes but received just one reply.

Highly skilled people in our communities face this every day: We have all been in taxis driven by lawyers, doctors, or engineers. We have the ability to change this. It begins when we open the door to diversity. But it flourishes when our work environments become places where everyone feels accepted, able to share, and encouraged to grow.

It is not enough to announce that we welcome diversity. Creating an inclusive workplace must be a key business objective—one pursued with the same energy we invest in developing new markets. Where do we start? By broadly redefining culture to include gender, ethnicity, sexual preference, immigration status, age, parental status, disability, and other characteristics that contribute to who we are. Then we identify leaders and set goals.

At Ernst & Young, all groups have inclusiveness champions. We take snapshots to measure our results. This helps us tailor our initiatives to the specific needs of all employees.

Cross-cultural coaching and workshops are a big part of our strategy. Employees need to be provided with practical skills for working in diverse teams and communicating across different cultures. Also, by developing professional networks that support women, companies can change the face of senior leadership and gain a valuable perspective.

By opening up companies to bright new Canadians, Canadian businesses gain a competitive edge and a better understanding of our increasingly diverse customers around the globe. At our firm, we have developed Succeeding in Canada workshops to help new Canadians, including skilled immigrants who make up 24 percent of our population, acclimatize to this business scene.

The threat of negative repercussions often hinders the lesbian-gay-bisexual-transgender (LGBT) population. By educating employees about vital issues, we give these individuals the chance to participate without fear. Ernst & Young's LGBT network addresses this.

By setting specific goals, building cross-cultural skills, implementing mentorship programs, and measuring results, we can all learn to leverage our differences to create better teams capable of achieving more.

Business is always evolving. But for those who stand out for being "different," the challenges remain largely the same. Canada is a diverse society. Imagine what we could achieve if our meeting rooms truly reflected this. We have the power to fully engage our workforce by welcoming people and building frameworks to help them succeed. The time to do that is now.

You Be the Manager

1. What else is required in addition to recruiting well?

expectancy theory
The theory that motivation will be high when employees believe that high levels of effort will lead to high performance and that high performance will lead to the attainment of desired outcomes.

expectancy
In expectancy theory, a perception about the extent to which effort will result in a certain level of performance.

Expectancy Theory

Expectancy theory, formulated by Victor H. Vroom in the 1960s, states that motivation will be high when employees believe that high levels of effort will lead to high performance and that high performance will lead to receiving desired outcomes. Expectancy theory is one of the most popular theories of work motivation because it focuses on all three parts of the motivation equation: inputs, performance, and outcomes. Expectancy theory identifies three major factors that determine a person's motivation: *expectancy, instrumentality,* and *valence* (see Figure 8.5).[16]

Expectancy

Expectancy is a person's perception about the extent to which effort (an input) will result in a certain level of performance.

Courtesy of Inco Ltd.
Inco Ltd. has rolled out a front-line planning and scheduling system at its Copper Cliff smelter in Sudbury, Ontario, in which the daily, weekly, and monthly goals for production and maintenance are clearly established every day.

■ **FIGURE 8.5** | **Expectancy, Instrumentality, and Valence**

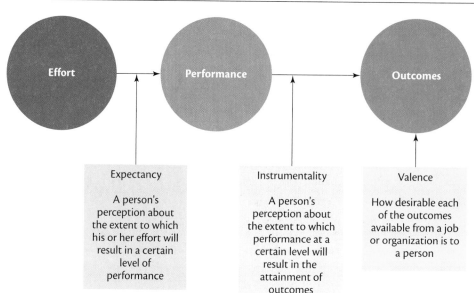

A person's level of expectancy determines whether he or she believes that a high level of effort will result in a high level of performance. People are motivated to put forth a lot of effort on their jobs only if they think that their effort will pay off in high performance—that is, if they have a high expectancy. Think about how motivated you would be to study for a test if you thought that no matter how hard you tried, you would get only a D. In this case, expectancy is low, so overall motivation is also low.

In trying to influence motivation, managers need to make sure that their subordinates believe that if they do try hard, they actually can succeed. For example, excessive criticism, as we know from our own experiences, leads to relatively low levels of expectancy on our part. We begin to doubt our own ability to succeed, which then leads to low motivation. In addition to expressing confidence in subordinates, another way for managers to boost subordinates' expectancy levels and motivation is by providing training so that people have all the expertise they need for high performance. At Irving Oil Ltd., at Saint John, New Brunswick, a family-owned company known for its tankers, truck stops, and refinery towers, managers eagerly look forward to leadership training with the workplace learning provider Forum Corp. of Boston, Massachusetts. Kenneth Irving, a senior executive, at Irving Oil, actively promotes the training and the need for more of such training.[17] NuComm International Inc., a privately held company based in St. Catherines, Ontario, which provides "customer care" services for North American companies in the cable, telecommunications, automotive, entertainment, and retail sectors, is another such company that believes in training. Linda Robichaud, who works as a telephone service representative, remarked that NuComm's training is comprehensive and professional, "I was on the phones for one week, and then I moved up. I'm training to be a trainer." The training increases Robichaud's expectancy by improving her ability to perform well.

From the point of view of how they are being managed, according to Greg Schinkel, of London, Ontario, speaker, trainer, and the co-author of *Employees Not Doing What*

You Expect,[18] we can see the 12 reasons why employees do not meet expectations and how these can be prevented

1. Employees do not know what managers expect.
2. Employees think what they are already doing is acceptable.
3. Employees think what they are doing is not important.
4. Employees feel overwhelmed and confused.
5. Employees do not know how to do it.
6. Employees do not have the resources.
7. Employees are being prevented by others.
8. Employees are not suited to the jobs.
9. Employees think: something to gain, nothing to lose.
10. Employees have given up trying.
11. Employees have personal problems.
12. Employees are trouble makers sometimes.[19]

Instrumentality

Expectancy captures a person's perceptions about the relationship between effort and performance. **Instrumentality**, the second major concept in expectancy theory, is a person's perception about the extent to which performance at a certain level will result in receiving outcomes or rewards (see Figure 8.5). According to expectancy theory, employees will be motivated to perform at a high level only if they think that high performance will lead to outcomes such as pay, job security, interesting job assignments, bonuses, or a feeling of accomplishment.

Managers promote high levels of instrumentality when they clearly link performance to desired outcomes and communicate this. By making sure that rewards are given to organizational members based on their performance, managers promote high instrumentality and motivation. When rewards are linked to performance in this way, high performers receive more than low performers. In the case of Cognos Inc., the Ottawa-based software company, (now a subsidiary of IBM) when employees realized there would be more feedback, more recognition, and more help in meeting their personal goals, they were more motivated to stay with the company. They see the link between performance and reward.

instrumentality
In expectancy theory, a perception about the extent to which performance will result in the attainment of outcomes.

http://www_01.ibm.com/ software/data/cognos

Valence

Expectancy theory acknowledges that people differ in their preferences for outcomes or rewards. For many people, pay is the most important outcome of working. For others, a feeling of accomplishment or enjoying one's work is more important. At Motorola's Malaysian plant, the rewards to employees reflect things that they value. Salaries are relatively high, as are job security and promotional opportunities, which makes employees feel that they are valued members of Motorola.[20] The term **valence** refers to how desirable each of the outcomes available from a job or organization is to a person. To motivate organizational members, managers need to determine which outcomes have high valence for them—are highly desired—and make sure that those outcomes are provided when members perform at a high level.

valence
In expectancy theory, how desirable each of the outcomes available from a job of organization is to a person.

Bringing It All Together

According to expectancy theory, high motivation results from high levels of expectancy, instrumentality, and valence (see Figure 8.6). If any one of these factors is low,

FIGURE 8.6 | Expectancy Theory

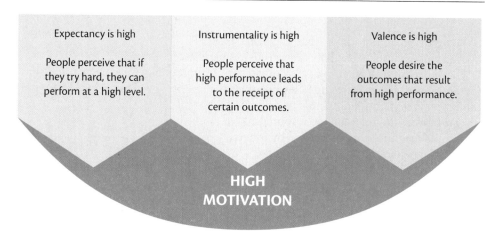

FIGURE 8.7 | How Managers Can Apply Expectancy Theory

To Increase Employee Motivation, Managers Can:		
Increase Expectancy Levels	**Increase Instrumentality Levels**	**Increase Valence**
• by providing proper training	• by keeping their word and being transparent in the distibution of outcomes (rewards)	• by individualizing outcomes and rewards

motivation is likely to be low. No matter how tightly desired outcomes are linked to performance, if a person thinks that it is practically impossible for him or her to perform at a high level, then motivation to perform at a high level will be exceedingly low. Similarly, if a person does not think that outcomes are linked to high performance, or if a person does not desire the outcomes that are linked to high performance, then motivation to perform at a high level will be low.

Managers of successful companies try to ensure that employees' levels of expectancy, instrumentality, and valence are high so that they will be highly motivated (see Figure 8.7), as is illustrated by Motorola's efforts at managing globally.

Goal-Setting Theory

"People do not always argue because they misunderstand one another; they argue because they hold different goals."
—William H. Whyte, author of *The Organization Man*[21]

goal-setting theory
A theory that focuses on identifying the types of goals that are most effective in producing high levels of motivation and performance and explaining why goals have these effects.

Goal-setting theory, developed by Ed Locke and Gary Latham, suggests that the goals that organizational members strive to achieve determine their motivation and subsequent performance. A *goal* is what a person is trying to accomplish through his or her efforts and behaviours.[22] Just as you may have a goal to get a good grade in this course, members of an organization have goals that they strive to meet. Psychologist Barbara Moses writes, "Without any goals, we drift. Take one 35-year-old man who has spent the past decade bouncing around among different occupational pursuits. With indulgent and wealthy parents behind him, he has never had any sense of urgency to commit to a particular career path; nor has he ever thought through what he wanted to achieve in his occupational pursuits, other than a vague feeling of "this might be it."

When you talk to him, you get a sense of a lost soul who has no belief in himself or his future."[23]

Goal-setting theory suggests that in order to result in high motivation and performance, goals must be *specific and difficult*.[24] Specific goals are often quantitative—a salesperson's goal to sell $200 worth of merchandise each day, a scientist's goal to finish a project in one year, a CEO's goal to reduce debt by 40 percent and increase revenues by 20 percent, a restaurant manager's goal to serve 150 customers each evening. In contrast to specific goals, vague goals such as "doing your best" or "selling as much as you can" do not have much motivational force. Difficult goals are ones that are hard but not impossible to attain.

Regardless of whether specific difficult goals are set by managers, workers, or managers and workers together, they lead to high levels of motivation and performance. As CEO of Eastman Kodak, George Fisher set specific, difficult goals for his employees but then left deciding how to meet the goals up to them. When managers set goals for their subordinates, it is important that their subordinates accept the goals or agree to work toward them and also that they are committed to them or really want to attain them. Some managers find that having subordinates participate in the actual setting of goals boosts their acceptance of and commitment to the goals. It is also important for organizational members to receive *feedback* about how they are doing; feedback can often be provided by the performance appraisal and feedback component of an organization's human resource management system (see Chapter 11).

Reinforcement Theory

THINK ABOUT IT

Take This Job and Shove It![25]

There are jobs, and then there are jobs! Have you ever had a job that you would classify as "less-than-perfect"? In fact, you had to "gear up" every day, so to speak, just to get to work. Many of us have had those jobs when first entering the workforce. Then, again, we might have such a job even later in order to pay the bills.

Some would consider night-shift work to be one of those "less-than-perfect" jobs. Take the jobs that many of us take for granted: taxi drivers, medical personnel at hospitals, emergency service personnel, and police officers. Many of these people do shift work. Abdul Said, a Royal Taxi night-shift driver in Toronto, who works seven days a week at 12-hour shifts that start late in the afternoon, says he needs to work such hours because his wife is only employed sporadically and he wants to give his growing children the advantages their friends have. "I feel guilty that I don't have a lot of time with my family. But I would feel more guilty if I abandoned my kids to the social system or left them alone. So I prefer to work to provide them with food and shelter," said Said, who has been on the night shift for three years. Somehow he has to find that motivational spark that will provide the energy to do what he has to do.

Sgt. Jim Adamson, with 26 years as a police officer, finds it very difficult to get his body "turned around again," as he puts it. "Often tired on the midnight shift, the police officer nonetheless tosses and turns when he has to try to get some sleep during the day—his body rebelling against its natural circadian rhythms. He pays extra attention to his health because he finds his body is more susceptible to illnesses when he is on midnights. The cyclical night-time absences from home have also taken a toll on his personal life. His marriage fell apart after 14 years and he blames the graveyard duty for contributing to the breakup."

You Be the Manager

1. What are the challenges that the following shift workers face in their jobs: police officers, taxi drivers, medical personnel?
2. How would you motivate yourself if you had to do shift work?

reinforcement theory
A motivation theory based on the relationship between a given behaviour and its consequence.

reinforcement
Anything that causes a given behaviour to be repeated or stopped.

Reinforcement theory is a motivation theory that looks at the relationship between behaviour and its consequences. **Reinforcement** is defined as anything that causes a certain behaviour to be repeated. Actions that receive reinforcement or stimulus (either positive or negative) will be repeated. Four reinforcements are generally discussed in the theory: *positive reinforcement, negative reinforcement, extinction,* and *punishment.* Positive reinforcement and punishment involve presenting a stimulus or reinforcer, while negative reinforcement and extinction involve removing the stimulus or reinforcer. See Table 8.3. Managers use these four techniques to modify the workplace behaviours of employees.

Positive Reinforcement

positive reinforcement
Giving people outcomes they desire when they perform organizationally functional behaviours well.

Positive reinforcement gives people outcomes they desire when they perform well. These outcomes, called positive reinforcers, include any outcome that a person desires, such as good pay, praise, or a promotion. Performing well might include producing high-quality goods and services, providing high-quality customer service, and meeting deadlines. By linking positive reinforcers to positive performance, managers motivate people to perform the desired behaviours. For instance, managers at Brandon's hog slaughterhouse offer a variety of incentives to encourage workers to show up for their shifts. To be eligible for a truck raffle, held every three months, employees have to show up for every one of their shifts during that period. Employees get bonuses of

TABLE 8.3 | *Four Reinforcement Techniques*

Action	Type of Stimulus	
	Positive	**Negative**
Present the Reinforcer or Stimulus	*Positive reinforcement*—increases the desired behaviour. Give a reward when desired actions are exhibited. **For example:** Jon arrives at work early (desired action) and is given praise (positive stimulus) by his manager.	*Punishment*—decreases the undesired behaviour. Take something of value away when the undesired action is exhibited. **For example:** Sarah arrives at work late consistently (undesired action) and is made to stay late (negative stimulus) by her manager to make up the time.
Remove the Reinforcer or Stimulus	*Extinction*—decreases the undesired behaviour. Ignore the undesired behaviour when it occurs to stop it from being repeated. **For example:** Ash constantly asks inappropriate questions at staff meetings. Rather than acknowledging Ash (positive stimulus is removed) and giving her a platform to be heard, her manager ignores her raised hand.	*Negative reinforcement*—increases the desired behaviour. Remove the unpleasant consequence or punishment when the desired behaviour is exhibited. **For example:** When Sarah arrives at work on time (desired action), her manager does not demand that she work late (negative stimulus is removed).

75 cents an hour for perfect attendance during shorter periods. Regular wages range from $8.25 to $13 an hour. The incentive program has paid off. Before the rewards, 12 percent of the employees skipped work each day. Since the rewards, absenteeism has dropped to about 7 to 8 percent.

Negative Reinforcement

Negative reinforcement also can be used to encourage members of an organization to perform well. Managers using negative reinforcement actually eliminate or remove undesired outcomes once the desired behaviour is performed. These undesired outcomes, called *negative reinforcers*, can include unpleasant assignments, a manager's constant nagging or criticism, or the ever-present threat of termination. When negative reinforcement is used, people are motivated to perform behaviours because they want to avoid or stop receiving undesired outcomes. For example, when a salesperson exceeds the quota, his or her manager cancels the pep-talk meetings. In this case, the reinforcer or negative stimulus is removed (the pep-talk lecture) because the salesperson has performed the desired behaviour (booked more than expected sales).

Whenever possible, managers should try to use positive reinforcement. Negative reinforcement can make for a very unpleasant work environment and even a negative culture in an organization. No one likes to be nagged, threatened, or exposed to other kinds of negative outcomes. The use of negative reinforcement sometimes causes subordinates to resent managers and try to get back at them.

> **negative reinforcement**
> Eliminating or removing undesired outcomes once people have performed organizationally functional behaviours.

Extinction

Sometimes members of an organization are motivated to engage in poor performance. One way for managers to stop dysfunctional behaviours is to eliminate whatever is reinforcing the behaviours. This process is called **extinction**.

Suppose a manager has a subordinate who frequently stops by the office to chat—sometimes about work-related matters but at other times about various topics ranging from politics to last night's football game. Though the chats are fun, the manager ends up working late to catch up. To extinguish this behaviour, the manager stops acting interested in these nonwork-related conversations and keeps responses polite and friendly but brief. No longer being reinforced with a pleasant conversation, the subordinate eventually ceases to be motivated to interrupt the manager during working hours to discuss nonwork issues.

> **extinction**
> Stopping the performance of dysfunctional behaviours by eliminating whatever is reinforcing them.

Punishment

When employees are performing dangerous behaviours or those that are illegal or unethical, the behaviours need to be stopped immediately. Therefore the manager will use **punishment**, administering undesired or negative consequences to subordinates when they perform the dysfunctional behaviours. Punishments used by organizations range from verbal reprimands to pay cuts, temporary suspensions, demotions, and terminations. Punishment, however, can have unintended side effects—resentment, loss of self-respect, a desire for retaliation, and so on—and should be used only when absolutely necessary.

> **punishment**
> Administering an undesired or negative consequence when dysfunctional behaviour occurs.

Organizational Behaviour Modification

When managers use reinforcement to encourage positive behaviours and discourage negative behaviours, they are engaging in **organizational behaviour modification (OB MOD)**.[26] OB MOD has been used successfully to improve productivity, efficiency, attendance, punctuality, compliance with safety procedures, and other important behaviours in a wide variety of organizations. The five basic steps in OB MOD are described in Figure 8.8.

> **organizational behaviour modification (OB MOD)**
> The systematic application of operant conditioning techniques to promote the performance of organizationally functional behaviours and discourage the performance of dysfunctional behaviours.

OB MOD works best for behaviours that are specific, objective, and countable—such as attendance and punctuality, making sales, or putting telephones together—which lend themselves to careful scrutiny and control. OB MOD may be questioned because of its lack of relevance to certain kinds of work behaviours (e.g., the many work behaviours that are not specific, objective, and countable). Some people also have questioned it on ethical grounds. Critics of OB MOD suggest that it is overly controlling and robs workers of their dignity, individuality, freedom of choice, and even their creativity. Supporters counter that OB MOD is a highly effective means of promoting organizational efficiency. Both sides of this argument have some merit. What is clear, however, is that when used appropriately, OB MOD provides managers with a technique to motivate the performance of at least some positive behaviours.

In trying to understand how all of these theories of motivation fit together, it may be helpful to remember that needs theories suggest that individuals have needs, and that they will be motivated to have these needs met. Expectancy, goal-setting, and reinforcement theories show the processes by which individuals can be encouraged to behave in ways that earn rewards. Job design, which we discussed in Chapter 6, can also be a way of motivating individuals. Job rotation, job enlargement, and job enrichment can increase an employee's job satisfaction and thus lead him or her to be more motivated in performing the job.

FIGURE 8.8 | Five Steps in OB MOD

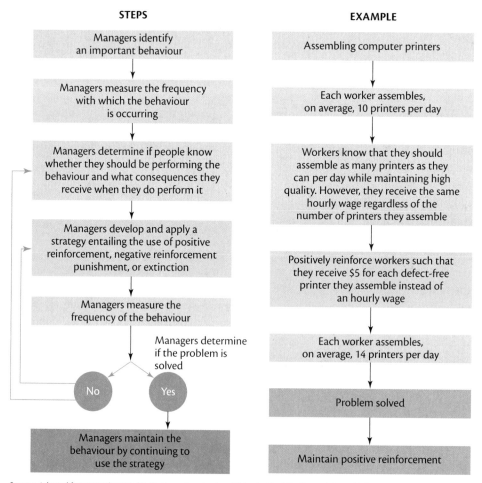

Source: Adapted from F. Luthans and R. Kreitner, *Organizational Behavior Modification and Beyond* (Glenview, IL: Scott, Foresman, 1985).

Equity Theory

Women and the Labyrinth of Leadership[27]

Alice H. Eagly and Linda L. Carli, authors of the *Harvard Business Review* article, "Women and the Labyrinth of Leadership," write, "When you put all the pieces together, a new picture emerges for why women don't make it into the C-suite, that is, the boardroom. It's not the glass ceiling, but the sum of many obstacles along the way." They say that the C-suite is "as rare as hens' teeth." They insist the expression, "the glass ceiling," described in 1986 by the *Wall Street Journal*'s Carol Hymowitz and Timothy Schellhardt, is now obsolete. The metaphor was effective at the time because barriers were, in fact, quite absolute; not so as much anymore. They refer to comments by then "President Richard Nixon, recorded on White House audiotapes and made public through the Freedom of Information Act. When explaining why he would not appoint a woman to the U.S. Supreme Court, Nixon said, 'I don't think a woman should be in any government job whatsoever ... mainly because they are erratic. And emotional. Men are erratic and emotional, too, but the point is a woman is more likely to be.' In a culture where such opinions were widely held, women had virtually no chance of attaining influential leadership roles."

Eagly and Carli state that it is time to rename the metaphor: "labyrinth." They go on to say: "As a contemporary symbol, it conveys the idea of a complex journey toward a goal worth striving for. Passage through a labyrinth is not simple or direct but requires persistence, awareness of one's progress, and a careful analysis of the puzzles that lie ahead. It is this meaning that we intend to convey. For women who aspire to top leadership, routes exist but are full of twists and turns, both unexpected and expected. Because all labyrinths have a viable route to the center, it is understood that goals are attainable. The metaphor acknowledges obstacles but is not ultimately discouraging."

It is the authors' contention that if "we can understand the various barriers that make up this labyrinth, and how some women find their way around them, we can work more effectively to improve the situation." There are still "vestiges of prejudice," as they put it. The 2006 Census in Canada, released on May 2, 2008, showed that women had yet to close the wage gap with men—a wage gap that had not changed in the past five years. "Statistics Canada said median earnings for young women experienced no growth in that period, and median earnings of young men also changed little between 2000 and 2005 after dropping substantially between 1980 and 2000. The median earnings—the level at which half a population falls above and half below—for full-time male workers aged 25 to 29 in 2005 was $37,680. For women, it was $32,104."[28]

You Be the Manager

1. Have you ever been paid unfairly compared with others you worked with? How did you feel? What did you do about the situation?
2. How could you "rebalance" the equity scales if you were a manager?

equity theory
A theory of motivation that focuses on people's perceptions of the fairness of their work outcomes relative to their work inputs.

Equity theory is a theory of motivation that concentrates on people's perceptions of the fairness of their work *outcomes* relative to, or in proportion to, their work *inputs*. Equity theory complements need and expectancy theories by focusing on how people perceive the relationship between the outcomes they receive from their jobs and organizations and the inputs they contribute.

Equity

equity
The justice, impartiality, and fairness to which all organizational members are entitled.

Equity exists when a person perceives his or her own outcome/input ratio to be equal to a referent's outcome/input ratio. The *referent* could be another person or a group of people who are perceived to be similar to oneself; the referent also could be oneself in a previous job or one's expectations about what outcome/input ratios should be. Under conditions of equity (see Table 8.4), if a referent receives more outcomes than you receive, the referent contributes proportionally more inputs to the organization, so his or her outcome/input ratio still equals your outcome/input ratio. Similarly, under conditions of equity, if you receive more outcomes than a referent, then your inputs are perceived to be proportionally higher. Maria Lau and Claudia King, for example, both work in a shoe store in a large mall. Lau is paid more per hour than King but also contributes more inputs, including being responsible for some of the store's bookkeeping, closing the store, and periodically depositing cash in the bank. When King compares her outcome/input ratio to Lau's (her referent's), she perceives the ratios to be equitable because Lau's higher level of pay (an outcome) is proportional to her higher level of inputs (bookkeeping, closing the store, and going to the bank). In a comparison of one's own outcome/input ratio to a referent's outcome/input ratio, one's *perceptions* of outcomes and inputs (not any objective indicator of them) are key.

When equity exists, people are motivated to continue contributing their current levels of inputs to their organizations in order to receive their current levels of outcomes. Under conditions of equity, if people wish to increase their outcomes, they are motivated to increase their inputs.

Inequity

inequity
Lack of fairness.

underpayment inequity
Inequity that exists when a person perceives that his or her own outcome/input ratio is less than the ratio of a referent.

Inequity, lack of fairness, exists when a person's outcome/input ratio is not perceived to be equal to a referent's. Inequity creates pressure or tension inside people and motivates them to restore equity by bringing the two ratios back into balance.

There are two types of inequity: underpayment inequity and overpayment inequity (see Table 8.4). **Underpayment inequity** exists when a person's own outcome/input ratio is perceived to be less than that of a referent: In comparing yourself to a referent,

---

TABLE 8.4 | *Equity Theory*

Condition	Person		Referent	Example
Equity	$\dfrac{\text{Outcomes}}{\text{Inputs}}$	$=$	$\dfrac{\text{Outcomes}}{\text{Inputs}}$	An engineer perceives that he contributes more inputs (time and effort), and receives proportionally more outcomes (a higher salary and choice job assignments) than his referent does.
Underpayment inequity	$\dfrac{\text{Outcomes}}{\text{Inputs}}$	$<$ (less than)	$\dfrac{\text{Outcomes}}{\text{Inputs}}$	An engineer perceives that he contributes more inputs but receives the same outcomes as his referent.
Overpayment inequity	$\dfrac{\text{Outcomes}}{\text{Inputs}}$	$>$ (greater than)	$\dfrac{\text{Outcomes}}{\text{Inputs}}$	An engineer perceives that he contributes the same inputs but receives more outcomes than his referent.

you think that you are not receiving the outcomes you should be receiving, given your inputs. For instance, in international assignments, this notion of fairness is absolutely critical: "Failure to establish a uniform compensation policy in an international alliance that requires high interaction among employees from different partners can lead to predictably adverse effects. Differences in compensation systems, especially for employees doing the same jobs, often lead to feelings of inequity among those receiving lower compensation and benefits. Morale and motivation therefore suffer among group members."[29]

Overpayment inequity exists when a person perceives that his or her own outcome/input ratio is greater than that of a referent: In comparing yourself to a referent, you think that the referent is receiving fewer outcomes than he or she should be receiving, given his or her inputs.

overpayment inequity
Inequity that exists when a person perceives that his or her own outcome/input ratio is greater than the ratio of a referent.

Ways to Restore Equity

According to equity theory, both underpayment inequity and overpayment inequity create tension that motivates most people to restore equity by bringing the ratios back into balance.[30] When people experience *underpayment* inequity, they may be motivated to lower their inputs by reducing their working hours, putting forth less effort on the job, or being absent, or they may be motivated to increase their outcomes by asking for a raise or a promotion. Take an employee like Mary Campbell, a financial analyst at a large corporation. She noticed that she was working longer hours and getting more work accomplished than a co-worker who had the same position, yet they both received the exact same pay and other outcomes. To restore equity, Campbell decided to stop coming in early and staying late. Alternatively, she could have tried to restore equity by trying to increase her outcomes by, for example, asking her boss for a raise.

When people experience *overpayment* inequity, they may try to restore equity by changing their perceptions of their own or their referents' inputs or outcomes. Equity can be restored when people "realize" that they are contributing more inputs than they originally thought. Equity also can be restored by perceiving the referent's inputs to be lower or the referent's outcomes to be higher than one originally thought. When equity is restored in this way, actual inputs and outcomes are unchanged. What is changed is how people think about or view their own or the referent's inputs and outcomes. For example, employee Susan Martineau experienced overpayment inequity when she realized that she was being paid $2 an hour more than a co-worker who had the same job as hers in a record store and who contributed the same amount of inputs. Martineau restored equity by changing her perceptions of her inputs. She "realized" that she worked harder than her co-worker and solved more problems that came up in the store.

By experiencing either overpayment or underpayment inequity, you might decide that your referent is not appropriate because, for example, the referent is too different from yourself. Choosing a more appropriate referent may bring the ratios back into balance. However, when people experience *underpayment* inequity and other means of equity restoration fail, they may leave the organization.

Motivation is highest when as many people as possible in an organization perceive that they are being equitably treated, that is, their outcomes and inputs are in balance. Top contributors and performers are motivated to continue contributing a high level of inputs because they are receiving the outcomes they deserve. Mediocre contributors and performers realize that if they want to increase their outcomes, they have to increase their inputs. Managers of effective organizations, such as Calgary-based

Telvent Canada Inc., which develops information management systems, with its dozens of professional mentoring relationships that benefit both its employees and profit margin,[31] and Regina-based Saskatchewan Power Corp., with its leadership succession planning,[32] realize the importance of equity for motivation and performance and continually strive to ensure that employees feel they are being equitably treated.

 Tips for Managers

EXPECTANCY AND EQUITY THEORIES

1. Express sincere confidence in your subordinates' capabilities, and let them know that you expect them to succeed.

2. Distribute outcomes based on important inputs and performance levels, and clearly communicate to your subordinates that this is the case.

3. Determine which outcomes your subordinates desire, and try to gain control over as many of these as possible (i.e., have the authority to distribute or withhold outcomes).

4. Provide clear information to your subordinates about which inputs are most valuable for them to contribute to their jobs and the organization in order to receive desired outcomes.

LO4

Reward Systems and Motivation

THINK ABOUT IT

Is Pay the "Be-All and End-All"?[33]

"It's not just about the best pay or the best benefits program anymore because all our peers do that," says Susan O'Dowd, vice-president of human resources at Hoffman-La Roche Ltd. "It's about engaging employees and finding out how engaged they are." O'Dowd continues, "Now CEOs are seeing that the next frontier for productivity enhancement is people. They know the next great $10-million or $100-million computer system isn't where they're going to get the next round of productivity increases. It's by getting their people truly engaged in helping them make the business more successful, whether that's cutting costs, employees helping them to drive more revenue, or whatever the avenue is."

What is also getting increased attention today for motivating employees is the notion of the *healthy workplace*. "Healthy" is not simply a company's occupational health and safety record or access to an employee assistance program (EAP). Bill Wilkerson, president of the Global Business and Economic Roundtable on Addiction and Mental Health, says, "Ambiguity, inconsistency, uncertainty, insecurity, arbitrariness, bad decision-making, self-centredness, rewarding the wrong things in the office, the fostering of office politics and rewarding political behaviours—that's the earmark of weak leadership. And if you're a lousy leader, you're making people sick." Joan Burton, manager of health strategy for the Industrial Accident Prevention Association (IAPA), writes, "A sense of fairness in the workplace is related to trust, which is key to employer–worker relations, high morale, and productivity. Feelings associated with a sense of unfairness are anger, depression, demoralization, and anxiety. These strong negative feelings translate chemically within workers into compromised immune systems, setting the stage for a variety of adverse physical and mental health problems."[34]

In 2008, it was estimated that work stress was costing $33 billion a year in lost productivity in Canada.[35] In the UK, mental health issues are now the largest cause of workplace absence.[36] And in June 2008, the Canadian public sector was described as a "toxic place to work"[37] so much so that disability claims in Canada were climbing with between 30 to 40 percent of the claims being for depression. The cost to the economy was estimated to be $51 billion, or 4 percent of the GDP.

You Be the Manager

1. What are the advantages for having a "healthy workplace"?
2. How would you create a healthy motivational work environment?

Once a pay level and structure are in place, managers can use pay to motivate employees to perform at a high level and attain their work goals. Pay is used to motivate entry-level workers, first-line and middle managers, and even top managers such as CEOs. Pay can be used to motivate people to perform behaviours that will help an organization achieve its goals.

Total Reward Strategies

As illustrated in Figure 8.9 pay is an important extrinsic motivating factor addressed by both *needs* and *process theories*.

- **Needs theories:** Physiological needs are satisfied through earning wages needed to purchase food, clothing, and shelter. Pay levels must be adequate to avoid feeling dissatisfaction but do not contribute to one's level of satisfaction, according to Herzberg.

FIGURE 8.9 | How Pay Motivates

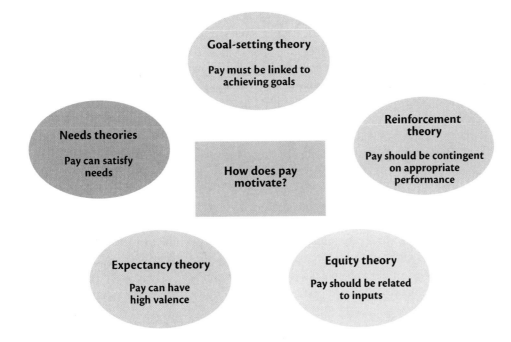

- **Expectancy theory:** Instrumentality, the linkage between performance and outcomes such as pay, must be high for motivation to be high. Pay is also an outcome that has a positive valence.

- **Goal-setting theory:** Outcomes such as pay should be linked to the attainment of goals.

- **Reinforcement theory:** The distribution of pay and other rewards should depend on the performance of desirable workplace behaviours.

- **Equity theory:** Outcomes such as pay should be distributed in proportion to the level of inputs.

total reward strategy
A total reward strategy encompasses both intrinsically and extrinsically motivating factors.

As these theories suggest, to promote high motivation, managers should base the distribution of pay on performance levels so that high performers receive more pay than do low performers (other things being equal).[38] It should be remembered that pay is, however, only one part of a **total reward strategy**. A total reward strategy encompasses both intrinsically and extrinsically motivating factors such as giving positive reinforcement, recognition, opportunities for advancement and personal growth, responsibility, adequate training to raise expectancy levels, flexible hours for work–life balance, and individualized benefits. Managers must recognize that reward systems must be tailored to individual needs if they are to be motivating.

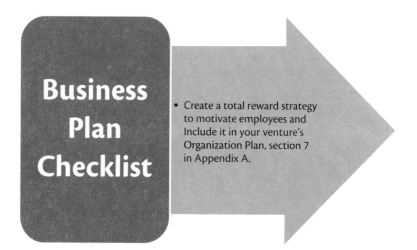

Business Plan Checklist

- Create a total reward strategy to motivate employees and Include it in your venture's Organization Plan, section 7 in Appendix A.

In deciding whether to pay for performance, managers also have to determine whether to use salary increases or bonuses. Thus some pay-for-performance programs (particularly those that use bonuses) are variable-pay programs. With variable pay, earnings go up and down annually based on performance.[39] Thus, there is no guarantee that an individual will earn as much this year as the last.

The number of employees affected by variable-pay plans has been rising in Canada. A 2002 survey of 191 firms by Hewitt Associates found that 76 percent of them have variable-pay plans in place, compared with 43 percent in 1994.[40] In 2006, Keri Humber, a senior compensation consultant with Hewitt, remarked, "In this economy, especially, employers must continue to ensure their corporate pay strategies are properly executed. … In order to remain competitive and continue to attract quality talent, organizations will need to look beyond base salary for ways to reward and motivate their employees. … Variable pay plans are one alternative."[41] These programs are more common among nonunionized workers, although more than 30 percent of unionized companies had such plans in 2002.[42] In Canada, pay-for-performance programs are more common for nonunionized workers than unionized ones. Prem Benimadhu from the Conference Board of Canada notes, "Canadian unions have been very allergic to variable compensation."[43] In addition to wage uncertainty, employees may object to pay for performance if they feel that factors out of their control might affect the extent to which bonuses are possible.

Summary and Review

1. **THE NATURE OF MOTIVATION** Motivation encompasses the psychological forces within a person that determine the direction of a person's behaviour in an organization, a person's level of effort, and a person's level of persistence in the face of obstacles. Managers strive to motivate employees to contribute their inputs to an organization, to focus these inputs in the direction of high performance, and to ensure that people receive the outcomes they desire when they perform at a high level.

2. **NEEDS THEORIES** Needs theories suggest that in order to have a motivated workforce, managers should determine what needs employees are trying to satisfy in organizations and then ensure that employees receive outcomes that will satisfy these needs when they perform at a high level and contribute to organizational effectiveness. **Maslow** suggests humans have five levels of needs arranged in a hierarchical order: physiological, safety, belongingness, esteem, and self-actualization. Once a set of needs is satisfied, it no longer acts as a motivator, and the next level of needs drives us to take action to satisfy it. **Herzberg's Two factor** theory suggests that hygiene needs must be met adequately to avoid feeling dissatisfaction, while motivator needs must be built into jobs to ensure employee satisfaction. **Hackman and Oldham's Job Characteristics Model** tells us that five core job dimensions—skill variety, task identity, task significance, autonomy, and feedback—give employees a sense of meaningfulness and responsibility that motivate high levels of performance depending on the employee's level of growth need.

3. **PROCESS THEORIES** Process theories help managers explain workplace behaviours and increase employee motivation. According to **expectancy theory**, managers can promote high levels of motivation in their organizations by taking steps to ensure that *expectancy* is high (employees think that if they try, they can perform at a high level), *instrumentality* is high (employees think that if they perform at a high level, they will receive certain outcomes), and *valence* is high (employees desire these outcomes).

   Goal-setting theory suggests that managers can promote high motivation and performance by ensuring that employees are striving to achieve specific, difficult goals. It also is important for employees to accept the goals, be committed to them, and receive feedback about how they are doing.

   Reinforcement theory suggests that managers can motivate employees to perform highly by using *positive reinforcement* or *negative reinforcement* (positive reinforcement being the preferred strategy). Managers can motivate employees to avoid performing dysfunctional behaviours by using *extinction* or *punishment.*

   According to **equity theory**, managers can promote high levels of motivation by ensuring that employees perceive that there is equity in the organization or that outcomes are distributed in proportion to inputs. *Equity* exists when an employee perceives that his or her own outcome/input ratio equals the outcome/input ratio of a referent. Inequity motivates people to try to restore equity.

4. **REWARDS AND MOTIVATION** Each of the motivation theories discussed in this chapter alludes to the importance of pay and suggests that pay should be based on performance. Pay is only one part of a *total reward strategy*, which includes both extrinsic elements such as pay, and intrinsic elements such as making work enjoyable.

Key Terms

equity, p. 260
equity theory, p. 259
expectancy, p. 251
expectancy theory, p. 251
extinction, p. 257
extrinsically motivated behaviour, p. 244
goal-setting theory, p. 254
Hackman and Oldham's job characteristics model, p. 248
Herzberg's motivator-hygiene theory, p. 247
inequity, p. 260
instrumentality, p. 253
intrinsically motivated behaviour, p. 244
Maslow's hierarchy of needs, p. 246

motivation, p. 244
need, p. 246
needs theories, p. 246
negative reinforcement, p. 257
organizational behaviour modification (OB MOD), p. 257
overpayment inequity, p. 261
positive reinforcement, p. 256
process theories, p. 250
punishment, p. 257
reinforcement, p. 256
reinforcement theory, p. 256
total reward strategy, p. 264
underpayment inequity, p. 260
valence, p. 253

SO WHERE DO YOU STAND?

Wrap-Up to Opening Case

We began this chapter with the late U.S. President John F. Kennedy's intention in the 1960s of firing up the imagination of the American people. He proposed that a person could land on the moon in a decade. It happened.

We saw that such inspirational intentions and words make up what are called "ideas that stick." Such ideas captivate the imagination and pull us into a future worth going to. In short, they are highly motivational.

We saw how six principles were necessary to accomplish such an inspirational goal: "Simple? Yes. Unexpected? Yes. Concrete? Amazingly so. Credible? The goal seemed like science fiction, but the source was credible. Emotional? Yes. Story? In miniature."

Great ideas need to be able "to stick" in order to create a motivational environment in the workplace. Saying that employees must create more shareholder value does not do that.

In *Firms of Endearment: How World-Class Companies Profit from Passion and Purpose*, the authors discuss why "share of heart" versus "share of market" will be the driving force and energy for employees now and for the future; and they have the research to back up their claim.[44] Writing in the foreword to the book, Warren Bennis, distinguished professor of Business Administration, University of Southern California, says, "The men and women cited in this book ... evidence keen self-knowledge and project candor and maturity—three essential elements of integrity—in their interactions with others. In return, stakeholders in every category place uncommon trust in their companies and products. Beyond this, stakeholders develop real affection for such companies. They literally love Firms of Endearment (FoEs). It is not too much of a stretch to see that as FoEs proliferate—and that they are doing—the principles of leadership that guide their destinies will be adopted by organizations of every stripe."[45]

These sentiments are in line with the more than 16 000 respondents to an ongoing online survey conducted by Career Systems International, the consulting firm run by Beverly Kaye, co-author of *Love 'Em or Lose 'Em* to the question: "What makes employees stick with an employer?"[46] Here are the top 10 reasons:

1. Exciting work and challenge
2. Career growth, learning, and development
3. Working with great people
4. Fair pay
5. Supportive management or good boss
6. Being recognized, valued, and respected
7. Benefits
8. Meaningful work and making a difference
9. Pride in an organization and its product
10. Great work environment and culture

Management in Action

Topics for Discussion and Action

Level 1

1. Define motivation, and describe how it is related to behaviours that concern managers in organizations.
2. Describe Maslow's Hierarchy of Needs *or* Herzberg's Two Factor theory *or* the Job Characteristics Model, and suggest what managers could do to apply them in the workplace.
3. What are the qualities of organizational goals that make them motivating?

Level 2

4. From the point of view of Expectancy theory, evaluate what managers should do to have a highly motivated workforce.
5. From the point of view of Equity theory, assess what managers should do to have a highly motivated workforce.

6. Discuss how each theory of motivation treats wages and salary as a part of a Total Reward Strategy.

Level 3

7. Listen to the podcast at http://positivesharing.com/media/motivation.mp3 by Alex Kjerulf (23 minutes). Describe the four types of motivation discussed. Which one works over the long term, and why?
8. Discuss why two people with similar abilities may have very different expectancies for performing at a high level. What steps could a manager take to influence people's levels of expectancy, instrumentality, and valence?
9. Under what circumstances should a manager use each of the techniques in Reinforcement theory? Which technique is the best for long-term changes in behaviour?

Building Management Skills

Answer the following questions of the organization you have chosen to follow:

1. What evidence can you find on the types of motivation theories that are at work in this organization? For example, if it has an "employee of the month" award, what needs does this fulfill?
2. What kinds of things does the management do to increase the expectancy levels of employees? What about levels of instrumentality?

3. What practices does the management engage in to ensure there is a perception of equity within the organization? Do the outcomes appear to be distributed fairly?

Management for You

The following is a typical situation that students often face: you are in a team with six other management students, and you have a major case analysis due in four weeks. This assignment will count for 25 percent of your course mark. *You are the team's leader.*

The problem: Several of your team members are having difficulty getting motivated to start work on the project.

The task: Identify ways you could motivate your team members by using the following theories of motivation as studied in this chapter:

1. Needs theories
2. Expectancy theory
3. Goal setting

4. Reinforcement theory
5. Equity theory

Small Group Breakout Exercise

Assume you are the manager of a small company that hired five employees, two of them at minimum wage. One of these employees, Khan, tends to slack off when you are not around to directly supervise his work. When you are around, he puts out more work effort to avoid being disciplined, but he just does not seem motivated. Jack is the company clown. He spends most of the day telling jokes and making the other employees laugh. Jack is almost always late for work. The last time he was late you reprimanded him in front of all the other staff, and Jack felt very uncomfortable but made a joke out of it anyway. Lately, Khan has been taking a lot of sick time. Something is not right.

1. What can you do to motivate high performance from Khan and Jack?
2. Identify the behaviours you would like to see Khan increase and Jack decrease.
3. Design a program using Reinforcement theory to:
   a. Increase the frequency of the functional behaviours you want the employees to exhibit, and
   b. Decrease the frequency of the undesirable behaviours.

Business Planning Exercise

You and your business plan writing team find yourselves in a typical situation. The Business Plan is due in four weeks, and several of the team members are having difficulty getting motivated to finish the work that needs to be done for the project.

1. Identify ways you could motivate your team members by using the following theories of motivation as studied in this chapter:
   • Maslow's Hierarchy of Needs
   • Herzberg's Motivator-Hygiene Theory
   • Expectancy Theory
   • Goal-Setting Theory
   • Reinforcement Theory

Managing Ethically

You are the new CEO of a pharmaceutical company that has a reputation for compensating managers well but not employees. Top and middle managers get a 15-percent across-the-board increase, while the employees receive a 4-percent increase annually. The justification is that managers take the risks, make the decisions, and figure out the strategies. But, in fact, for years the company has been using teams to make many of the most crucial decisions for the company. And everyone has input into strategic planning. Employees also have to work extra-long hours during the busiest seasons with no overtime pay. You find that employee morale is very low. While they seem motivated because they have a passion for the work, developing drugs to help cure major diseases, many are threatening to leave if they are not rewarded more fairly. What would you do?

Exploring the World Wide Web

SPECIFIC ASSIGNMENT

Enter Hewlett-Packard Canada's website at: www.hp.com/country/ca/en/welcome.html. Click on "About Us" under Company Information; then click on "Jobs at HP Canada," then "HP Benefits Canada" and "Training and Development Canada."

1. What kinds of things in "Jobs at HP Canada" would motivate you to want to work there?
2. Describe some of the extrinsic motivator factors at HP Canada.
3. What does the company offer that would strengthen your level of instrumentality and perception of equity?

GENERAL ASSIGNMENT

Find the website of a company that bases pay on performance for some or all of its employees. Describe the pay-for-performance plan in use at this company. Which employees are covered by the plan? Do you think this pay plan will foster high levels of motivation? Why, or why not?

McGraw-Hill Connect™—Available 24/7 with instant feedback so you can study when you want, how you want, and where you want. Take advantage of the Study Plan—an innovative tool that helps you customize your learning experience. You can diagnose your knowledge with pre- and post-tests, identify the areas where you need help, search the entire learning package for content specific to the topic you're studying, and add these resources to your personalized study plan. Visit www.mcgrawhillconnect.ca to register—take practice quizzes, search the e-book, and much more.

Be the Manager

HANDING OVER THE REINS

Recently a former colleague at a company of 100 employees called you in. You know this company very well because you worked there for seven years before becoming a motivational consultant. It is a family-owned business. Your former colleague is the daughter of the founder who is very reluctant to hand over the reins of management completely to his daughter. He knows he must, but he keeps saying that he needs that "little extra push"! Your former colleague believes that you have the "motivational key" for this transfer of power.

Questions

1. Using the motivational theories from this chapter, what theory or theories would you utilize to try to work this current challenge?
2. What motivational plan are you reasonably comfortable with that you can present to your former colleague?

Management Case

Motivating Your Team "Spirits"[47]

Investing in the skills of your people makes smart business sense. If you do not motivate your team, the good people leave, and worse still, the poor ones stay!

Profitable bars and contented customers depend upon motivated, enthusiastic people, and that takes good management. Are you giving your staff something to smile about?

It is an old but proven fact in running any business that people buy people first. Great decor, good prices, and fine food will not bring in the customers without friendly, efficient people on hand who enjoy what they do. If staff are ill-tempered, ill-equipped, or ill-trained, customers definitely notice and then vote with their feet. So, what steps can astute managers take to ensure that their bar is delivering the positive atmosphere and service that matters to customers?

Recognition

There is a whole lot of skill involved in being a good barperson, but how often is that recognized? Ben Reed of IPBartenders in England said, "On the continent, bartenders are seen as professionals and held in high esteem. But that's not always the case in the UK."

Bar work is often seen as a casual, unskilled job, with staff being treated accordingly. Low status leads to low morale, so the effective manager is always looking to encourage staff to develop their skills and take pride in their work. Recognition for a job well done is a key factor in developing staff satisfaction.

Information

Ben Reed also said that to have happy, successful staff, they need to be empowered and inspired. That goes beyond telling staff what to do and how to do it, it is also explaining why things are done in a particular way. For example, demonstrating the perfect serve will make far more sense to people when they know why it is important to customers and how it helps encourage repeat orders. Empowerment is also about giving people reasonable control over how they do their job and how they respond to customers. But if you want them to make good decisions, then you need to invest in your people.

Training

"A good bartender will have four main areas of expertise," says Ben. "Knowledge, speed, style, and etiquette. Each requires training to develop."

Ben feels that bar owners and managers should look at training as a sound business investment. Staff who understand wines, for example, are in a much stronger position to influence customer choice, and customers will appreciate that knowledge. Upselling is a great profit opportunity, but it requires staff who understand the products. You cannot sell an expensive cocktail if you do not know how to mix it and serve it with style and without keeping your other customers waiting for their orders.

There are always difficult customers, but how serious a problem they will be also depends on the people skills of barstaff. Staff need to recognize and know how to refuse to serve someone who is at their limit or possibly underage. Training can play a vital role in helping staff

become confident and capable of dealing with tricky situations.

Equipment

Good-quality service also depends on having the right materials on hand, the right glasses, the ice, the lemons, and so on. Making sure the bar area is sensibly organized and uncluttered will also help the staff work more effectively.

Teamwork

Job satisfaction is closely related to the success of working relationships. Smart managers should be on the lookout for ways of stimulating team work and cooperation. Team incentives and rewards possibly linked to a manufacturer's promotion can be used in this way. Work needs to have an element of fun to it. If your staff do not enjoy their job, your customers will not enjoy your bar or pub.

Questions

1. What are some motivation challenges outlined in this case?
2. What theories of motivation would work more seamlessly to develop a motivating environment?
3. As a manager, what kind of a training program would you set up to get the best out of the employees?

Video Management

Johnson & Johnson

Johnson & Johnson (J&J) is a family-oriented health care and personal products company with about 330 operating units and more than 150,000 employees around the world. The company is well known for "the Credo", a set of values statements introduced in 1938 to help J&J's executives and employees make better decisions. The Credo helps J&J staff to continuously be aware of and serve the needs of its core stakeholders. It also serves as the glue that holds the company's geographically and industrially diverse operating units together. This program introduces Johnson & Johnson's

credo and shows how the company instills those values in its managers.

Questions to consider

1. Why does Johnson & Johnson place so much importance on The Credo"?
2. How does Johnson & Johnson ensure that managers understand and apply The Credo in their daily decisions and actions?

Managing Leadership

Learning Outcomes

1. Describe what leadership is and on what bases of power leaders influence others.

2. Describe the early trait and behavioural theories of leadership and their limitations.

3. Describe the contingency theories of leadership.

4. Compare and contrast transactional and transformational leadership.

5. Explain how gender, culture, and emotional intelligence affect leadership.

Unto the Seventh Generation[1]

How has it come that we cannot see the value of a forest? And, what does this mean to leaders of our organizations? We live in a time when our corporate leaders manage quarter by quarter and our political leaders tell us they can't be bound by three year plans. Yet, the most pressing problem faced by our planet—the current decline of every living system—requires a multi-generational strategy.—**Gabriel Draven**[2]

In what is called the Cathedral of Temagami, in the near north of Ontario, lies an old growth forest of 150 year-old trees. Plans had been approved to commence clear-cutting of the trees. An elder of the Teme-Augama Anishnabai, the last of his people to homestead on ancestral lands, invited writer Gabriel Draven to visit this area that has served as a gathering place for the elder's people for a thousand years as they sought wisdom and communed with their elders. The area contains the Spirit Forest that lies between Lake Temagami and Lake Obakika. Draven asks why it is that people cannot see the value of a forest and, for our purpose, what does this "not seeing" mean to leaders of today's organizations?

Toronto author Thomas Homer-Dixon,[3] past director of the Trudeau Centre for Peace and Conflict Studies at the University of Toronto, says that our institutions are failing us because they are unable to deal with complex crises like global environmental meltdown, world hunger, peace and conflict, and the gap between the rich and the poor. According to Draven:

> Our religions have become efficiency and consumption. We fall to the myth of perpetual economic growth while the only organism in nature, which is governed by such an imperative, is the cancer cell that eventually kills its host. We have traded compassion and replaced it with competition. Somewhere along the way we forgot people live in communities and neighborhoods, not marketplaces. In our organizations, I see workplaces that are over-managed and under-led. I see corporations that would rather make decisions for the casino of the stock market than long-term value creation. I see a world where we demand compliance in our people rather than inspiring their commitment and engaging them in a process of co-creating a positive vision of the future. Is it any wonder most Fortune 500 corporations last no longer than 40 years. Is it any wonder that worker disengagement costs US corporations $350B a year according to

Comstock/Punch Stock

According to Gabriel Draven, we can no longer see the forest for the trees: "Our religions have become efficiency and consumption."

Gallop Research? Is it any wonder that disability represents up to 12% of payroll costs in Canada with mental health claims as the fastest growing category of disability, or so according to a major roundtable study completed in 2000 looking at depression in the Canadian workplace?

To be disengaged is to show up physically for work but to be absent mentally.[4] This state of affairs, or disengagement, is called "presenteeism."[5] There is even a website devoted to teaching and helping people to slack off from work. Slackersguild.com bills itself as an "online community made up of people who generally dislike work." It appeals to such a broad range of people that it has offered access to everything from music to contests and interviews. "Our main goal is simple: to give you something to do instead of working," it boasts.[6] Sometimes presenteeism occurs because employees show up for work, even though they may be quite ill! Not only is this an organizational health issue, but the Harvard Business School estimates that costs associated with this type of presenteeism to be about US$150 billion per year.[7] Some employees even work at honing their presenteeism! In his book, *Hardly Work*, which the author claims he wrote "on company time," author Chris Morran—referred to by www.amazon.ca as "an idol of idleness"—claims that overachieving underperformers get all the credit for everyone else's effort.[8]

Warren Bennis reminds us that what is really needed are leaders who will do the right thing.[9] Robert Greenleaf (1904–1990) founded the Center for Applied Ethics, Inc. in 1964, which was then renamed the Robert K. Greenleaf Center in 1985.[10] Today it is known as The Robert K. Greenleaf Center for Servant-Leadership, or the Greenleaf Center for Servant-Leadership. In 1970, he published *The Servant as Leader*. Draven writes that the most powerful lessons on leadership do not come from the business schools or from such notables as Donald Trump or Rudy Giuliani of 9/11 fame.

Rather, it is a piece of wisdom that guided leaders in the Iroquois Confederacy, instructing them to consider the impact of their decisions on the seven generations around them. Our indigenous people knew that one man, one leader, could only hope to know the seven generations around him: the three that preceded him—to his great grandparents—and the three that will follow—to his great grandchildren. The leader was bound by a moral duty to care for the Seven Generations.

For Draven, in reflecting on this notion of the Seventh Generation, he asks the question: "What would Seventh Generation Leadership look like in our organizations?" He lists the following implications of Seventh Generation leadership:

1. Corporations would be principle-based.

2. Leadership would be spiritual, not religious.

3. Leaders would intuitively understand the power of inclusion, the power of conversation.

4. Leadership would be transformed into stewardship, and leaders roles would be as keepers of dialogue, the proverbial village elder and sage.

5. Leaders would be earth-affirming.

Draven finishes his reflection this way: "The hallmark of leadership is when old men and old women plant trees they know they will not live long enough to enjoy. Our world needs such leaders. For, one thousand years from now, I want my descendents to be able to worship in a cathedral of trees. It does not look hopeful."

Now It's Your Turn

What are some leadership implications of the Seventh Generation vision for today's managers and their organizations?[11]

1. _____

2. _____

3. _____

4. _____

5. _____

6. _____

Overview

In the opening scenario, we see perhaps a new vision of leadership, one that goes beyond simply the traditional model of leader–follower and looks at the vision a manager or person in authority brings to the organization. Draven reminds us that leadership, from the big picture point of view, is a vision of "seven generations." As such, the implications by and for organizations are immense. In Chapter 1, we explained that one of the four principal tasks of managers is leading. Thus, it should come as no surprise that leadership is a key ingredient in effective management. When leaders are effective, their subordinates or followers are highly motivated, committed, and high-performing. When leaders are ineffective, chances are good that their subordinates do not perform up to their capabilities, are demotivated, and may be dissatisfied as well. Leadership is an important ingredient for managerial success at all levels of an organization: top management, middle management, and first-line management. Moreover, leadership is a key ingredient for managerial success for organizations large and small.

In this chapter, we describe what leadership is and examine the major leadership models that shed light on the factors that help make a manager an effective leader. *Trait and behaviour models* focus on what leaders are like and what they do. *Contingency models*—Fiedler's contingency model, Hersey-Blanchard's situational leadership theory, path-goal theory, and the leader substitutes model—take into account the complexity surrounding leadership and the role of the situation in leader effectiveness. We describe how managers can have dramatic effects in their organizations by means of transformational leadership. We also examine the relationship between gender and leadership, culture and leadership, and social intelligence and leadership. By the end of this chapter, you will have a good appreciation of the many factors and issues that managers face in their quest to be effective leaders.

L O 1

The Nature of Leadership

THINK ABOUT IT

Finding Our Way: Leadership for an Uncertain Time[12]

We first think in images. One of the most embedded images we have of the organization—since the time of the Industrial Age—is that the organization, to work well, should be like a well-oiled machine. Everything, then, would be in its place; everything would fit; and a manager's job would be making sure that all the parts continue to work well together. That is one image. It is called the "command and control" image.

But what if we were to choose another image of how organizations work? What if we, as Dr. Margaret Wheatley suggests, looked at organizations as "living systems" and as "self-organizing systems"? Such systems would be without command and control and would structure themselves organically, that is, leadership would *emerge*, and the best ways to work and organize would become self-evident as people experimented freely through their networks of communication, values and meaning, behaviour and norms. Dr. Wheatley points out that there is a clear correlation between participation and productivity and that in truly self-managed work environments, productivity is at least 35 percent higher than in traditionally managed organizations.

The question is, if this reality of self-managed teams is so obvious, why don't leaders choose to nurture and develop self-organizing systems? The answer, according to Wheatley, is that leaders keep choosing power over productivity and control over trust. The excuses for such behaviour will range from "these are turbulent times" to "somebody has to be in charge." The problem with this kind of thinking, for Wheatley, is that when the risks are high, leaders need everyone's commitment and intelligence, not easily evoked with power and control. The net result is that leaders prevent intelligent work from being accomplished, or in Wheatley's own words, "guaranteed levels of performance are preferable to surprising breakthroughs. In our machine-like organizations, we try to extinguish individuality in order to reach our goal of compliance. We trade uniqueness for control, and barter our humanness for petty performance measures."

You Be the Manager

1. What has your experience been in working for a "command-and-control" type manager or leader?
2. How realistic is Dr. Margaret Wheatley's idea that if leaders were to foster self-organizing teams, there would be higher productivity as a result?

leadership
The process by which an individual exerts influence over other people and inspires, motivates, and directs their activities to help achieve group or organizational goals.

leader
An individual who is able to exert influence over other people to help achieve group or organizational goals.

personal leadership style
The ways a manager chooses to influence others and how they approach planning, organizing, and controlling.

Leadership is the process by which a person exerts influence over other people and inspires, motivates, and directs their activities to help achieve group or organizational goals.[13] The person who exerts such influence is a **leader**. When leaders are effective, the influence they exert over others helps a group or organization achieve its performance goals. When leaders are ineffective, their influence does not contribute to, and often detracts from, goal attainment. Dee Hock, founder of Visa International, was an effective leader. From its inception in 1970 to 1996 alone, Visa had grown "by something like 10,000 percent."[14] He did this in exercising his leadership ability in setting up Visa International, thus enabling a "seventh generation" leadership vision to become real. Or, in Gabriel Draven's words, "The leader was bound by a moral duty to care for the Seven Generations."[15] Visa International continues to exist today all around the world.

Effective leadership increases an organization's ability to meet a variety of challenges, including the need to obtain a competitive advantage, the need to foster ethical behaviour, and the need to manage a diverse workforce fairly and equitably. Leaders who exert influence to help meet these goals increase their organization's chances of success.

A manager's **personal leadership style**—that is, the specific ways in which a manager chooses to influence other people—shapes the way that the manager approaches planning, organizing, and controlling (the other principal tasks of managing).

Dee Hock, cited above, describes leadership this way:

Here is the very heart and soul of the matter. If you look to lead, invest at least 40 percent of your time managing yourself—your ethics, character, principles, purpose, motivation, and conduct. Invest at least 30 percent managing those with authority over you, and 15 percent managing your peers. Use the remainder to induce those you "work for" to understand and practice the theory. I use the terms "work for" advisedly, for if you don't understand that you should be working for your mislabeled "subordinates," you haven't understood anything. Lead yourself, lead your superiors, lead your peers, and free your people to do the same. All else is trivia.[16]

Managers at all levels and in all kinds of organizations have their own personal leadership styles. Ricardo Semler, management expert and CEO of Brazilian-based Semco, found it stressful to manage his company if he created fear in his employees, even though other traditional Brazilian companies were still managing employees in that fashion.[17] What is interesting about Semler is that he never wanted to run his father's industrial machinery company (Semco has now expanded into a diverse federation of companies). He was a musician who played in rock bands and could not fathom a life of babysitting employees, making sure they punched the clock on time.

Today, Semco has no official structure. It does not have any five-year business plans, mission statements, vice-presidents or chief officers, human resources department or job descriptions, among other things. Employees are encouraged to set their own salaries, choose their own bosses, and work wherever and whenever they want.

"People are considered adults in their private lives, at the bank, at their children's schools, with family and among friends—so why are they suddenly treated like adolescents at work?" writes Semler.[18]

While some would say that he has a "loose leadership style," given that the "proof is in the pudding," from 1984 to 2004, his company grew from $4 million a year to $212 million! And he maintains, this all happened *because* of his leadership.[19]

In considering the nature of leadership, the age-old question for management thought arises: How do you get other people to follow and carry out tasks and orders effectively? Max Weber and his three main historical paradigms of authority written early in the twentieth century was one of the first social scientists to deal with this issue.[20] Henri Fayol also writing in the same period was very clear about the chain of command and believed in centralized control and decision-making.[21] Mary Parker Follett addressed the issue of "giving orders" and obedience in a series of lectures published around the same time.[22] In fact, the entire Classical era of managerial thought, and most notably, Fredrick W. Taylor's scientific management theory, was consumed by this central question.[23]

Henry Mintzberg and other contemporary leadership theorists agree that no matter what one's leadership style, a key component of effective leadership is found in the *power* the leader has to affect other people's behaviour and to get them to act in certain ways.[24]

Power: The Key to Leadership

French and Raven depict five types of social power: *legitimate, reward, coercive, expert,* and *referent* (see Figure 9.1).[25]

Legitimate Power

Legitimate power is the authority a manager has by virtue of his or her position in an organization's hierarchy. This is the power, for instance, that allows managers to hire new employees, assign projects to individuals, monitor their work, and appraise their performance.

legitimate power
The authority that a manager has by virtue of his or her position in an organization's hierarchy.

FIGURE 9.1 | Sources of Managerial Power

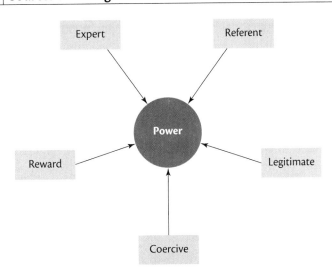

reward power
The ability of a manager to give or withhold tangible and intangible rewards.

Reward Power

Reward power is the ability of a manager to give or withhold tangible rewards (pay raises, bonuses, choice job assignments) and intangible rewards (verbal praise, a pat on the back, respect). As you learned in Chapter 8, members of an organization are motivated to perform at a high level by a variety of rewards. Being able to give or withhold rewards based on performance is a major source of power that allows managers to have a highly motivated workforce.

Effective managers use their reward power in such a way that subordinates feel that they are doing a good job and their efforts are appreciated. Ineffective managers use rewards in a more controlling manner (wielding the "stick" instead of offering the carrot"), which signals to subordinates that the manager has the upper hand. One example of effective use of reward power was with the New York firefighters who "were heralded as heroes for their acts on 9-11-01."[26] Rewards need to be aligned also with ethics and corporate governance. Craig Johnston of Canada Post was rewarded for his bright idea with a $10 000 cheque, the respect of his bosses, and the admiration of his peers. He developed a time-saving device so that Canada Post could revamp its sorting line by jury-rigging its existing machinery to generate mail barcodes on the fly. Before his suggestion, packages without barcodes had to be manually sorted by clerks; this labour-intensive activity contributed to clogging up of the machines. The $10 000 was part of Canada Post's employee involvement award program—an initiative designed to encourage and reward innovation on the job.[27] Charles Schwab & Co., the discount broker, is another example. The company

pays its brokers a straight salary, unlike other brokerage firms that offer commissions on the basis of the number of transactions that a client makes—an incentive that can lead to brokers encouraging customers to buy and sell stocks excessively. Moreover, Schwab has no investment banking division and is thus free to offer unbiased ratings of company stocks.[28]

As Wolfe J. Rinke, Ph.D. points out, trust is also very central to creating a leadership and rewarding environment.[29] *Chief Executive Perspectives* magazine has described the key challenge facing CEO leaders of the twenty-first century: *people* issues in the workplace.[30] They estimate that "people costs" account for some 65 percent of corporate spending, indicating an obvious impact issue for the bottom line. Mark A. Huselid, who is an associate professor in the Department of Human Resource Management at Rutgers University and the editor of *Human Resource Management Journal*, puts things this way: "The ability to execute strategy well is a source of competitive advantage, and 'people' are the linchpin of effective strategy execution." The key skills needed for effective leaders? "Hiring the right people, training them, paying them, rewarding them, supporting them, and promoting them appropriately."

Coercive Power

coercive power
The ability to force someone to do something against his or her will.

Coercive power is the ability of a manager to force someone to do something against his or her will. It includes psychological and physical threats and actual physical and mental harm. Sexual harassment is a form of coercive power. Other forms of power can be used in a coercive way. For example, reward power can be used to punish employees by withholding valuable outcomes like pay when the employee demonstrates undesirable behaviour such as frequent absenteeism. Referent power can become coercive if it is used to deceive people as is found in some religious cults. Managers who rely heavily on coercive power tend to be ineffective as leaders.

Excessive use of coercive power seldom produces high performance and is questionable ethically. Sometimes it amounts to a form of mental abuse, robbing workers of their dignity and causing excessive levels of stress. Better results are obtained with reward power.

Expert Power

Expert power is based in the special knowledge, skills, and expertise that a leader possesses. The nature of expert power varies, depending on the leader's level in the hierarchy. First-line and middle managers often have technical expertise relevant to the tasks that their subordinates perform. Their expert power gives them considerable influence over subordinates.

Some top managers derive expert power from their technical expertise. Dee Hock, described in Chapter 6 and in the opening scenario to this chapter, is one of these, with his experience, strategic intelligence, and his ability to envision what needed to be done to eventually build and lead a dynamic organization such as Visa International. Many top-level managers lack technical expertise, however, and derive their expert power from their abilities as decision makers, planners, and strategists. Expert power tends to be best used in a guiding or coaching manner rather than in an arrogant, high-handed manner.

expert power
Power that is based in the special knowledge, skills, and expertise that a leader possesses.

Referent Power

Referent power is more informal than the other kinds of power. **Referent power** is a function of the personal characteristics of a leader. It is the power that comes from subordinates' and co-workers' respect, admiration, and loyalty. Leaders who are likeable and whom subordinates wish to use as a role model are especially likely to possess referent power.

In addition to being a valuable asset for top managers, referent power can help first-line and middle managers be effective leaders.

referent power
Power that comes from subordinates' and co-workers' respect, admiration, and loyalty.

> *Referent power is the power that you derive from the trust and commitment given to you by your colleagues because of who you are and how you are perceived. Celebrities are often used in marketing campaigns because they have referent power. You have to be seen as a role model, someone whom others like and admire. This is a precarious power source because if the respect and trust afforded to you falters, you can easily lose it.*[31]

Managers can take steps to increase their referent power—or other powers— for example, by taking time to get to know their subordinates and showing interest and concern for them, thus demonstrating also emotional intelligence in action. Mario F. Heilmann of the University of California at Los Angeles reminds us that there is an ethical implication to referent power as well, "Referent power facilitates learning from positive models and therefore enhances inclusive fitness."[32] Prof. Hugh Gunz, professor of organizational behaviour at the Rotman School of Management at the University of Toronto, makes the suggestion that one should look at the different sources of power and ask how they apply to oneself. Where there are gaps, one can then develop a plan to fill what he calls one's "power gap."

Empowerment: An Ingredient in Modern Management

More and more managers today are incorporating in their personal leadership styles an aspect that at first glance seems to be the opposite

The McGraw-Hill Companies, Inc./Gary He, photographer
Hilary Duff endorsing a video game is an example of referent power. How can managers increase their own referent power?

empowerment
The process of giving employees the authority to make decisions and be responsible for their outcomes.

of being a leader. **Empowerment**—the process of giving employees at all levels in the organization the authority to make decisions, be responsible for their outcomes, improve quality, and cut costs—is becoming increasingly popular in organizations. When leaders empower their subordinates, the subordinates typically take over some of the responsibilities and authority that used to reside with the leader or manager, such as the right to reject parts that do not meet quality standards, the right to check one's own work, and the right to schedule work activities. Empowered subordinates are given the power to make some of the decisions that their leaders or supervisors used to make.

At first glance, empowerment might seem to be the opposite of effective leadership because managers allow subordinates to take a more active role in leading themselves. In actuality, however, empowerment can contribute to effective leadership for several reasons:

- Empowerment increases a manager's ability to get things done because the manager has the support and help of subordinates who may have special knowledge of work tasks.

- Empowerment often increases workers' involvement, motivation, and commitment, which helps ensure that they will be working toward organizational goals.

- Empowerment gives managers more time to concentrate on their pressing concerns because they spend less time on day-to-day supervisory activities.

Effective managers realize the benefits of empowerment; ineffective managers try to keep control over all decision making and force agreement from subordinates. The personal leadership style of managers who empower subordinates often includes developing subordinates so that they can make good decisions and being subordinates' guide, coach, and source of inspiration. Empowerment is a popular trend in Canada and the United States at companies as diverse as United Parcel Service of America Inc. (a package delivery company), Dominion Information Services Inc. (at Burnaby, BC, which publishes *Super Pages* in BC, Alberta, Ontario, and Quebec), and Redwood Plastics Corp. (a manufacturing company based in Langley, BC), and it is also taking off around the world.[33] Even companies in South Korea (such as Samsung, Hyundai, and Daewoo), in which decision making typically was centralized with the founding families, are empowering managers at lower levels to make decisions.[34]

Not every employee is a good candidate for empowerment, however. A study that Professor Jia Lin Xie, of the University of Toronto's Joseph L. Rotman School of Management, conducted with several others found that people who lack confidence can get ill from being put in charge of their own work. The researchers found that "workers who had high levels of control at work but lacked confidence in their abilities or blamed themselves for workplace problems were more likely to have lower antibody levels and experienced more colds and flus."[35]

Some of the difficulty with empowerment is that not all companies introduce it properly. Professor Dan Ondrack at the Rotman School of Management notes that for employees to be empowered, four conditions need to be met: (1) There must be a clear definition of the values and mission of the company; (2) the company must help employees acquire the relevant skills; (3) employees need to be supported in their decision making, and not criticized when they try to do something out of the ordinary; and (4) workers need to be recognized for their efforts.[36] Thus, according to Gail Rieschi, president of Toronto-based vpi, a firm specializing in career and employment management, autonomy and empowerment "are two elements essential to job satisfaction—which, in turn, engenders greater commitment to the organization. It becomes, if managed correctly, a real win-win situation."[37]

Early Models of Leadership

Is there a difference between leadership and management? Harvard Business School Professor John Kotter suggests that "managers promote stability, while leaders press for change and only organizations that embrace both sides of the contradiction can survive in turbulent times."[38] Professor Rabindra Kanungo of McGill University reports growing agreement "among management scholars that the concept of 'leadership' must be distinguished from the concept of 'supervision/management.'"[39] Leaders look to the big picture, providing vision and strategy. Managers are charged with implementing vision and strategy; they coordinate and staff the organization, and handle day-to-day problems.

Below we discuss these early models of leadership.

THINK ABOUT IT

Building a Company to Last[40]

Art Phillips is a retired investment manager and former mayor of Vancouver, British Columbia. He points out that building a company in order to sell it has been a dominant theme and trait among BC entrepreneurs and accounts for the fact that there are so few corporate head offices in Vancouver. Just across the border, in nearby Seattle, such is not the case. The ethos there has bred such companies as Starbucks and Microsoft. However, Jim Pattison, founder of the Pattison Group[41] and "the last great tycoon still standing in British Columbia," is one leader who still oversees a company that grosses $5.7 billion a year, contains $3.3 billion in assets, and employs 28 000 people in total. He is an exception to this entrepreneurial trait of a "cash-out" style of leadership. Another example is Pattison who had increased investment stake to 29 percent in Canfor Corp., North America's third-largest lumber producer in December 2007. What was surprising is that Pattison made this move in a downturn economy in the wood industry. "He's truly a contrarian," said Don Roberts, forest products analyst at CIBC World Markets.[42] Pattison's traits are reflected in his instinct for being a long-term leader.

You Be the Manager

1. What would be your suggestions for traits that leaders should have?
2. How do managers act in a company that has a long-term vision?

Leadership theories developed before 1980 focused on the supervisory nature of leadership. Thus they were concerned with managing the day-to-day functions of employees. These theories took three different approaches to how supervision could be viewed: (1) Do leaders have traits different from nonleaders? (2) Should leaders engage in particular behaviours? (3) Does the situation a leader faces matter? We briefly examine these approaches below.

The Trait Model

The trait model of leadership focused on identifying the personal characteristics that are responsible for effective leadership. Decades of research (beginning in the 1930s)

TABLE 9.1 | *Traits and Personal Characteristics Related to Effective Leadership*

Trait	Description
Intelligence	Helps managers understand complex issues and solve problems
Knowledge and expertise	Help managers make good decisions and discover ways to increase efficiency and effectiveness
Dominance	Helps managers influence their subordinates to achieve organizational goals
Self-confidence	Contributes to managers' effectively influencing subordinates and persisting when faced with obstacles or difficulties
High energy	Helps managers deal with the many demands they face
Tolerance for stress	Helps managers deal with uncertainty and make difficult decisions
Integrity and honesty	Help managers behave ethically and earn their subordinates' trust and confidence
Maturity	Helps managers avoid acting selfishly, control their feelings, and admit when they have made a mistake

and hundreds of studies indicate that certain personal characteristics do appear to be associated with effective leadership (see Table 9.1 for a list of these).[43] Traits alone, however, are not the key to understanding leader effectiveness. Some effective leaders do not possess all of these traits, and some leaders who do possess them are not effective in their leadership roles. This lack of a consistent relationship between leader traits and leader effectiveness led researchers to search for new explanations for effective leadership. Researchers began to turn their attention to what effective leaders actually do—in other words, to the behaviours that allow effective leaders to influence their subordinates to achieve group and organizational goals.

The Behavioural Models

There are a variety of behavioural models of leadership, including the Ohio Studies,[44] the Michigan Studies,[45] and Blake and Mouton's Managerial Grid.[46] These models identify two basic kinds of leader behaviours that many leaders in the United States, Germany, and other countries used to influence their subordinates: *consideration behaviours*, also known as concern for people and employee-centred behaviours; and *initiating structure*, also known as concern for production or task oriented behaviours.

All of the behavioural theories suggest that leaders need to consider the nature of their subordinates when trying to determine the extent to which they should perform these two types of behaviours.

Leaders engage in **consideration** or **employee-centred behaviour** when they show subordinates that they trust, respect, and care about them. This behavioural leadership modelling is borne out with enthusiastic employees.[47] According to the company Sirota Survey Intelligence, specialists in attitude research, employees start out with a company by being enthusiastic. What eventually gets in the way is management! For example, about diversity in the workplace, Nick Starritt, European managing director for Sirota Survey Intelligence, says:

> *Although compliance with the relevant diversity laws is obviously a "must" for every organization, what's important to realize is that what people want from their work is essentially the same, the world over. Our data shows overwhelmingly that if employers create an inclusive environment—where everyone feels respected and performance expectations are the same, irrespective of skin colour, gender or ethnicity, then it's more likely that enthusiasm at work will be high.*[48]

consideration or employee-centred behaviour
Behaviour indicating that a manager trusts, respects, and cares about subordinates.

In addition, according to Starritt, at the end of the day, employees want three things from their work: (1) achievement, or being proud of one's work and employer; (2) camaraderie, or having an opportunity to have positive, productive relationships at work; and (3) equity, or feeling treated justly in relation to the basic conditions of employment, such as pay benefits and job security. Managers, therefore, who truly look out for the well-being of their subordinates and do what they can to help subordinates feel good and enjoy their work are performing consideration behaviours. With the increasing focus on the importance of high-quality customer service, many managers are realizing that when they are considerate to subordinates, subordinates are more likely to be considerate to customers and vice versa. Leaders engage in **initiating structure** or **task-oriented behaviours** when they focus on the goal rather than the process by taking steps to make sure that work gets done, subordinates perform their jobs acceptably, and the organization is efficient and effective. Assigning tasks to individuals or work groups, letting subordinates know what is expected of them, deciding how work should be done, making schedules, encouraging adherence to rules and regulations, and motivating subordinates to do a good job are all examples of initiating structure.[49]

initiating structure or task-oriented behaviours Behaviours that managers engage in to ensure that work gets done, subordinates perform their jobs acceptably, and the organization is efficient and effective.

The Managerial Grid

The managerial grid developed by Blake and Mouton provides a useful framework for managers to assess which set of behaviours have a propensity to dominate in their leadership style. See Figure 9.2. Five different leadership styles emerge from plotting behavioural dimensions on a simple grid. Concern for people is the degree to which the leader shows consideration, while concern for production is the degree to which the leader initiates structure. If a leader's behaviour is high in showing concern for people and low in showing concern for production, they fall into the **Country Club** style. While this type of leadership style may provide a fun and supportive environment for employees, the accomplishment of tasks and goals suffers. The **Impoverished** style shows a low concern for consideration behaviours on the part of the leader and a low concern for production. Needless to say, this type of leadership style tends to be ineffective. When leaders

FIGURE 9.2 | The Managerial Grid[50]

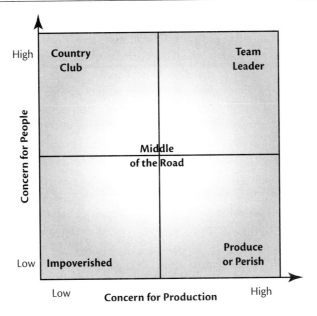

show a high concern for people and a high concern for production, they have the **Team Leader** management style. This creates an atmosphere of trust and respect that leads to high motivation and satisfaction and as a result high performance levels. According to Blake and Mouton, this combination exhibits the optimal leadership behaviours for effectiveness and efficiency. **Produce or Perish** leadership is the style that shows a strong emphasis on goal attainment at the expense of showing concern for the well-being of the employees. Formal rules and regulations as well as the fear of punishment tend to be used by these autocratic leaders. And finally, the **Middle of the Road** leadership style appears to show medium concern for people and production. This style, however, is not optimal, according to the model, because it requires compromise on both sets of concerns so as to leave them both unfulfilled resulting in average levels of performance.

Behavioural theories of leadership which assert that the most effective managers are high on both dimensions have been criticized for ignoring the particular circumstances in which the leader is operating. Just as the behavioural theories emerged as a critique of trait theory—by saying it is not the characteristics of the leader that matter but what they do—so too were the behavioural models criticized for assuming one style of leadership behaviours were appropriate in all situations. Realizing this, researchers began building more complicated models of leadership that focused not only on the leader's traits and behaviours but also on the situation or context in which leadership occurs. In the evolution of leadership theory, this led to the development of **contingency models of leadership.**

contingency models of leadership
Models of leadership that take into account the variables in the situation or context in which leadership occurs.

L O 3

Contingency Models of Leadership

Managers lead in a wide variety of situations and organizations and have various kinds of subordinates performing diverse tasks in many environmental contexts. Given the wide variety of situations in which leadership occurs, what makes a manager an effective leader in one situation (such as certain traits or certain behaviours) is not necessarily what that manager needs in order to be equally effective in a different situation. An effective army general might not be an effective university president, an effective manager of a restaurant might not be an effective manager of a clothing store, an effective coach of a football team might not be an effective manager of a fitness centre, and an effective first-line manager in a manufacturing company might not be an effective middle manager. The traits or behaviours that may contribute to a manager being an effective leader in one situation might actually result in the same manager being an ineffective leader in another situation.

Contingency models of leadership take into account the situation or context within which leadership occurs. So, for instance, while behavioural theories explored whether managers should be more employee-centred or more task-centred, contingency theories answer: It depends (or is contingent) on the situation. According to contingency models, whether or not a manager is an effective leader is the result of the interplay between what the manager is like, what he or she does, and the situation in which leadership takes place. In this section, we discuss four prominent contingency models that shed light on what makes managers effective leaders: Fiedler's contingency model, Hersey-Blanchard's situational leadership theory, House's path-goal theory, and the leader substitutes model. As you will see, these leadership models are complementary. Each focuses on a somewhat different aspect of effective leadership in organizations.

Fiedler's Contingency Model

Fred E. Fiedler was among the first leadership researchers to acknowledge that effective leadership is contingent on, or depends on, the characteristics of the leader and of the situation. Fiedler's contingency model helps explain why a manager may be an effective leader in one situation and ineffective in another; it also suggests which kinds of managers are likely to be most effective in which situations.[51]

Drawing from the previous behavioural studies, Fiedler identified two basic leadership styles: *relationship-oriented* and *task-oriented*. All managers can be described as having one style or the other.

Relationship-oriented leaders are mainly concerned with developing good relationships with their subordinates and being liked by them. The quality of interpersonal relationships with subordinates is a prime concern for relationship-oriented leaders. Task-oriented leaders are mainly concerned with ensuring that subordinates perform at a high level. Task-oriented managers focus on task accomplishment and making sure the job gets done.

Fiedler identified three situational characteristics that are important determinants of how favourable a situation is for leading:

- **Leader-Member Relations**. The extent to which followers like, trust, and are loyal to their leader. Situations are more favourable for leading when leader-member relations are good.

- **Task Structure**. The extent to which the work to be performed is clear-cut so that a leader's subordinates know what needs to be accomplished and how to go about doing it. When task structure is high, situations are favourable for leading. When task structure is low, goals may be vague, subordinates may be unsure of what they should be doing or how they should do it, and the situation is unfavourable for leading.

- **Position Power**. The amount of legitimate, reward, and coercive powers a leader has by virtue of his or her position in an organization. Leadership situations are more favourable for leading when position power is strong.

When a situation is favourable for leading, it is relatively easy for a manager to influence subordinates so that they perform at a high level and contribute to organizational efficiency and effectiveness. Therefore it makes the most sense to be task-oriented because the relationship is already going well. In a situation unfavourable for leading, it is much more difficult for a manager to exert influence. This makes being task-oriented the most desirable behaviour for the leader. After extensive research, Fiedler determined that relationship-oriented leaders are most effective in moderately favourable situations (IV, V, VI, and VII in Figure 9.3) and task-oriented leaders are most effective in very favourable situations (I, II, and III) or very unfavourable situations (VIII).

leader-member relations
The extent to which followers like, trust, and are loyal to their leader. They can be good or poor.

task structure
The extent to which the work to be performed is clear-cut so that a leader's subordinates know what needs to be accomplished and how to go about doing it; a determinant of how favourable a situation is for leading. The task structure can be high or low.

position power
The amount of legitimate, reward, and coercive power that a leader has by virtue of his or her position in an organization; a determinant of how favourable a situation is for leading. Position power can be strong or weak.

FIGURE 9.3 | Fiedler's Contingency Theory of Leadership

SITUATIONAL CHARACTERISTICS	Leader–Member Relations	GOOD				POOR			
	Task Structure	High		Low		High		Low	
	Position Power	Strong	Weak	Strong	Weak	Strong	Weak	Strong	Weak
		I	II	III	IV	V	VI	VII	VIII
	Kinds of leadership situations	Very favourable situation							Very unfavourable situation

Relationship-oriented leaders are most effective in moderately favourable situations for leading (IV, V, VI, VII).
Task-oriented leaders are most effective in very favourable situations (I, II, III) or very unfavourable situations (VIII) for leading.

According to Fiedler, individuals cannot change their leadership style. Therefore, managers need to be placed in leadership situations that fit their style, or situations need to be changed to suit the manager. Situations can be changed, for example, by giving a manager more position power or by taking steps to increase task structure such as by clarifying goals. Research studies tend to support Fiedler's model but also suggest that, like most theories, it needs to be adjusted.[52] Some researchers also find fault with the model's premise that leaders cannot alter their styles

Hersey-Blanchard's Situational Leadership Theory

Paul Hersey and Ken Blanchard's **situational leadership theory** (SLT)[53] has been incorporated into leadership training programs at numerous Fortune 500 companies. More than one million managers a year are taught its basic elements.[54]

SLT compares the leader–follower relationship to that between a parent and a child. Just as parents needs to give more control to a child as the child becomes more mature and responsible, so too should leaders do this with employees. Hersey and Blanchard identify four specific leadership behaviours that managers can use to lead their employees: telling, selling, participating, and delegating. The styles vary in their degree of task-oriented behaviour and relationship-oriented behaviour. The appropriate style depends on the follower's ability and motivation:

- *Telling.* If a follower is *unable* and *unwilling* to do a task, the leader needs to give clear and specific directions (in other words, the leader needs to be highly directive).

- *Selling.* If a follower is *unable* but *willing*, the leader needs to display both high task orientation and high relationship orientation. The high task orientation will compensate for the follower's lack of ability. The high relationship orientation will encourage the follower to "buy into" the leader's desires (in other words, the leader needs to "sell" the task).

- *Participating.* If the follower is *able* but *unwilling*, the leader needs to use a supportive and participative style.

- *Delegating.* If the employee is both *able* and *willing*, the leader does not need to do much (in other words, a laissez-faire approach will work).

Figure 9.4 illustrates the relationship of leader behaviours to follower readiness.

Path-Goal Theory

Developed by Rotman School of Management professor Martin Evans in the late 1960s, and then expanded on by Robert House, **path-goal theory** focuses on what leaders can do to motivate their subordinates to reach group and organizational goals.[55] The premise of path-goal theory is that effective leaders motivate subordinates to achieve goals by (1) clearly identifying the outcomes that subordinates are trying to obtain from the workplace, (2) rewarding subordinates with these outcomes for high performance and the attainment of work goals, and (3) clarifying for subordinates the paths leading to the attainment of work goals. Path-goal theory is a contingency model because it proposes that the steps that managers should take to motivate subordinates depend on both the nature of the subordinates and the type of work they do.

Based on the expectancy theory of motivation (see Chapter 8), path-goal theory provides managers with three guidelines to follow to be effective leaders:

1. *Find out what outcomes your subordinates are trying to obtain from their jobs and the organization.* These outcomes can range from satisfactory pay and job security

FIGURE 9.4 | Hersey-Blanchard's Situational Leadership Styles

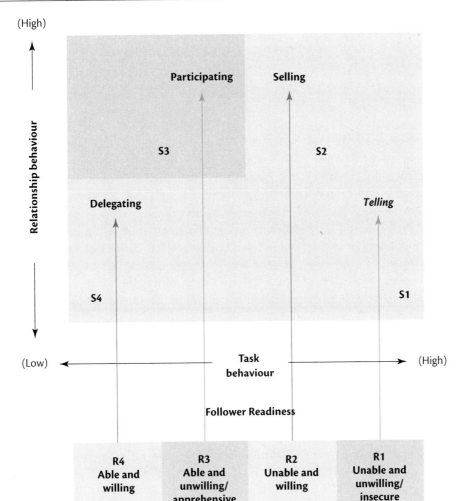

to reasonable working hours and interesting and challenging job assignments. After identifying what these outcomes are, the manager should make sure that he or she has the reward power needed to distribute or withhold them.

2. *Reward subordinates for high performance and goal attainment with the outcomes they desire.*

3. *Clarify the paths to goal attainment for subordinates, remove any obstacles to high performance, and express confidence in subordinates' capabilities.* This does not mean that a manager needs to tell his or her subordinates what to do. Rather, it means that a manager needs to make sure that subordinates are clear about what they should be trying to accomplish and have the capabilities, resources, and confidence levels they need to be successful.

Path-goal theory identifies four kinds of behaviours that leaders can use to motivate subordinates:

- *Directive behaviours* include setting goals, assigning tasks, showing subordinates how to complete tasks, and taking concrete steps to improve performance.

- *Supportive behaviours* include expressing concern for subordinates and looking out for their best interests.

- *Participative behaviours* give subordinates a say in matters and decisions that affect them.

- *Achievement-oriented behaviours* motivate subordinates to perform at the highest level possible by, for example, setting very challenging goals, expecting that they be met, and believing in subordinates' capabilities.

Which of these behaviours should managers use to lead effectively? The answer to this question depends, or is contingent, on the nature of the subordinates and the kind of work they do.

Directive behaviours may be beneficial when subordinates are having difficulty completing assigned tasks, but they might be detrimental when subordinates are independent thinkers who work best when left alone. *Supportive* behaviours are often advisable when subordinates are experiencing high levels of stress. *Participative* behaviours can be particularly effective when subordinates' support of a decision is required. *Achievement-oriented* behaviours may increase motivation levels of highly capable subordinates who are bored from having too few challenges, but they might backfire if used with subordinates who are already pushed to their limits.

Effective managers seem to have a knack for determining the kinds of leader behaviours that are likely to work in different situations and result in increased efficiency and effectiveness.

To illustrate the importance of understanding that situations are different, and can require different styles, consider the fate of some of the Americans who have been recruited to run Canadian companies. Retailer Millard Barron was brought north to turn Zellers around, and American Bill Fields was supposed to save Hudson's Bay Co. Neither could replicate their American successes in Canada. Texas oilman J.P. Bryan was given the chance to restore profitability at two Canadian companies—Gulf Canada Resources Ltd. (now ConocoPhillips Company) and Canadian 88 Energy Corp. (now Esprit Exploration Limited)—and failed at both attempts.[56] Chief operating officer Gary Daichendt and chief technology officer Gary Kunis walked away from Nortel Corp. over management differences or "divergent management styles and different views of the future of the business" with the then CEO Bill Owens. These examples show the importance of understanding that one's leadership style may need to be adjusted for different companies, for different employees, and perhaps even for different countries.

The Leader Substitutes Model

The leader substitutes model suggests that leadership is sometimes unnecessary because substitutes for leadership are present. A **leader substitute** is something that acts in place of the influence of a leader and makes leadership unnecessary. This model suggests that under certain conditions managers do not have to play a leadership role—that members of an organization sometimes can perform highly without a manager exerting influence over them.[57] The leader substitutes model is a contingency model because it suggests that in some situations leadership is unnecessary.

Both the *characteristics of subordinates*—such as their skills, abilities, experience, knowledge, and motivation—and the *characteristics of the situation or context*—such as the extent to which the work is interesting and enjoyable—can be substitutes for leadership.[58] When work is interesting and enjoyable, job holders do not need to be coaxed into performing because performing is rewarding in its own right. Similarly, when managers empower their subordinates or use *self-managed work teams* (discussed in detail in Chapter 10), the need for leadership influence from a manager is decreased because team members manage themselves.

leader substitute
Characteristics of subordinates or characteristics of a situation or context that act in place of the influence of a leader and make leadership unnecessary.

Substitutes for leadership can increase organizational efficiency and effectiveness because they free up some of managers' valuable time and allow managers to focus their efforts on discovering new ways to improve organizational effectiveness.

Bringing It All Together

Effective leadership in organizations occurs when managers take steps to lead in a way that is appropriate for the situation or context in which leadership occurs and the subordinates who are being led. The four contingency models of leadership just discussed help managers identify the necessary ingredients for effective leadership. They are complementary in that each one looks at the leadership question from a different angle. Fiedler's contingency model explores how a manager's leadership style needs to be matched to the leadership situation that the manager is in for maximum effectiveness. Hersey-Blanchard's situational leadership theory examines the need for leaders to adjust their style to match their followers' ability and motivation. House's path-goal theory focuses on how managers should motivate subordinates and describes the specific kinds of behaviours that managers can engage in to have a highly motivated workforce. The leadership substitutes model alerts managers to the fact that sometimes they do not need to exert influence over subordinates and thus can free up their time for other important activities. Table 9.2 recaps these four contingency models of leadership.

Tips for Managers

CONTINGENCY MODELS OF LEADERSHIP

1. Examine for yourself the kinds of situation where you feel you will be most effective as a leader.

2. Know how flexible you can be in choosing a different style to lead when the situation calls for such a difference.

3. Link your leadership style to the outcomes you want your employees to achieve; know how you will reward them; and make clear the paths for employees to follow to be successful.

4. Know when your subordinates can effectively manage and lead themselves.

TABLE 9.2 | *Contingency Models of Leadership*

Model	Focus	Key Contingencies
Fiedler's contingency model	Describes two leader styles, relationship-oriented and task-oriented, and the kinds of situations in which each kind of leader will be most effective	The favourableness for leading depends on three contingency factors: leader–member relations, task structure, and position power.
Hersey-Blanchard's situational leadership theory	Describes how leaders adjust their styles to match their followers' ability and motivation	The styles that managers should use are contingent on the ability and motivation of subordinates
House's path-goal theory	Describes how effective leaders motivate their followers	The behaviours that managers should engage in to be effective leaders are contingent on the nature of the subordinates and the work they do
Leader substitutes model	Describes when leadership is unnecessary	Whether or not leadership is necessary for subordinates to perform highly is contingent on characteristics of the subordinates and the situation

Transactional and Transformational Models of Leadership

THINK ABOUT IT

Seven Transformations of Leadership[59]

"The leader's voyage of development is not an easy one. Some people change little in their lifetimes; some change substantially. Despite the undeniably crucial role of genetics, human nature is not fixed. Those who are willing to work at developing themselves and becoming more self-aware can almost certainly evolve over time into truly transformational leaders."

So ends the article, "Seven Transformations of Leadership" by David Rooke, a partner at Harthill Consulting in Hewelsfield, England, and William R. Torbert, a professor at Boston College's Carroll School of Management in Massachusetts.[60] The authors based their research and applications on what they call "action inquiry": the process of transformational learning that individuals (and even whole organizations) can undertake to better assess current dangers and opportunities, act in a timely manner, and make future visions come true. What they discovered is that there is a transformational progression of leadership abilities in organizations: from opportunist to alchemist, with expert and achiever leadership styles being the most predominant. The seven styles of leadership, in their effectiveness, are: *opportunist* (wins any way possible), *diplomat* (avoids overt conflict), *expert* (rules by logic and expertise), *achiever* (meets strategic goals), *individualist* (interweaves competing personal and company action logics), *strategist* (generates organizational and personal transformations), or *alchemist* (generates social transformations).[61] What is significant about their work is the possibility of transforming oneself from one "action logic," or mindset, to a more refined one. For example, if a manager is seen to be an opportunist, he or she demonstrates a style that says: "I win at any cost. I am self-referencing and manipulative. I believe that 'might makes right.'" This is obviously a very undeveloped style, and the above-mentioned research found that only 5 percent of managers were described as such. At the other end of the spectrum is the alchemist, who is quite focused on social transformation and the integration of material, spiritual, and societal issues for transformation. This action logic individual accounts for only 1 percent of the managers. The bulk of managers (38 percent and 30 percent) turned out to be experts and achievers, respectively. What makes an individual manager transform from one action logic way of seeing and leading is attributed to a variety of reasons: personal changes, loss of faith in the system, external events, changes in the work environment—in other words, factors that challenge the status quo of the leader.

You Be the Manager

1. What factors have forced you to shift your view of the world?
2. What are some of the transformations you have experienced?

transactional leadership
Leaders who guide their subordinates toward expected goals with no expectation of exceeding expected behaviour.

The trait, behavioural, and contingency theories are transactional leadership theories developed when organizations were more hierarchical, with classic lines of command. **Transactional leadership** occurs when managers guide or motivate their subordinates in the direction of established goals. Some transactional leaders use rewards and recognize appropriate behaviour. Under this kind of leadership, employees will generally meet performance expectations, though rarely will they exceed expectations.[62] Other transactional leaders emphasize correction and possibly punishment rather than rewards and recognition. This style "results in performance below expectations, and discourages innovation and initiative in the workplace."[63] While leaders should not ignore poor performance, effective leaders emphasize how to achieve expectations, rather than dwelling on mistakes.

Hierarchical organizations still dominate Canada's "Most Respected Corporations,"[64] but some organizations are trying to be more innovative, faster moving, and more responsive to employees. These organizations have turned to a different style of leadership where leaders and managers are not expected to perform only supervisory tasks but also need to focus on vision-setting activities. These theories try to explain how certain leaders can achieve extraordinary performance from their followers, and they emphasize symbolic and emotionally appealing leadership behaviours.[65]

When managers have such dramatic effects on their subordinates and on an organization as a whole, they are engaging in transformational leadership. **Transformational leadership** occurs when managers change (or transform) their subordinates in three important ways:[66]

1. *Transformational managers make subordinates aware of how important their jobs are for the organization and how necessary it is for them to perform those jobs as best they can so that the organization can attain its goals.* At LG Electronics, Hun-Jo Lee opened new paths of communication between nonmanagerial employees and managers and openly shared the company's problems with employees. He made everyone feel responsible for helping to solve the problems. Decision making was decentralized, and all employees were encouraged to feel responsible for coming up with improvements, ideas for new products, and ways to increase quality.

2. *Transformational managers make their subordinates aware of the subordinates' own needs for personal growth, development, and accomplishment.* One of Lee's important steps at LG Electronics was to improve management relations with the union. He encourages union members to meet with him whenever they have ideas for improving things at LG Electronics.[67] He wants his employees to reach their full potential and is doing whatever he can think of to help them do that. He also empowers his employees, so they will feel free to consider new ways of doing things at the company.

3. *Transformational managers motivate their subordinates to work for the good of the organization as a whole, not just for their own personal gain or benefit.* In transforming LG Electronics, Lee explained to employees the need for change at the company and that growth and improvement in productivity would make the company much stronger, thus benefiting everyone.

Many transformational leaders engage in transactional leadership. They reward subordinates for a job well done and notice and respond to substandard performance. But they also have their eyes on the bigger picture of how much better things could be in their organizations, how much more their subordinates are capable of achieving, and how important it is to treat their subordinates with respect and to help them reach their full potential.

Influencing Others

How do managers like Lee transform subordinates and produce dramatic effects in their organizations? There are at least three ways in which managers and other transformational leaders can influence their followers: by being a charismatic leader, by stimulating subordinates intellectually, and by engaging in developmental consideration (see Table 9.3).

transformational leadership
Leadership that makes subordinates aware of the importance of their jobs and performance to the organization and aware of their own needs for personal growth, and that motivates subordinates to work for the good of the organization.

LG Electronics Inc.www. lg.co.kr/english/

Business Plan Checklist

- Determine the leadership style that is suitable for your venture.
- Make sure that it is reflected in your management team.

TABLE 9.3 | *Transformational Leadership*

Transformational Managers

- Tend to be charismatic
- Intellectually stimulate subordinates
- Engage in developmental consideration

Subordinates of Transformational Managers

- Have increased awareness of the importance of their jobs and high performance
- Are aware of their own needs for growth, development, and accomplishment
- Work for the good of the organization and not just their own personal benefit

Being a Charismatic Leader

charismatic leader
An enthusiastic, self-confident leader able to communicate clearly his or her vision of how good things could be.

Transformational managers tend to be **charismatic leaders**. They have a vision of how good things could be in their work groups and organizations, and it is in contrast with the status quo. Their vision usually entails dramatic improvements in group and organizational performance as a result of changes in the organization's structure, culture, strategy, decision making, and other critical processes and factors. This vision paves the way for gaining a competitive advantage.

Charismatic leaders are excited and enthusiastic about their vision and clearly communicate it to their subordinates. The excitement, enthusiasm, and self-confidence of a charismatic leader contribute to the leader's being able to inspire followers to enthusiastically support his or her vision.[68] People often think of charismatic leaders or managers as being "larger than life." The essence of charisma, however, is having a vision and enthusiastically communicating it to others. Thus, managers who appear to be quiet and earnest can also be charismatic.

The most comprehensive analysis of charismatic leadership was conducted by Professor Rabindra Kanungo at McGill University, together with Jay Conger.[69] Based on studies of managers from Canada, the United States, and India, they identified five dimensions that characterize charismatic leadership. These are shown in Table 9.4.

Does charismatic leadership really make a difference? An unpublished study by Robert House and some colleagues studying 63 American and 49 Canadian companies (including Nortel Networks, Molson [now Molson-Coors], Gulf Canada [now ConocoPhillips], and Manulife Financial) found that "between 15 and 25 percent of the variation in

TABLE 9.4 | *Key Characteristics of a Charismatic Leader*

1. *Vision and articulation*. Has a vision—expressed as an idealized goal—that proposes a future better than the status quo; is able to clarify the importance of the vision in terms that are understandable to others.
2. *Personal risk*. Willing to take on high personal risk, incur high costs, and engage in self-sacrifice to achieve the vision.
3. *Environmental sensitivity*. Able to make realistic assessments of the environmental constraints and resources needed to bring about change.
4. *Sensitivity to follower needs*. Perceptive of others' abilities and responsive to their needs and feelings.
5. *Unconventional behaviour*. Engages in behaviours that are perceived as novel and counter to norms.

Source: Based on J.A. Conger and R.N. Kanungo, *Charismatic Leadership in Organizations* (Thousand Oaks, CA: Sage, 1998), p. 94.

profitability among the companies was accounted for by the leadership qualities of their CEO."[70] Charismatic leaders led the more profitable companies.

An increasing body of research shows that people who work for charismatic leaders are motivated to exert extra work effort and, because they like their leaders, they express greater satisfaction.[71] One of the most cited studies of the effects of charismatic leadership was done at the University of British Columbia in the early 1980s by Jane Howell (now at the Richard Ivey School of Business, University of Western Ontario) and Peter Frost.[72] The two found that those who worked under a charismatic leader generated more ideas, produced better results, reported higher job satisfaction, and showed stronger bonds of loyalty. Howell, in summarizing these results, says, "Charismatic leaders know how to inspire people to think in new directions."[73]

The accounting scandals and high-profile bankruptcies of North American companies, including Enron and WorldCom, suggest some of the dangers of charismatic leadership. WorldCom Inc.'s Bernard Ebbers and Enron Corp.'s Kenneth Lay "seemed almost a breed apart, blessed with unique visionary powers" when their companies were increasing stock prices at phenomenal rates in the 1990s.[74] After the scandals, however, there was some desire for CEOs with less vision and more ethical and corporate responsibility.

Stimulating Subordinates Intellectually

Transformational managers openly share information with their subordinates so that subordinates are aware of problems and the need for change. The manager causes subordinates to view problems in their groups and throughout the organization from a different perspective, consistent with the manager's vision. Whereas in the past subordinates may not have been aware of some problems, may have viewed problems as a "management issue" beyond their concern, or may have viewed problems as insurmountable, the transformational manager's **intellectual stimulation** leads subordinates to view problems as challenges that they can and will meet and conquer. The manager engages and empowers subordinates to take personal responsibility for helping to solve problems.[75] For example, unlike other companies that often ask a team for an idea or to solve a problem and then tell them how much money they have to do it, Cirque du Soleil's leader Guy Laliberté instead would decide how much could be spent on a new show and then "expect the creative team to come up with their vision within its financial boundaries."[76]

intellectual stimulation
Behaviour a leader engages in to make followers aware of problems and view these problems in new ways, consistent with the leader's vision.

Engaging in Developmental Consideration

When a manager engages in **developmental consideration**, he or she not only performs the consideration behaviours described earlier, such as demonstrating true concern for the well-being of subordinates but also goes one step further. The manager goes out of his or her way to support and encourage subordinates, giving them opportunities to enhance their skills and capabilities and to grow and excel in their jobs.[77]

Research Support

The evidence supporting the superiority of transformational leadership is overwhelmingly impressive. For example, studies of Canadian, American, and German military officers found, at every level, that transformational leaders were considered more effective than their transactional counterparts (see Table 9.5).[78] Professor Jane Howell (at the University of Western Ontario) and her colleagues studied 250 executives and managers at a major financial-services company and found that "transformational leaders had 34 percent higher business unit performance results than other types of leaders."[79] Studies also find that when leaders engage in transformational leadership, their subordinates tend to have higher levels of job satisfaction and performance.[80] Additionally, subordinates of transformational leaders may be more likely to trust their leaders and their organizations and feel that they are being fairly treated, which, in turn, may positively influence their work motivation (see Chapter 8).[81]

 Tips for Managers

TRANSFORMATIONAL LEADERSHIP

1. Facilitate employee development and attainment of goals to ensure commitment and corporate goal attainment.

2. Develop ways for self-understanding so that you can be the very best.

3. Visualize what are ideal states of business operation and develop steps for their completion.

4. Let your employees know that you care for them, their well-being, and their productivity.

TABLE 9.5 | *Transactional versus Transformational leadership*

Transactional leadership	Transformational leadership
Managers guide and motivate subordinates to achieve organizational goals through conventional methods such as direct supervision.	Produce dramatic effects for the organization's performance by inspiring subordinates to go above and beyond stated goals by modelling desired behaviours.
The status quo daily activities of planning, leading, organizing, and controlling are carried out effectively and efficiently.	Have vision that goes beyond the status quo entailing changes in the organization's structure, culture, strategy, decision-making, and other critical variables for gaining a competitive advantage.
Subordinates meet performance expectations but rarely exceed them.	Perform at levels exceeding those of other types of leaders.
Formal rules, regulations, and the fear of punishment discourage risk-taking and innovation.	Show excitement and enthusiasm, trust and respect, and concern for subordinates' growth and development, encourage risk-taking and initiative.
Managers rely on legitimate and reward power to exercise authority and recognize high and low levels of performance.	Are charismatic, possess referent power, intellectually stimulate subordinates and engage in developmental consideration to foster high performance.
The model is effective and efficient in a stable organizational environment.	Is an effective model in an unstable, dynamic environment where a change in the organization's course is desired or necessary to gain a competitive advantage.

Gender, Culture, Emotional Intelligence, and Leadership

THINK ABOUT IT

Women and Leadership[82]

It is estimated that women now own 35 percent of all small businesses in Canada. When journalist Mary Teresa Bitti asked Dr. Lance Secretan, international bestselling author of 13 books on leadership, a corporate coach and a business adviser, about gender and leadership, he replied:

The landscape is changing very fast here, but the fact remains men have had a lot of forces working for them—clubs, old boy networks. They are swimming with the tide. Women, until very recently, have not typically had that. As a result, in some ways, they are better problem-solvers. They have had to work around things and create solutions that are innovative in order to get around the system. If a man wants to solve a financial problem, he will go to his pals in the financial world and ask for advice. Women don't have those pals and have to make it up themselves. They are more creative and collaborative.

Key success stories:

- Meg Whitman has transformed eBay Inc. from a trading post for collectors of Pez dispensers into the world's dominant online auctioneer.

- At Xerox Corp., Lucent Technologies Inc., and Avon Products Inc., successful turnaround CEOs Anne Mulcahy, Patricia Russo, and Toronto native Andrea Jung, respectively, have been cleaning up the mess left by ousted male predecessors.

- PepsiCo Inc. veteran Brenda Barnes was named the incoming CEO at food and apparel giant Sara Lee Corp. in early 2005.

- Business writer, David Olive, says that investors in women-led Fortune 500 companies enjoyed a 53.7-percent return on their stock in the past two years, compared with a 37.7-percent gain for the Standard & Poor's 500 index."[83]

You Be the Manager

1. What are the challenges that women face that men do not?

There are many questions about whether men and women have different leadership styles and whether observed differences have more to do with personality differences across people, rather than with explicit gender differences. Others consider whether leadership styles are the same cross-culturally and whether our North American leadership theories apply in other countries. More recently, the effects of moods and emotions of leaders on their effectiveness have gained notable attention. We consider these issues in the following sections.

Gender and Leadership

The increasing number of women entering the ranks of management as well as the problems some women face in their efforts to be hired as managers or promoted into management positions have prompted researchers to explore the relationship between gender and leadership. Although relatively more women are in management positions

CP Photo/P. Moczulski
Andrea Jung—CEO of Avon, the famous cosmetic producer—advanced to that rank after first serving as the company's president and chief operating officer.

today than 10 years ago, relatively few women are in top management in larger organizations, and, in some organizations, even in middle management. Although women make up 45 percent of the labour force in Canada, they fill only 32 percent of managerial roles, and only 12 percent of the senior management roles. In 2008, only 12 Fortune 500 companies had women CEOs.[84] In Canada, the growth of women-owned businesses is skyrocketing. In 2010, these businesses will exceed 1 million if the rate of growth stays consistent. Although female entrepreneurship is growing 60 percent faster than men's in Canada, just 4.3 percent of women's companies enjoy revenue of $1 million or more, while 10.7 percent of men's companies do.[85]

When women do advance to top-management positions, special attention is often focused on the fact that they are women, such as when Bobbi Gaunt was named to head Ford Motor Co. of Canada and Maureen Kempston Darkes was named to head General Motors of Canada.

A widespread stereotype of women is that they are nurturing, supportive, and concerned with interpersonal relations. Men are stereotypically viewed as being directive and focused on task accomplishment. Such stereotypes suggest that women tend to be more relationship-oriented as managers and engage in more consideration behaviours, whereas men are more task-oriented and engage in more initiating structure behaviours. Does the behaviour of actual male and female managers bear out these stereotypes? Do female managers lead in different ways than males? Are male or female managers more effective as leaders?

Research suggests that male managers and female managers who have leadership positions in organizations behave in similar ways.[86] Women do not engage in more consideration than do men, and men do not engage in more initiating structure than do women. Research does suggest, however, that leadership style may vary between women and men. Women tend to be somewhat more participative as leaders than men, involving subordinates in decision making and seeking their input.[87] Male managers tend to be less participative than female managers, making more decisions on their own and wanting to do things their own way.

There are at least two reasons why female managers may be more participative as leaders than are male managers.[88] First, subordinates may try to resist the influence of female managers more than they do the influence of male managers. Some subordinates may never have reported to a woman before, some may inappropriately see management roles as being more appropriate for men than for women, and some may just resist being led by a woman. To overcome this resistance and encourage subordinates' trust and respect, female managers may adopt a participative approach.

A second reason why female managers may be more participative is that they sometimes have better interpersonal skills than do male managers.[89] A participative approach to leadership requires high levels of interaction and involvement between a manager and his or her subordinates, sensitivity to subordinates' feelings, and the ability to make decisions that may be unpopular with subordinates but necessary for reaching goals. Good interpersonal skills may help female managers have the effective interactions with their subordinates that are crucial to a participative approach.[90] To the extent that male managers have more difficulty managing interpersonal relationships, they may shy away from the high levels of interaction with subordinates that are necessary for true participation.

Perhaps a question even more important than whether male and female managers differ in the leadership behaviours they perform is whether they differ in effectiveness. Consistent with the findings about leadership behaviours, research suggests that across different kinds of organizational settings, male and female managers tend to be *equally* effective as leaders.[91] Thus, there is no logical basis for stereotypes favouring male managers and leaders or for the existence of the glass ceiling (an invisible barrier that seems to prevent women from advancing as far as they should in some organizations). Because women and men are equally effective as leaders, the increasing number of women in the workforce should result in a larger pool of highly qualified candidates for management positions in organizations, ultimately enhancing organizational effectiveness.[92]

Leadership Styles Across Cultures

Some evidence suggests that leadership styles vary not only among individuals but also among countries or cultures. Some research suggests that European managers tend to be more humanistic or people-oriented than Japanese and American managers. The collectivistic culture in Japan places prime emphasis on the group rather than the individual, so the importance of individuals' own personalities, needs, and desires is minimized. Organizations in North America tend to be very profit-oriented and thus tend to downplay the importance of individual employees' needs and desires. Many countries in Europe have a more individualistic outlook than does Japan and a more humanistic outlook than does the United States, which may result in some European managers being more people-oriented than their Japanese or American counterparts. European managers, for example, tend to be reluctant to lay off employees, and when a layoff is absolutely necessary, they take careful steps to make it as painless as possible.[93]

Another cross-cultural difference that has been noted is in time horizons. Managers in any two countries often differ in their time horizons, but there also may be cultural differences. Canadian and American organizations tend to have a short-run profit orientation, which results in a leadership style emphasizing short-run performance. Many of the investors and creators of the dot-com companies that failed in 2000 and 2001 demonstrated very short-term objectives, along the lines of "get rich quick." Many of these companies failed to have a business plan that would guide them in a long-term strategy. By contrast, Japanese organizations tend to have a long-run growth orientation, which results in Japanese managers' personal leadership styles emphasizing long-run performance. Justus Mische, now chair at the European organization Aventis (formerly Hoechst) has suggested that "Europe, at least the big international firms in Europe, have a philosophy between the Japanese long term and the United States short term."[94] Research on these and other global aspects of leadership is in its infancy, but as it continues, more cultural differences in managers' personal leadership styles may be discovered.

Emotional Intelligence and Leadership

Do the moods and emotions leaders experience on the job influence their behaviour and effectiveness as leaders? Preliminary research suggests that this is likely to be the case. For example, one study found that when store managers experienced positive moods at work, salespeople in the stores they led provided high-quality customer service and were less likely to quit.[95]

Emotional intelligence is the ability to understand and manage one's own moods and emotions and the moods and emotions of other people. A leader's level of emotional intelligence may play a particularly important role in leadership effectiveness.[96] For example, emotional intelligence may help leaders develop a vision for their organizations, motivate their subordinates to commit to this vision, and energize them to enthusiastically work to achieve this vision. Moreover, emotional intelligence may enable leaders to develop a significant identity for their organization and instill high levels of trust and cooperation throughout the organization while maintaining the flexibility needed to respond to changing conditions.[97]

emotional intelligence
The ability to understand and manage one's own moods and emotions and the moods and emotions of other people.

THINK ABOUT IT

Social Intelligence: The "People Thing"

The acronym "EQ" was first coined by Dr. Reuven Bar-On in 1985 in his research while developing the Emotional Quotient-*Inventory*™ (or EQ-*i*™) from 1980–1997.[98] Dr. Daniel Goleman popularized the acronym in his 1995 book *Emotional Intelligence*.[99] The notion of emotional intelligence has caught the public's imagination quite dramatically. More and more scientific studies are being conducted to showcase its applicability as well as its predictability. As noted above, emotional intelligence is one's ability to recognize one's emotions and those of others to develop positive relational consequences at home and at work. Dr. Bar-On's latest research is now also focusing on a concept known as *social intelligence*: one's ability to deal with people.[100] In 2006, Dr. Daniel Goleman published another book, bringing the concept of social intelligence to the awareness of the general public.[101]

For management consultant Karl Albrecht, it is important to focus more intensely now on the role of social intelligence in the workplace.[102] He says that social intelligence can reduce conflict, create collaboration, replace bigotry and polarization with understanding, and mobilize people toward common goals. He even says that social intelligence may be the most important ingredient in our survival as a species. He outlines five key dimensions to social intelligence:

1. **Situational radar**: the ability to read the social context or situation and know what to do.
2. **Presence**: the ability to know how one comes across to others.
3. **Authenticity**: being honest with oneself and others.
4. **Clarity**: the ability to express oneself clearly, use language effectively, explain concepts clearly, and persuade others with ideas.
5. **Empathy**: the ability to create a sense of connectedness with others, to get emotionally in sync with them and to invite them to move with and toward you, rather than away from you.

You Be the Manager

1. As you review the outlined five key dimensions to social intelligence, which dimension(s) do you feel competent in?
2. Where was the biggest discrepancy on the five dimensions between your *self* and *other* assessment?

Becoming a Leader

Ask yourself:

1. What is important to me? What are my values, beliefs, ethics?
2. How am I demonstrating those values, beliefs, and ethics every day?
3. Is the larger organization designed to support my values, beliefs, and ethics?
4. How do I manage my moods and emotions and those of others?
5. How can I align my behaviours with my convictions and vision?
6. What steps can I take to build a collaborative culture based on organizational goals?

Take the following steps:

- Seek input from your employees and colleagues about what their needs and dreams are for their jobs and the organization

- Seek input from other stakeholders such as customers and suppliers about their needs

- Find out what you can do to create personal growth and organizational success

- Engage in conversation; actively listen to others; look for trends and themes

- Explore possibilities and opportunities

- Develop your full potential and help others develop theirs

Summary and Review

1. **THE NATURE OF LEADERSHIP** Leadership is the process by which a person exerts influence over other people and inspires, motivates, and directs their activities to help achieve group or organizational goals. Leaders are able to influence others because they possess power. The five types of power available to managers are *legitimate power, reward power, coercive power, expert power,* and *referent power.* Many managers are using empowerment as a tool to increase their effectiveness as leaders.

2. **EARLY MODELS OF LEADERSHIP** The *trait model* of leadership describes personal characteristics or traits that contribute to effective leadership. However, some managers who possess these traits are not effective leaders, and some managers who do not possess all the traits are nevertheless effective leaders. The *behaviour models* of leadership describes two kinds of behaviour that most leaders engage in: consideration and initiating structure, or concern for people and concern for production. The Managerial Grid represents five styles of leadership based on the degree of behaviour along these two dimensions.

3. **CONTINGENCY MODELS OF LEADERSHIP** Contingency models take into account the complexity surrounding leadership and the role of the situation in determining whether a manager is an effective or ineffective leader. *Fiedler's contingency model* explains why managers may be effective leaders in one situation and ineffective in another. *Hersey-Blanchard's situational leadership theory* examines the need for leaders to adjust their style to match their followers' ability and motivation. *House's path-goal theory* describes how effective managers motivate their subordinates by determining what outcomes their subordinates want, rewarding subordinates with these outcomes when they achieve their goals and perform at a high level, and clarifying the paths to goal attainment. The *leader substitutes model* suggests that sometimes managers do not have to play a leadership role because their subordinates perform highly without the manager having to exert influence over them.

4. **TRANSACTIONAL AND TRANSFORMATIONAL LEADERSHIP:** Leading with vision Transactional leaders generally only get their subordinates to meet expectations. Transformational leadership occurs when managers have dramatic effects on their subordinates and on the organization as a whole and inspire and energize subordinates to solve problems and improve performance. These effects include making subordinates aware of the importance of their own jobs and high performance; making subordinates aware of their own needs for personal growth, development, and accomplishment; and motivating subordinates to work for the good of the organization and not just their own personal gain. Managers can engage in transformational leadership by being charismatic leaders, by stimulating subordinates intellectually, and by engaging in developmental consideration. Charismatic leaders rely on referent power to influence others.

5. **GENDER, CULTURE, EMOTIONAL INTELLIGENCE AND LEADERSHIP** Female and male managers do not differ in the leadership behaviours that they perform, contrary to stereotypes suggesting that women are more relationship-oriented

and men more task-oriented. Female managers sometimes are more participative than are male managers, however. Research has found that women and men are equally effective as managers and leaders. Studies have found differences in leadership styles across cultures. European leaders tend to be more people-oriented than either American or Japanese leaders. Leaders also differ in their time orientations, with American and Canadian leaders being highly oriented toward the short term in their approach. The moods and emotions leaders experience on the job may affect their leadership effectiveness. Moreover, emotional intelligence has the potential to contribute to leadership effectiveness in multiple ways.

Key Terms

charismatic leader, p. 292

coercive power, p. 278

consideration or employee-centred behaviour, p. 282

contingency models of leadership, p. 284

developmental consideration, p. 294

emotional intelligence, p. 297

empowerment, p. 280

expert power, p. 279

initiating structure or task-oriented behaviours, p. 283

intellectual stimulation, p. 293

leader, p. 276

leader-member relations, p. 285

leader substitute, p. 288

leadership, p. 276

legitimate power, p. 277

path-goal theory, p. 286

personal leadership style, p. 276

position power, p. 285

referent power, p. 279

reward power, p. 278

situational leadership theory (SLT), p. 286

task structure, p. 285

transactional leadership, p. 290

transformational leadership, p. 291

SO WHERE DO YOU STAND?

Wrap-Up to Opening Case

We began this chapter on leadership with what could be called "the long view" of leadership. That is, we looked at leadership "unto the seventh generation." There is definitely a need among leaders and society at large to build organizations that serve not only shareholders but also stakeholders, or the wider community. The effect of numerous business scandals has drawn attention to the negative effects of short-term leadership decision making. For example, Ivanhoe Mines Ltd. of Vancouver, believes it has discovered a gigantic copper and gold deposit in South Gobi, Mongolia, and is spending US$10 million a month drilling holes, testing results, and pouring a gigantic concrete shaft in preparation for production in about two years. Like other companies in similar situations, time and money are being spent because the consequences of not consulting all the stakeholders can simply be too costly in terms of money and corporate reputation.

Dr. Warren Bennis reminded us that true leaders want to do the right thing. One model that was described in our opening scenario was that of the Iroquois Confederacy. Leaders in the Confederacy consider the impact of their decisions on the seven generations of people around them: the three that preceded them, the current one, and the three that will follow each leader. In this way, care was a moral duty because of these seventh generation considerations. "Our world is crying—even dying—for such leaders." John Kotter[103] says that "the ultimate act of leadership is to create a culture of leadership."[104] In the spirit of Dr. Margaret Wheatley's thoughts on leader, she believes that in tune with such a culture of leadership is the presence of "the leader-as-host," not the hero-leader. The cult of the hero-leader has created much of the corporate malfeasance that the beginning years of the twenty-first century have experienced from business.[105] Charles Elson, a corporate governance expert at the University of Delaware, puts matters this way: "We're seeing the outcome of a real dramatic shift. It's the destruction of the myth of the imperial CEO."[106]

Much has been researched in the twentieth century regarding leadership styles, approaches, traits, and so on. What is becoming more and more critical, however, in order to build a future worth going to, is the presence of what Richard Branson, famed British entrepreneur and founder of the Virgin Group, calls "living life to its full."[107] It is this "leadership authenticity" that will decide the new winners and losers in business.

Management in Action

Topics for Discussion and Action

Level 1

1. What is meant by "leadership," and on what bases of power do leaders influence others to take action that achieves organizational goals?
2. Describe trait and behavioural theories of leadership and their limitations.
3. Describe the leadership styles that evolve from the managerial grid. Which one is deemed to be optimal, and why? Is this style suitable in every situation?

Level 2

4. Think of specific situations in which it might be especially important for a manager to engage in consideration and in initiating structure.
5. Interview a manager to find out how the three situational characteristics that Fiedler identified are affecting the manager's ability to provide leadership.

6. Discuss why substitutes for leadership can contribute to organizational effectiveness.

Level 3

7. Listen to the following podcast by Jack Welch, former CEO of General Electric, "What are 'Agents of Change' in Organizations?": www.businessweek.com/mediacenter/qt/podcasts/welchway/welchway_10_10_08.mp3. Discuss the three characteristics of a "change agent" in organizations.
8. Compare and contrast transactional and transformational leadership styles.
9. Discuss why some people still think that men make better managers than do women, even though research indicates that men and women are equally effective as managers and leaders.

Building Management Skills

Answer the following questions about the organization you have chosen to follow:

1. How would you characterize the leadership style of the CEO?
2. Do you consider the CEO to be a transactional or transformative leader, and why? Is the style appropriate for the environmental context in which the organization is situated?
3. What sources of power does he or she rely on most heavily?

Management for You

Your school is developing a one-day orientation program for new students majoring in business. You have been asked to consider leading the group of students who will design and implement the orientation program. Develop a two- or three-page "handout" that shows whether the position is a natural fit for you. To do this, (1) identify your strengths and weaknesses in the sources of power you can bring to the project, and (2) discuss whether you would be a transactional leader or a transformation leader and why. Provide a strong concluding statement about whether or not you would be the best leader for this task.

Small Group Breakout Exercise

IMPROVING LEADERSHIP EFFECTIVENESS

Form groups of three to five, and appoint one member as the spokesperson who will communicate your findings and conclusions to the whole class when called on by the instructor. Then discuss the following scenario:

You are a team of human resource consultants who have been hired by Carla Caruso, an entrepreneur who started her own interior decorating business. At first, she worked on her own as an independent contractor. Then, because of a dramatic increase in the number of new homes being built, she decided to form her own company.

She hired a secretary/bookkeeper and four interior decorators. Caruso still does decorating jobs herself and has adopted a hands-off approach to leading the four decorators because she feels that interior design is a very personal, creative endeavour. Rather than paying the decorators on some kind of commission basis, she pays them a higher-than-average salary so that they are motivated to do what is best for their customers, not what will result in higher billings and commissions.

Caruso thought everything was going smoothly until customer complaints started coming in. These complaints were about the decorators being hard to reach, promising unrealistic delivery times, being late for or failing to keep appointments, and being impatient and rude when customers had trouble making up their minds. Caruso knows that her decorators are competent people and is concerned that she is not effectively leading and managing them. She has asked for your advice.

1. What advice can you give Caruso to either increase her power or use her existing power more effectively?
2. Does Caruso seem to be performing appropriate leadership behaviours in this situation? What advice can you give her about the kinds of behaviours she should perform?
3. How can Caruso increase the decorator's motivation to deliver high-quality customer service?
4. Would you advise Caruso to try engage in transformational leadership in this situation? If not, why not? If so, what steps would you advise her to take?

Business Planning Exercise

Your team is thinking about the management team for your new venture. You have to include a section in the business plan on what roles and responsibilities the management will undertake and what qualifies them to lead the organization.

1. Identify the traits you think the managers should possess for your venture.
2. Choose a functional area. Do you think a people-oriented leader or a production-oriented leader would best suit the situation? Why?
3. Would a transactional or transformational leader be more appropriate as the head of your organization?

Managing Ethically

One of your subordinates has noticed that your expense account reports have repeatedly overstated your expenses because you always bill for an extra day, at the "daily rate," when you go out of town on company business. Your assistant knows that you have always been in town and working from home on that extra day. He has questioned your reports, as you have now submitted 15 of these for the year. How would you use your knowledge of power to resolve this dilemma? Which use of power would be most ethical, and why?

Exploring the World Wide Web

SPECIFIC ASSIGNMENT

Go to the official website of Jack and Suzy Welch at www.welchway.com, and click on "Management in Action." Read "What Makes a Leader."[108]

1. Are leaders born or made, according to Welch?
2. What are the five characteristics that make a successful leader? Which are inherent, and which are learned?

GENERAL ASSIGNMENT

Find the website of a company that provides information on the company's missions, goals, and values, and on the company's top managers and their personal leadership styles. How might the company's missions, goals, and values impact the process of leadership in this company?

McGraw-Hill Connect™—Available 24/7 with instant feedback so you can study when you want, how you want, and where you want. Take advantage of the Study Plan—an innovative tool that helps you customize your learning experience. You can diagnose your knowledge with pre- and post-tests, identify the areas where you need help, search the entire learning package for content specific to the topic you're studying, and add these resources to your personalized study plan. Visit www.mcgrawhillconnect.ca to register—take practice quizzes, search the e-book, and much more.

Be the Manager

NAPOLEON ON LEADERSHIP[109]

Jim Warthin is a friend of yours; he is also CEO of a small plastics firm and has invited you in to discuss a new book he has recently read on leadership and Napoleon Bonaparte.[110] He tells you in an email that the author of this text has identified Napoloeon's six winning leadership principles. Jim wants to discuss these principles in the context of the leadership course that you both took when in business school together. He wants your trusted feedback.

1. **Exactitude:** He sought pinpoint precision through extensive research, continuous planning, and constant awareness of the situation he faced, which included meditating on what might occur—in other words, awareness, research, and continuous planning.
2. **Speed:** He recognized that momentum—mass times velocity—applied to achieving goals with people as well. "He knew that resistance causes momentum to fade. Increasing speed is about reducing resistance, increasing urgency, and providing focus by employing concentration of force and economy of force," the author says—in other words, reducing resistance, increasing urgency, and providing focus.

3. **Flexibility:** Napoleon ensured that his armies could react quickly to situation, yet operate according to a strategic plan. He organized his troops into mobile units and empowered them by providing knowledge of the mission and structuring them to operate independently; yet he also made sure they were operating under a unified doctrine and serving one ultimate leader—in other words, building teams that are adaptable, empowered, and unified.

4. **Simplicity**: He ensured his objectives were simple, his messages were simple, and his processes were simple, reducing confusion. "The art of war does not require complicated manoeuvre. The simplest are the best," Napoleon declared—in other words, clear simple objectives, messages, and processes.

5. **Character**: While driven by his ambition, Napoleon always maintained honour and integrity, calmness and responsibility, and encouraging respect of other cultures.

6. **Moral Force**: "In war, everything depends upon morale," Napoleon said. People do their best work when they have self-confidence, feel what they are doing is worthwhile, and are recognized for their effort—in other words, providing order, purpose recognition, and rewards.

Question

1. Are Napoleon's six principles more suited to a transformational leader or a transactional leader? Why?

Management Case

Leadership to the Seventh Generation[111]

'I wish to speak for nature ...... for there are enough champions of civilization'—Henry David Thoreau

"In September [2004] I am invited to celebrate the changing of the seasons in the cathedral of Temagami, an old growth forest of 150-year-old trees in the near north of Ontario. I am invited by an elder of the Teme-Augama Anishnabai, among the last of his people homesteading on ancestral lands, to visit an area that has served as a gathering place for his people for a thousand years as they seek wisdom and commune with their elders.

This may not be possible in the near future. For anyone. Plans have been approved to commence clear-cutting in the area that contains the Spirit Forest that lies between Lake Temagami and Lake Obakika. It is this area that contains the old growth forest and the Spirit Rock I have been invited to visit.

I sit here late at night, consider this trip, and write this article. How has it come that we cannot see the value of a forest? And, what does this mean to leaders of our organizations?

We live in a time when our corporate leaders manage quarter by quarter and our political leaders tell us they cannot be bound by three-year plans. Yet, the most pressing problem faced by our planet—the current decline of every living system—requires a multigenerational strategy.

Our institutions are failing us. Our organizations are crying for leaders who will help us do the right thing.

The most powerful leadership philosophy I know of does not come from our leading business schools, our leading corporations. It is not from celebrity authors like Donald Trump or Rudy Giuliani. Rather, it is a piece of wisdom that guided leaders in the Iroquois Confederacy, instructing them to consider the impact of their decisions on the seven generations around them. Our indigenous people knew that one man, one leader, could only hope to know the seven generations around him: the three that preceded him— to his great grandparents—and the three that will follow—to his great grandchildren. The leader was bound by a moral duty to care for the Seven Generations.

And this begs the question. What would Seventh Generation Leadership look like in our organizations? For just as the economy of nature requires long-term perspectives, so too does the economy of men.

First, I believe Seventh Generation leadership in our corporations would be principle-based. Principle-based leaders would create organizations that are aligned with the principles of their people. The challenge is not to align people with the principles of our workplaces but to create workplaces that enable people to live in accordance with their core values and beliefs. This is not mysticism. This is a competitive imperative. Our people and their innate values become our compass in times of great complexity rather than our directives and corporate statements of ethics. Company-destroying malfeasance is simply not possible in organizations where people work in accordance with their core values and beliefs.

I believe Seventh Generation leadership would be spiritual. Not religious, but spiritual. For too long we have viewed spirituality as akin to voodoo. Yet, as people, we are spiritual beings. What's more, we struggle for meaning in times of incredible turbulence. Amid such turbulence and complexity, our natural instinct is to seek control. Yet, chaos cannot be controlled; complexity cannot be controlled. Our science tells us this is the case. Leadership based on spirituality better prepares us to cope with the inevitable question of *why*? Leadership based on trying to control the uncontrollable is doomed to failure. Too much of what is around us is simply beyond our control. Rather than trying to control the uncontrollable, far better that we act paradoxically and relinquish control by enabling our people to act in accordance with the factors that surround them locally. Again, a paradox. By relinquishing control we actually build capacity that enables us to better respond to rapid change. How do we do this? We do so by sharing power and leading through inclusion.

I believe Seventh Generation leaders would intuitively understand the power of inclusion, the power of conversation. Their leadership style would be participative, involving and inclusive, not exclusive. As Margaret Wheatley has said, we no longer need hero-leaders, we need the leader-as-host. The leader-as-hero model is an insult to our people. It confirms our suspicion that they need saving from their own ineptitude. The leader-as-host by comparison would be the person who invites plurality and diversity into the conversation. Such a leader would understand the incredible wisdom that resides in the diversity of our organizations and that the power of such wisdom can be honoured and captured through inclusive dialogue.

This is not some feel-good directive, it is a corporate survival imperative. The research indicating that successful organizations fail to evolve in changing competitive environments is overwhelming. The evidence is that these successful companies fail because they fail to consider new perspectives and new ways of doing things. Their dialogue becomes one-dimensional and exclusive rather than inclusive. Seventh Generation leadership would be about inclusive dialogue that seeks and honours the wisdom in diversity. It is this diversity of opinion that will bring new perspectives to our organizations, thus ensuring our ability to evolve.

I believe Seventh Generation leaders would see themselves not as being in roles of prestige and privilege but as in roles of burden and responsibility. Such is a principle found in our religious and martial arts traditions where elders are expected to carry the heaviest of loads. As Margaret Wheatley has proposed, this changes the definition of leadership to *stewardship*.

Finally, I believe Seventh Generation leadership would be earth affirming. As one institutional investor recently said to me, the money she makes her clients is meaningless if the planet fails their children. Pretty much every piece of peer-reviewed research coming out today indicates that every living system on our planet is in a state of decline. We are failing our unborn children. And one day, we will learn that all our money is meaningless if our planet fails them. One day, maybe our leaders will learn that the money you get is not worth the price you pay.

Our world is crying—even dying—for such leaders. John Kotter says that the ultimate act of leadership is to create a culture of leadership. This is one of the best and clearest definitions of the duty of a leader I have come across. But to this, I would suggest an alternative that is more abstract, metaphorical: The hallmark of leadership is when old men and old women plant trees they know they will not live long enough to enjoy.

Our world needs such leaders. For, one thousand years from now, I want my descendents to be able to worship in a cathedral of trees. It does not look hopeful."

Questions

1. How would you describe Gabriel Draven's personal leadership style?
2. What leadership behaviours does Draven engage in?
3. Is Draven a transformational leader? Why, or why not?

Video Management Case

Daniel Goleman Interview

Emotional intelligence (EI) is considered the measure of how well people manage themselves and their relationships. Goleman, in his new book *Working with Emotional Intelligence*, claims that while IQ might help predict abilities and appropriate employment based on skills and knowledge, EI gauges competence in the workplace in its application. EI helps articulate, Goleman says, what sets an outstanding performer apart from others in work settings.

Questions to consider

1. What does Goleman mean when he says that EI skills are *learnable* and can be improved upon?
2. How does Goleman differentiate between personality or maturity and specific EI skills?

Managing Teams

Learning Outcomes

1. Explain why groups and teams are key contributors to organizational effectiveness.

2. Identify the different types of groups and teams that help managers and organizations achieve their goals.

3. Explain how different elements of group dynamics influence the functioning and effectiveness of groups and teams.

4. Explain how group decision making can be improved by minimizing groupthink and fostering creativity and innovation.

5. Describe how managers can create high-performing teams by motivating group members to achieve organizational goals, reducing social loafing, and managing conflict effectively.

The Teams That Bond[1]

Groups of people who work together often develop deep friendships. The magic, experts say, is a byproduct of the intensity of the work.

Michael Angrove knows how powerful teamwork can be. A senior technical specialist at Fujitsu Transaction Solutions,[2] Angrove recalls the friendships formed when he headed a workplace team seven years ago that was developing software for the supermarket self-checkout systems his company produces: "We had a 50-member team that was broken into smaller teams, but everyone in the group worked closely together. We used to go out to celebrate each other's birthdays and we'd go bowling together in the evenings. If someone on the team threw a Halloween party, half the group would be there."

Angrove was no stranger to teamwork when he arrived at Fujitsu. Between 1979 and 1981, he was a leading seaman in the Canadian Navy, where teamwork is de rigueur. "Your life depends on the guy beside you in the military," he says. "You develop lifetime friendships with people. And when they get transferred to another unit, you miss them. There's a hole in the unit."

The contemporary workplace is driven by teamwork, by teams that assemble for special short-term projects, such as product development, and those that exist indefinitely.

The experience of performing on a well-functioning team can, indeed, produce lifetime friendships. "Sometimes, you have that magic, in which everyone working together develops those bonds," said Barbara Moses, a Toronto-based career expert with BBM Career Development and the author of *What Next? The Complete Guide to Taking Control of Your Working Life.*[3]

The bonds of friendship often form on teams that work on deadline-driven projects in which there is an intensity in the work itself. "The intensity of the

(c) Masterfile (Royalty-Free Division)

experience gives you a heady feeling," Moses said. "People associate the task at hand with how well they work with others on the team. And they don't separate the two." The result, she said, is that workplace teams can experience a form of grief once a project is completed and the participants disband. "The experience of working on a team gives people a sense of identity and purpose," she said. "After they disband, they can get depressed."

Successful teams are those in which the participants trust each other, said Michel Daigle, a business coach with Communic.Aide. "It's the trust factor that builds bonds," he said. "If, after a team disbands, nothing happens, it's because there's an absence of trust and the bonds are more professional than emotional." But team members who forge that trust, he said, continue to affiliate socially. He cited 3M as a company that fosters teamwork, which leads to innovation. "They create teams that compete with each other. The higher the stakes, the bigger the bond between team members. People have to commit to the project. If they don't, they let the team down."

Moses says team members often grieve the disbanding of great teams. Angrove knows how that feels. "When a project ends and the team breaks up, it is like the passing of a good friend, maybe even a brother or sister. The feeling is that you don't want it to end. We'd form a team to work toward a common goal of as many as 10 people or fewer, each from a different department," he said.

Daigle recalls a workplace team he belonged to when he was employed in an American company. "I was learning about people every day," he said. "Whenever there was an obstacle, we would find solutions together. It was about never being alone. These are the highlights of teamwork."

Now It's Your Turn

1. What are some of the highlights of teamwork, as outlined in our opening scenario?

2. Ken Ingram, a professional business coach with the Montreal office of the Achievement Centre, says that once employees have collaborated on a team, "you can never go back to a position of isolation in the company." Why do you think this is so?

■■■■ Overview

Companies such as Zellers, Xerox Canada, Arcelor Mittal, Dofasco, Toyota Canada, Westinghouse Canada, and Sears Canada are all relying on teams to help them gain a competitive advantage.[4] In this chapter, we look in detail at how groups and teams can contribute to organizational effectiveness and at the types of groups and teams used in organizations. We discuss how different elements of group dynamics influence the functioning and effectiveness of groups, and we describe how managers can motivate group members to achieve organizational goals and reduce social loafing in groups and teams. By the end of this chapter, you will appreciate why the effective management of groups and teams is a key ingredient for organizational performance and a source of competitive advantage.

LO 1

Key Elements That Make a Team Approach Successful

It is difficult to escape reading about teams if you pick up almost any business magazine. Teams are widely used these days. A Conference Board of Canada report found that more than 80 percent of its 109 respondents used teams in the workplace.[5] In the United States, at least half of the employees at 80 percent of Fortune 500 companies work on teams, while 68 percent of small manufacturers use teams in their production areas.[6]

Teams increase an organization's competitive advantage (see Figure 10.1) by:

- *Enhancing its performance.* People working in teams are able to produce more or higher quality outputs than would have been produced if each person had worked separately and all their individual efforts had been combined.

- *Increasing its responsiveness to customers.* Bringing salespeople, research and development experts, and members of other departments together in a group or cross-functional team can enhance responsiveness to customers by increasing the skills and expertise available.

- *Increasing innovation.* Managers can better encourage innovation by creating teams of diverse individuals who together have the knowledge relevant to a particular type of innovation, rather than by relying on individuals working alone.

- *Increasing employees' motivation and satisfaction.* Members of teams are likely to be more highly motivated and satisfied than they would have been while working on their own. The experience of working alongside other highly charged and motivated people can be very stimulating.

FIGURE 10.1 | Groups' and Teams' Contributions to Organizational Effectiveness

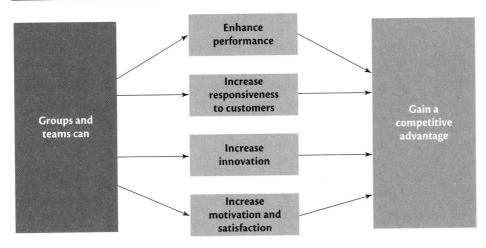

Types of Groups and Teams

THINK ABOUT IT

Emotionally Intelligent and Self-Managed Teams

Dr. Reuven Bar-On, author and developer of the now-standard *Emotional Quotient-Inventory*™ (or *EQ-i*™), defined emotional intelligence as an array of personal, emotional, and social competencies and skills that influence one's ability to succeed in coping with environmental demands and pressures.[7] These competencies and skills are critical when it comes to working in a team-based environment, a reality that is ever-increasing in today's workplaces. Emotional intelligence, therefore, becomes the hidden advantage. Groups often know *what* it is they must accomplish. Where the difficulties arise are in *how* the tasks are to be accomplished. This is where the emotional intelligence capability of the team members and the group as a whole play the major part. "Emotions impact everything we do. In an office setting, emotions can lead to team camaraderie and increased productivity. Likewise, emotions can also prove destructive. Not surprisingly, it is an individual's emotional intelligence that dictates interpersonal relationships."[8]

The important difference between effective teams and ineffective ones lies in the emotional intelligence of the group. Teams have an emotional intelligence of their own. It is comprised of the emotional intelligence of individual members, plus a collective competency of the group. Everyone contributes to the overall level of emotional intelligence, and the leader has more influence. The good news is that teams can develop greater emotional intelligence and boost their performance. ... To be most effective, the team needs to create emotionally intelligent norms—the attitudes and behaviors that eventually become habits—that support behaviors for building trust, group identity and group efficacy. Group identity is described as a feeling among members that they belong to a unique and worthwhile group. A sense of group efficacy is the belief that the team can perform well and that group members are more effective working together than apart.[9]

When we apply these notions to the self-managed team process, we realize each team member must play his or her part. It is important each individual team member assume a sense of responsibility for the team effort, well-being and outcome. This process of working *with* and *for* the team include the following:

- Making sure the team stays on topic and keeps its focus
- Contributes to facilitating input from group members
- Stays aware of procedures that will help the group function more intelligently and smoothly, such as clarifying questions and summaries of key points
- Fostering effective listen skills so that each member has a chance to contribute and gets heard, in short, nurturing a collaborative team norm for working together

You Be the Manager

1. Why are emotionally intelligent self-managed teams effective?
2. What do you personally have to develop in order to be a more emotionally intelligent member of a self-managed team?[10]

group
Two or more people who interact with each other to reach certain goals or meet certain needs.

team
A group whose members work intensely with each other to achieve a specific common goal or objective.

top-management team
A group composed of the CEO, or the president, and the heads of the most important departments.

cross-functional team
A group of individuals from different departments brought together to perform organizational tasks.

A **group** may be defined as two or more people who interact with each other to reach certain goals or meet certain needs.[11] A **team** is a group whose members work intensely with each other to achieve a specific common goal or objective. As these definitions imply, all teams are groups, but not all groups are teams. The two characteristics that distinguish teams from groups are the *intensity* with which team members work together and the presence of a *specific, overriding team goal or objective*. Organizations use a variety of groups and teams in the workplace. We describe a few of these in the next few pages (see Figure 10.2).

The Top-Management Team

A central concern of the CEO and president of a company is to form a **top-management team** to help the organization achieve its mission and goals. Top-management teams are responsible for developing the strategies that produce an organization's competitive advantage; most have between five and seven members. In forming their top-management teams, CEOs are well advised to stress diversity—in expertise, skills, knowledge, and experience. Thus, many top-management teams are **cross-functional teams**: They include members of different departments, such as finance, marketing, production, and engineering. Diversity helps ensure that the top-management team will have all the background and resources it needs to make good decisions.

FIGURE 10.2 | Types of Groups and Teams in Organizations

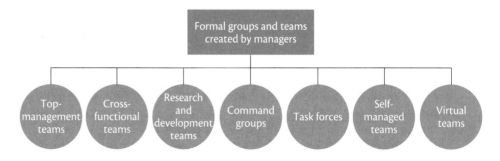

Research and Development Teams

Managers in pharmaceuticals, computers, electronics, electronic imaging, and other high-tech industries often create **research and development teams** to develop new products. Managers select R&D team members on the basis of their expertise and experience in a certain area. Sometimes R&D teams are cross-functional teams with members from departments such as engineering, marketing, and production in addition to members from the research and development department.

research and development team
A team whose members have the expertise and experience needed to develop new products.

Command Groups

Subordinates who report to the same supervisor form a **command group**. When top managers design an organization's structure and establish reporting relationships and a chain of command, they are essentially creating command groups. Command groups, often called *departments* or *units*, perform a significant amount of the work in many organizations. In order to have command groups that help an organization gain a competitive advantage, managers need to motivate group members to perform at a high level, and managers need to be effective leaders. Examples of command groups include the salespeople at the Bay who report to the same supervisor, the employees of a small swimming pool sales and maintenance company who report to a general manager, the telephone operators at Manulife Financial insurance company who report to the same supervisor, and workers on an automobile assembly line at Ford Canada who report to the same first-line manager.

command group
A group composed of subordinates who report to the same supervisor; also called a department or unit.

Task Forces

Managers form task forces to accomplish specific goals or solve problems in a certain period; task forces are sometimes called ad hoc committees. When Vancouver Island-based Myra Falls copper and zinc mine was purchased in 1998 by Swedish-controlled Boliden AB, the mine had been facing labour strife for years.[12] Boliden sent over a new mine manager to help get things in order. His first job was to set up five task forces geared to key problem areas. For instance, the ground support task force found that the previous owners had neglected a number of safety problems. The task forces' recommendations were followed, and $15-million worth of improvements were done. This sent a strong signal to employees that the new management team was concerned about its employees. Task forces can be a valuable tool for busy managers who do not have the time to explore an important issue in depth on their own.

Sometimes organizations need to address a long-term or enduring problem or issue facing an organization, such as how to contribute most usefully to the local community or how to make sure that the organization provides opportunities for potential employees with disabilities. **Task forces** that are relatively permanent are often referred to as **standing committees**. Membership in standing committees changes over time. Members may have, for example, a two, or three-year term on the committee and then rotate off. Memberships expire at varying times so that there are always some members with experience on the committee. Managers form and maintain standing committees to make sure that important issues continue to be addressed.

task force
A cross-functional team charged with solving a specific problem or addressing a specific issue within a fixed timeframe.

standing committee
A relatively permanent task force charged with addressing long-term, enduring problems or issues facing an organization.

Finally, after the 2005 South Asia's Boxing Day tsunami devastation, then UN Secretary-General Kofi Annan launched the Millennium Project. He set up 10 international task forces to come up with concrete, innovative proposals to achieve the agreed-on goals originally envisioned in the 2002 *Investing in Development* report.[13] Eight goals were set to be achieved by 2015. While some saw all of this as visionary, others, of course, saw the effort more cynically. As you read the list below, reflect back to the discussion on emotional and social intelligence from Chapter 9. While goals and targets may be envisioned and articulated, it takes courage, emotional and social intelligence, an ability to deal with conflict and political forces, and a leadership vision to make such efforts fruitful.

The eight goals set up to be achieved by 2015 were:

1. To halve the number of people living on less than $1 a day.
2. To make primary education available to every child.
3. To reduce child mortality by two-thirds.
4. To cut maternal mortality by three-quarters.
5. To promote gender equality.
6. To reverse the spread of HIV/AIDS and malaria.
7. To halt the loss of environmental resources.
8. To create a global partnership for development.

Self-Managed Work Teams[14]

self-managed (or self-directed) work teams
Groups of employees who supervise their own activities and monitor the quality of the goods and services they provide.

Self-managed (or self-directed) work teams are teams whose members are empowered and have the responsibility and autonomy to complete identifiable pieces of work. On a day-to-day basis, team members decide what the team will do, how it will do it, and which team members will perform specific tasks.[15] Managers provide self-managed work teams with their overall goals (such as assembling defect-free computer keyboards) but let team members decide how to meet those goals. Managers usually form self-managed work teams to improve quality, increase motivation and satisfaction, and lower costs. Often, by creating self-managed work teams, they combine tasks that individuals used to perform on their own, so the team is responsible for the whole set of tasks that yield an identifiable output or end product. The Conference Board of Canada found that self-directed work teams are used in a variety of manufacturing environments (e.g., the auto and chemicals industries) and service environments (e.g., hotels, banks, and airlines).[16]

Managers can take a number of steps to ensure that self-managed work teams are effective and help an organization gain a competitive advantage:[17]

- Give teams enough responsibility and autonomy to be truly self-managing. Refrain from telling team members what to do or solving problems for them even if you (as a manager) know what should be done.

- Make sure that a team's work is sufficiently complex so that it entails a number of different steps or procedures that must be performed and results in some kind of finished end product.

- Carefully select members of self-managed work teams. Team members should have the diversity of skills needed to complete the team's work, have the ability to work with others, and want to be part of a team.

- Recognize that self-managed work teams need guidance, coaching, and support, not direct supervision. Managers should be a resource for teams to turn to when needed.

- Analyze what type of training team members need, and provide it. Working in a self-managed work team often requires that employees have more extensive technical and interpersonal skills.

Managers in a wide variety of organizations have found that self-managed work teams help the organization achieve its goals.[18] However, self-managed work teams can run into trouble. Members are often reluctant to discipline one another by withholding bonuses from members who are not performing up to par or by firing members.[19]

They are also reluctant to evaluate each other's performance and determine pay levels. One reason for team members' discomfort may be the close personal relationships they sometimes develop with each other. In addition, sometimes members of self-managed work teams actually take longer to accomplish tasks, such as when team members have difficulties coordinating their efforts.

Virtual Teams

Virtual teams are teams whose members rarely or never meet face to face and instead interact by using various forms of information technology such as email, computer networks, telephones, faxes, and video conferences. As organizations become increasingly global and have operations in far-flung regions of the world, and as the need for specialized knowledge increases due to advances in technology, virtual teams allow managers to create teams to solve problems or explore opportunities without being limited by the need for team members to be working in the same geographic location.[20]

Take the case of an organization that has manufacturing facilities in Australia, Canada, the United States, and Mexico, and is encountering a quality problem in a complex manufacturing process. Each of its manufacturing facilities has a quality control team that is headed by a quality control manager. The vice-president for production does not try to solve the problem by forming and leading a team at one of the four manufacturing facilities; instead, she forms and leads a virtual team composed of the quality control managers of the four plants and the plants' general managers. Team members communicate via email and video conferencing, and a wide array of knowledge and experience is utilized to solve the problem.

The principal advantage of virtual teams is that they enable managers to disregard geographic distances and form teams whose members have the knowledge, expertise, and experience to tackle a particular problem or take advantage of a specific opportunity.[21] Virtual teams can include members who are not employees of the organization itself. For example, a virtual team might include members of an organization that is used for outsourcing. More and more companies—including Hewlett-Packard, Pricewaterhouse Coopers, and Kodak—are either using or exploring the use of virtual teams.[22]

Beware! Teams Are Not Always the Answer

Though we have given a lot of information about how teams are used in the workplace, teams are not always the best way to get work done. Because teams have increased communication demands, have more conflicts to manage, and need more meetings, the benefits of using teams have to exceed the costs.

When trying to determine if a team is appropriate to the situation, consider the following:[23]

- Can the work be performed better by an individual? If so, it is not necessary to form a team.

- Can the team provide more value than the individual can? For instance, new-car dealer service departments have introduced teams that link customer service staff, mechanics, parts specialists, and sales representatives. These teams can better manage customer needs.

virtual team
A team whose members rarely or never meet face to face and interact by using various forms of information technology such as email, computer networks, telephones, faxes, and video conferences.

- Are there interdependent tasks so that employees have to rely on each other to get work completed? Teamwork often makes interdependent work go more smoothly.

Other situations where organizations would find teams more useful include:

When work processes cut across functional lines; when speed is important (and complex relationships are involved); when the organization mirrors a complex, differentiated and rapidly changing market environment; when innovation and learning have priority; when the tasks that have to be done require online integration of highly interdependent performers.[24]

LO3

Group Dynamics

THINK ABOUT IT

Team Operating Agreements (TOAs)

How does professional corporate trainer Claire Sookman build a virtual team that works seamlessly together? After all, she has coached over 1000 project managers across North America. She creates what she calls a "team operating agreement" (or TOA)[25] through brainstorming, clarification, and discussion and knows that in a global work environment, dedicated teams of skilled employees need expert managers who create effective communication channels. An interesting comment she makes is that if such a norm is not created by the project manager, team members will do so on their own, opening up the possibility of potential problems or misunderstanding. What needs to be managed well are geographic, ethnic, and cultural differences especially so that the team can be as effective as possible. Says Sookman, "The more inclusive it is, the less chance for miscommunication, conflict, and lost opportunities. Ideally, the TOA should be created at the beginning of a project or when a new team forms." A TOA is also *not* a stagnant document and will possibly be modified during the course of the project.

Sookman's suggestions for a TOA include the following categories:

1. **Meeting Protocols:**
   a. Beginning and ending meetings on time
   b. Scheduling meetings to accommodate people in different time zones
   c. Taking into consideration holidays of the different cultures
   d. Respecting and listening to what other people are saying on the call and not holding sidebar conversations
   e. Giving one week's notice to the team if a member is unable to attend

2. **Communication:**
   a. Checking emails twice a day
   b. Call in to the office once a day
   c. Handling conflict directly with the person concerned and working to resolve it by identifying and communicating possible conflicts clearly and immediately
   d. Giving feedback in a timely manner, respecting cultural sensitivities
   e. Valuing confidentiality

You Be the Manager

1. What factors are important when virtual teams need to work together?
2. How effective would you be in working on a virtual team?

How groups and teams function and how effective they will ultimately be depends on a number of characteristics and processes known collectively as **group dynamics**. In this section, we discuss five key elements of group dynamics: group size and roles; group leadership; group development; group norms; and group cohesiveness. As we mentioned earlier in the chapter, teams and groups are not the same thing, though some of their processes are similar. Thus, much of what we call group dynamics here also applies to teams.

group dynamics
The ways in which group members interact determines their effectiveness.

Group Size and Roles

Managers need to take group size and group roles into account as they create and maintain high-performing groups and teams.

Group Size

The number of members in a group can be an important determinant of members' motivation and commitment and of group performance. There are several advantages to keeping a group relatively small—between two and nine members. Compared with members of large groups, members of small groups tend to

- interact more with each other and find it easier to coordinate their efforts;

- be more motivated, satisfied, and committed;

- find it easier to share information; and

- be better able to see the importance of their personal contributions for group success.

Recognizing these advantages, Nathan Myhrvold, former chief technology officer at Microsoft Corporation, found that eight is the ideal size for the types of R&D teams he would form to develop new software.[26] A disadvantage of small groups is that members have fewer resources available to accomplish their goals.

Large groups—with 10 or more members—also offer some advantages. They have at their disposal more resources to achieve group goals than do small groups. These resources include the knowledge, experience, skills, and abilities of group members as well as their actual time and effort. Large groups also have advantages stemming from the **division of labour**—splitting the work to be performed into particular tasks and assigning tasks to individuals. Individuals who specialize in particular tasks are likely to become skilled at performing those tasks and contribute significantly to high group performance.

division of labour
Splitting the work to be performed into particular tasks and assigning tasks to individual workers.

Large groups suffer a number of problems, including greater communication and coordination difficulties and lower levels of motivation, satisfaction, and commitment. It is clearly more difficult to share information and coordinate activities when you are dealing with 16 people rather than 8. Moreover, members of large groups might not feel that their efforts are really needed and sometimes might not even feel a part of the group.

As a general rule of thumb, groups should have no more members than necessary to achieve a division of labour and provide the resources needed to achieve group goals. Group size is too large when[27]

- members spend more time communicating what they know to others rather than applying what they know to solve problems and create new products;

- individual productivity decreases; and

- group performance suffers.

Group Roles

In forming groups and teams, managers need to communicate clearly the expectations for each group role, what is required of each member, and how the different roles in the group fit together to accomplish group goals. A **group role** is a set of behaviours and tasks that a member of a group is expected to perform because of his or her position in the group. Members of cross-functional teams, for example, are expected to perform roles relevant to their special areas of expertise. Managers also need to realize that group roles change and evolve as a group's tasks and goals change and as group members gain experience and knowledge. Thus, to get the performance gains that come from experience or "learning by doing," managers should encourage group members to take the initiative to modify their assigned roles by taking on extra responsibilities as they see fit. This process, called **role making**, can enhance individual and group performance.

Beyond the simple roles that each person fulfills in order to complete the task at hand, two major kinds of roles need to be discussed: task-oriented roles and maintenance roles. **Task-oriented roles** are performed by group members to make sure that the group accomplishes its tasks. **Maintenance roles** are carried out to make sure that team members have good relationships. For teams to be effective, there needs to be some balance between task orientation and relationship maintenance. Table 10.1 identifies a number of task-oriented and maintenance roles that you might find in a team.

In self-managed work teams and some other groups, group members themselves are responsible for creating and assigning roles. Many self-managed work teams also pick their own team leaders. When group members create their own roles, managers should be available in an advisory capacity, helping group members effectively settle conflicts and disagreements. At Johnsonville Foods, for example, the position titles of first-line managers were changed to "advisory coach" to reflect the managers' new role vis-à-vis the self-managed work teams they oversee.[28]

group role
A set of behaviours and tasks that a member of a group is expected to perform because of his or her position in the group.

role making
Taking the initiative to modify an assigned role by taking on extra responsibilities.

task-oriented roles
Roles performed by group members to make sure the task gets done.

maintenance roles
Roles performed by group members to make sure there are good relationships among group members.

Royalty-free/Corbis
Smaller groups allow for more interaction, improve motivation, and make it easier for members to share information.

TABLE 10.1 | *Roles Required for Effective Group Functioning*   ■ ■ ■

	Function	Description	Example
Roles that build task accomplishment	Initiating	Stating the goal or problem, making proposals about how to work on it, and setting time limits.	"Let's set up an agenda for discussing each of the problems we have to consider."
	Seeking information and opinions	Asking group members for specific factual information related to the task or problem, or for their opinions about it.	"What do you think would be the best approach to this, Jack?"
	Providing information and opinions	Sharing information or opinions related to the task or problems.	"I worked on a similar problem last year and found . . ."
	Clarifying	Helping one another understand ideas and suggestions that come up in the group.	"What you mean, Sue, is that we could . . .?"
	Elaborating	Building on one another's ideas and suggestions.	"Building on Don's idea, I think we could . . ."
	Summarizing	Reviewing the points covered by the group and the different ideas stated so that decisions can be based on full information.	Appointing a recorder to write notes on a blackboard.
	Consensus testing	Periodic testing about whether the group is nearing a decision or needs to continue discussion.	"Is the group ready to decide about this?"
Roles that build and maintain a group	Harmonizing	Mediating conflict among other members, reconciling disagreements, and relieving tensions.	"Don, I don't think you and Sue really see the question that differently."
	Compromising	Admitting error at times of group conflict.	"Well, I'd be willing to change if you provided some help on . . ."
	Gatekeeping	Making sure all members have a chance to express their ideas and feelings and preventing members from being interrupted.	"Sue, we haven't heard from you on this issue."
	Encouraging	Helping a group member make his or her point and establishing a climate of acceptance in the group.	"I think what you started to say is important, Jack. Please continue."

Source: D. Ancona, T. Kochan, M. Scully, J. Van Maanen, D.E. Westney. "Team Processes," in *Managing for the Future* (Cincinnati, OH: South-Western College. Publishing 1996).

Group Leadership

All groups and teams need leadership. Indeed, as we discussed in detail in Chapter 9, effective leadership is a key ingredient for high-performing groups, teams, and organizations. Sometimes managers assume the leadership role, as is the case in many command groups and top-management teams. Or a manager may appoint a member of a group who is not a manager to be group leader or chairperson, as is the case in a task force or standing committee. In other cases, group or team members may choose their own leaders, or a leader may emerge naturally as group members work together to achieve group goals. When managers empower members of self-managed work teams, they often let group members choose their own leaders. Some self-managed work teams find it effective to rotate the leadership role among their members. Whether leaders of groups and teams are managers or not and whether they are appointed by managers or emerge naturally in a group, they play an important role in ensuring that groups and teams perform up to their potential.

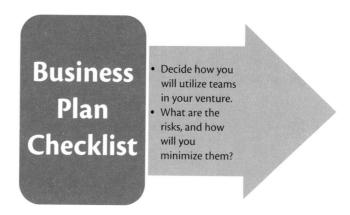

Group Development Over Time

Every group's development over time is somewhat unique. However, researchers have identified five stages of group development that many groups seem to pass through (see Figure 10.3):[29]

- *Forming.* Members try to get to know each other and reach a common understanding of what the group is trying to accomplish and how group members should behave. During this stage, managers should strive to make each member feel like a valued part of the group.

- *Storming.* Group members experience conflict and disagreements because some members do not wish to submit to the demands of other group members. Disputes may arise over who should lead the group. Self-managed work teams can be particularly vulnerable during the storming stage. Managers need to keep an eye on groups at this stage to make sure that the conflict does not get out of hand.

- *Norming.* Close ties between group members develop, and feelings of friendship and camaraderie emerge. Group members arrive at a consensus about what goals they should be aiming to achieve and how group members should behave toward one another.

- *Performing.* The real work of the group gets accomplished during this stage. Depending on the type of group in question, managers need to take different steps at this stage to help ensure that groups are effective. Managers of command groups need to make sure that group members are motivated and that they are effectively leading group members. Managers overseeing self-managed work teams have to empower team members and make sure that teams are given enough responsibility and autonomy at the performing stage.

- *Adjourning.* This stage applies only to groups that eventually are disbanded, such as task forces. During adjourning, a group is dispersed. Sometimes, adjourning takes place when a group completes a finished product, such as when a task force evaluating the pros and cons of providing on-site child care produces a report supporting its recommendation.

FIGURE 10.3 | Five Stages of Group Development

Managers need a flexible approach to group development and need to keep attuned to the different needs and requirements of groups at the various stages.[30] Above all else, and regardless of the stage of development, managers need to think of themselves as *resources* for groups. Thus, managers always should be trying to find ways to help groups and teams function more effectively.

Group Norms

All groups, whether top-management teams, self-managed work teams, or command groups, need to control their members' behaviour to ensure that the group performs well and meets its goals. Roles as well as group norms control behaviour in groups.[31] **Group norms** are shared guidelines or rules for behaviour that most group members follow. Groups develop norms for a wide variety of behaviours, including working hours, the sharing of information among group members, how certain group tasks should be performed, and even how members of a group should dress.

group norms
Shared guidelines or rules for behaviour that most group members follow.

Managers should encourage members of a group to develop norms that contribute to group performance and the attainment of group goals. These could include group norms that dictate that each member of a cross-functional team should always be available for the rest of the team when his or her input is needed, return phone calls as soon as possible, inform other team members of travel plans, and give team members a phone number at which he or she can be reached when travelling on business. Virtual teams such as those at Ryder System Inc. in Mississauga, Ontario, establish such norms as how often to have conference calls and how often they should meet face to face in order to increase their ability to communicate effectively.

Conformity and Deviance

Group members conform to norms for three reasons:[32]

- They want to obtain rewards and avoid punishments.

- They want to imitate group members whom they like and admire.

- They have internalized the norm and believe it is the right and proper way to behave.

Failure to conform, or deviance, occurs when a member of a group violates a group norm. Deviance signals that a group is not controlling one of its members' behaviours. Groups generally respond to members who behave deviantly in one of three ways:[33]

- The group might try to get the member to change his or her deviant ways and conform to the norm. Group members might try to convince the member of the need to conform, or they might ignore or even punish the deviant.

- The group might expel the member.

- The group might change the norm to be consistent with the member's behaviour.

That last alternative suggests some deviant behaviour can be functional for groups when performance norms are low. Deviance is functional for a group when it causes group members to stop and evaluate norms that may be dysfunctional but that are taken for granted by the group. Often, group members do not think about why they behave in a certain way or why they follow certain norms. Deviance can cause group members to reflect on their norms and change them when appropriate, such as when a new employee comes up with a new procedure because she was not aware of "the right way" to do something, and everyone realizes her suggestion is a better way.

Encouraging a Balance of Conformity and Deviance

In order for groups and teams to be effective and help an organization gain a competitive advantage, they need to have the right balance of conformity and deviance (see Figure 10.4). A group needs a certain level of conformity to ensure that it can control members' behaviour and channel it in the direction of high performance and group goal accomplishment. A group also needs a certain level of deviance to ensure that dysfunctional norms are discarded and replaced with functional ones. Balancing conformity and deviance is a pressing concern for all groups, whether they are top-management teams, R&D teams, command groups, or self-managed work teams.

Managers can take several steps to ensure that there is enough tolerance of deviance in groups so that group members are willing to deviate from dysfunctional norms:

• Be role models by not rigidly insisting on existing norms and procedures.

• Encourage openness to new norms and procedures.

• Encourage the evaluation of existing norms.

FIGURE 10.4 | Balancing Conformity and Deviance in Groups

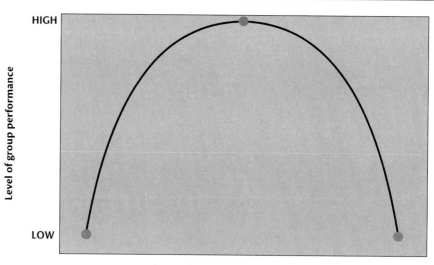

Low conformity/
high deviance

Too much deviance and
a lack of conformity
result in low
performance because
the group cannot
control its members'
behaviours.

Moderate conformity/
moderate deviance

Good balance results
in high performance.

High conformity/
low deviance

Too much conformity
and a lack of deviance
result in low
performance because
the group fails to
change dysfunctional
norms.

Group Cohesiveness

Another important element of group dynamics that affects group performance and effectiveness is **group cohesiveness**, the degree to which members are attracted or loyal to their group or team.[34] When group cohesiveness is high, individuals strongly value their group membership, find the group very appealing, and have strong desires to remain part of the group. When group cohesiveness is low, group members do not find their group particularly appealing and have little desire to retain their group membership. Research suggests that managers should aim to have a moderate level of cohesiveness in the groups and teams they manage because that is most likely to contribute to an organization's competitive advantage.

group cohesiveness
The degree to which members are attracted or loyal to a group.

Consequences of Group Cohesiveness

There are three major consequences of increasing group cohesiveness: level of participation within a group, level of conformity to group norms, and emphasis on group goal accomplishment (see Figure 10.5).[35]

As group cohesiveness grows, the extent of group members' participation within the group increases. A moderate level of group cohesiveness helps ensure that group members take an active part in the group and communicate effectively with each other. Increasing levels of group cohesiveness result in increasing levels of conformity to group norms. This is a good thing for the organization when the performance norms are high. But when performance norms are low, groups need a good dose of deviance to shake things up and adopt better working habits. Thus a moderate degree of cohesiveness often yields the best outcome. And finally, as group cohesiveness grows, emphasis on group goal accomplishment also increases within a group. A moderate level of cohesiveness motivates group members to accomplish both group and organizational goals.

Note of caution: In 1972 psychologist Janis Irving named a phenomenon called "groupthink."[36] The group cohesiveness in this case becomes dysfunctional. In other words, the group's decision-making processes become faulty because members do not consider all the alternatives and seek unanimity at the expense of quality decisions. The group may see themselves as invulnerable and hence are not open to any criticism at all or seek any outside expertise. Of course, when the group's processes are later

FIGURE 10.5 | Sources and Consequences of Group Cohesiveness

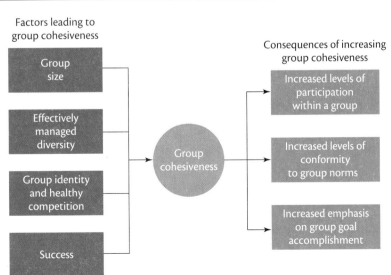

examined, the illusion the group thinks it has is shown for what it is: an illusion. To challenge such groupthink, a critical analysis of how the group functions and its decisions needs to occur because its efforts to minimize conflict only results in a shallow sense of consensus.

Group Decision Making

THINK ABOUT IT

Emotional Intelligence and Teams[37]

Can we say that groups make better decisions than do individuals? We can, if that group is an emotionally intelligent one. What does that mean? In 1988, psychologists Williams and Sternberg defined group intelligence as "the functional intelligence of a group of people working as a unit."[38] In their research study, interpersonal skills of group members and compatibility were found to be the key to group performance. While the traditional marker known as IQ was there, the more important marker called "EQ," or emotional intelligence, was more critical. EQ referred to such social skills as empathy, motivation, the ability to resolve differences, and effective communication. The noted author Steven Covey said, "When teams achieve synergy, gain momentum, and 'get on a roll,' they become virtually unstoppable."[39] The net result is that teams that are competent in personal and interpersonal skills are more effective. They simply have high problem-solving abilities and better performance.

In their book *The Emotionally Intelligent Team*,[40] authors Marcia M. Hughes and James Bradford Terrell outline seven emotional competencies of emotionally intelligent teams:

- Team Identity
- Motivation
- Emotional Awareness
- Communication
- Stress Tolerance
- Conflict Resolution
- Positive Mood

Steven J. Stein, Ph.D., founder and CEO of MHS, Toronto, Canada, and co-author of the bestseller *The EQ Edge: Emotional Intelligence and Your Success* and of *Make Your Workplace Great: The 7 Keys to an Emotionally Intelligent Organization*, writes that "Marcia and James provide a good lens for the way people view others in a team environment. This insight, when combined with measuring one's own EQ through a test such as the Emotional Quotient inventory (EQ-*i*®),[41] provides a powerful lever for improving team performance."[42]

You Be the Manager

1. What are the differences you have experienced when you were in an emotionally intelligent group?
2. What are the differences you have experienced when you were in a group with low emotional intelligence?

Many, perhaps most, important organizational decisions are made by groups of managers rather than by individuals. Group decision making is superior to individual decision making in several respects. When managers work as a team to make decisions and solve problems, their choices of alternatives are less likely to fall victim to the biases and errors discussed previously. They are able to draw on the combined skills, competencies, and accumulated knowledge of group members, and thereby improve their ability to generate feasible alternatives and make good decisions. Group decision making also allows managers to process more information and to correct each other's errors. In the implementation phase, all managers affected by the decisions agree to cooperate. When a group of managers makes a decision, as opposed to one top manager making a decision and imposing it on subordinate managers, it is more probable that the decision will be implemented successfully.

Nevertheless, some disadvantages are associated with group decision making. Groups often take much longer than individuals to make decisions. Getting two or more managers to agree to the same solution can be difficult because managers' interests and preferences are often different. In addition, just like decision making by individual managers, group decision making can be undermined by biases. A major source of group bias is groupthink.

The Perils of Groupthink

Groupthink is a pattern of faulty and biased decision making that occurs in groups whose members strive for agreement among themselves at the expense of accurately assessing information relevant to a decision.[43] When individuals are subject to groupthink, they collectively embark on a course of action without developing appropriate criteria to evaluate alternatives. Typically, a group rallies around a strong individual and the course of action that the individual supports. Group members become blindly committed to that course of action without evaluating its merits. Commitment is often based on an emotional—rather than objective—assessment of the best course of action.

We have all seen the symptoms of the groupthink phenomenon:[44]

groupthink
A pattern of faulty and biased decision making that occurs in groups whose members strive for agreement among themselves at the expense of accurately assessing information relevant to a decision.

- *Illusion of invulnerability.* Group members become overconfident, and this causes them to take extraordinary risks.

- *Assumption of morality.* Group members believe that the group's objectives are morally right, and so they do not debate the ethics of their actions.

- *Rationalized resistance.* No matter how strongly the evidence may contradict their basic assumptions, group members rationalize that their assumptions are correct and that the negative evidence is faulty.

- *Peer pressure.* Members who express doubts about any of the group's shared views are pressured to ignore their concerns and to support the group.

- *Minimized doubts.* Members who have doubts or hold differing points of view may keep silent about their misgivings and even minimize to themselves the importance of their doubts.

- *Illusion of unanimity.* If someone does not speak, it is assumed that he or she agrees with the group. In other words, silence becomes viewed as a "yes" vote.

Pressures for agreement and harmony within a group have the unintended effect of discouraging individuals from raising issues that run counter to majority opinion. For example, a colourful character named Sherman Kent, a onetime history professor at Yale, known as "Buffalo Bill, the Cultured Cowboy" because he wore red suspenders, could tell bawdy jokes, and use barnyard language, had also previously taught CIA personnel for 17 years how important it was for intelligence analysts to challenge their assumptions, to acknowledge uncertainty and ambiguity, to watch for their own biases, and to meet the needs of policymakers without being seduced by them. When the U.S. Senate Select Committee on Intelligence brought out its paper in July 2004, it cited Professor Kent as the person whose admonitions had been ignored, so much so that "intelligence officials did not explain the uncertainties behind their judgment that Iraq was pursuing biological, chemical, and nuclear weapons." Instead, intelligence analysts fell into "groupthink."[45]

There is considerable anecdotal evidence to suggest the negative implications of groupthink in organizational settings, but very little empirical work has been conducted in organizations on the subject of groupthink.[46] In fact, more recently, groupthink has been criticized for overestimating the link between the decision-making process and its outcome[47] and for suggesting that its effect is uniformly negative.[48] A study of groupthink in five large corporations reported that elements of groupthink may affect decision making differently. For instance, the illusion of vulnerability, the belief in inherent group morality, and the illusion of unanimity often led to greater team performance, counter to what the original groupthink proposals suggest.[49]

Improving Group Decision Making

A variety of steps can be taken to improve group decision making.[50] Managers should encourage group leaders to be impartial in their leadership, and actively seek input from all group members. Leaders should avoid expressing their own opinions in the early stages of discussion.

devil's advocacy
Critical analysis of a preferred alternative, made by a group member who plays the role of devil's advocate to defend unpopular or opposing alternatives for the sake of argument.

Another strategy to improve group decision making is to encourage one group member to play the role of the devil's advocate. **Devil's advocacy** is a critical analysis of a preferred alternative to pinpoint its strengths and weaknesses before it is implemented (see Figure 10.6).[51] Typically, one member of the decision-making group plays the role of the devil's advocate. The devil's advocate critiques and challenges the way the group evaluated alternatives and chose one over the others. The purpose of devil's advocacy is to identify all the reasons that might make the preferred alternative unacceptable after all. In this way, decision makers can be made aware of the possible perils of recommended courses of action.

FIGURE 10.6 | Devil's Advocacy

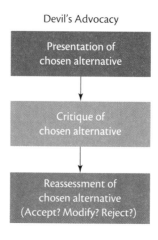

Devil's Advocacy

Presentation of chosen alternative

Critique of chosen alternative

Reassessment of chosen alternative (Accept? Modify? Reject?)

Another way to improve group decision making is to promote diversity in decision-making groups.[52] Bringing together male *and* female managers from various ethnic, national, and functional backgrounds broadens the range of life experiences and opinions that group members can draw from as they generate, assess, and choose among alternatives. Moreover, diverse groups are sometimes less prone to groupthink because group members already differ from each other and thus are less subject to pressures for uniformity. The Swiss firm The BrainStore takes advantage of diversity to improve decision making by mixing children and managers together.

www.brainstore.com

Promoting Group Creativity

To encourage creativity at the group level, organizations can make use of group problem-solving techniques that promote creative ideas and innovative solutions. These techniques can also be used to prevent groupthink and to help managers and employees uncover biases. Here, we look at three group decision-making techniques: *brainstorming*, the *nominal group technique*, and the *Delphi technique*.

Brainstorming

Brainstorming is a group problem-solving technique in which individuals meet face to face to generate and debate a wide variety of alternatives from which to make a decision.[53] Generally, from 5 to 15 individuals meet in a closed-door session and proceed like this:

- One person describes in broad outline the problem the group is to address.

- Group members then share their ideas and generate alternative courses of action.

- As each alternative is described, group members are not allowed to criticize it, and everyone withholds judgment until all alternatives have been heard. One member of the group records the alternatives on a flip chart.

- Group members are encouraged to be as innovative and radical as possible. Anything goes; and the greater the number of ideas put forth, the better. Moreover, group members are encouraged to "piggyback"—that is, to build on each other's suggestions.

- When all alternatives have been generated, group members debate the pros and cons of each and develop a short list of the best alternatives.

Brainstorming is very useful in some problem-solving situations—for example, when trying to find a new name for a perfume or for a model of car. But sometimes individuals working alone can generate more alternatives. The main reason, it seems, is the **production blocking** that occurs in groups because members cannot always simultaneously make sense of all the alternatives being generated, think up additional alternatives, and remember what they were thinking.[54]

Nominal Group Technique

To avoid production blocking, the **nominal group technique** is often used. It provides a more structured way of generating alternatives in writing and gives each individual more time and opportunity to generate alternative solutions. The nominal group technique is especially useful when an issue is controversial and when different people might be expected to champion different courses of action. Generally, a small group of people meet in a closed-door session and adopt the following procedures:

- One person outlines the problem to be addressed, and 30 or 40 minutes are allocated for each group member to write down ideas and solutions. Group members are encouraged to be innovative.

brainstorming
A group problem-solving technique in which individuals meet face to face to generate and debate a wide variety of alternatives from which to make a decision.

production blocking
A loss of productivity in brainstorming sessions due to the unstructured nature of brainstorming.

nominal group technique
A decision-making technique in which group members write down ideas and solutions, read their suggestions to the whole group, and discuss and then rank the alternatives.

- Individuals take turns reading their suggestions to the group. One person writes the alternatives on a flip chart. No criticism or evaluation of alternatives is allowed until all alternatives have been read.

- The alternatives are then discussed, one by one, in the sequence in which they were first proposed. Group members can ask for clarifying information and critique each alternative to identify its pros and cons.

- When all alternatives have been discussed, each group member ranks all the alternatives from most preferred to least preferred, and the alternative that receives the highest ranking is chosen.[55]

Delphi Technique

Both nominal group technique and brainstorming require people to meet together to generate creative ideas and engage in joint problem solving. What happens if people are in different cities or in different parts of the world and cannot meet face to face? Videoconferencing is one way to bring distant people together to brainstorm. Another way is to use the **Delphi technique**, a written approach to creative problem solving.[56] The Delphi technique works like this:

Delphi technique
A decision-making technique in which group members do not meet face to face but respond in writing to questions posed by the group leader.

- The group leader writes a statement of the problem and a series of questions to which participating individuals are to respond.

- The questions are sent to the managers and departmental experts who are most knowledgeable about the problem; they are asked to generate solutions and mail the questionnaire back to the group leader.

- The group leader records and summarizes the responses. The results are then sent back to the participants, with additional questions to be answered before a decision can be made.

- The process is repeated until a consensus is reached and the most suitable course of action is clear.

Tips for Managers
IMPROVING DECISION MAKING

1. Make sure you know what biases you bring to your decision making.
2. Identify your strongest bias when you have to make an important decision.
3. Cite two examples of your experience with groupthink.
4. Describe how important creativity is for you in your job.
5. List ways that creativity could be improved in your workplace.

LO 5

Managing Groups and Teams for High Performance

Now that you have a good understanding of the reasons why groups and teams are so important for organizations, the types of groups that managers create, and group dynamics, group decision making and the perils of groupthink, we consider additional steps that managers can take to make sure groups and teams perform highly and contribute to organizational effectiveness. Managers who want top performing groups and teams need to (1). Motivate group members to achieve organizational goals, (2). Reduce social loafing, and (3) help groups manage conflict effectively.

Motivating Group Members to Achieve Organizational Goals

Managers can motivate members of groups and teams to reach organizational goals and create a competitive advantage by making sure that the members themselves benefit when the group or team performs highly. If members of a self-managed work team know that they will receive a percentage of any cost savings that the team discovers and implements, they probably will try to cut costs. For example, Canadian Tire offers team incentives to employees of its gas bars. "Secret" retail shoppers visit the outlets on a regular basis and score them on such factors as cleanliness, manner in which the transaction was processed, and the types of products offered, using a 100-point scoring system. Scores above a particular threshold provide extra compensation that is shared by the team. Xerox Canada, through its XTRA program, rewards districts for achieving profit and customer satisfaction targets. Everyone in the district shares equally in the bonuses.

Managers often rely on some combination of individual and group-based incentives to motivate members of groups and teams to work toward reaching organizational goals and a competitive advantage. When individual performance within a group can be assessed, pay is often determined by individual performance or by both individual and group performances. When individual performance within a group cannot be assessed accurately, then group performance should be the key determinant of pay levels.

Benefits that managers can make available to group members when a group performs highly could also include equipment and computer software, awards and other forms of recognition, and choice future work assignments. For example, members of self-managed work teams that develop new software at companies such as Microsoft often value working on interesting and important projects, and so members of teams that perform highly are rewarded with interesting and important new projects.

CP/Darcy Cheek
"Neither rain nor sleet nor snow ...." Canada Post delivers 50 million pieces of mail per day during the Christmas season. What yearly managerial challenges does this present?

Reducing Social Loafing in Groups

Social loafing is the tendency of individuals to put forth less effort when they work in groups than when they work alone.[57] Have you ever watched one or two group members who never seemed to be pulling their weight?

Social loafing can occur in all kinds of groups and teams and in all kinds of organizations. It can result in lower group performance and may even prevent a group from reaching its goals. Fortunately, managers can take steps to reduce social loafing by making sure that individual contributions are recognizable, emphasizing the valuable contributions of each individual, and making sure that the group size is not too large (see Figure 10.7). Individuals who feel their contributions matter will be less likely to engage in social loafing.

social loafing
The tendency of individuals to put forth less effort when they work in groups than when they work alone.

FIGURE 10.7 | Three Ways to Reduce Social Loafing

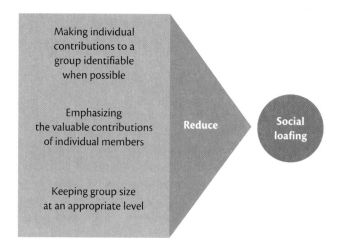

Helping Groups to Manage Conflict Effectively

At some point or other, practically all groups experience conflict either within the group (intragroup conflict) or with other groups (intergroup conflict). In Chapter 12, we discuss conflict in depth and explore ways to manage it effectively. As you will learn there, managers can take several steps to help groups manage conflict and disagreements.

For the purposes of this discussion, we focus on the types of conflict that emerge within groups and what managers can do to manage it effectively.

Task-related conflict *(or constructive conflict)* occurs when the members of the group perceive a problem or have a disagreement about the nature of the task or project, not in the way the members are relating to one another. This type of conflict is relatively easy to resolve by seeking clarification about the nature of the task or problem to be solved. **Relationship conflict** on the other hand, occurs when members of the group perceive each other's attitudes as the problem. Differences in opinions are viewed as personal attacks that threaten to derail the project. Managers should practise the following four strategies to diminish and discourage relationship conflict:

1. Reduce interpersonal hostility by developing high levels of *emotional intelligence* (see Chapter 9). Team members with high levels of emotional intelligence are less likely to fly off the handle when disagreements arise.
2. *Promote cohesiveness:* Teams with high levels of loyalty and commitment are more tolerant of emotional outbreaks and tend not to become personally offended when the conversation gets heated.
3. *Promote positive group norms:* Supportive group norms such as encouraging open and honest discussion and practising maintenance roles such as "gatekeeping" that promotes participation can diminish relationship conflict.
4. *Collaborating conflict-handling behaviour:* When conflicting members of the group can collaborate by asserting their interests and point of view clearly, without being aggressive, and genuinely desire to have a positive outcome to the disagreement, a win-win situation can result. On the other hand, if group members' conflict-handling behaviours focus on competing or forcing their own take on the situation, relationship conflict will likely escalate.

task-related conflict
Members of the group perceive a problem or have a disagreement about the nature of the task or project.

relationship conflict
Members of the group perceive each other's attitudes as a problem.

Tips for Managers

BUILDING TEAMS FOR HIGH PERFORMANCE[58]

1. Build and manage teams that live up to their promise of higher productivity and greater problem-solving ability.

2. Clarify roles and responsibilities for team members so they work together effectively.

3. Manage interpersonal conflicts among team members.

4. Maximize team productivity by encouraging group discussion and problem-solving.

5. Overcome organizational, management, and employee barriers to teamwork through the focus on enhancing the emotional intelligence of team members.

6. Identify and manage team rewards effectively.

Summary and Review

1. **WHY THE POPULARITY OF GROUPS AND TEAMS IN THE WORKPLACE?** A group is two or more people who interact with each other to reach certain goals or meet certain needs. A team is a group whose members work intensely with each other to achieve a specific common goal or objective. Groups and teams can contribute to organizational effectiveness by enhancing performance, increasing responsiveness to customers, increasing innovation, and being a source of motivation for their members.

2. **TYPES OF GROUPS AND TEAMS** Managers can establish a variety of groups and teams to reach organizational goals. These include cross-functional teams, top-management teams, research and development teams, command groups, task forces, self-managed work teams, and virtual teams. Teams may not always be the answer for reaching a goal, however.

3. **GROUP DYNAMICS** Key elements of group dynamics are group size and roles, group leadership, group development, group norms, and group cohesiveness. The advantages and disadvantages of large and small groups suggest that managers should form groups with no more members than are needed to provide the human resources the group needs to reach its goals and use a division of labour. A group role is a set of behaviours and tasks that a member of a group is expected to perform because of his or her position in the group. All groups and teams need leadership. Five stages of development that many groups pass through are *forming, storming, norming, performing,* and *adjourning*. Group norms are shared rules of behaviour that most group members follow. To be effective, groups need a balance of conformity and deviance. Conformity allows a group to control its members' behaviours in order to achieve group goals; deviance provides the impetus for needed change. Group cohesiveness is the attractiveness of a group or team to its members. As group cohesiveness increases, so, too, do the level of participation and communication within a group, the level of conformity to group norms, and the emphasis on group goal accomplishment. Managers should strive to achieve a moderate level of group cohesiveness in the groups and teams they manage.

4. **GROUP DECISION MAKING** Managers can minimize *groupthink* by playing the *devil's advocate* and foster creativity and innovation to improve decision making by using three techniques. (1). *Brainstorming* involves generating lots of innovative alternatives, without judgment, in a face-to-face environment. The assessment of the alternatives comes after the brainstorm (2). The *nominal group technique* allows group members to generate alternatives individually and write them down for later consideration by the whole group (3). The *delphi technique* is used to solve problems by allowing experts to generate and debate appropriate solutions and courses of action.

5. **MANAGING GROUPS AND TEAMS FOR HIGH PERFORMANCE** Managers who want top-performing groups and teams need to motivate members of groups and teams to achieve goals, reduce social loafing and help groups manage conflict effectively. Managers can motivate members of groups and teams to work toward the achievement of organizational goals by making sure that members personally benefit when their group or team performs well.

Key Terms

SO WHERE DO YOU STAND?

Wrap-Up to Opening Case

We began this chapter by looking at how powerful teamwork can be. Key examples were acknowledged. One of the key realities of effective teams was the experience of friendships and how important they are to the team functioning well. This became particularly obvious whenever the team had to disband or move on to other things. There tended to be a period of grief because the closeness of working together was no more. Dr. Barbara Moses said, "The intensity of the experience gives you a heady feeling. People associate the task at hand with how well they work with others on the team. And they don't separate the two." As well, according to Moses, "The experience of working on a team gives people a sense of identity and purpose. After they disband, they can get depressed." We saw that it was the trust factor that held the team together; it was the glue that bonded the members.

We saw, however, that there is also a shadow side to teams. Moses pointed out that not all teams operate well. "Because of people's divergent personalities, they don't always work out. Working intensely with people brings their personalities into high relief. There are those who want to hijack a project and others who want to dot the Is and cross the Ts. And sometimes, you'll have a person on a team who targets one other person with his dislike. A great team can make people soar, and a bad one can be very dispiriting."

And now, let us summarize with a story called "To the Beat of the Same Drummer."

The Drum Café in British Columbia has an interesting tag line: "Building Teams ... One Beat at a Time."[59] Danny Aaron, president of Vancouver-based Drum Café Canada, teaches Canadian executives how to make their companies pulsate. How does he do this? His method is to bring their employees together in a big room where he entices them to bang away on African drums. By the end of the hour, even the most timid or pessimistic of the bunch is in the groove, with values such as teamwork and collaboration coming across loud and clear.

According to Aaron, companies, like music, are made up of a variety of different rhythms. "You can have sales, marketing, accounting. You can have Vancouver, Calgary, and Toronto. But as long as those different rhythms can play to that same beat—the foundation—and can listen to each other—the communication—then as an organization they can make music."

A conference held at Georgian College's Kempenfelt Conference Centre, just outside Barrie, Ontario, in 1999, demonstrated the effectiveness of drumming and teamwork. One hundred casually dressed businesspeople were in attendance. Lance Secretan, former professor, author, and leadership guru, remarked, "Most people will go home and forget 80 percent of the things that have happened here, but they won't forget the drumming."

Drumming, therefore, is a metaphor and a practice for some companies, to synchronize efforts, to get individuals to work together as a team, and to develop a sense of shared responsibility. Sue Anderson, who was director of Internal Communication at Xerox Canada, had already organized two such sessions. In her words: "Doing something like this in a large corporate environment is a risk because you don't know how anybody in that room is going to react. But for us it's about getting into a new kind of rhythm, a rhythm that allows you to reach new kinds of heights."

The new reality is that everyone must work together to be effective.

(c) Brand X Pictures/Punch Stock

Management in Action

Topics for Discussion and Action

Level 1

1. Describe how teams can increase an organization's competitive advantage.
2. Describe the different types of groups and teams found in organizations.
3. Describe the three techniques managers can use to improve group decision-making and promote creativity.

Level 2

4. Explain why and how managers would use self-managed teams to achieve organizational goals. What are some of the disadvantages to using self-managed teams?
5. Listen to the BusinessWeek podcast at www.businessweek.com/mediacenter/qt/podcasts/climbing/climbing_01_29_08.mp3 called "Climbing the Ladder." Describe the four archetypal personalities found in organizations and what roles they play in a high-performing team.
6. Describe the task and maintenance roles for effective group functioning. Which do you think are the most important, and why?

Level 3

7. Teams should have a moderate level of cohesiveness and a balance of conformity and deviance from group norms. Why are these levels important to the performance of the team?
8. Imagine that you are the manager of a hotel. What steps will you take to reduce social loafing by members of the cleaning staff who are responsible for keeping all common and guest rooms spotless?
9. Analyze the pitfalls of groupthink. How can group conflict be resolved?

Building Management Skills

Answer the following questions about the organization you have chosen to follow:

1. What type of groups and teams can you identify in this organization?
2. Does this organization use self-managed teams? How are they organized?
3. Does this organization use virtual teams? If so, in what areas of the operation do they function?
4. Can you identify any conflicts in this organization? What caused them, and how would you resolve them?

Management for You

DIAGNOSING GROUP FAILURES

Think about the last dissatisfying or discouraging experience you had as a member of a group or team. Perhaps the group did not accomplish its goals, perhaps group members could agree about nothing, or perhaps there was too much social loafing. Now answer the following questions.

1. What type of group was this?
2. Were group members motivated to achieve group goals? Why, or why not?
3. What were the group's norms? How much conformity and deviance existed in the group?
4. How cohesive was the group? Why do you think the group's cohesiveness was at this level? What consequences did this level of group cohesiveness have for the group and its members?
5. Was social loafing a problem in this group? Why, or why not?
6. What could the group's leader or manager have done differently to increase group effectiveness?
7. What could group members have done differently to increase group effectiveness?

Small Group Breakout Exercise

CREATING A CROSS-FUNCTIONAL TEAM

Form groups of three or four, and appoint one member as the spokesperson who will communicate your findings to the whole class when called on by the instructor. Then discuss the following scenario:

You are a group of managers in charge of food services for a large university. Recently, a survey of students, faculty, and staff was conducted to evaluate customer satisfaction with the food services provided by the university's eight cafeterias. The results were disappointing, to put it mildly. Complaints ranged from dissatisfaction with the type and range of meals and snacks provided, operating hours, and food temperature, to unresponsiveness to current concerns about the importance of low-carb/high-protein diets and the preferences of vegetarians. You have decided to form a cross-functional team to further evaluate reactions to the food services and to develop a proposal for changes that can be made to increase customer satisfaction.

1. Indicate who should be on this important cross-functional team and why.
2. Describe the goals the team should be trying to achieve.
3. Describe the different roles team members will need to perform.
4. Describe the steps you will take to help ensure that the team has a good balance between conformity and deviance and a moderate level of cohesiveness.

Business Planning Exercise

You and your business planning team realize that you might have to operate as a virtual team because it turns out that each of you has a different work and class schedule, so there is almost no time when more than three people could meet face-to-face. As you know, virtual teams have benefits, but they also face problems.

1. How will you build group cohesiveness in this team?
2. Write out a "team effectiveness contract" that includes how the group will divide the labour of writing the business plan, (what roles and responsibilities will each member take on), what norms might help the group function, how the team will prevent social loafing and what will be the consequences for not meeting commitments.

Managing Ethically

Strana Corporation uses self-managed teams to develop and produce new greeting cards. Some of the members of the team are engaged in social loafing, and other members of the team are reluctant to say anything. Team members are supposed to provide performance evaluations of each other at the end of each project, but some rate everyone equally, to avoid conflict. This practice has caused low morale on the team because hard work results in the same pay as does loafing. Some team members are complaining that it is unethical to rate everyone the same way when individual performances differ so much. One team member has come to you for advice because you are an expert in team performance and ethics. What would you advise this team member to do? How could the team's performance be improved?

Exploring the World Wide Web

SPECIFIC ASSIGNMENT

Many companies are committed to the use of teams, including Sears Canada. Visit Sears' website to learn more about this company (www.sears.ca). Then click on "Corporate Information," "Careers at Sears," and "Mission, Vision & Values."

1. What principles or values underlie Sears' use of teams?
2. How does Sears use teams to build employee commitment?

GENERAL ASSIGNMENT

Find the website of a company that relies heavily on teams to accomplish its goals. What kinds of teams does this company use? What steps do managers take to ensure that team members are motivated to perform at a high level?

McGraw-Hill Connect™—Available 24/7 with instant feedback so you can study when you want, how you want, and where you want. Take advantage of the Study Plan—an innovative tool that helps you customize your learning experience. You can diagnose your knowledge with pre- and post-tests, identify the areas where you need help, search the entire learning package for content specific to the topic you're studying, and add these resources to your personalized study plan. Visit www.mcgrawhillconnect.ca to register—take practice quizzes, search the e-book, and much more.

Be the Manager

BUILDING TEAM SPIRIT[60]

Jim Clemmer, based in Kitchener, Ontario, is a professional speaker, workshop/retreat leader, and author of *Growing the Distance* and *The Leader's Digest*. He says that "team spirit is the catalyst every organization needs to achieve outstanding performance." Indeed, he goes to say that the "emotional commitment of the people using the tools and executing the plans is what determines whether companies sink or soar." He further explains how companies can kill or build spirit.

Because of your knowledge and skill in team-based performance, you have been called into discussions with the two founding partners and 10 employees of a new specialty tire company about to open its doors in Winnipeg, Manitoba. Many of these people have been friends to this point, but the owners want to get the company going on the right footing, especially because during the planning stage, owners had tolerated the use of wireless devices in the meetings. They notice now that some members are beginning to resent this "extra presence" while the team is doing its best to communicate. The owners have discovered that bored staff are simply emailing one another "under the table," literally.

Questions

1. What do you think is the problem here?
2. What is your best advice regarding team-building for this group?

Management Case

The Seven Habits of Winning Teams[61]

When I ask executives to recall an experience when they and their management team were performing at their best, their answers often include the same themes: At the top of their game, the team worked intensely to achieve a shared, deeply meaningful business objective. Free of hierarchy, they enjoyed open communication, constructive debate, and mutual support. It was "exhilarating" and "rewarding."

But when I ask them whether their teams perform at their best when the stakes are at their highest—for instance, during a major transaction—the answer is almost always, "no."

How can business leaders recreate that "winning team" experience? Research across hundreds of executive teams worldwide reveals that the best-performing teams share seven common characteristics that enable them to bring out the best in each other and their entire organization.

Winning teams focus on a few critical objectives. High-performing teams focus their efforts on the handful of fundamentals that make the biggest difference. For example, the management team at one of the best-performing utilities in North America focuses most of its collective efforts on regulatory strategy and business development. Operations are important but will not fundamentally shift the company's value, so the team dedicates less time to this. Often, how the team functions, for example, in making critical strategic decisions, can be as important as setting strategic priorities, and consequently targeted investments in team effectiveness can move to the top of the agenda.

Winning teams have a flexible working style, within a clear set of operating norms. When faced with a new challenge, high-performing teams are able to transform themselves, adopting a style that the new situation demands. For instance, during times of organizational change or while executing an acquisition, teams need a much greater degree of collaboration and alignment than when they are simply running the day-to-day business. However, even in these exceptional circumstances, the working style respects a few commonly understood norms such as how working sessions are conducted and how team members relate to each other.

Winning teams have a CEO who is "first among equals." Too many leaders tend either to step back and delegate decision making or to rule by decree.

The best leaders have an impressive command of all aspects of their business and are able to get deep into the substance of an issue to help the team draw out new and unexpected insights. Rather than having the answer themselves, they build an environment for open dialogue free from the frictions of ego, thereby facilitating more rapid decision-making.

Winning teams capitalize on their unique position as integrators. The best teams take on work that only the team can do as a collective, focusing on pivotal issues that cannot be pursued by individual executives alone. On such topics, they break out of organizational silos to develop an integrated view of the business and discover new commercial opportunities or find better ways of running the business.

Winning teams create a "high challenge, high support" environment. The ideal environment is one that enables a constructive debate based on facts and free of anecdotes, emotions, and politics. Team members cannot achieve peak performance when they fear provoking disagreements or emotional debates, when they mistrust the motivations of colleagues, or when there is a history of hurt feelings. On the other hand, an absence of challenge leads to false consensus, needless grumbling, or worse.

Winning teams set farsighted goals that are stretching on multiple dimensions. The best teams set high standards for both business results and team performance. While ensuring that financial results are on track, they maintain a relentless focus on long-term performance and health indicators, including quality of the business portfolio, excellence in operational execution, relationships with external audiences such as customers, investments to broaden and deepen organizational capabilities, and the professional satisfaction of their most talented leaders.

Winning teams invest in building the team's effectiveness. Star-studded teams often fail when top performers dive into the business issues without recognizing that the team's performance is the real challenge. Instead, the best teams invest in the skills of individual members as well as the team itself.

Instilling these seven habits in a management team is not easy, but it is critical to achieving a track record in developing and executing winning business strategies successfully over the long term.

Questions

1. What are the seven habits of winning teams that reflect your best experience of working in a team? Use the chart below to develop your answer.

2. What would be your personal challenges in developing each of these seven challenges to the maximum?

Habit	Winning teams ...	My best experience with this habit ...
#1	focus on a few critical objectives	
#2	have a flexible working style, within a clear set of operating norms	
#3	have a CEO (or person in charge) who is "first among equals"	
#4	capitalize on their unique position as integrators	
#5	create a "high challenge, high support" environment	
#6	set farsighted goals that are stretching on multiple dimensions	
#7	invest in building the team's effectiveness	

Video Management Case

Pike Place Fish

Teaching Objective: To provide an example of synergy within a high-performing team. To show how such a team can enhance work performance and increase innovation, motivation, job satisfaction, and responsiveness to customers.

Video Summary: This video chronicles the Pike Place Fish Co.'s effort to become world famous. After working with a consultant, the owner decides to abandon his autocratic management style for one that is team-focused. The interviews of the owner, consultant, and manager and the scenes inside the market provide an excellent example of a high-performing, self-managed work team and the dynamics that occur within it.

Questions to consider

1. What does it mean at Pike Place Fish to be world famous?

2. What roles do teams play in Pike Place Fish's quest to be world famous? Why does it take new employees time, in some cases three months, to become effective team members?

3. How does Pike Place Fish create the context for workers to reach their maximum potential? What role do managers play in creating and nurturing this atmosphere?

Managing Human Resources

CHAPTER 11

Learning Outcomes

1. Describe the legal framework of human resource management in Canada.

2. Explain why strategic human resource management and human resources planning can help an organization gain a competitive advantage.

3. Describe the five components of human resources management and how they fit together with the strategy and structure of the organization.

    i.   Recruitment and Selection
    ii. Training and Development
    iii. Performance Appraisal and feedback
    iv. Pay and Benefits
    v.   Labour relations

Business Ill-Prepared for Aging Workshop[1]

Abstract (Summary)

The aging of the workforce is "unprecedented" in Canada and around the world, said Bill Gleberzon, director of government relations with Canada's Association for the 50-Plus. Businesses are not prepared and governments are "only beginning to become aware," he said.

In the meantime, younger workers may experience the upside of an aging workforce. Andrew Jackson, chief economist at the Canadian Labour Congress, said the situation could "tip the scales in the favour of labour" and bring higher wages. "Bring it on," he said of a tight labour market.

"The opportunity for the younger crowd is incredible," said Prem Benimadhu. "It's great to be young today."

Canadian businesses and governments are not ready to deal with the upcoming deluge of older employees leaving the workforce, a situation that presents opportunities and challenges, experts agree.

In its latest 2006 Census report on the age and sex of the population, Statistics Canada said ... that the number of people aged 55 to 64 in the workforce was an unprecedented 3.7 million last year, or 16.9 percent. By 2016, people in that age group could form more than one-fifth of the working-age population, it added.

"With workers generally leaving the workforce between the ages of 55 and 64, Canada has never had so many people close to retirement," the report said. In about 10 years, "Canada may have more people at the age where they can leave the labour force than people at the age where they can begin working," it noted.

Businesses are aware of the situation, but most have done nothing about it, said Prem Benimadhu, vice-president of Governance and Human Resource Management at the Conference Board of Canada.

"The practices and policies we have were created for ... the labour surplus of the 1970s," he said. "Policies have to change, we have to extend the working lives of people 55-plus."

Economic growth will be limited by businesses not being able to hire and expand and not being able to invest in operations if wages increase, Mr. Benimadhu said. "When we hit the huge crunch, companies are going to get inventive, we will be forced to adapt."

Garth Whyte, executive vice-president of the Canadian Federation of Independent Business, said labour shortages being experienced in booming Western Canada are a preview of what is to come. "There's a tidal wave coming at us from west to east, and over time it's going to get worse," he said.

Federation members, mostly owners of small- and medium-sized businesses, will be forced to hire underqualified people, ignore business opportunities, or put in longer hours themselves, Mr. Whyte said.

"It's going to hit Canada and all Canadians," he said, adding policies that need to be reviewed include the Canada Pension Plan, mandatory retirement age, employment insurance, immigration legislation, and the education system.

"This is not being done in a minority government situation," Whyte added.

Adam Crowley/Getty Images
Commitment makes the difference between "good" decisions and "great" decisions.

Benimadhu said government has a very important role in offering incentives for older people to stay in the workforce, perhaps by allowing them to earn a certain portion of income tax-free.

Businesses must get past "Freedom 55" thinking, at which age people are expected to retire soon, he said. This is "insane" when people are healthier and living longer, he added.

"The 9-to-5, five days a week, rigid, inflexible schedules are not appropriate for older workers. We're stuck in a quagmire of old thinking ... . We have to change the mindset of both older and younger workers," Benimadhu said.

The aging of the workforce is "unprecedented" in Canada and around the world, said Bill Gleberzon, director of Government Relations with Canada's Association for the 50-Plus. Businesses are not prepared and governments are "only beginning to become aware," he said.

Most retirees do not want to sit on the porch, he added, and could be enticed by measures such as phased retirement, flexible work hours, and, perhaps above all, a little respect.

"Ageism is rampant in the workplace," Gleberzon said, with the common belief that people are "played out" after age 58. But governments should not consider replacing mandatory retirement with mandatory employment, adjusting the age when workers can access their pension.

"They will face a huge revolt," he said. "This (baby boomers) is a large, vocal, politically active group of people."

In the meantime, younger workers may experience the upside of an aging workforce. Andrew Jackson, chief economist at the Canadian Labour Congress, said the situation could "tip the scales in the favour of labour" and bring higher wages. "Bring it on," he said of a tight labour market.

"The opportunity for the younger crowd is incredible," said Benimadhu. "It's great to be young today."

Now It's Your Turn!

1. Prem Benimadhu, vice-president of Governance and Human Resource Management at the Conference Board of Canada, remarked that "practices and policies we have were created for ... the labour surplus of the 1970s." What are a strength and a weakness of these practices and policies?

2. When you look over the opening scenario, what are some advantages and disadvantages that you see for yourself in relation to the aging workforce?

■■■■ Overview

Managers are responsible for acquiring, developing, protecting, and using the resources that an organization needs to be efficient and effective. One of the most important resources in all organizations is human resources—the people involved in the production and distribution of goods and services. Human resources include all members of an organization, ranging from top managers to entry-level employees. In our opening scenario, we saw how the aging of the workforce is "unprecedented." At the same time, younger workers may experience the upside of an aging workforce. Effective human resource managers will need to be ready to deal with the opportunities and challenges of all segments of Canada's workforce.

This chapter examines how managers can tailor their human resource management system to their organization's strategy and structure. We discuss in particular the major components of human resource management: recruitment and selection, training and development, performance appraisal, pay and benefits, and labour relations in the context of the Canadian legal framework. By the end of this chapter, you will understand the central role that human resource management plays in creating a high-performing organization.

L O 1

The Legal Framework of Human Resource Management in Canada

intentional discrimination
The illegal practice of deliberately using prohibited grounds, such as race, religion and sex, when making employment decisions.

unintentional discrimination
Unfair practices and policies that have an adverse impact on specific groups for reasons unrelated to the job.

Canadian Human Rights Commission
www.chrc-ccdp.ca

There are several key pieces of legislation that govern the management of human resources (HR) in Canada. The laws have been developed to protect the rights of employers and employees. HR managers must be aware of the legal and political environment in which they do their work. Failure to adhere to the legislation governing employment standards, labour relations, health and safety, employment equity, and other employment-related regulations, such as the Charter of Rights and Freedoms, knowingly or unknowingly, can result in severe penalties to managers and employers. The HR manager has the responsibility to avoid **intentional discrimination** (deliberately using prohibited grounds, such as race, religion, and sex, when making employment decisions) and **unintentional discrimination** (unfair practices and policies that have an adverse impact on specific groups for reasons that are unrelated to the job). In this chapter, we look at two of the pieces of legislation that make up the legal environment of HR management in Canada: the Employment Standards Act and the Canadian Human Rights Act.

The Employment Standards Act sets out minimum standards for the private sector in federal, provincial, and territorial legislation. It deals with the minimum age for employment, hours of work and overtime pay, minimum wages, equal pay, the weekly rest-day, general holidays with pay, annual vacations with pay, parental leave, and individual and group terminations of employment. It also deals with mandatory retirement and whistleblower protection rights. Minimum employee entitlements are established for each element covered by the Act.

The Canadian Human Rights Act covers all businesses under federal jurisdiction. Each province and territory has its own human rights legislation that prohibits discrimination based on specific grounds. There are differences across the nation. For example, in British Columbia, Prince Edward Island, Quebec, and Yukon, it is considered discriminatory to reject an applicant for employment based on a record of criminal conviction. This is not a prohibited ground of discrimination in any other of the 14 jurisdictions in Canada. All jurisdictions prohibit discrimination on the grounds of race, colour, religion or creed, physical and mental disability, sex (including pregnancy and childbirth), and marital status. All areas have policies related to discrimination on the basis of age; however, the protected age groups differ.

It is important to note that this legislation does not restrict the employers' right and ability to reward high-performing employees and discipline employees for not meeting productivity standards or following company rules, as long as such rewards and punishments are based on job-related criteria and not on prohibited grounds. We now turn to the activities that managers engage in to attract, develop, and retain high-performing employees.

L O 2

Strategic Human Resource Management

human resource management (HRM)
Activities that managers engage in to attract and retain employees and to ensure that they perform at a high level and contribute to the accomplishment of organizational goals.

Human resource management (HRM) includes all the activities that managers engage in to attract and retain employees and to ensure that they perform at a high level and contribute to the accomplishment of organizational goals. **Strategic human resource management** is the process by which managers design the components of an HRM system to be consistent with each other, with other elements of organizational architecture, and with the organization's strategy and goals.[2] The objective of strategic HRM is the development of an HRM system that enhances an organization's efficiency, quality, innovation, and responsiveness to customers—the four building blocks of competitive advantage, which we discussed in Chapter 2.

Michael Stern, president and CEO of Michael Stern Associates Inc., an executive search firm headquartered in Toronto, puts the matter succinctly:

> *Human resources has to come up with ways to retain top people—without giving away the store. These challenges are tailormade for HR leaders who understand strategic business. If they want to join the executive committee, they have to go beyond their "personnel" mindset and see their role in the big picture: preparing the workforce for tomorrow's challenges, changing the culture, or filling senior management gaps with proactive hiring and cutting-edge training. The good news is businesses that give HR a seat at the table tend to outperform the competition. Pepsico companies have long benefited from aligning their people processes with their business processes.*[3]

strategic human resource management
The process by which managers design the components of a human resource management system to be consistent with each other, with other elements of organizational architecture, and with the organization's strategy and goals.

Human Resource Planning

THINK ABOUT IT

Chain of Knowledge: Boomers Filling the Gaps[4]

"It's a bit of a paradigm shift," says David Lathrop, president of Grey Fox Associates Inc.[5] "The world is slowly coming to realize there is a real need (for senior management expertise) that isn't a full-time need." And so a growing number of baby boomers with senior-level business experience will be recruited to fill a niche created by their retiring colleagues, who are leaving a skills gap in their wake.

David Lathrop and Bob Eccleston, 57-year-old information technology executives, felt the sting of downsizing. They wanted to capitalize on their expertise in a way that gave them the work flexibility they wanted—and could afford—at this stage in life. So they set up a consulting business that allows them to work 40 or 50 hours a month on a contract basis to client companies that need to develop the skills of current, and often much more inexperienced, leaders. "It's about providing very senior level help, but in very small and manageable quantities in a way that a customer can see great value," says Eccleston, who was "downsized" three times before deciding to venture in a different direction.

Most human resource experts agree there will be a relatively sudden lack of senior experience in the market once the majority of baby boomers retire, leaving unprepared companies scrambling to find the qualified talent to replace them. Increasingly, firms such as Grey Fox are offering their services by coaching and mentoring up-and-coming leaders while keeping their own hands in the business world, Eccleston says. "You get so much satisfaction out of taking what you've learned over 35 years and helping these people get through those bumps in their careers." Lathrop says the goal is to recruit more partners with the same amount of experience and wisdom so the chain of knowledge continues moving along to the next generation of business leaders. The trend has also given rise to the increased use of interim managers, or contract executives who take over the helm of a department or company until a replacement can be groomed or recruited. "What [more junior executives] really need is just a few hours a week of someone with 30-plus years behind them who has kind of seen it all to hold them by the hand and get them through those difficult moments," Eccleston says.

You Be the Manager

1. Why is the recruitment of older employees important in managing the skills gap?
2. What is the paradigm shift that David Lathrop refers to?

human resource planning
Activities that managers use to forecast their current and future needs for human resources.

Human resource planning includes all the activities that managers use to forecast their current and future needs for human resources. Current human resources are the employees an organization needs today to provide high-quality goods and services to customers. Future human resources are the employees the organization will need at some later date to achieve its longer-term goals. As part of human resource planning, managers must make both demand forecasts and supply forecasts. *Demand forecasts* estimate the qualifications and numbers of employees an organization will need given its goals and strategies. *Supply forecasts* estimate the availability and qualifications of current employees now and in the future and the supply of qualified workers in the external labour market. One of the factors facing some amusement parks is that not enough teenagers are available or willing to work at them. With low supply, they have had to look to senior citizens as an alternative supply of labour.

The assessment of both current and future human resource needs helps managers determine whom they should be trying to recruit and select to achieve organizational goals now and in the future. See Figure 11.1. As we saw in our previous *Think About It* case example, some baby boomers are creating companies to fulfill this leadership talent need. According to Statistics Canada, the average retirement age in Canada is now 62. Older workers are still in demand, of course. Dan Ondrack, academic director of executive programs at the University of Toronto's Joseph L. Rotman School of Management, says that older workers "have a lot of tacit knowledge about the ins and outs of getting a job done, which makes them valuable employees. And many will take jobs that pay less than their earlier careers."[6] However, succession planning is also becoming a critical need as more and more companies actively search for talent that will provide the leadership and direction for future organizational success. In recent years, Montreal-based BCE has created a new position, "chief talent officer," and appointed Léo Houle to the post. Houle reports directly to BCE's CEO Michael Sabia. Houle is responsible for executive recruitment, compensation, and succession planning to make sure that BCE's companies have the right leadership and talent as BCE looks toward the future.[7]

BCE Inc. www.bce.ca

Succession planning must be well thought out. Human resources managers often use **personnel replacement charts** as tools in this process. A personnel replacement chart is an examination of all current positions, along with who holds them, what their skills and qualifications are, and whether or not their performance levels make them suitable for promotion as positions become available. In order to create a replacement chart, a thorough analysis of each position is required.

personnel replacement charts
A graphic illustration of current positions, who holds them, and whether they have the skills and qualifications necessary for succession planning.

Job Analysis

job analysis
Identifying the tasks, duties, and responsibilities that make up a job and the knowledge, skills, and abilities needed to perform the job.

Job analysis is the process of identifying (1) the tasks, duties, and responsibilities that make up a job (the *job description*), and (2) the knowledge, skills, and abilities needed to perform the job (the *job specifications*).[8] For each job in an organization, a job analysis needs to be done.

◼ FIGURE 11.1 | HRM Planning and Job Analysis

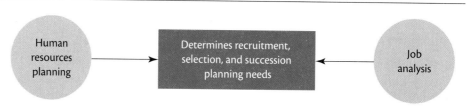

A job analysis can be done in a number of ways, including by observing current employees as they perform the job or by interviewing them. Often, managers rely on questionnaires completed by job holders and their managers. The questionnaires ask about the skills and abilities needed to perform the job, job tasks and the amount of time spent on them, responsibilities, supervisory activities, equipment used, reports prepared, and decisions made.[9]

When managers complete human resource planning and job analyses for all jobs in an organization, they know their human resource needs and the jobs they need to fill. They also know what knowledge, skills, and abilities potential employees will need to perform those jobs. At this point, recruitment and selection can begin.

Irrespective of the province or federal jurisdiction, an employer must keep in mind the Employment Standards Act[10] and their respective Human Rights Code.[11] "The Canadian Human Rights Commission administers the Canadian Human Rights Act and is responsible for ensuring compliance with the Employment Equity Act. Both laws ensure that the principles of equal opportunity and nondiscrimination are followed in all areas of federal jurisdiction."[12]

L O **3**

Overview of the Components of HRM

An organization's human resource management system has five major components: (1) recruitment and selection, (2) training and development, (3) performance appraisal and feedback, (4) pay and benefits, and (5) labour relations (see Figure 11.2). Managers use *recruitment and selection*, the first component of an HRM system, to attract and hire new employees who have the abilities, skills, and experiences that will help an organization achieve its goals. For example, Cirque du Soleil recruits its members from all over the world. About 70 percent of recruits come from a sports background, which is well suited for training in acrobatics, a core part of their entertainment experience.

FIGURE 11.2 │ Components of a Human Resource Management System

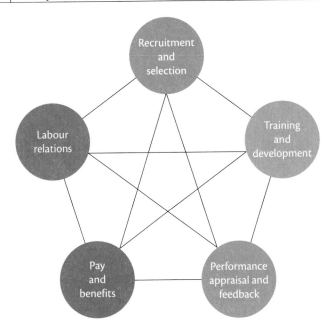

**Each component of an HRM system influences
the others, and all five must fit together**

After recruiting and selecting employees, managers use the second component, *training and development*, to ensure that organizational members develop skills and abilities that will enable them to perform their jobs effectively in the present and the future. Training and development is an ongoing process because changes in technology and the environment, as well as in an organization's goals and strategies, often require organizational members to learn new techniques and ways of working.

At Cirque, new recruits have the discipline and technical skills but usually lack the acrobatic and artistic skills. Extensive training removes this gap and positions the company to gain a competitive advantage.

The third component, *performance appraisal and feedback*, serves two purposes in HRM. First, performance appraisal can provide managers with the information they need to make good human resources decisions—decisions about how to train, motivate, and reward organizational members.[13] Thus, the performance appraisal and feedback component is a kind of control system that can be used with management by objectives (discussed in Chapters 5 and 13). Second, performance feedback from performance appraisal serves a developmental purpose for the members of an organization. When managers regularly evaluate their subordinates' performance, they can provide subordinates with valuable information about their strengths and weaknesses and the areas in which they need to concentrate. On the basis of performance appraisals, managers distribute pay to employees.

In the fourth component of HRM, *pay and benefits*, managers distribute pay to employees, first by determining their starting salaries, and later by determining whether raises or bonuses should be given. By rewarding high-performing organizational members with pay raises, bonuses, and the like, managers increase the likelihood that an organization's most valued human resources are motivated to continue their high levels of contribution to the organization. Moreover, when pay is linked to performance, high-performing employees are more likely to stay with the organization, and managers are more likely to be able to fill open positions with highly talented individuals. Benefits such as health insurance are important outcomes that employees receive by virtue of their membership in an organization.

Last but not least, *labour relations* includes the steps that managers take to develop and maintain good working relationships with the labour unions that may represent their employees' interests. For example, an organization's labour relations component can help managers establish safe working conditions and fair labour practices in their offices and plants.

Managers must ensure that all five of these components fit together and complement their companies' structure and control systems.[14] For example, if managers decide to decentralize authority and empower employees, they need to invest in training and development to ensure that lower-level employees have the knowledge and expertise they need to make the decisions that top managers would make in a more centralized structure.

Each of the five components of HRM influences the others (see Figure 11.2).[15] The kinds of people that the organization attracts and hires through recruitment and selection, for example, determine (1) the training and development that are necessary, (2) the way performance is appraised, and (3) the appropriate levels of pay and benefits.

A note on health and safety: Every human resource manager must pay attention to maintaining a healthy and safe working environment. It is estimated that indirect costs can be as much as two to 10 times more than the direct costs of an accident. The Canadian government has recognized this importance of health and safety as well. However, in Canada, unlike in the United States, there is no federal body to which organizations report. Rather, Canada has health and safety regulations and enforcement agencies by province and territory. What can be called Canadian health and safety net legislation would include the following: the Canada Labour Code,[16] WHMIS (Workplace Hazardous Materials Information System),[17] Workers' Compensation,[18] Canadian Centre for Occupational Health and Safety,[19] and Occupational Health and Safety Act.[20]

Recruitment and Selection

Recruitment includes all the activities that managers use to develop a pool of qualified candidates for open positions.[21] **Selection** is the process by which managers determine the relative qualifications of job applicants and their potential for performing well in a particular job.

External and Internal Recruitment

Late in 2006, *The Economist* magazine devoted a 15-page special report to what it called "The Search for Talent: Why It's Getting Harder to Find."[22] They speak about the world's most valuable commodity—talent—getting more and more difficult to find. Brainpower is the *intangible asset* that now describes the word "talent." What are making things difficult in finding "talent" is the collapse of loyalty and the shortage of "trained brains," as *The Economist* refers to the term. Even in countries where seemingly workers are plenty, "the training budget at Infosys, an Indian tech giant, is now well above $100m."[23] While in times past, discussions were on the "balance of power," today, in business and with HR managers, globally, the emphasis is on the "balance of brains."[24] The skills shortages that are the most acute are among managers.[25] Because of such factors, the balance of power is now shifting from companies to workers. The old social and corporate contract has gone; would-be employees know that. Given that China is now in the global economy only accentuates this difficulty of finding the "balance of brains." *The Economist* refers to Clyde Prestowitz's book *Three Billion New Capitalists: The Great Shift of Wealth and Power to the East*, where he quotes a Chinese friend: "We've had a couple of hundred bad years, but now we're back."[26] Welcome to the challenge and race for talent! HR managers generally use two types of recruiting: external and internal.

External Recruiting

When managers do external recruiting to fill open positions, they look outside the organization for people who have not worked for the organization before. There are many ways in which managers can recruit externally—advertisements in newspapers and magazines, open houses for students, career counsellors at high schools and colleges, career fairs at colleges, recruitment meetings with groups in the local community, and notices on the web.

External recruitment can also take place through informal networks, such as when current employees inform friends about open positions in their companies or recommend people they know to fill vacant spots. Some organizations use employment agencies for external recruitment, and some external recruitment takes place simply through walk-ins, where job hunters come to an organization and inquire about employment possibilities.

External recruiting has both advantages and disadvantages for managers. Advantages include having access to a potentially large applicant pool; being able to hire people who have the skills, knowledge, and abilities the organization needs to achieve its goals; and being able to bring in newcomers who may have a fresh approach to problems and

recruitment
Activities that managers use to develop a pool of qualified candidates for open positions.

selection
The process that managers use to determine the relative qualifications of job applicants and the individuals' potential for performing well in a particular job.

be up to date on the latest technology. These advantages have to be weighed against the disadvantages, however, including lower morale if current employees feel that there are individuals within the company who should be promoted. External recruitment also has high costs. Employees recruited externally lack knowledge about the inner workings of the organization and may need to receive more training than those recruited internally. InSystems uses its website to inform potential employees about its culture and strategic plans. Finally, with external recruitment, there is always uncertainty about whether the new employees actually will be good performers. Vancouver-based Angiotech Pharmaceuticals, Inc. solves this problem by working with potential employees years before they are ready to be hired. The company provides research money to graduate students at the University of British Columbia who are working on projects closely related to Angiotech's needs.

Some of the disadvantages of finding viable candidates from external sources are diminished when managers **outsource** their human resources needs. Although outsourcing human resources needs instead of doing the work in-house can save a company money by taking advantage of cheaper labour available elsewhere, there are several disadvantages to consider as outlined in Table 11.1.

Internal Recruiting

When recruiting is internal, managers turn to existing employees to fill open positions. Employees recruited internally want either **lateral moves** (job changes that entail no major changes in responsibility or authority levels) or promotions. Internal recruiting has several advantages. First, internal applicants are already familiar with the organization (including its goals, structure, culture, rules, and norms). Second, managers already know internal candidates; they have considerable information about their skills and abilities and actual behaviour on the job. Third, internal recruiting can help boost levels of employee motivation and morale, both for the employee who gets the job and for other workers. Those who are not seeking a promotion or who may not be ready for a promotion can see that it is a possibility for the future, or a lateral move can alleviate boredom once a job has been fully mastered and also provide a useful way to learn new skills. Finally, internal recruiting is normally less time-consuming and expensive.

Given the advantages of internal recruiting, why do managers rely on external recruiting as much as they do? The answer is that there are disadvantages to internal recruiting—among them, a limited pool of candidates and a tendency among those candidates to be "set" in the organization's ways. Often, the organization simply does not have suitable internal candidates. Sometimes, even when suitable internal applicants

Angiotech Pharmaceuticals, Inc.
www.angiotech.com

outsourcing
Using outside suppliers and manufacturers to produce goods and services.

lateral move
A job change that entails no major changes in responsibility or authority levels.

TABLE 11.1 | *Advantages and Disadvantages of Outsourcing Human Resources*

Examples	Advantages	Disadvantages
Computer software companies out-sourcing programming work to India	Takes advantage of lower labour costs	Lose control over the quality of goods and services.
Contracting out activities to companies that specialize in HRM	Provides flexibility by allowing the company to focus on core competencies	Companies hired to do the work have less knowledge of organizational practices, procedures, and goals.
	Reduces costs When a company outsources, it does not have to provide benefits to full-time workers or invest in training	Outsourced employees have less commitment to an organization than do regular, full-time employees. The potential to eliminate members' jobs creates resistance to outsourcing by labour unions.

are available, managers may rely on external recruiting to find the very best candidate or to help bring new ideas and approaches into the organization. When organizations are in trouble and performing poorly, external recruiting is often relied on to bring in managerial talent with a fresh approach. Thus, while David Nish was the financial director at Standard Life in the UK since 2006, he was appointed CEO in 2009 after a six month global search. He is the first CEO to be appointed who hasn't been with the company for decades.

The Selection Process

Once managers develop a pool of applicants for open positions through the recruitment process, they need to find out whether each applicant is qualified for the position and whether he or she is likely to be a good performer. If more than one applicant meets these two conditions, managers must further determine which applicants are likely to be better performers than others. They have several selection tools to help them sort out the relative qualifications of job applicants and to appraise applicants' potential for being good performers in a particular job. Those tools include background information, interviews, tests, and references.[27]

All selection techniques must be **valid** and **reliable**. To be valid, a selection technique must determine the candidates' likely performance (success or failure) on the job. If the test is unrelated to performing the job, it is invalid and managers can be subject to charges of discrimination if the candidate is not chosen. For example, it would be invalid for a manager to use a test of strength to select a candidate for a word processing job. The test of strength has no relation to how the candidate will perform the tasks of a word processor. Women have long been unable to access many of the jobs traditionally held by men because of invalid selection techniques. In order for a selection technique to be reliable, it must yield consistent results when repeated. In the previous example, if the word-processing candidate is given a typing test, it should yield similar performance results, without a significant deviation, when repeated to be reliable.

> **valid selection techniques**
> Must relate to the candidates' likely success or failure on the job.

> **reliable selection techniques**
> Must yield consistent results when repeated.

Background Information

To aid in the selection process, managers obtain background information from job applications and from résumés. Such information might include highest levels of education obtained, university or college majors and minors, type of college or university attended, years and type of work experience, and mastery of foreign languages. Background information can be helpful both to screen out applicants who are lacking key qualifications (such as a post-secondary degree) and to determine which qualified applicants are more promising than others (e.g., applicants with a BSc may be acceptable, but those who also have an MBA are preferable).

Interviews

Virtually all organizations use interviews during the selection process. Two general types of interviews are structured and unstructured. In a structured interview, managers ask each applicant the same standard questions (such as "What are your unique qualifications for this position?" and "What characteristics of a job are most important for you?"). Particularly informative questions may be those where the actual answering allows an interviewee to demonstrate skills and abilities needed for the job. Sometimes called **situational interview questions**, these questions present interviewees with a scenario that they would likely encounter on the job and ask them to indicate how they would handle it.[28] For example, applicants for a sales job may be asked to indicate how they would respond to a customer who complains about waiting too long for service, a customer who is indecisive, and a customer whose order is lost.

> **situational interview questions**
> Ask candidates how they would deal with a situation they might encounter on the job.

behavioural interview questions
Ask candidates how they dealt with a situation they encountered on the job.

unstructured interview
Unplanned questions asked as points of interest arise in the conversation.

structured interview
Formal questions asked in a set sequence.

Behavioural interview questions focus on relevant past job-related behaviours. It involves describing a situation and asking the candidate how they handled it. While situational interview questions ask candidates how they would deal with a specific situation *in the future*, behavioural interview questions ask them to describe how they reacted to a specific situation *in the past*. See Figure 11.3.

An **unstructured interview** proceeds more like an ordinary conversation. The interviewer feels free to ask probing questions to discover what the applicant is like and does not ask a fixed set of questions prepared in advance. In general, **structured interviews**, where questions are asked in set sequence, are superior to unstructured interviews because they are more likely to yield information that will help identify qualified candidates and they are less subjective. Also, evaluations based on structured interviews may be less likely to be influenced by the biases of the interviewer than evaluations based on unstructured interviews.

Even when structured interviews are used, however, there is always the potential for the biases of the interviewer to influence his or her judgment. The similar-to-me effect can cause people to perceive others who are similar to themselves more positively than they perceive those who are different and how stereotypes can result in inaccurate perceptions. It is important for interviewers to be trained to avoid these biases and sources of inaccurate perceptions as much as possible. Many of the approaches to increasing diversity awareness and diversity skills described in Chapter 3 can be used to train interviewers to avoid the effects of biases and stereotypes. In addition, using multiple interviewers can be advantageous, for their individual biases and idiosyncrasies may cancel one another out.[29]

When conducting interviews, managers have to be careful not to ask questions that are irrelevant to the job in question, or their organizations run the risk of costly lawsuits. It is inappropriate and illegal, for example, to inquire about an interviewee's spouse or to ask questions about whether an interviewee plans to have children. Questions such as these, which are irrelevant to job performance, may be viewed as discriminatory and as violating human rights legislation. Thus, interviewers also need to be instructed in what is required under the legislation and informed about questions that may be seen as violating those laws. See Figure 11.3.

Testing

Potential employees may be asked to take ability tests, personality tests, physical ability tests, or performance tests. **Ability tests** assess the extent to which applicants possess skills necessary for job performance, such as verbal comprehension or numerical skills. Keep in mind that all selection techniques must be both valid (predict job performance)

ability tests
Assess the skills necessary to perform the job well.

▇ **FIGURE 11.3 | Examples of Interview Question Types**

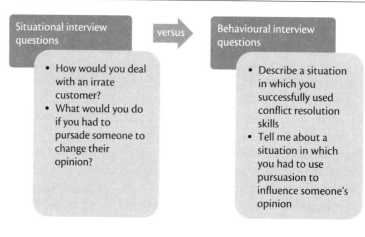

and reliable (yield consistent results). Also, giving a **realistic job preview (RJP)** is a useful technique to prevent the mismatching of employee expectations and the reality of the job, thereby minimizing high turnover.

Personality tests measure personality traits and characteristics relevant to job performance. Employers keen to find and retain the right workers are turning to personality testing to help everything from recruiting to promoting to team building. Proponents call them essential, but critics worry that they sometimes can be invasive, ineffective, even borderline illegal.[30] Some retail organizations, for example, give job applicants honesty tests to determine how trustworthy they are. The use of personality tests (including honesty tests) for hiring purposes is controversial. Some critics maintain that honesty tests do not really measure honesty (i.e., they are not valid) and can be subject to faking by job applicants. For jobs that require physical abilities—such as firefighting, garbage collecting, and package delivery—managers' selection tools include physical ability tests that measure physical strength and stamina.

Performance tests measure job applicants' performance on actual job tasks. Applicants for secretarial positions, for example, are typically required to complete a typing test that measures how quickly and accurately they are able to type. Applicants for middle- and top-management positions are sometimes given short-term projects to complete—projects that mirror the kinds of situations that arise in the job being filled—to assess their knowledge and problem-solving capabilities.[31]

References

Applicants for many jobs are required to provide references from former employers or other knowledgeable sources (such as a college instructor or adviser) who know the applicants' skills, abilities, and other personal characteristics. These individuals are asked to provide candid information about the applicants. References are often used at the end of the selection process to confirm a decision to hire. Yet, the fact that many former employers are reluctant to provide negative information in references sometimes makes it difficult to interpret what a reference is really saying about an applicant.

In fact, several recent lawsuits filed by applicants who felt that they were unfairly denigrated or had their privacy invaded by unfavourable references from former employers have caused managers to be increasingly wary of providing any kind of negative information in a reference, even if it is accurate. For jobs in which the job holder is responsible for the safety and lives of other people, however, failing to provide accurate negative information in a reference does not just mean that the wrong person might get hired but may also mean that other people's lives will be at stake. See Figure 11.4 for a summary of the typical steps in the hiring process.

realistic job preview (RJP)
Communicating the good and bad aspects of a job to a candidate to prevent mismatched expectations and high turnover.

personality tests
Measure personality traits and characteristics relevant to job performance.

performance tests
Measure the candidate's ability to perform actual job tasks.

Tips for Managers

RECRUITMENT AND SELECTION

1. Use human resource planning and job analysis as the basis to know what your human resource needs are.
2. Be transparent with potential new recruits as to the advantages and disadvantages of a job.
3. Be aware that older workers may be your solution to a skills gap in your company.
4. Think through the leadership talent you will need to build future organizational success.
5. Make sure your selection tools are reliable and valid.

■ **FIGURE 11.4** | **Typical Steps in the Hiring Process**

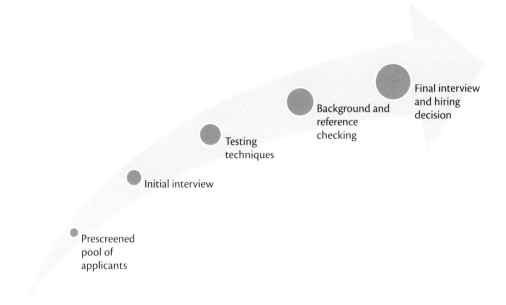

Final interview
and hiring
decision

Background and
reference
checking

Testing
techniques

Initial interview

Prescreened
pool of
applicants

Training and Development

Training and development help ensure that organizational members have the knowledge and skills they need to perform their jobs effectively, take on new responsibilities, and adapt to changing conditions. **Training** focuses mainly on teaching organizational members how to perform their current jobs and on helping them acquire the knowledge and skills they need to be effective performers.

Development focuses on building the knowledge and skills of organizational members so that they will be prepared to take on new responsibilities and challenges. Training tends to be used more often at lower levels of an organization; development tends to be used more often with professionals and managers. As we saw with our opening case scenario, the Online Performance Evaluation and Learning Support (OPELS) software and process provides the needed training and feedback information both for employee learners and managers. The program aims at ongoing training and development and employee-manager targets, action plans, and check-off points.

Before creating training and development programs, managers should perform a **needs assessment** in which they determine which employees need training or development and what type of skills or knowledge they need to acquire (see Figure 11.5).[32]

Issues in Career Development

A career is "the evolving sequence of a person's work experiences over time."[33] As individuals progress through their lives, they may get promoted, change employers, or even become self-employed. All of this constitutes one's career. There are benefits to effective career development: It improves satisfaction and self-esteem, reduces stress, and strengthens an individual's psychological and physical health.[34] It also helps the organization because employees become better suited to meet organizational needs.

training
Teaching organizational members how to perform their current jobs and helping them acquire the knowledge and skills they need to be effective performers.

development
Building the knowledge and skills of organizational members so that they will be prepared to take on new responsibilities and challenges.

needs assessment
An assessment to determine which employees need training or development and what type of skills or knowledge they need to acquire.

FIGURE 11.5 | Training and Development

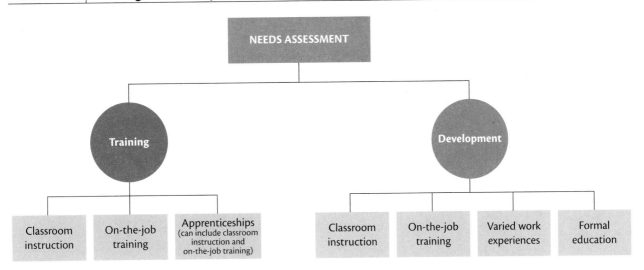

One of the new realities over the past few years is the social networking capabilities of websites such Facebook, Friendster, and MySpace, which are evolving at tremendous speed. These sites "are becoming, for some users, platforms from which to network for job leads, to forge professional contacts, or even to announce to friends that you are out of work." In addition, "savvy users say the sites can be effective tools for promoting one's job skills and all-around business networking. Even human resource professionals are encouraging people to log on." Marilyn Mackes, the executive director for the U.S. National Association of Colleges and Employers, published that whereas in the past employers used social-networking sites "to check profiles of potential hires," today "more than half will use the sites to network with potential candidates."[35]

The issue of career development and who is responsible for making sure it happens has become a national issue. The federal government is predicting "a looming national employment crisis" because of an aging and shrinking labour force.[36] Within 10 to 15 years, there will not be enough employable young people to replace those who are retiring. There is also concern that employees need to develop more job-related skills due to the increase in technology and the demands of the information economy. There is no single answer as to who should take action to resolve the issue of skills training: government, employers, or employees.

Human Resources Development Canada (HRDC) proposed, in 2001, a plan to increase the skills of Canada's workforce. The plan's main proposals included encouraging individuals to retrain and pursue lifelong learning; giving incentives to private industry to make employee training a top priority; increasing the numbers of skilled immigrants and speeding up their accreditation; and bringing traditionally unemployed groups into the labour force. The HRDC proposal faced serious controversy and is only one way of trying to resolve the skills crisis in Canada.

Organizations benefit when they offer career development programs:[37] They can make sure that the right people will be available for changing staffing needs, increase workforce diversity, and help employees get a better understanding of what is expected in various positions, that is, to have more realistic job expectations. At SaskPower, the leadership training program was started because management

Human Resources Development Canada
www.hrdc-drhc.gc.ca

SaskPower Corporation
www.saskpower.com

recognized that an aging workforce and rapid turnover in the executive ranks would otherwise lead to a lack of leadership experience in the company. The training program also helps individuals see whether they really want to move up the management ranks.

Performance Appraisal and Feedback

THINK ABOUT IT

Performance Review Ritual[38]

"Here we go again! It's that time of year!"

One can almost hear these voices as the time for the annual or semiannual performance review time comes around.

Ideally, this is a time for managers and their direct reports to "agree on what is important, how to measure success or failure in the future, and how to reward it," says Akhil Bhandari, chief information officer at CCL Industries Inc. What often happens instead can be the exact opposite: demotivation, frustration, dread, and cynicism.

To avoid the downsides and the ritualistic feeling often accompanying performance appraisals, here is a checklist to keep them effective:[39]

1. Align objectives specifically to the job and its contribution to corporate value.
2. Provide regular and consistent feedback so that the review does not come as a surprise to the employee.
3. Do your homework so that you know what you are talking about and can provide encouragement and competency.
4. Shorten the review process to a short checklist that shows everyone what they need to do and by what date.
5. Weigh your criticism to keep it balanced, fair, and remotivating.
6. Use flexible rating systems so that employees do not feel they are boxed in.
7. Reward star performers because they are the ones who need recognition.
8. Listen *and* respond so that the review process is simply not one-sided.
9. Do not invent "weaknesses" just because there is an area on the performance review sheet for "improvement".
10. Support transparency by sharing average statistics, similar to what happens when students receive their grades.
11. Be honest, by being appreciative, direct, and constructive.
12. Follow up, that is, do what you said you would do, no later than a month after the review.

You Be the Manager

1. After reviewing the above performance review checklist, what factors are important to you? Why?
2. What areas would give you the most challenge? Why?

---

performance appraisal
The evaluation of employees' job performance and contributions to their organization.

The recruitment and selection and the training and development components of a human resource management system ensure that employees have the knowledge and skills they need to be effective now and in the future. Performance appraisal and feedback complement recruitment, selection, training, and development. **Performance appraisal** is the evaluation of employees' job performance and contributions to their organization. **Performance feedback** is the process through which managers share performance appraisal information with their subordinates, give subordinates an opportunity to reflect on their own performance, and develop, with subordinates, plans for the future. In order for performance feedback to occur, performance appraisal must take place. Performance appraisal could take place without providing performance feedback, but wise managers are careful to provide feedback because it can contribute to employee motivation and performance.

Performance appraisal and feedback contribute to the effective management of human resources in two ways. Performance appraisal gives managers important information on which to base human resource decisions.[40] Decisions about pay raises, bonuses, promotions, and job moves all hinge on the accurate appraisal of performance. Performance appraisal also can help managers determine which workers are candidates for training and development and in what areas. Performance feedback encourages high levels of employee motivation and performance. It alerts good performers that their efforts are valued and appreciated and alerts poor performers that their lacklustre performance needs improvement. Performance feedback can provide both good and poor performers with insight into their strengths and weaknesses and ways in which they can improve their performance in the future.

Graphic Rating Scale Method

The most popular method of employee performance appraisal is called the graphic rating scale method. In this method, the appraiser scores the employee on a number of characteristics that reflect performance levels in such areas as quality, productivity, job knowledge, reliability, availability, and ability to work independently or in a team. Specific behavioural descriptions are used for each area that relate to the current job requirements. Points are assigned for each rating and are totalled and averaged for an overall performance score. See Figure 11.6.

performance feedback
The process through which managers share performance appraisal information with subordinates, give subordinates an opportunity to reflect on their own performance, and develop, with subordinates, plans for the future.

FIGURE 11.6 | **Elements Included in a Graphic Rating Scale Performance Appraisal**

Factors	Rating	Scale	Points and comments
Quality—The degree of excellence and thoroughness of the work performed	**Outstanding**—Performance is exceptional and superior to others	100–90	☐
Productivity—The amount of work done in a specific period	**Very good**—High levels of performance that consistently exceed requirements	90–80	☐
Job knowledge—The specialized skills and information used on the job	**Good**—Competent and reliable level of performance	80–70	☐
Reliability—The degree of trustworthiness to complete the task and follow up	**Improvement needed**—Performance falls below requirements in some areas	70–60	☐
Availability—The rate of absenteeism and punctuality of the employee	**Unsatisfactory**—Performance levels are unacceptable	Below 60	☐
Independence—The degree to which the employee must be supervised			☐
Team work—The ability to work well as a member of a group			☐

Who Appraises Performance?

We have been assuming that managers or the supervisors of employees evaluate performance. This is a pretty fair assumption, as supervisors are the most common appraisers of performance. Performance appraisal is an important part of most managers' job duties. It is managers' responsibility to motivate their subordinates to perform at a high level, and managers make many of the decisions that hinge on performance appraisals, such as decisions about pay raises or promotions. Appraisals by managers can, however, be usefully supplemented by appraisals from other sources (see Figure 11.7).

Although appraisals from each of these sources can be useful, managers need to be aware of potential issues that may arise when they are used. Subordinates sometimes may be inclined to inflate self-appraisals, especially if organizations are downsizing and they are worried about their job security. Managers who are appraised by their subordinates may fail to take needed but unpopular actions for fear that their subordinates will appraise them negatively.

360-Degree Performance Appraisals

360-degree appraisal
A performance appraisal by peers, subordinates, superiors, and sometimes clients who are in a position to evaluate a manager's performance.

To improve motivation and performance, some organizations include **360-degree appraisals** and feedback in their performance appraisal systems, especially for managers. In a 360-degree appraisal, an individual's performance is appraised by a variety of people, such as self, peers or co-workers, subordinates, superiors, and sometimes even customers or clients. The individual receives feedback based on evaluations from these multiple sources.

The growing number of companies using 360-degree appraisals and feedback includes Celestica (Toronto); InSystems (Markham, Ontario); Dominion Information Services (Burnaby, BC); and Hudson's Bay (Toronto). A 360-degree appraisal and feedback is not always as clear-cut as it might seem. On the one hand, some subordinates may try to get back at their managers by giving them negative evaluations, especially when evaluations are anonymous (to encourage honesty and openness). On the other hand, some managers may coach subordinates to give—or even threaten punishment if they fail to give—positive evaluations.

FIGURE 11.7 | Who Appraises Performance?

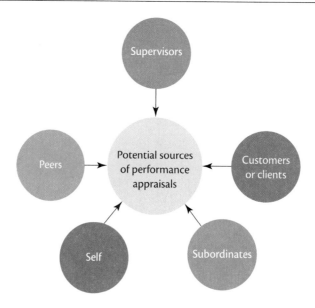

Peers often are very knowledgeable about performance but may be reluctant to provide an accurate and negative appraisal of someone they like or a positive appraisal of someone they dislike. In addition, whenever peers, subordinates, or anyone else evaluates an employee's performance, managers must be sure that the evaluators are actually knowledgeable about the performance dimensions being assessed. For example, subordinates should not evaluate their supervisor's decision-making if they have little opportunity to observe this dimension of his or her performance.

These potential problems with 360-degree appraisals and feedback do not mean that they are not useful. Rather, they suggest that in order for 360-degree appraisals and feedback to be effective, trust is needed throughout the organization. More generally, trust is a critical ingredient in any performance appraisal and feedback procedure. Managers using 360-degree appraisals and feedback also have to consider carefully the pros and cons of using anonymous evaluations and of using the results of the appraisals for decision-making about important issues such as pay raises.[41]

Effective Performance Feedback

In order for the performance appraisal and feedback component of a human resource management system to encourage and motivate high performance, managers must provide their subordinates with performance feedback. To generate useful information to pass on to subordinates, managers can use both formal and informal appraisals. **Formal appraisals** are conducted at set times during the year and are based on performance dimensions and measures that have been specified in advance. A salesperson, for example, may be evaluated by his or her manager twice a year on the performance dimensions of sales and customer service, sales being measured from sales reports and customer service being measured by the number of complaints received. **Informal appraisals**—unscheduled appraisals of ongoing progress and areas for improvement—may occur at the request of the employee.

An integral part of a formal appraisal is a meeting between the manager and the subordinate in which the subordinate is given feedback on his or her performance.

Managers often dislike providing performance feedback, especially when the feedback is negative, but doing so is an important managerial activity. Here are some guidelines for effectively giving performance feedback that will contribute to employee motivation and performance:

- Be specific and focus on behaviours or outcomes that are correctable and within a worker's ability to improve. *Example:* Telling a salesperson that he or she is too shy when interacting with customers is likely to do nothing more than lower the person's self-confidence and prompt him or her to become defensive. A more effective approach is to give the salesperson feedback about specific behaviours to engage in—greeting customers as soon as they enter the department, asking customers whether they need help, and volunteering to help customers find items if they seem to be having trouble.

- Approach performance appraisal as an exercise in problem-solving and solution-finding, not criticizing. *Example:* Rather than criticizing a financial analyst for turning reports in late, the manager helps the analyst determine why the reports are late and identify ways to better manage time.

- Express confidence in a subordinate's ability to improve. *Example:* Instead of being skeptical, a first-level manager tells a subordinate in confidence that the subordinate can increase quality levels.

formal appraisal
An appraisal conducted at a set time during the year and based on performance dimensions and measures that were specified in advance.

informal appraisal
An unscheduled appraisal of ongoing progress and areas for improvement.

- Provide performance feedback both formally and informally. *Example:* The staff of a preschool receives feedback from formal performance appraisals twice a year. The director of the school also provides frequent informal feedback such as complimenting staff members on creative ideas for special projects, noticing when they do a particularly good job of handling a difficult child, and pointing out when they provide inadequate supervision.

- Praise instances of high performance and areas of a job in which an employee excels. *Example:* Rather than focusing on just the negative, a manager discusses the areas the subordinate excels in as well as areas in need of improvement.

- Avoid personal criticisms, and treat subordinates with respect. *Example:* An engineering manager acknowledges subordinates' expertise and treats them as professionals. Even when the manager points out performance problems to subordinates, it is important to refrain from criticizing them personally.

- Agree to a timetable for performance improvements. *Example:* A first-level manager and subordinate decide to meet again in one month to determine whether quality has improved.

In following these guidelines, managers need to keep in mind why they are giving performance feedback: to encourage high levels of motivation and performance. Moreover, the information that managers gather through performance appraisal and feedback helps them determine how to distribute pay raises and bonuses.

Tips for Managers

BUILDING TEAMS FOR HIGH PERFORMANCE[42]

1. Do performance appraisals on a more or less frequent basis so that the formal occurrence will not bring up surprises.

2. Make sure you have adequate training in administering a performance appraisal process.

3. Focus on making the performance review process a problem-solving process.

4. Minimize defensiveness to the best of your ability.

Pay and Benefits

In Chapter 8, we discussed the ways in which pay can be used to motivate organizational members to perform at a high level. Here we focus on how organizations determine their pay levels and pay structures.

Pay Level

Pay includes employees' base salaries, pay raises, and bonuses and is determined by a number of factors, including characteristics of the organization and of the job and levels of performance. **Pay level** is a broad comparative concept that refers to how an organization's pay incentives compare, in general, to those of other organizations in the same industry employing similar kinds of workers. Managers must decide whether they want to offer relatively high wages, average wages, or relatively low wages. High wages help ensure that an organization is going to be able to recruit, select, and retain high performers, but high wages also raise costs. Low wages give an organization a

pay level
The relative position of an organization's pay incentives in comparison with those of other organizations in the same industry employing similar kinds of workers.

cost advantage but may undermine the organization's ability to select and recruit high performers and motivate current employees to perform at a high level. Either of these situations may lead to inferior quality or inferior customer service.

In determining pay levels, managers should take their organization's strategy into account. A high pay level may prohibit managers from effectively pursuing a low-cost strategy. But a high pay level may be well worth the added costs in an organization whose competitive advantage lies in superior quality and excellent customer service. As one might expect, hotel and motel chains with a low-cost strategy, such as Days Inn and Hampton Inns, have lower pay levels than do chains striving to provide high-quality rooms and services, such as Four Seasons and Hyatt Regency.

Business Plan Checklist

- Conduct a job analysis for each employee position.
- Determine how you will recruit, select, train, appraise, and compensate your employees. Include this in the Human Resources section of the Operation plan in Appendix A.
- What are the risks, and how will you minimize them?
- Use this information for section 7 of the business plan, the Organization Plan in Appendix A.

Pay Structure

After deciding on a pay level, managers have to establish a pay structure for the different jobs in the organization. A **pay structure** clusters jobs into categories that reflect their relative importance to the organization and its goals, levels of skills required, and other characteristics that managers consider important. Pay ranges are established for each job category. Individual job holders' pay within job categories is then determined by such factors as performance, seniority, and skill levels.

There is quite a difference between public and private sector pay structures. On average, governments at all three levels (federal, provincial, and local) pay a premium of about 9 percent to their employees, compared with private sector jobs. Public sector employees are also more likely to be covered by pension plans. Despite the seeming differences between public and private sector wages, it is generally women and less-skilled workers who get higher wages for working in the public sector. Managers, especially male managers, do not get paid much more for working in the public sector. Moreover, at the federal level, senior managers are paid less than they might earn in the private sector. There is also far more wage compression in the public sector. In the private sector, on average, individuals in managerial, administrative, or professional occupations are paid 41-percent more than those in service occupations. In the public sector, it is not uncommon for managers to be paid only 10-percent more than other employees.[43]

pay structure
The arrangement of jobs into categories that reflect their relative importance to the organization and its goals, levels of skill required, and other characteristics.

Benefits

Employee benefits are based on membership in an organization (and not necessarily on the particular job held) and include sick days, vacation days, and medical and life insurances. Organizations are legally required to provide certain benefits to their employees, including workers' compensation, social insurance, and employment insurance. Workers' compensation provides employees with financial assistance if they become unable to work because of a work-related injury or illness. Social insurance provides financial assistance to retirees and disabled former employees. Employment insurance provides financial assistance to employees who lose their jobs through no fault of their own.

Other benefits—such as extended health insurance, dental insurance, vacation time, pension plans, life insurance, flexible working hours, company-provided daycare, and employee assistance and wellness programs—are provided at the option of employers. Benefits mandated by public policy and benefits provided at the option of employers cost organizations a substantial amount of money.

In some organizations, top managers decide which benefits might best suit the organization and employees and offer the same benefit package to all employees. Other organizations, realizing that employees' needs and desires for benefits might differ, offer **cafeteria-style benefit plans** that let employees themselves choose the benefits they want, from among such options as flextime, tuition credits, and extended medical and dental plans. Some organizations have success with cafeteria-style plans, while others find them difficult to manage.

cafeteria-style benefit plan
A plan from which employees can choose the benefits that they want.

Labour Relations

Labour relations are the activities that managers engage in to ensure that they have effective working relationships with the labour unions that represent their employees' interests. As a way to deal with unethical and unfair treatment of workers, the federal and provincial governments created and enforce the Canada Labour Code, the Canadian Human Rights Act, and provincial Employment Standards laws so that unions are more effective than codes and laws in protecting their rights. However, some employees believe that unions will be more effective than codes and laws in protecting their rights.

The first step in the labour relations process is for workers to seek collective representation to further their interests in the organization. The reasons they might desire to unionize are many:

labour relations
The activities that managers engage in to ensure that they have effective working relationships with the labour unions that represent their employees' interests.

- Shareholder interests overshadow those of the workers
- Dissatisfaction with wages, benefits, and working conditions
- Lack of a safe work environment
- Lack of job security
- Lack of proper training
- Perceived inequities in pay
- Unfair policies and practices
- Dissatisfaction with management
- Inability to communicate concerns and effect change
- Lack of opportunities for advancement, growth, and role in decision-making

FIGURE 11.8 | The Process of Labour Relations

- The belief that unionization may improve working conditions

- The belief that a united group wields more power than an individual

There are also forces that can resist the campaign to organize a union. Individual workers may reject unionization for a number of reasons, including the perception that the leaders are corrupt, or they simply do not want to pay union dues. In order for a union to become the bargaining unit for a group of employees, it must attain acceptance by the majority of eligible employees and be certified by the Labour Relations Board (LRB). See Figure 11.8. Employers must make sure they do not question employees about their union activities or use "undue influence" by promising to increase wages and benefits in a way that could be perceived as a bribe for remaining nonunionized or, for that matter, by threatening employee's jobs if they support unionization.

Once a union is recognized by the employer and the LRB as the bargaining unit for a group of employees, negotiations then take place between the labour union and the employer to arrive at a mutually acceptable **collective agreement** pertaining to the terms and conditions of employment for a specified period of time. Once a collective agreement is signed, both the union members and the management are required to abide by the provisions. When disagreements over the administration of the agreement or violations of the terms arise, they are handled and settled by the *grievance procedure*. When the timeframe of the agreement has ended and a new collective agreement has not been reached, neither party is bound by its terms and conditions. In such a case, the union is in a legal strike position, and the employer has the potential to lock out the workers. In 2009, the management of the popular daily newspaper *Le Journal de Montreal* locked out 250 editorial and office workers.[44] Both *strikes* and *lockouts* involve work stoppages. In 2008, there were 14 work stoppages involving 500 or more employees in Canada.[45]

collective agreement
A mutually agreed upon set of provisions that govern working conditions between a union and an employer for a set period of time.

Trends in Labour Relations

Canada and the United States have differential rates of unionization. Statistics Canada shows that in 2003, 31 percent of the Canadian workforce was unionized, down from the 38 percent in 1981. In the United States, only 14.8 percent of the workers are unionized. Declines in the industrial sectors of the economy, such as manufacturing, where unions have traditionally been strong are often viewed as the reasons for declining unionization in the United States. The growth in service sector employment, which is often viewed as more difficult to organize is also seen as a reason. In Canada, however, almost 40 percent of service workers are unionized, while approximately 7 percent belong to unions in the United States. On the macro level, the main argument for differences between the countries is labour law and the structure of the political system in each country.[46]

Several provincial governments have passed legislation in the last decade that hinders the impact of unions. In late 2001, Ontario changed its Labour Relations Act to require employers to post information in the workplace about how a union can be decertified. In the 2000–2001 fiscal year in Ontario, there were 521 certifications and 59 decertifications. In the next year, there were 307 certifications and 85 decertifications. In Quebec, the government managed to push through legislation to force the reduction of the number of unions bargaining in such institutions as hospitals. In one case, the number of unions dropped from 88 to 4. Other legislation, despite strong union objections, made it easier for public institutions such as hospitals to outsource some services, for example, food and laundry services.[47] In Saskatchewan, Bill 6, Trade Union Amendment Act, 2008, came into force on May 14, 2008, and made significant amendments to the Trade Union Act (TUA). Any application for certification or decertification of a union must now be determined by a mandatory secret ballot vote. Furthermore, the level of employee support necessary for an application for certification or decertification, previously unspecified in the TUA (except in the case of an application to displace a certified union, which was set at 25 percent), is now fixed at 45 percent. Finally, the timeframe within which evidence of employee support must be obtained has been reduced to 90 days and employers have been given more leeway to communicate facts and opinions to their employees during union drives.[48]

The impact of labour relations on human resource management is considerable. Once a collective agreement is signed, the HR department typically expands to include a labour relations specialist and thus affects the organizational structure of the company. Managers may have their power to make decisions diminished as union leaders typically increase their participation in issues that affect their members. Reward power is lessened, as pay levels and pay structures are set out in the terms of the collective agreement. Some managers resent the loss of authority that having to abide by the collective agreement sometimes entails. HR managers tend to keep more paper records of employee assignments and behaviours, as this is crucial at grievance and arbitration hearings. Overall, union leaders and managers must recognize the need to build effective cooperative working relationships in order to remain competitive long before they get to the bargaining table to negotiate a collective agreement. It is in their mutual interests to ensure that labour strife is avoided.

Summary and Review

1. **THE LEGAL FRAMEWORK OF HRM** There are several key pieces of legislation that govern the management of human resources in Canada. The Canadian Human Rights Act and the Employment Standards Act ensure minimum employee entitlements are standardized across the country and that *intentional and unintentional discrimination* is prohibited based on specific grounds.

2. **STRATEGIC HUMAN RESOURCE MANAGEMENT** *Human resource management* (HRM) includes all the activities that managers use to ensure that their organizations are able to attract, retain, and utilize human resources effectively. *Strategic HRM* is the process by which managers design the components of an HRM system to be consistent with each other, with other elements of organizational architecture, and with the organization's strategies and goals. *Human resource planning* includes all the activities managers engage in to forecast their current and future needs for human resources. *Job analysis* is the process of identifying (1) the tasks,

duties, and responsibilities that make up a job and (2) the knowledge, skills, and abilities needed to perform the job.

3. **MAJOR COMPONENTS OF HRM** *Recruitment and selection* includes all the activities that managers engage in to develop a pool of qualified applicants for open positions. *Selection* is the process by which managers determine the relative qualifications of job applicants and their potential for performing well in a particular job. *Training and Development* focuses on teaching organizational members how to perform effectively in their current jobs. Development focuses on broadening organizational members' knowledge and skills so that employees will be prepared to take on new responsibilities and challenges. As part of the training and development process, organizations and individuals need to consider the career development of employees. *Performance Appraisal and Feedback* is the evaluation of employees' job performance and contributions to their organization. *Performance feedback* is the process through which managers share performance appraisal information with their subordinates; give subordinates an opportunity to reflect on their own performance; and help subordinates develop plans for the future. Performance appraisal provides managers with useful information for decision making. Performance feedback can encourage high levels of motivation and performance. *Pay and Benefits* is the relative position of an organization's pay incentives in comparison with those of other organizations in the same industry employing similar kinds of employees. A *pay structure* clusters jobs into categories that reflect their relative importance to the organization and its goals, levels of skill required, and other characteristics. Pay ranges are established for each job category. Organizations are legally required to provide certain benefits to their employees; other benefits are provided at the discretion of employers. *Labour Relations* are the activities that managers engage in to ensure that they have effective working relationships with the labour unions that represent their employees' interests.

Key Terms

360-degree appraisal, p. 354

ability tests, p. 348

behavioural interview questions, p. 348

cafeteria-style benefit plan, p. 358

collective agreement, p. 359

development, p. 350

formal appraisal, p. 355

human resource management (HRM), p. 340

human resource planning, p. 342

informal appraisal, p. 355

intentional discrimination, p. 340

job analysis, p. 342

labour relations, p. 358

lateral move, p. 346

needs assessment, p. 350

outsourcing, p. 346

pay level, p. 356

pay structure, p. 357

performance appraisal, p. 352

performance feedback, p. 353

performance tests, p. 349

personality tests, p. 349

personnel replacement charts, p. 342

realistic job preview (RJP), p. 349

recruitment, p. 345

reliable selection techniques, p. 347

selection, p. 345

situational interview questions, p. 347

strategic human resource management, p. 341

structured interview, p. 348

training, p. 350

unintentional discrimination, p. 340

unstructured interview, p. 348

valid selection techniques, p. 347

Wrap-Up to Opening Case

We began this chapter by examining what Prem Benimadhu, vice-president of governance and HRM at the Conference Board of Canada, pointed out—how ill-prepared business is in relation to the aging of the workforce. This is an HR issue not only from the perspective of the problem but also from the planning that HR and business need to do to manage it.

For Benimadhu there is a real opportunity here for younger people today. He says, "It's great to be young today."[49] If by 2016, as Statistics Canada points out, roughly 20 percent of the workforce will be in the 55–64 years age range, HR practitioners have only a few short years to plan effectively for this reality. There is the possibility of a real imbalance: more employees in the aging category than those entering the workforce! Benimadhu says that businesses are aware of the situation but doing very little about it.

To compensate for fewer younger employees—hence, the term "war on talent" or "talent gap"—and greater numbers of aging employees, in addition to planning, HR must consider issues such as developing effective retention strategies for existing employees who make a considerable contribution; designing health, safety, and ergonomic strategies for older employees; and implementing effective retention and training strategies.[50] In other words, "Managing talent is the most critical human resources (HR) challenge worldwide and will remain at or near the top of executive agendas in every region and industry for the foreseeable future, according to a new global study conducted by the Boston Consulting Group (BCG) and the World Federation of Personnel Management Associations (WFPMA)/Canadian Council of Human Resources Associations (CCHRA).[51]

Of course, a key for HR in managing the new workplace will be how two different groupings of employees—aging and younger—will be able to interact well. Garth Whyte, executive vice-president of the Canadian Federation of Independent Business, pointed out in the opening case that his "federation members, mostly owners of small and medium-sized businesses, will be forced to hire underqualified people, ignore business opportunities, or put in longer hours themselves."

Peter B. Vaill coined the term "permanent white water" to refer to the "complex, turbulent, changing environment in which we are all trying to operate." He writes, "Permanent white water conditions are regularly taking us out of our comfort zones and asking things of us that we never imagined would be required. Permanent white water means permanent life outside one's comfort zone."[52]

Knowledge is the competitive advantage today. Recruiting the right people, training and developing them, rewarding them appropriately, providing feedback, and building succession plans are the key human resource steps to ensure this competitive advantage. Managers must adopt planned approaches to HRM. In today's new economy, learning is the basis for ongoing organizational success. Managers need to subscribe, both in theory and in practice, to developing a corporate culture that is deeply embedded in the learning process. Again, Vaill provides us insight:

> Learning as a way of being is a whole mentality. It is a way of being in the world.... More than just a skill, learning as a way of being is a whole posture toward experience, a way of framing or interpreting all experience as a learning opportunity or learning process. 'Why must anyone seek for new ways of acting?' asked the biologist J.Z. Young. "The answer is that in the long run the continuity of life itself depends on the making of new experiments. ... [T]he continuous invention of new ways of observing man's [sic] special secret of living."[53]

Authors Daniel H. Kim and Eileen Mullen describe what they call the spirit of the learning organization. "In a 'spirited' learning organization," say these authors, "the energy released with this kind of freedom is infectious. People like to come into this kind of space. When we do not have to censor what we really think and care about, we have more energy to devote to creating something that really matters to us."[54]

Learning a living: the heart-and-soul of today's management of human resources.

Management in Action

Topics for Discussion and Action

Level 1

1. Describe the five components of an HRM system.
2. Discuss the reasons why an organization might outsource its human resources. What problems can arise?
3. Describe the best way for managers to give performance feedback to subordinates.

Level 2

4. Discuss why it is important for the components of the HRM system to be in sync with an organization's strategy and goals and with each other.
5. Interview a manager in a local organization to determine how that organization recruits and selects employees.

6. How can managers avoid charges of discrimination in their hiring practices? Describe the legal framework of HRM in Canada.

Level 3

7. Evaluate the pros and cons of 360-degree performance appraisals and feedback. Would you like your performance to be appraised in this manner? Why, or why not?
8. Discuss why two restaurants in the same community might have different pay levels.
9. Listen to Jack and Suzy Welch's podcast called "Team Building: Wrong and Right" at www.businessweek.com/mediacenter/qt/podcasts/welchway/welchway_11_14_08%201.mp3. What three things do they argue a leader should not do when hiring and putting together a high-performing team?

Building Management Skills

Answer the following questions about the organization you have chosen to follow:

1. Find out and report on how your organization plans for its human resources. What are the forces operating on this firm that make it easy or difficult to forecast its future supply of and demand for employees?
2. Describe the training and development programs for employees and managers in this organization.
3. What methods of employee performance appraisals are used in this company? How are they different for different categories of employees?

4. Describe the company's compensation and benefits system. Would this system motivate you to work for this company? Why, or why not?
5. Discuss whether or not the company's HRM system is compatible with its strategy and organizational structure. If not, make recommendations as to how to reach a better fit.
6. If the organization is unionized, describe the state of its labour relations.

Management for You

ANALYZING HUMAN RESOURCES MANAGEMENT SYSTEMS

Think about your current job or a job that you had in the past. If you have never had a job, then interview a friend or family member who is currently working. Answer the following questions about the job you have chosen:

1. How are people recruited and selected for this job? Are the recruitment and selection procedures that the organization uses effective or ineffective? Why?
2. What training and development do people who hold this job receive? Is it appropriate? Why, or why not?

3. How is performance of this job appraised? Does performance feedback contribute to motivation and high performance on this job?
4. What levels of pay and benefits are provided for this job? Are these levels of pay and benefits appropriate? Why, or why not?

Small Group Breakout Exercise

BUILDING A HUMAN RESOURCES MANAGEMENT SYSTEM

Form groups of three or four, and appoint one group member as the spokesperson who will communicate your findings to the whole class when called upon by the instructor. Then discuss the following scenario:

You and your two or three partners are engineers with a business minor who have decided to start a consulting business. Your goal is to provide manufacturing-process engineering and other engineering services to large and small organizations. You forecast that there will be an increased use of outsourcing for these activities. You have discussed with managers in several large organizations the services you plan to offer, and they have expressed considerable interest. You have secured funding to start the business and are now building the HRM system. Your human resources planning suggests that you need to hire between five and eight experienced engineers with good communication skills, two clerical/secretarial workers, and two MBAs who between them will have financial, accounting, and human resources skills. You are striving to develop an in-house approach to building your human resources that will enable your new business to prosper.

1. Describe the steps you will take to recruit and select (a) the engineers, (b) the clerical/secretarial workers, and (c) the MBAs.
2. Describe the training and development the engineers, the clerical/secretarial workers, and the MBAs will receive.
3. Describe how you will appraise the performance of each group of employees and how you will provide feedback.
4. Describe the pay level and pay structure of your consulting firm.

Business Planning Exercise

After reading this chapter, you and your business planning team realize that you must develop a human resources plan for your venture and include this in your business plan. Using the HRM tools in this chapter, answer the following:

1. How will you
   a. recruit,
   b. select, and
   c. train and develop your employees?
2. Write a job description and specification for a bartender (if appropriate) and other personnel you will need to hire in your first year of operation.
3. How you will appraise your employees' performances?
   - Refer to the material in the chapter to determine the methods of appraising employee performance that would be appropriate for your organization.
4. How much should you pay each category of employees for their inputs?
   - Will you offer wages at, above, or below the industry standards? Justify your answer in terms of the strategy of the venture.
5. What, if any, benefits will you offer aside from the mandatory benefits?
   - Determine the mandatory benefits you must provide as an employer in your province. Describe these and others you intend to provide. What are the costs of these benefits, and why would you offer them to your employees?

Managing Ethically

Nadia Burowsky has recently been promoted to a managerial position in a large downtown bank. Before her promotion, she was one of a group of bank tellers who got together weekly and complained about their jobs. Burowsky enjoyed these get-togethers because she is recently divorced, and they provided a bit of a social life for her. In Burowsky's new role, she will be conducting performance appraisals and making decisions about pay raises and promotions for these same tellers. Burowsky reports to you, and you are aware of her former weekly get-togethers with the tellers. Is it ethical for her to continue attending these social functions? How might she effectively manage having relationships with co-workers and evaluating them?

Exploring the World Wide Web

SPECIFIC ASSIGNMENT

Visit the official website of Cirque du Soleil at www.cirquedusoleil.com and click on "Jobs." Follow the links to learn about life at Cirque, working conditions, and other aspects of recruitment at this company. Report your findings.

GENERAL ASSIGNMENT

Find websites of two companies that try to recruit new employees by means of the World Wide Web. Are their approaches to recruitment on the web similar or different? What are the potential advantages of the approaches of each? What are the potential disadvantages?

McGraw-Hill Connect™—Available 24/7 with instant feedback so you can study when you want, how you want, and where you want. Take advantage of the Study Plan—an innovative tool that helps you customize your learning experience. You can diagnose your knowledge with pre- and post-tests, identify the areas where you need help, search the entire learning package for content specific to the topic you're studying, and add these resources to your personalized study plan. Visit www.mcgrawhillconnect.ca to register—take practice quizzes, search the e-book, and much more.

Be the Manager

As Canada's economy grew stronger after the recession of 2008–2009, a new power emerged in the executive suite. Many companies began shifting from cutback-survival mode to embracing such enlightened concepts as growth, expansion, and a healthy corporate culture. Canada's human resource specialists finally began getting away from planning layoffs and calculating severance packages to building productive teams, enhancing employee motivation, and creating a winning corporate culture. In some companies, HR's new role is not just evolutionary but revolutionary. A prominent medical products company, for instance, recently appointed its HR vice-president as VP of marketing. One large retailer promoted its former head of HR to country manager. In a recovering economy, it figured its biggest challenge is not merchandising, but improving the quality of customer service and building staff morale. Similarly, a high-tech firm created a senior HR position to forge a new corporate culture. The company knew it had more than enough software engineers on staff (most of them recruited right out of college) but realized it now needed more people who could challenge the culture—develop new markets, build relationships, and foster risk-taking in a company that had always talked things to death. The HR executive's mandate: Find tech-savvy business leaders and hire them now, even if their job does not exist yet. Because of your expertise, your advice is now being sought by a well-known mid-sized company in your area.

Question

1. What course of action would you recommend to the executives to fulfill their mandate?

Management Case

The Brazen Careerist Speaks Out![55]

Generation Y is moving up in the professional world; and they are bringing a new set of ideals, values, tech tools, and perspectives that may upset the status quo.

Penelope Trunk, author, blogger, and *Boston Globe* columnist, shares her insight on the generational differences shaping the workspace on *The Brazen Careerist*. But be forewarned that you never know what to expect on Trunk's blog: part career advice, part entrepreneurialism, part marketing, part techy, and many times personal, controversial, and opinionated, she writes as if the filter is off and seemingly without regard to the reactions in the comments section.

Trunk's "10 Reasons Why Generation Y's Conservatism is Mistaken for Craziness" might help people understand that generation better:

1. More than 60 percent of Generation Y goes back home to their parents after college or university. If they go home to their parents and give themselves a buffer, the more likely they will find a job that is suitable for them. They are willing to trade freedom for a great job.
2. Those between the ages 18 and 32 change jobs every 18 months. Job hopping makes them more engaged because they are always trying something new. It keeps the learning curve high, increases their skill set, and grows their network.
3. They have no loyalty to a company, but they have a lot of loyalty to the project they are on. If you are a good manager, they will be loyal to you.
4. They ignore school. They think getting good grades does not help them and good grades are not relevant to school. They may not be reading great literature, but 80 percent are getting good internships.
5. Entrepreneurship is a safety net for them. If they hate their job, they think they can start a company in their parents' basements.

6. They will not take entry-level work. Do not have them do stupid, meaningless work to climb the ladder because there are no ladders anymore. There is no reason to pay your dues if you are job hopping.
7. They want to leave work early a lot and use family as a justification. They will ask you, "Don't you think family is more important than work?" Workplaces talk about family being important; but if the company does not support their family needs, Generation Y think work is lying to them.
8. They demand nonhierarchical structures, and they think everyone is a team. Everyone plays on the soccer team, even if they do not play well. They think anyone should hear their ideas—even the CEO.
9. Generation Y demands constant feedback. They want to be told they are doing well and not doing well in a delicate way. They want everyone to know that they are great. They want mentors and to be helped and that can only happen with feedback.
10. Baby boomers stage a protest and sign petitions when they do not like something, but Generation Y is conservative. They do not protest, they just leave. Be honest with them, and they will tell you what they need and what engages them. They put everything on the table and expect you to do the same.

Questions

1. After you review Trunk's "10 Reasons Why Generation Y's Conservatism is Mistaken for Craziness," which ones relate to you and why? Be honest with your self-assessment.
2. What would be your recommendations for an HR manager regarding these "Reasons"?

Video Management Case

Balancing work and life

Work-life balance is the hottest topic among human resource executives these days, and for a good reason. Most Canadians have a serious lack of balance, which is costing employers plenty. Companies have

introduced several practices to minimize the damage to time-stressed staff, such as fitness programs, career breaks, daycare centres, flex-time, job sharing, telework, and so on. But a major Canadian study has reported that Canadians are still stressed. University of Guelph professor Peter Hausdorf says that part of the problem is that employers do not want to deal with the main cause of poor work-life balance: workload. Carleton University professor Linda Duxbury asks how companies can afford not to help employees maintain a work/life balance. This CBC video program investigates these and other issues regarding work/life balance among Canadian employees.

Questions to consider

1. Explain how companies that encourage work-life balance might be more successful than those pushing more hours of work out of their staff.

2. Looking through other chapters in this book, identify topics that might explain why work/life balance is linked to employee performance and workplace productivity.

12

Managing Communication, Conflict, and Negotiation

Learning Outcomes

1. Describe the communication process.

2. Define information richness, and describe the information richness of communication media available to managers.

3. Describe important communication skills that individuals need as senders and receivers of messages.

4. Identify the sources of organizational conflict and how conflict is handled by individuals.

5. Describe conflict management strategies that managers can use to resolve individual and organizational conflict effectively.

6. Describe how distributive and integrative bargaining can be used to resolve intergroup conflict.

The Remote Communicator[1]

How does one avoid becoming a faceless and forgotten employee from a distance? With a robotic stand-in at the office.

If you are a teleworker, that is, you work in Halifax but your manager and company are in Waterloo, Ontario, how do you "show your face" and still communicate?

The answer is, you have a robot communicator stand in for you!

Software developer Ivan Bowman popped into his boss's office to discuss the latest computer code he was working on. His manager, Glenn Paulley, surprised him by closing the door and staring him straight in the eye. "Effective July 1, you're being promoted to distinguished engineer," said Paulley, the director of engineering.

Bowman smiled. It was a welcome step up at Sybase iAnywhere, the technology company in Waterloo, Ontario, where both work. "Wow," he said. "Thank you."

After discussing the fine print of the new position, manager and employee might have shaken hands to seal the deal. But Bowman was not exactly in hand-shaking range. Rather, he was about 1900 kilometres away, working from his home office in Halifax. It was not Bowman in the flesh who had swung by Paulley's office but a robotic version of him.

While more and more companies are trying to be flexible, what is known as "face-time" is still an important reminder of times past. In other words, even though you might be a teleworker, or working from home, "out of sight, out of mind" is a natural human tendency, in spite of everyone's best intentions. The difficulty is creating a presence for yourself, even though you are not physically at work. Hence the robot named IvanAnywhere!

How does this work for Bowman?

Sitting in front of a computer equipped with a Webcam, microphone, and a video game controller in his Halifax home, Bowman sends his face and voice to a robot roaming the Waterloo halls of Sybase iAnywhere, a subsidiary of Sybase Inc., based in Dublin, California.

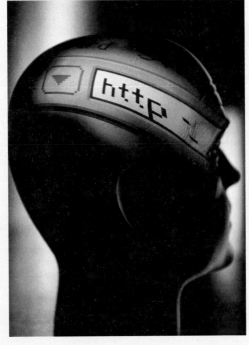

Nick Koudis/Getty Images

Dubbed IvanAnywhere, the robot, standing 1.7 metres tall, looks like a coat rack on four wheels. About halfway up an aluminum pole is a tablet computer, whose screen displays Bowman's face to his co-workers. Two speakers below it project his voice.

Above the tablet computer are a Webcam and microphone, which are used to transmit the co-workers' faces and voices back to Bowman in Halifax. *Skype software allows free, two-way communication over the Internet.*[2]

There is also a digital camera on the robot that Bowman can operate to snap photos of whiteboards in Waterloo for viewing in Halifax.

The robot usually remains stationary at a cubicle at Sybase iAnywhere's office while Bowman works. But if he needs to hop over to a co-worker's cubicle or swing by his boss's office, he can send the 36-kilogram robot anywhere around the floor on which his team is stationed at a top speed of almost 2½ kilometres an hour.

In the past 30 years, robotic technology has made leaps and bounds in fields as diverse as medicine, emergency rescue, and the space industry. Now, some employers have begun to examine how robotic technology can help remote workers feel closer to the office.

"I think that there's going to be a real push in this technology over the next little while," Paulley predicts.

There are now about 1.4 million Canadian teleworkers, according to Statistics Canada. A problem they still face is feeling part of the team from afar. "One of the things that people give up when they [work remotely] is the interaction you get from being in the office," says Jenny Burke, a research scientist and director of the human-robot interaction lab at the University of South Florida's Institute for Safety Security Rescue Technology. "In the old times, they would call it being around the water cooler. But just being physically present there—a lot of things go on, and sometimes if you're not there you can feel disconnected ... So [robotic technology] has the potential to allow you to gain some of that back," she says.

Now It's Your Turn

1. If you had a chance to be a teleworker and use a technology like IvanAnywhere, how would you respond to the opportunity?

◼◼◼◼ Overview

We can see from our opening scenario that distance does not always have to be an insurmountable problem in communicating with one another. We already know this from our experience with the telephone, Internet chat lines, and so on, but now we see it in action with teleworking: an employee living in one part of the country and still being "present" in the office via a robot.

In the office, communication is an essential component in the fabric of a healthy workplace. In addition to warding off toxic work environments, effective communication can be the lifeblood of work each day. Ineffective communication is detrimental for managers, employees, and organizations; it can lead to conflict, poor performance, strained interpersonal relations, poor service, and dissatisfied customers. Managers at all levels need to be good communicators in order for an organization to be effective and gain a competitive advantage.

In this chapter, we describe the nature of communication and the communication process and explain why it is so important for all managers and their subordinates to be effective communicators. We describe the communication media available to managers, and the factors that managers need to consider in selecting a communication medium for each message they send. We describe the communication skills that help individuals be effective senders and receivers of messages. We describe conflict, and the strategies that managers can use to resolve it effectively. We discuss one major conflict resolution technique—negotiation—in detail, outlining the steps managers can take to be good negotiators. By the end of this chapter, you will have a good appreciation of the nature of communication and the steps that all organizational members can take to ensure that they are effective communicators. You will also become aware of the skills necessary to manage organizational conflict.

L O 1

Communication and Organizations

THINK ABOUT IT ◼◼◼◼◼

Acting with Honesty and Empathy: Communicating in a Crisis[3]

Dr. Daniel F. Muzyka, dean and RBC Financial Group professor of entrepreneurship at the Sauder School of Business at the University of British Columbia, discusses communicating with honesty and empathy.

"Last month [May 2008], I was in China shortly after that country's devastating earth-quake, and witnessed the aftermath of this tragedy. The actions and communications of the Chinese government stood in stark contrast to the reaction of Myanmar's government after the recent cyclone, or the difficult situation following Hurricane Katrina. It all led me to consider the question: What makes for effective communications in a crisis situation?

The first thing to ensure is that primary communications in a crisis are undertaken by people on or near the ground in question: call it locality. We all know the difficulties inherent in relaying the truth through a room half a world away. Hurricane Katrina was a classic demonstration of this point.

It's also important to note how effective crisis communication relates to immediacy and energy. Crises and their evolution commonly "get away" from those who are not ready to deal with them—no matter what reluctance the legal department may have to get involved. You cannot wish a crisis away. Henry Kissinger once observed, wryly: "There cannot be a crisis next week. My schedule is already full." Alas, there is no such luxury.

If you are part of the crisis, you are involved and need to dedicate immediate and adequate effort to understanding and communicating the issues. And this has to be done with transparency. Even if it hurts, you must be open, telling what you know, what you don't know, and what you would like to know. You must be willing to answer all questions openly and permit others access so that they may share their observations. Help the media to ensure accurate reporting, through and including accurate, up-to-date background information and graphics.

A crisis is not the place to try to "frame the message"; it is not the time for the marketing department to reinforce the brand pyramid. Rather, it is a time for the organization to live the values behind the organization and brand through its actions. Yes, you can influence what people see, but mostly by being open. American Airlines recently faced this issue when many planes were pulled out of service for safety checks as a result of an FAA ruling. American's management realized the key issue wasn't about them or the perception of their safety, but the travel disruption it caused.

Honesty is the best—and only—policy. When people are trying to deal with the immediate impact of an unfolding negative event, being disingenuous or incomplete in order to guard future legal options only sows the seeds of something that may blow up in the short term but will backfire in the long run. Present the correct facts and corrected "facts."

Along with the truth, clarity is key. Those who have faced a crisis situation will recognize that Oscar Wilde's statement, that "Truth is rarely pure and never simple," is certainly operative. The reality is that the most successful communicators are those who can simplify and clarify.

Another element of successful communications is constancy. Communicating in a crisis is not about a single transaction or statement. Similarly, it is a mistake to say "we are busy now because we are dealing first with the victims." There are always additional interested stakeholders, such as family members, friends, and others.

You need to keep reinforcing what you know and keep feeding information out. In the wake of last month's [May 2008] earthquake, the Chinese government has performed superbly in this dimension.

A critical element of effective crisis communication is empathy. There are usually many victims, real and felt, in a crisis. Your ability as an organization to relate to the human tragedy in a crisis is important. Your spokespeople and those involved in dealing with the crisis should understand this. Empathy is best communicated through continuing respect and human caring for all affected.

Combined with the need to realize that people have physical and emotional needs in a crisis is the need for all of our organizations to realize that these special situations may require quick, appropriate action: Actions speak louder than words. Even if something doesn't fit with corporate procedure, but it is the right thing to do, you should do it quickly.

Beyond all of this are a few more important elements. A key to successful crisis communication is the choice of a spokesperson. Obviously, given the requirements noted above, communications style, combined with the need for emotional connection, is important. We have all been reading the burgeoning literature on messages conveyed through physical expression, language and voice.

Another suggestion made by some experts is to ensure that a trusted, but arm's-length, adviser is brought into the communications process. This individual can maintain objectivity and watch the formation of "group think."

And be mindful of the entire picture. Many organizations fail in their communications by not managing the endgame. When the immediate crisis is dealt with, they celebrate and walk off the field, not noticing that the clock is still running. Stakeholders want to know the follow-up, especially since new information is continually revealed.

Finally, remember that with every crisis and the communications surrounding it, there is opportunity. It's often noted that the Chinese use two brush strokes to write the word crisis. One stands for danger; the other represents opportunity. We may recognize the danger but fail to capture the opportunity—to strengthen or improve our organizations, or to avoid a future, larger crisis—by not taking the time to learn.

As the old adage goes, 'A person has no more character than they can command in a time of crisis.'"

You Be the Manager

1. According to Dr. Daniel F. Muzyka, what makes for effective communications in a crisis situation?
2. What is your personal experience to the old adage at the end of the story: "A person has no more character than they can command in a time of crisis"?

communication
The sharing of information between two or more individuals or groups to reach a common understanding.

Communication is the sharing of information between two or more individuals or groups to reach a common understanding.[4] Some organizations are more effective at doing this than are others. Even though a manager's knowledge of the parent company, for example, is limited because of distance or corporate politics, the manager must still have a plan: to ensure that all employees remain focused on what needs to be done and to keep everyone communicating with everybody as effectively as possible. Communication is the lifeblood of any organization.

Good communication is essential for organizations to function effectively. Managers spend about 85 percent of their time engaged in some form of communication, whether in meetings, in telephone conversations, through email, or in face-to-face interactions. Employees also need to be effective communicators.[5] When all members of an organization are able to communicate effectively with each other and with people outside the organization, the organization is much more likely to perform highly and gain a competitive advantage.

FIGURE 12.1 | The Communication Process

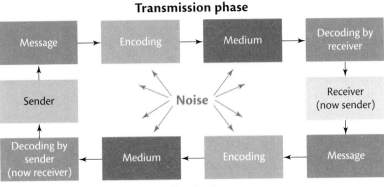

The Communication Process

The communication process consists of two phases. In the *transmission phase*, information is shared between two or more individuals or groups. In the *feedback phase*, a common understanding is reached. In both phases, a number of distinct stages must occur for communication to take place (see Figure 12.1).[6]

The **sender** (the person or group wishing to share information with some other person or group) starts the transmission phase by deciding on the **message** (the information to communicate). Then the sender translates the message into symbols or language, a process called **encoding**. Often, messages are encoded into words but they could also be symbols, such as :-) or a stop sign. **Noise** is a general term that refers to anything that hampers any stage of the communication process.

Once encoded, a message is transmitted through a medium to the **receiver**, the person or group for which the message is intended. A **medium** is simply the pathway—such as a phone call, a letter, a memo, or face-to-face communication in a meeting—through which an encoded message is transmitted to a receiver. At the next stage, the receiver interprets and tries to make sense of the message, a process called **decoding**. This is a critical point in communication.

The feedback phase is begun by the receiver (who becomes a sender). The receiver decides what message to send to the original sender (who becomes a receiver), encodes it, and transmits it through a chosen medium (see Figure 12.1). The message might contain a confirmation that the original message was received and understood, a restatement of the original message to make sure that it was correctly interpreted, or a request for more information. The original sender decodes the message and makes sure that a common understanding has been reached. If the original sender determines that a common understanding has not been reached, the sender and receiver go through the whole process as many times as needed to reach a common understanding. Failure to listen to employees prevents many managers from receiving feedback and reaching a common understanding with their employees. Feedback eliminates misunderstandings, ensures that messages are correctly interpreted, and enables senders and receivers to reach a common understanding.

Nonverbal Communication

The encoding of messages into words, written or spoken, is **verbal communication**. We also encode messages without using written or spoken language. **Nonverbal communication** shares information by means of facial expressions (smiling, raising

sender
The person or group wishing to share information.

message
The information that a sender wants to share.

encoding
Translating a message into understandable symbols or language.

noise
Anything that hampers any stage of the communication process.

receiver
The person or group for which a message is intended.

medium
The pathway through which an encoded message is transmitted to a receiver.

decoding
Interpreting and trying to make sense of a message.

verbal communication
The encoding of messages into words, either written or spoken.

nonverbal communication
The encoding of messages by means of facial expressions, body language, and styles of dressing.

an eyebrow, frowning, dropping one's jaw), body language (posture, gestures, nods, shrugs), and even style of dressing (casual, formal, conservative, trendy). "People make judgments about you based on how you look. If you're sloppily dressed or look like you're going to the beach, you'll leave a negative impression on clients and other employees," warns Natasha vandenHoven, senior vice-president of human resources, at Aon Consulting in Toronto.[7]

Nonverbal communication can reinforce verbal communication. Just as a warm and genuine smile can support words of appreciation for a job well done, a concerned facial expression can support words of sympathy for a personal problem. In such cases, similarity between verbal and nonverbal communication helps ensure that a common understanding is reached. This is not always as straightforward as it appears. Nonverbal gestures are culturally constructed, that is, different cultures perceive and interpret the symbols differently. For example, the thumbs up sign in Western cultures indicates "all is good," but in the Middle East it is a gesture of insult. Similarly, maintaining eye contact is viewed as a sign of engagement and attentiveness in Canada, but in Japan it is viewed as rude behaviour and invasion of privacy.[8]

People tend to have less control over nonverbal communication, and often a verbal message that is withheld gets expressed through body language or facial expressions. For instance, a manager who agrees to a proposal that she or he actually is not in favour of may unintentionally communicate disfavour by grimacing.

It is important to be aware of nonverbal aspects of communication, as well as the literal meaning of the words. You should particularly be aware of contradictions between the messages. A manager may say it is a good time to discuss a raise but then keep looking at the clock. This nonverbal signal may indicate that this is really *not* a good time to talk. Thus actions can speak louder (and more accurately) than words. A variety of popular books help one interpret body language. However, do use some care. For instance, while it is often thought that crossing your arms in front of your chest conveys resistance to a message, you might do this simply because you feel cold.

The Role of Perception in Communication

Perception plays a central role in communication and affects both transmission and feedback. **Perception** is the process through which people select, organize, and interpret sensory input to give meaning and order to the world around them. But it is inherently subjective and influenced by people's personalities, values, attitudes, and moods, as well as by their culture, experience, and knowledge. Thus, when senders and receivers communicate with each other, they are doing so based on their own subjective perceptions. The encoding and decoding of messages and even the choice of a medium hinge on the perceptions of senders and receivers.

In addition, perceptual biases can hamper effective communication. Recall from Chapter 3 that *biases* are systematic tendencies to use information about others in ways that result in inaccurate perceptions. In Chapter 3, we described a number of biases that can result in diverse members of an organization being treated unfairly. These same biases also can lead to ineffective communication. For example, **stereotypes**—simplified and often inaccurate beliefs about the characteristics of particular groups of people—can interfere with the encoding and decoding of messages.

One group that has suffered extensively over the years from unwarranted stereotyping has been Canada's Aboriginal population. However, today, Aboriginal entrepreneurs are growing in number and moving beyond their roots.[9] In 2017, visible minorities will become Canada's majority. It is one of the reasons that Orrin Benn,

perception
The process through which people select, organize, and interpret sensory input to give meaning and order to the world around them.

stereotypes
Simplified and often inaccurate beliefs about the characteristics of particular groups of people.

president of the newly formed Canadian Aboriginal and Minority Supplier Council (CAMSC), is working hard to make sure Aboriginal entrepreneurs succeed in growing their businesses. Otherwise, as he points out, given the stereotypical perceptions, "Canada loses." John Bernard, president and founder of Donna Cona Inc., Canada's largest Aboriginal-owned technology firm, has experienced first hand the unique challenges facing Aboriginal and minority entrepreneurs. He readily admits that being Aboriginal makes it that much harder gaining access to the supply chains of major corporations. For example,

> *Six months after beating out IBM and CGI to design the infrastructure for Nunavut residents to communicate across the two million-square-kilometre expanse of Canada's largest territory, Mr. Bernard learned that the fact he was aboriginal could have cost him the contract. "I was at an event with the CIO of the Nunavut project and he asked if I was aboriginal. I said, 'Yes, isn't that one of the reasons we won.' And he said, 'Oh God, no. You won because you had the best proposal. 'In fact,' he said, 'if we had known you were aboriginal that would have gone against you.' Why? Because of the stereotype that aboriginal firms do not deliver. If an aboriginal company makes a mistake, it reflects on the entire community. That is a huge obstacle to overcome."*

Instead of relying on stereotypes, effective communicators strive to perceive other people accurately by focusing on their actual behaviours, knowledge, skills, and abilities. Accurate perceptions, in turn, contribute to effective communication.

Information Richness and Communication Media

THINK ABOUT IT

Cultural Differences—Eyes and Mouth: Are the Windows to the Soul the Same in the East and West?[10]

The images, which featured photos of real humans as well as computerized icons known as "emoticons," were manipulated to produce irregular combinations—such as a picture of someone with melancholy eyes and a big grin, or a neutral mouth mixed with happy eyes.

"We found, in general, Japanese people are strongly influenced by the eyes—so even though a mouth is showing a sad expression, if that person has happy eyes, Japanese people are more likely to think that person must be happy," said Takahiko Masuda. Psychology professor Takahiko Masuda, co-author of a study that examined how people in Japan and North America interpret different expressions.

In the final moments of *Pretty Woman*, when Richard Gere climbs the fire escape into the waiting arms of Julia Roberts, she gives him a smile so bright it lights up the screen. In *Silence of the Lambs*, a distinctly more chilling look is offered by Anthony Hopkins when he stares at Jodie Foster from his prison cell.

While such expressions may seem a simple matter of how the actors position their mouths, eyes, and cheek muscles, new research from the University of Alberta suggests that the power they hold is also dependent on the cultural background of the audience.

"Many people likely think that a facial expression is the same everywhere and there are no cultural differences, but there can be many connotations involved," said Masuda.

The research, conducted jointly with scholars in Hokkaido (Japan) and Ohio (US), could eventually have big benefits for multicultural countries such as Canada, where it is becoming increasingly important and challenging for people to learn how to understand each other, he said.

Study subjects in Japan and North America were presented with a variety of facial images and asked to evaluate the level of happiness or sadness in each image. "North American judgments, in general, are more strongly influenced by the shape of the mouth. If a person has a wide-open smile, they are likely to think that person is happy, even if they have sad eyes."

Masuda believes the differences in interpretation can be explained, in part, by cultural experiences. For example, in North American society, where it is common for people to show emotions, it seems natural to express delight or revulsion with the mouth, since that is the biggest feature on the face. Japanese culture tends to be more restrained, so people focus on the eyes, which are smaller and more subtle.

Because of these subdued displays, Masuda suspects, Japanese people are highly sensitive to slight changes in people's expressions. This suggests the possibility that they are better at sensing when someone is lying or giving a false smile, though more study is needed to prove this.

You Be the Manager

1. How have the eyes been of help to you in your communication experiences?

To be effective communicators, individuals need to select an appropriate communication medium for *each* message they send. Should a change in procedures be communicated to subordinates in a memo or sent as email? Should a congratulatory message about a major accomplishment be communicated in a letter, in a phone call, or over lunch? Should a layoff announcement be made in a memo or at a plant meeting? Should the members of a purchasing team travel to Europe to finalize a major agreement with a new supplier, or should they do this through faxes?

There is no one best communication medium. In choosing a communication medium for any message, individuals need to consider three factors:

- *The level of information richness that is needed.* **Information richness** is the amount of information a communication medium can carry and the extent to which the medium enables sender and receiver to reach a common understanding.[11] The communication media that managers use vary in their information richness (see Figure 12.2).[12] Media high in information richness are able to carry a lot of information and generally enable receivers and senders to come to a common understanding.

- *The time needed for communication.* Managers' and other organizational members' time is valuable, and this affects the way messages should be sent.

- *The need for a paper or electronic trail.* An individual may want written documentation that a message was sent and received.

In the remainder of this section, we examine four types of communication media that vary along these three dimensions: information richness, time, and need for a paper or electronic trail.[13]

information richness
The amount of information that a communication medium can carry and the extent to which the medium enables sender and receiver to reach a common understanding.

FIGURE 12.2 | **The Information Richness of Communication Media**

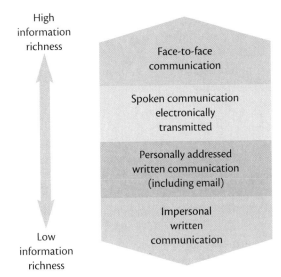

High
information
richness

Face-to-face
communication

Spoken communication
electronically
transmitted

Personally addressed
written communication
(including email)

Impersonal
written
communication

Low
information
richness

Face-to-Face Communication

Face-to-face communication has the highest information richness. When individuals communicate face to face, they not only can take advantage of verbal communication but also can interpret each other's nonverbal signals, such as facial expressions and body language. A look of concern or puzzlement can sometimes tell more than a thousand words, and individuals can respond to these nonverbal signals on the spot. Face-to-face communication also enables instant feedback. Points of confusion, ambiguity, or misunderstanding can be resolved, and individuals can cycle through the communication process as many times as they need to in order to reach a common understanding.

Because face-to-face communication is highest in information richness, you might think that it should always be the medium of choice. This is not the case, however, because of the amount of time it takes and the lack of a paper or electronic trail resulting from it. For messages that are important, personal, or likely to be misunderstood, it is often well worth the time to use face-to-face communication and, if need be, supplement it with some form of written communication documenting the message.

Many organizations are using videoconferences to capture some of the advantages of face-to-face communication (such as access to facial expressions), while saving time and money because individuals in different locations do not have to travel to meet with one another. In addition to saving travel costs, videoconferences can speed up decisions, shorten new product development time, and lead to more efficient meetings. Some managers have found that meetings are 20- to 30-percent shorter when they use videoconferences instead of face-to-face meetings.[14]

Spoken Communication Electronically Transmitted

After face-to-face communication, spoken communication electronically transmitted over the phone is second-highest in information richness (see Figure 12.2). Although individuals communicating over the phone do not have access to body language and facial expressions, they do have access to the tone of voice in which a message is delivered, the parts of the message the sender emphasizes, and the general manner in which the message is spoken, in addition to the actual words themselves. Thus, phone conversations have the capacity to convey extensive amounts of information. Individuals also can ensure that mutual understanding is reached because they can get quick feedback over the phone and can answer questions.

Voice mail systems and answering machines also allow people to send and receive verbal electronic messages. Such systems are obviously a necessity when managers or employees are frequently out of the office, and those on the road are well advised to check their voice mail periodically.

Personally Addressed Written Communication

Lower than electronically transmitted verbal communication in information richness is personally addressed written communication (see Figure 12.2). One of the advantages of face-to-face communication and verbal communication electronically transmitted is that they both tend to demand attention, which helps ensure that receivers pay attention. Personally addressed written communication such as a memo or letter also has this advantage. Because it is addressed to a particular person, the chances are good that the person will actually pay attention to (and read) it. Moreover, the sender can write the message in a way that the receiver is most likely to understand it. Like voice mail, written communication does not enable a receiver to have his or her questions answered immediately, but when messages are clearly written and feedback is provided, common understanding can still be reached. Even if managers use face-to-face communication, a follow-up in writing is often needed for messages that are important or complicated and need to be referred to later on.

Business Plan Checklist

- Determine the most appropriate medium or channel of communication to present your business plan to potential investors.
- Make sure the plan is concise and well thought out.
- Include the key ideas in the Executive Summary, such as who you are, the nature of the venture, the strengths of the management team, the strategy for achieving your goals, your financial projections, any funding sought, and how you will handle the main risks facing the venture.

E-Mail Etiquette
www.emailreplies.com

Email

Email also fits into this category of communication media because senders and receivers are communicating through personally addressed written words. The words are appearing on their personal computer screens, however, rather than on pieces of paper. Email is becoming so widespread in the business world that managers are even developing their own email etiquette. For instance, messages in capital letters are often perceived as being shouted or screamed. Some guidelines from polite emailers follows

- Always punctuate messages.

- Do not ramble on or say more than you need to.

- Do not act as though you do not understand something when, in fact, you do understand it.

- Pay attention to spelling and format (put a memo in memo form).

While the growing use of email has enabled better communication within organizations, not all benefits have been positive. Many individuals complain of "email overload," and being unable to keep up with all the email that arrives, even personally addressed messages. In addition, some employees sexually harass co-workers through email, and employees often find their electronic mailboxes clogged with junk mail. In a recent survey, more than half of the organizations surveyed acknowledged some problems with their email systems.[15]

To avoid these and other costly forms of email abuse, managers need to develop a clear policy specifying what company email can and should be used for and what is out of bounds. Managers also should clearly communicate this policy to all members of an organization as well as describe both the procedures that will be used when email abuse is suspected and the consequences that will result when email abuse is confirmed.

The increasing use of voice mail and email in companies large and small has led to some ethical concerns. These forms of communication are not necessarily private. The federal Privacy Act and Access to Information Act apply to all federal government departments, most federal agencies, and some federal Crown corporations, but many private sector employees are not covered by privacy legislation. Only Quebec's privacy act applies to the entire private sector.

The ethics of listening to other people's voice mail or reading their email are likely to be a growing concern for many managers. While no comparable Canadian data are available, a recent survey of more than 2000 large American firms found that 38 percent reported that they "store and review" employee email messages. This was up from 27 percent in 1999 and just 15 percent in 1997.[16] The Ontario, Manitoba, and British Columbia governments have told their employees that email will be monitored if abuse is suspected. The governments' positions are that the Internet and email should be used only for business purposes.

Ryan McVay/Getty Images
Videoconferencing can effectively facilitate meetings by retaining a personal feeling

Impersonal Written Communication

Impersonal written communication is lowest in information richness and is well suited for messages that need to reach a large number of receivers. Because such messages are not addressed to particular receivers, feedback is unlikely, so managers must make sure that messages sent by this medium are written clearly in language that all receivers will understand.

Managers can use impersonal written communication, including company newsletters, for various types of messages, including rules, regulations, policies, newsworthy information, and announcements of changes in procedures or the arrival of new organizational members. Impersonal written communication also can be used to communicate instructions about how to use machinery or how to process work orders or customer requests. For these kinds of messages, the paper trail left by this communication medium can be invaluable for employees. Much of this information is also being posted to company intranets. The danger with impersonal communication, however, is that some individuals will not read it, so it is important that employees are made aware of important messages.

Tips for Managers
INFORMATION RICHNESS AND COMMUNICATION MEDIA

1. When you have something to communicate that is important, emotion-based, and personal, use face-to-face communication.

2. Use videoconferencing when distance, weather, or cost hinders face-to-face communication, although convenience, price, the practical number of people, and the need for some participants to be more concerned with how they look may be problematic.

3. Consider introducing "Email-Free Friday," recommended by Sport England, as part of its Everyday Sport campaign. Dr. Dorian Dugmore, an international heart expert in the UK, said: "We need the nation to get behind Email-Free Friday as we are losing millions of hours of exercise through the explosion of email."[17]

4. Be clear with employees about the company policy on the use of email in the office.

5. Whether or not privacy is protected by law or contract, foster a workplace culture where privacy is valued and respected, contributes to morale and mutual trust, and makes good business sense.[18]

L O 3

Developing Communication Skills

THINK ABOUT IT

When Communications Go Ka-Boom!!!

Have you ever been in a work situation where you felt quite angry and wanted to write an email and "give the person a piece of your mind"? We all have those feelings once in awhile. But you might want to take a deep breath, count to 10, and wait before you hit the "Send" button! If you are a manager, you could be creating not only serious human relations and communication problems for yourself and the office, you just might also be putting your company in economic turmoil. If you are the CEO and go on an email rampage, be prepared for the "ka-boom effect."

This is exactly what happened at Cerner Corporation, a health-care software development company in Kansas City, Missouri, on March 13, 2001, when Neal L. Patterson, the CEO, blew his stack and let loose his emotional torrent of frustration in an email he thought was going to 400 of his managers. Instead, he sent it to 3100 employees![19] When this happened, the email was leaked and posted on Yahoo! The stock price of the US$1.5-billion company dropped 22 percent in three days! In effect, the CEO put himself at war with his abusive email language and threats ... all in the hope of getting his managers to be more responsible—at least, as he interpreted responsibility: a parking lot "substantially full" at 7:30 a.m. till 6:30 p.m. and half-full on Saturdays! He gave the managers two weeks to get on his schedule and said, "Tick, tock," indicating that his clock (time bomb) was running.

The *Wall Street Journal* wrote that the Cerner Corp., for the 2009 second quarter that ended July 4, 2009, had "strong levels of bookings, earnings, and cash flow." As well, "bookings in the second quarter of 2009 were $394.0 million. Second quarter revenue was $403.8 million, which [was] flat over the year-ago period."[20]

Of course, we need to ask if CEO Neal L. Patterson (one of the three founders of the company, Paul Gorup and Cliff Illig being the other two[21]) and his very direct communication style present a management liability. Obviously, since earnings are strong eight years after his original outburst, some might say that it worked. Others, on the other hand, would want to examine the personal effect on employees, especially managers, for his impulsive behaviour. In 1998 and 2000, Cerner did meet *Fortune* magazine's list of best companies to work for in America.

You Be The Manager

1. What are some key communication errors in this story?

There are various kinds of barriers to effective communication in organizations. Some barriers have their origins in senders. When messages are unclear, incomplete, or difficult to understand, when they are sent over an inappropriate medium, or when no provision for feedback is made, communication suffers. Other communication barriers have their origins in receivers. When receivers pay no attention to, do not listen to, or make no effort to understand the meaning of a message, communication is likely to be ineffective.

To overcome these barriers and effectively communicate with others, managers (as well as other organizational members) must possess or develop certain communication skills. Some of these skills are particularly important when individuals send messages, and others are critical when individuals receive messages. These skills help ensure not only that individuals will be able to share information but also that they will have the information they need to make good decisions and take action and be able to reach a common understanding with others.

Communication Skills for Senders

Individuals can make sure that they consider all of the steps of the communication process when they are engaging in communication. They can also develop their skills in giving feedback. We discuss each of these issues in turn.

Improving the Communication Process

Table 12.1 summarizes seven communication skills that help ensure that when individuals send messages, they are properly understood and the transmission phase of the communication process is effective. Let us see what each skill entails.

TABLE 12.1 | *Seven Communication Skills for Managers as Senders of Messages*

1. Send messages that are clear and complete.
2. Encode messages in symbols that the receiver understands.
3. Select a medium that is appropriate for the message.
4. Select a medium that the receiver monitors.
5. Avoid filtering and information distortion.
6. Ensure that a feedback mechanism is built into messages.
7. Provide accurate information to ensure that misleading rumours are not spread.

1. **Send Clear and Complete Messages** Individuals need to learn how to send a message that is clear and complete. A message is clear when it is easy for the receiver to understand and interpret, and it is complete when it contains all the information that the sender and receiver need to reach a common understanding. In trying to send messages that are both clear and complete, managers must learn to anticipate how receivers will interpret messages and adjust messages to eliminate sources of misunderstanding or confusion.

2. **Encode Messages in Symbols the Receiver Understands** Individuals need to appreciate that when they encode messages, they should use symbols or language that the receiver understands. When sending messages in English to receivers whose native language is not English, for example, it is important to use commonplace vocabulary and to avoid clichés that, when translated, may make little sense and in some cases are unintentionally comical or insulting.

   Jargon, specialized language that members of an occupation, group, or organization develop to facilitate communication among themselves, should never be used to communicate with people outside the occupation, group, or organization. For example, truck drivers refer to compact cars as "roller skates," highway dividing lines as "paints," and orange barrels around road construction areas as "Schneider eggs." Using this jargon among themselves results in effective communication because they know precisely what is being referred to. But if a truck driver used this language to send a message (such as "That roller skate can't stay off the paint") to a receiver who did not drive trucks, the receiver would not know what the message meant.[22]

3. **Select a Medium Appropriate for the Message** When choosing among communication media, individuals need to take into account the level of information richness required, time constraints, and the need for a paper or electronic trail. A primary concern in choosing an appropriate medium is the nature of the message. Is it personal, important, nonroutine, and likely to be misunderstood and in need of further clarification? If it is, face-to-face communication is likely to be in order.

4. **Select a Medium that the Receiver Monitors** Another factor that individuals need to take into account when selecting a communication medium is whether it is one that the receiver uses. Not everyone checks voice mail and email routinely. Many people simply select the medium that they themselves use the most and are most comfortable with, but doing this can often lead to ineffective communication. No matter how much an individual likes email, sending an email message to someone else who never checks his or her email is useless. Learning which individuals like things in writing and which prefer face-to-face interactions and then using the appropriate medium enhances the chance that receivers will actually receive and pay attention to messages.

   A related consideration is whether receivers have disabilities that limit their ability to decode certain kinds of messages. A visually impaired receiver, for example, cannot read a written message. Managers should ensure that their employees with disabilities have resources available to communicate effectively with others.

5. **Avoid Filtering and Information Distortion Filtering** occurs when senders withhold part of a message because they (mistakenly) think that the receiver does not need the information or will not want to receive it. Filtering can occur at all levels in an organization and in both vertical and horizontal communication. Rank-and-file employees may filter messages they send to first-line managers, first-line managers may filter messages to middle managers, and middle managers may filter messages to top managers. Such filtering is most likely to take place when messages contain bad news or problems that subordinates are afraid they will be blamed for.

   Information distortion occurs when the meaning of a message changes as the message passes through a series of senders and receivers. Some information

jargon
Specialized language that members of an occupation, group, or organization develop to facilitate communication among themselves.

filtering
Withholding part of a message out of the mistaken belief that the receiver does not need or will not want the information.

information distortion
Changes in the meaning of a message as the message passes through a series of senders and receivers.

distortion is accidental—due to faulty encoding and decoding or to a lack of feedback. Other information distortion is deliberate. Senders may alter a message to make themselves or their groups look good and to receive special treatment. The **grapevine** is the informal way of communicating information throughout an organization that is based on a gossip network. Surprisingly, much of the information that is sent and received through the grapevine is seldom distorted. Managers can use the grapevine to their advantage by floating new ideas and gauging the reaction of employees before actually implementing change.

Managers themselves should avoid filtering and distorting information. But how can they eliminate these barriers to effective communication throughout their organization? They need to establish trust throughout the organization. Subordinates who trust their managers believe that they will not be blamed for things beyond their control and will be treated fairly. Managers who trust their subordinates provide them with clear and complete information and do not hold things back.

6. **Include a Feedback Mechanism in Messages** Because feedback is essential for effective communication, individuals should build a feedback mechanism into the messages they send. They either should include a request for feedback or indicate when and how they will follow up on the message to make sure that it was received and understood. When writing letters and memos or sending faxes, one can request that the receiver respond with comments and suggestions in a letter, memo, or fax; schedule a meeting to discuss the issue; or follow up with a phone call. Building feedback mechanisms such as these into messages ensures that messages are received and understood.

7. **Provide Accurate Information Rumours** are unofficial pieces of information of interest to organizational members but with no identifiable source. Rumours spread quickly once they are started, and usually they concern topics that organizational members think are important, interesting, or amusing. Rumours, however, can be misleading and can cause harm to individual employees and to an organization when they are false, malicious, or unfounded. Managers can halt the spread of misleading rumours by providing organizational members with accurate information on matters that concern them.

grapevine
An informal communication network among people in organizations.

rumours
Unofficial pieces of information of interest to organizational members but with no identifiable source.

Giving Feedback

We have discussed the importance of feedback in making sure that communication is understood. We can also talk about providing feedback more generally, because communicating feedback is an important task for managers. While positive feedback is easier to give, many individuals do not provide such feedback. Most people find giving negative feedback more difficult. Individuals can learn from feedback, whether it is positive or negative, so providing it in a timely fashion is important. The following suggestions can lead to more effective feedback:

-   *Focus on specific behaviours.* Individuals should be told what it was that they did well or poorly, rather than simply being told that they did a good job. They can learn more from comments such as "You were very organized in your presentation," or "You managed your time effectively on this project," than when told simply, "Great job."

-   *Keep feedback impersonal.* When giving feedback, you should describe the behaviour rather than judge or evaluate the person.[23] Particularly when giving negative feedback, it is easy to focus on personal characteristics (rudeness, laziness, incompetence, etc.), but this rarely helps the person learn from mistakes. It is better to explain that the report was late, it contained a number of errors, and was missing an important section.

- *Keep feedback goal-oriented.* Feedback should not be given just because it will make you feel better. Rather, it should have a goal, such as improving performance the next time.

- *Make feedback well-timed.* Feedback should be given shortly after the behaviour occurs. This ensures that the individual remembers the event and also is more likely to result in change if change is needed. Giving feedback to someone six months later, during a performance review, is usually not helpful. If a situation has provoked an emotional response in you, however, delaying feedback until you have had time to lessen the emotional impact is wise.

- *Direct negative feedback toward behaviour that the receiver can control.* When giving negative feedback, consider which things the individual can fix and which are out of his or her control. Criticizing someone's writing skills and then suggesting that the person take a writing course focuses on behaviour that can be controlled. Criticizing someone for not sending an important email when the company's network was down is not likely a situation the individual can fix or control.

Communication Skills for Receivers

Senders also receive messages, and thus they must possess or develop communication skills that allow them to be effective receivers of messages. Table 12.2 summarizes three of these important skills, which we examine in greater detail.

1. Pay Attention

When individuals are overloaded and forced to think about several things at once, they sometimes do not pay sufficient attention to the messages they receive. To be effective, however, individuals should always pay attention to messages they receive, no matter how busy they are. For example, when discussing a project with a subordinate, an effective manager focuses on the project and not on an upcoming meeting with his or her own boss. Similarly, when individuals are reading written forms of communication, they should focus their attention on understanding what they are reading and not be sidetracked into thinking about other issues.

2. Be a Good Listener

Part of being a good communicator is being a good listener. This is an essential communication skill for all organizational members. Being a good listener is surprisingly more difficult than you might realize, however. The average person speaks at a rate of 125 to 200 words per minute, but the average listener can effectively process up to 400 words per minute. Therefore listeners are often thinking about other things when someone is speaking to them.

It is important to engage in active listening, which requires paying attention, interpreting, and remembering what was said. Active listening requires making a conscious effort to hear what a person is saying and interpreting it to see that it makes sense.

TABLE 12.2 | *Three Communication Skills for Managers as Receivers of Messages*

1. Pay attention.
2. Be a good listener.
3. Be empathetic.

Being a good listener is an essential communication skill in many different kinds of organizations, from small businesses to large corporations.

Organizational members can practise the following behaviours to become active listeners:[24]

1. *Make eye contact if it is culturally appropriate.* Eye contact lets the speaker know that you are paying attention, and it also lets you pick up nonverbal cues. Making eye contact in Japan is considered rude behaviour, and so being a good listener requires being culturally sensitive.
2. *Exhibit affirmative nods and appropriate facial expressions.* By nodding your head and exhibiting appropriate facial expressions, you further show the speaker that you are listening.
3. *Avoid distracting actions or gestures.* Do not look at your watch, shuffle papers, play with your pencil, or engage in similar distractions when you are listening to someone. These actions suggest to the speaker that you are bored or uninterested. The actions also mean that you probably are not paying full attention to what is being said.
4. *Ask questions.* The critical listener analyzes what he or she hears and asks questions. Asking questions provides clarification and reduces ambiguity, leading to greater understanding. It also assures the speaker that you are listening.
5. *Paraphrase.* Paraphrasing means restating in your own words what the speaker has said. The effective listener uses such phrases as "What I hear you saying is ..." or "Do you mean ... ?" Paraphrasing is a check on whether you are listening carefully and accurately.
6. *Avoid interrupting the speaker.* Interruptions can cause the speaker to lose his or her train of thought and cause the listener to jump to wrong conclusions based on incomplete information.
7. *Do not overtalk.* Most of us prefer talking to listening. However, a good listener knows the importance of taking turns in a conversation.
8. *Make smooth transitions between the roles of speaker and listener.* The effective listener knows how to make the transition from listener role to speaker role, and then back to being a listener. It is important to listen rather than plan what you are going to say next.

3. Be Empathetic

Receivers are empathetic when they try to understand how the sender feels and try to interpret a message from the sender's perspective, rather than viewing a message from only their own point of view.

Organizational Conflict

Organizational conflict often arises as the result of communication breakdowns among individuals or units. **Organizational conflict** is the discord that arises when the goals, interests, or values of different individuals or groups are incompatible and those individuals or groups block or thwart each other's attempts to achieve their objectives.[25] Conflict is an inevitable part of organizational life because the goals of different stakeholders such as managers and workers are often incompatible. Organizational conflict also can exist between departments and divisions that compete for resources or even between managers who may be competing for promotion to the next level in the organizational hierarchy.

Though many people dislike conflict, it is not always dysfunctional. Too little conflict can be as bad as too much conflict, but a medium level of conflict can encourage

organizational conflict
The discord that arises when the goals, interest, or values of different individuals or groups are incompatible and those individuals or groups block or thwart each other's attempts to achieve their objectives.

a variety of perspectives that improve organizational functioning and effectiveness and help decision making. Conflict is a force that needs to be managed rather than eliminated.[26] Managers should never try to eliminate all conflict but rather should try to keep conflict at a moderate and functional level to promote change efforts that benefit the organization. To deal with conflict effectively, managers should understand the sources of conflict in organizations and understand how individuals behave when they are engaged in conflict.

Conflict Handling Behaviours

Organizational conflict can happen between individuals, within a group or department, between groups or departments, or even across organizations. Conflict can arise for a variety of reasons. Within organizations conflict occurs for such reasons as incompatible goals and time horizons, overlapping authority, task interdependencies, incompatible evaluation or reward systems, scarce resources, and status inconsistencies (see Figure 12.3).[27] Regardless of the source of the conflict, knowing how individuals handle conflict is an important skill for the manager who may have to intervene to resolve it.

The behaviours for handling conflict fall along two dimensions: *cooperativeness* (the degree to which one party tries to satisfy the other party's concerns) and *assertiveness* (the degree to which one party tries to satisfy his or her own concerns).[28] This can be seen in Figure 12.4. From these two dimensions emerge five conflict-handling behaviours:

- *Avoiding.* Withdrawing from conflict.

- *Competing.* One person tries to satisfy his or her own interests, without regard to the interests of the other party.

- *Compromising.* Each party is concerned about its own goal accomplishment and the goal accomplishment of the other party and is willing to engage in a give-and-take exchange and to make concessions until a reasonable resolution of the conflict is reached.

FIGURE 12.3 | Sources of Conflict in Organizations

FIGURE 12.4 | Dimensions of Conflict-Handling Behaviours

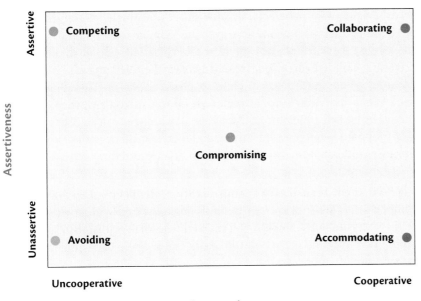

Source: K.W. Thomas, "Conflict and Negotiation in Organizations," in M.D. Dunnette and L.M. Hough (eds), *Handbook of Industrial Psychology*, 2nd ed, vol. 3 (Palo Alto, CA: Consulting Psychologists Press, 1992), p. 668. Copyright 2001 by Acad. of Mgmt. Reproduced with permission of Acad. of Mgmt. in the format Textbook via Copyright Clearance Center.

- *Accommodating.* One person tries to please the other person by putting the other's interests ahead of his or her own.

- *Collaborating.* The parties to a conflict try to satisfy their goals without making any concessions and instead come up with a way to resolve their differences that leaves them both better off.

When the parties to a conflict are willing to cooperate with each other and devise a solution that each finds acceptable (through compromise or collaboration), an organization is more likely to achieve its goals.

LO5

Conflict Management Strategies

Conflict management strategies that ensure conflicts are resolved in a functional manner focus on individuals, groups, and on the organization as a whole. Below, we describe strategies that focus on individuals: increasing awareness of the sources of conflict, increasing diversity awareness and skills, practising job rotation or temporary assignments, and using permanent transfers or dismissals when necessary. We also describe two strategies that focus on the organization as a whole: changing an organization's structure or culture and directly altering the source of conflict. Finally, distributive and integrative negotiation techniques are analyzed as methods to resolve intergroup conflict.

Strategies Focused on Individuals

1. Strategies Focused on Individuals Much conflict arises because individuals are not aware of how differences in linguistic styles, personalities, backgrounds, and job requirements affect interactions. For example, differences in linguistic styles may lead some men in work teams to talk more and take more credit for ideas than would women in those teams. These communication differences can result in conflict when the men incorrectly assume that the women are uninterested or less capable because they participate less and the women incorrectly assume that the men are being bossy and are not interested in their ideas because they seem to do all the talking. Conflict can also arise when co-workers are unaware of the demands of each other's jobs and place unrealistic expectations on someone to complete a project. When individuals are aware of the source of conflict, they can take steps to interact with each other more effectively. Awareness can be increased through diversity training, open communication, and job rotation or temporary assignments that increase understanding of the work activities and demands that others in the organization face.

2. Using Permanent Transfers or Dismissals Strategies Focused on the Organization Sometimes when other conflict resolution strategies do not work, managers may need to take more drastic steps, including permanent transfers or dismissals.

Suppose two first-line managers who work in the same department are always at each other's throats; frequent bitter conflicts arise between them, even though they both seem to get along well with the other people they work with. No matter what their supervisor does to increase their understanding of each other, these conflicts keep occurring. In this case, the supervisor may want to transfer one or both managers so that they do not have to interact as frequently.

When dysfunctionally high levels of conflict occur among top managers who cannot resolve their differences and understand each other, it may be necessary for one of them to leave the company.

Strategies Focused on the Organization

1. Changing Structure or Culture Conflict can signal the need for changes in an organization's structure or culture. Sometimes, managers can effectively resolve conflict by changing the organizational structure they use to group people and tasks.[29] As an organization grows, for example, the *functional structure* that was effective when the organization was small may no longer be effective, and a shift to a product structure might effectively resolve conflicts (see Chapter 6).

Managers also can effectively resolve conflicts by increasing levels of integration in an organization. When individuals from different departments are assigned to the same team, they can directly resolve issues on the spot, rather than going through departments.

Sometimes managers may need to take steps to change an organization's culture to resolve conflicts (see Chapter 7). Norms and values in an organizational culture might inadvertently promote dysfunctionally high levels of conflicts that are difficult to resolve. For instance, norms that stress respect for formal authority may create conflict that is difficult to resolve when an organization creates self-managed work teams. Values stressing individual competition may make it difficult to resolve conflicts when organizational members need to put others' interests ahead of their own. In circumstances such as these, taking steps to change norms and values can be an effective conflict resolution strategy.

2. Altering the Source of Conflict When conflict is due to overlapping authority, status inconsistencies, and incompatible evaluation or reward systems, managers can sometimes effectively resolve the conflict by directly altering the source of conflict—the overlapping authority, the status inconsistency, or the evaluation or reward system. For example, managers can clarify the chain of command and reassign tasks and responsibilities to resolve conflicts due to overlapping authority.

Tips for Managers

HANDLING CONFLICT[30]

1. Use compromise or collaboration as much as you can to resolve conflict.
2. Identify the factors of a conflict that cause you the most difficulty, and seek to resolve them.
3. Identify factors that may be contributing to unhealthy workplace conflict.
4. Examine the organizational structure to see if it is causing unnecessary conflict.
5. Maintain neutrality when handling conflicts.

Negotiation Strategies

L O 6

THINK ABOUT IT

Women *Can* Ask for It! The Negotiation Gym![31]

Mary was a successful plant biologist at a U.S. university, one of the few women at the top ranks of her profession. She did not feel she had ever been treated unfairly as a woman, encountering few obstacles in her rise to prominence.

So, it came as a shock when, after making a grant proposal for a study with six colleagues, she saw the salary requests from the other scientists and realized they all earned much more than she did—including three who were junior to her.

She had assumed the university had a salary scale and accepted what her department head proposed annually. But it turned out that the men routinely asked for more—and got it. When she confronted the department head—insisting that her salary be raised to US$10 000 more than her best-paid colleagues—he was confused. "I thought you were comfortable with what you were getting," he said. "I figured—I don't know—that you weren't especially materialistic."

In *Ask For It*,[32] Linda Babcock, a professor at Carnegie-Mellon University, and writer Sara Laschever cite Mary as one of many examples where women fail to negotiate for better treatment and lose out to men. It starts with their initial job—where female university graduates tend to take what is offered, whereas many men press for more—and continues through annual pay raises, bonuses, and the unwillingness to ask for everything from time off to use of a company apartment on vacation.

Men feel entitled, whereas women feel more constrained. In every study reviewed by Babcock, men initiated negotiations to advance their interests about four times as frequently as women did.

"If you're very successful, you may assume that you've experienced fair treatment along the way, otherwise you wouldn't have done so well or risen so high. Unfortunately, no. Even very successful women often discover that equally qualified men have been rewarded far more extravagantly or allowed to jump steps as they ascend the corporate ladder or enjoyed special treatment not offered to their female peers," Babcock and Laschever write.

This book is a sequel to *Women Don't Ask*,[33] in which they first documented the failure of women to negotiate and explored the psychology behind it. *Ask For It* is a negotiation guide but, unlike others, is rooted in gender.

Women feel guilty about asking, the authors contend. They have, on average, a less extravagant sense of self-worth than do men. They view negotiations as scarier, more difficult, and even more agonizing than do men, who see negotiations as easier, less threatening, and more fun.

So, the first phase in negotiations for women is to realize everything is negotiable, to acknowledge what they would truly like, and accept that they are worth it. Only then can they begin to learn the basics of negotiation, although, again, this must be according to their psychology and what is expected of them in a society where women cannot be too aggressive, the book says.

They must first frame a negotiation plan. That includes the well-known BATNA, or "best alternative to a negotiated agreement," but also the reservation value (bottom line) and target zone (what you would be thrilled to achieve). It is easy to give in and accept the first offer or counteroffer if you have not outlined these benchmarks beforehand.

Next, you must negotiate. The authors take readers through a "negotiation gym," where you tackle increasingly tougher negotiation situations until you become more skilled. It starts with an easy warm-up over the course of a week when you ask various people you deal with for simple things you know you will get. It then goes on to include a week of asking people for things you know you will not get—in order to become accustomed to being rebuffed. Finally, the third week involves trying to ask for something that is not okay to ask for from somebody close to you.

The book offers suggestions on how to negotiate with a softer style, since the authors say that men will penalize women if they appear aggressive in asking. So women have to combine likeability with polite assertiveness. They also need to keep focusing on their target—indeed, asking for more than their target, as a negotiation strategy to win what they deserve. Often, that will mean asking for a break in the negotiation for everyone to reassess.

The last chapter has a warning: If you never hear "no" in negotiations, you are not asking for enough. "When you aim high in a negotiation, you adjust other people's perceptions of you," they write. "You communicate that you expect to be treated fairly and that you're willing to stand up for yourself (in a friendly and likeable way, of course)." This is an excellent book, nicely weaving the psychological aspects that hurt women in negotiations, along with academic studies, examples from real-life women, and the negotiation advice.

You Be the Manager

1. According to the article, what are the phases in negotiations the authors suggest for women?

negotiation
A method of conflict resolution in which the parties in conflict consider various alternative ways to allocate resources to each other in order to come up with a solution acceptable to them all.

distributive negotiation
Adversarial negotiation in which the parties in conflict compete to win the most resources while conceding as little as possible.

A particularly important conflict resolution technique for managers and other organizational members to use in situations in which the parties to a conflict have approximately equal levels of power is negotiation. During **negotiation**, the parties to a conflict try to come up with a solution acceptable to themselves by considering various alternative ways to allocate resources to each other.[34]

There are two major types of negotiation—distributive negotiation and integrative bargaining.[35] In **distributive negotiation**, the parties perceive that they have a "fixed pie" of resources that they need to divide up.[36] They take a competitive, adversarial stance. Each party realizes that he or she must concede something but is out to get the lion's share of resources.[37] The parties see no need to interact with each other in the future and do not care if their interpersonal relationship is damaged or destroyed by their competitive negotiations.[38] Take, for example, the situation of the 2300 bus drivers, dispatchers, and maintenance employees of the Ontario

Amalgamated Transit Union who work for the City of Ottawa's public transportation services, OC Transpo. In January 2009, city councillor Clive Doucet described the 35-day transit strike in classic distributive bargaining language: "Both sides are frozen in their corners, nothing is moving forward, and the city is suffering."[39] In this case, the union had a responsibility to its members whose jobs were under threat from the proposal to contract out and change the scheduling practices. The city of Ottawa had a responsibility to its 850 000 residents to increase the efficiency of the system.

In **integrative bargaining**, the parties perceive that they might be able to increase the resource pie by trying to come up with a creative solution to the conflict. They do not view the conflict competitively, as a win-or-lose situation; instead, they view it cooperatively, as a win-win situation in which all parties can gain. Integrative bargaining is characterized by trust, information sharing, and the desire of all parties to achieve a good resolution of the conflict.[40] For the OC Transpo workers and the City of Ottawa to show a commitment to integrative bargaining, each side would need to figure out ways to address some of the needs of the other, rather than simply taking an adversarial position.

integrative bargaining
Cooperative negotiation in which the parties in conflict work together to achieve a resolution that is good for them all.

There are five strategies that individuals can rely on to increase the odds of a win-win solution:[41]

- *Emphasize the big-picture goals.* This reminds individuals that they are working together for a larger purpose or goal despite their disagreements.

- *Focus on the problem, not the people.* All parties to a conflict need to keep focused on the source of the conflict and avoid the temptation to discredit each other by personalizing the conflict.

- *Focus on interests, not demands.* Demands are what a person wants, and interests are why the person wants them. When two people are in conflict, it is unlikely that the demands of both can be met. Their underlying interests often can be met, creating a win-win solution.

- *Create new options for joint gain.* Rather than having a fixed set of alternatives from which to choose, the parties can come up with new alternatives that might even expand the resource pie.

- *Focus on what is fair.* Emphasizing fairness will help the parties come to a mutual agreement about what the best solution to the problem is.

Any and all of these strategies would help the OC Transpo workers and the City of Ottawa negotiate with each other more effectively. When managers pursue these five strategies and encourage other organizational members to do so, they are more likely to resolve their conflicts effectively, through integrative bargaining. In addition, throughout the negotiation process, managers and other organizational members need to be aware of, and on their guard against, the biases that can lead to faulty decision making (see Chapter 4).[42]

Amalgamated Transit
Union Canada
www.atucanada.ca

Collective Bargaining

Collective bargaining is negotiation between labour unions and managers to resolve conflicts and disputes about important issues such as working hours, wages, benefits, working conditions, and job security. Once an agreement that union members support has been reached (sometimes with the help of a neutral third party called a *mediator*), union leaders and managers sign a contract spelling out the terms of the collective bargaining.

collective bargaining
Negotiation between labour unions and managers to resolve conflicts and disputes about issues such as working hours, wages, benefits, working conditions, and job security.

Collective bargaining is an ongoing consideration in labour relations. After signing an agreement, it must be administered, and the rules governing working conditions must be followed by both parties. However, disagreement and conflicts can arise over the interpretation of the contract. In these cases, a neutral third party known as an *arbitrator* is usually called in to resolve the conflict. An important component of a collective agreement is a *grievance procedure* through which workers who feel they are not being fairly treated are allowed to voice their concerns and have their interests represented by the union. Employees who feel they were unjustly fired in violation of a union contract, for example, may file a grievance, have the union represent them, and get their jobs back if an arbitrator agrees with them. See Chapter 11 for more on Labour relations.

 Tips for Managers

NEGOTIATION[43]

1. Separate the people in the conflict negotiation from the problem.

2. Negotiate about interests, not positions which parties cling to.

3. Invent options for mutual gain, and be mutually creative.

4. Insist on objective decision criteria.

5. Know your BATNA (best alternative to a negotiated agreement).

6. Do not jump to conclusions.

Summary and Review

1. **COMMUNICATION IN ORGANIZATIONS** Communication is the sharing of information between two or more individuals or groups to reach a common understanding. Good communication is necessary for an organization to gain a competitive advantage. Communication takes place in a cyclical process that has two phases: *transmission* and *feedback.*

2. **INFORMATION RICHNESS AND COMMUNICATION MEDIA** Information richness is the amount of information a communication medium can carry and the extent to which the medium enables the sender and receiver to reach a common understanding. Four categories of communication media in descending order of information richness are *face-to-face communication* (includes videoconferences), *spoken communication electronically transmitted* (includes voice mail), *personally addressed written communication* (includes email), and *impersonal written communication.*

3. **DEVELOPING COMMUNICATION SKILLS** There are various barriers to effective communication in organizations. To overcome these barriers and effectively communicate with others, individuals must possess or develop certain communication skills. As senders of messages, individuals should send messages that are clear and complete, encode messages in symbols the receiver understands, choose a medium that is appropriate for the message and monitored by the receiver,

avoid filtering and information distortion, include a feedback mechanism in the message, and provide accurate information to ensure that misleading rumours are not spread. Communication skills for individuals as receivers of messages include paying *attention*, being a *good listener*, and being *empathetic*.

4. **ORGANIZATIONAL CONFLICT** Organizational conflict is the discord that arises when the goals, interests, or values of different individuals or groups clash, and those individuals or groups block or thwart each other's attempts to achieve their objectives. Sources of organizational conflict include incompatible goals and time horizons, overlapping authority, task interdependencies, incompatible evaluation and reward systems, scarce resources and status inconsistencies. Individuals handle conflict along two dimensions, their level of cooperativeness and their level of assertiveness, which give rise to five types of conflict-handling behaviours: *competing, avoiding, compromising, accommodating and collaborating*. The collaboration behaviour tends to yield a win-win resolution.

5. **CONFLICT MANAGEMENT STRATEGIES** Conflict management strategies focused on individuals include increasing awareness of the sources of conflict, increasing diversity awareness and skills, practising job rotation or temporary assignments, and using permanent transfers or dismissals when necessary. Strategies focused on the whole organization include changing an organization's structure or culture and altering the source of conflict.

6. **NEGOTIATION STRATEGIES** Negotiation is a conflict resolution technique used when parties to a conflict have approximately equal levels of power and try to come up with an acceptable way to allocate resources to each other. In *distributive negotiation*, the parties perceive that there is a fixed level of resources for them to allocate, and each competes to receive as much as possible at the expense of the others, not caring about their relationship in the future. In *integrative bargaining*, the parties perceive that they may be able to increase the resource pie by coming up with a creative solution to the conflict, trusting each other, and cooperating with each other to achieve a win-win resolution. Five strategies that managers can use to facilitate integrative bargaining are to emphasize big-picture goals; focus on the problem, not the people; focus on interests, not demands; create new options for joint gain; and focus on what is fair. *Collective bargaining* is the process through which labour unions and managers negotiate agreements.

Key Terms

collective bargaining, p. 391
communication, p. 372
decoding, p. 373
distributive negotiation, p. 390
encoding, p. 373
filtering, p. 382
grapevine, p. 383
information distortion, p. 382
information richness, p. 376
integrative bargaining, p. 391
jargon, p. 382
medium, p. 373

message, p. 373
negotiation, p. 390
noise, p. 373
nonverbal communication, p. 373
organizational conflict, p. 385
perception, p. 374
receiver, p. 373
rumours, p. 383
sender, p. 373
stereotypes, p. 374
verbal communication , p. 373

Wrap-Up to Opening Case

We began this chapter by examining the use of the "robotic communicator" for someone who is a teleworker. In view of the critical importance of communication in the workplace, this robot was an innovative piece of technology to bridge the 1900-kilometre distance between an employee in Halifax and the head office in Waterloo, Ontario. While there are pros and cons to such a tool, in the case selected, it seems to work rather well.

A reality of communication is that it is considered a "soft skill" versus a "hard skill" such as accounting. Many today would argue over such traditional terminology because it is often the "hard stuff" that gets a person *hired* but usually the "soft stuff" that gets a person *fired*. In other words, it is the *way* we communicate about what we know, how we manage conflict, and how skillful we are in negotiations that determines much. We saw with emotional intelligence that it is metaphorically the "oxygen" for getting what needs to be accomplished at work.

Lisa Fried of OfficeTeam in Surrey, B.C., said technical skills are "cut and dried," but interpersonal skills are more "situational and complex."

In a May 2007 survey by OfficeTeam, HR.com and the International Association of Administrative Professionals (IAAP), 67 percent of human resource managers (300 administrative professionals and 400 HR managers) polled said they would hire an applicant with strong soft skills whose technical abilities were lacking; only 9 percent would hire someone who had strong technical expertise but weak interpersonal skills. The survey was released to coincide with the Administrative Professionals Week.[44] Valued soft skills, with the percentage of managers who rated them as most in demand, were as follows:

- Organizational skills (87)

- Verbal communication (81)

- Teamwork and collaboration (78)

- Problem solving (60)

- Tact and diplomacy (59)

- Business writing (48)

- Analytical skills (45)

Sandra P. Chandler, international president for IAAP, said in a statement that the survey results indicate an increasingly complex administrative world. "Today's professionals often negotiate with vendors, plan meetings and special events, create presentations, and interview and supervise other employees. While office technology skills are very important, excellent interpersonal abilities are invaluable and usually difficult to teach."

Management in Action

Topics for Discussion and Action

Level 1

1. Describe the communication process. Why is perception important?
2. Why do some managers find it difficult to be good listeners?
3. Describe the sources of organizational conflict. Which type of strategies—those that focus on the individual or those that focus on the structure and culture of the organization—are suitable to diminish each source?

Level 2

4. Explain why subordinates might filter and distort information about problems and performance shortfalls when communicating with their managers.
5. Interview a manager to determine the kinds of conflicts that occur in the organization and the strategies that are used to manage them.
6. Which medium (or media) do you think would be appropriate for a manager to use when sending the following messages to a subordinate?
   a. Getting a raise
   b. Not receiving a promotion
   c. Disciplining an employee for being consistently late
   d. Adding job responsibilities
   e. Creating the schedule for company holidays for the upcoming year.
   Explain your choices.

Level 3

7. Why is integrative bargaining a more effective way of resolving conflicts than is distributive negotiation?
8. Explain why linguistic differences can lead to ineffective communication.
9. Listen to the podcast by Jack and Suzy Welch, called "The Connected Leader: How Will the Internet Change Leadership?" at www.businessweek.com/mediacenter/qt/podcasts/welchway/welchway_06_13_08.mp3. How do they describe the changes to the manager's job in the way that information is communicated via the Internet?

Building Management Skills

Answer the following questions about the organization you have chosen to follow:

1. What kinds of communication media are commonly used in this organization for the various types of messages? Are the media appropriate for the messages?

2. Have there been any examples of organizational conflict? What was the nature of the conflict, and how was it resolved?

Management for You

Consider a person with whom you have had difficulty communicating. Using the communication skills for senders as a start, analyze what has gone wrong with the communication process with that person. What can be done to improve communication? To what extent did sender and receiver problems contribute to communication breakdown?

Small Group Breakout Exercise

NEGOTIATING A SOLUTION

Form groups of three or four. One member of your group will play the role of Jane Rister, one member will play the role of Michael Schwartz, and one or two members will be observer(s) and spokesperson(s) for your group.

Jane Rister and Michael Schwartz are assistant managers in a large department store. They report directly to the store manager. Today they are meeting to discuss important problems that they need to solve but on which they disagree.

The first problem hinges on the fact that either Rister or Schwartz needs to be on duty whenever the store is open. For the last six months, Rister has taken most of the least desirable hours (nights and weekends). They are planning their schedules for the next six months. Rister hopes Schwartz will take more of the undesirable times, but Schwartz has informed Rister that his wife has just started a nursing job that requires her to work weekends, so he needs to stay home on weekends to take care of their infant daughter.

The second problem concerns a department manager who has had a hard time retaining sales people in his department. The turnover rate in his department is twice that of the other departments in the store. Rister thinks the manager is ineffective and wants to fire him. Schwartz thinks the high turnover is a fluke and the manager is effective.

The last problem concerns Rister's and Schwartz's vacation schedules. Both managers want to take off the week of July 1, but, as mentioned above, one of them needs to be in the store whenever it is open.

1. The group members playing Rister and Schwartz assume their roles and negotiate a solution to these three problems.
2. Observers take notes on how Rister and Schwartz negotiate solutions to their problems.
3. Observers determine the extent to which Rister and Schwartz use distributive negotiation or integrative bargaining to resolve their conflicts.
4. When called on by the instructor, observers communicate to the rest of the class how Rister and Schwartz resolved their conflicts, whether they used distributive negotiation or integrative bargaining, and their actual solutions.

Business Planning Exercise

After reading this chapter you and your team realize that you will have to negotiate with many different people when operating your venture.

1. Make a list of all the parties you will have to negotiate with in order to operate the venture.
2. Which negotiation strategy will you use with each of the parties, and why?

Managing Ethically

About 75 percent of medium and large companies that were surveyed engaged in some kind of monitoring of employees' email and Internet activities. Critics say this is an invasion of privacy. Proponents say that Web surfing costs millions of dollars in lost productivity. What is your opinion of Web surfing? To what extent should it be allowed? When does Internet use at work become unethical? To what extent should it be monitored? When does monitoring become unethical?

Exploring the World Wide Web

SPECIFIC ASSIGNMENT

Many companies use the World Wide Web to communicate with prospective employees, including Ford Motor Company of Canada, Ltd. Scan the Ford website (www.ford.ca) to learn more about this company and the kinds of information it communicates to prospective employees through its website. Then click on "More About Ford" and "Career Centre." Click on the various selections in this location of the website, such as "Ford in Canada," "Career Starting Points," "Empowerment, Diversity, Teamwork," and "Sharing in the Rewards."

1. What kinds of information does Ford communicate to prospective employees through its website?
2. How might providing this information on the web help Ford Canada attract new employees?

GENERAL ASSIGNMENT

Find the website of a company that you know very little about. Scan the website of this company. Do you think it effectively communicates important information about the company? Why, or why not? Can you think of anything that customers or prospective employees might want to see on the website that is not currently there? Is there anything on the website that you think should not be there?

McGraw-Hill Connect™—Available 24/7 with instant feedback so you can study when you want, how you want, and where you want. Take advantage of the Study Plan—an innovative tool that helps you customize your learning experience. You can diagnose your knowledge with pre- and post-tests, identify the areas where you need help, search the entire learning package for content specific to the topic you're studying, and add these resources to your personalized study plan. Visit www.mcgrawhillconnect.ca to register—take practice quizzes, search the e-book, and much more.

Be the Manager

Assume you are a middle-level manager at a data processing company. After monitoring the online user statistics, it is evident that several employees are using company time to send personal emails. You have been asked by your boss to create a company policy on personal emails at work and send a memo to the employees describing it. Share your thoughts with two other students, and consolidate everyone's thoughts on the policy into one memo.

Integrated Case

Three Strikes and You're Out[45]

To save Chrysler Group LLC, chief executive Sergio Marchionne has to create a mid-size sedan that can compete with the world's best. It is a three- to five-year job, and he may have two years to do it.

Chrysler, which got a US$15-billion government bailout, may be out of cash in 24 months if he does not return the Auburn Hills (MI)–based company to profitability. Developing a car to rival perennial top sellers Toyota Camry and Honda Accord would normally take at least three years, analysts say.

Marchionne, 57, the Italian-Canadian CEO of Fiat SpA who brought that company back from near ruin, stepped into the toughest challenge of his career by taking control of Chrysler. Failure may mean not only the demise of the third-largest U.S. automaker and tens of thousands of jobs, it may prevent Marchionne from turning Fiat (Turin, Italy) into a global player.

"He's going to have a much harder-time than at Fiat," said Maryann Keller, president of consulting firm Maryann Keller & Associates in Stamford, Connecticut. She has covered the auto industry since 1972 and said the question is "whether they have time to fix the product problem before they run out of money."

The company must sell at least one million cars in the United States to break even, people familiar with the matter said. It is a hurdle Chrysler may not clear this year after topping two million as recently as 2007, according to researcher Autodata Corp. of Woodcliff Lake, New Jersey. Chrysler can make about US$1-billion operating profit for every 100 000 additional vehicles it sells, one person said. According to bankruptcy documents, Chrysler lost US$16-billion in 2008, the most recent numbers available. Without a quick turnaround, it has about 24 months of cash left, said one person familiar with the finances.

Chrysler may gain time if a rebounding U.S. economy pushes auto sales higher, giving it a better chance of exceeding its break-even point. U.S. auto sales ran at less than a 10-million annual rate during the first half of 2009 after finishing at more than 16 million every year from 1999 through 2007.

Marchionne, who bought a condominium in Birmingham for his Michigan visits, is trying to turn around Chrysler after two previous owners failed. DaimlerAG sold 80.1 percent of Chrysler to Cerberus Capital Management LP in August 2007 after an unsuccessful nine-year merger.

Marchionne's attention to detail amazes colleagues. In 2004, he visited CNH's Chicago-area offices. Near the end of two days of 10-hour slide presentations, he halted the proceedings and asked the presenter to flip back four slides and explain a numerical discrepancy, according to a person who attended.

The presenter admitted the mistake. The room full of executives sat up, stunned that their boss caught such minutiae after 20 hours of PowerPoint, this person said.

Fiat has a 20-percent stake in Chrysler and can get up to 35 percent by reaching performance milestones set in the bankruptcy agreement, such as building a car in the United States that gets 40 miles per gallon or more. The United Auto Workers union retiree health care trust owns more than two-thirds of Chrysler, and the American and Canadian governments own the rest.

"We don't have a car that can compete in the largest segment of the market."

Adding to Chrysler's urgency is a consumer shift toward smaller vehicles as volatile gasoline prices and rising U.S. fuel-economy standards push buyers toward passenger cars, which now outsell light trucks in the United States. As of August 2009, the sales breakdown is 53 percent cars to 47 percent trucks, according to researcher Autodata Corp. As recently as 2007, that ratio was 53 percent trucks to 47 percent cars.

In the U.S. government's just-ended program to get consumers to trade in older gas-guzzlers for new fuel-efficient vehicles, 6 percent of purchases were Chrysler-made, 13 percent were Hondas.

Chrysler's U.S. market share is 9.2 percent, down from 11 percent a year earlier. Kristin Dziczek, an analyst at the Center of Automotive Research in Ann Arbor, Michigan, said Chrysler needs Fiat-based products to prevent further erosion.

"If fuel prices rise and there's a car-buying resurgence next year, and they don't have anything out there, they could be getting down into the 6-percent market share range," said Mr. Dziczek. "Then they're toast."

"He needs to stage a revolution at Chrysler and turn it from a maker of light trucks to a maker of passenger cars and probably electric cars," said Pierre Bergeron, a credit analyst at Societé Generale SA in Paris.

Fiat has focused on small cars. Its most recognizable model, the Cinquecento or 500, is just under 12 feet long—about six inches shorter than the Mini Cooper, and almost three feet shorter than the Dodge Caliber, Chrysler's smallest. It also gets more than 40 miles to the gallon in city driving.

Marchionne, who was born in Italy and educated in Canada and speaks Italian and English fluently, is already changing Chrysler's philosophy.

"You can't just keep shoving stuff down the customer's throat," he said in an interview on June 30, 2009. "You don't put as much iron on dealers' lots—you make quality products that people will wait a day to get."

"He wants a cultural change," said Ken Lewenza, president of the Canadian Auto Workers union. "He's demanding more accountability. He's giving workers more responsibility, and trying to get people working with a sense of pride. There are people in the plants from Fiat, measuring, engaging, following it up."

Fiat was on the brink of collapse when the Agnelli family, which controls 30 percent of the Italian conglomerate, hired Marchionne in 2004 to be the fifth CEO in two years. It had lost US$11.7-billion in four years and was facing a debt payment it probably could not make. Marchionne fired top managers and sped up development.

At Fiat, Marchionne could be both generous and tough. He would throw weekend barbecues for his team at Fiat headquarters after flying in a load of steaks, fries, and beer from the United States, said a person who attended. He plays cards, drinks with executives, and sleeps on a Fiat corporate jet, when his travel schedule is intense.

As he did at Fiat, Marchionne began his tenure at Chrysler by skimming off layers of management and promoting younger leaders into top positions.

On June 10, 2009, the day he took over Chrysler, he installed a new set of 23 managers—average age just under 45—he had identified during visits to Auburn Hills. According to people familiar with his early days at Chrysler, Marchionne, in his usual black sweater and sometimes smoking Muratti cigarettes, would walk the 5.3 million-square-foot headquarters complex, introducing himself to executives.

Some of his 23 direct reports were promoted several pay grades. Peter Fong used to be the sales manager of the mid-Atlantic region and is now the top sales executive. Others changed jobs entirely. Mike Keegan was in charge of sales incentives; now he plans auto production. Marchionne also visited some U.S. plants, fired the top managers and promoted the people under them.

If Marchionne does not successfully rebuild Chrysler, the automaker may not get another chance.

"It has to work this time," said a Chrysler board member. "A patient can only be operated on so many times before he dies."

Discussion Questions

1. What aspects of the different needs theories could apply to this case?

2. "No matter what one's leadership style, a key component of effective leadership is found in the *power* the leader has to affect other people's behaviour and get them to act in certain ways."[46] How are the different types of power illustrated in this case?

3. In what ways does CEO Sergio Marchionne engage in teamwork?

4. How does communication play a role in this case?

Video Management Case

Could You Go Without Technology for a Week?

Teaching Objective: To consider the role of electronic communication media in work and personal lives.

Video Summary: In this NBC feature, *Forbes* editor Dennis Neal tries to go a week without his cell phone, Blackberry, and email and finds it nearly impossible to do his job, communicate with his family, and manage personal business. His notion that living with technology would help increase face-to-face interaction gives way to total frustration at being unconnected. His experience illustrates how dependent people can become on electronic media and begs the question: Do such media provide convenient communication tools, or do they rule our lives?

Questions to consider

1. How do cell phones and email rank on the information richness scale? When would making a phone call be more effective than sending an email, and vice versa?

2. What are the advantages and disadvantages of using email to communicate?

3. What are some indications—from Dennis Neal's experience and your observations—that people may be too dependent on communications technology?

CHAPTER

13

Managing Organizational Control

Learning Outcomes

1. Define organizational control, and discuss why it is important to overall performance.

2. Describe the four steps in the process of control.

3. Describe three systems of control managers use in operations management.

4. Identify how output, behavioural, and clan controls coordinate and motivate employees to achieve organizational goals.

5. Explain how *innovative* and *conservative* cultures control managerial behaviour.

Organizational Control During a Recession: Winning Case Examples[1]

It is fair to say no one has come out a "winner" from the Great Recession in the conventional sense. Mere survival counts as winning in the worst economic downturn since the Dirty Thirties.

Tuesday will mark the anniversary of the collapse of Lehman Brothers, the giant New York securities firm whose demise turned a bad case of bankerly jitters into a full-blown global financial meltdown.

While the American recession began in December 2007, the great bulk of about 7.3 million North American jobs lost in this epic downturn occurred with stunning severity after September 15, 2008, the day Lehman went down. That is when corporate employers, fearful of running out of cash and no longer having a bank or healthy stock market from which to raise day-to-day operating funds, began slashing payrolls at a pace unprecedented since the Great Depression.

Yet, unlikely as it seems, there have been a few winners, by any definition of that term, in the midst of these remarkably trying times. They include such major business figures as Jim Balsillie and Mike Lazaridis of Research In Motion Ltd.—as well as lesser-known leaders such as Cora Tsouflidou, whose Montreal-based restaurant franchise operation has grown in the past year.

Now that the recessionary forces at last appear to be ebbing, it is time to note how some leaders have been able to rise to the occasion.

1. Jim Balsillie and Mike Lazaridis, co-CEOs, Research In Motion Ltd., Waterloo, Ontario

How do you make the cover of *Fortune* magazine as the fastest-growing company in North America when you are not a start-up and boast 12 800 employees? You are relentless in developing new products—the Curve, Bold, Storm, and Tour among the latest—that are ahead of the curve in design and features, quintupling revenues and profits over four years. Having U.S. President Barack Obama as an unpaid endorser does not hurt.

2. Alain Bouchard, Chairman, President and CEO, Alimentation Couche-Tard Inc., Laval, Quebec

In the guts of a recession, Bouchard pulled off the always difficult feat of integrating his Canadian convenience store chain, whose banners include Mac's and Couche-Tard (roughly translated as "night owl") with a huge acquisition, the huge Circle K chain in the United States. Most recently, the No. 2 convenience store operator in North America, trailing only 7-Eleven, snapped up the On the Run convenience outlets at Exxon, Mobil, and Esso filling stations, bringing the Couche-Tard empire up to 5906 stores.

3. Mark Carney, Governor, Bank of Canada

The neophyte governor, stepping into the large shoes left by highly regarded predecessor David Dodge, arrived just in time for the worst global financial collapse since the Great Depression—putting him front and centre in the rescue mission. Working easily with his American and European counterparts, the personable Carney quietly made an unprecedented amount of liquidity available to financial institutions, moving with alacrity after the Lehman collapse last fall. Unusually transparent for a central banker, Carney has played a "Rudy Giuliani 9/11" role in keeping Canadians informed about remaining challenges and signs of recovery.

4. Rick George, CEO, Suncor Energy Inc., Calgary, Alberta

Already the cream of the crop among oilpatch CEOs, George seized on the sudden plunge in world oil prices to merge with the far larger Petro-Canada, creating an integrated giant (production and retailing) to rival mighty Imperial Oil Ltd. The Brush, Colorado, native, long a Canadian citizen, has so enlarged the combined firms that their foreign takeover is less likely and ended their over-reliance on production (Suncor's Athabasca tarsands) and the downstream (Petrocan's refineries and coast-to-coast retail operations).

Lourens Smak/Alamy
RIM's co-CEOs Mike Laxaridis, left, and Jim Balsillie share top-spot on David Olive's list of recessions winners. (July 14, 2009)

5. Steve Jobs, CEO, Apple Inc., Cupertino, California

Just returned from a successful liver transplant, Apple's mascot is back and girding for the rollout of a jumbo-sized iPod Touch that promises more long lineups of "early adopters" eager to upgrade. The iPhone remains the smartphone gold standard, dominating the consumer market as BlackBerry does the corporate. Together, Apple and RIM have pushed pioneers Nokia, Motorola, and Samsung into second-tier status in the North American market.

6. Alan Mulally, President and CEO, Ford Motor Co., Dearborn, Michigan

It took this outsider to Detroit, recruited from Boeing Co., to mortgage Ford to the eyeballs just before the credit crunch so that Ford alone escaped bankruptcy and government bailout. Ford has eclipsed General Motors as the No. 1 American automaker and will strengthen that hold by replacing as much as 90 percent of its North American models by 2012. Ford was the big Detroit winner in the U.S. cash-for-clunkers program, with August sales up 17 percent, while GM and Chrysler were down 20 percent and 15 percent, respectively.

7. Gord Nixon, President and CEO, Royal Bank of Canada

Like most of his Big Five peers, Gord Nixon has been inundated with offers to acquire struggling American banks. Nixon's insistence on high-quality assets at Royal Bank of Canada, the country's largest lender, has so far kept temptation at bay to use the assets of troubled American banks to bulk up RBC's foothold in the U.S. southeast. Such caution paid off again in RBC's most recent quarter, when the bank exceeded Bay Street expectations with a 24-percent increase in profits, to a record $1.6 billion in the third quarter of 2009, and a 21-percent drop in loan-loss provisions from the previous quarter.

8. Donald Schroeder, President and CEO, Tim Hortons Inc., Oakville, Ontario

Tim Hortons has powered through the recession with new store openings and menu offerings, not letting a downturn get in the way of snapping up high-traffic locations in Canada and the United States, moving into inner-city districts and kiosk locations in office towers, hospitals, and other institutional settings. This accounts for "Tim's" status as North America's fourth-largest publicly traded quick-service restaurant chain, with 2939 outlets in Canada and 536 in the United States. The American market has been tough for Tim's, but it has persisted for more than a decade, this summer opening more than a dozen high-profile stores in Times Square, Madison Square Garden, and other New York locations.

9. Jim Skinner, CEO, McDonald's Corp., Oak Brook, Illinois

The Golden Arches "experience," thoroughly criticized in the films *Fast Food Nation* and *Supersize Me*, is so cheap and ubiquitous that consumers trading down since 2008 have found it less expensive than eating at home. The successful McCafé line has created a new revenue stream for a 54-year-old company that long ago lost its "growth stock" status. New "tiered menus" of cheap to expensive food options have been a hit in Europe. The firm has 66 percent of its stores outside the United States, many in such countries as China (1000 stores alone), where McDonald's is an "aspirational" experience for those enamoured of Western culture. Thus Big M's stock shared company only with that of Wal-Mart Stores Inc. among members of the Dow Jones industrial average in posting gains last year. Its shares have outperformed the S&P 500 over the past three years.

10. Cora Tsouflidou, Founder, Cora's, Montreal, Quebec

This homestyle eatery, launched in 1987 and still run by Montreal's Cora Tsouflidou, 62, has been among Canada's fastest-growing restaurant operations through the recession, with 100 locations in Quebec, Ontario, Atlantic Canada, and the Prairies. Tsouflidou's formula is friendly service, cheap food piled high (one dish is called the Construction Workers' Plate), and limited hours of operation (6 a.m. to 3 p.m.), a boon to franchisees balancing work and family. Each proposed new menu item is first tested in Tsouflidou's home kitchen. Tsouflidou hopes for 200 outlets but says "no" much more often than "yes" on locations that are too pricey or under-trafficked, more assurance that her franchisees will thrive.

Now It's Your Turn

1. Sometimes when students hear the word "control," negative images come to mind. But it does not have to be that way. Review the "Recession Winners" list. Select three examples of how positive control made the difference.

2. Select one "winning" company for background reading. What additional information did you find to support the "recession winners" label?

■■■■ Overview

Organizations are always trying to manage the delicate balance of too much and too little control. Stress is caused by conflict that people cannot handle, loss of control, uncertainty and lack of information. Wendy Poirier, a consultant with Towers Perrin in Calgary, says, "There's still a lot of lip service to the issue of stress management, especially at the most senior levels. But there is more awareness. Especially since the issue of employee engagement has become so hot. It's being seen as the key to improved productivity."

As discussed in Chapter 6, one major task facing managers is organizing—that is, establishing the structure of task and reporting relationships that allows organizational members to use resources most efficiently and effectively. Structure alone, however, does not provide the incentive or motivation for people to behave in ways that help achieve organizational goals. The purpose of organizational control is to provide managers with a means of motivating subordinates to work toward achieving organizational goals, and to provide managers with specific feedback on how well an organization and its members are performing. Organizational structure provides an organization with a skeleton, to which organizational control and culture add the muscles, sinews, nerves, and sensations that allow managers to regulate and govern the organization's activities. The managerial functions of organizing and controlling are inseparable, and effective managers must learn to make them work together harmoniously.

In this chapter, we look in detail at the nature of organizational control and describe the steps in the control process. We discuss three systems of control available to managers for controlling and influencing operations and supply chain management. We then look at types of controls managers can use to motivate and control resources and people: *output, behavioural, and clan controls*. Finally, we discuss the how innovative and conservative cultures control managerial behaviour.[2] By the end of this chapter, you will appreciate the rich variety of control systems available to managers and understand why developing an appropriate control system is vital to increasing the performance of an organization and its members.

L O **1**

What Is Organizational Control?

THINK ABOUT IT

A Husky Solution for Organizational Control[3]

One company that has become a poster child for progressive employee management is Husky Injection Mouldings of Aurora, Ontario. Reflecting the personal values of the company's founder and CEO Robert Schad, the company has constructed a culture that proactively addresses stress in the workplace. In addition to a 150-child on-site daycare centre, Husky also offers workers a subsidized cafeteria, where only healthy foods are served.

Although red meat is not served, chicken, fish, and tofu are available along with a customized salad bar. Herbal teas are free.

Husky also has a wellness centre that employs a naturopath and a full-time massage therapist and a chiropractor. At the fitness centre, tai chi and yoga are among the daily classes on offer.

"We take the view that if it's good for quality of life, it's good for business," says Dirk Schlimm, Husky's director of human resources. "We mean well, but we also measure our return on investment."

He says the savings come in the fact that his firm's rate of absenteeism is 40 percent below the national average. Spending on its drug plan, which also covers naturopathic remedies, comes in at half the natural average. Workers' Compensation Board claims are 1.5 percent for every 200 000 hours of operation, compared with the average 7.2 percent. Adds Schlimm, "We also offer the usual employee assistance programs for those who are in distress—which takes a burden off managers. The paycheque will always be a motivator, but we also want people to feel like they are part of something meaningful. That's a very basic human desire."

You Be the Manager

1. What is Husky doing to create organizational control?

controlling
Evaluating how well an organization is achieving its goals and taking action to maintain or improve performance; one of the four principle functions of management.

As noted in Chapter 1, *controlling* is the process that managers use to monitor and regulate how efficiently and effectively an organization and its members are performing the activities necessary to achieve organizational goals. As discussed in previous chapters, in *planning* and *organizing*, managers develop the organizational strategy and then create the structure that they hope will allow the organization to use resources most effectively to create value for customers. In *controlling*, managers monitor and evaluate whether their organization's strategy and structure support the plans they have created. On the basis of this evaluation, they determine what could be improved or changed. In the case of Husky, the whole company is proactively geared to managing that effective balance of too much/too little control. Managers create a healthy corporate culture and minimize conflict that people cannot handle—loss of control, uncertainty and lack of information. Husky will not only have that healthy work culture but also an effective bottom line. Husky managers are proactive and participative in their culture; organizing is seen in their flexible structures that can respond effectively to employee well-being and business demands; leading is demonstrated because managers truly support and build an organizational culture

FIGURE 13.1 | The Importance of Control

that leads by example; and controlling is illustrated in their ability to balance the too much/too little organizational control process. By investing in their employees, managers build self-controls and organizational controls in a mutually satisfying manner.

The Importance of Organizational Control

Control systems are intended to make organizations more successful. As we see in Figure 13.1, they help managers do the following:[4]

1. *Adapt to change and uncertainty.* We described in Chapter 2 how managers face uncertain task and external environments. New suppliers and customers can appear, as well as new technologies and regulations. Control systems help managers anticipate these changes and be prepared for them.
2. *Discover irregularities and errors.* There may be problems with quality control, customer service, or even human resource management. Control systems help managers uncover these problems before they become too serious to overcome.
3. *Reduce costs, increase productivity, or add value.* Control systems can be used to reduce labour or production costs, to improve productivity, or to add value to a product, making it more attractive to a customer.
4. *Detect opportunities.* Control systems can help managers identify new markets, demographic changes, new suppliers, and other opportunities.
5. *Deal with complexity.* When organizations become large, it sometimes becomes impossible to know what the different units are doing. This is particularly the case when two companies merge. There may be redundancies in product lines or employees. Control systems help managers deal with these complexities.
6. *Decentralize decision making, and facilitate teamwork.* When control systems are in place, managers can allow employees to make more decisions, and work in teams.

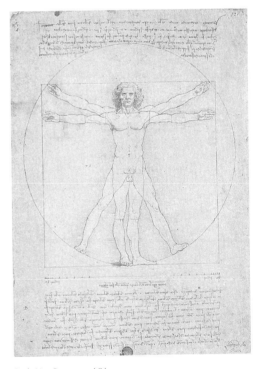

Scala/Art Resource, NY
This famous Leonardo da Vinci drawing illustrates the artist's concern for understanding how the human body controls its own movements and how the different parts of the body work together to maintain the body's integrity. The interconnection of the body is similar to the way in which various departments operate in an organization.

LO 2

Steps in the Control Process

The control process can be broken down into four steps: establishing standards of performance, then measuring, comparing, and evaluating actual performance (see Figure 13.2).[5]

Step 1: *Establish the standards of performance*

At Step 1 in the control process, managers decide on the standards of performance, goals, or targets that they will use to evaluate the performance of either the entire organization or some part of it, such as a division, a function, or an individual. The standards of performance that managers select measure efficiency, quality, responsiveness to customers, and innovation.[6] If managers decide to pursue a low-cost strategy, for example, they need to measure efficiency at all levels in the organization.

At the corporate level, a standard of performance that measures efficiency is *operating costs*—the actual costs associated with producing goods and services, including all employee-related costs. Top managers might set a corporate goal of "reducing operating costs by 10 percent for the next three years" to increase efficiency. Corporate managers might then evaluate divisional managers for their ability to reduce operating costs within their respective divisions, and divisional managers might set cost-savings targets for functional managers. Thus, performance standards selected at one level affect those at the other levels, and ultimately individual managers are evaluated for their ability to reduce costs. For example, S.I. Newhouse, the owner of Condé Nast Publications Inc., which produces magazines such as *GQ*, *Vanity Fair*, *Vogue*, and *Wired*, started an across-the-board attempt to reduce costs so that he could reverse the company's losses and instructed all divisional managers to begin a cost-cutting

Condé Nast
Publications Inc.
www.condenast.com

FIGURE 13.2 | Steps in Organizational Control

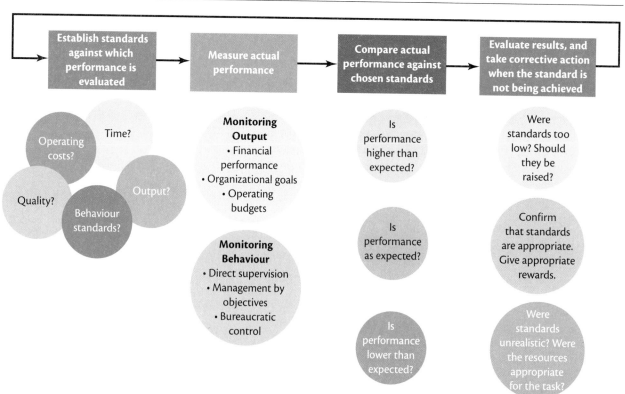

program. When Newhouse decided to retire, he chose Steven T. Florio to replace him. Florio had been the division head who had been most successful in reducing costs and increasing efficiency at *The New Yorker* magazine.

Managers can set a variety of standards, including time, output, quality, and behaviour standards. *Time standards* refer to how long it is supposed to take to complete a task. Some companies, for instance, instruct staff that all emails must be answered within 24 hours. *Output standards* refer to the quantity of the service or product the employee is to produce. *Quality standards* refer to the level of quality expected in the delivery of goods or services. For instance, a company might set what it considers an acceptable level of defects. Or a retail store might set a standard of one complaint per thousand customers served. Finally, a company might set *behaviour standards*, which can govern such factors as hours worked, dress code, or how one interacts with others.

Managers must be careful to choose standards of performance that are not harmful in unintended ways. If managers focus on just one issue (such as efficiency) and ignore others (such as determining what customers really want and innovating a new line of products to satisfy them), managers may end up hurting their organization's performance. Being aware of this threat, managers at Husky take a proactive approach to organizational control and not only emphasize efficiency (what needs to get done), but also effectiveness (how it is done) by creating an organizational culture that supports their employees' well-being.

Step 2: *Measure actual performance*

Once managers have decided which standards or targets they will use to evaluate performance, the next step in the control process is to measure actual performance. In practice, managers can measure or evaluate two things: (1) the actual *outputs* that result from the behaviour of their members and (2) the *behaviours* themselves (hence the terms *output* control and *behaviour control*).[7]

Sometimes both outputs and behaviours can be easily measured. Measuring outputs and evaluating behaviour are relatively easy in a fast-food restaurant, for example, because employees are performing routine tasks. Managers of a fast-food restaurant can measure outputs quite easily by counting how many customers their employees serve and how much money customers spend. Managers can easily observe each employee's behaviour and quickly take action to solve any problems that may arise.

When an organization and its members perform complex, nonroutine activities that are difficult to measure, it is much more difficult for managers to measure outputs or behaviour.[8] It is very difficult, for example, for managers in charge of R&D departments at Merck or Microsoft to measure performance or to evaluate the performance of individual members because it can take 5 or 10 years to determine whether the new products that scientists are developing are going to be profitable. Moreover, it is impossible for a manager to measure how creative a research scientist is by watching his or her actions.

In general, the more nonroutine or complex organizational activities are, the harder it is for managers to measure outputs or behaviours.[9] Outputs, however, are usually easier to measure than behaviours because they are more tangible and objective. Therefore, the first kind of performance measures that managers tend to use are those that measure outputs. Then managers develop performance measures or standards that allow them to evaluate behaviours in order to determine whether employees at all levels are working toward organizational goals. Some simple behaviour measures are: Do employees come to work on time? Do employees consistently follow the established rules for greeting and serving customers? Each type of output and behaviour control and the way it is used at the different organizational levels—corporate, divisional, functional, and individual—is discussed in detail later in the chapter.

Step 3: *Compare actual performance against chosen standards of performance*

During Step 3, managers evaluate whether—and to what extent—performance deviates from the standards of performance chosen in Step 1. If performance is higher than expected, managers might decide that performance standards are too low and may raise them for the next period to challenge subordinates.[10] Managers at Japanese companies are well known for the way they try to raise performance in manufacturing settings by constantly raising performance standards to motivate managers and employees to find new ways to reduce costs or increase quality.

However, if performance is too low and standards were not reached, or if standards were set so high that employees could not achieve them, managers must decide whether the deviation is substantial enough to warrant taking corrective action.[11] See Figure 13.3. If managers are to take any form of corrective action, Step 4 is necessary.

Step 4: *Evaluate the result and initiate corrective action if necessary*

The final step in the control process is to evaluate the results. Whether performance standards have been met or not, managers can learn a great deal during this step. If managers decide that the level of performance is unacceptable, they must try to solve the problem. Sometimes, performance problems occur because the standard was too high—for example, a sales target was too optimistic and impossible to achieve. In this case, adopting more realistic standards can reduce the gap between actual

FIGURE 13.3 | Variance Analysis

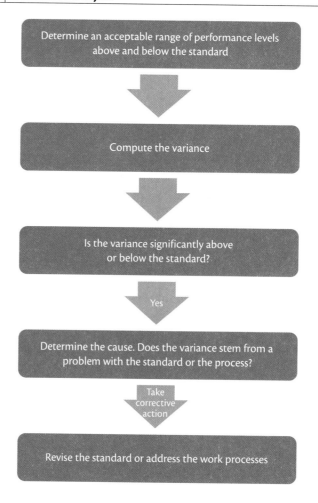

performance and desired performance. However, if managers determine that something in the situation is causing the problem, then to raise performance they will need to change the way in which resources are being used.[12] Perhaps the latest technology is not being used, perhaps workers lack the advanced training they need to perform at a higher level, perhaps the organization needs to buy its inputs or assemble its products abroad to compete against low-cost rivals, or perhaps it needs to restructure itself or re-engineer its work processes to increase efficiency. If managers decide that the level has been achieved or exceeded, they can consider whether the standard set was too low. However, they might also consider rewarding employees for a job well done.

Establishing targets and designing measurement systems can be difficult for managers. Because of the high level of uncertainty in the organizational environment, managers rarely know what might happen. Thus it is vital for managers to design control systems to alert them to problems so that these can be dealt with before they become threatening. Another issue is that managers are not just concerned with bringing the organization's performance up to some predetermined standard; they want to push that standard forward, to encourage employees at all levels to find new ways to raise performance.

Control Systems

L O 3

As we see from the control process described above, managers need effective control systems to help them evaluate whether they are staying on target with their planned performance. **Control systems** are formal target-setting, monitoring, evaluation, and feedback systems that provide managers with information about whether the organization's strategy and structure are working efficiently and effectively.[13] Effective control systems alert managers when something is going wrong and give them time to respond to opportunities and threats. An effective control system has three characteristics:

control systems
Formal target-setting, monitoring, evaluation, and feedback systems that provide managers with information about how well the organization's strategy and structure are working.

- It is flexible enough to allow managers to respond, as necessary, to unexpected events.

- It provides accurate information and gives managers a true picture of organizational performance.

- It provides managers with the information in a timely manner because making decisions on the basis of outdated information is a recipe for failure.

New forms of information technology have revolutionized control systems because they ease the flow of accurate and timely information up and down the organizational hierarchy and between functions and divisions. Today, employees at all levels of the organization routinely feed information into a company's information system or network and start the chain of events that affect decision making at some other part of the organization. This could be the department-store clerk whose scanning of purchased clothing tells merchandise managers what kinds of clothing need to be reordered; or the salesperson in the field who uses a wireless laptop to send information about customers' changing needs or problems.

Controlling Operations

Operations management is the process of managing the use of materials and other resources in producing an organization's goods and services. Operations managers include titles such as manufacturing managers, purchasing managers, and logistics (transportation) managers. These managers focus on the five "Ps" of the organizations' operations: *people* (the labour force), *plants* (facilities), *parts* (inputs), *processes* (technology and work flow), and *planning and control systems* (standards and measures for quality control).

operations management
The process of managing the use of materials and other resources in producing an organization's goods and services.

FIGURE 13.4 | Three Systems of Control

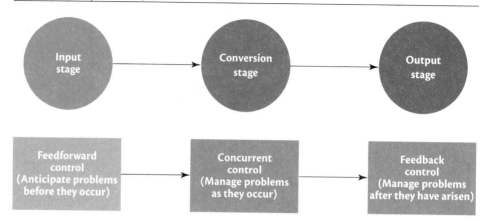

In managing a production (or service) process, managers focus on the three stages of the process of taking the raw materials and transforming them into a useable finished product or service. Control systems are developed to measure performance at each stage (see Figure 13.4).

Feedforward Control

feedforward control
Control that allows managers to anticipate and deal with potential problems.

Before the work begins, managers use **feedforward control** to anticipate possible problems that they can then avoid once the work is underway.[14] For example, by giving stringent product specifications to suppliers in advance (a form of performance target), an organization can control the quality of the inputs it receives from its suppliers and thus avoid potential problems at the conversion stage (see Figure 13.4). Similarly, by screening job applicants and using several interviews to select the most highly skilled people, managers can lessen the chance that they will hire people who lack the skills or experience needed to perform effectively. Another form of feedforward control is the development of management information systems that provide managers with timely information about changes in the task and general environments that may impact their organization later on. Effective managers always monitor trends and changes in the external environment to try to anticipate problems.

Concurrent Control

concurrent control
Control that gives managers immediate feedback on how efficiently inputs are being transformed into outputs so that managers can correct problems as they arise.

During the actual production phase, **concurrent control** gives managers immediate feedback on how efficiently inputs are being transformed into outputs so that managers can correct problems as they arise. Concurrent control alerts managers to the need for quick reaction to the source of the problem, be it a defective batch of inputs, a machine that is out of alignment, or an employee who lacks the skills necessary to perform a task efficiently. Concurrent control is at the heart of total quality management programs, in which employees are expected to constantly monitor the quality of the goods or services they provide at every step of the production process and inform managers as soon as they discover problems. One of the strengths of Toyota's production system, for example, is that individual employees are given the authority to push a button to stop the assembly line whenever they discover a quality problem. When all problems have been corrected, the result is a finished product that is much more reliable.

Feedback Control

feedback control
Control that gives managers information about customers' reactions to goods and services so that corrective action can be taken if necessary.

Once the work is completed, managers use **feedback control** to provide information about customers' reactions to goods and services so that corrective action can be taken if necessary. For example, a feedback control system that monitors the number of customer returns alerts managers when defective products are being produced, and a system that measures increases or decreases in product sales alerts managers to changes in customer tastes so they can increase or reduce the production of specific products.

To summarize, all processes of production (and service provision) have control mechanisms at each stage to measure performance and determine if standards are being met. If significant deviations between the actual performance and the objective are found, managers can take action to correct the situation anywhere along the supply chain. **Supply chain management** involves all the activities in procuring materials, transforming them into parts or finished products, and delivering them to consumers.

supply chain management
The activities involved in procuring raw materials, transforming them into parts or finished products and delivering them to consumers.

Types of Control to Coordinate and Motivate Employees

Managers need to determine internal control measures that will motivate employees and ensure that they perform effectively. In the following sections, we consider the three most important types of control that managers use to coordinate and motivate employees: *output control*, *behaviour control*, and *clan control*. Managers use all three to govern and regulate organizational activities, no matter what specific organizational structure is in place.

THINK ABOUT IT

Over the Top CEO Compensation Leaves Investors in the Cold[15]

"Just because the spate of mergers and acquisitions in recent years keeps some investors up at night doesn't mean CEOs are losing any sleep over the rash of Wall Street deals.

That's because large new grants of stock and options offset the effects of poor performance on CEO wealth following an acquisition. It's a situation that raises the question: How effective are current compensation schemes in controlling the conflicts of interests between corporate managers and shareholders?

Given the flurry of mergers and acquisitions in recent months, investors have good reason to be disturbed by this trend. It's time to pay heed to their demand for greater corporate governance.

From Wall Street to Main Street, corporate governance is a hot topic in light of this decade's accounting scandals in companies such as Enron and WorldCom. This is underscored by a new wave of emboldened shareholder activists and company watchdogs, who demand greater transparency and management accountability in this climate of market volatility and recessionary fears.

The bottom line is that corporate governance is about investor protection. And if there's one topic that gets investors grumbling in 2008, it's the lavish salaries, stock option packages, and over-the-top perks reserved for today's CEOs.

So it is interesting to explore the interplay of corporate governance and executive compensation in one very important arena: the market for corporate control.

In 2007, global mergers-and-acquisitions activity reached record proportions, from technology to mining to media. And the deal making shows no signs of letting up in 2008—in Canada or internationally.

All of this is playing out against a backdrop of economic volatility, and an escalating concern about the growing gap between CEO salaries and compensation levels for the rest of us.

Past research has shown that many acquisitions destroy value. So shareholders might assume that CEOs' large equity portfolios may discourage them from making bad acquisitions.

Here's where those shareholders are misled. Even in mergers where bidding shareholders are worse off, bidding CEOs are better off three-quarters of the time.

Think about the bonuses and other financial considerations a CEO receives in exchange for sanctioning a merger. It turns out the value of this compensation after an acquisition could swamp any incentive effect provided by the CEO's preacquisition portfolio.

This is not the news most investors will want to hear.

In 2007, I investigated the role of executive compensation in corporate acquisition decisions in my joint work with Professor Jarrad Harford of the University of Washington (*Journal of Finance*, 2007). We looked at all completed U.S. mergers announced between 1993 and 2000.

It turns out that following the acquisition, company performance suffers, market to book value, return on assets and stock return all drop, and leverage increases. At the same time, the acquiring CEO's compensation and wealth increased substantially.

And there is a clear and increasing relationship between the change in acquiring CEO pay, particularly CEO total pay (which includes long-term incentive payouts), and the size of transaction value.

Next up: the question of whether acquiring CEOs are overpaid relative to industry, time, and economic factors. Our research showed that indeed, acquiring CEOs are overpaid even before making acquisitions.

Then there's the issue of how pay-to-performance sensitivity evolves around the time of acquisition. While non-acquiring CEOs normally are penalized for poor performance, acquiring CEOs are not penalized in the post-merger period.

It's a scenario where many CEOs have low exposure to the downside of mergers, but high exposure to the upside.

Lastly, it's important to consider the long-term wealth effect from making acquisitions.

We divided the acquiring companies into two groups: the overperformers, whose stock increased faster than the broader markets; and yes, the underperformers, whose stock failed to keep pace.

For shareholders, the news is equally grim with the passage of time: One year after a merger, shares of the underperformers lagged the broader market by an average of 52 percent. But thanks largely to new stock and option grants, three quarters of the CEOs at the underperformers ended up richer.

Oddly enough, there is almost zero CEO wealth-to-performance sensitivity when the post-merger performance is poor.

No wonder, then, that investors have become such a jaded lot in 2008."

You Be the Manager

1. Why is organization control and corporate governance such a challenge?

Output Control

All managers develop a system of output control for their organizations. First, they choose the goals or output performance standards or targets that they think will best measure factors such as efficiency, quality, innovation, and responsiveness to customers. Then they measure to see whether the performance goals and standards are being achieved at the corporate, divisional or functional, and individual levels of the organization. If the goals are being met, usually organizations give rewards to employees and managers. If goals are not being met, senior management needs to evaluate the reasons why performance standards are missed.

Financial Measures of Performance

Top managers are most concerned with overall organizational performance and use various financial measures to evaluate performance. The most common are *profit ratios*, *liquidity ratios*, *leverage ratios*, and *activity ratios*. They are discussed below and summarized in Table 13.1.[16]

Profit Ratios

Profit ratios measure how efficiently managers are using the organization's resources to generate profits. *Return on investment (ROI)*, an organization's net profit after taxes divided by its total assets, is the most commonly used financial performance measure because it allows managers of one organization to compare performance with that of other organizations. ROI allows managers to assess an organization's competitive advantage. *Gross profit margin* is the difference between the amount of revenue generated by a product and the resources used to produce the product. This measure provides managers with information about how efficiently an organization is using

TABLE 13.1 | *Four Measures of Financial Performance*

Profit Ratios		
Return on investment	$= \dfrac{\text{Net profit after taxes}}{\text{Total assets}}$	Measures how well managers are using the organization's resources to generate profits.
Gross profit margin	$= \dfrac{\text{Sales revenue} - \text{cost of goods sold}}{\text{Sales revenue}}$	The difference between the amount of revenue generated from the product and the resources used to produce the product.
Liquidity Ratios		
Current ratio	$= \dfrac{\text{Current assets}}{\text{Current liabilities}}$	Do managers have resources available to meet claims of short-term creditors?
Quick ratio	$= \dfrac{\text{Current assets} - \text{Inventory}}{\text{Current liabilities}}$	Can managers pay off claims of short-term creditors without selling inventory?
Leverage Ratios		
Debt-to-assets ratio	$= \dfrac{\text{Total debt}}{\text{Total assets}}$	To what extent have managers used borrowed funds to finance investments?
Times-covered ratio	$= \dfrac{\text{Profit before interest and taxes}}{\text{Total interest charges}}$	Measures how far profits can decline before managers cannot meet interest charges. If ratio declines to less than 1, the organization is technically insolvent.
Activity Ratios		
Inventory turnover	$= \dfrac{\text{Cost of goods sold}}{\text{Inventory}}$	Measures how efficiently managers are turning inventory over so excess inventory is not carried.
Days sales outstanding	$= \dfrac{\text{Accounts receivable}}{\text{Total Sales}}$	Measures how efficiently managers are collecting revenues from customers to pay expenses.

its resources and about how attractive customers find the product. It also provides managers with a way to assess how well an organization is building a competitive advantage.

Liquidity Ratios

Liquidity ratios measure how well managers have protected organizational resources so as to be able to meet short-term obligations. The *current ratio* (current assets divided by current liabilities) tells managers whether they have the resources available to meet the claims of short-term creditors. The *quick ratio* tells whether they can pay these claims without selling inventory.

Leverage Ratios

Leverage ratios such as the *debt-to-assets ratio* and the *times-covered ratio* measure the degree to which managers use debt (borrow money) or equity (issue new shares) to finance ongoing operations. An organization is highly leveraged if it uses more debt than equity. Debt can be very risky when profits fail to cover the interest on the debt.

Activity Ratios

Activity ratios provide measures of how well managers are creating value from organizational assets. *Inventory turnover* measures how efficiently managers are turning inventory over so that excess inventory is not carried. *Days sales outstanding* provides information on how efficiently managers are collecting revenue from customers to pay expenses.

The objectivity of financial measures of performance is the reason why so many managers use them to assess the efficiency and effectiveness of their organizations. When an organization fails to meet performance standards such as ROI, revenue, or stock price targets, managers know that they must take corrective action. Thus, financial controls tell managers when a corporate reorganization might be necessary, when they should sell off divisions and exit from businesses, or when they should rethink their corporate-level strategies.[17] For example, Starbucks had to rethink their corporate strategy after profits declined by 53 percent in 2008.[18]

While financial information is an important output control, on its own it does not provide managers with all the information they need about whether the plans they have made are being met. Financial results inform managers about the results of decisions they have already made; they do not tell managers how to find new opportunities to build competitive advantage in the future. To encourage a future-oriented approach, top managers, in their planning function, establish organizational goals that provide direction to middle and first-line managers. As part of the control function, managers evaluate whether those goals are being met.

Organizational Goals

Once top managers, in consultation with lower-level managers, have set the organization's overall goals, they then establish performance standards for the divisions and functions. These standards specify for divisional and functional managers the level at which their units must perform if the organization is to reach its overall goals.[19] For instance, if the goals for the year include improved sales, quality, and innovation, sales managers might be evaluated for their ability to increase sales, materials managers for their ability to increase the quality of inputs or lower their costs, and R&D managers for the number of products they innovate or the number of patents they receive. By evaluating how well performance matches up to the goals set, managers at all levels can determine whether the plans they had made are being met, or whether adjustments need to be made in either the plans or the behaviours of managers and employees. Thus goals can be a form of control by providing the framework for what is evaluated and assessed.

Operating Budgets

Once managers at each level have been given a goal or target to achieve, the next step in developing an output control system is to establish operating budgets that regulate how managers and employees reach those goals. An **operating budget** is a blueprint that states how managers intend to use organizational resources to achieve organizational goals efficiently. Typically, managers at one level allocate to subordinate managers a specific amount of resources to produce goods and services. Once they have been given a budget, these lower-level managers must decide how to allocate resources for different organizational activities. They are then evaluated for their ability to stay within budget and to make the best use of available resources. The failure of many dot-com companies illustrates what happens when organizations do not emphasize control. It would appear that many dot-com companies focused more on spending whatever money came in (i.e., had a high "burn rate") without consideration of developing and then staying within a budget. This practice proved to be disastrous when investors decided to stop pouring money into these companies after they had little in the way of performance that they could show investors.

> **operating budget**
> A budget that states how managers intend to use organizational resources to achieve organizational goals.

Large organizations often treat each division as a singular or stand-alone responsibility centre. Corporate managers then evaluate each division's contribution to corporate performance. Managers of a division may be given a fixed budget for resources and evaluated for the amount of goods or services they can produce using those resources (this is a *cost* or *expense* budget approach). Or managers may be asked to maximize the revenues from the sales of goods and services produced (a *revenue* budget approach). Or managers may be evaluated on the difference between the revenues generated by the sales of goods and services and the budgeted cost of making those goods and services (a *profit* budget approach). Japanese companies' use of operating budgets and challenging goals to increase efficiency is instructive in this context.

In summary, three components—objective financial measures, performance standards derived from goals, and appropriate operating budgets—are the essence of effective output control. Most organizations develop sophisticated output control systems to allow managers at all levels to maintain an accurate picture of the organization so that they can move quickly to take corrective action as needed.[20] Output control is an essential part of management.

Problems with Output Control

Boards of directors have to adopt new organizational output accounting control systems with managers and executives in order to reduce potential ethical conflicts. When designing an output control system, managers must be careful to avoid some pitfalls, as shown in Figure 13.5. First, they must be sure that their output standards motivate managers at all levels and do not cause managers to behave in inappropriate ways to achieve organizational goals. ScotiaMcLeod's system of rewarding for each individual trade ended up creating "churning." Brokers advised clients to trade too much, and this led to investigations by regulatory bodies, as well as fines and discipline against the brokerages and individual brokers.

FIGURE 13.5 | Pitfalls of Output Control

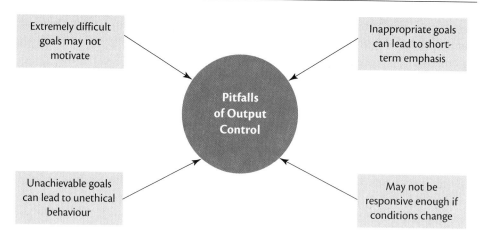

Problems can also occur if the standards that are set turn out to be unrealistic. Suppose that top managers give divisional managers the goal of doubling profits over a three-year period. This goal seems challenging and reachable when it is jointly agreed upon, and in the first two years profits go up by 70 percent. In the third year, however, an economic recession hits and sales plummet. Divisional managers think it is increasingly unlikely that they will meet their profit goal. Failure will mean losing the substantial monetary bonus tied to achieving the goal. How might managers behave to try to preserve their bonuses?

One course of action they might take is to find ways to reduce costs, since profit can be increased either by raising revenues or by reducing costs. Thus, divisional managers might cut back on expensive research and development activities, delay maintenance on machinery, reduce marketing expenditures, and lay off middle managers and employees to reduce costs so that at the end of the year they will make their target of doubling profits and will receive their bonuses. This tactic might help them achieve a short-term goal—doubling profits—but such actions could hurt long-term profitability or ROI (because a cutback in R&D can reduce the rate of product innovation, a cutback in marketing will lead to the loss of customers, and so on).

The long term is what corporate managers should be most concerned about. Thus, top managers must consider carefully how flexible they should be when using output control. If conditions change (as they will because of uncertainty in the task and general environments), it is probably better for top managers to communicate to managers lower in the hierarchy that they are aware of the changes taking place and are willing to revise and lower goals and standards. Indeed, most organizations schedule yearly revisions of their five-year plan and goals.

Second, the inappropriate use of output control measures can lead managers and employees to behave unethically. If goals are too challenging, employees may be motivated to behave unethically toward customers, as sometimes happens in brokerage firms. ScotiaMcLeod has moved to a fee-based system to change the way in which its brokers are rewarded in order to reduce potential ethical conflicts.

The message is clear: Although output control is a useful tool for keeping managers and employees at all levels motivated and the organization on track, it is only a guide to appropriate action. Output controls need to be flexible enough to accommodate changes in the organization's environment. Therefore, managers must be sensitive to how they use output control and constantly monitor its effects at all levels in the organization.

Behaviour Control

Control and the Call Centre: Quebec-Based Multimedia Vidéotron[21]

Scattered atop tables and counters in an employees' cafeteria is a wide selection of magazines and tabloids ranging in topic from pop culture and entertainment to daily news.

It is not unusual for companies to provide reading material for employees to read on their break, but for the staff of the division of Quebec-based multimedia company Vidéotron, which is located in Egypt, perusing the publications is a requisite.

"We want to make sure that if they are asked questions when they talk to customers that they understand what kind of culture we have in Quebec," says Isabelle Dessureault, vice-president of corporate affairs for Vidéotron, which recently outsourced call centre work to Egypt. "Say if we have a big snow storm, the people there can understand more about what people are [going through] here. It can be 30°C and sunny there but someone here might phone and say they have a problem and maybe it's snow on the fibre optics," she says. "We want to make sure people are on the same page even though they're far away."

Sharing magazines and newspapers is only one means companies use to ensure outsourced operations fit in with the corporate culture. Vidéotron, for example, incorporated training about Quebec's culture and the colloquialisms of the French spoken in the province when training Egypt-based employees.

Dessureault says Egypt was chosen because of the prevalence of French there. Planning and logistics for the outsourced offices began a year in advance after Vidéotron partnered with Egyptian call centre company Xceed, a division of Telecom Egypt that specializes in outsourced business solutions.

A team of managers from Vidéotron's IT department, human resources, and customer service travelled to Egypt four times during the planning stages and five employees from the customer service division arrived in Egypt a month before the pilot project was launched.

Employees in Egypt receive more than a month of training before taking calls. "We're the only company in Canada that has a real one-stop shop in our call centres," Dessureault says. "All our agents can answer questions on all of our products."

The company turned to outsourcing to augment its Quebec call centre staff of 2000. "Our surprise is we have the same challenge of not being able to recruit enough," she says.

A growing shortage of employees and an eye to cost-savings is prompting more companies to outsource operations overseas. But there is a lot involved in facilitating a seamless work environment between two geographically separated locations. "One of the key factors in outsourcing, to make sure that the agents are aligned with the culture of the company, is really constant communications at different levels," says Halim Gabra, head of business development for Xceed in North America, who is based in Montreal.

While Xceed is relatively new to outsourcing, it manages 3.5 million calls a month in eight languages for clients from information technology, telecommunication, automotive, travel, and tourism. Due to the multilingual capabilities of its population, one of Xceed's flagship clients is Microsoft Europe, and Bill Gates has personally provided a testimonial on Xceed's website.

Gabra says if there is one single advantage Egypt has over competitors such as India it is the stability of its workforce. He says, "It has become a very high cost for attrition because there's high training costs involved" in outsourcing. For Egyptians, however, "it's more of a prestige to be dealing with international clients and we tend to have much higher retention." But retaining workers is only one challenge in outsourcing, says Lisa Abe, a senior partner at Fasken Martineau's business law practice, who advises clients on drafting contractual agreements for outsourcing arrangements and workplace best practices.

"One of the things that is not focused on as much is the corporate policies. There's a lot of focus on doing the contract and looking at payment and pricing and the scope of the service," she says. "But they forget about the softer aspects," such as conflict resolution measures, complaints procedures, and other internal guidelines and policies integral to running a workplace that must be harmonized.

"It also means doing the due diligence on the country itself. The economics, the laws … You have to make sure your contract is enforceable, that the local laws and judicial system will support your contract" to deal with the protection of information, intellectual property, and even employee fraud, she says.

"It really comes down to people and relationships," says Michael Manson, chief executive of Ottawa-based TaraSpan Group, which facilitates outsourcing for software developers, largely to India. Many of its clients require middle-management personnel from the Indian outsourcer to live in Canada and work at head office for several months before the overseas division is launched to absorb the workplace culture. He says firms that outsource to India also have huge opportunities to market their products there. "When choosing your outsourcing partner, one question you should ask is: 'What can you do for me in India, and how can you help potentially sell my products in India?'"

Manson says software developers in particular, are increasingly outsourcing operations, which demands a skill set that has a higher retention rate. "One of the big issues in India is attrition, and the more you move up the knowledge curve, the lower the rate of attrition," he says of the higher-skilled jobs. "They become an extended part of your team."

You Be the Manager

1. What factors have to be controlled in call centres?

Organizational structure is often viewed as a way of achieving control by designating who reports to whom and what the responsibilities of each individual are. However, structure by itself does not provide any mechanism that motivates managers and nonmanagerial employees to behave in ways that make the structure work or even improve the way it works—hence the need for control. Output control is one way to motivate people; behaviour control is another. In this section, we begin by examining the ways that managerial behaviour can be held accountable through *corporate governance* principles. We end with a discussion of three mechanisms that managers can use to keep subordinates on track and make organizational structures work as they are designed to work: *direct supervision, management by objectives,* and *bureaucratic rules and operating procedures* (see Figure 13.6).

Corporate Governance and Control

After the Enron and WorldCom scandals arose in the early twenty-first century around corporate financial reporting, the ways that top managers account for and report their

FIGURE 13.6 | Types of Control Measures to Coordinate and Motivate Employees

Type of Control	Mechanisms of Control
Output control	Financial measures of performance Organizational goals Operating budgets
Behaviour control	Corporate Governance Direct supervision Management by objectives Bureaucratic rules
Clan control	Values Norms Socialization

performance has been called into question. Canadian-born CEO of WorldCom, Bernard Ebbers, made dubious accounting judgments that misrepresented the actual performance level of the company in an effort to keep the share price high and investors happy. Instead, the fraudulent activity landed him in jail, and the company went bankrupt. In the case of Enron, the CFO Andrew Fastow set up accounting practices that allowed him to defraud investors as well as disguise the declining performance to shareholders. These and other more recent financial scandals around the world, such as Satyam in India in 2009, have resulted in reforms to the way that corporations approach **corporate governance** and accountability. The failure of the self-governing practices of corporations has lead shareholders, particularly institutional investors, to become more active in controlling the management of their assets and scrutinizing top managerial behaviour.

How do companies make managerial behaviour accountable?

corporate governance
The processes companies use to be accountable to its stakeholders, including investors, employees, the environment, and communities.

RIM Governance and Compliance

Research In Motion's annual income grew by 45 000 percent in just 10 years of operation. With such rapid growth, how did the company maintain control and compliance to regulatory standards in accounting?

In 2006, RIM undertook a voluntary internal review of its stock option granting practices. Accounting errors were found in connection with the administration of certain stock options to acquire 4 581 000 common shares between February 2002 and August 2006. The audit's findings resulted in some significant changes to RIM's governance structure. First the roles of chairman of the board and CEO were separated. The chair became a nonexecutive role after Jim Balsillie voluntarily stepped down and maintained the position of co-CEO with Mike Lazaridis, who also holds the position of president of the company. Second, an Oversight Committee of the board of directors was formed to implement changes to the company's board, Audit Committee, Compensation Committee, and Nominating Committee and to change various management roles. In 2009, the Oversight Committee's role would be reviewed to determine if it had completed its mandate of examining executive compensation, the use of stock options as a compensation mechanism, trading by insiders, hiring practices, and a general review of activities within the accounting and finance groups and whether or not it should continue or cease to function. Although no employees were asked to leave the company as a result of the uncovering of errors in governance, RIM did have to restate several years of financial statements and made significant changes to its organizational structure as a result.

"We are satisfied with the thoroughness of the review and we believe that the resulting enhancements to governance and controls will make RIM even stronger as it continues to grow and lead in the thriving market it pioneered," said Estill and Richardson, who sat on the Special Committee investigating the issue in a joint statement. "It must also be said that we have the utmost confidence in Jim Balsillie and the senior management team. Over the last 10 years, incredible results have been accomplished under their stewardship, including an increase in RIM's annual revenue by more than 45 000 percent and an increase in RIM's share price by more than 10 000 percent. In addition, RIM just achieved another important corporate milestone in the fourth quarter ended March 3, 2007, by adding one million BlackBerry subscriber accounts within a single quarter for the first time. These results speak loudly about the management team and the value of their leadership to RIM and its shareholders."[22]

In light of these developments, the role of the board of directors has undergone substantial reform (see Figure 13.7). Nell Minow, the editor of The Corporate Library, an independent U.S.-based research firm that rates boards of directors of public companies and compiles research on corporate governance issues put the matter like this, "boards of directors are like subatomic particles—they behave differently when they are observed."[23] To encourage boards and top managers to do their jobs in a more transparent and effective way government legislation and guidelines set out by stakeholder groups have been developed. In 2002, the Sarbanes–Oxley Act was passed in the United States, imposing considerable demands on board members of publicly traded companies with respect to accountability. Similar, but far less tough, rules were adopted in Canada in 2004 by the Canadian Securities Commission. Principles and guidelines go beyond promoting accountability in financial matters. Figure 13.8 illustrates the Ceres 14-point Climate Change Governance Checklist used by the largest pension fund in the United States, the California Public Employees Retirement System (calPERS), to decide in which companies to invest. Transparent corporate governance systems and adopting a sustainability strategy are increasingly important control measures for creating a competitive advantage as more vigilant shareholders are also more socially responsible in terms of adding economic, environmental, and social values (triple bottom line returns).

Direct Supervision

The most immediate and potent form of behaviour control is direct supervision by managers who actively monitor and observe the behaviour of their subordinates,

FIGURE 13.7 | **Reforms to the Role of the Board of Directors**

Old versus New Corporate Governance Roles

CEO also holds Chair of the Board of Directors (BoD) position	**Top Management is independent from the Board of Directors**
• BoD self governs decisions and practices • BoD members held close professional and/or personal ties to the corporation • BoD relied on top management expertise • BoD met infrequently with little access to relevant information needed to perform their duties • Insider trading and other activities not publically disclosed	• BoD monitors the CEO and control systems • BoD members are independent of the corporation • BoD members possess relevant industry, company, governance and functional area expertise • BoD meets frequently with all required resources • Activities and transactions are communicated in a timely and transparent manner • Independent internal audit committee

FIGURE 13.8 | **Ceres 14-Point Climate Change Governance Checklist**[24]

Board Oversight

- 1. Board is actively engaged in climate change policy and has assigned oversight responsibility to board member, board committee, or full board.

Management Execution

- 2. Chairman/CEO assumes leadership role in articulating and executing climate change policy.
- 3. Top executives and/or executive committees assigned to manage climate change response strategies.
- 4. Climate change initiatives are integrated into risk management and mainstream business activities.
- 5. Executive officers' compensation is linked to attainment of environmental goals and GHG targets.

Public Disclosure

- 6. Securities filings disclose material risks and opportunities posed by climate change.
- 7. Public communications offer comprehensive, transparent presentation of response measures.

Emissions Accounting

- 8. Company calculates and registers GHG emissions savings and offsets from operations.
- 9. Company conducts annual inventory of GHG emissions and publicly reports results.
- 10. Company has an emissions baseline by which to gauge future GHG emissions trends.
- 11. Company has third-party verification process for GHG emissions data.
- 12. Company sets absolute GHG emission reduction targets for facilities, energy use, business travel, and other operations (including direct emissions.)

Strategic Planning

- 13. Company participates in GHG emissions trading programs–up to 30.
- 14. Company pursues business strategies to reduce GHG emissions, minimize exposure to regulatory and physical risks, and maximize opportunities from changing market forces and emerging controls.

educate subordinates about the behaviours that are appropriate or inappropriate, and intervene to take corrective action as needed. When managers personally supervise subordinates, they lead by example and in this way can help subordinates develop and increase their own skill levels (leadership is the subject of Chapter 9). Thus, control through personal supervision can be a very effective way of motivating employees and promoting behaviours that increase efficiency and effectiveness.[25]

Nevertheless, certain problems are associated with direct supervision.

- It is very expensive. A manager can personally manage only a small number of subordinates effectively. Therefore, direct supervision requires a lot of managers, and this will raise costs.

- It can demotivate subordinates if they feel that they are not free to make their own decisions. Subordinates may avoid responsibility if they feel that their manager is waiting to reprimand anyone who makes the slightest error.

- For many jobs, direct supervision is simply not feasible. The more complex a job is, the more difficult it is for a manager to evaluate how well a subordinate is performing.

For all of these reasons, output control is usually preferred to behaviour control. Indeed, output control tends to be the first type of control that managers at all levels use to evaluate performance.

Management by Objectives

To provide a framework within which to evaluate subordinates' behaviour and, in particular, to allow managers to monitor progress toward achieving goals, many organizations implement some version of management by objectives (MBO), which we described in Chapter 5.

From a control perspective, the important element of MBO is that managers and their subordinates need to periodically review the subordinates' progress toward meeting goals. Normally, salary raises and promotions are linked to the goal-setting process, and managers who achieve their goals receive greater rewards than those who fall short. (The issue of how to design reward systems to motivate managers and other organizational employees is discussed in Chapter 8.)

In companies that decentralize responsibility for the production of goods and services to empowered teams and cross-functional teams, management would review the accomplishments of the team, and then the rewards would be linked to team performance as well as the performance of any one team member. For either the individual or team situation, MBO creates the conditions for providing standards that are evaluated.

Bureaucratic Rules and Standard Operating Procedures

bureaucratic control
Control of behaviour by means of a comprehensive system of rules and standard operating procedures.

standard operating procedures (SOPs)
Rules and policies that standardize behaviours.

When direct supervision is too expensive and management by objectives is inappropriate, managers might turn to another mechanism to shape and motivate employee behaviour: bureaucratic control. **Bureaucratic control** is control by means of a comprehensive system of rules and **standard operating procedures** (SOPs) that shape and regulate the behaviour of divisions, functions, and individuals. All organizations use bureaucratic rules and procedures, but some use them more than others.[26]

Rules and SOPs guide behaviour and specify what employees are to do when they confront a problem that needs a solution. It is the responsibility of a manager to develop rules that allow employees to perform their activities efficiently and effectively. When employees follow the rules that managers have developed, their behaviour is *standardized*—actions are performed in the same way time and time again—and the outcomes of their work are predictable. In addition, to the degree that managers can make employees' behaviour predictable, there is no need to monitor the outputs of behaviour because standardized behaviour leads to standardized outputs.

Suppose a worker at Toyota comes up with a way to attach exhaust pipes that reduces the number of steps in the assembly process and increases efficiency. Always on the lookout for ways to standardize procedures, managers make this idea the basis of a new rule: "From now on, the procedure for attaching the exhaust pipe to the car is as follows … " If all workers followed the rule to the letter, every car would come off the assembly line with its exhaust pipe attached in the new way, and there would be no need to check exhaust pipes at the end of the line. In practice, mistakes and lapses of attention do happen, so output control is used at the end of the line, and each car's exhaust system is given a routine inspection. However, the number of quality problems with the exhaust system is minimized because the rule (bureaucratic control) is being followed.

Service organizations such as retail stores and fast-food restaurants try to standardize the behaviour of employees by instructing them on the correct way to greet customers or the appropriate way to serve or bag food. Employees are trained to follow the rules that have proven to be most effective in a particular situation. The better trained the employees are, the more standardized is their behaviour and the more trust managers can have that outputs (such as food quality) will be consistent.

discipline
Managerial control through administering punishment when undesired workplace behaviours, such as absenteeism, lack of punctuality, and low performance, are exhibited, in an attempt to decrease their frequency.

Inconsistent behaviour and undesired behaviour on the part of employees such as not showing up for work, coming late and performing poorly should be formally addressed through discipline. **Discipline** is administering punishment when undesired

FIGURE 13.9 | Progressive Discipline

behaviours are exhibited, in an attempt to decrease the frequency of those actions. It is based on Reinforcement Theory (discussed in Chapter 8). Management introduces an unpleasant stimulus, such as a reprimand or withholding pay, when for example, an employee performs shoddy work. If discipline is given in an objective, fair, and consistent way that makes clear to the employee what the undesired behaviour is, it is a valuable from of managerial control. Management uses varying degrees of penalties when administering discipline according to the nature of the infraction. After a series of written reprimands for continually being late for work, the next step might be docking pay and then temporary suspension. Severe penalties, such as termination of employment would be used for behaviours such as theft and sabotage. The objective is to achieve compliance with the organization's goals and standards through the least severe reprimand possible. See Figure 13.9.

Problems with Bureaucratic Control

All organizations make extensive use of bureaucratic control because rules and SOPs effectively control routine organizational activities. With a bureaucratic control system in place, managers can manage by exception and intervene and take corrective action only when necessary. However, managers need to be aware of a number of problems associated with bureaucratic control because these problems can reduce organizational effectiveness.[27]

First, establishing rules is always easier than discarding them. Organizations tend to become overly bureaucratic over time if managers do everything according to the rule book. When the amount of "red tape" becomes too great, decision making slows, and managers react slowly to changing conditions. This slowness can harm an organization's survival if quicker new competitors emerge.

Second, because rules constrain and standardize behaviour and lead people to behave in predictable ways, people may become so used to automatically following rules that they stop thinking for themselves. By definition, new ideas do not come from blindly following standardized procedures. Similarly, the pursuit of innovation implies a commitment by managers to discover new ways of doing things; innovation, however, is incompatible with the use of extensive bureaucratic control.

Managers must therefore be sensitive about the way they use bureaucratic control. It is most useful when organizational activities are routine and well understood and employees are making programmed decisions such as in mass-production settings or in a routine service setting, for example, in restaurants and stores such as Tim Hortons, Canadian Tire, and Midas Muffler. Bureaucratic control is not nearly as useful in situations where nonprogrammed decisions have to be made and managers have to react quickly to changes in the organizational environment.

To use output control and behaviour control, managers must be able to identify the outcomes they want to achieve and the behaviours they want employees to perform to achieve these outcomes.

Tips for Managers

CONTROL

1. Make a list of "must-do" items that need to be accomplished to get the job done (an efficiency task).

2. Make another list of "must-do" items that need to be accomplished taking into consideration the people who will complete the work (an effectiveness task).

3. Involve employees in training programs that not only will help them do a better job but will meet your control targets (e.g., safety, better financial reporting, etc.) as well.

4. List the different ways you feel you can balance the challenge of too much control versus too little.

Clan Control

THINK ABOUT IT

"Scotiabank," Not "Brian Toda"[28]

Clan control primarily has an internal focus on the involvement and participation of employees to meet the expectations of a rapidly changing environment.[29] It emphasizes the values of cooperation, consideration, agreement, fairness, and social equality. The adaptability culture has strategic leaders that support values promoting autonomy, individual initiative and responsibility, creativity, risk-taking, learning, and entrepreneurship that allow the organization to interpret and translate signals from the environment into new goals and strategies. Both the clan and adaptability cultures place an emphasis on flexibility in meeting the demands of an uncertain and ever-changing environment.[30]

Brain Toda's willingness to share his office space reflects Scotiabank's team-oriented culture. "People who want to be part of a team do well here," says Brian Toda, vice-president of human resources for Scotiabank's compensation group. He has a huge office with upscale cherry wood furniture and a view. What makes Toda different from many other executives is that he invites his employees to use his office when he is not there for such activities as making conference calls from his comfortable, black leather chair or holding small meetings at a round table.

His objective: He wants the office to communicate "Scotiabank" rather than "Brian Toda." Because he has built such a strong organizational culture, staff members are able to carry on without him when he is not there. "It's not like employees are coming into my space. It's their space, too," he explains. He has built such a culture because his aim has always been to deliver "the best employment experience."

You Be the Manager

1. What are key communication errors in this story?
2. What is Brian Toda doing to build an employee self-responsibility and clan control culture?

For many of the most important organizational activities, output control and behaviour control are inappropriate for several reasons:

• Not all employees can be observed on a day-to-day basis.

- Rules and SOPs are of little use in crisis situations or in situations requiring innovation.
- Output controls can be a very crude measure of the quality of performance and could, in fact, harm performance in some instances.

Professionals such as scientists, engineers, doctors, and professors often have jobs that are relatively ambiguous in terms of standard operating procedures and which may require individualized response based on the situation.

How can managers try to control and regulate the behaviour of their subordinates when personal supervision is of little use, when rules cannot be developed to tell employees what to do, and when outputs and goals cannot be measured at all or can be measured usefully only over long periods? One source of control increasingly being used by organizations is clan control, which relies on a strong organizational culture. This form of control is also increasingly being used in organizations that value innovation and want to empower their employees.

How Clan Control Works

William Ouchi used the term **clan control** to describe the control exerted on individuals and groups in an organization by shared values, norms, standards of behaviour, and expectations. The control arising from clan control is not an externally imposed system of constraints, such as direct supervision or rules and procedures, but constraints that come from organizational culture (discussed in Chapter 7).

clan control
Control exerted on individuals and groups in an organization by shared values, norms, standards of behaviour, and expectations.

Clan control is an important source of control for two reasons. First, it makes control possible in situations where managers cannot use output or behaviour control. Second, and more importantly, when a strong and cohesive set of organizational values and norms is in place, employees focus on thinking about what is best for the organization in the long run—all their decisions and actions become oriented toward helping the organization perform well. For example, a teacher spends personal time after school coaching and counselling students; an R&D scientist works 80 hours a week, evenings and weekends, to help speed up a late project; a sales clerk at a department store runs after a customer who left a credit card at the cash register. Many researchers and managers believe that employees of some organizations go out of their way to help their organization because the organization has a strong and cohesive organizational culture—a culture that controls employee attitudes and behaviours. Strong bureaucratic control is less likely to foster positive attitudes and behaviours that encourage employees to go above and beyond. Brian Toda and Scotiabank are examples of how effective clan culture can be in encouraging effective behaviour from all employees. As Toda says, his objective is to deliver "the best employment experience."[31]

How Culture Controls Managerial Action

The way in which organizational culture shapes and controls behaviour is evident in the way managers perform their four main functions—planning, organizing, leading, and controlling—when they work in different types of organizations (see Table 13.2). As we consider these functions, we continue to distinguish between two kinds of top managers: (1) those who create organizational values and norms that encourage creative, *innovative* behaviour and (2) those who encourage a *conservative*, cautious approach in their subordinates. We noted earlier that both kinds of values and norms may be appropriate in different situations.

TABLE 13.2 | *How Culture Controls Managerial Functions*

Managerial Function	Type of Organization	
	Conservative	**Innovative**
Planning	Formal, top-down planning	All managers encouraged to participate in decision making
Organizing	Well-defined hierarchy of authority and clear reporting relationships	Organic, flexible structure
Leading	Rigid MBO and constant monitoring	Managers lead by example Encourage risk-taking
Controlling	Bureaucratic control Closed door corporate governance	Clan control Transparent corporate governance

Planning

Top managers in an organization with an *innovative* culture are likely to encourage lower-level managers to take part in the planning process and develop a flexible approach to planning. They are likely to be willing to listen to new ideas and to take risks involving the development of new products.

In contrast, top managers in an organization with *conservative* values are likely to emphasize formal top-down planning. Suggestions from lower-level managers are likely to be subjected to a formal review, which can significantly slow down decision making. Although this deliberate approach may improve the quality of decision making in a nuclear power plant, it also can have unintended consequences. At conservative IBM, for example, before its more recent turnaround, the planning process became so formalized that managers spent most of their time assembling complex slide shows and overheads to defend their current positions rather than thinking about what they should be doing to keep IBM abreast of the changes taking place in the computer industry.

Organizing

Valuing creativity, managers in an *innovative* culture are likely to try to create an organic structure, one that is flat, with few levels in the hierarchy, and in which authority is decentralized so that employees are encouraged to work together to find solutions to ongoing problems. A product team structure may be very suitable for an organization with an innovative culture.

In contrast, managers in a *conservative* culture are likely to create a well-defined hierarchy of authority and establish clear reporting relationships so that employees know exactly whom to report to and how to react to any problems that arise.

Leading

In an *innovative* culture, managers are likely to lead by example, encouraging employees to take risks and experiment. They are supportive regardless of employees succeeding or failing.

In contrast, managers in a conservative culture are likely to develop a rigid management by objectives system and to constantly monitor subordinates' progress toward goals, overseeing their every move.

Controlling

As this chapter makes clear, there are many control systems that managers can adopt to shape and influence employee behaviour. The control systems managers choose reflect how they want to motivate organizational members and keep them focused on organizational goals. Managers who want to encourage the development of *innovative* values and norms that encourage risk-taking choose output and behaviour controls that match this objective. They are likely to choose output controls that measure performance over the long run and develop a flexible MBO system suited to the long and uncertain process of innovation.

In contrast, managers who want to encourage the development of conservative values choose the opposite combination of output and behaviour controls. They develop specific, difficult goals for subordinates, frequently monitor progress toward these goals, and develop a clear set of rules that subordinates are expected to adhere to. Sometimes managers who are hired by a company do not fit into the existing culture. Calgary-based WestJet fired CEO Steve Smith, who was far more controlling than the company's culture warranted. WestJet's founders sent a strong message to the employees by firing Smith in a year when the company had done very well financially.

The values and norms of an organization's culture strongly affect the way managers perform their management functions. The extent to which managers buy into the values and norms of their organization shapes their view of the world and their actions and decisions in particular circumstances.[32] In turn, the actions that managers take can have an impact on the performance of the organization. Thus, organizational culture, managerial action, and organizational performance are linked together. Geoffrey Relph, IBM's director of services marketing, noted in an interview that his previous company (GE Appliances in Louisville, Kentucky) had a very different set of expectations from that in IBM Canada. "The priorities in GE are: 'Make the financial commitments. Make the financial commitments. Make the financial commitments.' At IBM, the company's attention is divided among customer satisfaction, employee morale, and positive financial results."[33] GE Appliances' focus on financial commitments may deter employees from looking at customer satisfaction also. Relph's experience at GE Appliances may also suggest that managers need to be concerned with employee morale.

GE Appliances Company
www.geappliances.com

Although organizational culture can give rise to managerial actions that ultimately benefit the organization, this is not always the case. Sometimes culture can become so much a part of the organization that it becomes difficult to improve performance.[34] For example, Wayne Sales, the former CEO of Canadian Tire, tried desperately to revitalize customer service in the company's stores. Canadians had become so used to poor service that employees did not see the need to change. However, with increased competition from Home Depot Canada, RONA, Home Hardware, and Lowe's Canada, lack of customer service is a big issue. Sales set out to "drive away the chain's 'crappy tire' image" by changing the control systems to encourage employees to be more customer-focused.[35]

Canadian Tire
www.canadiantire.ca

Summary and Review

1. **WHAT IS ORGANIZATIONAL CONTROL?** Controlling is the process that managers use to monitor and regulate how efficiently and effectively an organization and its members are performing the activities necessary to reach organizational goals. Controlling is a four-step process: (1) establishing performance standards, (2) measuring actual performance, (3) comparing actual performance against performance standards, and (4) evaluating the results and taking corrective action if needed.

2. **CONTROL SYSTEMS** Control systems set targets, monitor and evaluate performance, and help managers make sure the organization is working effectively and efficiently to reach its goals. Three systems of control are used by operations and supply chain managers: feedforward control used to control inputs; concurrent control, used during the conversion stage; and feedback control, used to provide information in the post-production stage.

3. **TYPES OF CONTROLS** To coordinate and motivate employees, *output controls* and *behavioural controls* are used. The main mechanisms to monitor output are financial measures of performance, organizational goals, and operating budgets. *Corporate governance practices* control managerial behaviour, while the main mechanisms to shape employee behaviour and induce them to work toward achieving organizational goals, are direct supervision, management by objectives, and bureaucratic rules and standard operating procedures. *Clan control* operates on individuals and groups through shared values, norms, standards of behaviour, and expectations.

4. **CULTURE CONTROLS MANAGERIAL BEHAVIOURS** Managers in organizations with *innovative cultures* carry out the managerial functions of planning, leading, organizing, and controlling very differently from managers in organizations with *conservative cultures*.

Key Terms

bureaucratic control, p. 422

clan control, p. 425

concurrent control, p. 410

controlling, p. 404

control systems, p. 409

corporate governance, p. 419

discipline, p. 422

feedback control, p. 410

feedforward control, p. 410

operating budget, p. 415

operations management, p. 409

standard operating procedures (SOPs), p. 422

supply chain management, p. 411

SO WHERE DO YOU STAND?

Wrap-Up to Opening Case

In this chapter, we discussed the three types of control: output, behaviour, and clan. *Output* control looks at such factors as financial measures of performance, organizational goals, and operating budget. *Behaviour* control examines direct supervision, management by objectives and rules, and standard operating procedures (SOP). Finally, *clan control* acknowledges values, norms, and socialization.

In each of these types of control, leadership must be present. It is fair to say that without a strong and healthy leadership, control becomes a matter of "power-and-control" versus control as shaping the vision, direction, and movement of people to agreed-upon goals.

The Management Snapshot we looked at— "Organizational Control During a Recession: Winning Case Examples"—provides us with 10 examples of companies, during the recent recession that came out as winners by using effective controls. But you will notice that in each example, leadership was present.

In 2007, Michael Maccoby, former professor at Harvard University, wrote a book called *Leaders We Need*.[36] Early in 2008, we learned that a "leadership gap at the world's largest companies is imminent for reasons far more reaching than a retiring Baby Boom generation."[37] This leadership gap stemmed from IBM's 2008 Global Human Capital Study. More than 75 percent of HR executives worldwide (more than 400 human resource executives in private, public, and not-for-profit organizations from 40 countries took part) reported they were concerned about their ability to develop future leaders. Approximately 52 percent are focused on their inability to rapidly develop employee skills and align those skills to future business needs. And only 13 percent of organizations say they have a clear understanding of the skills they will require in the next three to five years. "These are key issues worldwide, but it was a result that surprised us a little bit," Ringo, global leader, IBM global business services human capital management practice in London, said, "We knew there would be some theme that came out around leadership; we didn't expect to have that level of response."

The authors hope that this textbook has helped both students and professors to give ongoing thought, consideration, and practical efforts to closing the leadership gap. A balanced and positive sense of organizational control from leaders can do much to not only close this gap but also provide exciting opportunities for future work. This future depends on such efforts.

Management in Action

Topics for Discussion and Action

Level 1

1. Define organizational control and why it is important to overall performance.
2. Describe the four steps in the process of control.
3. Describe three systems of control manager's use in operations management.

Level 2

4. Identify the main methods of output and behaviour control, and discuss their advantages and disadvantages as means of coordinating and motivating employees.
5. Why is it important to involve subordinates in the control process?

6. What is clan control and how does it affect the way employees behave?

Level 3

7. What types of controls would you expect to find most used in (a) a hospital, (b) the Armed Forces, and (c) a city police force? Why?
8. Watch the following video or a similar one on YouTube at www.youtube.com/watch?v=aOZhbOhEunY. Describe the culture at Google. What types of control measures are evident in these videos? What kinds of green initiatives make up the culture at Google?
9. Explain how *innovative* and *conservative* cultures control managerial behaviour.

Building Management Skills

Answer the following questions about the organization you have chosen to follow:

1. What are the main types of control used by management to monitor and evaluate the performance of the organization and employees?

2. Are these methods of control appropriate, given the organization's strategy and culture?
3. What recommendations would you make with respect to the organizational control of this enterprise?

Management for You

Your parents have indicated that they are expecting a big party for their 25th wedding anniversary and that you are in charge of planning it. Develop a timeline for carrying out the project, and then identify ways to monitor progress in planning for the party. How will you know that your plans have been successful? At what critical points do you need to examine your plans to make sure that everything is on track?

Small Group Breakout Exercise

HOW BEST TO CONTROL THE SALES FORCE?

Form groups of three or four, and appoint one member as the spokesperson who will communicate your findings to the whole class when called on by the instructor. Then discuss the following scenario:

You are the regional sales managers of an organization that supplies high-quality windows and doors to building supply centres nationwide. Over the last three years, the rate of sales growth has slackened. There is increasing evidence that to make their jobs easier, salespeople are primarily servicing large customer accounts and ignoring small accounts. In addition, the salespeople are not dealing promptly with customer questions and complaints, and this inattention has resulted in a drop in after-sales service. You have talked about these problems, and you are meeting to design a control system to increase both the amount of sales and the quality of customer service.

1. What type of control do you think will best motivate the salespeople to achieve these goals?

2. What relative importance do you put on (1) output control, (2) behaviour control, and (3) organizational culture in this design?

Business Planning Exercise

You and your team realize that you must use a variety of control measures in your venture to monitor and evaluate the use of resources and make sure the goals of the organization are being met. In order to complete the financial plan component of your business plan, you know you must use output control techniques, including the financial ratios and equations in the text, to forecast the cash flow for one year and the break-even point. Angel investors or any bank will want to see the bottom line numbers on your expenses and expected revenues to determine if their ROI will be worthwhile. For the financial plan, you must create a pro-forma cash flow, income statement, opening balance sheet, and break-even analysis.

1. **Cash flow projections for year one**: At which points over the year will your expenses exceed your revenue? How will you make up the shortfall? Subtract all expenses in the cost of goods sold from all revenues to project a net gain or loss for one year. This is your pro-forma **Income Statement**.
2. **Opening balance sheet:** Are the assets and liabilities equal to the shareholders' equity?

3. **Break-even analysis:** When will the revenues exceed the expenses of the venture?
4. Identify the assumptions you will need to make to complete the financial plan section of your business plan such as interest rates, taxation rates, and other details on which to base your financial projections. These should be clearly stated with reference to the specific line item on the spreadsheet.

Managing Ethically

You are a manager of a group of 10 employees in their twenties. They are very innovative and are not accustomed to tight rules and regulations. Managers at the company want order and control on every front. Your team is fighting the rules and regulations, which is creating an ethical dilemma for you. They are being very productive and innovative but clearly not in the way top management wants things run. You have been asked to bring more order to your team. You really like your team and think they are effective but will leave if they are forced to conform. And the company needs their expertise and energy to remain competitive in the high-tech world. What would you do?

Exploring the World Wide Web

SPECIFIC ASSIGNMENT

Review the "Sustainable Competitive Advantage" website (www.1000ventures.com/business_guide/crosscuttings/sca_main.html). Read what the page says on the relationship between corporate culture and building a sustainable competitive advantage in business. Then on the left side of the screen, in a boxed area, click on "Organizational Culture" (www.1000ventures.com/business_guide/crosscuttings/culture_corporate.html), and read what is on this screen.

1. Compare and contrast an *adaptive* versus an *unadaptive* corporate culture in terms of core values and common behaviour.
2. How does this compare with an *innovative* versus a *conservative* culture outlined in this chapter?

GENERAL ASSIGNMENT

Search for the website of a company that actively uses organizational culture (or one of the other types of control) to build competitive advantage. What kind of values and norms is the culture based on? How does it affect employee behaviour?

McGraw-Hill Connect™—Available 24/7 with instant feedback so you can study when you want, how you want, and where you want. Take advantage of the Study Plan—an innovative tool that helps you customize your learning experience. You can diagnose your knowledge with pre- and post-tests, identify the areas where you need help, search the entire learning package for content specific to the topic you're studying, and add these resources to your personalized study plan. Visit www.mcgrawhillconnect.ca to register—take practice quizzes, search the e-book, and much more.

Be the Manager

SAVE THE CHILDREN PROJECT

Assume your professor has asked you to consult and manage the design of a special "Save the Children" innovative program that 10 teams of five students in your course will be working on. Save the Children Canada will be acting as final judge on the winning program submitted by different colleges and universities. You must manage 10 teams; because of the shortness of time for this request, the innovative program will need aspects designed by each team, as no one team can do it all. Hence, all 10 teams will have contributed to the finished product. Your professor will be grading you on how well you actually manage, motivate, and put into action controls to help each team function at optimal levels.

Question

1. What is your plan to control the operations of the teams in such a way that they function optimally?

Video Management Case

Trouble's Brewing[38]

CBC Marketplace makes a startling discovery: Coffee Time, a well-known coffee chain has double the major health violations than its competitors.

Questions to consider

1. What type of control system does the Health Inspection Agency use to determine if the coffee shops are meeting food safety standards?
2. Coffee Time faced twice as many unsafe food handling charges as other major competitors such as Tim Hortons, Starbucks, and Second Cup. What was the nature of those violations?
3. What is the obvious feedforward control measure that Coffee Time should be taking?
4. What kind of control systems is Tim Hortons using when employees fill out "time and temp" logs every two hours?
5. In the Wrap Up to this report, Marketplace suggests three things the consumers can do to minimize risks from poor food handling practices. Which type of control system does each represent?

Source: Aired on February 21, 2007.

Part 6: Integrated Case

Bruce Power: Its Control of Internet Use[39]

Nuclear operator Bruce Power assured today [September 10, 2009] that the abrupt dismissal of dozens of contract workers at its nuclear plant near Kincardine, Ontario, had nothing to do with nuclear safety or station security.

The company said the workers, who were not direct employees of Bruce Power, were found to have violated its code of conduct through inappropriate use of computer equipment, including email and Internet use.

Spokesman Ross Lamont would not confirm how many workers were affected but said the action stemmed from an earlier internal investigation.

"None of the information that we're dealing with here is business-related. There are no trade secrets, and absolutely no impact on operations, on security, on safety. It was just inappropriate behaviour," said Lamont.

Lamont explained that a few isolated code violations triggered a larger investigation that included more widespread monitoring.

"Any significant company has some monitoring of their systems," he said. "We're not confirming numbers, but it's significant enough for it to be alarming."

Earlier reports suggested that as many as 100 workers had been turned away from the Bruce work site, and that the police had been notified.

Lamont, however, told the *Star* that there has been no interaction between Bruce Power and the police and that he is not aware of any suspected criminal activity related to the dismissals.

One fired worker who spoke to the *Star* on the condition of anonymity said his dismissal took him "completely by surprise."

"It's just bizarre," said the former employee who has worked at Bruce Power for more than 20 years.

He acknowledged that some employees had been reprimanded in the past and some even received three-day suspensions for inappropriate Internet use but said he was never warned personally about his own Internet use.

When asked if he remembered reading the company's code of conduct pertaining to Internet use—which states all Internet use should be for company business only—the former employee said he did not.

Both the Power Workers' Union and the Society of Energy Professionals said none of their members were affected. A spokesman for the Canadian wing of the Building and Construction Trades Department, a group of 15 affiliate unions representing everyone from bricklayers to metals workers, declined to comment.

"We're not going to get involved with this one," he said.

Privately owned Bruce Power operates a nuclear plant three hours northwest of Toronto that supplies up to 4700 megawatts of power to Ontario's electricity system. The company is in the process of restarting two older reactors, a multibillion-dollar project that will contribute another 1500 megawatts to the provincial grid.

Discussion Questions

1. Review Figure 13.2, "Steps in Organizational Control." How do you imagine these steps were applied to "the workers, who were not direct employees of Bruce Power, [but who] were found to have violated its code of conduct through inappropriate use of computer equipment, including email and Internet use"?
2. What are your personal experiences with workplace computer use and control in places where you have worked?

Developing a Business Plan APPENDIX A

The Business Plan as an Exercise in the Processes of Management[1]

Writing a business plan may never be a more important exercise than in the context of today's rapidly changing environment. Even if you are not an entrepreneur and do not wish to develop a new original idea and bring it to market, developing a business plan is still a valuable exercise in practising the management processes. It provides a crucial foundation for managing an organization. In this section of the text, we will treat developing a business plan as an exercise in the management processes of planning, organizing, leading, and controlling. By doing the exercises at the end of each chapter, you will have the foundation to put together a plan that will help you develop as a manager. The experience you will gain is valid for profit and not-for-profit organizations as well as new and existing ventures. Writing a business plan gives you practice in thinking about managing activities such as:

- Developing an idea to solve a problem
- Tapping into opportunities and countering threats in competitive conditions
- Organizing resources to achieve goals
- Targeting potential customers with promotional opportunities
- Designing an effective organizational structure
- Securing sources of finance
- Controlling for risk

What Is a Business Plan?

A business plan is a recognized management tool used to document the organization's objectives and to set out how these objectives will be achieved within a specific timeframe. It is a written document that describes who you are, what you intend to accomplish, how you will organize resources to attain your goals, and how you will overcome the risks involved to provide the anticipated returns. In general, a business plan comprises several elements, each giving the reader a piece of the overall picture of the project you are undertaking, and provides convincing reasons why you will be successful in this undertaking. Managers and entrepreneurs use a business plan to seek support and financing to expand an existing business or to finance a new venture.

Putting It All Together

Throughout this course, you may have been asked to complete the end-of-chapter exercises on developing a business plan. Now is the time to start to put all the pieces together to create your comprehensive plan. Draw on the work that you have already done to write the major components of the business plan. See Table B.1.

At this point, you should familiarize yourself with a business planning software. There are several on the market. Your professor will instruct you as to which is appropriate for your course.[2] The software will help you compile the main elements in your plan and calculate the financial statements.

TABLE B.1 | *Major Business Plan Components*

	Check off and date when completed and add any notes of interest
1. Nondisclosure Statement	❑
2. Executive Summary	❑
3. Profile of the Organization	❑
4. Profile of the Industry or Sector	❑
5. Profile of the Product or Service	❑
6. Marketing Plan	❑
7. Organizational Plan	❑
8. Operating and Control Systems Plan	❑
9. Financial Plan	❑
10. Appendices	❑

1. Nondisclosure Statement

A nondisclosure agreement is optional in a business plan. When used, it usually states that the information in the plan is proprietary and not to be shared, copied, or disclosed. The agreement should have a unique "copy number" that is the same as a number on the title page of the plan and a place for the recipient's signature. The agreement should be either a loose-leaf page or a page that can be torn out of the plan and retained by you. See the following example:[3]

Copy Number _____ 123 _____

FFP Consulting Inc.'s business plan is confidential, containing information proprietary to FFP Consulting Inc. None of the information contained in this plan may be reproduced or disclosed to any person under any circumstances without express written permission of FFP Consulting Inc. I have accepted and will protect the confidentiality of this business plan.

_____
Recipient's signature

2. Executive Summary

The executive summary is the first thing, besides the Table of Contents and Title page, that the reader will view, but it is generally the last thing the writer creates. The executive summary is a maximum one-page précis of your business plan. It is based on this summary probably the most important part of your plan because readers will make a judgment as to whether or not they want to continue to examine your plan. The executive summary tells the reader the following information:

- Who you are and what your company/organization does
- The products and/or services that you provide or intend to provide
- Your target markets, that is, who are or will be your customers
- How you will promote your product/service to your customers
- What your financial projections are for a given period
- How you will achieve your goals, that is, your strategy for gaining a competitive advantage
- The strengths of your management team and why the reader should believe you can do what you are proposing
- Identify the major risks you expect and your solutions to minimize these threats

   The Executive summary should be no longer than one or one and a half pages.

3. Profile of the Organization

This section of the business plan tells the reader your vision, mission, and goals for the organization.
   Consider the following questions when preparing this section.

- What is the name of your company/organization?
- What is the legal structure and form of ownership?
- What are your reasons for going into business?
- What problem does your product or service solve, or what needs gap does it fill?
- What experience do you have that would enable you to pursue this venture successfully?
- Who makes up your management team, and what roles and responsibilities will they have?

Vision Statement

The vision for your company/organization is set out in a written statement telling the reader what direction or dream you wish your company to pursue for the next three to five years. Write this statement in the future tense. As stated in Chapter 5, Bill Gate's vision for Microsoft when it first began was to have "a computer on every desk, in every home, and in every office." The vision of the TD Bank is, simply, "to be the better bank."[4] The vision of the Australian company The Body Shop is "to be operating and recognised as the benchmark Company for the integration of Economic Success, Stakeholder Fulfillment, and Social and Environmental Change."[5] Cara Operations Ltd., founded by the Phelan family in 1883, is a privately owned Canadian company and the largest operator of full service restaurants and the leading caterer to the travel industry in Canada. Cara's vision is "to be Canada's leading integrated restaurant company."[6] The vision of Renée's, a Canadian gourmet food products company, is "to be the market leader in developing and delivering superior-quality, innovative fresh food products."[7]

For additional examples, refer to Chapter 5: Managing Planning and Strategy.

Refer to the exercise you did for Chapter 5: Managing Planning and Strategy. Write the vision statement for your venture. Keep it to 150 words or less.

Mission Statement

The mission statement tells the reader what the purpose of your company/organization is. Refer to the mission statement of The Body Shop outlined below (see Table B.2).[8] Ask yourself what the essence of your business is. What will the business really be doing? Why does it exist? What values is it premised on? Every noun, adjective, and verb in the statement is important and should explain the problem that will be solved or the need that will be fulfilled if your plan is implemented. Your mission statement should reflect your basic beliefs, values, and principles.

TABLE B.2 | *Mission Statement of The Body Shop*

Our reason for being is to:

- Dedicate our business to the pursuit of social and environmental change.
- Creatively balance the financial and human needs of our stakeholders: employees, customers, franchisees, suppliers, and shareholders.
- Courageously ensure that our business is ecologically sustainable, meeting the needs of the present without compromising the future.
- Meaningfully contribute to local, national, and international communities in which we trade, by adopting a code of conduct, which ensures care, honesty, fairness, and respect.
- Passionately campaign for the protection of the environment, human and civil rights, and against animal testing within the cosmetics and toiletries industry.
- Tirelessly work to narrow the gap between principle and practice, whilst making fun, passion, and care part of our daily lives.

- Refer to the value statement and code of ethics you created for the exercise you did for Chapter 3: Managing Ethics, Social Responsibility, and Diversity. Incorporate these values and principles into your mission statement.

- Refer to the mission statement you wrote for the exercise you did for Chapter 5: Managing Planning and Strategy.

Write the mission statement for your venture. Keep it to 150 words or less.

Organizational Goals

Organizational goals must be made for the business as a whole and for each functional area. Organizationwide goals are longer term and are strategic in nature, while functional level goals are shorter term and are more operational in nature. For example, corporate- and divisional-level goals are generally made in the areas of market share, profitability, and return on investment. Functional-level goals include how departments will add value for the customer and reduce costs in the production of a good or service. Goals and objectives are statements of the level of performance desired within a certain timeframe. Goals must be formulated so that they are S.M.A.R.T:

- **S**pecific

- **M**easurable

- **A**ttainable
- **R**ealistic, within a
- **T**imeframe

An example of a SMART goal relating to market share might look like the following:

"By the end of the first year of operation, ABC company will have a 20-percent market share for its product XYZ."

The Body Shop might formulate the goal of …

"giving 5 percent of gross profits to the major charitable organizations in the environmental movement by the year 2015."

This goal is consistent with the company's mission and strategic vision as stated above. Once goals are developed, plans must be formulated to achieve the objectives. These plans are generally referred to as strategies. The formulation of strategies depends upon the opportunities and threats facing your company from the forces in the organizational environment. You will formulate your strategy after doing an analysis of the current situation. The competitive analysis and strategy is analyzed in the context of the industry as a whole and detailed in the Marketing Plan component of the business plan.

Formulate the major goal for the venture as a whole, using a one-year timeframe.

Form of Ownership

If you are writing a business plan for an existing organization, the legal entity has no doubt been established already; however, it may make sense to consider a separate legal entity for the new product/service. If you are an entrepreneur or a group of entrepreneurs, you must decide what form of legal entity (form of ownership) will best suit the nature of the business, the competitive strategy, and the organizational structure of the business. Will you need a partner? Should you incorporate or simply operate as a sole proprietor? What advantages, if any, would be there in forming a cooperative structure? Refresh your memory about the advantages and disadvantages of each legal structure by reviewing an introductory business textbook. Now that you have developed your ideas and business plan up to this point, describe the legal form of your organization.

Which legal structure do you think is most appropriate, and why?

The Management Team

At the beginning of a new venture, the principal person who writes the business plan generally has overriding authority over the other members of the management team, if a team exists at all. In the case that several people are involved in the management team, the positions they will hold and roles they will play should be described and justified on the basis of their experience and expertise.

Provide a brief biography[9] of each member of the management team, and describe their roles and responsibilities in the venture.

4. Profile of the Industry or Sector

Industries are classified and coded according to specific criteria that are common across North America. The North American Industrial Classification System (NAICS)[10] (pronounced "Nakes") is used to codify industries and sectors. It is useful to know which NAICS code, and hence which industrial group, applies to your venture to research the changing trends from the forces acting in its organizational environment (Chapter 2). For example, if your business plan is to start a family restaurant, you would find that this type of venture is part of the Accommodation and Food Services Industry, NAICS 72211. From there, you can research the active forces within the industry that are providing opportunities for growth or proving to be a threat to your venture. Use *Porter's Five Forces Model* to analyze the threats to profitability within the industry (Chapter 5). Information on changing industrial trends can be found from Statistics Canada,[11] and industry associations. For our family restaurant example, we could go to the Canadian Restaurant and Food Services Association website to learn about industry trends.[12] From this site, we learn that "the average Canadian household spent $2017 on food and alcoholic beverages served from restaurants and licensed establishments in 2007, a $99—or 5.2 percent—increase over 2006. Household spending on food purchased from restaurants rose by $81 to $1715." This indicates that consumers are increasing the amount of their income spent on food and alcohol from establishments similar to what you are proposing. However, additional research indicates that Food Service sales are projected to drop by 1.4 percent in the recession of 2009. This gives evidence to the reader of your plan whether or not the trends support your proposal and what the risks are for your venture.

Describe the trends in the industry and whether or not they pose an opportunity for growth or a threat to the profitability of your venture.

State how you will minimize the risks.

5. Profile of the Product/Service

This part of the business plan provides the reader with a complete overview of all the products and services you will offer.

Product or Service Description

It is important to stress to the reader the uniqueness of your offering. What will you provide or do that is different from your competitors? Why would consumers purchase your product or service over someone else's?

Describe in as much detail as possible the uniqueness of the product or service you will be offering.

Regulations, Licences, and Permits

All businesses in Canada are subject to regulations at various levels of government. Consult BizPal,[13] a website designed to help businesspeople figure out all the regulations they must comply with and the permits and licences that are necessary to operate the venture. If you have developed a prototype of an original product or a modification of an existing product, you should apply for a patent and/or protection of your intellectual property. This can be done online:

http://strategis.ic.gc.ca/sc_mrksv/cipo/welcome/welcom-e.html

Describe the permits and licences that are required for your venture.

Future Product Development/Innovation

In this section, tell the reader how you expect your product or service offering to change in the future. Do you have plans for expansion? Will you bring new products and services on board, and when? How will you sustain your growth once the business reaches maturity? Give the reader a sense of how you will end the venture. Do you intend to sell the venture, franchise, or dissolve the company?

Describe your future product development and exit strategies.

6. Marketing Plan

This part of the business plan includes an analysis of your venture's strengths and weaknesses relative to your competition (SWOT) as well as an analysis of the four P's in the marketing mix: product, place (distribution channels), price, and promotion. Detailed research must be gathered on who will buy the product or service; what the potential size of the market is and whether there is potential for growth; the prices that should be charged; the distribution channel and the most effective promotion strategy to reach the target market.

SWOT Analysis

Referring to the SWOT analysis you did in Chapter 5, identify your strengths and weaknesses relative to one major competitor. Direct competitors can be found by searching the Yellow Pages and the websites of associations, trade magazines, chambers of commerce, and Statistics Canada. Things to compare might include:

Strengths
- Resources (assets/people)
- Experience
- Diversity
- Location
- Sustainability strategy
- Quality of product/service

Weaknesses
- Gaps in capabilities
- Reputation
- Poor customer responsiveness
- Resources (assets/people)
- Inexperience
- Lack of quality

Opportunities
- Market demand/changing trends
- Competitors' vulnerabilities
- Partnerships
- Innovation
- Competitive advantages

Threats
- Legal /political
- Demographic trends
- Competitive advantages
- Barriers to entry
- Suppliers

Strategies for a Competitive Advantage

After completing the SWOT analysis relative to your competition and remembering the analysis of the industry you did in section 4, you are now ready to articulate the kind of strategy that will gain you a competitive advantage. Refer to Chapter 5. Will you adopt a cost-leadership or a differentiation strategy? How will you focus that strategy?

Describe the business-level strategy you intend to use to gain a competitive advantage.

Target Market Profile(s)

Which segment of the market will buy your product or service? Demographic characteristics such as age, income, geographic location, and buyer behaviour need to be researched and documented. This is usually done through conducting focus groups, giving surveys, interviewing potential market segments, and through observing and recording pre- and postpurchase behavioural habits of customers. Association websites and Statistics Canada[14] are good sources of the 2006 Census data.

For each market segment, create a customer profile by researching the following:

- Demographic questions
- Customer attitudes on price and quality
- Where customers currently buy the product/service
- Where customers wish to buy the product/service
- The influence of advertising
- How much of the product/service the customer buys and how often
- Why the customer buys this product/service

Characteristics of the Customer	Customer Profile for Your Venture's Product/Service/Offering	Potential for Growth/Trends	Source
Demographic information			
Frequency of purchase			
No. of units purchased yearly			
Price sensitivity			
Lifestyle/personality			
Advertising influences			
Motivation			
Buying decisions based on:			
Other			

Describe your target market(s).

Pricing

Before setting the price of your product or service, you must evaluate your costs per unit, what the markup should be and what the competition charges for a similar product/service. Cost of goods should include material and labour overhead (utilities, rent, insurance, salaries), and costs from suppliers. You must add up the costs based on an estimate of the volume of sales. Markups or margins in your industry can be found by reading a trade journal or by asking the suppliers. The markup usually includes a degree of profit that represents the industry standard. Industry standards can be found from Statistic Canada, association websites, and organizations such as Dun and Bradstreet.[15]

If you plan to increase market penetration by using pricing specials or volume discounts, you should describe them. Before deciding to discount in order to undercut the competition and gain market share, you should consider that the competition could also lower its prices and therefore reduce the profit margins for everyone.

If you adopt a differentiation business level strategy for your product/service, you may be able to justify charging more than the competition. To do this, you will offer customers a product or service that is unique and/or of better quality such that people will pay the higher price relative to the competition.

Describe your pricing strategy and how that compares with the competition.

Distribution (Place)

How will you make it convenient for your customers to access your product/service? The market conditions, attributes of the product/service, cost benefits, and characteristics of the venture should all be considered when deciding on a channel of distribution.

It may be appropriate to sell directly to the customer or to a retailer if the target market is concentrated in a particular geographic area. If not, it may be appropriate to use a distributor or wholesaler. If the product is large, bulky, perishable, hazardous, or expensive, the rule of thumb is to channel the product through direct sales. If the cost of indirect sales (using a middle person such as a retailer or wholesaler) is minimal and the benefit is great in terms of reaching a dispersed market, it may be more appropriate to channel indirectly. And finally, if the venture has great financial strength, multiple channels may be considered.

If you intend to use dealers or distributors, discounts or commissions will be required and should be described.

Describe your distribution strategy.

When deciding on a *location* for your facilities, you must consider how much space you will need for the operation and whether or not the facility will be accessible to the consumer (direct sales). If you are considering purchasing or renting a building, further criteria may become relevant: Is it zoned for commercial use? Is it in need of renovation? Is there potential for expansion? Is there ample parking? What is the cost per square foot? How many competitors are in the area? Other criteria may be relevant to your location decision. Compare two or three sites against your criteria to come up with the best location for your venture.

Criteria	Site X	Site Y	Site Z
Cost per square foot			
Parking			
Accessibility			
History of the building			
Number of competitors in the area			
Zoning laws			
Potential for expansion			
Features of the area (specify)			
Other (specify)			

Describe the location of your venture.

Promotion

The success of your venture will largely depend on your promotional plan. Advertising, public relations, and Internet marketing are common ways of promoting your organization to your target market. Consider that each market segment may require different promotional activities. Also consider the degree to which your target market is influenced by advertising. Would a slogan be appropriate to capture the vision of your organization or capitalize on the uniqueness of your product/service?

Develop a slogan and/or logo that promotes the image you want to project about your organization/product/service.

Decide whether you will "pull" or "push" your promotions. Things to consider include:

- The pull strategy requires direct contact with the customer. This requires a major commitment to advertising. The objective is to attract the customers to every channel outlet for your product/service. If enough customers demand your product, the channels will want to carry it. The price and quality of your product is important here.

- The push strategy requires less investment in advertising. The push strategy maximizes the use of all available channels of distribution to "push" the offering into the marketplace, usually by giving large discounts or commissions as incentives to the channels to promote the offering. Research must be done into the channel discount requirements and the relationship that the competition has with the channel.

Create a list of public relations, Internet activities, and types of advertising that you can undertake to generate awareness of your venture in your target market(s). Expected returns include the audience reached and how this exposure will benefit you. Include the costs of the promotion plan in the financial plan section of the business plan.

Promotional Activity	Date and Contact Person	Cost and Length of Run	Expected Returns
Send a press kit with your company's profile, pictures, and press releases to newspapers and trade journals			
Host an open house			
Go to a trade show			
Write letters to the editors of various papers			
Develop a company website			
Blog			
Register with search engines			
Banner ads			
Billboard ads			
Radio/TV ads			
Other			

Write your promotional strategy for each market segment.

7. Organizational Plan

This section provides a description of the organizational structure, culture, and human resources plan for your venture.

Organizational Structure

When designing the *organizational structure,* some things to consider are:

- How should similar jobs be grouped together into units or departments?

- Who should be accountable to whom to ensure the coordination of activities?

- How many levels of authority are needed?

The relationships that jobs have with one another are depicted in an organizational chart. The organizational chart shows the positions of all members. Refer to the business planning exercise you did for Chapter 6.

Draw an organizational chart for year one of your venture.

Organizational Culture

The organizational structure creates the foundation for the coordination of work that needs to be done. But finding the right mix of people to assume the responsibilities outlined in the structure is just as critical to the success of the organization as having a marketable product.

When building *organizational culture,* the founder and management team will foster the values and principles embodied in your vision and mission statements. The desired culture must be consistently role-modelled for employees. It must be deliberately embodied in the symbols and practices of the organization if it is to be successful. Revisit the value statement you wrote in Chapter 3.

Describe the values, principles, and norms that underlie your organizational culture.

Human Resources Management Plan

The objective of human resources planning is to match the right people to the right job at the right time. This section of the business plan provides the reader with a job analysis of the key positions and how the management will recruit, select, train, appraise, and compensate employees. Things to consider are:

- What kinds of labour (specifications) are needed to fulfill the duties of the positions (descriptions)?
- How will they be recruited?
- What selection techniques will be used to determine the best candidates?
- What kind of training and development will be offered?
- How will you know if they have learned the jobs?
- What levels of pay and pay structures will you offer that are consistent with the strategy of the venture?

Job Analysis

In conducting a job analysis for the venture, consult Chapter 11 as well as industry and association websites to determine what you need to include for each position. Consider the degree of enrichment you build into each job as a motivating factor.

For each position in the organizational chart, research and write a job description and a set of job specifications.

Recruitment

Where will you find the employees you need for your venture? Is there a need for highly specialized/qualified human resources? If so, determine if there will be a shortage in supply for those positions in the first year of operation.

Make a list of the external sources of potential applicants for each position.

Selection

What methods will you use to pick the most qualified and best-suited applicant for a position? The techniques you use, such as interviews, ability testing, background checks and so on must be valid and reliable.

Describe the selection techniques you will use to hire new employees and why they are valid and reliable.

Training and Development

Once you have offered a candidate a job, you must orient and train them in the roles and responsibilities of the position. Referring to Chapter 11, determine what types of training and development programs are suitable for each position.

Describe the types of training you will provide for each position.

Performance Appraisals

In order to determine if the employee has learned how to do the job, their performance levels must be appraised by management. The Human Resources Plan section of the business plan should describe how performance appraisals will be conducted and in what timeframe.

How will employee performance appraisals be conducted and feedback given?

Pay and Compensation

Research the pay levels and structures for the types of occupations you need for your venture. Industry standards can be found from Statistics Canada.[16] The amount of pay you offer should be consistent with the *strategy* you have adopted. For example, if our family restaurant intends to differentiate itself from the competition by focusing on high-income households as a target market, it makes sense that it can pay its waitstaff higher wages than if it adopted a cost-leadership strategy focusing on low-income households. Generally, if the competitive advantage is derived from superior quality, customer service, and innovation, higher than industry wages can be paid. If, on the other hand, the competitive advantage is derived from efficiency, lower than standard industry wages generally will be paid.

Will you offer wages at, above, or below the industry standards? Justify your answer in terms of the strategy of the venture.

8. Operating and Control Systems Plan

This section of the business plan describes the flow of goods and services from the input stage, through the conversion stage, and in the postproduction stage. Standards must be set for the use of resources at every stage and control measures implemented to ensure that the standards are being met. This involves an analysis of the whole supply chain. In particular, a supplier analysis, an inventory control analysis, and an assessment of how the goods will flow to the customer must be considered, whether the venture is a retail operation, a service provider, or a manufacturer.

Retail Operation or Service Provider

If your venture is a retail operation or a service provider, you should consider the following questions:

1. From whom will merchandise be purchased?
    - Consider the supplier's reputation, past record, prices versus other suppliers, delivery methods, whether or not it supplies your competitors, and how important your business is to it.
2. How will the inventory and quality control system operate?
    - Consider how you will inspect the goods received and what you will do if materials are defective.
    - What are your storage and processing space needs?
    - What is your ordering materials process?
3. How will the goods flow to the customer?
    - What steps are involved in a business transaction?
    - What technology (debit machines, scanners) will you need to serve customers effectively?

Create standards for each phase of the operation, and describe what methods of control you will use to ensure they are met.

	Standard/Goal	Control measures
Supplier analysis		
Inventory and quality control		
Flow of goods to customers		
Customer satisfaction		

Manufacturing Operation

If you are proposing a manufacturing operation, you should describe the complete operations management process. Some of the issues will be the same as above, but some will be different. In the *supplier analysis* area, you would include how much, if any, of the manufacturing process is subcontracted out to another firm. Who will perform such work, and how will you decide what to outsource and what operations to keep in-house? What specialized machinery and equipment is needed, and who will supply this? What are the capital equipment needs and expenditures? Include the costs in your financial plan and a full list of equipment in the appendices. In analyzing the *flow of goods*, illustrate the layout and all the steps in the production process.

Both service providers and manufacturers should have standards set for being responsive to customers. For example, a goal for customer service might be, "100-percent satisfaction or your money back guaranteed!" Enterprises must build in feedback control measures that allow customers to complain and praise the service and/or products, such as questionnaires and surveys.

Describe the risks that could arise in managing the operations of the venture and how you can minimize them.

9. Financial Plan

The financial plan tells the reader what level of potential investment commitment is needed and whether or not the business plan is feasible. It details the needed capital requirements for starting the venture, or new strategy, the forecasted sales, and the expenses incurred in selling the product/service over a number of months and years.

Anyone reading your financial projections will want to know what assumptions went into the creation of the projections. This includes assumptions about, for example, the size of the market and your ability to penetrate it, staffing plans, management salaries, inventory turnover, receivables and payables periods, and expectations for investment or loans.

Refer to the exercise you did for Chapter 13: Managing Organizational Control and an accounting textbook to help you calculate the financial statements for your venture for a period of two years. Or simply follow the instructions in a business planning software program. This will create the spreadsheets for your plan.

Pro Forma Income Statement

The income statement subtracts all the costs incurred to operate your enterprise from the amounts received from selling goods and services. The result is a net income or a net loss for the year. You will be asked to enter revenue and expenses for each month of the first year, for each quarter of the second year.

Cash Flow Projections

The cash flow statement will show the amount of cash you have available at any given time during your business plan. If a negative cash balance occurs, you will have to examine your revenue and expense projections. To address the negative cash balance, you will have to increase revenues, decrease expenses, or arrange to get cash through a loan or capital investment. Cash flow is projected for each month of the first year and for each quarter of the second year.

Pro Forma Balance Sheet

The balance sheet is divided into two sections: assets and liabilities plus shareholders' equity. The two sections must always be in balance. A dollar amount or a "balance" represents each asset, liability, and component of shareholders' equity reported in the balance sheet. The balance sheet is projected for each month of the first year and for each quarter of the second year.

Break-Even Analysis

The projection of when the revenue will surpass the expenses of the venture is called the break-even point and is generally depicted graphically.

Alternative Scenarios

When presenting your business plan to an investor or to your management, it is of value to show projections for revenues and expenses that represent the best possible case and the worst possible case. It is recommended you provide some explanation for the circumstances that might precipitate either the best or worst case in the financial assumptions section.

Create a pro forma income statement, a cash flow statement, a balance sheet, and a break-even analysis for your business plan.

10. Appendices

The appendix of the business plan generally contains all the documents that are referenced in the plan itself and any backup material that is not necessary in the text of the document. You might consider including the following:

- Product/service samples
- Market research data
- Legal forms and documents
- Leases or contracts
- Price lists from suppliers, if applicable
- Promotional material examples
- Résumés of the management team
- Other backup material

Glossary

360-DEGREE APPRAISAL A performance appraisal by peers, subordinates, superiors, and sometimes clients who are in a position to evaluate a manager's performance.

A

ABILITY THESIS Assess skills necessary to perform the job well.

ACCOMMODATIVE APPROACH Moderate commitment to social responsibility; willingness to do more than the law requires, if asked.

ADMINISTRATIVE MANAGEMENT The study of ways to create an organizational structure that leads to high efficiency and effectiveness.

ADMINISTRATIVE MODEL An approach to decision making that explains why decision making is basically uncertain and risky and why managers usually make satisficing decisions rather than optimum decisions.

AGING POPULATION When the average age of a country's population increases; popularly known as the emerging "silver tsunami" to indicate a large wave of people with greying hair in the population.

AMBIGUOUS INFORMATION Information that can be interpreted in multiple and often conflicting ways.

ARTIFACTS Aspects of an organization's culture that one sees, hears, and feels.

ASSUMPTIONS The taken-for-granted notions of how something should be in an organization.

AUTHORITY The power to hold people accountable for their actions and to make decisions concerning the use of organizational resources.

B

BARRIERS TO ENTRY Factors that make it difficult and costly for an organization to enter a particular task environment or industry.

BEHAVIOURAL INTERVIEW QUESTIONS Ask candidates how they dealt with a situation they encountered on the job.

BEHAVIOURAL MANAGEMENT The study of how managers should behave in order to motivate employees and encourage them to perform at high levels and be committed to achieving organizational goals.

BELIEFS The understandings of how objects and ideas relate to each other.

BENCHMARKING Comparing performance on specific dimensions with the performances of high-performing organizations.

BIAS The systematic tendency to use information about others in ways that result in inaccurate perceptions.

BOTTOM-UP CHANGE Change that is introduced gradually and involves managers and employees at all levels of an organization.

BOUNDARYLESS ORGANIZATION An organization whose members are linked by computers, faxes, computer-aided design systems, and video teleconferencing and who rarely, if ever, see one another face to face.

BOUNDED EMOTIONALITY Sometimes called the management of emotion, that is, the inclusion of emotional expression in organizations for the purposes of productivity.

BOUNDED RATIONALITY Cognitive limitations that constrain one's ability to interpret, process, and act on information.

BRAINSTORMING A group problem-solving technique in which individuals meet face to face to generate and debate a wide variety of alternatives from which to make a decision.

BRAND LOYALTY Customers' preference for the products of organizations that currently exist in the task environment.

BUREAUCRACY A formal system of organization and administration designed to ensure efficiency and effectiveness.

BUREAUCRATIC CONTROL Control of behaviour by means of a comprehensive system of rules and standard operating procedures.

BUSINESS-LEVEL PLAN Divisional managers' decisions relating to divisions' long-term goals, overall strategy, and structure.

BUSINESS-LEVEL STRATEGY A plan that indicates how a division intends to compete against its rivals in an industry.

BUSINESS-TO-BUSINESS (B2B) NETWORKS A group of organizations that join together and use software to link themselves to potential global suppliers to increase efficiency and effectiveness.

C

CAFETERIA-STYLE BENEFIT PLAN A plan from which employees can choose the benefits that they want.

CERTAINTY The state of environmental forces that is stable enough to predict possible outcomes of decisions.

CHARISMATIC LEADER An enthusiastic, self-confident leader able to communicate clearly his or her vision of how good things could be.

CLAN CONTROL Control exerted on individuals and groups in an organization by shared values, norms, standards of behaviour, and expectations.

CLOSED SYSTEM A system that is self-contained and thus not affected by changes that occur in its external environment.

CODES OF ETHICS Formal standards and rules, based on beliefs about right or wrong, that managers can use to help themselves make appropriate decisions with regard to the interests of their stakeholders.

COERCIVE POWER The ability to force someone to do something against his or her will.

COLLECTIVE AGREEMENT A mutually agreed upon set of provisions that govern working conditions between a union and an employer for a set period.

COLLECTIVE BARGAINING Negotiation between labour unions and managers to resolve conflicts and disputes about issues such as working hours, wages, benefits, working conditions, and job security.

COMMAND ECONOMY An economic system in which the government owns all businesses and specifies which and how many goods and services are produced and the prices at which they are sold.

COMMAND GROUP A group composed of subordinates who report to the same supervisor; also called a department or unit.

COMMUNICATION The sharing of information between two or more individuals or groups to reach a common understanding.

COMPETITIVE ADVANTAGE The ability of one organization to outperform other organizations because it produces desired goods or services more efficiently and effectively than competitors do.

COMPETITIVE LANDSCAPE The competitive environment within which a company operates.

COMPETITORS Organizations that produce goods and services that are similar to a particular organization's goods and services.

COMPLEXITY THEORY Organizations respond best to change if they are not perfectly aligned with their environment.

CONCEPTUAL SKILLS The ability to analyze and diagnose a situation and to distinguish between cause and effect.

CONCURRENT CONTROL Control that gives managers immediate feedback on how efficiently inputs are being transformed into outputs so that managers can correct problems as they arise.

CONSIDERATION OR EMPLOYEE-CENTRED BEHAVIOUR Behaviour indicating that a manager trusts, respects, and cares about subordinates.

CONTINGENCY MODELS OF LEADERSHIP Models of leadership that take into account the variables in the situation or context in which leadership occurs.

CONTINGENCY THEORY The idea that managers' choice of organizational structures and control systems depends on and—is contingent on—characteristics of the external environment in which the organization operates.

CONTROL SYSTEMS Formal target-setting, monitoring, evaluation, and feedback systems that provide managers with information about how well the organization's strategy and structure are working.

CONTROLLING Evaluating how well an organization is achieving its goals and taking action to maintain or improve performance; one of the four principal functions of management.

CO-OPETITION Arrangements in which firms compete vigorously with one another, while also cooperating in specific areas to achieve economies of scale.

CORPORATE GOVERNANCE The processes companies use to be accountable to its stakeholders, including investors, employees, the environment, and communities.

CORPORATE-LEVEL PLAN Top management's decisions relating to the organization's mission, overall strategy, and structure.

CORPORATE-LEVEL STRATEGY A plan that indicates the industries and national markets in which an organization intends to compete.

COST-LEADERSHIP STRATEGY Driving the organization's costs down below the costs of its rivals.

CREATIVITY A decision maker's ability to discover original and novel ideas that lead to feasible alternative courses of action.

CRISIS MANAGEMENT Occurs when unanticipated and unplanned contingencies arise.

CROSS-FUNCTIONAL TEAM A group of individuals from different departments brought together to perform organizational tasks.

CUSTOMER-CENTRICITY The awareness and focus that a company has of a customer's needs, wants, desires, and behaviours.

CUSTOMERS Individuals and groups that buy the goods and services that an organization produces.

D

DATA Raw, unsummarized, and unanalyzed facts.

DECISION MAKING The process by which managers analyze the options facing them and make decisions about specific organizational goals and courses of action.

DECODING Interpreting and trying to make sense of a message.

DEFENSIVE APPROACH Minimal commitment to social responsibility; willingness to do what the law requires and no more.

DELPHI TECHNIQUE A decision-making technique in which group members do not meet face to face but respond in writing to questions posed by the group leader.

DEMOGRAPHIC FORCES Outcomes of changes in, or changing attitudes toward, the characteristics of a population, such as age, gender, ethnic origin, race, sexual orientation, and social class.

DEPARTMENT A group of people who work together and possess similar skills or use the same knowledge, tools, or techniques to perform their jobs.

DEVELOPMENT Building the knowledge and skills of organizational members so that they will be prepared to take on new responsibilities and challenges.

DEVELOPMENTAL CONSIDERATION Behaviour a leader engages in to support and encourage followers and help them develop and grow on the job.

DEVIL'S ADVOCACY Critical analysis of a preferred alternative, made by a group member who plays the role of the devil's advocate to defend unpopular or opposing alternatives for the sake of argument.

DIFFERENTIATION STRATEGY Distinguishing an organization's products from the products of competitors in dimensions such as product design, quality, or after-sales service.

DISCIPLINE Managerial control through administering punishment when undesired workplace behaviours such as absenteeism, lack of punctuality, and low performance are exhibited, in an attempt to decrease their frequency.

DISTRIBUTIVE JUSTICE A moral principle calling for the distribution of pay raises, promotions, and other organizational resources to be based on meaningful contributions that individuals have made and not on personal characteristics over which they have no control.

DISTRIBUTIVE NEGOTIATION Adversarial negotiation in which the parties in conflict compete to win the most resources while conceding as little as possible.

DISTRIBUTORS Organizations that help other organizations sell their goods or services to customers.

DIVERSIFICATION Expanding operations into a new business or industry and producing new goods or services.

DIVERSITY Differences among people in age, gender, race, ethnicity, religion, sexual orientation, socio-economic background, and capabilities or disabilities.

DIVISION A business unit that has its own set of managers and functions or departments and competes in a distinct industry.

DIVISION OF LABOUR Splitting the work to be performed into particular tasks and assigning tasks to individual workers.

DIVISIONAL MANAGERS Managers who control the various divisions of an organization.

DIVISIONAL STRUCTURE An organizational structure composed of separate business units within which are the functions that work together to produce a specific product for a specific customer.

DRIVING FORCES Forces that direct behaviour away from the status quo.

E

E-BUSINESS Using the Internet and intranet applications to communicate with employees, suppliers, customers, and other stakeholders.

ECONOMIC FORCES Interest rates, inflation, unemployment, economic growth, and other factors that affect the general health and well-being of a nation or the regional economy of an organization.

ECONOMIES OF SCALE Cost advantages associated with large operations.

EFFECTIVENESS A measure of the appropriateness of the goals an organization is pursuing and of the degree to which the organization achieves those goals.

EFFICIENCY A measure of how well or productively resources are used to achieve a goal.

EMOTIONAL INTELLIGENCE The ability to understand and manage one's own moods and emotions and the moods and emotions of other people.

EMPOWERMENT Expanding employees' tasks and responsibilities.

ENCODING Translating a message into understandable symbols or language.

ENTROPY The tendency of a system to dissolve and disintegrate because it loses the ability to control itself.

ENVIRONMENTAL CHANGE The degree to which forces in the task and general environments change and evolve over time.

ENVIRONMENTAL CONSCIOUSNESS The awareness that people have of environmental and ecological issues and realities and their dependence on ecosystems.

EQUITY The justice, impartiality, and fairness to which all organizational members are entitled.

EQUITY THEORY A theory of motivation that focuses on people's perceptions of the fairness of their work outcomes relative to their work inputs.

ESCALATING COMMITMENT A source of cognitive bias resulting from the tendency to commit additional resources to a project even if evidence shows that the project is failing.

ETHICAL DECISION A decision that reasonable or typical stakeholders would find acceptable because it aids stakeholders, the organization, or society.

ETHICS Moral principles or beliefs about what is right or wrong.

ETHICS OMBUDSPERSON An ethics officer who monitors an organization's practices and procedures to ensure that they are ethical.

EXPECTANCY In expectancy theory, a perception about the extent to which effort will result in a certain level of performance.

EXPECTANCY THEORY The theory that motivation will be high when employees believe that high levels of effort will lead to high performance and that high performance will lead to the attainment of desired outcomes.

EXPERT POWER Power that is based in the special knowledge, skills, and expertise that a leader possesses.

EXTERNAL ENVIRONMENT The forces operating outside an organization that affect how the organization functions.

EXTINCTION Stopping the performance of dysfunctional behaviours by eliminating whatever is reinforcing them.

EXTRINSICALLY MOTIVATED BEHAVIOUR Behaviour that is performed to acquire material or social rewards or to avoid punishment.

F

FEEDBACK CONTROL Control that gives managers information about customers' reactions to goods and services so that corrective action can be taken if necessary.

FEEDFORWARD CONTROL Control that allows managers to anticipate and deal with potential problems.

FILTERING Withholding part of a message out of the mistaken belief that the receiver does not need or will not want the information.

"FIRMS OF ENDEARMENT" Humanistic companies—companies with "soul"—that seek to maximize their value to society as a whole, not just to their shareholders.

FIRST-LINE MANAGERS Managers who are responsible for the daily supervision and coordination of nonmanagerial employees.

FOCUSED DIFFERENTIATION STRATEGY Serving only one segment of the overall market and trying to be the most differentiated organization serving that segment.

FOCUSED LOW-COST STRATEGY Serving only one segment of the overall market and being the lowest-cost organization serving that segment.

FORMAL APPRAISAL An appraisal conducted at a set time during the year and based on performance dimensions and measures specified in advance.

FREE-MARKET ECONOMY An economic system in which private enterprise controls production, and the interaction of supply and demand determines which and how many goods and services are produced and how much consumers pay for them.

FUNCTION A unit or department in which people have the same skills or use the same resources to perform their jobs.

FUNCTIONAL-LEVEL PLAN Functional managers' decisions relating to the goals that functional managers propose to pursue to help the division reach its business-level goals.

FUNCTIONAL-LEVEL STRATEGY A plan that indicates how a function is intended to achieve its goals.

FUNCTIONAL MANAGERS Managers who supervise the various functions—such as manufacturing, accounting, and sales—within a division.

FUNCTIONAL STRUCTURE An organizational structure composed of all the departments that an organization requires to produce its goods or services.

G

GANTT CHART A graphic bar chart managers use to schedule the tasks in a project showing what tasks need to be done who will do them, and by what time frame.

GENERAL ENVIRONMENT The economic, technological, socio-cultural, demographic, political and legal, and global forces that affect an organization and its task environment.

GENERATION Y Also known as Millennials refers to people born between 1981 and 1992.

GEOGRAPHIC STRUCTURE An organizational structure in which each region of a country or area of the world is served by a self-contained division.

GLOBAL FORCES Outcomes of changes in international relationships; changes in nations' economic, political, and legal systems; and changes in technology—such as falling trade barriers, the growth of representative democracies, and reliable and instantaneous communication.

GLOBAL ORGANIZATIONS Organizations that operate and compete in more than one country.

GLOBAL STRATEGY Selling the same standardized product and using the same basic marketing approach in each national market.

GOAL A desired future outcome that an organization strives to achieve.

GOAL-SETTING THEORY A theory that focuses on identifying the types of goals that are most effective in producing high levels of motivation and performance and on explaining why goals have these effects.

GRAPEVINE An informal communication network among people in organizations.

GROUP Two or more people who interact with each other to reach certain goals or meet certain needs.

GROUP COHESIVENESS The degree to which members are attracted or loyal to a group.

GROUP NORMS Shared guidelines or rules of behaviour that most group members follow.

GROUP ROLE A set of behaviours and tasks that a member of a group is expected to perform because of his or her position in the group.

GROUPTHINK A pattern of faulty and biased decision making that occurs in groups whose members strive for agreement among themselves at the expense of accurately assessing information relevant to a decision.

H

HACKMAN AND OLDHAM'S JOB CHARACTERISTICS MODEL States that when employee growth needs are strong, integrating core job dimensions into their work leads to positive personal and job outcomes.

HERZBERG'S MOTIVATOR-HYGIENE THEORY A needs theory that distinguishes between motivator needs (related to the nature of the work itself) and hygiene needs (related to the physical and psychological context in which the work is performed). Herzberg proposed that motivator needs must be met in order for motivation and job satisfaction to be high.

HEURISTICS Rules of thumb that simplify decision making.

HIERARCHY OF AUTHORITY An organization's chain of command, specifying the relative authority of each manager.

HOSTILE WORK ENVIRONMENT SEXUAL HARASSMENT Telling lewd jokes, displaying pornography, making sexually oriented remarks about someone's personal appearance, and other sex-related actions that make the work environment unpleasant.

HUMAN RESOURCE MANAGEMENT (HRM) Activities that managers engage in to attract and retain employees and to ensure that they perform at a high level and contribute to the accomplishment of organizational goals.

HUMAN RESOURCE PLANNING Activities that managers use to forecast their current and future needs for human resources.

HUMAN SKILLS The ability to understand, alter, lead, and control the behaviour of other individuals and groups.

I

ILLUSION OF CONTROL A source of cognitive bias resulting from the tendency to overestimate one's own ability to control activities and events.

IMPOSED CHANGE New institutional arrangements made to comply with regulations.

INDIVIDUAL ETHICS Personal standards that govern how individuals interact with other people.

INDUCED CHANGE New institutional arrangements made to gain a competitive advantage.

INEQUITY Lack of fairness.

INFORMAL APPRAISAL An unscheduled appraisal of ongoing progress and areas for improvement.

INFORMAL ORGANIZATION The system of behavioural rules and norms that emerge in a group.

INFORMATION Data that are organized in a meaningful fashion.

INFORMATION DISTORTION Changes in the meaning of a message as the message passes through a series of senders and receivers.

INFORMATION RICHNESS The amount of information that a communication medium can carry and the extent to which the medium enables sender and receiver to reach a common understanding.

INFORMATION TECHNOLOGY The means by which information is acquired, organized, stored, manipulated, and transmitted.

INITIATING STRUCTURE OR TASK-ORIENTED BEHAVIOURS Behaviours that managers engage in to ensure that work gets done, subordinates perform their jobs acceptably, and the organization is efficient and effective.

INNOVATION The process of creating new goods and services or developing better ways to produce or provide goods and services.

INTENTIONAL DISCRIMINATION The illegal practice of deliberately using prohibited grounds, such as race, religion, and sex, when making employment decisions.

INSTRUMENTALITY In expectancy theory, a perception about the extent to which performance will result in the attainment of outcomes.

INTEGRATIVE BARGAINING Cooperative negotiation in which the parties in conflict work together to achieve a resolution that is good for them all.

INTELLECTUAL STIMULATION Behaviour a leader engages in to make followers aware of problems and view these problems in new ways, consistent with the leader's vision.

INTERNAL ENVIRONMENT The forces operating within an organization and stemming from the organization's structure and culture.

INTRINSICALLY MOTIVATED BEHAVIOUR Behaviour that is performed for its own sake.

INTUITION Ability to make sound decisions based on past experiences and immediate feelings about the information at hand.

J

JARGON Specialized language that members of an occupation, group, or organization develop to facilitate communication among themselves.

JOB ANALYSIS Identifying the tasks, duties, and responsibilities that make up a job and the knowledge, skills, and abilities needed to perform the job.

JOB DESIGN The process by which managers decide how to divide tasks into specific jobs.

JOB ENLARGEMENT Increasing the number of different tasks in a given job by changing the division of labour.

JOB ENRICHMENT Increasing the degree of responsibility a worker has over his or her job.

JOB SIMPLIFICATION Reducing the number of tasks that each worker performs.

JOB SPECIALIZATION The process by which a division of labour occurs as different employees specialize in different tasks over time.

JOINT VENTURE A strategic alliance among two or more companies that agree to establish jointly and share the ownership of a new business.

JUDGMENT Ability to develop a sound opinion based on one's evaluation of the importance of the information at hand.

L

LABOUR RELATIONS The activities that managers engage in to ensure that they have effective working relationships with the labour unions that represent their employees' interests.

LATERAL MOVE A job change that entails no major changes in responsibility or authority levels.

LEADER An individual who is able to exert influence over other people to help achieve group or organizational goals.

LEADER-MEMBER RELATIONS The extent to which followers like, trust, and are loyal to their leader. They can be good or poor.

LEADER SUBSTITUTE Characteristics of subordinates or characteristics of a situation or context that act in place of the influence of a leader and make leadership unnecessary.

LEADERSHIP The process by which an individual exerts influence over other people and inspires, motivates, and directs their activities to help achieve group or organizational goals.

LEADING Articulating a clear vision and energizing and empowering organizational members so that everyone understands their individual roles in achieving organizational goals; one of the four principal functions of management.

LEARNING ORGANIZATION An organization in which managers try to maximize the ability of individuals and groups to think and behave creatively and thus maximize the potential for organizational learning to take place.

LEGITIMATE POWER The authority that a manager has by virtue of his or her position in an organization's hierarchy.

LINGUISTIC STYLE A person's characteristic way of speaking.

M

MAINTENANCE ROLES Roles performed by group members to make sure there are good relations among group members.

MANAGEMENT The planning, organizing, leading, and controlling of resources to achieve organizational goals effectively and efficiently.

MANAGEMENT BY OBJECTIVES A system of evaluating subordinates for their ability to achieve specific organizational goals or performance standards.

MANAGEMENT INFORMATION SYSTEMS (MIS) Electronic systems of interconnected components designed to collect, process, store, and disseminate information to facilitate management decision making, planning, and control.

MANAGEMENT SCIENCE THEORY An approach to management that uses rigorous quantitative techniques to help managers make full use of organizational resources.

MANAGER A person who is responsible for supervising the use of an organization's resources to achieve its goals.

MARKET STRUCTURE An organizational structure in which each kind of customer is served by a self-contained division; also called customer structure.

MASLOW'S HIERARCHY OF NEEDS An arrangement of five basic needs that, according to Maslow, motivate behaviour. Maslow proposed that the lowest level of unmet needs is the prime motivator and that only one level of needs is motivational at a time.

MATRIX STRUCTURE An organizational structure that simultaneously groups people and resources by function and by product.

MECHANISTIC STRUCTURE An organizational structure in which authority is centralized at the top of the hierarchy, tasks and roles are clearly specified, and employees are closely supervised.

MEDIUM The pathway through which an encoded message is transmitted to a receiver.

MESSAGE The information that a sender wants to share.

MIDDLE MANAGERS Managers who supervise first-line managers and are responsible for finding the best way to use resources to achieve organizational goals.

MISSION STATEMENT A broad declaration of an organization's purpose that identifies the organization's products and customers and distinguishes the organization from its competitors.

MIXED ECONOMY An economic system in which some sectors of the economy are left to private ownership and free-market mechanisms and others are owned by the government and subject to government planning.

MOTIVATION Psychological forces that determine the direction of a person's behaviour in an organization, level of effort, and level of persistence.

MULTIDOMESTIC STRATEGY Customizing products and marketing strategies to specific national conditions.

N

NEED A requirement or necessity for survival and well-being.

NEEDS ASSESSMENT An assessment of which employees need training or development and what type of skills or knowledge they need to acquire.

NEEDS THEORIES Theories of motivation that focus on what needs people are trying to satisfy at work and what outcomes will satisfy those needs.

NEGATIVE REINFORCEMENT Eliminating or removing undesired outcomes once people have performed organizationally functional behaviours.

NEGOTIATION A method of conflict resolution in which the parties in conflict consider various alternative ways to allocate resources to each other in order to come up with a solution acceptable to them all.

NETWORK STRUCTURE A series of strategic alliances that an organization creates with suppliers, manufacturers, and distributors to produce and market a product.

NOISE Anything that hampers any stage of the communication process.

NOMINAL GROUP TECHNIQUE A decision-making technique in which group members write down ideas and solutions, read their suggestions to the whole group, and discuss and then rank the alternatives.

NONPROGRAMMED DECISION MAKING Nonroutine decision making that occurs in response to unusual, unpredictable opportunities and threats.

NONVERBAL COMMUNICATION The encoding of messages by means of facial expressions, body language, and styles of dress.

NORMS Unwritten rules or guidelines for appropriate behaviour in particular situations.

O

OBSTRUCTIONIST APPROACH Disregard for social responsibility; willingness to engage in and cover up unethical and illegal behaviour.

OPEN SYSTEM A system that takes in resources from its external environment and converts them into goods and services that are then sent back to that environment for purchase by customers.

OPERATING BUDGET A budget that states how managers intend to use organizational resources to achieve organizational goals.

OPERATIONS MANAGEMENT The process of managing the use of materials and other resources in producing an organization's goods and services.

OPPOSABLE THINKING The ability to hold opposing viewpoints and be successful with "both-and" or integrative thinking.

OPTIMUM DECISION The best decision in light of what managers believe to be the most desirable future consequences for their organization.

ORGANIC STRUCTURE An organizational structure in which authority is decentralized to middle and first-line managers and tasks and roles are left ambiguous to encourage employees to cooperate and respond quickly to the unexpected.

ORGANIZATIONAL BEHAVIOUR The study of the factors that have an impact on how individuals and groups respond to and act in organizations.

ORGANIZATIONAL BEHAVIOUR MODIFICATION (OB MOD) The systematic application of operant conditioning techniques to promote the performance of organizationally functional behaviours and discourage the performance of dysfunctional behaviours.

ORGANIZATIONAL CONFLICT The discord that arises when the goals, interest, or values of different individuals or groups are incompatible and those individuals or groups block or thwart each other's attempts to achieve their objectives.

ORGANIZATIONAL CULTURE A system of shared meaning, held by organization members, that distinguishes the organization from other organizations.

ORGANIZATIONAL DESIGN The process by which managers make specific organizing choices that result in a particular kind of organizational structure.

ORGANIZATIONAL ENVIRONMENT The set of forces and conditions that operate beyond an organization's boundaries but affect a manager's ability to acquire and use resources.

ORGANIZATIONAL LEARNING The process through which managers seek to improve employees' desire and ability to understand and manage the organization and its task environment.

ORGANIZATIONAL PERFORMANCE A measure of how efficiently and effectively a manager uses resources to satisfy customers and achieve organizational goals.

ORGANIZATIONAL SOCIALIZATION The process by which newcomers learn an organization's values and norms and acquire the work behaviours necessary to perform jobs effectively.

ORGANIZATIONAL STAKEHOLDERS Shareholders, employees, customers, suppliers, and others who have an interest, claim, or stake in an organization and in what it does.

ORGANIZATIONAL STRUCTURE A formal system of both task and reporting relationships that coordinates and motivates organizational members so that they work together to reach organizational goals.

ORGANIZATIONS Collections of people who work together and coordinate their actions to achieve goals.

ORGANIZING Structuring workplace relationships in a way that allows members of an organization to work together to achieve organizational goals; one of the four principal functions of management.

OUTSOURCING Using outside suppliers and manufacturers to produce goods and services.

OVERPAYMENT INEQUITY Inequity that exists when a person perceives that his or her own outcome/input ratio is greater than the ratio of a referent.

OVERT DISCRIMINATION Knowingly and willingly denying diverse individuals access to opportunities and outcomes in an organization.

P

PATH-GOAL THEORY A contingency model of leadership proposing that leaders can motivate subordinates by identifying their desired outcomes, rewarding them for high performance and the attainment of work goals with these desired outcomes, and clarifying for them the paths leading to the attainment of work goals.

PAY LEVEL The relative position of an organization's pay incentives in comparison with those of other organizations in the same industry employing similar kinds of workers.

PAY STRUCTURE The arrangement of jobs into categories that reflect their relative importance to the organization and its goals, levels of skill required, and other characteristics.

PERCEPTION The process through which people select, organize, and interpret sensory input to give meaning and order to the world around them.

PERFORMANCE APPRAISAL The evaluation of employees' job performance and contributions to their organization.

PERFORMANCE FEEDBACK The process through which managers share performance appraisal information with subordinates, give subordinates an opportunity to reflect on their own performances, and develop, with subordinates, plans for the future.

PERFORMANCE TESTS Measure the candidates ability to perform actual job tasks.

PERSONAL LEADERSHIP STYLE The ways a manager chooses to influence others and how they approach planning, organizing, and controlling.

PERSONALITY TESTS Measure personality traits and characteristics relevant to job performance.

PERSONNEL REPLACEMENT CHARTS A graphic illustration of current positions, who holds them, and whether they have the skills and qualifications necessary for succession planning.

PLANNING Identifying and selecting appropriate goals and courses of action; one of the four principal functions of management.

POLICY A general guide to action.

POLITICAL AND LEGAL FORCES Outcomes of changes in laws and regulations, such as the deregulation of industries, the privatization of organizations, and increased emphasis on environmental protection.

PORTER'S FIVE FORDCES MODEL A technique managers use to analyze the potential profitability of entertaining and competing in a particular industry.

POSITION POWER The amount of legitimate, reward, and coercive powers that a leader has by virtue of his or her position in an organization; a determinant of how favourable a situation is for leading.

POSITIVE REINFORCEMENT Giving people outcomes they desire when they perform organizationally functional behaviours well.

PRIOR HYPOTHESIS BIAS A cognitive bias resulting from the tendency to base decisions on strong prior beliefs, even if evidence shows that those beliefs are wrong.

PROACTIVE APPROACH Strong commitment to social responsibility; eagerness to do more than the law requires and to use organizational resources to promote the interests of all organizational stakeholders.

PROCEDURAL JUSTICE A moral principle calling for the use of fair procedures to determine how to distribute outcomes to organizational members.

PROCESS THEORIES Theories of motivation that explore how one actually motivates someone.

PRODUCT STRUCTURE An organizational structure in which each product line or business is handled by a self-contained division.

PRODUCT TEAM STRUCTURE An organizational structure in which employees are permanently assigned to a cross-functional team and report only to the product team manager or to one of his or her direct subordinates.

PRODUCTION BLOCKING A loss of productivity in brainstorming sessions due to the unstructured nature of brainstorming.

PROFESSIONAL ETHICS Standards that govern how members of a profession are to make decisions when the way they should behave is not clear-cut.

PROGRAMMED DECISION MAKING Routine, virtually automatic decision making that follows established rules or guidelines.

PUNISHMENT Administering an undesired or negative consequence when dysfunctional behaviour occurs.

Q

QUID PRO QUO SEXUAL HARASSMENT Asking or forcing an employee to perform sexual favours in exchange for some reward or to avoid negative consequences.

R

RATIONAL DECISION-MAKING MODEL A prescriptive approach to decision making based on the idea that the decision maker can identify and evaluate all possible alternatives and their consequences and rationally choose the most suitable course of action.

REAL-TIME INFORMATION Frequently updated information that reflects current conditions.

REALISTIC JOB PREVIEW (RJP) Communicating the good and bad aspects of a job to a candidate to prevent mismatched expectations and high turnover.

RECEIVER The person or group for whom a message is intended.

RECRUITMENT Activities that managers use to develop a pool of qualified candidates for open positions.

REFERENT POWER Power that comes from subordinates' and co-workers' respect, admiration, and loyalty.

REINFORCEMENT Anything that causes a given behaviour to be repeated or stopped.

REINFORCEMENT THEORY A motivation theory based on the relationship between a given behaviour and its consequence.

RELATIONSHIP CONFLICT Members of the group perceive each other's attitudes as a problem.

RELATED DIVERSIFICATION Entering a new business or industry to create a competitive advantage in one or more of an organization's existing divisions or businesses.

RELIABLE SELECTION TECHNIQUES Must yield consistent results when repeated.

REPRESENTATIVE DEMOCRACY A political system in which representatives elected by citizens and legally accountable to the electorate form a government whose function is to make decisions on behalf of the electorate.

REPRESENTATIVENESS BIAS A cognitive bias resulting from the tendency to generalize inappropriately from a small sample or from a single vivid case or episode.

REPUTATION The esteem or high repute that individuals or organizations gain when they behave ethically.

RESEARCH AND DEVELOPMENT TEAM A team whose members have the expertise and experience needed to develop new products.

RESOURCES Assets such as people, machinery, raw materials, information, skills, and financial capital.

RESTRAINING FORCES Forces that prevent movement away from the status quo.

RESTRUCTURING Downsizing an organization by eliminating the jobs of large numbers of top, middle, and first-line managers and nonmanagerial employees.

REWARD POWER The ability of a manager to give or withhold tangible and intangible rewards.

ROLE The specific tasks that a person is expected to perform because of the position he or she holds in an organization.

ROLE MAKING Taking the initiative to modify an assigned role by taking on extra responsibilities.

RULE(S) A formal, written guide to action; formal written instructions that specify actions to be taken under different circumstances to achieve specific goals.

RUMOURS Unofficial pieces of information of interest to organizational members but with no identifiable source.

S

SATISFICING Searching for and choosing acceptable, or satisfactory, ways to respond to problems and opportunities, rather than trying to make the best decision.

SCENARIO PLANNING The generation of multiple forecasts of future conditions followed by an analysis of how to respond effectively to each of those conditions; also called contingency planning.

SCIENTIFIC MANAGEMENT The systematic study of relationships among people and tasks for the purpose of redesigning the work process to increase efficiency.

SELECTION The process that managers use to determine the relative qualifications of job applicants and the individuals' potential for performing well in a particular job.

SELF-FULFILLING PROPHECY A person's prediction in their way of thinking and feeling that actually causes, directly or otherwise, something to come true.

SELF-MANAGED (OR SELF-DIRECTED) WORK TEAMS Groups of employees who supervise their own activities and monitor the quality of the goods and services they provide.

SELF-MANAGED TEAMS Groups of employees who supervise their own activities and monitor the quality of the goods and services they provide.

SENDER The person or group wishing to share information.

SEXUAL HARASSMENT Unwelcome behaviour of a sexual nature in the workplace that negatively affects the work environment or leads to adverse job-related consequences for the employee.

SITUATIONAL INTERVIEW QUESTIONS Ask candidates how they would deal with a situation they might encounter on the job.

SITUATIONAL LEADERSHIP THEORY (SLT) A contingency model of leadership that focuses on the followers' readiness.

SOCIAL AUDIT A tool that allows managers to analyze the profitability and social returns of socially responsible actions.

SOCIAL LOAFING The tendency of individuals to put forth less effort when they work in groups than when they work alone.

SOCIAL RESPONSIBILITY A manager's duty or obligation to make decisions that promote the well-being of stakeholders and society as a whole.

SOCIETAL ETHICS Standards that govern how members of a society are to deal with each other on issues such as fairness, justice, poverty, and the rights of the individual.

SPAN OF CONTROL The number of subordinates who report directly to a manager.

STAKEHOLDERS Persons, groups and institutions directly affected by the activities and decisions of an organization.

STANDARD OPERATING PROCEDURES (SOPs) Specific sets of written instructions about how to perform a certain aspect of a task.

STANDING COMMITTEE A relatively permanent task force charged with addressing long-term, enduring problems or issues facing an organization.

STEREOTYPE Simplistic and often inaccurate beliefs about the typical characteristics of particular groups of people.

STRATEGIC ALLIANCE An agreement in which managers pool or share their organization's resources and know-how with a foreign company and the two organizations share the rewards and risks of starting a new venture.

STRATEGIC HUMAN RESOURCE MANAGEMENT The process by which managers design the components of a human resource management system to be consistent with each other, with other elements of organizational architecture, and with the organization's strategy and goals.

STRATEGY A cluster of decisions about what goals to pursue, what actions to take, and how to use resources to achieve goals.

STRATEGY FORMULATION Analysis of an organization's current situation followed by the development of strategies to accomplish the organization's mission and achieve its goals.

STRUCTURED INTERVIEW Formal questions asked in a set sequence.

SUPPLIERS Individuals and organizations that provide an organization with the input resources that it needs to produce goods and services.

SUPPLY CHAIN MANAGEMENT The activities involved in procuring raw materials, transforming them into parts or finished products and delivering them to consumers.

SUSTAINABILITY Decisions that protect the environment, promote social responsibility, respect cultural differences, and provide an economic benefit.

SWOT ANALYSIS A planning exercise in which managers identify organizational strengths (S) and weaknesses (W), and environmental opportunities (O) and threats (T).

SYNERGY Performance gains that result when individuals and departments coordinate their actions.

SYSTEMATIC ERRORS Errors that people make over and over again and that result in poor decision making.

T

TASK ENVIRONMENT The set of forces and conditions that start with suppliers, distributors, customers, and competitors and affect an organization's ability to obtain inputs and dispose of its outputs, because they influence managers on a daily basis.

TASK FORCE A committee of managers or nonmanagerial employees from various departments or divisions who meet to solve a specific, mutual problem; also called an *ad hoc committee*.

TASK-ORIENTED ROLES Roles performed by group members to make sure the task gets done.

TASK-RELATED CONFLICT Members of the group perceive a problem or have a disagreement about the nature of the task or project.

TASK STRUCTURE The extent to which the work to be performed is clear-cut so that a leader's subordinates know what needs to be accomplished and how to go about doing it; a determinant of how favourable a situation is for leading.

TEAM A group whose members work intensely with each other to achieve a specific common goal or objective.

TECHNICAL SKILLS Job-specific knowledge and techniques that are required to perform an organizational role.

TECHNOLOGICAL FORCES Outcomes of changes in the technology that managers use to design, produce, or distribute goods and services.

TECHNOLOGY The combination of skills and equipment that managers use in the design, production, and distribution of goods and services.

THEORY X Negative assumptions about employees that lead to the conclusion that a manager's task is to supervise them closely and control their behaviour.

THEORY Y Positive assumptions about employees that lead to the conclusion that a manager's task is to create a work setting that encourages commitment to organizational goals and provides opportunities for imagination, initiative, and self-direction.

TIME HORIZON The intended duration of a plan.

TOP-DOWN CHANGE Change that is introduced quickly throughout an organization by upper-level managers.

TOP-MANAGEMENT TEAM A group composed of the CEO, the president, and the heads of the most important departments.

TOP MANAGERS Managers who establish organizational goals, decide how departments should interact, and monitor the performance of middle managers.

TOTALITARIAN REGIME A political system in which a single party, individual, or group holds all political power and neither recognizes nor permits opposition.

TOTAL REWARD STRATEGY A total reward strategy that encompasses both intrinsically and extrinsically motivating factors.

TRAINING Teaching organizational members how to perform their current jobs and helping them acquire the knowledge and skills they need to be effective performers.

TRANSACTIONAL LEADERSHIP Leaders who guide their subordinates toward expected goals with no expectation of exceeding expected behaviour.

TRANSFORMATIONAL LEADERSHIP Leadership that makes subordinates aware of the importance of their jobs and performance to the organization and aware of their own needs for personal growth and that motivates subordinates to work for the good of the organization.

U

UNCERTAIN ENVIRONMENT The state of environmental forces that is so dynamic that managers cannot predict the probable outcomes of a course of action unpredictability.

UNDERPAYMENT INEQUITY Inequity that exists when a person perceives that his or her own outcome/input ratio is less than the ratio of a referent.

UNETHICAL DECISION A decision that a manager would prefer to disguise or hide from other people because it enables a company or a particular individual to gain at the expense of society or other stakeholders.

UNINTENTIONAL DISCRIMINATION Unfair practices and policies that have an adverse impact on specific groups for reasons unrelated to the job.

UNRELATED DIVERSIFICATION Entering a new industry or buying a company in a new industry that is not related in any way to an organization's current businesses or industries.

UNSTRUCTURED INTERVIEW Unplanned questions asked as points of interest arise in the conversation.

V

VALENCE In expectancy theory, how desirable each of the outcomes available from a job or organization is to a person.

VALID SELECTION TECHNIQUES Must relate to the candidates' likely success or failure on the job.

VALUES The stable, long-lasting beliefs about what is important.

VERBAL COMMUNICATION The encoding of messages into words, either written or spoken.

VERTICAL INTEGRATION A strategy that allows an organization to create value by producing its own inputs or distributing and selling its own outputs.

VIRTUAL TEAM A team whose members rarely or never meet face to face and interact by using various forms of information technology such as email, computer networks, telephones, faxes, and videoconferences.

VISION STATEMENT A broad declaration of the big picture of the organization and/or a statement of its dreams for the future.

W

WORKPLACE HARASSMENT Any behaviour directed toward an employee that is known to be or ought to be known to be offensive and unwelcome.

Endnotes

Chapter 1

1. Website: www.quoteworld.org/quotes/3649. Accessed May 11, 2008.

2. Neil King Jr. and Spencer Swartz, "Oil 'Superspike' Could Pummel World Economy," *The Globe and Mail*, Wednesday, May 7, 2008, B11.

3. Editorial, "Don't Panic," *National Post*, Saturday, April 26, 2008, A16.

4. David Crane, "Globalization Column Touched a Raw Nerve," *Toronto Star*, January 7, 2007. Website: www.thestar.com/comment/columnists/article/168600. Accessed May 11, 2008.

5. In January, United Nations Secretary-General Ban Ki-moon declared that 2008 should be "the year of the bottom billion."

6. Kevin Carmichael, "Soaring Food Prices Now Top Threat, IMF Says," *The Globe and Mail*, Monday, April 14, 2008, A1, 7.

7. Michael Coren, "Food Beyond the Reach of the Poor," *The Globe and Mail*, Saturday, April 12, 2008, A13; also, Kevin Libin, "Biofuels Seen as Problem, Not Solution," *National Post*, Saturday, April 12, 2008, A10.

8. Eric Reguly, "How the Cupboards Went Bare," *The Globe and Mail*, Saturday, April 12, 2008, A12–13.

9. Richard Gwyn, "Attitudes to Immigration Hardening in Britain," *Toronto Star*, Friday, March 18, 2005, A19.

10. Michael Rock, *Ethics: To Live By, To Work By* (Toronto: McGraw-Hill, 2005), p. 165.

11. David Olive, "GE Boss Brings Fresh Energy," *Toronto Star*, Sunday, June 24, 2007. Website: www.thestar.com/Business/article/228806. Accessed May 10, 2008.

12. Roger Martin, *The Opposable Mind: How Successful Leaders Win Through Integrative Thinking* (Boston, MA: Harvard Business School, 2007).

13. See Marcia M. Hughes and James Bradford Terrell, *The Emotionally Intelligent Team: Understanding and Developing the Behaviors of Success* (San Francisco: Jossey-Bass, 2007).

14. Darlene Mary O'Leary, *An Integral Vision of Economic Transformation: The Relevance of Bernard Lonergan to Debates in Canadian Social Ethics on the Relationship of Ethics and Economics and the Function of Profit*. Ph.D. Dissertation. Ottawa, Ontario: Saint Paul University, September 2007. See also Doug Saunders, "How to Fix the World? Make Aid Work for the 'Bottom Billion'," *The Globe and Mail*, Saturday, March 29, 2008, F3.

15. Tomi J. Kallio, "Taboos in Corporate Social Responsibility Discourse," *Journal of Business Ethics*, 74, no 2, August, 2007, pp. 165–175.

16. G.R. Jones, *Organizational Theory* (Reading, MA: Addison-Wesley, 1995).

17. "Engaging Our Stakeholders," Website: www.petro-canada.ca/en/socialresp/916.aspx.

18. J.P. Campbell, "On the Nature of Organizational Effectiveness," in P.S. Goodman, J.M. Pennings, and Associates, *New Perspectives on Organizational Effectiveness* (San Francisco: Jossey-Bass, 1977).

19. P. Drucker, *Management: Tasks, Responsibilities, Practices* (New York: Harper and Row, 1974).

20. Rita Trichur, "Reflecting a New Image in Banking," *Toronto Star*, March 17, 2008. Website: www.thestar.com/printArticle/349252.

21. Graeme Hamilton, "Visible Minorities the New Majority," *National Post*, Thursday, April 3, 2008, A1, 7.

22. It was estimated that the U.S. gay and lesbian market was worth US$600 billion in 2007.

23. H. Fayol, *General and Industrial Management* (New York: IEEE Press, 1984). Fayol's work was first published in 1916. Fayol actually identified five different managerial functions, but most scholars today believe these four capture the essence of Fayol's ideas.

24. P.F. Drucker, *Management Tasks, Responsibilities, and Practices* (New York: Harper and Row, 1974).

25. G. Dixon, "Clock Ticking for New CEOs," *The Globe and Mail*, May 8, 2001.

26. Adapted from Gordon Pitts, "As Tough as Her Father? Some Say Even Tougher," *The Globe and Mail*, Monday, August 13, 2007, B1, 8.

27. J. Kotter, *The General Managers* (New York: Free Press, 1992).

28. C.P. Hales, "What Do Managers Do? A Critical Review of the Evidence," *Journal of Management Studies*, January 1986, pp. 88–115; A.I. Kraul, P.R. Pedigo, D.D. McKenna, and M.D. Dunnette, "The Role of the Manager: What's Really Important in Different Management Jobs," *Academy of Management Executive*, November 1989, pp. 286–293.

29. A.K. Gupta, "Contingency Perspectives on Strategic Leadership," in D.C. Hambrick (ed.), *The Executive Effect: Concepts and Methods for Studying Top Managers* (Greenwich, CT: JAI Press, 1988), pp.147–178.

30. D.G. Ancona, "Top Management Teams: Preparing for the Revolution," in J.S. Carroll (ed.), *Applied Social Psychology and Organizational Settings* (Hillsdale, NJ: Erlbaum, 1990); D.C. Hambrick and P.A. Mason, "Upper Echelons: The Organization as a Reflection of Its Top Managers," *Academy of Management Journal*, 9, 1984, pp. 193–206.

31. T.A. Mahony, T.H. Jerdee, and S.J. Carroll, "The Jobs of Management," *Industrial Relations*, 4, 1965, pp. 97–110; L. Gomez-Mejia, J. McCann, and R.C. Page, "The Structure of Managerial Behaviours and Rewards," *Industrial Relations*, 24, 1985, pp. 147–154.

32. K. Labich, "Making Over Middle Managers," *Fortune*, May 8, 1989, pp. 58–64.

33. Deena Waisberg, "Bank Executive Proves He's a Stand-up Guy," *National Post*, Saturday, May 28, 2005, p. FW9.

34. Anthony Grnak, John Hughes and Douglas Hunter, *Building the Best, Lessons from Inside Canada's Best Managed Companies* (Toronto: Viking Canada, 2006), p. 91.

35. See James Collins, Ph.D. *Good to Great: Why Some Companies Make the Leap... and Others Don't*. New York: Harper Collins, 2001.

36. R.L. Katz, "Skills of an Effective Administrator," *Harvard Business Review,* September–October 1974, pp. 90–102.

37. Ibid.

38. Adapted from Harvey Schachter, "Being an MBA Doesn't Mean You Can Manage," *The Globe and Mail,* Wednesday, June 2, 2004, p. C6. See also Henry Mintzberg, "Forget Heroes: What We Really Need Are 'Engaging' Managers," *The Globe and Mail, Friday,* May 28, 2004, pp. C1, 4; also Henry Mintzberg. *Managers Not MBAs: A Hard Look at the Soft Practice of Managing and Management Development.* San Francisco: Berrett-Koehler Publishers, 2004.

39. R.H. Guest, "Of Time and the Foreman," *Personnel,* 32, 1955, pp. 478–486.

40. C.W.L. Hill, *Becoming a Manager: Mastery of a New Identity* (Boston: Harvard Business School Press, 1992).

41. H. Mintzberg, "The Manager's Job: Folklore and Fact," *Harvard Business Review,* July–August 1975, pp. 56–62.

42. H. Mintzberg, *The Nature of Managerial Work* (New York: Harper and Row, 1973).

43. Ibid.

44. Roger Martin. *The Opposable Mind: How Successful Leaders Win Through Integrative Thinking* (Boston, MA: Harvard Business School, 2007), p. 6.

45. Slightly edited; Website: http://phm3.blogspot.com/2007/12/opposable-mind.html. Accessed May 10, 2008; comment posted on December 28, 2007, 9:04 a.m.

46. Adapted from: Mark Kozak-Holland, "Plan for the Unthinkable," *Financial Post,* Monday, October 18, 2004, p. FE9.

47. The official Titanic site by Paramount Pictures and Twentieth Century Fox: www.titanicmovie.com.

48. Marcy Zitz, "The Anniversary of the Titanic Disaster: The Date the Titanic Sank," website: http://familyinternet.about.com/cs/entertainment/a/aatitanic.htm.

49. Adapted slightly from Mohammed Adam, "He Was the 'Wisest of the Old Mandarins'," *Ottawa Citizen,* Sunday, May 11, 2008, A1, 4.

50. Adapted from: "How Do I Manage a Mobile Workforce?" Special Feature to the *National Post:* Business Solutions. Presented by CISCO. *National Post,* Business Solutions, Monday, March 3, 2008, FP8. Website: www.financialpost.com/small_business/story.html?id=343859. Accessed May 11, 2008.

Chapter 2

1. Slightly edited from ENTREPRENEUR, Special Feature to the *National Post,* Monday, February 25, 2008, F12. Website: www.roynat.com/files/profiles/pdf/Floform-022508.pdf. Accessed May 13, 2008.

2. L.J. Bourgeois, "Strategy and Environment: A Conceptual Integration," *Academy of Management Review,* 5, 1985, pp. 25–39.

3. Brian Bergstein, "MIT Students Show Power of Open Cellphone Systems," *USA Today,* Tuesday, May 13, 2008. Website: www.usatoday.com/tech/products/2008-05-13-locale-mit_N.htm?csp=Daily%20Briefing. Accessed May 13, 2008.

4. Slightly adapted from: Warren Jestin, "Global Trends Effect Change," *National Post,* ENTREPRENEUR, Monday, March 12, 2007, EN1, 4. Warren Jestin is senior vice-president and chief economist of Scotiabank Group.

5. Don Tapscott and David Agnew, "Governance in the Digital Economy: The Importance of Human Development," *International Monetary Fund (IMF) Finance & Development,* December 1999, 36, No. 4, 9 printed pages. Website: www.imf.org/external/pubs/ft/fandd/1999/12/tapscott.htm.

6. Jacqueline Thorpe, "Mauled by China Inc.," *Financial Post,* Saturday, April 23, 2005, pp. FP1, 6.

7. M.E. Porter, *Competitive Strategy* (New York: Free Press, 1980).

8. Hollier Shaw, "Bowrings Files for Bankruptcy," *Financial Post,* Thursday, August 25, 2005, pp. FP1, 4. See also www.dnb.ca/news/2005-08-26.htm.

9. M.E. Porter, *Competitive Advantage* (New York: Free Press, 1985).

10. Paul Schwartz, "Great Expectations—Customers as Competitors," Posted on August 28, 2007. Website: customeru.wordpress.com/2007/08/28/great-expectations-customers-as-competitors/. Accessed May 15, 2008.

11. "Researching Your Competition," StatsLink Canada, © John White, GDSourcing—Research & Retrieval 2006. Website: www.stats-link-canada.com/Industry-Competitors.html. Accessed May 15, 2008.

12. For views on barriers to entry from an economics perspective, see M.E. Porter, *Competitive Strategy* (New York: Free Press, 1980). For the sociological perspective, see J. Pfeffer and G.R. Salancik, *The External Control of Organization: A Resource Dependence Perspective* (New York: Harper and Row, 1978).

13. M.E. Porter, *Competitive Strategy* (New York: Free Press, 1980); J.E. Bain, *Barriers to New Competition* (Cambridge, MA: Harvard University Press, 1956); R.J. Gilbert, "Mobility Barriers and the Value of Incumbency," in R. Schmalensee and R.D. Willig (eds.), *Handbook of Industrial Organization,* vol. 1 (Amsterdam: North Holland, 1989).

14. Brent Jang, "Leblanc on Sorrow, Remorse and His Little 'White Lie'" *The Globe and Mail,* Friday, March 18, 2005, pp. B1, 2.

15. C.W.L. Hill, "The Computer Industry: The New Industry of Industries," in C.W.L. Hill and G.R. Jones, *Strategic Management: An Integrated Approach,* 3rd ed. (Boston: Houghton Mifflin, 1995).

16. "Western Glove Works Ltd.," ENTREPRENEUR: Special Feature to *National Post, Financial Post,* Friday, June 10, 2005, p. FP20.

17. Adapted from Carly Weeks, "16¢ Pricey," *The Globe and Mail,* Monday, May 12, 2008, L1, 2. Website: www.theglobeandmail.com/servlet/story/RTGAM.20080512.wlfreebies12/BNStory/lifeMain/home. Accessed May 12, 2008.

18. Website: www.youtube.com/watch?v=5YGc4zOqozo. Accessed Tuesday, July 21, 2009.

19. Website: www.casttv.com/video/u8ey2k1/united-breaks-guitars-cnn-situation-room-wolf-blitzer-video. Accessed Tuesday, July 21, 2009.

20. Website: http://mktgcliks.blogspot.com/2009/07/united-breaks-guitars-united-airlines.html. Accessed Tuesday, July 21, 2009.

21. Website: http://beverages.recipefeeds.org/news/tims-eats-humble-pie-to-avert-pr-catastrophe/. Accessed May 15, 2008.

22. "When Fortune Frowned: A Special Report on the World Economy," *The Economist,* October 11, 2008, p. 3.

23. World Economic Forum.

24. www.canada.com/topics/news/story.html?id=c3a67e3b-1aef-4daf-a768-a54eedb80185. Accessed October 11, 2008.

25. J. Schumpeter, *Capitalism, Socialism and Democracy* (London: Macmillan, 1950), p. 68. Also see R.R. Winter and S.G. Winter, *An Evolutionary Theory of Economic Change* (Cambridge, MA: Harvard University Press, 1982).

26. "Demographic Time Bomb: Mitigating the Effects of Demographic Change in Canada," Report of the Standing Senate Committee on Banking, Trade and Commerce, June

2006. Website: www.parl.gc.ca/39/1/parlbus/commbus/senate/Com-e/bank-e/rep-e/rep03jun06-e.htm. Accessed May 15, 2008.

27. Wallace Immen, "The Way We Will Be," *The Globe and Mail*, October 1, 2007. Website: www.wrien.com/documents/TheWayWeWillBe.pdf. Accessed May 15, 2008.

28. Margaret Wente, "It's Manly at the Top," *The Globe and Mail*, Saturday, May 7, 2005, p. A21.

29. Ibid.

30. Mary Teresa Bitti, "A Champion of Women," *National Post*, Wednesday, May 14, 2008, FP13. Website: www.financialpost.com/working/story.html?id=512791. Accessed May 14, 2008.

31. For a detailed discussion of the importance of the structure of law as a factor explaining economic change and growth, see D.C. North, *Institutions, Institutional Change and Economic Performance* (Cambridge: Cambridge University Press, 1990).

32. Barbara Shecter, "Cineplex Snaps Up Rival," *Financial Post*, Tuesday, June 14, 2005, pp. FP1, 6. See also Richard Blackwell, "Movie Marriage Promises Blockbuster Savings," *The Globe and Mail*, Wednesday, June 22, 2005, p. B3; also Gayle MacDonald, "Movie Boss Has Best Seat in the House," *The Globe and Mail*, Wednesday, June 15, 2005, pp. B1, 4.

33. Marina Strauss, "Tribunal Rules Sears Broke Law by Inflating Tire Savings," *The Globe and Mail*, Tuesday, January 25, 2005, pp. B1, 8.

34. R.B. Reich, *The Work of Nations* (New York: Knopf, 1991).

35. Jagdish Bhagwati, *Protectionism* (Cambridge, MA: MIT Press, 1988).

36. P.M. Sweezy and H. Magdoff, *The Dynamics of US Capitalism* (New York: Monthly Review Press, 1972).

37. Peter Foster, "Vlad the Great," *Financial Post*, Friday, November 5, 2004, p. FP15.

38. The ideology is that of individualism, which dates back to Adam Smith, John Stuart Mill, and the like. See H.W. Spiegel, *The Growth of Economic Thought* (Durham, NC: Duke University Press, 1991).

39. M. Magnier, "Chiquita Bets Czechoslovakia Can Produce Banana Bonanza," *Journal of Commerce*, August 29, 1991, pp. 1, 3.

40. "In Praise of the Stateless Multinational," *The Economist*, September 20, 2008, p. 20.

41. Karl Moore, "Great Global Managers, They Don't Come From Great Powers. Here's

Where to Look" Website: www.conference-board.org/articles/atb_article.cfm?id=200. Accessed January 17, 2009.

42. Ibid.

43. Ibid.

44. Adapted from G.H. Hofstede, *Culture's Consequences: International Differences in Work-Related Values.* (Beverly Hills, CA: Sage Publications, 1984).

45. Karl Moore, "Great Global Managers, They Don't Come From Great Powers. Here's Where to Look," www.conference-board.org/articles/atb_article.cfm?id=200. Accessed January 17, 2009.

46. Rajendra S. Sisodia, David B. Wolfe, and Jagdish N. Sheth, *Firms of Endearment. How World-Class Companies Profit from Passion and Purpose.* (Upper Saddle River, NJ: Wharton School Publishing, 2007).

47. Website: www.cherwell.oxon.sch.uk/arcadia/outline0.htm. Accessed May 15, 2008.

48. Rajendra S. Sisodia, et al., *op. cit.*, p. 4.

49. Rajendra S. Sisodia, et al., *op. cit.*, p. 16.

50. Daniel Pink calls this the "Conceptual Age," *A Whole New Mind: Moving from the Information Age to the Conceptual Age* (New York: Riverhead Books division of Penguin, 2005).

51. The authors even use the word "metaphysical" in conjunction with "experiential" (Ibid., p. xxix).

52. "Roll-up-Rim Contest Wasteful, Critics Say," *The London Free Press*, March 2, 2005. Website: www.canoe.ca/NewsStand/LondonFreePress/News/2005/03/02/946850-sun.html.

53. Bill Mah, "Tim Hortons Contest a Litterbug, Critics Say: Roll Up the Rim Begins," *National Post*, March 1, 2005.

54. R.B. Duncan, "Characteristics of Organization Environment and Perceived Environment," *Administrative Science Quarterly*, 17, 1972, pp. 313–327.

55. See "McDonald's USA Food Allergens and Sensitivities Listing," Website: www.mcdonalds.com/app_controller.nutrition.categories.allergens.index.html.

56. "Former McDonald's CEO Charlie Bell Dies of Cancer," *USA Today*, Monday, January 17, 2005.

57. Mike Adams, "Former CEO of McDonald's Dies of Colon Cancer at Age of 44," *News Target*, January 16, 2005. Website: www.newstatget.com/003232.html.

58. Not everyone agrees with this assessment. Some argue that organizations

and individual managers have little impact on the environment. See M.T. Hannan and J. Freeman, "Structural Inertia and Organizational Change," *American Sociological Review*, 49, 1984, pp. 149–164.

59. Adapted from Marjo Johne, "Mobility and Flexibility Are Key in World of Increasing Globalization," *The Globe and Mail*, Monday, October 1, 2007, B12. Website: www.theglobeandmail.com/servlet/story/RTGAM.20071001.wsrworkplaceglobal01/BNStory/Technology/. Accessed May 11, 2008.

60. "Foreign Investment in Canada, Lie Back and Forget the Maple Leaf," *The Economist*, April 5, 2008, p. 42.

61. A. Shama, "Management Under Fire: The Transformation of Management in the Soviet Union and Eastern Europe," *Academy of Management Executive*, 1993, pp. 22–35.

62. Anthony Grnak, John Hughes, and Douglas Hunter, *Building the Best, Lessons from Inside Canada's Best Managed Companies* (Toronto: Viking Canada, 2006), p. 86.

63. Ibid, p. 37.

64. Website: www.hollandc.pe.ca/quality/. Accessed May 11, 2008.

65. Michael Rachlis, "Medicare Made Easy," *The Globe and Mail*, Monday, April 26, 2004, p. A13.

66. "Nortel blasts RIM over bid for its assets," by Jamie Sturgeon, *Canwest News Service* July 29, 2009. Website: www.canada.com/Nortel+blasts+over+assets/1840769/story.html. Accessed July 29, 2009.

67. K. Seiders and L.L. Berry, "Service Fairness: What It Is and Why It Matters," *Academy of Management Executive*, 12, 1998, pp. 8–20.

68. C. Anderson, "Values-Based Management," *Academy of Management Executive*, 11, 1997, pp. 25–46.

69. W.H. Shaw and V. Barry, *Moral Issues in Business*, 6th ed. (Belmont, CA: Wadsworth, 1995); and T. Donaldson, *Corporations and Morality* (Englewood Cliffs, NJ: Prentice-Hall, 1982).

70. D.R. Tobin, *The Knowledge Enabled Organization* (New York: AMACOM, 1998).

71. "Canadian Productivity Rising Because of High Tech Investment, Says Conference Board," *Canadian Press Newswire*, November 30, 2000.

72. Adapted from "Impersonal Approach Hurts Business, Study Says," *The Globe and Mail*, Wednesday, August 20, 2003, C3.

73. Alan M. Webber, "The Future of the Future," *Toronto Star*, Sunday, September 25, 2005, D4. Website: www.leighbureau.com/speakers/awebber/essays/future.pdf. Accessed May 15, 2008.

74. *A Whole New Mind: Moving from the Information Age to the Conceptual Age* (New York: Riverhead Books division of Penguin, 2005).

75. Cited in Rajendra S. Sisodia et al., p. xxix.

76. Cited in Rajendra S. Sisodia et al., p. xxxii.

Chapter 3

1. Edited and adapted from Donna Nebenzahl, "Don't Look Now," *National Post*, Wednesday, March 12, 2008, WK7. Website: www.financialpost.com/scripts/story.html?id=368504. Accessed May 18, 2008; Francesca Gino, Don A. Moore, and Max H. Bazerman, "See No Evil: When We Overlook Other People's Unethical Behavior," Working Papers (#08-045), Harvard Business School, January 11, 2008, 29 pages. Website: http://hbswk.hbs.edu/item/5839.html. Accessed May 18, 2008.

2. Website: www.hbs.edu/research/pdf/08-045.pdf. Accessed May 18, 2008.

3. See opening case in Chapter 3: Gareth R. Jones, Jennifer M. George, and Michael Rock, *Essentials of Contemporary Management*, 2nd ed. (Toronto: McGraw-Hill, 2007), pp. 61–62.

4. Francesca Gino, Don A. Moore, and Max H. Bazerman, *op. cit.*, p. 6.

5. Francesca Gino, Don A. Moore, and Max H. Bazerman, *op. cit.*, p. 5.

6. A book that features 45 activist women from around the world, Website: www.canada.com/montrealgazette/columnists/donna_nebenzahl.html. Accessed May 18, 2008.

7. Francesca Gino, Don A. Moore, and Max H. Bazerman, *op. cit.*, pp. 7, 8, 11.

8. Francesca Gino, Don A. Moore, and Max H. Bazerman, *op. cit.*, p. 10.

9. Francesca Gino, Don A. Moore, and Max H. Bazerman, *op. cit.*, p. 12.

10. Francesca Gino, Don A. Moore, and Max H. Bazerman, *op. cit.*, p. 29.

11. Website: http://hbswk.hbs.edu/item/5839.html.

12. Based on Richard Bloom, "How Parmalat Juggled the Struggle," *The Globe and Mail*, Monday, May 23, 2005, p. B3. Also, *New Cases in Management*, Quarter 4, 2006 Edition, p. 39. Website: www.ecch.com/uploads/ecchbib06-4.pdf. Accessed May 18, 2008.

13. Jennifer Wells, "'Aw Shucks' Defence Fails," *Toronto Star*, Wednesday, March 16, 2005, pp. A1, 15.

14. Adapted from Tu Thanh Ha, "Ad Executive Pays Back $1-Million," *The Globe and Mail*, Wednesday, August 17, 2005, p. A4.

15. "Gomery Report: Key Players," CTV News, Monday, October 31, 2005, 1:29 p.m. ET. Website: www.ctv.ca/servlet/ArticleNews/story/CTVNews/20051031/gomeryreport_sponsorshipplayers_20051031/20051031/. Accessed May 18, 2008.

16. On September 19, 2005, Paul Coffin was given a conditional sentence of two years less a day, to be served in the community. In sentencing him, Justice Jean-Guy Boilard of Quebec Superior Court said, "Mr. Coffin is genuinely contrite, but unfortunately he cannot turn the clock back. In my view, the risk of reoffending is extremely minimal, I would dare say inexistent." Les Perreaux, "Paul Coffin Avoids Prison Over Sponsorship Fraud," *The Globe and Mail*, Monday, September 19, 2005, p. 1.

17. T.L. Beauchamp and N.E. Bowie (eds.), *Ethical Theory and Business* (Englewood Cliffs, NJ: Prentice-Hall, 1979); and A. Macintyre, *After Virtue* (South Bend, IN: University of Notre Dame Press, 1981).

18. R.E. Goodin, "How to Determine Who Should Get What," *Ethics*, July 1975, pp. 310–321.

19. T.M. Jones, "Ethical Decision Making by Individuals in Organizations: An Issue Contingent Model," *Academy of Management Journal*, 16, 1991, pp. 366–395; and G.F. Cavanaugh, D.J. Moberg, and M. Velasquez, "The Ethics of Organizational Politics," *Academy of Management Review*, 6, 1981, pp. 363–374.

20. L.K. Trevino, "Ethical Decision Making in Organizations: A Person–Situation Interactionist Model," *Academy of Management Review*, 11, 1986, pp. 601–617; and W.H. Shaw and V. Barry, *Moral Issues in Business*, 6th ed. (Belmont, CA: Wadsworth, 1995).

21. Francesca Gino, Don A. Moore, and Max H. Bazerman, *op. cit.*, p. 26.

22. A.S. Waterman, "On the Uses of Psychological Theory and Research in the Process of Ethical Inquiry," *Psychological Bulletin*, 103, no. 3, 1988, pp. 283–298.

23. Website: www.canadiantimber.ca/code_ethics.html. Accessed May 18, 2008.

24. Website: www.ciri.org/about/policies/ethics/. Accessed May 18, 2008.

25. Tim Paradis and Sara Lepro, "Stocks Hit Five-Year Low Mark," *The Associated Press*, Website: www.kansascity.com/business/story/857209.html. Accessed October 25, 2008.

26. Website: http://blogs.mercurynews.com/docudrama/2008/10/24/ayn-rand-devotee-says-greenspans-philoshopy-not-anything-resembling-a-free-market/. Accessed October 25, 2008.

27. "Former Fed Chairman Greenspan Calls for More Regulation in Testimony to House." www.economicnews.ca/cepnews/wire/article/143992. Accessed October 25, 2008.

28. Lisa Schmidt, "Syncrude Charged for Duck Deaths at Tailings Pond," *Calgary Herald*, February 9, 2009. Website: www.calgaryherald.com/Health/Syncrude+charged+duck+deaths+tailings+pond/1270016/story.html. Accessed July 14, 2009.

29. J.A. Pearce, "The Company Mission as a Strategic Tool," *Sloan Management Review*, Spring 1982, pp. 15–24.

30. C.I. Barnard, *The Functions of the Executive* (Cambridge, MA: Harvard University Press, 1948).

31. R.E. Freeman, *Strategic Management: A Stakeholder Approach* (Marshfield, MA: Pitman, 1984).

32. Diane Francis, "Mining's New Frontier," *National Post*, Saturday, July 30, 2005, pp. FP1, 5.

33. M. McClearn, "African Adventure," *Canadian Business*, September 1, 2003.

34. "Corruption Still Tainting Asian Financial Picture, Study Says," *The Vancouver Sun*, March 20, 2001, p. D18.

35. Choe Sang-Hun, "Samsung Chairman Indicted," *National Post*, Saturday, April 19, 2008, FP15.

36. "Indicted Samsung Chairman Stepping Down," MSNBC, Monday, April 21, 2008. Website: www.msnbc.msn.com/id/24248167/. Accessed May 18, 2008.

37. Website: http://en.wikipedia.org/wiki/Lee_Myung-bak. Accessed May 18, 2008.

38. "Canadian Firms Ink New Ethics Code [for International Operations]," *Plant*, October 6, 1997, p. 4.

39. Transparency International, Global Corruption Report. Website: www.transparency.org/news_room/in_focus/2008/gcr2008. Accessed October 25, 2008.

40. "Focus on Small and Medium Businesses and Bribery," Transparency International. Website: www.transparency.org/news_room/in_focus/2008/sme_bribery. Accessed October 25, 2008.

41. B. Victor and J.B. Cullen, "The Organizational Bases of Ethical Work Climates," *Administrative Science Quarterly*, 33, 1988, pp. 101–125.

42. H. Demsetz, "Towards a Theory of Property Rights," *American Economic Review*, 57, 1967, pp. 347–359.

43. John Gray, "Time to Pay the Piper," *Canadian Business Online*, October 7, 2008. Website: www.canadianbusiness.com/. Accessed November 16, 2008.

44. C. Howes, "Ethics as More Than Just a Course: More Companies Are Promoting Ethical Practices in Work," *National Post*, October 28, 2000, p. D4.

45. Erin McClam, "Eight Former KPMG Executives Indicted," *The Globe and Mail*, Tuesday, August 30, 2005, p. B9.

46. KPMG FORENSIC Integrity Survey 2005–2006. Website: www.us.kpmg. com/RutUS_prod/Documents/9/ ForIntegritySurv_WEB.pdf, p. 5. Accessed May 18, 2008.

47. C. Howes, "Ethics as More Than Just a Course: More Companies Are Promoting Ethical Practices in Work," *National Post*, October 28, 2000, p. D4.

48. Ibid.

49. P.E. Murphy, "Creating Ethical Corporate Structure," *Sloan Management Review*, Winter 1989, pp. 81–87.

50. G.R. Jones, *Organizational Theory: Text and Cases* (Reading, MA: Addison-Wesley, 1997).

51. Website: http://news.bbc.co.uk/1/hi/ business/7636542.stm. Accessed: October 25, 2008.

52. "When It Comes to Ethics, Canadian Companies Are All Talk and Little Action, A Survey Shows," *Canadian Press Newswire*, February 17, 2000.

53. "India IT Boss Quits Over Scandal." Website: http://news.bbc.co.uk/2/hi/ business/7815031.stm. Accessed January 7, 2009.

54. Adapted from Julie Mason, "Sign of the Apocalypse," *Ottawa Citizen*, Sunday, April 20, 2008, A11. Website: www.canada.com/ ottawacitizen/story.html?id=21bc343b-3e54- 4136-9dab-30bea19ab541&p=2. Accessed May 18, 2008. See also "$15,000 Crib for Rich Kids," Website: www.pricy-spicy. com/15000-crib-for-rich-kids/ and www. trendhunter.com/trends/baby-fairy-tale- 15000-carriage-crib. Accessed Wednesday, July 22, 2009.

55. Website: www.poshtots.com/. Accessed May 18, 2008.

56. E. Gatewood and A.B. Carroll, "The Anatomy of Corporate Social Response," *Business Horizons*, September–October 1981, pp. 9–16.

57. M. Friedman, "A Friedman Doctrine: The Social Responsibility of Business Is to Increase Its Profits," *New York Times Magazine*, September 13, 1970, p. 33.

58. "Mining Could Be More Resourceful," *The Economist*, August 16, 2008, p. 64.

59. "Wal-Mart Canada Says Imports From Myanmar Ended in Spring," *Canadian Press Newswire*, July 18, 2000.

60. Danielle Sacks, "Working with the Enemy," *Fast Company*, September 2007, 74–81. Website: www.fastcompany.com/ magazine/118/working-with-the-enemy.html.

61. Colby Cosh, "In Wal-Mart We Trust," *National Post*, Tuesday, April 1, 2008. Website: www.nationalpost.com/opinion/ columnists/story.html?id=b65bd77e-511f- 4e00-88a7-a53a2a5ea4ca&k=68939. Accessed May 18, 2008.

62. Steven Horwitz, "Making Hurricane Response More Effective: Lessons from the Private Sector and the Coast Guard during Katrina," The Mercatus Center's Global Prosperity Initiative. Website: www.mercatus. org/repository/docLib/20080319_Making HurricaneReponseEffective_19Mar08.pdf. Accessed May 18, 2008.

63. Colby Cosh, *op. cit.*

64. "What," *National Post*, Saturday, June 11, 2005, p. WP3.

65. Paul Tsaparis, "This Quarter's Profit Isn't All There Is to Life," *National Post*, Monday, February 21, 2005, p. FP19.

66. For an interesting discussion of ethical perceptions of business students and other cultures, see Kun Young Chung, John W. Eichenseher, and Teruso Taniguchi, "Ethical Perceptions of Business Students: Differences Between East Asia and the USA and Among 'Confucian' Cultures," *Journal of Business Ethics*, 79, 2008, pp. 121–132. DOI 10.1007/s10551-007-9391-7--Springer 2007. Website: www.springerlink.com/content/ q305874w0g9961h6/fulltext.pdf. Accessed May 22, 2008.

67. Paul Tsaparis, "Canada's Best Bet for Global Competitiveness: CSR," April 25, 2005, 12:00 p.m. Website: www.canadianclub. org/do/event;jsessionid=E0ADD74FF4F6A D4E46A99C14D2F07ACE?event_id=2942. Accessed May 18, 2008.

68. CSR Case Study: Husky Injection Moulding Determined to Make a Contribution. Website: www.fivewinds. com/uploadedfiles_shared/CSRHusky.pdf. Accessed August 4, 2009.

69. W.G. Ouchi, *Theory Z: How American Business Can Meet the Japanese Challenge* (Reading, MA: Addison-Wesley, 1981).

70. J.B. McGuire, A. Sundgren, and T. Schneewis, "Corporate Social Responsibility and Firm Financial Performance," *Academy of Management Review*, 31, 1988, pp. 854–872.

71. J. Jedras, "Social Workers," *Silicon Valley NORTH*, July 30, 2001, p. 1.

72. M. Friedman, "A Friedman Doctrine: The Social Responsibility of Business Is to Increase Its Profits," *New York Times Magazine*, September 13, 1970, pp. 32, 33, 122, 124, 126.

73. E.D. Bowman, "Corporate Social Responsibility and the Investor," *Journal of Contemporary Business*, Winter 1973, pp. 49–58.

74. Prithi Yelaja, "Business with an Indian Twist," *Toronto Star*, Sunday, May 22, 2005, p. A19.

75. Ethnic Origin and Visible Minorities, Release no. 7, April 2, 2008. Website: www12. statcan.ca/census-recensement/2006/rt-td/ eth-eng.cfm. Accessed October 25, 2008.

76. Taken from "Employers Access to Support and Employees." Website: www. toronto.ca/yep/ease/myths.htm. Accessed August 22, 2008.

77. Colin Perkel, "Highly Educated Immigrants Still Lag in Earnings," *Toronto Star*, May 1, 2008. Website: www.thestar.com/Canada/ Census/article/420336. Accessed May 18, 2008.

78. Calgary Economic Development, "The Changing Profile of Calgary's Workforce Labour Force Profile," *CalgaryWorks*, June 2006, p. 32. Website: www.calgaryeconomic development.com/files/CED%20reports/ LabourForce_SP04.pdf. Accessed May 18, 2008.

79. Ibid. See also Derek Sankey, "The Many Faces of Diversity," *National Post*, FP WORKING, Wednesday, April 9, 2009, WK3.

80. Noor Javed and Nicholas Keung, "Visible Minorities Gaining," *Toronto Star*, April 3, 2008. Website: www.thestar.com/Canada/ Census/article/409455. Accessed May 18, 2008.

81. "Near Half in GTA Minorities," *Toronto Star*, April 2, 2008. Website: www.thestar. com/News/Canada/article/409112. Accessed May 18, 2008.

82. John Ivison, "Ottawa Moves to Slash Immigrant Backlog," *National Post*, Thursday, March 13, 2008. Website: www.nationalpost. com/news/canada/story.html?id=370894. Accessed May 18, 2008.

83. Quoted in Michael Adams, "Whose Conventional Wisdom?" *The Globe and Mail*, Monday, May 16, 2005, p. A15.

84. Gordon Nixon, "Unleashing Canada's People Power," *National Post*, Tuesday, June 21, 2005, p. A16.

85. R. Folger and M.A. Konovsky, "Effects of Procedural and Distributive Justice on Reactions to Pay Raise Decisions," *Academy of Management Journal*, 32, 1989, pp. 115–130; and J. Greenberg, "Organizational Justice: Yesterday, Today, and Tomorrow," *Journal of Management*, 16, 1990, pp. 399–402.

86. Website: www.canadastop100.com/diversity/chapters/Enbridge.pdf. Accessed October 25, 2008.

87. MediaCorp Inc. Website: www.canadastop100.com/diversity/. Accessed October 25, 2008.

88. J. Greenberg, "Organizational Justice: Yesterday, Today, and Tomorrow," *Journal of Management*, 16, 1990, pp. 399–402.

89. Website: www.newagecanada.com/eventmarketing.html. Accessed January 17, 2009.

90. D. Calleja, "Equity or Else," *Canadian Business*, March 19, 2001, p. 31.

91. G. Robinson and K. Dechant, "Building a Case for Business Diversity," *Academy of Management Executive*, 1997, pp. 3, 32–47.

92. Anthony Grnak, John Hughes, and Douglas Hunter, *Building the Best, Lessons from Inside Canada's Best Managed Companies* (Toronto: Viking Canada, 2006).

93. K. Kalawsky, "US Group Wants Royal's Centura Buy Delayed: Alleges Takeover Target Discriminates Against Minorities," *Financial Post (National Post)*, April 10, 2001, p. C4.

94. Stefan Christoff, "Racism and Reasonable Accommodation in Quebec: The Debate is A Farce," Website: www.nationalpost.com/news/story.html?id=d39d491c-f74c-4409-8e4a-e04798faaca9&k=1284. Accessed July 14, 2009.

95. Marina Strauss, *Globe and Mail* Update, July 24, 2009. Website: www.theglobeandmail.com/report-on-business/loblaw-buys-asian-grocery-chain/article1229762/.

96. H. Branswell, "When Nestlé Canada Said Last Month It Would No Longer Be Making Chocolate Bars in a Nut-Free Facility, Thousands Wrote in to Protest," *Canadian Press Newswire*, May 14, 2001.

97. Ibid.

98. A.P. Carnevale and S.C. Stone, "Diversity: Beyond the Golden Rule," *Training & Development*, October 1994, pp. 22–39.

99. Website: www.rcmp-grc.gc.ca/clet/cletweb/mssn_e.htm.

100. Website: www.rcmp-grc.gc.ca/clet/cletweb/orntn/ornt_40_e.htm.

101. "Selling Equity," *Financial Post Magazine*, September 1994, pp. 20–25.

102. Donna Seale, LL.B., "Diversity: Human Rights in the Workplace: Discussing Canadian Human Rights Law Issues Affecting Today's Workplaces," September 24, 2007. Website: http://donnasealeconsulting.typepad.com/workplacehumanrights/diversity/. Accessed May 18, 2008. See also Yosie Saint-Cyr, LL.B., "Ramadan and the Workplace—A Guide for Human Resources," HRinfodesk.com, *Canadian Payroll and Employment Law News*, September 2007. Website: www.hrinfodesk.com/preview.asp?article=23263. Accessed May 18, 2008.

103. "Study Shows Women Who Are Unhappy with Corporate Life Plan to Start Own Businesses," *Women in Management*, December–January 1999, pp. 1–3.

104. Website: www.canadastop100.com/diversity/. Accessed October 25, 2008.

105. Website: www.servicecanada.gc.ca/eng/cs/fas/as/contracting/harass_policy.shtml. Accessed July 13, 2009.

106. Ibid.

107. Website: www.safety-council.org/info/OSH/bullies.html. Accessed July 13, 2009.

108. B. Carton, "Muscled Out? At Jenny Craig, Men Are Ones Who Claim Sex Discrimination," *The Wall Street Journal*, November 29, 1994, pp. A1, A7.

109. R.L. Paetzold and A.M. O'Leary-Kelly, "Organizational Communication and the Legal Dimensions of Hostile Work Environment Sexual Harassment," in G.L. Kreps (ed.), *Sexual Harassment: Communication Implications* (Cresskill, NJ: Hampton Press, 1993).

110. M. Galen, J. Weber, and A.Z. Cuneo, "Sexual Harassment: Out of the Shadows," *Fortune*, October 28, 1991, pp. 30–31.

111. "Employers Underestimate Extent of Sexual Harassment, Report Says," *The Vancouver Sun*, March 8, 2001, p. D6.

112. A.M. O'Leary-Kelly, R.L. Paetzold, and R.W. Griffin, "Sexual Harassment as Aggressive Action: A Framework for Understanding Sexual Harassment," paper presented at the annual meeting of the Academy of Management, Vancouver, August 1995.

113. "Employers Underestimate Extent of Sexual Harassment, Report Says," *The Vancouver Sun*, March 8, 2001, p. D6.

114. Information in this paragraph based on Ian Jack, "Magna Suit Spotlights Auto Industry Practices," *The Financial Post Daily*, September 10, 1997, p. 1.

115. "Sexual Harassment in the Workplace," Website: www.metrac.org/programs/info/prevent/har_book.pdf. Accessed May 18, 2008.

116. S.J. Bresler and R. Thacker, "Four-Point Plan Helps Solve Harassment Problems," *HR Magazine*, May 1993, pp. 117–124.

117. http://hbswk.hbs.edu/item/5839.html.

118. Francesca Gino, Don A. Moore, and Max H. Bazerman, *op. cit.*, p. 12.

119. Website: http://en.wikipedia.org/wiki/Boiling_frog. Accessed May 18, 2008.

120. Adapted from Howard Levitt, "Spurning Lover or Workplace Harasser?" *National Post*, Wednesday, March 9, 2005, p. FP10.

121. Slightly adapted from Patrick White, "Generation NGO," *The Globe and Mail*, Saturday, March 21, 2008, L1, 2.

122. To see a video and listen to Jesse Harmonic explain what Student Harvest is, and the good that the charity does, visit Website: http://torontosun.feedroom.com/?fr_story=6a91378cd1fa3cf3bd8f422c9ea0d6e11da45fed&rf=sitemap.

123. Veronica Carr, "Fight Against Poverty Hits the Campus," *Manitoban Online*, 94, no. 11, The Official University of Manitoba Students' Newspaper Website, November 1, 2006. Website: www.themanitoban.com/2006-2007/1101/106.Fight.against.poverty.hits.the.campus.php. Accessed May 18, 2008.

124. The Website has the following message: "StudentCharities.ca (SC) was created by Jesse G. Hamonic to help assist students who want to give back to this great country. SC acts as an intermediary between major charitable organizations and students. StudentCharities.ca manages a large student volunteer registry that assists in the implementation of charitable campaigns on campuses across the country. In doing so, StudentCharities.ca now works with many major charitable organizations such as Habitat for Humanity and the Canadian Association of Food Banks. StudentCharities.ca also operates its own aid organizations, WaveofHope.ca and StudentHarvest.ca. WaveofHope.ca organizes trips to New Orleans to help out with the reconstruction effort and StudentHarvest.ca runs the "One Tin Challenge" where all students are encouraged to donate at least one can of food to their local food bank. StudentCharities.ca believes that students can make a great

positive change in the world and is proud to be a national organization uniting students all across Canada."

125. Visit Website: waveofhope.ca/.

Chapter 4

1. Known as Quintus Horatius Flaccus. Website: http://en.wikipedia.org/wiki/Horace. Accessed May 22, 2008.

2. See "Oil Mania Takes Hold," *Financial Post*, Thursday, May 22, 2008, pp. FP1, 5.

3. Jacqueline Thorpe, "US$133 Oil Shows No Signs of Stopping," *Financial Post*, Thursday, May 22, 2008, pp. FP1, 5. Website: www.financialpost.com/story.html?id=530271. Accessed May 22, 2008.

4. Scott Deveau, "Air Canada Puts Surcharge into Its Ads," *Financial Post*, Thursday, May 22, 2008, p. FP16. See also, Linda Nguyen and Grant Ellis, "Air Canada Adds Surcharges," *The Windsor Star*, Saturday, May 10, 2008. Website: www.canada.com/windsorstar/news/story.html?id=e2869fd1-5053-4f7a-b2ef-eb577e349d5a. Accessed May 22, 2008.

5. "Air Canada Fails Transparency Test in Adopting Fuel Surcharges, Observers Say," *canoe.ca*, Friday, May 16, 2008. Website: http://money.canoe.ca/News/Other/2008/05/16/5591541-cp.html. Accessed May 22, 2008.

6. Transparency International writes, "Corruption is the abuse of entrusted power for private gain. It hurts everyone whose life, livelihood or happiness depends on the integrity of people in a position of authority." Website: www.transparency.org/about_us. Accessed May 22, 2008.

7. Bruce J. Avolio and William L. Gardner, "Promoting More Integrative Strategies for Leadership Theory-Building," *The Leadership Quarterly*, 16, no. 3, June 2005, pp. 315–338. Website: www.ncbi.nlm.nih.gov/pubmed/17209677. Accessed May 22, 2008.

8. Herbert Simon, "Making Management Decisions: The Role of Intuition and Emotion," In W. H. Agor (Ed.), *Intuition in Organizations*. (Newbury Park, CA: Sage, 1989), pp. 23–39. See also Website: www2.agsm.edu.au/agsm/web.nsf/AttachmentsByTitle/read42.pdf/$FILE/read42.pdf. Accessed May 22, 2008.

9. "Herbert A. Simon, 1916–2001," The History of Economic Website: Website: http://cepa.newschool.edu/het/profiles/simon.htm. Accessed May 22, 2008.

10. Dennis K. Mumby and Linda L. Putnam, "The Politics of Emotion: A Feminist Reading of Bounded Rationality," *The Academy of Management Review*, 17, no. 3, July, 1992, pp. 465–486. See also Website: www. jstor. org/sici?sici=0363-7425 (199207)17%3A3%3C465%3ATPOEAF%3E2.0.CO%3B2-A.

11. Ibid., p. 466.

12. Ibid., p. 474.

13. Ibid., p. 475.

14. H.A. Simon, *The New Science of Management* (Englewood Cliffs, NJ: Prentice-Hall, 1977).

15. Michael Kesterton, "Social Studies," *The Globe and Mail*, Monday, August 29, 2005, p. A14.

16. Sandra E. Martin, "Staff Stay at Companies with Heart," *Financial Post*, Monday, August 16, 2004, p. FP10.

17. Robert Burns writes, "The best laid schemes o' mice an' men/Gang aft a-gley." E.D. Hirsch, Jr., Joseph F. Kett, and James Trefil (Eds.). *The New Dictionary of Cultural Literacy*. Third Edition. Houghton Mifflin Company, 2002. Website: www.bartleby.com/59/3/bestlaidplan.html.

18. Risha Gottlieb, "Is Collaboration the Next Big Web Thing?" *Backbone*, July/August 2004, pp. 20–21.

19. See Jon Husband's Wirerarchy home page. Website: http://blog.wirearchy.com/blog. Accessed May 22, 2008.

20. H.A. Simon, *Administrative Behavior* (New York: Macmillan, 1947), p. 79.

21. H.A. Simon, *Models of Man* (New York: Wiley, 1957).

22. K.J. Arrow, *Aspects of the Theory of Risk Bearing* (Helsinki: Yrjo Johnssonis Saatio, 1965).

23. R.L. Daft and R.H. Lengel, "Organizational Information Requirements, Media Richness and Structural Design," *Management Science*, 32, 1986, pp. 554–571.

24. R. Cyert and J. March, *Behavioral Theory of the Firm* (Englewood Cliffs, NJ: Prentice-Hall, 1963).

25. Alan Kearns, "The Big Career Decisions," *National Post*, Wednesday, May 4, 2005, p. FP9. See also the website: www.econlib.org/library/Enc/bios/Simon.html.

26. J.G. March and H.A. Simon, Organizations (New York: Wiley, 1958).

27. H.A. Simon, "Making Management Decisions: The Role of Intuition and Emotion," *Academy of Management Executive*, 1, 1987, pp. 57–64.

28. See Trevor Curnow, *Wisdom, Intuition, and Ethics.* (Aldershot, England and Brookfield, VT USA: Ashgate 1999); see also, Kwame Anthony Appiah. *Experiment in Ethics* (Harvard University Press, 2008).

29. Margaret Somerville, "Different Ways of Knowing," *Ottawa Citizen*, Monday, July 23, 2007, A9. Website: www.canada.com/ottawacitizen/news/opinion/story.html?id=3e69bb15-6aad-42d0-96fc-05c0e125f321. Accessed May 22, 2008.

30. Katie Rook, "Record Now, Experience Later," BIG IDEAS Series, *National Post*, Wednesday, January 2, 2008, A1, 6.

31. M.H. Bazerman, *Judgment in Managerial Decision Making* (New York: Wiley, 1986); G.P. Huber, *Managerial Decision Making* (Glenview, IL: Scott, Foresman, 1993); and J.E. Russo and P.J. Schoemaker, *Decision Traps* (New York: Simon and Schuster, 1989).

32. M.D. Cohen, J.G. March, and J.P. Olsen, "A Garbage Can Model of Organizational Choice," *Administrative Science Quarterly*, 17, 1972, pp. 1–25.

33. P.C. Nutt, *Why Decisions Fail: Avoiding the Blunders and Traps That Lead to Debacles* (San Francisco: Berrett-Koehler Publishers, 2002); and M.H. Bazerman, *Judgment in Managerial Decision Making* (New York: Wiley, 1986).

34. J.E. Russo and P.J. Schoemaker, *Decision Traps* (New York: Simon and Schuster, 1989).

35. M.H. Bazerman, *Judgment in Managerial Decision Making* (New York: Wiley, 1986).

36. P.C. Nutt, *Why Decisions Fail: Avoiding the Blunders and Traps That Lead to Debacles* (San Francisco: Berrett-Koehler Publishers, 2002).

37. Ibid.

38. J.E. Russo and P.J. Schoemaker, *Decision Traps* (New York: Simon and Schuster, 1989).

39. Connie Guglielmo and Dina Bass, "The HP Way Revival," *National Post*, Thursday, March 31, 2005, p. FP8.

40. Daniel Goleman, Richard Boyatzis and Annie McKee. *Primal Leadership: Realizing the Power of Emotional Intelligence*, Boston: Harvard Business School Press, 2002.

41. Eric Bonabeau, Dan Lovallo, Daniel Kahneman, John S. Hammond III, Ralph L. Keeney, and Howard Raiffa, "Make Better Decisions—Faster," (HBR OnPoint Enhanced Edition) *Harvard Business Review*, July 2003, 35 pages. Product Number: 3582.

42. "Heuristic," www.wikipedia.com, Accessed: April 20, 2007.

43. Quote BD. Website: www.quotedb.com/quotes/2332. Accessed May 22, 2008.

44. Dr. J. Edward Russo and Dr. Paul J. H. Schoemaker, *Decision Traps: Ten Barriers to Brilliant Decision-Making and How to Overcome Them* (New York: Simon and Schuster, 1990).

45. D. Kahneman and A. Tversky, "Judgment Under Scrutiny: Heuristics and Biases," *Science*, 185, 1974, pp. 1124–1131.

46. C.R. Schwenk, "Cognitive Simplification Processes in Strategic Decision Making," *Strategic Management Journal*, 5, 1984, pp. 111–128.

47. Prof. Ray Titus, "Prior Hypothesis Bias," Monday, June 4, 2007. Website: http://Prof/2007/06/prior-hypothesis-bias.html. Accessed May 22, 2008.

48. The Quotations Page. Website: www.quotationspage.com/quote/34608.html. Accessed May 22, 2008.

49. Mary Jo Foley, "Microsoft Bails Out Rival Corel," *ZDNet.co.uk*, October 3, 2000. Website: http://news.zdnet.co.uk/software/0,1000000121,2081744,00.htm. Accessed May 22, 2008.

50. An interesting example of the illusion of control is Richard Roll's hubris hypothesis of takeovers. See R. Roll, "The Hubris Hypothesis of Corporate Takeovers," *Journal of Business*, 59, 1986, pp. 197–216.

51. J. Tullberg, "Illusions of Corporate Power: Revisiting the Relative Powers of Corporations and Governments," *Journal of Business Ethics*, 52, 2004, pp. 325–333.

52. B.M. Staw, "The Escalation of Commitment to a Course of Action," *Academy of Management Review*, 6, 1981, pp. 577–587.

53. John C. Edwards, "Self-Fulfilling Prophecy and Escalating Commitment," *The Journal of Applied Behavioral Science*, 37, no. 3, 2001, pp. 343–360. Website: http://jab.sagepub.com/cgi/content/abstract/37/3/343. Accessed May 22, 2008. See also Marc Street and Vera .L. Street, "The Effects of Escalating Commitment on Ethical Decision-Making," *Journal of Business Ethics*," 64, 2006, pp. 343–356. Website: www.springerlink.com/content/g0u1r47kv975w272/. Accessed May 22, 2008.

54. J.E. Russo and P.J. Schoemaker, *Decision Traps* (New York: Simon and Schuster, 1989).

55. Timberland Company Podcast, posted October 31, 2008 on JustMeans Website: www.justmeans.com/company podcasts/23/10-29-09---Responsible-Sourcing.html. Accessed November 6, 2008.

56. Russo and Schoemaker.

57. Website: www.crestaurant.com.

58. Website: www.vanaqua.org/oceanwise/ Jack MacDonald, CEO Compass Food Canada, Press Release May 9, 2008. Compass Group Canada takes leading role in sustainable seafood purchasing.

59. Website: www.compass-canada.com/home/media/sustainability_purchasing.pdf.

60. Website: www.environmentalleader.com/2008/05/10/green-marketing-campaigns-not-sticking/.

61. Website: www.imc2.com/Documents/StateOfSustainabilityCommunications.pdf. Accessed November 5, 2008.

62. Website: www.justmeans.com/index.php?action=viewcompanyprofile&id=122&sublinkid=33. Accessed November 5, 2008.

63. See P. Senge, The *Fifth Discipline: The Art and Practice of the Learning Organization* (New York: Doubleday, 1990).

64. Richard Saul Wurman, Information Anxiety in Ian Mitroff, Ph.D. *Smart Thinking for Crazy Times: The Art of Solving the Right Problems.* (San Francisco: Berrett-Koehler Publishers, Inc., 1998)

65. Quoted in Chris Young, "Copy Rights and Copy Wrongs," *Toronto Star*, Sunday, May 22, 2005, pp. D1, 10.

66. Arthur H. Bell and Dayle M. Smith. *Developing Leadership Abilities.* (Upper Saddle River, New Jersey: Prentice Hall, 2002) p. 127.

67. Wynn Quon, "Music Loss Leader," *National Post*, Friday, July 29, 2005, p. FP17.

68. Lynn Moore, "Corporate Fool Too Funny for Workplace Fired," *National Post*, Saturday, February 19, 2005, p. FW5.

69. T.A. Stewart, "3M Fights Back," *Fortune*, February 5, 1996, pp. 94–99; and T.D. Schellhardt, "David in Goliath," *The Wall Street Journal*, May 23, 1996, p. R14.

70. R.W. Woodman, J.E. Sawyer, and R.W. Griffin, "Towards a Theory of Organizational Creativity," *Academy of Management Review*, 18, 1993, pp. 293–321.

71. M. Ullmann, "Creativity Cubed: Burntsand Has Found a Novel Program to Motivate Its Most Creative Employees. Can It Work for You?" *SVN Canada*, February 2001, pp. B22–B23+.

72. William M. Bulkeley, "Women the Focus of Kodak's Digital Moment," *The Globe and Mail*, Saturday, July 9, 2005, B13. The quote is originally from William M. Bulkeley, "Kodak Sharpens Digital Focus on Female Customers," *The Wall Street Journal*, Wednesday, July 06, 2005, 6 printed pages.

Alternate website: www.post-gazette.com/pg/05187/533671.stm.

73. Cover Story: "Special Report: The Art of Foresight: Preparing for a Changing World," *The Futurist*, May–June 2004, 38(3), 31–38.

74. N.B. Macintosh, *The Social Software of Accounting Information Systems* (New York: Wiley, 1995).

75. R.I. Benjamin and J. Blunt, "Critical IT Issues: The Next Ten Years," *Sloan Management Review*, Summer 1992, pp. 7–19; W.H. Davidow and M.S. Malone, *The Virtual Corporation* (New York: Harper Business, 1992).

76. C.A. O'Reilly, "Variations in Decision Makers' Use of Information: The Impact of Quality and Accessibility," *Academy of Management Journal*, 25, 1982, pp. 756–771.

77. G. Stalk and T.H. Hout, *Competing Against Time* (New York: Free Press, 1990).

78. R. Cyert and J. March, *Behavioral Theory of the Firm* (Englewood Cliffs, NJ: Prentice-Hall, 1963).

79. "A Special Report on Corporate IT," *The Economist*, October 25–31, 2008, p. 10.

80. Ibid., p. 4.

81. EMC2 Corporate Social Responsibility, Website: www.imc2.com/AboutUs/PR50.aspx. Accessed November 6, 2008.

82. Harriet Rubin, "The Power of Words," *Fast Company*, Issue 21, January 1999, 142ff.

83. Jennifer Newman and Darryl Grigg, "Manager's Struggle with Ethical Questions," *Vancouver Sun*, June 21, 2008.

84. See Mark Hollingworth, "Resolving the Dilemma of Work-Life Balance: Developing Life-Maps," *IVEY Business Journal*, November/December 2005, 6 pages. Website: www.iveybusinessjournal.com/view_article.asp?intArticle_ID=593. Accessed May 22, 2008. The abstract of the article reads: "If the Balanced Scorecard or a Strategic Map can help an organization track its performance and goals, then why not develop a similar tool that enables an individual to achieve that most elusive of goals, a work-life balance? Enter the Life Map, which allows an individual to achieve his or her personal objectives and to balance the work-life equation. This author/developer explains how and why a Life Map works."

85. Website: www.cbc.ca.thehour. Accessed November 12, 2008.

86. Harvey Schachter, "Stay Cool in the Face of Competitive Arousal," Monday Morning Manager, *The Globe and Mail*, Monday,

May 19, 2008, B8. Website: www.theglobeand
mail.com/servlet/story/RTGAM.20080519.
WBwschachter20080519092356/WBStory/
WBwschachter. Accessed May 20, 2008.

87. Deepak Malhotra, Gillian Ku, and
J. Keith Murnighan, "When Winning is
Everything," *Harvard Business Review*, 86,
no. 5, May 2008.

Chapter 5

1. Adapted from Chris Sorenson, "Rogers
Still Doing It His Way," *Toronto Star*,
Saturday, May 24, 2008; and Grant Robertson
and Catherine McLean, "Out of the Shadow,"
The Globe and Mail, Saturday, May 24, 2008,
B4-B5. Websites: www.thestar.com/Business/
article/429412; www.theglobeandmail.com/
servlet/story/LAC.20080524.RCOVER24//
TPStory/Business.

2. As reported on October 17, 2007, in
"Technology Fast 50: 2006 Results Analysis."
Website: www.deloitte.com/dtt/article/0,1002,
cid%253D175729,00.html.

3. Wallace Immen, "In the Shadow of the
One Who Went Before You," *The Globe and
Mail*, Wednesday, April 30, 2008, C1, 5.

4. Laura Fowlie, "The Ultimate Test,"
SPECIAL REPORT: FP EDGE, *Financial Post*,
Monday, May 3, 2004, p. FE4.

5. A. Chandler, *Strategy and Structure:
Chapters in the History of the American
Enterprise* (Cambridge, MA: MIT Press, 1962).

6. F.J. Aguilar, "General Electric: Reg Jones
and Jack Welch," in *General Managers in
Action* (Oxford: Oxford University Press,
1992).

7. Ibid.

8. C.W. Hofer and D. Schendel, *Strategy
Formulation: Analytical Concepts* (St. Paul,
MN: West, 1978).

9. H. Fayol, *General and Industrial
Management* (New York: IEEE Press, 1984).
Fayol's work was first published in 1916.

10. Ibid., p. 18.

11. R. Phelps, C. Chan, S.C. Kapsalis, "Does
Scenario Planning Affect Firm Performance?"
Journal of Business Research, March 2001,
pp. 223–232.

12. George Day and Paul Schoemaker,
Peripheral Vision (Cambridge, MA: Harvard
Business School Press).

13. Paul J. H. Schoemaker, "Are You
Ready for Global Turmoil?" *BusinessWeek*,
April 25, 2008. Website: www.businessweek.
com/print/managing/content/apr2008/
ca20080429_312634.htm.

14. Hill and McShane, Principles of
Management (New York: McGraw-Hill/Irwin,
2008), p. 111.

15. "How Maple Leaf Foods is Handling
the Listeria Outbreak." Website: www.cbc.
ca/money/story/2008/08/27/f-crisisresponse.
html. Accessed November 13, 2008.

16. Ibid.

17. M. Ingram, "Our Job Is to Be Better,"
The Globe and Mail, May 12, 2001, p. F3.

18. A. Chandler, *Strategy and Structure:
Chapters in the History of the American
Enterprise* (Cambridge, MA: MIT Press,
1962).

19. Daniel Dale, "Tim Hortons in a
New PR Jam," *Toronto Star*, Friday,
May 23, 2008. Website: www.thestar.com/
printArticle/429178. See also Melly Alazraki,
"Tim Hortons' (THI) Homeless Policy?"
bloggingstocks.com, May 23, 2008. Website:
www.bloggingstocks.com/2008/05/23/tim-
hortons-thi-homeless-policy/.

20. J.A. Pearce, "The Company Mission as a
Strategic Tool," *Sloan Management Review*,
Spring 1992, pp. 15–24.

21. P.C. Nutt and R.W. Backoff, "Crafting
Vision," *Journal of Management Inquiry*,
December 1997, p. 309.

22. D.F. Abell, *Defining the Business:
The Starting Point of Strategic Planning*
(Englewood Cliffs, NJ: Prentice-Hall, 1980).

23. George T. Doran. "There's a S.M.A.R.T.
Way to Write Management's Goals and
Objectives," *Management Review (AMA
Forum)*, November 1981, pp. 35–36.

24. G. Hamel and C.K. Prahalad, "Strategic
Intent," *Harvard Business Review*, May–June
1989, pp. 63–73.

25. E.A. Locke, G.P. Latham, and M. Erez,
"The Determinants of Goal Commitment,"
Academy of Management Review, 13, 1988,
pp. 23–39.

26. Website: www.justmeans.com/index.
php?action=viewcompanyprofile&id=122.
Accessed November 15, 2008.

27. P.F. Drucker, *The Practice of Management*
(New York: Harper and Row, 1954).

28. S.J. Carroll and H.L. Tosi, *Management
by Objectives: Applications and Research*
(New York: Macmillan, 1973).

29. R. Rodgers and J.E. Hunter, "Impact of
Management by Objectives on Organizational
Productivity," *Journal of Applied Psychology*,
76, 1991, pp. 322–326.

30. M.B. Gavin, S.G. Green, and
G.T. Fairhurst, "Managerial Control

Strategies for Poor Performance Over Time
and the Impact on Subordinate Reactions,"
*Organizational Behaviour and Human
Decision Processes*, 63, 1995, pp. 207–221.

31. Adapted from Marketing Teacher Website:
www.marketingteacher.com/SWOT/eBay_
swot.htm. Disclaimer: This case study has been
compiled from information freely available
from public sources. It is merely intended to be
used for educational purposes only.

32. "eBay Completes Acquisition of
Skype," eBay Inc., October 14, 2005.
Website: investor.ebay.com/releasedetail.
cfm?ReleaseID=176402.

33. K.R. Andrews, *The Concept of Corporate
Strategy* (Homewood, IL: Irwin, 1971).

34. "Starbucks Reports Fourth Quarter and
Fiscal 2008 Results." Website: www.starbucks.
com/aboutus/pressdesc.asp?id=950. Accessed
November 16, 2008.

35. Adapted from Marketing Teacher
Website: www.marketingteacher.com/SWOT/
starbucks_swot.htm. Accessed November 15,
2008. Disclaimer: This case study has been
compiled from information freely available
from public sources. It is intended to be used
for educational purposes only.

36. Andrea James, "Starbucks Profit
Takes Bitter Shot for the Year," *Seattle P-I*,
November 11, 2008. Website: http://seattlepi.
nwsource.com/business/387203_sbuxearns11.
html. Accessed November 15, 2008.

37. Adapted from Website: www.timhortons.
com/en/about/index.html. Accessed
December 20, 2008.

38. Website: www.timhortons.com/
en/about/news.html?c=195616&p=irol-
newsArticle&ID=1232902&highlight=.
Accessed December 20, 2008.

39. Website: www.freep.com/article/
20081211/BUSINESS06/812110368/1051/
sports03. Accessed December 21, 2008.

40. Adapted from Haris Anwar, "Chief Risk
Officer: A Valuable Addition to the C-Suite,"
The Globe and Mail, Monday, June 20, 2005,
B13; and "The Rise and Rise of the Chief
Risk Officer," May 2, 2005. Website: www.
continuitycentral.com/news01881.htm. See also
the CRO Forum Website: www.croforum.org/.

41. "The CRO is a revolutionary position
created in the wake of the Basel Accord,
the Sarbanes-Oxley Act, the Turnbull
Report, and other pieces of legislation.
A main priority for the CRO is to ensure
that the organization is in full compliance
with applicable regulations. They may
also deal with topics regarding insurance,

internal auditing, corporate investigations, fraud, and information security. CROs typically have post-graduate education and 20+ years of business experience, with actuarial, accounting, and legal backgrounds common," from "Chief Risk Officer," *Wikipedia* Website: en.wikipedia.org/wiki/Chief_risk_officer.

42. Peter Drucker, "The Next Society," *The Economist*, 2001.

43. Cited in *The Economist*, "Dealing with the Downturn: Make Love—and War," August 9, 2008, p. 57; Adam M. Brandenburger and Barry J. Nalebuff, *Co-opetition: A Revolution Mindset* (New York: Bantam Double Day) 1997.

44. *The Economist*, "Dealing with the Downturn: Make Love—and War," August 9, 2008, p. 57.

45. Ibid.

46. D. Baines, "BC Hydro Unit Cited for Blame in California's Electricity Crisis," *The Vancouver Sun*, April 12, 2001, F1, F5.

47. Adapted from Harvey Schachter, "Challenging the Conventions of Strategy One Bite at a Time," *The Globe and Mail*, Wednesday, April 13, 2005, C4; and Editorial Review—*From the Inside Flap*, Amazon.ca. Website: www.amazon.ca/exec/obidos/tg/detail/-/books/0273693468/reviews/ref=cm_rev_more_2/702-7104076-7622461.

48. John Kotter. *The Heart of Change*. (Boston, MA.: Harvard Business School Press, 2002), p. x. Note: This was an interesting observation by one of the world's most noted scholars of organizational behaviour and corporate culture. He had originally written *Leading Change* (Cambridge, MA.: Harvard University Press, 1996), 187 pages and realized its incompleteness.

49. Tom Peters and Robert H. Waterman, Jr., *In Search of Excellence. Lessons from America's Best-Run Companies* (Toronto: HarperCollins Canada, 2004).

50. See Manitoba Chamber of Commerce note. Website: www.mbchamber.mb.ca/mbawards/awardrecipients.htm#OMA.

51. Catherine McLean and Gordon Pitts, "Bell Adopts a New Party Line," *The Globe and Mail*, Saturday, May 14, 2005, B4.

52. E. Penrose, *The Theory of the Growth of the Firm* (Oxford: Oxford University Press, 1959).

53. M.E. Porter, "From Competitive Advantage to Corporate Strategy," *Harvard Business Review*, 65, 1987, pp. 43–59.

54. Derek DeCloet, "Can This Molson-Coors Combo Bring Back the Fizz?" *The Globe and Mail*, Friday, July 23, 2004, B1, 21.

55. "Success Story," Electronic Data Systems Corporation, 2008. Website: www.eds.com/sites/success/coors.aspx.

56. Website: http://web.linix.ca/pedia/index.php/E.D._Smith.

57. "Jam Today: Imperial Capital Merchant Bank Takes Over E.D. Smith," *Canadian Press Newswire*, January 28, 2002.

58. Website: Report on Business Company, www.globeinvestor.com/snapshots/B0003334.htm.

59. Website: www.brascancorp.com/AboutBrascan/BoardofDirectors.html.

60. G. Pitts, "Small Is Beautiful, Conglomerates Signal," *The Globe and Mail*, April 1, 2002, pp. B1, B4.

61. For a review of the evidence, see C.W.L. Hill and G.R. Jones, *Strategic Management: An Integrated Approach*, 3rd ed. (Boston: Houghton Mifflin, 2000), Ch. 10.

62. V. Ramanujam and P. Varadarajan, "Research on Corporate Diversification: A Synthesis," *Strategic Management Journal*, 10, 1989, pp. 523–551. Also see A. Shleifer and R.W. Vishny, "Takeovers in the 1960s and 1980s: Evidence and Implications," in R.P. Rumelt, D.E. Schendel, and D.J. Teece, *Fundamental Issues in Strategy* (Boston: Harvard Business School Press, 1994).

63. J.R. Williams, B.L. Paez, and L. Sanders, "Conglomerates Revisited," *Strategic Management Journal*, 9, 1988, pp. 403–414.

64. H. Shaw, "Fish, Dairy Units Sacrificed to Help Raise Cash for Baked Goods: Bestfoods Deal," *Financial Post (National Post)*, February 20, 2001, pp. C1, C6.

65. Doug Krumrei, "Corporate Profiles: George Weston Bakeries, Inc.," *Milling & Baking News*, December 1, 2001.

66. C.A. Bartlett and S. Ghoshal, *Managing Across Borders* (Boston: Harvard Business School Press, 1989).

67. C.K. Prahalad and Y.L. Doz, *The Multinational Mission* (New York: Free Press, 1987).

68. Website: www.mhhe.com/business/management/thompson/11e/case/starbucks-2.html. Accessed December 29, 2008.

69. M.K. Perry, "Vertical Integration: Determinants and Effects," in R. Schmalensee and R.D. Willig, *Handbook of Industrial Organization*, vol. 1 (New York: Elsevier Science Publishing, 1989).

70. Website: www.mhhe.com/business/management/thompson/11e/case/starbucks-2.html. Accessed December 29, 2008.

71. Tony Keller, "Reinventing the Firm," *National Post Business*, June 2000, pp. 68–70, 72, 74, 76, 78, 81.

72. T. Muris, D. Scheffman, and P. Spiller, "Strategy and Transaction Costs: The Organization of Distribution in the Carbonated Soft Drink Industry," *Journal of Economics and Management Strategy*, 1, 1992, pp. 77–97.

73. "Matsushita Electric Industrial (MEI) in 1987," Harvard Business School Case #388-144.

74. P. Ghemawat, *Commitment: The Dynamic of Strategy* (New York: Free Press, 1991).

75. D. McMurdy, "The Human Cost of Mergers," *Maclean's*, November 20, 2000, p. 128.

76. Hollie Shaw, "Metro's Lessard Will Stick to Grocer's Recipe for Success," *Financial Post*, Friday, August 19, 2005, p. FP3.

77. "Metro Inc. Profit Jumps on Acquisition of A&P Canada," *CBC News*, Tuesday, April 11, 2006. Website: www.cbc.ca/money/story/2006/04/11/metro-060411.html.

78. M.E. Porter, *Competitive Strategy* (New York: Free Press, 1980).

79. Gordon Pitts, "Ganong Boss Aims for Sweet Spot," *The Globe and Mail*, March 3, 2003, p. B4.

80. Marina Strauss, "Watt to Light Up Wal-Mart Private Label," *The Globe and Mail*, Tuesday, April 19, 2005, pp. B1, 22.

81. Carolyn Leitch, "Best Buy's Secret: Sales Staff," *The Globe and Mail*, Friday, June 17, 2005, p. B12.

82. C.W.L. Hill, "Differentiation Versus Low Cost or Differentiation and Low Cost: A Contingency Framework," *Academy of Management Review*, 13, 1988, pp. 401–412.

83. For details see J.P. Womack, D.T. Jones, and D. Roos, *The Machine That Changed the World* (New York: Rawson Associates, 1990).

84. M.E. Porter, *Competitive Strategy* (New York: Free Press, 1980).

85. C.W.L. Hill and G.R. Jones, *Strategic Management: An Integrated Approach*, 3rd ed. (Boston: Houghton Mifflin, 2000).

86. See D. Garvin, "What Does Product Quality Really Mean?" *Sloan Management Review*, 26, Fall 1984, pp. 25–44; P.B. Crosby, *Quality Is Free* (New York: Mentor Books, 1980); and A. Gabor, *The Man Who Discovered Quality* (New York: Times Books, 1990).

87. Website: www.camh.net/pdf/camh_strategicplan2003.pdf.

88. Nickels et al., Understanding Canadian Business (Toronto: McGraw-Hill Ryerson, 2005).

89. Tara Perkins, "Legacy At a Crossroads," *Globe and Mail*, August 15, 2009, B1.

90. Adapted from: David George-Cosh, "Rogers Hoping Clients Cut Land Lines," *Financial Post*, Wednesday, May 7, 2008. Website: www.nationalpost.com/related/topics/story.html?id=498617; and Grant Robertson and Catherine McLean, "Out of the Shadow," *The Globe and Mail*, Saturday, May 24, 2008, B4-B5. Website: www.theglobeandmail.com/servlet/story/LAC.20080524.RCOVER24//TPStory/Business.

91. Moira Welsh, "Media Mogul Ted Rogers Dies," *Toronto Star*, December 2, 2009. Website: www.thestar.com/article/546983#Comments. Accessed July 26, 2009.

92. Website: www.thegreendoor.ca/.

93. Website: http://web.ustpaul.uottawa.ca/en/.

94. Website: www.ottawaplus.ca/portal/profile.do?profileID=45275.

95. Adapted from: Cathal Kelly, "Moses Znaimer's Second Act," *Toronto Star*, Sunday, July 26, 2009. Website: www.thestar.com/printArticle/671940. Accessed July 26, 2009.

96. Adapted slightly from: David Olive, "Sour Notes for Bronfman Jr.," *Toronto Star*, Sunday, May 25, 2008. Website: www.thestar.com/printArticle/429648.

Chapter 6

1. "Flexibility 'Benefits Both Employer and Employee'." Accessed May 29, 2008. Website: www.freshbusinessthinking.co.uk/news.php?NID=834&Title=Flexibility+%27benefits+both+employer+and+employee%27.

2. "Offer Flexible Working 'To Reach the Best People'." Accessed May 29, 2008. Website: www.freshbusinessthinking.co.uk/news.php?NID=832&Title=Offer+flexible+working+%27to+reach+the+best+people%27.

3. Adapted from Gary Neilson and Jack McGrath, "Exercising Common Sense," *Strategy + Business Resilience Report*, September 11, 2007. Website: www.strategy-business.com/resiliencereport/resilience/rr00050.

4. Slightly adapted from Ian I. Mitroff and Richard O. Mason, "Radical Surgery: What Will Tomorrow's Organizations Look Like?" *Academy of Management Executive*, 8, no. 2, 1994, pp. 11–12. Website: www.valdosta.edu/~mschnake/MitroffMasonPearson1994.

5. G.R. Jones, *Organizational Theory: Text and Cases* (Reading, MA: Addison-Wesley, 1995).

6. J. Child, *Organization: A Guide for Managers and Administrators* (New York: Harper and Row, 1977).

7. Bill Breen, "Soundoff," *Fast Company*, Issue 85, August 2004, 10. Website: http://pf.fastcompany.com/magazine/83/mod.html.

8. F.W. Taylor, *The Principles of Scientific Management* (New York: Harper, 1911).

9. R.W. Griffin, *Task Design: An Integrative Approach* (Glenview, IL: Scott, Foresman, 1982).

10. Ibid.

11. Ubisoft and Allen Carr's Easyway Team Up to Help Smokers Quit: Ubisoft to Bring Allen Carr's Easyway to Stop Smoking to the Nintendo DS™ System in November 2008. Website: ubisoftgroup.com/index.php?p=59&art_id=60&vars=Y29tX2lkPTU2NCZzZW5kZXI9SE9NRSZzZW5kZXJJfdXJsPWluZGV4LnBocCUzRnNpdF9pZCUzRDImZ mlsdGVyX3R5cGU9JmZpbHRlcl9tb250aD0mZmlsdGVyX3llYXI9&PHPSESSID=80e36bd07144cbef44e95388ff97ca39. Accessed June 15, 2008.

12. Emily Chung, "Dream Jobs—in Hell," *Toronto Star*, Monday, August 15, 2005, pp. C1, 5.

13. Roger Martin, "The Design of Business," *Rotman Management*, Winter 2004, 7–10. Website: www.rotman.utoronto.ca/rogermartin/DesignofBusiness.pdf.

14. Roger Martin, "The Design of Business," *Rotman Management*, Winter 2004, 9. Website: www.rotman.utoronto.ca/rogermartin/DesignofBusiness.pdf.

15. J.R. Galbraith and R.K. Kazanjian, *Strategy Implementation: Structure, System, and Process*, 2nd ed. (St. Paul, MN: West, 1986).

16. P.R. Lawrence and J.W. Lorsch, *Organization and Environment* (Boston: Graduate School of Business Administration, Harvard University, 1967).

17. G.R. Jones, *Organizational Theory: Text and Cases* (Reading, MA: Addison-Wesley, 1995).

18. P.R. Lawrence and J.W. Lorsch, *Organization and Environment* (Boston: Graduate School of Business Administration, Harvard University, 1967).

19. R.H. Hall, *Organizations: Structure and Process* (Englewood Cliffs, NJ: Prentice-Hall, 1972); and R. Miles, *Macro Organizational Behaviour* (Santa Monica, CA: Goodyear, 1980).

20. A.D. Chandler, *Strategy and Structure* (Cambridge, MA: MIT Press, 1962).

21. G.R. Jones and C.W.L. Hill, "Transaction Cost Analysis of Strategy–Structure Choice," *Strategic Management Journal*, 9, 1988, pp. 159–172.

22. Michael Maccoby, "Knowledge Workers Need New Structures," *Research Technology Management*, Vol. 30, No. 3 January–February 1996, pp. 56–58. Website: www.maccoby.com/Articles/KnowledgeWorkers.html.

23. See also the Website: www.amo.on.ca/AM/Template.cfm?Section=Home&CONTENTID=10555&TEMPLATE=/CM/ContentDisplay.cfm. Accessed June 15, 2008. For a job overview that was published for April 1, 2008, as an "Application and Technical Support Specialist (PCS)," see wx.toronto.ca/inter/hr/jobs.nsf/d581a4b0e644918285256fe7005fa2b2/C10884705868C9F58525740800734B40?opendocument. Accessed July 15, 2008.

24. Kaya Morgan, "RED SMITH—Federal Express Renegade." Website: www.islandconnections.com/edit/smith.htm. Accessed July 15, 2008.

25. S.M. Davis and P.R. Lawrence, *Matrix* (Reading, MA: Addison-Wesley, 1977); and J.R. Galbraith, "Matrix Organization Designs: How to Combine Functional and Project Forms," *Business Horizons*, 14, 1971, pp. 29–40.

26. L.R. Burns, "Matrix Management in Hospitals: Testing Theories of Matrix Structure and Development," *Administrative Science Quarterly*, 34, 1989, pp. 349–368.

27. C.W.L. Hill, *International Business* (Homewood, IL: Irwin, 1997).

28. C.A. Bartlett and S. Ghoshal, *Transnational Management* (Homewood, IL: Irwin, 1992).

29. G.R. Jones, *Organizational Theory: Text and Cases* (Reading, MA: Addison-Wesley, 1995).

30. Barbara Shecter, "Banking on Bands," *National Post*, Tuesday, August 23, 2005, pp. FP1, 3.

31. B. Kogut, "Joint Ventures: Theoretical and Empirical Perspectives," *Strategic Management Journal*, 9, 1988, pp. 319–332.

32. See, for example, B. Hedberg, G. Dahlgren, J. Hansson, and N.-G. Olve, *Virtual Organizations and Beyond: Discovering Imaginary Systems* (New York: Wiley, 2001); N.A. Wishart, J.J. Elam, and D. Robey, "Redrawing the Portrait of a Learning Organization Inside Knight-Ridder, Inc.," *Academy of Management Executive*, 10, (1) 1996, pp. 7–20; G.G. Dess, A.M.A. Rasheeed, K.J. McLaughlin, and R.L. Priem, "The New Corporate Architecture," *Academy of Management Executive*, 9, (3) 1995, p. 720; and R. Keidel, "Rethinking Organizational Design," *Academy of Management Executive*, November 1994, pp. 12–27.

33. B. Hedberg, G. Dahlgren, J. Hansson, and N.-G. Olve, *Virtual Organizations and Beyond: Discovering Imaginary Systems* (New York: Wiley, 2001).

34. Anthony Grnak, John Hughes, and Douglas Hunter, *op. cit.*, p. 154.

35. "World's Top Outsourcing Countries." Website: http://images.businessweek.com/ss/09/01/0114_top_outsourcers/1.htm. Accessed January 16, 2009.

36. Study: Multipliers and outsourcing: How industries interact with each other and affect GDP, January 12, 2006. Website: www.statcan.gc.ca/daily-quotidien/060112/dq060112b-eng.htm. Accessed December 21, 2008.

37. "World's Top Outsourcing Countries." Website: http://images.businessweek.com/ss/09/01/0114_top_outsourcers/1.htm. Accessed January 16, 2009.

38. Poonam Khanna, "CP Rail Jumps Aboard Outsourcing Train," *Computing Canada*, December 10, 2004, p. 30. For more on outsourcing, visit www.ezgoal.com/outsourcing/c.asp?a=Canada&outsourcing.

39. Grant Buckler, "Economies of Scale a Big Hit for IT Managers," *Computing Canada*, February 15, 2002. Website: www.findarticles.com/p/articles/mi_m0CGC/is_4_28/ai_83056527#continue.

40. Beth Ellyn Rosenthal, "Outsourcing Manages Risk While Transforming Processes for Canada's Central Bank," June 2007. Website: www.outsourcing-canada.com/canadian2.html. Accessed December 21, 2008.

41. J. Barthelemy and D. Adsit, "The Seven Deadly Sins of Outsourcing," *Academy of Management Executive*, 17, (2), 2003, pp. 87–100.

42. Adapted from Paul Vieira, "Bureaucracy's Radical Reno," *National Post*, Thursday, March 3, 2005, p. FP3.

43. P. Blau, "A Formal Theory of Differentiation in Organizations," *American Sociological Review*, 35, 1970, pp. 684–695.

44. J. Child, *Organization: A Guide for Managers and Administrators* (New York: Harper and Row, 1977).

45. Information about Ducks Unlimited from "Salute! Celebrating the Progressive Employer," advertising supplement, *Benefits Canada*, March 1999, p. Insert 1–23; and www.ducksunlimited.ca.

46. Adapted from "How Do I Manage a Mobile Workforce?" Special Feature to the *National Post:* BUSINESS SOLUTIONS. Presented by CISCO. *National Post*, Business Solutions Advertisement, Monday, March 3,

2008, FP8. Website: www.financialpost.com/small_business/businesssolutions/story.html?id=343859. Accessed June 15, 2008.

47. P.M. Blau and R.A. Schoenherr, *The Structure of Organizations* (New York: Basic Books, 1971).

48. G.R. Jones, *Organizational Theory: Text and Cases* (Reading, MA: Addison-Wesley, 1995).

49. Adapted from Andrew Duffy, "The Lonely Grindstone," *Ottawa Citizen*, Sunday, June 15, 2008, A8. Website: www.canada.com/ottawacitizen/news/story.html?id=f073bc50-175a-4011-971b-b7758d0b2384. Accessed July 15, 2008; also, Andrew Duffy, "'I Just Want a Bit More Breathing Room'," *Ottawa Citizen*, Sunday, June 15, 2008, A8. Website: www.canada.com/ottawacitizen/news/story.html?id=a844cccb-8ced-4440-89fa-b54281488b68. Accessed July 15, 2008. See also Statistics Canada, "Hours Polarization Revisited," by Jeannine Usalcas; "Control Over Time and Work-Life Balance: An Empirical Analysis," a report prepared for the Federal Labour Standards Review Committee by Graham S. Lowe. Website: www.statcan.ca/Daily/English/080318/d080318b.htm. Accessed June 15, 2008.

50. Those figures represented the combined efforts of both full- and part-time workers, which mean the average workweek has continued its decline even as more Canadians secured full-time jobs.

51. T. Burns and G.M. Stalker, *The Management of Innovation* (London: Tavistock, 1961).

52. L.A. Perlow, G.A. Okhuysen, and N.P. Repenning, "The Speed Trap: Exploring the Relationship Between Decision Making and Temporal Context, *Academy of Management Journal*, 45, 2002, pp. 931–955.

53. P.R. Lawrence and J.W. Lorsch, *Organization and Environment* (Boston: Graduate School of Business Administration, Harvard University, 1967).

54. R. Duncan, "What Is the Right Organizational Design?" *Organizational Dynamics*, Winter 1979, pp. 59–80.

55. T. Burns and G.R. Stalker, *The Management of Innovation* (London: Tavistock, 1966).

56. Scott Peterson, "Good Leaders Empower People," *National Post*, Wednesday, May 18, 2005, p. FP9.

57. D. Miller, "Strategy Making and Structure: Analysis and Implications for Performance," *Academy of Management Journal*, 30, 1987, pp. 7–32.

58. A.D. Chandler, *Strategy and Structure* (Cambridge, MA: MIT Press, 1962).

59. J. Stopford and L. Wells, *Managing the Multinational Enterprise* (London: Longman, 1972).

60. J. Woodward, *Management and Technology* (London: Her Majesty's Stationery Office, 1958).

61. "Flexibility 'Benefits Both Employer and Employee'." Website: www.freshbusinessthinking.co.uk/news.php? NID=834&Title=Flexibility+%27benefits+both+employer+and+employee%27; also, "Offer flexible working 'to reach the best people'." Website: www.freshbusinessthinking.co.uk, May 29, 2008. Website: www.freshbusinessthinking.co.uk/news.php?NID=832&Title=Offer+flexible+working+%27to+reach+the+best+people%27. Accessed May 29, 2008 also, adapted from Gary Neilson and Jack McGrath, "Exercising Common Sense," *Strategy + Business Resilience Report*, September 11, 2007. Website: www.strategy-business.com/resiliencereport/resilience/rr00050.

62. Jones, Gareth, Essentials of Contemporary Management 2ce, McGraw-Hill Ryerson, 2007.

63. Website: www.onex.com/index.taf?pid=49&_UserReference=DC9773E6122AC2DA44A1B665.

64. George Day and Paul Schoemaker. *Peripheral Vision* (Cambridge, MA: Harvard Business School Press).

65. Editorial review, amazon.ca. Website: www.amazon.ca/exec/obidos/ASIN/1422101541/sr=8-1/qid=1151507093/ref=sr_1_1/701-8310829-0022710?%5Fencoding=UTF8&s=gateway&v=glance.

66. Harvey Schacter, "Strategy Gleaning from the Corner of Your Eye," *The Globe and Mail*, Wednesday, June 28, 2005, p. C3.

67. Slightly adapted from Kali Saposnick, "The People Who Really Shape Our Organizations: An Interview with Art Kleiner," *Leverage Points Newsletter*, July 24, 2003, Issue 40. Website: www.pegasuscom.com/levpoints/kleinerint.html.

68. *Italics* added. This is the opening paragraph of the article.

Chapter 7

1. W. Chan Kim and Renée Mauborgne, *Blue Ocean Strategy: How to Create Uncontested Market Space and Make the Competition Irrelevant* (Boston, MA: Harvard Business School Press, 2006), p. 171.

2. W. Chan Kim and Renée Mauborgne, *op. cit.*, p. 4.

3. John Kotter and James L. Heskett. *Corporate Culture and Performance.* (New York: Simon and Schuster, 1992), 224 pages.

4. Marilyn Linton, "The 'New Worker' Needs New Employer," FP EDGE, *Financial Post*, Monday, April 13, 2004, pp. FP1, 10.

5. See, for example, H.S. Becker, "Culture: A Sociological View," *Yale Review*, Summer 1982, pp. 513–527; and E.H. Schein, *Organizational Culture and Leadership* (San Francisco: Jossey-Bass, 1985), p. 168.

6. T.E. Deal and A.A. Kennedy, "Culture: A New Look Through Old Lenses," *Journal of Applied Behavioral Science*, November 1983, p. 501.

7. M. Rokeach, *The Nature of Human Values* (New York: Free Press, 1973).

8. John Ralston Saul, *The Collapse of Globalism and the Reinvention of the World* (Toronto: Viking Canada, 2005).

9. Peter McKenna, "Defying the Gods of Globalization," *National Post*, Saturday, May 28, 2005, WP16.

10. E.H. Schein, "Leadership and Organizational Culture," in F. Hesselbein, M. Goldsmith, and R. Beckhard (eds.), *The Leader of the Future* (San Francisco: Jossey-Bass, 1996), pp. 61–62.

11. J.B. Sorensen, "The Strength of Corporate Culture and the Reliability of Firm Performance," *Administrative Science Quarterly*, 47, no. 1, 2002, pp. 70–91.

12. D.C. Feldman, "The Development and Enforcement of Group Norms," *Academy of Management Review*, 9, 1984, pp. 47–53.

13. Paul Brent, "Culture Shock May Be Brewing," *National Post*, Saturday, February 5, 2005, pp. FP1, 5.

14. D. Yedlin, "Merging Corporate Cultures Not Always Easy," *Calgary Herald*, June 2, 2001, p. E1.

15. G.R. Jones, *Organizational Theory: Text and Cases* (Reading, MA: Addison-Wesley, 1995).

16. H. Schein, "The Role of the Founder in Creating Organizational Culture," *Organizational Dynamics*, 12, 1983, pp. 13–28.

17. Anthony Grnak, John Hughes, and Douglas Hunter, op. cit.

18. J.M. George, "Personality, Affect, and Behaviour in Groups," *Journal of Applied Psychology*, 75, 1990, pp. 107–116.

19. J. Van Maanen, "Police Socialization: A Longitudinal Examination of Job Attitudes in an Urban Police Department," *Administrative Science Quarterly*, 20, 1975, pp. 207–228.

20. P.L. Berger and T. Luckman, *The Social Construction of Reality* (Garden City, NY: Anchor Books, 1967).

21. H.M. Trice and J.M. Beyer, "Studying Organizational Culture Through Rites and Ceremonials," *Academy of Management Review*, 9, 1984, pp. 653–669.

22. "Bonding and Brutality: Hazing Survives as a Way of Forging Loyalty to Groups," *Maclean's*, January 30, 1995, p. 18.

23. "Employer, Directors Held Liable for Workplace Assault," *hrreporter.com*, May 11, 2004.

24. B. Ortega, "Wal-Mart's Meeting Is a Reason to Party," *The Wall Street Journal*, June 3, 1994, p. A1.

25. Website: www.senecac.on.ca/.

26. A. Rafaeli and M.G. Pratt, "Tailored Meanings: On the Meaning and Impact of Organizational Dress," *Academy of Management Review*, January 1993, pp. 32–55.

27. J. Greenwood, "Job One: When Bobbie Gaunt Became Ford of Canada President Earlier This Year, the Appointment Put a Spotlight on the New Rules of the Auto Industry: It's Less About Manufacturing These Days Than About Marketing and Sales," *Financial Post Magazine*, June 1997, pp. 18–22.

28. D. Akin, "Big Blue Chills Out: A Canadian Executive Leads the Campaign to Turn IBM into Cool Blue," *Financial Post (National Post)*, October 11, 1999, pp. C1, C6.

29. Taken and adapted slightly from www.pluralism.org/about/people.php.

30. Douglas A. Hicks, *Religion and the Workplace: Pluralism, Spirituality, Leadership* (Cambridge, MA: Cambridge University Press, 2003).

31. Website: www.pluralism.org/about/eck_cv.php. Accessed June 23, 2008. See also www.pluralism.org/about/people.php.

32. Website: www.EIU.com. Accessed July 22, 2009.

33. Adapted slightly from Marty Parker, "Are You Ready for Corporate Culture?" *National Post*, FP WORKING, Wednesday, March 5, 2008, WK4. Website: www.financialpost.com/working/story.html?id=353601. Accessed June 23, 2008.

34. The author of this article had used the word "codependency." In light of its linkage to "addiction," the present author has omitted it and used the word "interdependency" to convey the mutual support that staff employ, one with the other.

35. L. Brown, "Research Action: Organizational Feedback, Understanding and Change," *Journal of Applied Behavioral Research*, 8, 1972, pp. 697–711; P.A. Clark, *Action Research and Organizational Change* (New York: Harper and Row, 1972); and N. Margulies and A.P. Raia (eds.), *Conceptual Foundations of Organizational Development* (New York: McGraw-Hill, 1978).

36. W.L. French and C.H. Bell, *Organizational Development* (Englewood Cliffs, NJ: Prentice-Hall, 1990).

37. Economist Intelligence Unit, E-Business Transformation. Website: http://store.eiu.com/product/313436031.html. Accessed August 18, 2009.

38. W.L. French, "A Checklist for Organizing and Implementing an OD Effort," in W.L. French, C.H. Bell, and R.A. Zawacki (eds.), *Organizational Development and Transformation* (Homewood, IL: Irwin, 1994), pp. 484–495.

39. K. Lewin, *Field Theory in Social Science* (New York: Harper and Row, 1951).

40. Ian Turner, "Strategy, Complexity and Uncertainty." Website: www.poolonline.com/archive/iss1fea5.html. Accessed August 2, 2009. Based on Ralph Stace.

41. Robert Townsend. *Up the Organization.* New York: Knopf, 1970, 93. *Italics* added for emphasis.

42. Website: www.answers.com/topic/featherbedding.

43. Colby Cosh, "Do Unions Still Matter?" *National Post*, Wednesday, August 3, 2005, p. A16.

44. Workplace Information Directorate. Website: www.hrsdc.gc.ca/en/lp/wid/union_membership.shtml.

45. Paul Vieira, "Canada Faces Productivity Crisis: Professor," *Financial Post*, Monday, April 11, 2005, p. FP4. See also Gilles Paquet, "Productivity and Innovation in Canada: A Case of Governance Failure," *Policy Options*, March–April 2005. Download .pdf document. Website: www.irpp.org/po/. The summary at the website reads: *While there is broad agreement on the benefits of productivity growth and innovation, Canada has not done very well on these fronts, trailing behind all its major trading partners. This, says Gilles Paquet, has to do with the fact that Canada is a risk-averse society "plagued by social rigidities that prevent it from adapting to the evolving context." Despite efforts to put these issues on the public agenda, Canadians have remained largely unconcerned, due to three mental blocks: the very little knowledge we have about the*

sources and causes of productivity gains and innovation, the growing anti-economic-growth sentiment, and the lack of leadership of public officials in educating individuals about their central importance. Paquet reviews the steps that Canada has to take in order to rise to the challenge of innovation and productivity and capture the accruing benefits: "This will entail a major reframing of Canadian perspectives, much restructuring and a fair bit of retooling," he says.

46. J.R. Stepp and T.J. Schneider, "Fostering Change in a Unionized Environment," *Canadian Business Review*, Summer 1995, pp. 13–16.

47. Ibid.

48. Susan Bourette, "10 Dirty Secrets of a Bay Street Temp," *Report on Business Magazine*, September 2005, pp. 28–29, 31, 33–34, 36.

49. Jim Collins, "Level 5 Leadership: The Triumph of Humility and Fierce Resolve," *Harvard Business Review*, HBR OnPoint, 15 pages. Product No. 5831.

50. Adapted from "Impersonal Approach Hurts Business, Study Says," *The Globe and Mail*, Wednesday, August 20, 2003, p. C3.

51. Slightly adapted from Marilyn Linton, "The 'New Worker' Needs New Employer," FP EDGE, *Financial Post*, Monday, April 13, 2004, pp. FP1, 10.

52. Slightly adapted from Barbara Moses, "Who Wants to Work for a 'Stinky' Employer?" *The Globe and Mail*, Wednesday, June 9, 2004, p. C3.

Chapter 8

1. Edited and slightly adapted from Donna Nebenzahl, "An Idea to Stick By," *Financial Post*, Wednesday, May 28, 2008, WK2. Website: www.financialpost.com/working/story.html?id=545960. Accessed June 24, 2008.

2. Apollo program. John F. Kennedy, "Address at Rice University on the Nation's Space Effort." Website: http://en.wikipedia.org/wiki/Apollo_program#cite_note-Rice_Speech-15.

3. Chip Heath and Dan Heath, *Made to Stick: Why Some Ideas Survive and Others Die* (New York: Random House, 2007).

4. www.cohnwolfe.ca/.

5. "Management Tip From the Top," *FP EDGE*, *Financial Post*, Monday, May 10, 2004, FE2.

6. R. Kanfer, "Motivation Theory and Industrial and Organizational Psychology,"

in M.D. Dunnette and L.M. Hough (eds.), *Handbook of Industrial and Organizational Psychology*, 2nd ed., vol. 1 (Palo Alto, CA: Consulting Psychologists Press, 1990), pp. 75–170.

7. Based on Barbara Moses, "Coddled, Confident and Cocky: The Challenges of Managing Gen Y," *The Globe and Mail*, Friday, March 11, 2005, C1, 2.

8. A.H. Maslow, *Motivation and Personality* (New York: Harper and Row, 1954); and J.P. Campbell and R.D. Pritchard, "Motivation Theory in Industrial and Organizational Psychology," in M.D. Dunnette (ed.), *Handbook of Industrial and Organizational Psychology* (Chicago: Rand McNally, 1976), pp. 63–130.

9. R. Kanfer, "Motivation Theory and Industrial and Organizational Psychology," in M.D. Dunnette and L.M. Hough (eds.), *Handbook of Industrial and Organizational Psychology*, 2nd ed., vol. 1 (Palo Alto, CA: Consulting Psychologists Press, 1990), pp. 75–170.

10. S. Ronen, "An Underlying Structure of Motivational Need Taxonomies: A Cross-Cultural Confirmation," in H.C. Triandis, M.D. Dunnette, and L.M. Hough (eds.), *Handbook of Industrial and Organizational Psychology*, vol. 4 (Palo Alto, CA: Consulting Psychologists Press, 1994), pp. 241–269.

11. N.J. Adler, *International Dimensions of Organizational Behavior*, 2nd ed. (Boston: P.W.S.-Kent, 1991); G. Hofstede, "Motivation, Leadership and Organization: Do American Theories Apply Abroad?" *Organizational Dynamics*, Summer 1980, pp. 42–63.

12. F. Herzberg, *Work and the Nature of Man* (Cleveland: World, 1966).

13. N. King, "Clarification and Evaluation of the Two-Factor Theory of Job Satisfaction," *Psychological Bulletin*, 74, 1970, pp. 18–31; and E.A. Locke, "The Nature and Causes of Job Satisfaction," in M.D. Dunnette (ed.), *Handbook of Industrial and Organizational Psychology* (Chicago: Rand McNally, 1976), pp. 1297–1349.

14. R.A. Clay, "Green Is Good for You," *Monitor on Psychology*, April 2001, pp. 40–42.

15. Fiona McFarlane, "Hiring Is Just the First Step," *National Post*, FP WORKING, Wednesday, April 9, 2008, WK1, 7. Website: http://working.canada.com/national/resources/sectors/story.html?id=33394ab9-7505-4a32-a7f4-630d7e61637f. Accessed June 24, 2008. Fiona Macfarlane is a managing partner, Tax, at Ernst & Young*

and executive sponsor of the firm's Canadian Gender Equity Advisory Group (*limited partner of Ernst &Young L.P., under Ernst &Young LLP). Website: www.ey.com/ca.

16. T.R. Mitchell, "Expectancy-Value Models in Organizational Psychology," in N.T. Feather (ed.), *Expectations and Actions: Expectancy-Value Models in Psychology* (Hillsdale, NJ: Erlbaum, 1982), pp. 293–312; V.H. Vroom, *Work and Motivation* (New York: Wiley, 1964).

17. Kevin Cox, "Irving Oil Fuels Its Leaders," *The Globe and Mail*, Wednesday, April 21, 2004, C1, 3.

18. Greg Schinkel and Irwin Schinkel, *Employees Not Doing What You Expect: Find Out Why, Fix It, Prevent It in the Future, Turn Negative Situations Into Positive Relationships* (Toronto: Hushion House, 2005).

19. Greg Schinkel, "Employees Not Up to Par? Here's Why," *The Globe and Mail*, Friday, July 1, 2005, B15.

20. P. Engardio and G. DeGeorge, "Importing Enthusiasm," *Business Week/21st Century Capitalism*, 1994, pp. 122–123.

21. Quoted in Michael Kesterton, "Social Studies," *The Globe and Mail*, Wednesday, May 19, 2004, A22.

22. E.A. Locke and G.P. Latham, *A Theory of Goal Setting and Task Performance* (Englewood Cliffs, NJ: Prentice-Hall, 1990).

23. Barbara Moses, "Make Sure Goals Really Do Serve You," *The Globe and Mail*, Friday, October 15, 2004, C1.

24. E.A. Locke and G.P. Latham, *A Theory of Goal Setting and Task Performance* (Englewood Cliffs, NJ: Prentice-Hall, 1990); J.J. Donovan and D.J. Radosevich, "The Moderating Role of Goal Commitment on the Goal Difficulty–Performance Relationship: A Meta-Analytic Review and Critical Analysis," *Journal of Applied Psychology*, 83, 1998, pp. 308–315; and M.E. Tubbs, "Goal Setting: A Meta-Analytic Examination of the Empirical Evidence," *Journal of Applied Psychology*, 71, 1986, pp. 474–483.

25. Charles Mitchell, "A Night in the Life of 'Graveyard Shift' Workers," *Toronto Star*, Saturday, March 12, 2005, D1, 15. The picture is the second image at www2.lut.fi/~garrido/unpleasant_jobs.htm.

26. F. Luthans and R. Kreitner, *Organizational Behavior Modification and Beyond* (Glenview, IL: Scott, Foresman, 1985); A.D. Stajkovic and F. Luthans, "A Meta-Analysis of the Effects of Organizational Behavior Modification on Task Performance,

1975–95," *Academy of Management Journal*, 40, 1997, pp. 1122–1149.

27. Adapted from Alice H. Eagly and Linda L. Carli, "Women and the Labyrinth of Leadership," *Harvard Business Review*, September 2007. Reprint: R0709C. Website: http://harvardbusinessonline.hbsp.harvard.edu/hbsp/hbr/articles/article.jsp?ml_action=get-article&articleID=R0709C&ml_page=1&ml_subscriber=true. Accessed June 24, 2008.

28. "Women Yet to Close Gender Earning Gap," *Ottawa Citizen*, Friday, May 2, 2008, A4.

29. Wayne F. Cascio, "Human Resources Systems in an International Alliance: The Undoing of a Done Deal?" Vol. 20, *Organizational Dynamics*, January 1, 1991, pp. 63ff.

30. J.S. Adams, "Toward an Understanding of Inequity," *Journal of Abnormal and Social Psychology*, 67, 1963, pp. 422–436; J. Greenberg, "Approaching Equity and Avoiding Inequity in Groups and Organizations," in J. Greenberg and R.L. Cohen (eds.), *Equity and Justice in Social Behavior* (New York: Academic Press, 1982), pp. 389–435; J. Greenberg, "Equity and Workplace Status: A Field Experiment," *Journal of Applied Psychology*, 73, 1988, pp. 606–613; and R.T. Mowday, "Equity Theory Predictions of Behavior in Organizations," in R.M. Steers and L.W. Porter, (eds.), *Motivation and Work Behavior* (New York: McGraw-Hill, 1987), pp. 89–110.

31. Katherine Harding, "Your New Best Friend," *The Globe and Mail*, Wednesday, March 12, 2003, C1, 10.

32. Katherine Harding, "Once and Future Kings," *The Globe and Mail*, Wednesday, April 9, 2003, C1, 6.

33. Based on Suzanne Wintrob, "Reward a Job Well Done," *FP EDGE, Financial Post*, Monday, May 10, 2004, FE7 and Janis Foord Kirk, "Unfair Rule Destroys Productivity," *Toronto Star*, Sunday, March 12, 2005, D1, 13.

34. *Creating Healthy Workplaces*, IAPA, November 2004. Website: www.iapa.ca/resources/resources_downloads.asp#healthy.

35. Ray Williams, "Tell-Tale Signs of Job Turning 'Extreme'," *Financial Post*, Wednesday, May 28, 2008, WK2. Website: www.financialpost.com/working/story.html?id=545962. Accessed June 24, 2008.

36. "Keeping Minds Working," *hrlook.com*, Monday, July 16, 2007.

37. Kathryn May, "Public Sector 'A Toxic Place to Work'," *Ottawa Citizen*, Monday, June 16, 2008.

38. E.E. Lawler III, *Pay and Organization Development* (Reading, MA: Addison-Wesley, 1981).

39. Based on S.E. Gross and J.P. Bacher, "The New Variable Pay Programs: How Some Succeed, Why Some Don't," *Compensation & Benefits Review*, January–February 1993, p. 51; and J.R. Schuster and P.K. Zingheim, "The New Variable Pay: Key Design Issues," *Compensation & Benefits Review*, March–April 1993, p. 28.

40. Peter Brieger, "Variable Pay Packages Gain Favour: Signing Bonuses, Profit Sharing Taking Place of Salary Hikes," *Financial Post (National Post)*, September 13, 2002, p. FP5.

41. "Calgary Salary Increases Outpace Rest of Canada, According to Hewitt," May 9, 2006. Website: www.hewittassociates.com/Intl/NA/en-CA/AboutHewitt/Newsroom/PressReleaseDetail.aspx?cid=3505. Accessed June 24, 2008.

42. E. Beauchesne, "Pay Bonuses Improve Productivity, Study Shows," *The Vancouver Sun*, September 13, 2002, p. D5.

43. "Hope for Higher Pay: The Squeeze on Incomes Is Gradually Easing Up," *Maclean's*, November 25, 1996, pp. 100–101.

44. Rajendra S. Sisodia, David B. Wolfe, and Jagdish N. Sheth, *Firms of Endearment: How World-Class Companies Profit from Passion and Purpose* (Upper Saddle River, N.J.: Wharton School Publishing, 2007).

45. Cited from the Website: www.firmsofendearment.com/.

46. www.keepem.com. Also, Beverly Kaye with Sharon Jordan-Evans. *Love 'em or Lose 'em: Getting Good People to Stay.* (San Francisco, CA: Berrett-Koehler, 2002), 244 pages.

47. Adapted from "Case Studies: Motivating Your Team." Website: www.cokepubandbar.co.uk/lic_casestudy_07.html.

Chapter 9

1. Adapted from Gabriel Draven, "Leadership and the Duty to the Seventh Generation," *hr.com*, Sunday, September 20, 2004. Website: www.hr.com; see also the website: www.hr.com/SITEFORUM?&t=/Default/gateway&i=1116423256281&b=1116423256281&application=story&active=no&ParentID=1119278182413&StoryID=1119654493515&xref=http%3A//www.google.ca/search%3Fhl%3Den%26q%3DSeventh+Generation+Leadership%26meta%3D. Accessed July 4, 2008.

2. Gabriel Draven is a Canadian-based thinker who works with clients to improve their organizational effectiveness by helping them align their people with organizational purpose. He conducts his work amidst a community of practice comprising of senior experts in the disciplines of marketing, strategy, technology, innovation, organizational behaviour, organizational design, and change management.

3. Director of the Trudeau Centre for Peace and Conflict Studies at the University of Toronto, and associate professor in the Department of Political Science at the University of Toronto, author of *The Ingenuity Gap* (Knopf, 2000), which won the 2001 Governor General's Non-fiction Award, and *Environment, Scarcity, and Violence* (Princeton University Press, 1999). Website: www.homerdixon.com/index.html.

4. Virginia Galt, "Disengagement Said 'Common' in Workplace," *The Globe and Mail*, Saturday, July 31, 2004, B7.

5. Janis Foord-Kirk, "Showing Up to Work, But Not Really There," *Toronto Star*, Saturday, February 12, 2005, D1, 11.

6. Julie Smith, "Internet Sites Celebrate the Art of Pretending to Work," *National Post*, Monday, February 2, 2004, A1, 9.

7. Paul Hemp, "Presenteeism: At Work-But Out of It," *Harvard Business Review*, October 2004, 49–58. Product Number: R0410B. Website: http://harvardbusinessonline.hbsp.harvard.edu/b01/en/common/item_detail.jhtml; jsessionid=T5APMMQIPZOBYAKRGWDR5VQBKE0YIISW?id=R0410B&referral=7855. Accessed July 4, 2008.

8. Bryony Gordon, "Slacking Off Can Be Such Hard Work," *National Post*, Tuesday, November 9, 2004, A1, 2.

9. Website: www.phd.antioch.edu/Pages/APhDWeb_Program/bennis.

10. Website: www.greenleaf.org/.

11. Visit the website: www.seventhgeneration.com/site/pp.asp?c=coIHKTMHF&b=90085.

12. Based on Margaret Wheatley. *Finding Our Way: Leadership For An Uncertain Time.* (San Francisco: Berrett-Koehler, 2005), 300 pages. See also Harvey Schachter, "Command and Control Mentality Hurts Living Organizations," *The Globe and Mail*, Wednesday, May 18, 2005, C3.

13. G. Yukl, *Leadership in Organizations*, 2nd ed. (New York: Academic Press, 1989); and R.M. Stogdill, *Handbook of Leadership: A Survey of the Literature* (New York: Free Press, 1974).

14. M. Mitchell Waldrop, "The Trillion-Dollar Vision of Dee Hock," *Fast*

Company.com, 5, October 1996. Website: www.fastcompany.com/magazine/05/deehock.html. Accessed July 4, 2008.

15. "Leadership and the Duty to the Seventh Generation," *hr.com*, Sunday, September 20, 2004. Website: www.hr.com.

16. "Dee Hock on Management," *Fast Company.com*, Issue 5, October/November 1996, 79. Website: www.fastcompany.com/online/05/dee2.html.

17. J. Fierman, "Winning Ideas From Maverick Managers," *Fortune*, February 6, 1995, p. 70.

18. Samantha Grick, "When Your Work Life Is Not Your Life's Work," *National Post*, Wednesday, May 5, 2004, AL1, 6.

19. Ricardo Semler, *The Seven-Day Weekend: Changing the Way Work Works* (Portfolio, 2004).

20. Max Weber, "The Types of Authority and Imperative Coordination," *The Theory of Social and Economic Organization* (NY: Oxford University Press), translated by A.M. Henderson and Talcott Parsons, 1949.

21. Henri Fayol, *General and Industrial Management* (Belmont CA: David S. Lake Publisher, 1987). First published in 1916.

22. Mary Parker Follett, "Giving of Orders and the Psychology of Control," in L. Urwick, ed., *Freedom and Coordination: Lectures in Business Organisation by Mary Parker Follett* (London Management Trust Publications Ltd., 1949). The lectures were delivered in January 1933 at the London School of Economics.

23. Fredrick W. Taylor, *The Principles of Scientific Management*, public domain from Project Gutenberg. First published in 1911.

24. H. Mintzberg, *Power in and Around Organizations* (Englewood Cliffs, NJ: Prentice-Hall, 1983); and J. Pfeffer, *Power in Organizations* (Marshfield, MA: Pitman, 1981).

25. R.P. French Jr. and B. Raven, "The Bases of Social Power," in D. Cartwright and A.F. Zander (eds.), *Group Dynamics* (Evanston, IL: Row, Peterson, 1960), pp. 607–623.

26. Ken Petress, Ph.D., "Power: Definition, Typology, Description, Examples, and Implications," Website: http://bliss.umpi.maine.edu/~petress/power.pdf.

27. Rob Shaw, "Reward Employee Ideas–Literally," *The Globe and Mail*, Friday, August 19, 2005, C1, 2.

28. Glen L. Urban, "The Elements of Customer Advocacy," Part 2 of 3, *FP EDGE, Financial Post*, Monday, March 8, 2004, FE2.

29. Wolf J. Rinke, Ph.D., *Don't Oil the Squeaky Wheel and 19 Other Contrarian Ways to Improve Your Leadership Effectiveness*, (New York: McGraw-Hill, 2004), 224 pages. ISBN: 007142993X. See also Wolf J. Rinke, "The Squeaky Wheels Deserve No Oil," *The Globe and Mail*, Friday, August 13, 2004, C1, 5.

30. "Meeting the Challenges of Tomorrow's Workplace," *Chief Executive Perspectives*, August/September 2002.

31. Sharda Prashad, "Fill Your Power Gap," *The Globe and Mail*, Wednesday, July 23, 2003, C3.

32. Mario F. Heilmann, "Social Evolution and Social Influence: Selfishness, Deception, Self-deception," from "V. Some Aspects of Raven's Power Interaction Model Under an Evolutionary Point of View, p. 28," Website: www.a3.com/myself/ravenpap.htm.

33. T.M. Burton, "Visionary's Reward: Combine 'Simple Ideas' and Some Failures; Result: Sweet Revenge," *The Wall Street Journal*, February 3, 1995, pp. A1, A5.

34. L. Nakarmi, "A Flying Leap Toward the 21st Century? Pressure from Competitors and Seoul May Transform the Chaebol," *Business Week*, March 20, 1995, pp. 78–80.

35. J. Schaubroeck, J.R. Jones, and J.L. Xie, "Individual Differences in Utilizing Control to Cope with Job Demands: Effects on Susceptibility to Infectious Disease," *Journal of Applied Psychology*, 86, no. 2, 2001, pp. 265–278; and A.M. Owens, "Empowerment Can Make You Ill, Study Says," *National Post*, April 30, 2001, pp. A1, A8.

36. "Delta Promotes Empowerment," *The Globe and Mail*, May 31, 1999, advertising supplement, p. C5.

37. "How Do I Manage a Mobile Workforce?" Special Feature to the *National Post: BUSINESS SOLUTIONS*. Presented by CISCO. *National Post*, Business Solutions Advertisement, Monday, March 3, 2008, FP8. Website: www.financialpost.com/small_business/story.html?id=343859. Accessed July 4, 2008.

38. J.P. Kotter, "What Leaders Really Do," *Harvard Business Review*, May–June 1990, pp. 103–111.

39. R.N. Kanungo, "Leadership in Organizations: Looking Ahead to the 21st Century," *Canadian Psychology*, 39, no. 1–2, 1998, p. 77. For more evidence of this consensus, see N. Adler, *International Dimensions of Organizational Behavior*, 3rd ed., (Cincinnati, OH: South Western College Publishing), 1997; R.J. House, "Leadership in the Twenty-First Century,"

in A. Howard (ed.), *The Changing Nature of Work* (San Francisco: Jossey-Bass), 1995, pp. 411–450; R.N. Kanungo and M. Mendonca, *Ethical Dimensions of Leadership* (Thousand Oaks, CA: Sage Publications, 1996); and A. Zaleznik, "The Leadership Gap," *Academy of Management Executive*, 4, no. 1, 1990, pp. 7–22.

40. Gordon Pitts, "Invisible Billionaire Casts a Huge Shadow," *The Globe and Mail*, Monday, April 18, 2004, JB3.

41. Website: www.jimpattison.com/.

42. "Jim Pattison Raises Stake in Canfor," Canada.com. Website: www.canada.com/vancouversun/news/business/story.html?id=4365d7e1-882b-473d-959d-5d57a9a98e98&k=67988. Accessed, August 30, 2009.

43. B.M. Bass, Bass and Stogdill's *Handbook of Leadership: Theory, Research, and Managerial Applications*, 3rd ed. (New York: Free Press, 1990); R.J. House and M.L. Baetz, "Leadership: Some Empirical Generalizations and New Research Directions," in B.M. Staw and L.L. Cummings (eds.), *Research in Organizational Behavior*, vol. 1 (Greenwich, CT: JAI Press, 1979), pp. 341–423; S.A. Kirpatrick and E.A. Locke, "Leadership: Do Traits Matter?" *Academy of Management Executive*, 5, no. 2, 1991, pp. 48–60; and G. Yukl, *Leadership in Organizations*, 2nd ed. (New York: Academic Press, 1989); and G. Yukl and D.D. Van Fleet, "Theory and Research on Leadership in Organizations," in M.D. Dunnette and L.M. Hough (eds.), *Handbook of Industrial and Organizational Psychology*, 2nd ed., vol. 3 (Palo Alto, CA: Consulting Psychologists Press, 1992), pp. 147–197.

44. E.A. Fleishman, "Performance Assessment Based on an Empirically Derived Task Taxonomy," *Human Factors*, 9, 1967, pp. 349–366; E.A. Fleishman, "The Description of Supervisory Behavior," *Personnel Psychology*, 37, 1953, pp. 1–6; A.W. Halpin and B.J. Winer, "A Factorial Study of the Leader Behavior Descriptions," in R.M. Stogdill and A.I. Coons (eds.), *Leader Behavior: Its Description and Measurement* (Columbus Bureau of Business Research, Ohio State University, 1957); and D. Tscheulin, "Leader Behavior Measurement in German Industry," *Journal of Applied Psychology*, 56, 1971, pp. 28–31.

45. R. Likert, *New Patterns of Management* (New York: McGraw-Hill, 1961); and N.C. Morse and E. Reimer, "The Experimental Change of a Major Organizational Variable," *Journal of Abnormal and Social Psychology*, 52, 1956, pp. 120–129.

46. R.R. Blake and J.S. Mouton, *The New Managerial Grid* (Houston: Gulf, 1978).

47. David Sirota, Louis A. Mischkind, and Michael Irwin Meltzer, "Nothing Beats an Enthusiastic Employee," *The Globe and Mail*, Friday, July 29, 2005, C1.

48. Edited slightly from "Diversity Lies in Workplace Environment Not People Selection," Website: www.personnelzone.com/WebSite/WebWatch.nsf/ArticleListHTML/02548FEC0EAE4D63802570970037DE87.

49. E.A. Fleishman and E.F. Harris, "Patterns of Leadership Behavior Related to Employee Grievances and Turnover," *Personnel Psychology*, 15, 1962, pp. 43–56.

50. This graphic is taken from website: www.mindtools.com/pages/article/newLDR_73.htm. Accessed January 3, 2009.

51. F.E. Fiedler, *A Theory of Leadership Effectiveness* (New York: McGraw-Hill, 1967); and F.E. Fiedler, "The Contingency Model and the Dynamics of the Leadership Process," in L. Berkowitz (ed.), *Advances in Experimental Social Psychology* (New York: Academic Press, 1978).

52. R.J. House and M.L. Baetz, "Leadership: Some Empirical Generalizations and New Research Directions," in B.M. Staw and L.L. Cummings (eds.), *Research in Organizational Behavior*, vol. 1 (Greenwich, CT: JAI Press, 1979), pp. 341–423; L.H. Peters, D.D. Hartke, and J.T. Pohlmann, "Fiedler's Contingency Theory of Leadership: An Application of the Meta-Analysis Procedures of Schmidt and Hunter," *Psychological Bulletin*, 97, 1985, pp. 274–285; and C.A. Schriesheim, B.J. Tepper, and L.A. Tetrault, "Least Preferred Co-Worker Score, Situational Control, and Leadership Effectiveness: A Meta-Analysis of Contingency Model Performance Predictions," *Journal of Applied Psychology*, 79, 1994, pp. 561–573.

53. P. Hersey and K.H. Blanchard, "So You Want to Know Your Leadership Style?" *Training and Development Journal*, February 1974, pp. 1–15; and P. Hersey and K.H. Blanchard, *Management of Organizational Behavior: Utilizing Human Resources*, 6th ed. (Englewood Cliffs, NJ: Prentice-Hall, 1993).

54. Cited in C.F. Fernandez and R.P. Vecchio, "Situational Leadership Theory Revisited: A Test of an Across-Jobs Perspective," *Leadership Quarterly*, 8, no.1, 1997, p. 67.

55. M.G. Evans, "The Effects of Supervisory Behavior on the Path–Goal Relationship," *Organizational Behavior and Human Performance*," 5, 1970, pp. 277–298; M.G. Evans, "Leadership and Motivation: A Core Concept," *Academy of Management Journal*, 13, 1970, pp. 91–102; R.J. House, "A Path–Goal Theory of Leader Effectiveness," *Administrative Science Quarterly*, September 1971, pp. 321–338; R.J. House and T.R. Mitchell, "Path–Goal Theory of Leadership," *Journal of Contemporary Business*, Autumn 1974, p. 86; M.G. Evans, "Leadership," in S. Kerr (ed.), *Organizational Behavior* (Columbus, OH: Grid Publishing, 1979); R.J. House, "Retrospective Comment," in L.E. Boone and D.D. Bowen (eds.), *The Great Writings in Management and Organizational Behavior*, 2nd ed. (New York: Random House, 1987), pp. 354–364; M.G. Evans, "Fuhrungstheorien, Weg-ziel-theorie" (trans. G. Reber), in A. Kieser, G. Reber, and R. Wunderer (eds.) *Handworterbuch Der Fuhrung*, 2nd ed. (Stuttgart, Germany: Schaffer Poeschal Verlag, 1995), pp. 1075–1091; and J.C. Wofford and L.Z. Liska, "Path–Goal Theories of Leadership: A Meta-Analysis," *Journal of Management*, 19, 1993, pp. 857–876.

56. R. McQueen, "The Long Shadow of Tom Stephens: He Branded MacBlo's Crew as Losers, Then Made Them into Winners," *Financial Post (National Post)*, June 22, 1999, pp. C1, C5.

57. S. Kerr and J.M. Jermier, "Substitutes for Leadership: Their Meaning and Measurement," *Organizational Behavior and Human Performance*, 22, 1978, pp. 375–403; P.M. Podsakoff, B.P. Niehoff, S.B. MacKenzie, and M.L. Williams, "Do Substitutes for Leadership Really Substitute for Leadership? An Empirical Examination of Kerr and Jermier's Situational Leadership Model," *Organizational Behavior and Human Decision Processes*, 54, 1993, pp. 1–44.

58. S. Kerr and J.M. Jermier, "Substitutes for Leadership: Their Meaning and Measurement," *Organizational Behavior and Human Performance*, 22, 1978, pp. 375–403; and P.M. Podsakoff, B.P. Niehoff, S.B. MacKenzie, and M.L. Williams, "Do Substitutes for Leadership Really Substitute for Leadership? An Empirical Examination of Kerr and Jermier's Situational Leadership Model," *Organizational Behavior and Human Decision Processes*, 54, 1993, pp. 1–44.

59. Adapted from David Rooke and William R. Torbert, "Transformations of Leadership," *Harvard Business Review*, April 2005, 66–76. Reprint R0504D. *Italics* added to opening quote.

60. See also Bill Torbert. *Action Inquiry: The Secret of Timely and Transforming Leadership.* (San Francisco: Berrett-Koehler, 2004), 300 pages. Also, "WEB Links To Participatory Action Research Sites: An Action-Research Resource for Both Students and Practitioners," Website: www.goshen.edu/soan/soan96p.htm.

61. David Rooke and William R. Torbert, "Seven Transformations of Leadership," *Harvard Business Review*, April 2005, 12 pages. Reprint R0504D. Website for the pdf file: www.iecoaching.com/docs/Seven%20Transformations%20of%20Leadership.pdf. Accessed August 30, 2009.

62. J.M. Howell and B.J. Avolio, "The Leverage of Leadership," in *Leadership: Achieving Exceptional Performance*, supplement prepared by the Richard Ivey School of Business, *The Globe and Mail*, May 15, 1998, pp. C1, C2.

63. Ibid.

64. V. Smith, "Leading Us On," *Report on Business Magazine*, April 1999, pp. 91–96.

65. A. Bryman, "Leadership in Organizations," in S.R. Clegg, C. Hardy, and W.R. Nord (eds.), *Handbook of Organization Studies* (London: Sage Publications, 1996), pp. 276–292.

66. B.M. Bass, *Leadership and Performance Beyond Expectations* (New York: Free Press, 1985); B.M. Bass, *Bass and Stogdill's Handbook of Leadership: Theory, Research, and Managerial Applications*, 3rd ed. (New York: Free Press, 1990); and G. Yukl and D.D. Van Fleet, "Theory and Research on Leadership in Organizations," in M.D. Dunnette and L.M. Hough (eds.), *Handbook of Industrial and Organizational Psychology*, 2nd ed., vol. 3 (Palo Alto, CA: Consulting Psychologists Press, 1992), pp. 147–97.

67. L. Nakarmi, "Goldstar is Burning Bright," *Business Week*, September 26, 1994, p. 129.

68. J.A. Conger and R.N. Kanungo, "Behavioral Dimensions of Charismatic Leadership," in J.A. Conger, R.N. Kanungo, and Associates, *Charismatic Leadership* (San Francisco: Jossey-Bass, 1988).

69. J.A. Conger and R.N. Kanungo, *Charismatic Leadership in Organizations* (Thousand Oaks, CA: Sage, 1998).

70. "Building a Better Boss," *Maclean's*, September 30, 1996, p. 41.

71. T. Dvir, D. Eden, B.J. Avolio, and B. Shamir, "Impact of Transformational Leadership on Follower Development and Performance: A Field Experiment,"

Academy of Management Journal, 45, no. 4, 2002, pp. 735–744; R.J. House, J. Woycke, and E.M. Fodor, "Charismatic and Noncharismatic Leaders: Differences in Behavior and Effectiveness," in J.A. Conger and R.N. Kanungo, *Charismatic Leadership in Organizations,* (Thousand Oaks, CA: Sage, 1998), pp. 103–104; D.A. Waldman, B.M. Bass, and F.J. Yammarino, "Adding to Contingent-Reward Behavior: The Augmenting Effect of Charismatic Leadership," *Group & Organization Studies,* December 1990, pp. 381–394; S.A. Kirkpatrick and E.A. Locke, "Direct and Indirect Effects of Three Core Charismatic Leadership Components on Performance and Attitudes," *Journal of Applied Psychology,* February 1996, pp. 36–51; and J.A. Conger, R.N. Kanungo, and S.T. Menon, "Charismatic Leadership and Follower Outcome Effects," paper presented at the 58th Annual Academy of Management Meetings, San Diego, CA, August 1998.

72. J.M. Howell and P.J. Frost, "A Laboratory Study of Charismatic Leadership," *Organizational Behavior & Human Decision Processes,* 43, no. 2, April 1989, pp. 243–269.

73. "Building a Better Boss," *Maclean's,* September 30, 1996, p. 41.

74. A. Elsner, "The Era of CEO as Superhero Ends Amid Corporate Scandals," globeandmail.com, July 10, 2002.

75. B.M. Bass, *Leadership and Performance Beyond Expectations* (New York: Free Press, 1985); B.M. Bass, Bass and Stogdill's *Handbook of Leadership: Theory, Research, and Managerial Applications,* 3rd ed. (New York: Free Press, 1990); and G. Yukl and D.D. Van Fleet, "Theory and Research on Leadership in Organizations," in M.D. Dunnette and L.M. Hough (eds.), *Handbook of Industrial and Organizational Psychology,* 2nd ed., vol. 3 (Palo Alto, CA: Consulting Psychologists Press, 1992), pp. 147–197.

76. Anthony Grnak, John Hughes, and Douglas Hunter, *op.cit.,* p. 195.

77. *Op cit.,* note 75.

78. Cited in B.M. Bass and B.J. Avolio, "Developing Transformational Leadership: 1992 and Beyond," *Journal of European Industrial Training,* January 1990, p. 23.

79. J.M. Howell and B.J. Avolio, "The Leverage of Leadership," in *Leadership: Achieving Exceptional Performance,* supplement prepared by the Richard Ivey School of Business, *The Globe and Mail,* May 15, 1998, p. C2.

80. B.M. Bass, Bass and Stogdill's *Handbook of Leadership;* B.M. Bass and B.J. Avolio,

"Transformational Leadership: A Response to Critiques," in M.M. Chemers and R. Ayman (eds.), *Leadership Theory and Research: Perspectives and Directions* (San Diego: Academic Press, 1993), pp. 49–80; B.M. Bass, B.J. Avolio, and L. Goodheim, "Biography and the Assessment of Transformational Leadership at the World Class Level," *Journal of Management,* 13, 1987, pp. 7–20; J.J. Hater and B.M. Bass, "Supervisors' Evaluations and Subordinates' Perceptions of Transformational and Transactional Leadership," *Journal of Applied Psychology,* 73, 1988, pp. 695–702; R. Pillai, "Crisis and Emergence of Charismatic Leadership in Groups: An Experimental Investigation," *Journal of Applied Psychology,* 26, 1996, pp. 543–562; J. Seltzer and B.M. Bass, "Transformational Leadership: Beyond Initiation and Consideration," *Journal of Management,* 16, 1990, pp. 693–703; and D.A. Waldman, B.M. Bass, and W.O. Einstein, "Effort, Performance, Transformational Leadership in Industrial and Military Service," *Journal of Occupation Psychology,* 60, 1987, pp. 1–10.

81. R. Pillai, C.A. Schriesheim, and E.S. Williams, "Fairness Perceptions and Trust as Mediators of Transformational and Transactional Leadership: A Two-Sample Study," *Journal of Management,* 25, 1999, pp. 897–933.

82. Mary Teresa Bitti, "If You Play the Game to Get Rich Quickly, You Will Lose," *National Post,* Monday, December 13, 2004, FP10. See also Anne Cummings, "The 'Masculine' and 'Feminine' Sides of Leadership and Culture: Perception vs. Reality Workers," *Knowledge@ Wharton,* September 21–October 4, 2005.

83. David Olive, "Wrong Person for the Job," *Toronto Star,* Sunday, February 13, 2005, A20.

84. Website: http://mutual-funds.us/magazines/fortune/fortune500/2008/womenceos/. Accessed January 3, 2009.

85. Website: www.canadianbusiness.com/rankings/w100/list.jsp?pageID=article&year=2006&content=overview&type=overview. Accessed January 3, 2009.

86. A.H. Eagly and B.T. Johnson, "Gender and Leadership Style: A Meta-Analysis," *Psychological Bulletin,* 108, 1990, pp. 233–256.

87. Ibid.

88. Ibid.

89. A.H. Eagly and B.T. Johnson, "Gender and Leadership Style: A Meta-Analysis," *Psychological Bulletin,* 108, 1990, pp. 233–256.

90. Ibid.

91. A.H. Eagly, S.J. Karau, and M.G. Makhijani, "Gender and the Effectiveness of Leaders: A Meta-Analysis," *Psychological Bulletin,* 117, 1995, pp. 125–145.

92. Ibid.

93. R. Calori and B. Dufour, "Management European Style," *Academy of Management Executive,* 9, no. 3, 1995, pp. 61–70.

94. Ibid.

95. J.M. George and K. Bettenhausen, "Understanding Prosocial Behavior, Sales Performance, and Turnover: A Group-Level Analysis in a Service Context," *Journal of Applied Psychology,* 75, 1990, pp. 698–709.

96. N.M. Ashkanasy and C.S. Daus, "Emotion in the Workplace: The New Challenge for Managers," *Academy of Management Executive,* 16, no. 1, 2002, pp. 76–86; and J.M. George, "Emotions and Leadership: The Role of Emotional Intelligence," *Human Relations,* 53, 2002, pp. 1027–1055.

97. J.M. George, "Emotions and Leadership: The Role of Emotional Intelligence," *Human Relations,* 53, 2000, pp. 1027–1055.

98. Reuven Bar-On, *Bar-On Emotional Quotient Inventory (EQ-i): Technical Manual* (Toronto, ON: Multi-Health Systems. 1997).

99. Daniel Goleman, *Emotional Intelligence* (New York: Bantam, 1995).

100. Reuven Bar-On, "Emotional and Social Intelligence: Insights from the Emotional Quotient Inventory (EQ-i)," in Reuven Bar-On and James D.A. Parker, eds., *Handbook of Emotional Intelligence* (San Francisco: Jossey-Bass, 2000), pp. 363–388. See also Reuven Bar-On, Daniel Tranel, Natalie L. Denburg, and Antoine Bechara, "Exploring the Neurological Substrate of Emotional and Social Intelligence," *Brain,* 126, no. 8, August 2003, pp. 1790–1800.

101. Daniel Goleman, *Social Intelligence: The New Science of Human Relationships* (New York: Bantam Books, 2006).

102. Slightly adapted from Harvey Schachter, "Social Intelligence New Gauge of Abilities," *The Globe and Mail,* Friday, February 4, 2005, C1, 2. See also Karl Albrecht, "Social Intelligence: The New Science of Success," website: http://karlalbrecht.com/articles/socialintelligence.shtml. Accessed July 4, 2008.

103. Harvard Business School professor. Website: www.johnkotter.com/bio.html.

104. Gabriel Draven, "Leadership and The Duty to The Seventh Generation," *hr.com,* Sunday, October 17, 2004.

105. Keith Kalawsky, "Trash a Fallen Star," *The Globe and Mail Report on Business Magazine*, April 2005, 21–22.

106. Joshua Chaffin, "Vanishing Imperial CEOs," *Financial Post*, Monday, March 21, 2005, FP20.

107. Brian Banks, "Life Wish," *National Post Business Magazine*, August 2005, 30–34, 36, 38, 40.

108. First published in *BusinessWeek*, December 19, 2005.

109. Adapted from: Harvey Schachter, "Monday Morning Manager," *The Globe and Mail*, Monday, July 3, 2006, p. B2 and Amazon.com website: www.amazon.com/gp/product/078521285X/002-5716207-3409632?v=glance&n=283155.

110. Jerry Manas. *Napoleon on Project Management: Timeless Lessons in Planning, Execution, and Leadership*. Toronto: Nelson Business, 2006, 288 pages.

111. Adapted from Gabriel Draven, "Leadership and The Duty to The Seventh Generation," *hr.com*, Sunday, October 17, 2004. Website: www.hr.com/servlets/sfs;jsessionid=16DD76DFE8F4F1A1954FEF8BD11F2D73?s=GDpdoD1wICmIkSP9y&t=/contentManager/onStory&i=1116423256281&b=1116423256281&l=0&e=UTF-8&StoryID=1119654493515.

Chapter 10

1. Stephanie Whittaker, "The Teams That Bond," *The Montreal Gazette*, Saturday, June 30, 2007. Website: http://working.canada.com/national/resources/career/story.html?id=c212103d-dfcc-4ae7-87fd-ea77112a0a22. Accessed July 5, 2008.

2. Website: www.fujitsu.com/ca/en/services/retailing/about/index_ca.html.

3. Barbara Moses, *What Next? The Complete Guide to Taking Control of Your Working Life* (Toronto: Dorling Kindersley Ltd., 2003).

4. W.R. Coradetti, "Teamwork Takes Time and a Lot of Energy," *HR Magazine*, June 1994, pp. 74–77; and D. Fenn, "Service Teams That Work," Inc., August 1995, p. 99; "Team Selling Catches on, but Is Sales Really a Team Sport?" *The Wall Street Journal*, March 29, 1994, p. A1.

5. P. Booth, Challenge and Change: Embracing the Team Concept, Report 123-94, Conference Board of Canada, 1994.

6. Cited in C. Joinson, "Teams at Work," *HRMagazine*, May 1999, p. 30; and P. Strozniak, "Teams at Work," *Industry Week*, September 18, 2000, p. 47.

7. Reuven Bar-On. EQ-i. *BarOn Emotional Quotient Inventory. A Measure of Emotional Intelligence. Technical Manual.* Toronto: Multi-Health Systems Inc., 1997.

8. Pamela R. Johnson and Julie Indvik, "Organizational Benefits of Having Emotionally Intelligent Managers and Employees," *Journal of Workplace Learning*, Vol. 11, Issue 3, 1999, 84ff.

9. Website: www.leadershipadvantage.com/emotionalIntelligence.shtml.

10. For additional information and ideas, see the following website: www.elsevier.com/wps/find/bookdescription.cws_home/680342/description#description.

11. T.M. Mills, *The Sociology of Small Groups* (Englewood Cliffs, NJ: Prentice-Hall, 1967); M.E. Shaw, *Group Dynamics* (New York: McGraw-Hill, 1981).

12. P. Willcocks, "Yours and Mine? Can the New Owner of the Once-Troubled Myra Falls Copper and Zinc Mine Near Campbell River Forge a New Relationship With Workers and Their Union to Create a True Partnership?" *BCBusiness Magazine*, September 2000, pp. 114–120.

13. Website: www.unmillenniumproject.org.

14. For additional research and papers on the top of self-managed work teams, see *Conference Proceedings: Anniversary Collection: The Best of 1990–1994*. Center for Collaborative Organizations (Center for the Study of Work Teams, University of North Texas, Denton, Texas. Website: www.workteams.unt.edu/old/literature/proceedings/Anver-contents.htm.

15. J.A. Pearce II and E.C. Ravlin, "The Design and Activation of Self-Regulating Work Groups," Human Relations, 11, 1987, pp. 751–782.

16. P. Booth, *Challenge and Change: Embracing the Team Concept*, Report 123–94, Conference Board of Canada, 1994.

17. B. Dumaine, "Who Needs a Boss?" *Fortune*, May 7, 1990, pp. 52–60; and J.A. Pearce II and E.C. Ravlin, "The Design and Activation of Self-Regulating Work Groups," *Human Relations*, 11, 1987, pp. 751–782.

18. B. Dumaine, "Who Needs a Boss?" *Fortune*, May 7, 1990, pp. 52–60; and A.R. Montebello and V.R. Buzzotta, "Work Teams That Work," *Training & Development*, March 1993, pp. 59–64.

19. T.D. Wall, N.J. Kemp, P.R. Jackson, and C.W. Clegg, "Outcomes of Autonomous Work Groups: A Long-Term Field Experiment," *Academy of Management Journal*, 29, 1986, pp. 280–304.

20. W.R. Pape, "Group Insurance," Inc. (Inc. Technology Supplement), June 17, 1997, pp. 29–31; A.M. Townsend, S.M. DeMarie, and A.R. Hendrickson, "Are You Ready for Virtual Teams?" *HRMagazine*, September 1996, pp. 122–126; and A.M. Townsend, S.M. DeMarie, and A.M. Hendrickson, "Virtual Teams: Technology and the Workplace of the Future," *Academy of Management Executive*, 12, no. 3, 1998, pp. 17–29.

21. A.M. Townsend, S.M. DeMarie, and A.R. Hendrickson, "Are You Ready for Virtual Teams?" *HRMagazine*, September 1996, pp. 122–126.

22. W.R. Pape, "Group Insurance," Inc. (Inc. Technology Supplement), June 17, 1997, pp. 29–31; and A.M. Townsend, S.M. DeMarie, and A.R. Hendrickson, "Are You Ready for Virtual Teams?" *HRMagazine*, September 1996, pp. 122–126.

23. A.B. Drexler and R. Forrester, "Teamwork—Not Necessarily the Answer," *HRMagazine*, January 1998, pp. 55–58.

24. R. Forrester and A.B. Drexler, "A Model for Team-Based Organization Performance," *Academy of Management Executive*, August 1999, p. 47. See also S.A. Mohrman, with S.G. Cohen and A.M. Mohrman Jr., *Designing Team-Based Organizations* (San Francisco: Jossey-Bass, 1995); and J.H. Shonk, *Team-Based Organizations* (Homewood, IL: Business One Irwin, 1992).

25. Claire Sookman, "Building Your Virtual Team," *ITWorldCanada*, March 2004. Website: www.itworldcanada.com/a/search/55dd71fe-030c-4487-8d27-e0e237b9ec49.html. *Claire Sookman specializes in 'virtual team' building, helping project managers who work remotely to collaborate more effectively to increase productivity and efficiency. She can be reached at csookman@sympatico.ca.*

26. A. Deutschman, "The Managing Wisdom of High-Tech Superstars," *Fortune*, October 17, 1994, pp. 197–206.

27. Ibid.

28. J.S. Lublin, "My Colleague, My Boss," *The Wall Street Journal*, April 12, 1995, pp. R4, R12.

29. B.W. Tuckman, "Developmental Sequences in Small Groups," *Psychological Bulletin*, 63, 1965, pp. 384–399; and B.W. Tuckman and M.C. Jensen, "Stages of Small Group Development," *Group and Organizational Studies*, 2, 1977, pp. 419–427.

30. C.J.G. Gersick, "Time and Transition in Work Teams: Toward a New Model of Group Development," *Academy of Management Journal*, 31, March 1988, pp. 9–41;

C.J.G. Gersick, "Marking Time: Predictable Transitions in Task Groups," *Academy of Management Journal*, 32, June 1989, pp. 274–309.

31. J.R. Hackman, "Group Influences on Individuals in Organizations," in M.D. Dunnette and L.M. Hough (eds.), *Handbook of Industrial and Organizational Psychology*, 2nd ed., vol. 3 (Palo Alto, CA: Consulting Psychologists Press, 1992), pp. 199–267.

32. Ibid.

33. Ibid.

34. L. Festinger, "Informal Social Communication," *Psychological Review*, 57, 1950, pp. 271–282; and M.E. Shaw, *Group Dynamics* (New York: McGraw-Hill, 1981).

35. J.R. Hackman, "Group Influences on Individuals in Organizations," in M.D. Dunnette and L.M. Hough (eds.), *Handbook of Industrial and Organizational Psychology*, 2nd ed., vol. 3 (Palo Alto, CA: Consulting Psychologists Press, 1992), pp. 199–267; and M.E. Shaw, *Group Dynamics* (New York: McGraw-Hill, 1981).

36. Janis Irving, *Victims of Groupthink* (Boston: Houghton Mifflin, 1972). See also Janis Irving, *Groupthink: Psychological Studies of Policy Decisions and Fiascos,* 2nd ed. (Boston: Houghton Mifflin, 1982).

37. Christine A. Yost and Mary L. Source, "Are Effective Teams More Emotionally Intelligent? Confirming the Importance of Effective Communication in Teams," *Delta Pi Epsilon Journal*, Vol. 42, No. 2, Spring 2000, 101–09.

38. Williams, W., & Sternberg, R., "Group Intelligence: Why Some Groups Are Better Than Others," *Intelligence*, 1988, 12, (4), 351–377.

39. S.R. Covey, S. R. "Unstoppable Teams," *Executive Excellence*, July 1996, 13, pp. 7–9. Website: http://proquest.umi.com/pqdlink.

40. Marcia M. Hughes and James Bradford Terrell, *The Emotionally Intelligent Team: Understanding and Developing the Behaviors of Success* (San Francisco: Jossey-Bass, 2007).

41. MHS owns the world rights to the EQ-*i*™ or (Emotional Quotient-Inventory™), which was originally research, designed, and validated by Dr. Reuven Bar-On who now refers to EQ as emotional-social intelligence. Website: http://www.reuvenbaron.org/. Accessed May 22, 2008.

42. Editorial review, amazon.ca. Website: www.amazon.ca/Emotionally-Intelligent-Team-Understanding-Developing/dp/0787988340/

ref=sr_1_1?ie=UTF8&s=books&qid=1211482054&sr=8-1. Accessed May 22, 2008.

43. I.L. Janis, *Groupthink: Psychological Studies of Policy Decisions and Fiascoes,* 2nd ed. (Boston: Houghton Mifflin, 1982).

44. Ibid.

45. Robert Pear, "He Wrote the Book on Intelligence," *The New York Times*, Sunday, July 11, 2004, p. WK12.

46. J.N. Choi and M.U. Kim, "The Organizational Application of Groupthink and Its Limitations in Organizations," *Journal of Applied Psychology*, 84, 1999, pp. 297–306.

47. C. McCauley, "The Nature of Social Influence in Groupthink: Compliance and Internalization," *Journal of Personality and Social Psychology*, 57, 1989, pp. 250–260; P.E. Tetlock, R.S. Peterson, C. McGuire, S. Chang, and P. Feld, "Assessing Political Group Dynamics: A Test of the Groupthink Model," *Journal of Personality and Social Psychology*, 63, 1992, pp. 781–796; S. Graham, "A Review of Attribution Theory in Achievement Contexts," *Educational Psychology Review*, 3, 1991, pp. 5–39; and G. Moorhead and J.R. Montanari, "An Empirical Investigation of the Groupthink Phenomenon," *Human Relations*, 39, 1986, pp. 399–410.

48. J. Longley and D.G. Pruitt, "Groupthink: A Critique of Janis' Theory," in L. Wheeler (ed.), *Review of Personality and Social Psychology* (Newbury Park, CA: Sage, 1980), pp. 507–513; and J.A. Sniezek, "Groups Under Uncertainty: An Examination of Confidence in Group Decision Making," *Organizational Behavior and Human Decision Processes*, 52, 1992, pp. 124–155.

49. J.N. Choi and M.U. Kim, "The Organizational Application of Groupthink and Its Limitations in Organizations," *Journal of Applied Psychology*, 84, 1999, pp. 297–306.

50. See N.R.F. Maier, *Principles of Human Relations* (New York: Wiley, 1952); I.L. Janis, *Groupthink: Psychological Studies of Policy Decisions and Fiascoes,* 2nd ed. (Boston: Houghton Mifflin, 1982); and C.R. Leana, "A Partial Test of Janis' Groupthink Model: Effects of Group Cohesiveness and Leader Behavior on Defective Decision Making," *Journal of Management*, Spring 1985, pp. 5–17.

51. See R.O. Mason, "A Dialectic Approach to Strategic Planning," *Management Science*, 13, 1969, pp. 403–414; R.A. Cosier and J.C. Aplin, "A Critical View of Dialectic Inquiry in Strategic Planning," *Strategic Management Journal*, 1, 1980, pp. 343–356; I.I. Mitroff and R.O. Mason, "Structuring III—Structured Policy Issues: Further

Explorations in a Methodology for Messy Problems," *Strategic Management Journal*, 1, 1980, pp. 331–342.

52. Mary C. Gentile, *Differences That Work: Organizational Excellence Through Diversity* (Boston: Harvard Business School Press, 1994).

53. T.J. Bouchard Jr., J. Barsaloux, and G. Drauden, "Brainstorming Procedure, Group Size, and Sex as Determinants of Problem Solving Effectiveness of Individuals and Groups," *Journal of Applied Psychology*, 59, 1974, pp. 135–138.

54. L. Thompson and L.F. Brajkovich, "Improving the Creativity of Organizational Work Groups," *Academy of Management Executive*, 17, no. 1, 2003, pp. 96–111, B. Mullen, C. Johnson, and E. Salas, "Productivity Loss in Brainstorming Groups: A Meta-Analytic Integration," *Basic and Applied Social Psychology*, 12, no. 1, 1991, pp. 3–23; and M. Diehl and W. Stroebe, "Productivity Loss in Brainstorming Groups: Towards the Solution of a Riddle," *Journal of Personality and Social Psychology*, 53, 1987, pp. 497–509.

55. D.H. Gustafson, R.K. Shulka, A. Delbecq, and W.G. Walster, "A Comparative Study of Differences in Subjective Likelihood Estimates Made by Individuals, Interacting Groups, Delphi Groups, and Nominal Groups," *Organizational Behavior and Human Performance*, 9, 1973, pp. 280–291.

56. N. Dalkey, *The Delphi Method: An Experimental Study of Group Decision Making* (Santa Monica, CA: Rand Corp., 1989).

57. P.C. Earley, "Social Loafing and Collectivism: A Comparison of the United States and the People's Republic of China," *Administrative Science Quarterly*, 34, 1989, pp. 565–581; J.M. George, "Extrinsic and Intrinsic Origins of Perceived Social Loafing in Organizations," *Academy of Management Journal*, 35, 1992, pp. 191–202; S.G. Harkins, B. Latane, and K. Williams, "Social Loafing: Allocating Effort or Taking it Easy," *Journal of Experimental Social Psychology*, 16, 1980, pp. 457–465; B. Latane, K.D. Williams, and S. Harkins, "Many Hands Make Light the Work: The Causes and Consequences of Social Loafing," *Journal of Personality and Social Psychology*, 37, 1979, pp. 822–832; and J.A. Shepperd, "Productivity Loss in Performance Groups: A Motivation Analysis," *Psychological Bulletin*, 113, 1993, pp. 67–81.

58. Adapted from the American Management Association, "How to Build High-Performance

Teams," Self-Study Course. Website: www.amanet.org/selfstudy/b13759.htm.

59. Website: www.corporatedrumcircles.com/.

60. Adapted from Jim Clemmer, "Team Spirit Built From the Top," *The Globe and Mail*, Friday, November 26, 2004, C1.

61. Jiri Maly, "The Seven Habits of Winning Teams," *The Globe and Mail*, Monday, August 13, 2007, B6. Jiri Maly is a Principal of McKinsey & Company. Website: www.soulzatwork.com/pdfs/team/The_seven_habits_of_winning_teams.pdf. Accessed July 5, 2008.

Chapter 11

1. Ann Howland, "Business Ill-Prepared for Aging Workshop," *Ottawa Citizen*, Wednesday, July 18, 2007, E1, 4.

2. J.E. Butler, G.R. Ferris, and N.K. Napier, *Strategy and Human Resource Management* (Cincinnati, OH: South Western, 1991); P.M. Wright and G.C. McMahan, "Theoretical Perspectives for Strategic Human Resource Management," *Journal of Management*, 18, 1992, pp. 295–320.

3. Michael Stern, "Expanding Role for HR Executives," *Financial Post*, August 1, 2004, FP10. Michael Stern is president and CEO of Michael Stern Associates Inc. (www.michaelstern.com), an executive search firm headquartered in Toronto and a founding member of AEA International Search with offices in major business centres worldwide.

4. Derek Sankey, "Boomers Aim to fill the Gaps in Management Expertise," *FP EDGE, Financial Post*, Monday, May 10, 2004, FE3.

5. http://greyfox.ca/.

6. Rosemary McCracken, "No Time to Retire," *FP EDGE, Financial Post*, Monday, March 8, 2004, FE1, 4.

7. M. Lewis, "BCE Appoints Alcan Recruit 'Chief Talent Officer,'" *Financial Post (National Post)*, May 24, 2001, p. C11.

8. E.L. Levine, *Everything You Always Wanted to Know About Job Analysis: A Job Analysis Primer* (Tampa, FL: Mariner, 1983).

9. R.L. Mathis and J.H. Jackson, *Human Resource Management*, 7th ed. (St. Paul, MN: West, 1994).

10. For example, see Employment Standards Act [RSBC 1996] c. 113, Website: www.bclaws.ca/Recon/document/freeside/--%20E%20--/Employment%20Standards%20Act%20%20RSBC%201996%20%20c.%20113/00_96113_01.xml. Posted August 19,

2009. Accessed August 31, 2009. See also *Your Guide to the Employment Standards Act, 2000*. Website: www.labour.gov.on.ca/english/es/guide/index.html, updated January 2009. Accessed August 31, 2009.

11. For example, The Saskatchewan Human Rights Code. Website: www.qp.gov.sk.ca/documents/English/Statutes/Statutes/S24-1.pdf. Accessed August 31, 2009.

12. Website: www.chrc-ccdp.ca/default-en.asp. Accessed August 31, 2009.

13. C.D. Fisher, L.F. Schoenfeldt, and J.B. Shaw, *Human Resource Management* (Boston: Houghton Mifflin, 1990).

14. P.M. Wright and G.C. McMahan, "Theoretical Perspectives for Strategic Human Resource Management," *Journal of Management*, 18, 1992, pp. 295–320.

15. L. Baird and I. Meshoulam, "Managing Two Fits for Strategic Human Resource Management," *Academy of Management Review*, 14, 1989, pp. 116–128; J. Milliman, M. Von Glinow, and M. Nathan, "Organizational Life Cycles and Strategic International Human Resource Management in Multinational Companies: Implications for Congruence Theory," *Academy of Management Review*, 16, 1991, pp. 318–339; R.S. Schuler and S.E. Jackson, "Linking Competitive Strategies With Human Resource Management Practices," *Academy of Management Executive*, 1, 1987, pp. 207–219; P.M. Wright and S.A. Snell, "Toward an Integrative View of Strategic Human Resource Management," *Human Resource Management Review*, 1, 1991, pp. 203–225.

16. Website: www.fedpubs.com/subject/legis/clc.htm. Accessed August 31, 2009.

17. Website: www.hc-sc.gc.ca/ewh-semt/occup-travail/whmis-simdut/index-eng.php. Accessed August 31, 2009.

18. See the various provincial and territorial documents.

19. Website: www.ccohs.ca/. Accessed August 31, 2009.

20. For example, website: www.gov.pe.ca/law/statutes/pdf/o-01_01.pdf. Accessed August 31, 2009.

21. S.L. Rynes, "Recruitment, Job Choice, and Post-Hire Consequences: A Call for New Research Directions," in M.D. Dunnette and L.M. Hough (eds.), *Handbook of Industrial and Organizational Psychology*, vol. 2 (Palo Alto, CA: Consulting Psychologists Press, 1991), pp. 399–444.

22. Special Report, "The Battle for Brainpower: A Survey of Talent," *The*

Economist, October 7, 2006, p. 1, 3–5, 8–9, 12–14, 16, 18, 20, 22–24.

23. Editorial, "The Search for Talent," *The Economist*, October 7, 2006, p. 11

24. "The Battle for Brainpower," *The Economist*, October 7, 2006, p. 3.

25. "The World Is Our Oyster," *The Economist*, October 7, 2006, p. 9.

26. "Nightmare Scenarios," *The Economist*, October 7, 2006, p. 14.

27. R.M. Guion, "Personnel Assessment, Selection, and Placement," in M.D. Dunnette and L.M. Hough (eds.), *Handbook of Industrial and Organizational Psychology*, vol. 2 (Palo Alto, CA: Consulting Psychologists Press, 1991), pp. 327–397.

28. R.A. Noe, J.R. Hollenbeck, B. Gerhart, and P.M. Wright, *Human Resource Management: Gaining a Competitive Advantage* (Burr Ridge, IL: Irwin, 1994); J.A. Wheeler and J.A. Gier, "Reliability and Validity of the Situational Interview for a Sales Position," *Journal of Applied Psychology*, 2, 1987, pp. 484–487.

29. R.A. Noe, J.R. Hollenbeck, B. Gerhart, and P.M. Wright, *Human Resource Management: Gaining a Competitive Advantage* (Burr Ridge, IL: Irwin, 1994).

30. Tavia Grant, "Colour Them Controversial," *The Globe and Mail*, Wednesday, May 21, 2008, C1, 4. See also Caitlin Crawshaw, "Questionnaires Test Job Seeker's Patience," *National Post*, Wednesday, May 14, 2008, FP15.

31. "Wanted: Middle Managers, Audition Required," *The Wall Street Journal*, December 28, 1995, p. A1.

32. I.L. Goldstein, "Training in Work Organizations," in M.D. Dunnette and L.M. Hough (eds.), *Handbook of Industrial and Organizational Psychology*, vol. 2 (Palo Alto, CA: Consulting Psychologists Press, 1991), pp. 507–619.

33. M.B. Arthur, D.T. Hall, and B.S. Lawrence (eds.), *Handbook of Career Theory* (Cambridge: Cambridge University Press, 1989), p. 8.

34. S.L. McShane, *Canadian Organizational Behaviour*, 4th ed. (Whitby, ON: McGraw-Hill Ryerson, 2001), p. 548.

35. Stephanie Rosenbloom, "Savvy Job Hunters Work the Web," *National Post*, FP WORKING, Wednesday, May 7, 2008, WK2.

36. L. Chwialkowska, "Ottawa Plan Targets Jobs Crisis," *National Post*, June 18, 2001, p. A1.

37. See, for example, P.O. Benham Jr., "Developing Organizational Talent: The Key to Performance and Productivity," *SAM Advanced Management Journal,* January 1993, pp. 34–39.

38. Sanjiv Purba, "When Reviews Deserve a Failing Grade," *The Globe and Mail,* Friday, June 11, 2004, C1.

39. Sources on the Internet that offer useful performance review forms, tools and human resource-related best practices: www.opm.gov/perform/monitor.asp; www.hr.com; www.businesstown.com/people/reviews-overview.asp; www.toolpack.com/performance.html; www.workplacetoolbox.com/index.jsp.

40. C.D. Fisher, L.F. Schoenfeldt, and J.B. Shaw, *Human Resource Management* (Boston: Houghton Mifflin, 1990).

41. M.A. Peiperl, "Getting 360° Feedback Right," *Harvard Business Review,* January 2001, pp. 142–147.

42. Adapted from the American Management Association, "How to Build High-Performance Teams," Self-Study Course. Website: www.amanet.org/selfstudy/b13759.htm.

43. L. Duxbury, L. Dyke, and N. Lam, "Career Development in the Federal Public Service: Building a World-Class Workforce," Treasury Board of Canada, January 1999.

44. "Montreal's Popular French-Language Daily Locks Out 253 Employees," *The Canadian Press,* 2009. Website: www.google.com/hostednews/canadianpress/article/ALeqM5jRH1t6anN2e6oBCrk098PPXMpvAQ. Accessed January 25, 2009.

45. Website: www1.servicecanada.gc.ca/eng/labour/labour_relations/info_analysis/work_stoppages/2008.shtml. Accessed January 14, 2009.

46. Ishak Saporta, "Managers' and Workers' Attitudes Toward Unions in the U.S. and Canada." Relations Industrielles/Industrial Relations. Website: http://findarticles.com/p/articles/mi_hb4388/is_n3_v50/ai_n28662583/. Accessed August 2, 2009.

47. "Union Membership and Public Attitudes Towards Unions Have Changed Dramatically in the Last 20 Years," James Ferrabee. Website: www.irpp.org/ferrabee/archive/0805.htm. Accessed August 2, 2009.

48. "Union Membership in Canada—2008, Strategic Policy, Analysis, and Workplace Information Directorate Labour Program, Human Resources and Skills Development Canada, Accessed August 2, 2009. Website: www.hrsdc.gc.ca/eng/labour/labour_relations/info_analysis/union_membership/index.shtml.

49. For an interesting and short blog on this reality, see Rick Beaudry, "War for Talent or War on Talent," B Wyze Solutions, January 4, 2009. Website: www.bwyze.com/blog/war-for-talent-or-war-on-talent/. Accessed September 1, 2009.

50. For an interesting overview, see "The Aging Workforce and Human Resources Development Implications For Sector Councils," prepared for The Alliance of Sector Councils by R.A Malatest & Associates Ltd., February 2003, 38 pages, esp. pp. 21–26. Website: www.cpsc-ccsp.ca/PDFS/Aging%20Workforce%20Final%20Report.pdf. Accessed September 1, 2009.

51. See "Canada Experiences a Global Phenomenon: Aging Workforce Creates Talent Gap." Website: www.consultant-news.com/article_display.aspx?p=adp&id=4751. Accessed September 1, 2009.

52. Peter B. Vaill, Ph.D. *Learning as a Way of Being. Strategies for Survival in a World of Permanent White Water.* (San Francisco: Jossey-Bass Publishers, 1966), 4, 14. See also http://gseweb.harvard.edu/~hepg/HER-BookRev/Articles/1997/1-Spring/Vaill.html.

53. Ibid. See also J.Z. Young. *Doubt and Certainty in Science.* New York: Oxford University Press, 1960.

54. Daniel H. Kim and Eileen Mullen, "The Spirit of the Learning Organization," LEVERAGE POINTS for a New Workplace, New World, August 26, 2004, Issue 53. This article, excerpted from *The Systems Thinker Newsletter,* appears in the Pegasus anthology, "Reflections on Creating Learning Organizations." Website: www.pegasuscom.com/levpoints/spiritlearn.html, or see *The Systems Thinker,* Vol. 4, No. 4, May 1993. Also, www.pegasuscom.com/levpoints/lp53.html.

55. Adapted slightly from Robyn Greenspan, "The Brazen Careerist," *Executive Insider Newsletter,* ExecuNet, June 30, 2008. Website: www.execunet.com/e_resources.cfm. Accessed July 6, 2008.

Chapter 12

1. Adapted from Matthew Trevisan, "Remote Worker? Try Remote-Controlled," *The Globe and Mail,* Friday, July 11, 2008, C1, 6. Website: www.theglobeandmail.com/servlet/ArticleNews/freeheadlines/LAC/20080711/CAROBOT11/business/ROB_Managing. Accessed July 11, 2008. For a video display of IvanAnywhere's capabilities, see website: www.today.com/video/view/episode_4ivananywheres_performance_review/play-ytIO1OoLFTTS0/. Accessed July 12, 1008.

2. Bold and *italics* added.

3. Slightly adapted from Daniel F. Muzyka, "Communicating in a Crisis: Act With Honesty and Empathy," *The Globe and Mail,* Monday, June 9, 2008, B8. Website: www.theglobeandmail.com/servlet/story/LAC.20080609.RSTRATEGYMUZYKA09/TPStory/Business. Accessed June 9, 2008.

4. C.A. O'Reilly and L.R. Pondy, "Organizational Communication," in S. Kerr (ed.), *Organizational Behavior* (Columbus, OH: Grid, 1979).

5. D.A. Adams, P.A. Todd, and R.R. Nelson, "A Comparative Evaluation of the Impact of Electronic and Voice Mail on Organizational Communication," *Information & Management,* 24, 1993, pp. 9–21.

6. E.M. Rogers and R. Agarwala-Rogers, *Communication in Organizations* (New York: Free Press, 1976).

7. Deena Waisberg, "Dress Code Still in Force Though It's Stinking Hot," *National Post,* Saturday, August 6, 2005, FW3.

8. Kamal Fatehi, *International Management* (Upper Saddle River, NJ: Prentice Hall, 1996).

9. Mary Teresa Bitti, "The New Face of Canadian Business," FP ENTREPRENEUR: Strategies for Small and Mid-Size Businesses, *National Post,* Monday, May 2, 2005, FP110.

10. Slightly adapted from Keith Green, "Study Reveals Emotions Not as Plain as the Smile on Your Face," *Ottawa Citizen,* Monday, May 21, 2007, A6. For the original article, see William W. Maddux and Takahiko Masuda, "Are the Windows to the Soul the Same in the East and West? Cultural Differences in Using the Eyes and Mouth as Cues to Recognize Emotions in Japan and the United States," *Journal of Experimental Social Psychology,* 43, March 2007, pp. 303–311. Website: http://eprints.lib.hokudai.ac.jp/dspace/handle/2115/22527. Accessed June 12, 2008.

11. R.L. Daft, R.H. Lengel, and L.K. Trevino, "Message Equivocality, Media Selection, and Manager Performance: Implications for Information Systems," *MIS Quarterly,* 11, 1987, pp. 355–366; R.L. Daft and R.H. Lengel, "Information Richness: A New Approach to Managerial Behavior and Organization Design," in B.M. Staw and L.L. Cummings (eds.), *Research in Organizational Behavior* (Greenwich, CT: JAI Press, 1984).

12. R.L. Daft, *Organization Theory and Design* (St. Paul, MN: West, 1992).

13. Ibid.

14. "Lights, Camera, Meeting: Teleconferencing Becomes a Time-Saving

Tool," *The Wall Street Journal,* February 21, 1995, p. A1.

15. "E-Mail Abuse: Workers Discover High-Tech Ways to Cause Trouble in the Office," *The Wall Street Journal,* November 22, 1994, p. A1; and "E-Mail Alert: Companies Lag in Devising Policies on How It Should Be Used," *The Wall Street Journal,* December 29, 1994, p. A1.

16. J. Kay, "Someone Will Watch Over Me: Think Your Office E-Mails are Private? Think Again," *National Post Business,* January 2001, pp. 59–64.

17. "Office Workers Urged to Go 'Email Free'," *Health & Beauty: News,* Monday, 17th October 2005. Website: www.manchesteronline.co.uk/healthandbeauty/news/s/178/178139_office_workers_urged_to_go_email_free.html.

18. "Fact Sheet: Privacy in the Workplace," Office of the Privacy Commissioner of Canada. Website: www.privcom.gc.ca/fs-fi/02_05_d_17_e.asp.

19. To see the actual email, go to website: http://technocrat.net/d/2006/8/28/7262/index.html; see also Edward Wong, "A Stinging Office Memo Boomerangs: Chief Executive is Criticized After Upbraiding Workers by E-Mail," *The New York Times,* April 5, 2001. Website: www.nytimes.com/2001/04/05/business/stinging-office-memo-boomerangs-chief-executive-criticized-after-upbraiding.html. Accessed September 17, 2009.

20. "Cerner Reports Second Quarter 2009 Results," *The Wall Street Journal,* July 29, 2009. Website: http://online.wsj.com/article/PR-CO-20090729-909997.html. Accessed September 21, 2009.

21. "Cerner," Wikipedia website: http://en.wikipedia.org/wiki/Cerner. Accessed September 21, 2009.

22. "On the Road," *Newsweek,* June 6, 1994, p. 8.

23. C.R. Mill, "Feedback: The Art of Giving and Receiving Help," in L. Porter and C.R. Mill (eds), *The Reading Book for Human Relations Training* (Bethel, ME: NTL Institute of Applied Behavioral Science, 1976), pp. 18–19.

24. Based on S.P. Robbins and P.L. Hunsaker, *Training in Interpersonal Skills: TIPS for Managing People at Work,* 2nd ed. Upper Saddle River, NJ: Prentice-Hall, 1996), Ch 3.

25. J.A. Litterer, "Conflict in Organizations: A Reexamination," *Academy of Management Journal,* 9, 1966, pp. 178–186; S.M. Schmidt and T.A. Kochan, "Conflict: Towards Conceptual Clarity," *Administrative Science Quarterly,* 13, 1972, pp. 359–370; and

R.H. Miles, *Macro Organizational Behavior* (Santa Monica, CA: Goodyear, 1980).

26. S.P. Robbins, *Managing Organizational Conflict: A Nontraditional Approach* (Englewood Cliffs, NJ: Prentice-Hall, 1974); and L. Coser, *The Functions of Social Conflict* (New York: Free Press, 1956).

27. L.R. Pondy, "Organizational Conflict: Concepts and Models," *Administrative Science Quarterly,* 2, 1967, pp. 296–320; and R.E. Walton and J.M. Dutton, "The Management of Interdepartmental Conflict: A Model and Review," *Administrative Science Quarterly,* 14, 1969, pp. 62–73.

28. K.W. Thomas, "Conflict and Negotiation Processes in Organizations," in M.D. Dunnette and L.M. Hough (eds.), *Handbook of Industrial and Organizational Psychology,* 2nd ed., vol. 3 (Palo Alto, CA: Consulting Psychologists Press, 1992), pp. 651–717.

29. P.R. Lawrence, L.B. Barnes, and J.W. Lorsch, *Organizational Behavior and Administration* (Homewood, IL: Irwin, 1976).

30. Adapted from the American Management Association, "How to Build High-Performance Teams," Self-Study Course. Website: www.amanet.org/selfstudy/b13759.htm.

31. Adapted slightly from Harvey Schachter, "What Women Want (But Don't Know How to Get It)," *The Globe and Mail,* Wednesday, March 19, 2008, C3. Website: http://wiseblog.usask.ca/?p=22. Accessed July 12, 2008.

32. Linda Babcock and Sara Laschever, *Ask For It. How Women Can Use the Power of Negotiation to Get What They Really Want* (New York: Bantam, 2008).

33. Linda Babcock and Sara Laschever, *Women Don't Ask. The High Cost of Avoiding Negotiation—and Positive Strategies for Change* (New York: Bantam, 2007).

34. R.J. Lewicki and J.R. Litterer, *Negotiation* (Homewood, IL: Irwin, 1985); G.B. Northcraft and M.A. Neale, *Organizational Behavior* (Fort Worth, TX: Dryden, 1994); J.Z. Rubin and B.R. Brown, *The Social Psychology of Bargaining and Negotiation* (New York: Academic Press, 1975).

35. L. Thompson and R. Hastie, "Social Perception in Negotiation," *Organizational Behavior and Human Decision Processes,* 47, 1990, pp. 98–123.

36. K.W. Thomas, "Conflict and Negotiation Processes in Organizations," in M.D. Dunnette and L.M. Hough (eds.), *Handbook of Industrial and Organizational Psychology,* 2nd ed., vol. 3 (Palo Alto, CA: Consulting Psychologists Press, 1992), pp. 651–717.

37. R.J. Lewicki, S.E. Weiss, and D. Lewin, "Models of Conflict, Negotiation and Third Party Intervention: A Review and Synthesis," *Journal of Organizational Behavior,* 13, 1992, pp. 209–252.

38. G.B. Northcraft and M.A. Neale, *Organizational Behavior* (Fort Worth, TX: Dryden, 1994).

39. "Ottawa Councillor Slams City's Transit Bargaining Team, Mayor." Website: www.cbc.ca/canada/ottawa/story/2009/01/13/ot-090113-scheduling.html?ref=rss. Accessed January 14, 2009.

40. R.J. Lewicki, S.E. Weiss, and D. Lewin, "Models of Conflict, Negotiation and Third Party Intervention"; G.B. Northcraft and M.A. Neale, *Organizational Behavior* (Fort Worth, TX: Dryden, 1994); and D.G. Pruitt, "Integrative Agreements: Nature and Consequences," in M.H. Bazerman and R.J. Lewicki (eds.), *Negotiating in Organizations* (Beverly Hills, CA: Sage, 1983).

41. R. Fischer and W. Ury, *Getting to Yes* (Boston: Houghton Mifflin, 1981); and G.B. Northcraft and M.A. Neale, *Organizational Behavior* (Fort Worth, TX: Dryden, 1994).

42. P.J. Carnevale and D.G. Pruitt, "Negotiation and Mediation," *Annual Review of Psychology,* 43, 1992, pp. 531–582.

43. Adapted from "Negotiation," *Negotiation Strategies,* International Online Training Program On Intractable Conflict, Conflict Research Consortium, University of Colorado, Copyright ©1998. Website: www.colorado.edu/conflict/peace/treatment/negotn.htm.

44. Website: www.iaap-hq.org/APW/apwindex.htm. Accessed July 12, 2008.

45. Website: http://archives.cbc.ca/war_conflict/peacekeeping/topics/659-3734/. Accessed January 24, 2009.

46. Mike Ramsey and Sara Gay Forden, "Three Strikes You're Out," *Financial Post,* Friday, Sepember 18, 1994, p. FP3.

Chapter 13

1. "David Olive's 10 Recession Winners," *Toronto Star,* Saturday, September 12, 2009. Website: www.thestar.com/specialsections/recession/article/694614. Accessed Saturday, July 1, 2009.

2. W.G. Ouchi, "Markets, Bureaucracies, and Clans," *Administrative Science Quarterly,* 25, 1980, pp. 129–141.

3. Slightly adapted from Diedre McMurdy, "People Get Stress Relief Express-Style," *Financial Post,* Saturday, January 15, 2005, IN1, 2.

4. A. Kinicki and B.K. Williams, "Management: A Practical Introduction" (Boston: McGraw-Hill Irwin, 2003).

5. E.E. Lawler III and J.G. Rhode, *Information and Control in Organizations* (Pacific Palisades, CA: Goodyear, 1976).

6. C.W.L. Hill and G.R. Jones, *Strategic Management: An Integrated Approach*, 4th ed. (Boston: Houghton Mifflin, 1997).

7. W.G. Ouchi, "The Transmission of Control Through Organizational Hierarchy," *Academy of Management Journal*, 21, 1978, pp. 173–192.

8. W.G. Ouchi, "The Relationship Between Organizational Structure and Organizational Control," *Administrative Science Quarterly*, 22, 1977, pp. 95–113.

9. W.G. Ouchi, "Markets, Bureaucracies, and Clans," *Administrative Science Quarterly*, 25, 1980, pp. 129–141.

10. W.H. Newman, *Constructive Control* (Englewood Cliffs, NJ: Prentice-Hall, 1975).

11. J.D. Thompson, *Organizations in Action* (New York: McGraw-Hill, 1967).

12. R.N. Anthony, *The Management Control Function* (Boston: Harvard Business School Press, 1988).

13. P. Lorange, M. Morton, and S. Ghoshal, *Strategic Control* (St. Paul, MN: West, 1986).

14. H. Koontz and R.W. Bradspies, "Managing Through Feedforward Control," *Business Horizons*, June 1972, pp. 25–36.

15. Kai Li, "'Over the Top' CEO Compensation Leaves Investors in the Cold," *The Globe and Mail*, Monday, June 2, 2008, B2.

16. W.G. Ouchi, "Markets, Bureaucracies, and Clans," *Administrative Science Quarterly*, 25, 1980, pp. 129–141.

17. C.W.L. Hill and G.R. Jones, *Strategic Management: An Integrated Approach*, 4th ed. (Boston: Houghton Mifflin, 1997).

18. Andrea James, "Starbucks Profit Takes Bitter Shot for the Year," *Seattle P-I*, November 11, 2008. Website: http://seattlepi.nwsource.com/business/387203_sbuxearns11.html. Accessed November 15, 2008.

19. R. Simons, "Strategic Orientation and Top Management Attention to Control Systems," *Strategic Management Journal*, 12, 1991, pp. 49–62.

20. J.A. Alexander, "Adaptive Changes in Corporate Control Practices," *Academy of Management Journal*, 34, 1991, pp. 162–193.

21. Daryl-Lynn Carlson, "Vidéotron Fine-Tunes Egypt Staff," *Financial Post*, Wednesday, May 28, 2008, WK1, 7.

Website: www.financialpost.com/working/story.html?id=545959. Accessed July 13, 2008.

22. "RIM Provides Status Update and Reports on Results of Internal Review of Stock Option Grants by Special Committee." Website: http://press.rim.com/financial/release.jsp?id=1193. Accessed July 29, 2009.

23. Quoted in www.corpgov.net/. Accessed August 1, 2009.

24. "Global Principles of Accountable Corporate Governance." Website: www.calpers-governance.org/docs-sof/marketinitiatives/2009-04-01-corp-governance-pub20-final-glossy.pdf. Accessed August 1, 2009.

25. G.H.B. Ross, "Revolution in Management Control," *Management Accounting*, 72, 1992, pp. 23–27.

26. D.S. Pugh, D.J. Hickson, C.R. Hinings, and C. Turner, "Dimensions of Organizational Structure," *Administrative Science Quarterly*, 13, 1968, pp. 65–91.

27. P.M. Blau, *The Dynamics of Bureaucracy* (Chicago: University of Chicago Press, 1955).

28. Adapted from Deena Waisberg, "Bank Executive Proves He's a Stand-up Guy," *Financial Post*, Saturday, May 28, 2005, FW9.

29. W. G. Ouchi, *Theory Z: How Americans Can Meet the Japanese Challenge* (New York: Warner, 1981).

30. Louis W. Fry, "Toward a Theory of Spiritual Leadership," *The Leadership Quarterly*, 14, no. 6, 2003, p. 696. *Italics* added to quote.

31. Deena Waisberg, "Bank Executive Proves He's a Stand-up Guy."

32. S. Mcgee, "Garish Jackets Add to Clamor of Chicago Pits," *The Wall Street Journal*, July 31, 1995, p. C1.

33. T. Cole, "How to Stay Hired," *Report on Business Magazine*, March 1995, pp. 46–48.

34. K.E. Weick, *The Social Psychology of Organization* (Reading, MA: Addison-Wesley, 1979).

35. J. McCann, "Cutting the Crap," *National Post Business*, March 2001, pp. 47–57.

36. Michael Maccoby, *Leaders We Need* (Toronto: McGraw-Hill Ryerson Agency, 2007).

37. Mary Teresa Bitti, "Where Will Future CEOs Come From?" *Financial Post*, FP WORKING, Wednesday, February 6, 2008, pp. WK1, 7. For partial access, visit website: www.immersionactive.com/html/resources/Where-will-future-CEOs-come-from.cfm.

38. Website: www.cbc.ca/marketplace/2007/02/coffee_shops.html. Accessed January 23, 2009.

39. Tyler Hamilton and Kenyon Wallace, "Dozens Fired at Bruce Power over Web, E-mail Use," *Toronto Star*, September 10, 2009. Website: www.thestar.com/printArticle/693525. Accessed September 12, 2009.

Appendix A

1. Written by J.W. Haddad, Professor, School of Business Management, Seneca College of Applied Arts and Technology, Toronto, Canada.

2. I suggest using *PlanWrite Business Plan Writer Deluxe 2006*, McGraw-Hill Irwin, ISBN-13: 978-0-07-328146-9, ISBN-10: 0-07-328146-8.

3. *PlanWrite Business Plan Writer Deluxe.*

4. TD Bank Financial Group, 150th Annual Report 2005, p. 4.

5. Website: www.thebodyshop.com.au/infopage.cfm?topicID=20.

6. Website: www.cara.com.

7. Website: www.renees.com/vision.asp.

8. Website: www.thebodyshop.com.au/infopage.cfm?pageID=53.

9. This is not a full résumé. The full résumés of the management team can be included in the Appendices. For this section of the business plan, simply state what experience and/or credentials make the manager suitable for the role they are taking on within the venture.

10. Website: www.statcan.gc.ca/subjects-sujets/standard-norme/naics-scian/2002/naics-scian02l-eng.htm.

11. Website: www.statcan.gc.ca.

12. Website: www.crfa.ca/research/statistics/.

13. Website: www.bizpal.ca/index_e.shtml.

14. Website: www.statcan.gc.ca/start-debut-eng.html.

15. Website: www.dnb.ca/default.htm.

16. Op. cit.

Appendix B

(Available Online)

Index

Name/Company/URL

Subject